Frommer's®
Croatia

My Croatia
by Karen Torme Olson

QUESTIONS INEVITABLY SURFACE WHEN PEOPLE FIND OUT THAT I WRITE about Croatia. Is it safe? Did the war leave anything worth seeing? How do Croatians feel about Americans? I had the same questions (and a healthy dose of motherly concern) in 1999, when my son Greg announced he was moving to Croatia to work on a rebuilding project. Within a few months, Greg had lost his heart to the land, its people, and a beautiful girl named Sanja, and I grudgingly headed for this central European country to see what my kid was up to. What I found was an achingly beautiful land that pulled me into its thrall in a nanosecond.

In just one visit I found myself poking around Istria's hilltop towns, floating off Pag's shore in water so clear I could see sand crabs having lunch 9m (30 ft.) down, relishing the sound of Andrea Bocelli's magnificent voice from a vantage point on an ancient stone bench in Pula's Roman amphitheater, sipping wine in a Striga vineyard, and catching cooling spray from the tumbling waterfalls at Plitvice. But what captivated me even more than gorgeous landscapes and historical sites was the warmth and hospitality of Croatia's people. Check out the photos that follow, and my "Best of Croatia" chapter, and you'll get the idea.

ROVINJ (left) wins my vote for the prettiest town in Croatia. It was founded by Romans, was deeply influenced by Venetians, and is still home to an Italian majority, which is reflected in the food and street signs. Must-see attractions are the hilltop church of St. Euphemia (visible in this photo), the art galleries on Grisia Street, and Balbi's Arch, next to the Town Museum.

Turquoise lakes, rushing water, and a tranquil forest are the setting for **PLITVICE LAKES NATIONAL PARK (above).** Whether you explore this UNESCO Heritage site for an hour or a day, you'll see spectacular waterfalls of every size and intensity, woodland gardens, and the occasional critter. When your hike is over, nothing tastes better than *janjetina,* lamb roasted on a spit. Get it hot off the fire just outside the park.

Evidence of Croatia's Homeland War has largely disappeared from most of the country, with the exception of the town of **VUKOVAR (left)**. Mortar-ravaged churches, pock-marked houses, and roofless structures still stand as testament to the 1991 destruction that hit this once-robust town on the Danube. Some say politicians have left the damage unrepaired deliberately, as a reminder of the attack.

By day, the **PERISTIL AREA OF DIOCLETIAN'S PALACE (above)** is a popular meeting place, an outdoor cafe, and one of the biggest remaining chunks of the Emperor's former digs. At night, especially during Split's Summer Fest, it becomes an open-air opera house. Tickets are difficult to find. If you can't snag a seat, book Room 302 on the top floor of the adjacent Peristil Hotel and open the window. The music will float up to you as you listen in comfort.

Poreč is home to the fabulous St. Euphrasius Basilica and its eye-popping mosaics, which still glow with gold, gems, and brilliant color after 14 centuries. The **APSE MOSAICS (above)** depict Christ and His Apostles and compare favorably with celebrated mosaics in Ravenna, Italy. My tip: Don't miss the mosaics displayed in outdoor courtyards *in situ*—not as vibrant as the Apse Mosaics but still amazing.

Almost every Croatian church and museum of religious art has a few ornate gold or silver arm, leg, or head sculptures. Each sculpture is a **RELIQUARY (right)** containing human relics from a saint or saintly person. I recommend seeing Zadar's exhibit and, if you have time, Vodjnan's in Istria.

LADIES SELLING LACE (right), lavender sachets, homemade cheese, and rakija and other sundries are commonplace in Croatia. If you are looking for genuine Pag lace, do some research—check out photos online or seek advice at the local tourist agency. Once you see the real article, you won't be fooled by imitations.

It's just a short walk up a set of stairs behind central Zagreb's Jelačić Square to Dolac, one of the most colorful **OPEN-AIR MARKETS (below)** anywhere. Dolac is more than a place to buy groceries, however: It is ringed with cafes and "diners" and behind it you'll find kiosks selling embroidery, toys, and some apparel.

Smaller and a little newer than Rome's Colosseum, **PULA'S ROMAN AMPHI-THEATER (above)** is also in much better shape. Here, you can walk on the same soil where Christians fought lions and even go beneath the arena where gladiators waited to prove their strength. The amphitheater's "basement" is now a fine museum dedicated to Istrian history. In the summer, you can take in films and concerts by big-name music stars in the coliseum, sometimes at no charge.

Visiting a cemetery on a vacation might seem odd, but **MIROGOJ (right)** is much more than a graveyard. Famous Croatian sculptors created the monuments that mark the graves of notables, soldiers, and common folk alike. Even more unusual: There's no religious segregation here. You'll find Christians, Jews, and Muslims buried side by side. Don't miss the ivy-covered Herman Bollé façade and the Neo-Renaissance arcades (shown here) that lead to the ornate burial chambers of Croatian society.

Frommer's®

Croatia
2nd Edition

by Karen Tormé Olson

with Sanja Bažulić Olson

Here's what the critics say about Frommer's:

"Amazingly easy to use. Very portable, very complete."
—*Booklist*

"Detailed, accurate, and easy-to-read information for all price ranges."
—*Glamour Magazine*

"Hotel information is close to encyclopedic."
—*Des Moines Sunday Register*

"Frommer's Guides have a way of giving you a real feel for a place."
—*Knight Ridder Newspapers*

WILEY
Wiley Publishing, Inc.

Wiley Publishing, Inc.

111 River St.
Hoboken, NJ 07030-5774

ISBN: 978-0-470-18185-0

Editor: Linda Barth
Production Editor: Eric T. Schroeder
Cartographer: Roberta Stockwell
Photo Editor: Richard Fox
Production by Wiley Indianapolis Composition Services

Front cover photo: Tower & coastline, Dubrovnik
Back cover photo: Diners at outdoor cafe, Hvar Town

For information on our other products and services or to obtain technical support, please contact our Customer Care Department within the U.S. at 800/762-2974, outside the U.S. at 317/572-3993 or fax 317/572-4002.

Wiley also publishes its books in a variety of electronic formats. Some content that appears in print may not be available in electronic formats.

Manufactured in the United States of America

5 4 3 2 1

Contents

8 Istria   206

9 Zagreb   249

10 Excursions From Zagreb   282

11 Inland Croatia   313

Appendix: Croatia in Context   346

Index   365

List of Maps

About the Authors

Karen Tormé Olson and her daughter-in-law, Sanja Bažulić Olson, have spent every summer and holiday since 2003 traveling Croatia as a two-person writer-translator team to gather material for this Frommer's guide. Karen is a photographer, freelance travel writer, and former *Chicago Tribune* editor. She recently earned her doctorate in administration and currently holds a day job as a high school counselor and fencing coach. She lives in a Chicago suburb with her husband, son, and three large dogs.

Sanja Bažulić Olson is a Croatian national who was born in Denmark, but has lived in Croatia all her life. She graduated from Zagreb University with a degree in agricultural engineering. She currently is working as a project manager for the U.S. Agency for International Development in Kabul, Afghanistan.

Acknowledgments

Thanks to Nada Kožul, Goran Kožul, Sanda Sokol, Mitchell Tocher, Marića Matkovic, Igor Mareovic and all the wonderful Croatian people who graciously shared their advice, time, and encouragement during research for this guide. Special thanks (again) to Mirko and Finka Bažulić, who opened their home and hearts to the author. Thanks, too, to my husband Randall Weissman, who joined us in Istria and added his journalistic perspective to our research. Finally, kudos to Linda Barth for her editorial diligence and insight.

An Invitation to the Reader

In researching this book, we discovered many wonderful places—hotels, restaurants, shops, and more. We're sure you'll find others. Please tell us about them, so we can share the information with your fellow travelers in upcoming editions. If you were disappointed with a recommendation, we'd love to know that, too. Please write to:

Frommer's Croatia, 2nd Edition
Wiley Publishing, Inc. • 111 River St. • Hoboken, NJ 07030-5774

An Additional Note

Please be advised that travel information is subject to change at any time—and this is especially true of prices. We therefore suggest that you write or call ahead for confirmation when making your travel plans. The authors, editors, and publisher cannot be held responsible for the experiences of readers while traveling. Your safety is important to us, however, so we encourage you to stay alert and be aware of your surroundings. Keep a close eye on cameras, purses, and wallets, all favorite targets of thieves and pickpockets.

Other Great Guides for Your Trip:

Frommer's Europe
Frommer's European Cruises & Ports of Call
Frommer's Budapest & the Best of Hungary

Frommer's Star Ratings, Icons & Abbreviations

Every hotel, restaurant, and attraction listing in this guide has been ranked for quality, value, service, amenities, and special features using a **star-rating system.** In country, state, and regional guides, we also rate towns and regions to help you narrow down your choices and budget your time accordingly. Hotels and restaurants are rated on a scale of zero (recommended) to three stars (exceptional). Attractions, shopping, nightlife, towns, and regions are rated according to the following scale: zero stars (recommended), one star (highly recommended), two stars (very highly recommended), and three stars (must-see).

In addition to the star-rating system, we also use **seven feature icons** that point you to the great deals, in-the-know advice, and unique experiences that separate travelers from tourists. Throughout the book, look for:

Finds	Special finds—those places only insiders know about
Fun Fact	Fun facts—details that make travelers more informed and their trips more fun
Kids	Best bets for kids and advice for the whole family
Moments	Special moments—those experiences that memories are made of
Overrated	Places or experiences not worth your time or money
Tips	Insider tips—great ways to save time and money
Value	Great values—where to get the best deals

The following **abbreviations** are used for credit cards:

AE	American Express	DISC	Discover	V	Visa
DC	Diners Club	MC	MasterCard		

Frommers.com

Now that you have the guidebook to a great trip, visit our website at **www.frommers.com** for travel information on more than 3,600 destinations. We update features regularly to give you instant access to the most current trip-planning information available. At Frommers.com, you'll find scoops on the best airfares, lodging rates, and car rental bargains. You can even book your travel online through our reliable travel booking partners. Other popular features include:

- Online updates of our most popular guidebooks
- Vacation sweepstakes and contest giveaways
- Newsletters highlighting the hottest travel trends
- Online travel message boards with featured travel discussions

The Best of Croatia

Until recently, July and August in Croatia belonged to German and Italian tourists, who clogged border crossings in their annual "migration" to the country's endless beaches and clear blue sea. Today, the rest of the world has discovered Croatia's charms: its wealth of Roman ruins, medieval hilltop castles, and staggering cache of natural wonders. Even though the summer crowd is now larger and more diverse and tourism is one of the country's biggest sources of income, it still is possible to find a secluded cove or patch of beach where it seems you're the only person on Earth. When all the name-brand hotels are filled, there is always a room with personality waiting in a private home where the landlord welcomes you like a long-lost friend.

Every town and village has at least one restaurant where the locals hang out and where the slice of life you get with your meal is the best dessert there is. In Croatia, each building has a story that adds another facet to this gem of a country.

This chapter is a "road map," meant to provide insight to the delights that await you in Croatia. All you have to do is fill in the blanks as you make discoveries of your own.

1 The Best Travel Experiences

- **Listening to the Sea Organ** (Zadar): Waves move water through this organ's undersea pipes, creating music. Add a set of white stone steps descending into the crystal water above the organ and a sky full of stars, and you have a matchless venue to enjoy the moonlight. Let the water lap at your feet, and luxuriate in the organ's haunting sounds. See p. 149.
- **Viewing Mummies** (Vodjnan): They are billed as the bodies of holy people who died centuries ago and miraculously never decomposed. They look a little like skeletons shrink-wrapped in leather, but they are compelling. You can't get too close to these relics, but you'll get close enough to recognize them as being human. They're stored in the curtained-off area behind the altar of St. Blaise Church, where the light is dim, the music

soulful, and the piped-in commentary a little exaggerated. The setting contributes to the atmosphere, which is creepy but riveting. See p. 219.
- **Exploring the Village of Hum** (Istria): It calls itself the smallest town in the world, and population-wise, it might be. But so many people visit this village high in the Istrian interior that it always seems crowded. The village fathers have done a wonderful job of restoring the buildings in town and making it tourist-friendly. See p. 246.
- **Strolling Through Mirogoj Cemetery** (Zagreb): As much sculpture garden as burial ground, this 19th-century cemetery was designed by Herman Bollé. It is home to Croatian patriots, common folk, and people of all faiths and nationalities. The tombstones range from small and simple to enormous and elaborate, but each is a

story in itself. Don't miss the black granite slab at the grave of former president Franjo Tuđman or the sculpture-rich arcades on either side of the entrance. See p. 277.

- **Descending Into Iločki Podrumi** (Ilok): You'll get the chills in this second-oldest wine cellar in Croatia from two sources: the temperature and the history. The cellar was looted by the Serbs during the Homeland War, but not before the owners concealed bottles of the best vintages behind a false wall. Today those bottles are out of hiding and on display along with the barrels and vats used to store the winery's newest vintages. See p. 344.

2 The Best Natural Wonders

- **Plitvice Lakes National Park** (145km/90 miles southwest of Zagreb): Plitvice is Croatia's best-known natural wonder. The park's 16 crystal-clear, turquoise lakes and countless waterfalls put on a great show. The lakes flow into one another and tumble over deposits of travertine, creating waterfalls that may drop a few feet or plunge as much as 64m (210 ft.). All this beauty is set in a dense forest accessed via footpaths and populated by bears and wild boar. See p. 293.

- **Kornati National Park** (part of the Zadar Archipelago): Kornati's 140 islands are really the tops of mountains that were above sea level 20,000 years ago but now are mostly submerged. One side of each island consists of land that is rocky and lightly blanketed with vegetation (a few grapevines and olive trees). The side facing the sea is a sheer rock wall known as a "crown" that plunges almost 76m (250 ft.) straight into the water. Sixty-nine species of butterflies live here. Perhaps the most interesting part is Kornati's offshore underwater landscape. Its rock formations support flourishing flora and fauna. See p. 163.

- **Paklenica National Park** (between Zadar and Karlobag): Paklenica's raw beauty is best appreciated by hikers and nature lovers. But even motorists respect the imposing Velebit peaks because the limestone cliffs that soar above deep gorges and dense vegetation are visible for miles from nearby highways. Even from afar you can see cave openings and imagine what's inside the chambers. See p. 157.

- **Krka National Park** (less than half an hour from Šibenik): The park was formed to protect the Krka River, which runs from its source near Knin to the sea near Šibenik. The river has created a series of spectacular gorges, waterfalls, lakes, and rapids on its trip through the mountains. The most spectacular falls are the jaw-droppingly steep Skradinski Buk and Roški Slapovi. Between the two are Lake Visovac and Visovac Island, home to a Franciscan monastery. See p. 166.

3 The Best Open-Air Markets

- **Dolac** (Zagreb): The market is above the main square at the foot of Old Town but it is more than just a place to buy fruit and veggies. This urban market is a crossroads where people come to see and be seen; to trade gossip; and to relax with a cup of coffee. Early morning is the best time to visit because that's when the bread is freshest, the displays the prettiest, and the people the most interesting. See p. 270.

- **Pazarin** (Split): Pazarin is reminiscent of a Turkish bazaar in looks, sounds, and smells. Booths and tables line both sides of Hrvojeva Street outside the east wall of Diocletian's Palace from the Riva to the Silver Gate. You'll find the usual assortment of produce plus a large variety of textiles and some of the most persuasive vendors anywhere. See p. 89.

- **Bjelovar's** (Bjelovar): This market is quite civilized and partially covered. It is noteworthy as the place where farmers from Croatia's agricultural belt bring their best produce, dairy products, fish, and meat every day. The market is at its busiest from 7am to noon, but a few vendors stay open until 6pm or so. The later it gets, the lower the prices go. See p. 323.

4 The Best Small Hotels & Inns

- **Hotel San Rocco** (Brtonigla): San Rocco's location deep in Istria adds to the romance you'll find in its lovingly restored stone buildings and grounds. Flowers, olive groves, and an assortment of ruins comprise the hotel's sensual "curb appeal." But it's really the beautifully put together guest rooms with their mélange of antique and modern touches, the inviting pool, and the magnificent gourmet restaurant that seal the deal. See p. 233.

- **Hotel Waldinger** (Osijek): It packs a lot of elegance into its 18 rooms, each of which drips with elegance in the heart of a city that has not altogether recovered from the 1991 war. From here you can easily walk to the banks of the Drava, shop the city market, and explore medieval Tvrđa. See p. 336.

- **Hotel Korana-Srakovčić** (Karlovac): The Korana's sleek guest rooms are a nice surprise in Karlovac, which is still putting itself back together after the 1991 war. The hotel's big porch overlooking the river and riverwalk is a vacation all by itself. See p. 291.

- **Hotel Vestibul Palace** (Split): The Roman Empire meets the 21st century at the Palace, where most rooms share at least part of a wall built by Diocletian. History and gourmet delights align to make this one of the best hotel experiences in Croatia. Each room has a personality of its own, complete with cleverly designed windows carved into the stone walls to reveal views of various aspects of Old Town. See p. 93.

- **Valsabbion** (Pula): This hedonistic experience is not to be missed. The hotel's seven rooms and three suites are decorated with flair in a breezy, romantic style that carries over to its exquisite restaurant, one of the best in Croatia. There is also a spa with a long menu of beauty treatments. You might come here for the beach, but you'll stay for the food and the pampering. See p. 214.

5 The Best Big Luxury Hotels

- **The Regent Esplanade** (Zagreb): The most gracious hotel in Croatia compares favorably with luxury hotels in New York and Paris for a fraction of the cost. From rich furnishings in the guest rooms to a concierge who is a gallant repository of Croatian history, a stay at the Esplanade is an experience you'll never forget. See p. 256.

- **Hilton Imperial** (Dubrovnik): This is the U.S. chain's first foray into Croatia. Rather than build a hotel from scratch, Hilton had the wisdom to restore what was salvageable from

Dubrovnik's historic 19th-century Imperial and graft a modern hotel onto the base. Every detail has been taken care of, and you'll be treated as an honored guest here. See p. 62.

- **Le Meridien Lav** (Split): Le Meridien's seaside location in Podstrana, 20 minutes from Split's Old Town, gives it a resort feel. Its spacious, well-appointed rooms, spa, casino, and high-design public areas contribute luxury, and its marina, tennis courts, and pools make it a destination hotel. If you are looking for a place you don't have to leave to have fun, this is it. See p. 92.

- **Diamant** (Poreč): Though it looks like one of those impersonal '70s package-style hotels from the outside,

it is much more—management has thought of everything, and the hotel has an activity to match guests' every whim. The Diamont deserves special kudos for its efforts to cater to guests with disabilities. Every room can accommodate wheelchairs; even the pool and locker rooms are outfitted to allow access for guests with disabilities. See p. 229.

- **Funimation** (Zadar): The ultimate resort hotel. Funimation is elegant, all-inclusive with excellent restaurants. It is right on the beach, and scheduled up the wazoo with activities to keep kids busy and out of their parents' hair. This is as close as it gets to a Disney World hotel in Croatia. See p. 151.

6 The Best Roman Ruins

- **Pula Amphitheater** (Pula): Smaller than Rome's coliseum but in much better shape, the amphitheater is a lot more accessible to tourists than its Rome counterpart. Don't miss the newly restored underground chambers and their exhibits featuring Istrian history. And if you're in town when a concert is scheduled there, get a ticket no matter who is headlining. See p. 212.

- **Salona** (Solin): The grandeur that was Rome is still evident in the crumbling buildings and foundations that grace this former outpost of the empire. It isn't difficult to imagine what Salona looked like in its prime, but it is tough to imagine why this magnificent city was left to sink into the Earth for a couple of centuries.

Do not approach without sturdy walking shoes, sunscreen, and a full water bottle. See p. 99.

- **Diocletian's Palace** (Split): It isn't what you think of when you hear the word "palace." Diocletian built his estate on a scale so grand it was converted into a city after he died. And the city's landscape has been tinkered with so much during the last 15 centuries that the character of the original complex has been all but obliterated. However, what remains of the palace and what has been built on its footprint is now Split's Old Town. If you walk around it, through it, and under it enough, you'll begin to understand Diocletian's enormous ego. See p. 87.

7 The Best Beaches

- **Baška** (Krk Island): This is a sunlover's paradise, with more than 30 beaches of varying size and a promenade that skirts most of them. Baška's

beaches once were sand, but today the sand is covered with pebbles that extend a few feet into the water. That doesn't diminish their appeal because beach chairs, umbrellas, and padded mats are readily available on the promenade. See p. 192.

- **Novalja** (Pag Island): Any cove off Novalja can be a private beach. The water just a few feet offshore is so clear you can see the white, sandy bottom 6m (20 ft.) below. If you have a boat, drop anchor for a while, take a dip, and let your stress float away. See p. 139.

- **Zlatni Rat** (Brač Island): You must visit this beach just so you can say you did. This is the famous strip, usually photographed from the air, that appears in all the Croatia ads. From above, Zlatni Rat resembles a green finger rimmed with sand and tipped with a curling tendril extending into the sapphire sea. From ground level, it is a sun-blasted, pebbled landscape covered with a huge international crowd soaking up the rays and the local culture. See p. 107.

- **Orebić** (Pelješac Peninsula): This is a civilized place where families linger together and, at the end of the day, Mom brings covered bowls full of fruit down to kids who don't want to leave their sand castles and snorkels for dinner. The water is warm, the sun constant, and the people as nice as they come. See p. 127.

8 The Best Promenades

- **Tkalčićeva Street** (Zagreb): This is a designer's runway, a shopper's paradise, a gourmet's delight, and a historian's fascination. This is where Zagreb's cafe society holds court and where everyone—including tourists—takes a stroll in the evening to see what's happening. See p. 270.

- **Riverwalk** (Osijek): The promenade along the mighty Drava is never empty. People walk their dogs, couples take romantic strolls, kids ride skateboards, and tourists stretch their legs at all hours of the day and night as they follow the river from Tvrđa to the winter harbor. Near Tvrđa, a little bridge leads to the opposite bank and Copacabana, a popular swimming area. See p. 332.

- **Stradun** (Dubrovnik): The walled city's main thoroughfare is broad and bricked and lined with shops and cafes. During the day, the Stradun is a tourist path crowded with hordes rushing to and from Old Town's famous churches and monuments. Once the sun sinks into the sea, the traffic slows to promenade pace, and the crowd's style changes from comfortably dressed to their showy best. See p. 57.

- **Lungomare** (Volosko to Lovran): This Kvarner Bay promenade is Croatia's longest at 12km (7.2 miles). It is a winding flagstone walkway along the shore from **Volosko** to **Lovran** that cuts through restaurants, snakes along rocky outcrops, and even crosses a couple of hotel terraces. It's always crowded and never boring. See p. 179.

- **Obala Hrvatskog Naradnog Preporoda—The "Riva"** (Split): Split's Riva is caught between the city's two busiest places: Diocletian's Palace and the ferry landing. Consequently, foot traffic is shoulder-to-shoulder, with the occasional detours to cafe tables and portable ice-cream stands. The Riva abuts the palace's south wall and was once under water, but today it is the location of some of Split's liveliest nightlife. See p. 87.

- **Riva** (Trogir): Croatia's most entertaining promenade may be the Riva, especially during the summer. Besides the restaurants that line this path between the city walls and the sea, fire-eating dancers, vendors selling candy by the kilo, and other entrepreneurs mingle with strollers taking in the sights. For a visual treat, go to the top of Kamerlengo Fortress at the end of the Riva and take a picture of the lights and action swirling below. See p. 87.

9 The Most Charming Rustic Villages

• **Kumrovec** in the Zagorje region is like a Croatian Williamsburg, Va. with restored cabins and barns furnished as they were when Croatia's most famous son, Josip Broz Tito, was born in the early 20th century. Some of the rustic buildings in this open-air museum contain photos and displays, while others feature docents in traditional costumes who explain weaving, candle making, and some of the crafts of the times. See p. 297.

• **Čigoć** is known as the "Stork Place" because of the long-legged birds that perch atop roofs in this Lonjsko Polje village. The storks are the hook that gets tourists to stop in the middle of the marsh, but the historic cabins and natural surroundings are what keep them there for hours. See p. 317.

• **Štrigova** itself isn't exceptionally rustic, but it is a quaint launching pad for a visit to the surrounding Međimurje region. From here you can explore the rolling vineyards and wineries of northern Croatia. See p. 296.

• **Hlebine** in the north-central part of inland Croatia is home to a colony of nearly 200 painters and sculptors, the country's naive art movement, and Josip and Ivan Generalić, all of whom give it the largest concentration of proponents of naive art in Croatia. Many works from these artists are on display in the town's galleries, one of which is the Generalić home. See p. 320.

10 The Best Cathedrals/Churches

• **Holy Cross Church** (Nin): Holy Cross is the oldest church in Croatia and also the world's smallest cathedral, according to signs posted outside. According to one scientist, the little white stone church is also a giant sun dial and was constructed according to mathematical calculations. See p. 159.

• **Euphrasian Basilica Complex** (Poreč): A must-see sight in this city of superlatives, the UNESCO World Heritage church is the final of four that were built on top of each other. One of its premier attractions is the collection of Byzantine mosaics on display. This is not just one church, but a series of church buildings, each with its own story. See p. 226.

• **St. Donatus** (Zadar): Notable for its unusual shape (circular inside), St. Donatus has a dearth of decoration. The church is no longer used for Mass, but its great acoustics make it a hot venue for classical concerts. Like other churches of its time (9th c.), Donatus is one of several buildings in a clerical complex. See p. 149.

• **Church of St. Mary** (Beram): This chapel in the woods is so small and so remote that you would never notice it if it weren't in a guidebook. But its very remoteness is what protected the eye-popping frescoes that dance on St. Mary's walls. You'll need to pick up one of the church's keepers in Beram and drive to the chapel in the woods so she can unlock it, but it's worth it. See p. 239.

11 The Best Castles

- **Pazin Kaštel** (Istria): One of the best-preserved castles in Istria, this is a surprising "must-see" in the Istrian interior. Pazin Kaštel is built next to one of the scariest-looking gorges ever, a feature that was conveniently utilized as a dumping ground (literally) for enemies of whomever controlled the castle at the time. What may be Croatia's best ethnographic museum is inside. See p. 238.

- **Stari Grad** (Varaždin): The Gothic Renaissance defensive complex includes a castle and the Varaždin Town Museum. As a whole, Stari Grad is one of this baroque town's best attractions. The museum is an excellent showcase for the town's artwork and historical items. Multi-lingual docents are happy to help visitors. See p. 307.

- **Veliki Tabor** (Zagorje Region): North of Zagreb is an imposing, solid brick fortress that looks like the place Rapunzel might have let down her hair. Veliki Tabor has its own legends, including murder, mayhem, and a ghost. While the exterior of the 12th-century structure looks like it could withstand a nuclear attack, the inside is still a ruin in search of renovation. Veliki Tabor was closed for renovation in 2007, so call ahead to see if it's open. See p. 299.

- **Trakošćan Castle** (near Varaždin): North of Zagreb is one of Croatia's most visited sites and one of its most impressive castles—from the outside. The grounds are extensive and the structure itself is everything you'd expect a storybook castle to be—stone walls, turrets, a drawbridge—but inside, renovations have been less than meticulous and sometimes border on the ridiculous. However, Trakošćan is worth the trip if for no other reason than to ponder the plastic deer mounted on the walls outside the entrance. See p. 304.

12 The Best Town Squares

- **The Forum** (Zadar): The city's main square, the Forum is notable for the Roman ruins that lie *in situ* just outside the St. Donatus church complex. The ruins are used daily. Merchants display their wares on what's left of the walls; kids ride their trikes over them; and people sit anywhere. This is the heart of the city. See p. 148.

- **The Peristil** (Split): Once Diocletian's reception room, the Peristil is just inside the Silver Gate. It is perhaps the one spot in what's left of the palace (besides the cellar) where you can grasp the scope of the place and how it looked in its prime. The Peristil is also where Split puts on its famous opera performances during its celebrated summer festival. See p. 88.

- **Forum Square** (Pula): This is the city's center and the site of its second-best Roman ruin, the Temple of Augustus. The 2nd-century B.C. temple is now a museum. Extensively restored after severe damage during World War II, it still is an exceptional example of Roman engineering. See p. 210.

- **Čakovec:** Čakovec's newly renovated town square is home to shops and cafes, a salmon-colored Secessionist-style building, and a conversation-piece fountain that spits arching streams of lighted water at night.

This is a gathering place for the whole town when the sun goes down, and you'll be in the company of families, dogs, couples, and tourists, all enjoying the scene and refreshing night air. See p. 309.

13 The Best Restaurants

- **Valsabbion** (Pula): This is one of those restaurants that defies categorization. It is innovative yet traditional; stylish yet not overly so; a mecca of haute cuisine but not at all intimidating. Valsabbion is a temple to Istrian ingredients and Istrian dishes that are a perfect match for its talented chef. Together they make magic. See p. 215.

- **Mala Hiza** (Mačkovec): This is one of the finest restaurants in the country. The building itself built in 1887 and once stood outside Zagreb—it was later reassembled 4km (2.5 miles) outside Čakovic. The menu is full of creative interpretations of regional Croatian cuisine, and the chef will prepare old-time recipes not on the menu if you call ahead with your request. The surrounding garden is gorgeous, and there is a well-protected non-smoking section, a rarity in Croatia. See p. 311.

- **Zigante** (Livade): Behold truffle king Giancarlo Zigante's gourmet palace. Almost everything on the extensive menu here utilizes the truffle, the precious fungus with which Zigante made his fortune. The restaurant is not a gimmick, however: Everything on the menu is expertly prepared and even flirts with creativity. See p. 245.

- **Gallo** (Zagreb): Tucked in the courtyard of a drab building in downtown Zagreb, Gallo is an oasis of fine dining that relies on freshly made pasta, just-caught fish, a strong wine list, and superb service. Both the terrace and the dining room are perfect settings for the beautiful food. See p. 266.

- **Bitoraj** (Fužine): Bitoraj is a 75-year-old restaurant in a brand new building, which only enhances the dining experience. The menu offers game dishes available nowhere else plus a huge selection of traditional delicacies. From bear and deer ham to Bitoraj's signature dish of young wild boars baked under a lid on an open fire (peka), all dishes utilize the best ingredients the surrounding woods can offer.

- **Porat** (Dubrovnik): The Hilton Imperial's signature restaurant offers a menu that pushes the creativity envelope. The food is Dalmatian fare with complex sauces and side dishes that surprise you. Both the dining room and the piano bar (which serves light snacks) are very sophisticated spaces. See p. 71.

- **Riblji Restaurant Foša** (Zadar): Foša has one of the best locations in Croatia. It is right at the water outside the Zadar wall and it has a view and sea breeze that make the food taste that much better. The restaurant is a favorite hangout for locals. See p. 153.

- **Palača Paladini** (Hvar Town): This restaurant appeals to all five senses: It is set in a beautiful garden with blooming lavender and orange trees frequented by songbirds. It has a great list of wines and it offers superb Dalmatian cuisine that tastes as good as it smells and looks. See p. 117.

2

Planning Your Trip to Croatia

Croatia is generously endowed with natural and man-made wonders, a rich culture cache, a complicated history, and people who are warm and welcoming. It is a European destination like no other.

1 The Regions in Brief

There are many ways to designate Croatia's regions—coastal and inland, islands and mainland, northern and southern—but the best way to get a feel for the country's geography is to look at each destination from several perspectives.

DALMATIAN COAST Croatia's Dalmatian Coast is characterized by extremes. From **Zadar** in the north to **Dubrovnik** in the south, the terrain that rolls westward toward the sea from the rugged Dinaric mountain range is a sun-washed, 3-D mosaic of red-tiled roofs, graceful bell towers, lush vegetation, and shimmering beaches. The region is a repository of history with very visible Roman and Venetian influences plus a mild Mediterranean climate that supports a thriving fishing industry, an agricultural economy rich in olives and grapes, and tourism. Offshore, Croatia's islands (1,185) lure boating and water sports enthusiasts, sun worshipers, celebrities, and ordinary visitors who just want to get away from it all.

The eastern side of the Dinaric range is a world away from the glitzy coast in terrain and personality. Inland Dalmatia is a mix of stark, rocky hills and verdant valleys, a sparse local population, and few tourists. This is an area that has not recovered from being on the front line during the 1991 Homeland War.

INLAND CROATIA Inland Croatia is home to a melting-pot of cultures. Each is distinct, but each is unmistakably Croatian. The country's largest city, **Zagreb,** is a thriving inland metropolis of nearly one million people. Zagreb is the economic and political center of Croatia and it is a gateway to spectacular natural wonders in southern Croatia and to the hilly wine-growing regions in the north. The extreme northern part of the country is home to many Hapsburg-inspired towns and castles set at regular intervals across the rolling farmland east of Zagreb all the way to the Danube River and the border. The expanse east of Zagreb is Croatia's breadbasket and it is characterized by historic towns and villages that have been fought over for centuries, especially during the 1991 war.

ISTRIA Istria is a peninsula in Croatia's northwest corner that hangs into the northern Adriatic. It is the part of the country that abuts Western Europe, and its identity is complex thanks to cultural osmosis and a long history of occupation by Romans, Venetians, Austro-Hungarians, Italians, and Yugoslavs. Part of Istria's charm is due to its occupiers' foresight in letting the region's coastal towns and interior medieval settlements retain their personalities through the centuries. These places still possess unique architecture and customs that draw visitors from both

Croatia

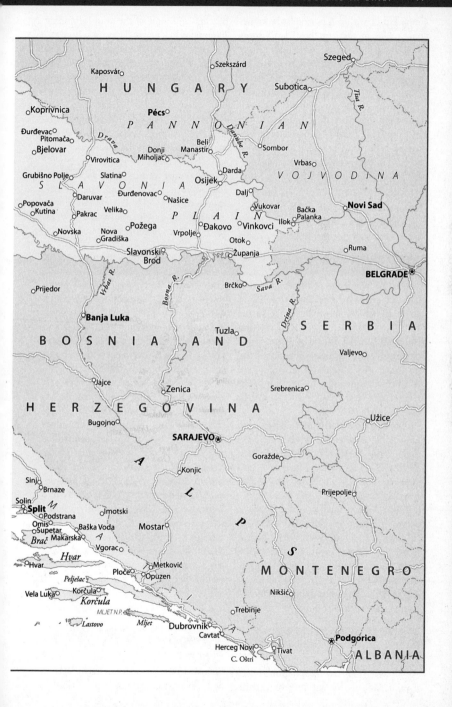

outside and within Croatia. Istria knows how to be an excellent host and visitors have been flocking to its seaside resorts and Roman ruins from western Europe—and now from everywhere—for more than a century. Istria also has a reputation as one of Croatia's gastronomic capitals thanks to the wines produced in its vineyards, the rich supply of truffles found in its forests, and the refined cuisine served in its restaurants, a mix that reflects the region's cultural past and optimistic future.

KVARNER GULF   The **Kvarner Gulf** lies between Istria and northern Dalmatia, and includes a mélange of stark island landscapes, sophisticated resorts, excellent beaches, and some of the most forbidding mountains in Croatia. The area is home to Croatia's largest islands and its biggest resorts. Rijeka, Croatia's busiest port and one of the country's biggest transportation hubs is here, as is Opatija, one of the country's most developed holiday cities. The Kvarner islands of Krk, Cres, Losinj, Rab, and Pag are easily accessed from Rijeka and other points on the mainland, which insures that they are especially busy with tourists during the summer months. Croatia's unpredictable wild and wooly northeastern wind *(bura)* is the only deterrent to enjoying this part of the country. When the *bura* blows, tourists flee.

2 Visitor Information

The home Web page of the **Republic of Croatia** (www.hr/index.en.shtml) offers potential visitors numerous links to the country's attractions. The **Croatian National Tourist Board website,** www.croatia.hr, contributes specifics about trip planning, with a focus on transportation and accommodations. In addition, each region, city, and most towns have their own websites.

The **Croatian National Tourist Board** has a U.S. office at 350 Fifth Ave., Suite 4003, New York, NY 10118 (© **212/279-8672**); and a U.K. office at 2 Lanchesters, 162–164 Fulham Palace Rd., London W6 9ER (© **020/8563-7979**).

Dubrovnik's tourist office (www.tz dubrovnik.hr) is located at Ante Starčevića 7, © **020/427-591. Zagreb** maintains several tourist offices. The most centrally located (www.zagreb-touristinfo.hr) is at Trg Jelačaća 11, © **01/48-14-051. Istria** maintains an extensive tourism network with links to individual towns' pages. Go to www.istra.hr for info and connections to the town sites. The website for **Adriatica** (www.adriatica.net) not only gives information on places and events, but also has links to hotels, restaurants, sports agencies, boat and car rental agencies, and tour companies.

The Croatian National Tourist Board, www.croatia.hr can supply a free, decent tourist road map published by HAK (Hvratski Auto Klub), but for more detailed maps, go to Amazon.com where you can get Michelin's *"Slovenia, Croatia, Bosnia And Herzegovina, Serbia, Montenegro, Yugoslava. Republic Of Macedonia"* for about $10. Rand-McNally also stocks Croatia maps in its nearly 3 dozen stores across the U.S. Check www.rand mcnally.com for the store nearest you. *Tip:* Algoritam bookstores and every large supermarket in Croatia sell fine region-specific maps for about $6 each and tourist offices in almost every city and town provide free city-specific maps.

3 Entry Requirements

PASSPORTS

All foreign (non-Croatian) nationals need a valid passport for entrance to Croatia. Citizens of the U.S., U.K., Australia, Canada, New Zealand, Israel, Ireland, and Singapore do not need visas for

Tips   Destination Croatia: Pre-Departure Checklist

- If you plan to attend a summer festival performance in Split or Dubrovnik or at the Pula amphitheater, it is a good idea to secure tickets in advance. Space is limited, and these events are very popular. Go to the following websites for information: **Pula**: www.histriafestival.com; **Split**: www.splitsko-ljeto.hr; and **Dubrovnik**: www.dubrovnik-festival.hr for details.

- Always call ahead for attraction opening and closing times. Almost everything on the coast is open with extended hours during July and August, but if you visit any other time, be sure to check specific opening and closing times. Sometimes on-site impromptu hours will be posted that contradict published schedules.

- Call your bank card and bank representatives before heading to Croatia to let them know you will be using credit cards and ATM cards out of the country. Almost every village in the Croatia has at least one ATM and credit cards are accepted at most upscale hotels and restaurants. You will need cash for private accommodations and at smaller restaurants and shops.

- Know your PIN numbers. Most ATMs accept credit cards, ATM cards, and debit cards for cash withdrawals and most have an English option in the onscreen instructions. Note: Croatian ATMs accept 4-digit PIN numbers exclusively, so convert any 5- or 6-digit PINs to that format before you travel.

- Hostilities in Croatia ended in 1995, but removal of land mines from areas along the fronts is not complete. Be sure you know how to recognize land mine warning signs, especially in eastern Slavonia, eastern Dalmatia, and in the Zadar region.

tourist/business trips of fewer than 90 days within a 6-month period. For a stay over 90 days, a visa is required and should be obtained in advance. South Africans do require a visa. For more information on visas, go to **www.croatiaemb.org**. For U.S. citizens: Go to "Passports" in the "Fast Facts: Croatia" section, later in this chapter—the websites listed provide downloadable passport applications as well as the current fees for processing passport applications. For an up-to-date country-by-country listing of passport requirements around the world, go to the "Foreign Entry Requirement" Web page of the U.S. State Department at **http://travel.state.gov**.

CUSTOMS
WHAT YOU CAN BRING INTO CROATIA

Foreign visitors can bring in foreign currency in any amount, but you must declare in writing anything above 40,000kn ($7,400). Local currency is limited to 15,000kn ($2,800). Visitors also may bring in 200 cigarettes, 1 liter of spirits, 2 liters of wine, and 2 liters of liqueur duty-free. Foreign visitors can bring in boats without duty or taxes for private use while in Croatia as long as they take them home when they leave.

WHAT YOU CAN TAKE HOME FROM CROATIA

Returning **U.S. citizens** who have been away for at least 48 hours are allowed to bring back, once every 30 days, $800 worth of merchandise duty-free. You'll be charged a flat rate of duty on the next $1,000 worth of purchases. Any dollar amount beyond that is dutiable at whatever rates apply. On mailed gifts, the duty-free limit is $200. Be sure to have your receipts or purchases handy to expedite the declaration process. *Note:* If you owe duty, you are required to pay on your arrival in the United States, by cash, personal check, government or traveler's check, or money order, and in some locations, by Visa or MasterCard.

To avoid paying duty on foreign-made personal items you owned before you left on your trip, bring along a bill of sale, insurance policy, jeweler's appraisal, or receipts of purchase. Or you can register items that can be readily identified by permanently affixed serial numbers or markings—think laptop computers, cameras, and CD players—with Customs before you leave. Take the items to the nearest Customs office or register them with Customs at the airport from which you're departing. You'll receive, at no cost, a Certificate of Registration, which allows duty-free entry for the life of each item.

With few exceptions, you cannot bring fresh fruits and vegetables into the United States. For specifics on what you can bring back, download the invaluable free pamphlet *Know Before You Go* online at **www.cbp.gov**. (Click on "Travel," and then click on "Know Before You Go! Online Brochure.") Or contact the **U.S. Customs & Border Protection (CBP)**, 1300 Pennsylvania Ave. NW, Washington, DC 20229 (© **877/287-8667**) and request the pamphlet.

For a clear summary of **Canadian** rules, write for the booklet *I Declare,* issued by the **Canada Border Services Agency** (© **800/461-9999** in Canada, or 204/983-3500; www.cbsa-asfc.gc.ca). Canada allows its citizens a C$750 exemption, and they are allowed to bring back, duty-free, one carton of cigarettes, 1 can of tobacco, 40 imperial ounces of liquor, and 50 cigars. In addition, mailed gifts to Canada valued at less than C$60 a day are allowed, provided they're unsolicited and don't contain alcohol or tobacco. (Write on the package: "Unsolicited gift, under $60 value.") All valuables should be declared on the Y-38 form before departure from Canada, including serial numbers of valuables you already own, such as expensive foreign cameras. *Note:* The C$750 exemption can be used only once a year and only after an absence of 7 days.

U.K. citizens returning from a **non-E.U. country** have a Customs allowance of 200 cigarettes; 50 cigars; 250 grams of smoking tobacco; 2 liters of still table wine; 1 liter of spirits or strong liqueurs (over 22% alcohol by volume); 2 liters of fortified wine, sparkling wine, or other liqueurs; 60cc (ml) perfume; 250cc (ml) toilet water; and £145 worth of all other goods, including gifts and souvenirs. People under 17 cannot have the tobacco or alcohol allowance. For more information, contact HM Customs & Excise at © **0845/010-9000** (from outside the U.K., © 020/8929-0152), or consult their website at **www.hmce.gov.uk**.

The duty-free allowance in **Australia** is A$400 or, for those under 18, A$200. Citizens can bring in 250 cigarettes or 250 grams of loose tobacco, and 1,125 milliliters of alcohol. If you're returning with valuables you already own, such as foreign-made cameras, you should file form B263. A helpful brochure available from Australian consulates or Customs offices is *Know Before You Go.* For more information, call the **Australian Customs Service** at © **1300/363-263**, or log on to **www.customs.gov.au**.

The duty-free allowance for **New Zealand** is NZ$700. Citizens over 17 can bring in 200 cigarettes, 50 cigars, or 250 grams of tobacco (or a mixture of all three if their combined weight doesn't exceed 250g); plus 4.5 liters of wine and beer, or 1.125 liters of liquor. New Zealand currency does not carry import or export restrictions. Fill out a certificate of export, listing the valuables you are taking out of the country; that way, you can bring them back without paying duty. Most questions are answered in a free pamphlet available at New Zealand consulates and Customs offices: *New Zealand Customs Guide for Travellers, Notice no. 4.* For more information, contact **New Zealand Customs,** The Customhouse, 17–21 Whitmore St., Box 2218, Wellington (© **04/473-6099** or 0800/428-786; www.customs.govt.nz).

For further information on what you can bring into and take out of Croatia, go to "**Customs**" in the "**Fast Facts**" section of this chapter.

4 When to Go

WEATHER

Summer, specifically July and August, is the busiest time on the Croatian coast and on the islands. This is Croatia's "season," a time when the sun is the hottest, the sea the bluest, and traffic endless. The coast is at its best—and worst—during midsummer. Hotel room rates top out; restaurant tables are always full, and crowds can be overwhelming. This is the period that makes or breaks many Croatian businesses that depend on tourism for a year's income, and it can be tough on unsuspecting travelers.

Much of the madness is due to traditional European July and August vacation schedules which coincide with the Croatian coast's glorious summer weather.

Weather in Croatia generally can be divided into two mini-climates. Northern Croatia has a Continental climate, with average temperatures ranging from near freezing in January to about 70°F (21°C) in August. The coastal areas have a more Mediterranean climate, with average temperatures ranging from the mid-40s in January to near 100°F (38°C) in August. Spring and autumn are pleasant and mild along the coast; winter inland can be cold and snowy.

The bottom line is that in July and August, good weather is almost a certainty and tourism is in full swing, but prices and availability on the coast can be prohibitive. Conversely, in the interior, crowds are minimal and prices can reach their lowest levels in summer. Zagreb and other interior cities can be real bargains then because many residents will be on the coast. However, that means many Zagreb restaurants and shops may be closed. A word of warning: The weather on the coast is usually nice, the sea warm, and prices lower in May, June, September, and October, but some establishments, especially those on the islands, might be shuttered and some ferry routes might be canceled or on reduced schedules.

Croatia's Average Temperatures (°F/°C)

Interior	Jan	Feb	Mar	Apr	May	June	July	Aug	Sept	Oct	Nov	Dec
High	38/3	43/6	52/11	61/16	70/21	76/24	79/26	77/25	70/21	59/15	49/9	40/4
Low	29/-2	32/0	38/3	47/8	54/12	58/14	61/16	61/16	56/13	47/8	38/3	31/-1
Coastal												
High	50/10	52/11	56/13	63/17	72/22	79/26	85/29	85/29	77/25	68/20	58/14	52/11
Low	41/5	43/6	45/7	52/11	59/15	65/18	70/21	70/21	65/18	58/14	49/9	43/6

CALENDAR OF EVENTS

The festivals mentioned in this section, unless otherwise specified, fall on different dates every year. Inquire at the Croatian National Tourist Office (www.croatia.hr) or at local tourist offices for event contact information and for an updated calendar.

January

Old Christmas: On January 7, Croatians who follow Eastern Orthodox rules celebrate Christmas and take a day off from work.

February

Rijeka Carnival: This pre-Lenten celebration begins in mid-February and ends at midnight on Shrove Tuesday. It is celebrated all over the country, lavishly so in Rijeka (and Samobor) with parades, masquerades, and merrymaking similar to those of New Orleans's Mardi Gras.

Feast of St. Blaise: This day is celebrated by Catholics all over the world with the blessing of throats in honor of St. Blaise. In Dubrovnik, there is also a parade and lots of eating and drinking in the name of the city's patron saint.

March

Vukovar Puppet Festival: During the last week of March, this city in eastern Croatia becomes a venue for puppet shows, workshops, and demonstrations.

April

Biennale: An international festival of contemporary music, Biennale is held in April in odd-numbered years in Zagreb. Contemporary classical musicians are the focus. For more information, go to www.biennale-zagreb.hr.

May

Dubrovnik International Film Festival: The annual cinema festival showcases the work of Croatian filmmakers as well as internationally produced films. Showings are in theaters across the city in late May.

One-Minute Movie Cup: Požega in east-central Croatia is the setting for screenings of these obviously short, usually avant-garde films, which are shown the last weekend in May.

1,001 Delights: Split hosts an annual 2-day food festival at the end of May that includes workshops, tastings, and exhibits related to Croatian cuisine. Go to www.1001delicija.com for details.

June

International Children's Festival: Šibenik is home to this annual festival, which encourages creativity in children. Programs showcasing youthful talents are presented in venues across the city from mid-June to early July.

Contemporary Dance Week: Zagreb is the main stage for this dance and choreography showcase held in the first week of June, but there are parallel events in Rijeka and Zadar.

Histria Festival: Pula Amphitheater is a magnificent venue for open-air concerts. Big names in pop, opera, and dance sign up for this cultural series, which runs from late June to early September. Go to www.histriafestival.com for dates and info.

July

Rab Festival: Every year for a week at the end of July, the island of Rab goes medieval with a costumed festival celebrating the customs, traditional crafts, and lifestyles of that era. The festival begins in the afternoon daily during this week and lasts until after midnight.

Motovun Film Festival: This tiny medieval town in the heart of Istria hosts an annual film festival in late July to celebrate independent films. Go to www.motovunfilmfestival.com for more information.

Split Summer Festival: From mid-July to mid-August, the Split Summer Festival takes over the city's historic core with exhibitions, concerts, dance, theater, and especially opera performed in the Peristil of Diocletian's former palace.

Dubrovnik Summer Festival: Well-known artists from all over the world perform during this annual event, which takes place from early July to late August. This summer festival, dubbed "Libertas," has taken place every year—even during wartime—since 1950.

International Folklore Festival: For a week in mid-July, Zagreb comes alive with dancing, song, musical performances, workshops, and exhibitions that celebrate Croatia's cultural heritage.

Extreme Sports Festival: Brač is known for its fine windsurfing and that's just one of the competitions held during the island's weeklong Extreme Sports Festival near Supetar. Take the half hour ferry ride from Split and besides windsurfing, you can see athletes vie for medals in skateboarding, rock climbing, dirt bike riding, and diving. Go to www.sutivan.hr for more information.

Zagreb Baroque Festival: As part of its Summer Nights series, Zagreb includes almost 30 baroque concerts at venues around the city, including concerts at Zagreb Cathedral. Go to www.kdz.hr for more information.

August

Street Art Festival Poreč: For 10 days in August, the streets of Poreč become a stage for music and dance performances, and a gallery for clowns, acrobats, and jugglers. The annual event starts the second week of August. Go to www.porec.hr for more information.

International Puppet Festival: European ensembles demonstrate their puppetry skills in venues all over Zagreb during this festival, which occurs at the end of August. Go to www.srce.hr/piffestival for more information.

Grisia Street Art Festival: For one glorious week, Rovinj's "art street" becomes an indoor-outdoor gallery. Anyone can set up shop at this time and the narrow, cobbled street is crammed with browsers and artists until the wee hours. Go to www.tzgrovinj.hr/eng/home.asp for more information.

Zadar Dreams Festival: The second week of August is a time for whimsy in Zadar. Admission to events is free for anyone into alternative drama or performance art. For more information go to www.zadarsnova.hr.

September

Varaždin Festival of Baroque Music: Listen to baroque music in one of Europe's most baroque cities through early October. Performances are mostly in Varaždin's churches. Go to www.vbv.hr for more information.

Zagreb International Trade Fair: You won't be able to get into this huge fair without credentials, but you won't be able to get a hotel room in Zagreb during the second week of September when the trade fair is in town, either.

October

Marunada (Chestnut Festival): For three weekends in October, the tiny town of Lovran near Opatija in the Kvarner region celebrates everything chestnut-related with food, merrymaking, and even cook-offs, all in honor of the chestnut and its many culinary uses.

International Jazz Days: Zagreb is host for this fall jazz festival, one of two (the other is in spring) yearly events. Go to www.jazz.hr for more information.

November

Martinje (St. Martin's Day): Besides being a church feast day, November 11 is also the day when the new wine is blessed and "tested" in unlimited amounts. The ceremony, conducted in almost all grape-growing regions of

Croatia, begins with a song in honor of St. Martin and ends with a prayer for a good year for all. If possible, the blessing is in a vineyard, but wherever it is held, it is followed by a party that includes eating, drinking, and singing well into the night. Most Croatian restaurants mark the occasion by offering special dinners (much as the French do when celebrating the *nouveau Beaujolais*).

Comic Book Festival: Anime and comic book aficionados will enjoy this weekend celebration of cartoons and music in Zagreb. Go to www.crs-festival.com for more information.

December

St. Nicholas Day: Komiža on the island of Vis honors the town's patron saint on December 6, his feast day, with a huge party that opens with the burning of an old fishing boat in front of St. Nicholas Church. Go to www.dalmatia.hr for more information.

New Year's Regatta: This event from December 28 to December 31 features wild small-boat races off the island of Hvar.

For an exhaustive list of events beyond those listed here, check http://events.frommers.com, where you'll find a searchable, up-to-the-minute roster of what's happening in cities all over the world.

5 Getting There

BY PLANE

Croatia Air (© 385/1487-2727; www.croatiaairlines.hr) flies to and from many of the major cities of Europe, among them Amsterdam, Berlin, Brussels, Dusseldorf, Frankfurt, Moscow, Munich, Paris, Prague, Rome, Sarajevo, and Vienna.

A number of Europe's discount carriers, such as Ryanair, Easyjet, and SkyEurope, serve Croatia via smaller European cities such as Venice. For details, see specific destination chapters.

ARRIVING AT THE AIRPORT

Airport security procedures at most U.S. terminals are more stable and consistent than ever. Generally, you'll be fine if you arrive at the airport **1 hour** before a domestic flight and **2 hours** before an international flight; if you show up late, tell an airline employee, who probably will whisk you to the front of the line.

Bring a **current, government-issued photo ID** such as a driver's license or passport. Keep your ID at the ready to show at check-in, at the security checkpoint, and sometimes even at the gate. (Children under 18 do not need government-issued photo IDs for domestic flights, but they do for international flights to most countries.)

In 2003, the Transportation Security Administration (TSA) phased out **gate check-in** at all U.S. airports. And **e-tickets** have made paper tickets nearly obsolete. Passengers with e-tickets can beat the ticket-counter lines by using airport **electronic kiosks** or even **online check-in** from their home computers. Online check-in involves logging on to your airline's website, accessing your reservation, and printing out your boarding pass—and the airline may even offer you bonus miles to do so! If you're using a kiosk at the airport, bring the credit card with which you booked the ticket, or bring your frequent-flier card. Print out your boarding pass from the kiosk and proceed to the security checkpoint with your pass and a photo ID. If you're checking bags or looking to snag an exit-row seat, you will be able to do so using most airline kiosks. Even the smaller airlines are employing the kiosk system, but always call your airline to make sure these alternatives are available. **Curbside check-in** is a good way to avoid lines, although a few airlines ban curbside check-in; call before you go.

Security checkpoint lines vary in length from country to country and from airport to airport. If you have trouble standing for long periods of time, tell an airline employee; the airline will provide a wheelchair. Speed up security by **not wearing metal objects** such as big belt buckles. If you have metallic body parts, a note from your doctor can prevent a long chat with the security screeners. Keep in mind that only **ticketed passengers** are allowed past security, except for folks escorting passengers with disabilities, or children.

Federalization has stabilized **what you can carry on** and **what you can't.** The rules keep changing, but in general sharp things such as knives are out, nail clippers are okay, and food and beverages must be purchased AFTER you clear security. Liquids are limited to 3-ounce containers that fit in one, 1-quart plastic bag. Keep this bag outside your suitcase to show screeners as you pass through security. *Note:* In Croatia, battery-operated devices equipped with working batteries are not allowed in checked luggage, so take out that alarm clock before you check your bag. Otherwise, you may waste valuable time scrambling to repack those items in your carry-on luggage.

Bring food in your carry-on rather than check it in, as explosive-detection machines used on checked luggage have been known to mistake food (especially chocolate, for some reason) for bombs. Travelers in the U.S. are allowed one carry-on bag, plus a "personal item" such as a purse, briefcase, or laptop computer bag. Carry-on hoarders can stuff all sorts of things into a laptop bag; as long as it has a laptop in it, it's considered a personal item. The TSA has issued a list of restricted items; check its website (www.tsa.gov/public/index.jsp) for details.

Airport screeners may decide that your checked luggage needs to be searched by hand. You can now purchase luggage locks that allow screeners to open and re-lock a checked bag if hand-searching is necessary. Look for Travel Sentry certified locks at luggage or travel shops and Brookstone stores (you can buy them online at www.brookstone.com). These locks, approved by the TSA, can be opened by luggage inspectors with a special code or key. For more information on the locks, visit www.travelsentry.org. If you use something other than TSA-approved locks, your lock will be cut off your suitcase if a TSA agent needs to hand-search your luggage.

BY CAR

The highways that connect Croatia to its neighbors (Slovenia, Hungary, Bosnia and Hercegovina, and Serbia-Montenegro) are good and getting better as miles of new pavement are poured. This is especially true of the span between Ljubljana and Zagreb, a route that takes just 2 hours to complete. The route from Budapest to Zagreb running across Croatia's northern border is also popular. It takes about 5 hours to reach Zagreb (362km/225 miles) from the Hungarian capital.

Visitors coming from Italy and Austria must pass through Slovenia to get to Croatia's border, but Slovenia's roads are excellent, too.

In addition, the E.U. countries that abut Croatia (Slovenia, Hungary) anticipate subscribing to the Schengen protocol, under which internal borders among E.U. countries are dissolved. Croatia is in the process of applying for E.U. membership, which could put the country in the Schengen territory and make crossing national lines seamless.

But even if border checks disappear, you should always have your passport, insurance card, and any rental car papers (including the car's registration) available when you travel through Europe. This is especially true if you are traveling through Serbia or Montenegro, countries that are not yet in the E.U. membership pipeline.

Car rental: Car rental in Croatia is expensive, and it can be tricky. Even if you use a global agency like Hertz or Avis, it is best to reserve a car by contacting a local agency branch in the city where you plan to rent rather than through the agency's parent company.

In our experience, on two occasions, car rental companies at the Zagreb airport had "no record" of our reservation and we had to rebook on the spot at a higher rate. We also witnessed the "we-have-no-record" scenario played out with a couple from Italy who had prepaid for the car via an Italian travel agency.

It is a good idea to take the "full insurance" package offered with your car rental even though it can add considerable cost to your rental. You will be given a chance to inspect your vehicle with your car rental rep, and you should be certain he documents any existing scratches or other damage before you take the keys. Any dings incurred thereafter, not to mention major damage, will be charged to you at full rate. *Note:* Most cars rented in Croatia are stick shift. Vehicles with automatic transmissions are scarce and you will pay extra if you need this feature.

Warning: In most cases, liability coverage from your domestic auto insurance policy **will not** cover you on vehicles rented outside the U.S. That is also true of the auto coverage that comes with most major bank cards. Check with your insurance agent and credit card companies to be sure.

BY TRAIN

Trains connect all major Croatian cities north of Split. There is no train service to cities between Split and Dubrovnik in southern Dalmatia.

The country does have convenient railway links with Slovenia, Hungary, Italy, Austria, Switzerland, Slovakia, France, Germany, and Bosnia and Hercegovina. The railway links to and from other European countries can be extremely time-consuming. The train ride from Paris to Zagreb, for example, takes 18-plus hours, while a rail trip from Frankfurt to Split will take almost 24 hours. If you must get to Croatia from another European city by rail, check schedules, fares, and details on rail passes at **Rail Europe,** www.raileurope.com. For trains within Croatia, check **Croatia Railways,** www.hznet.hr.

BY FERRY

There are four ferry lines with regular service from Bari, Ancona, Pescara, and Venice in Italy to major ports in Croatia. Several other lines operate seasonal routes. In most cases, you hop on a cruise ship after 9pm and arrive in Croatia just as the sun is rising. Routes, fares, schedules, and booking information for all ferry lines listed below are available at www.cemar.it.

Jadrolinija: Croatia's national ferry line has three international routes. Jadrolinija ships travel twice a week between Ancona and Zadar and Ancona and Split in central Dalmatia and once a week between Bari and Dubrovnik. Round-trip deck passage for two adults without a vehicle runs 74€ ($104) for the overnight trip between Bari and Dubrovnik, while the fare on the same route for two in an external cabin with toilet plus a vehicle runs 419€ ($587). Prices are the same for Ancona-Split and slightly less for Ancona-Zadar.

Blue Line International: This ferry line has daily overnight service between Ancona and Split. Round-trip deck accommodations for two without a vehicle run 176€ ($246) while a deluxe cabin for two with a vehicle runs 594€ ($832) round-trip during the summer. Weekend departures from late July through late August are even higher as a 25% surcharge is added to the bill if you travel Friday to Sunday at that time and a 50% surcharge is added if you travel alone in a double cabin.

In addition to the ferry options above, **SNAV** operates several "express" routes between Italy and Croatia, and it is the only international connection to popular Hvar Island. The SNAV Hvar "Jet" catamaran service departs from Pescara, Italy, and deposits passengers at Hvar's Stari Grad port. The trip takes about 3½ hours, but service is seasonal (mid-June through early Sept). A round-trip between Pescara and Hvar for two costs 366€ ($512).

Prices and schedule information are available from April through September on the cemar.hr website (above).

Last, **Venezia Lines** travels between Venice in Italy and cities such as Rovinj, Poreč, and Pula on Istria's western coast. Current schedule and fare information is available at the website listed above or at www.venezialines.com from April through September.

6 Money & Costs

It's always advisable to bring money in a variety of forms on a vacation: a mix of cash, credit cards, and traveler's checks. You should also exchange enough petty cash to cover airport incidentals, tipping, and transportation to your hotel before you leave home, or withdraw money upon arrival at an airport ATM.

In many international destinations, ATMs offer the best exchange rates. Avoid exchanging money at commercial exchange bureaus and hotels, which often have the highest transaction fees.

CURRENCY

The Croatian national currency is the kuna, which is made up of 100 lipa. With Croatia's anticipated E.U. membership in process, many Croatian businesses are beginning to express their prices in euros and kuna, though euros are not yet widely accepted. Foreign currency can be exchanged at post offices, banks, and exchange offices. Numerous hotels and travel agencies also will exchange currency, but beware of the service charges, which can be as high as 3%. To convert prices in kunas to prices in U.S. dollars, go to www.xe.com/ucc.

ATMs

The easiest and best way to get cash away from home is from an ATM (automated teller machine, aka Bankomat in Croatia). The **Cirrus** (© 800/424-7787; www.mastercard.com) and **PLUS**

(© 800/843-7587; www.visa.com) networks span the globe; look at the back of your bank card to see which network you're on, then call or check online for ATM locations at your destination. Be sure you know your personal identification number (PIN) before you leave home, and be sure to find out your daily withdrawal limit before you depart. Also keep in mind that many banks impose a fee every time a card is used at another bank's ATM, and that fee can be higher for international transactions ($5 or more) than for domestic ones (where they're rarely more than $3). On top of this, the bank from which you withdraw cash may charge its own fee. To compare banks' ATM fees within the U.S., use www.bankrate.com. For international withdrawal fees, ask your bank.

TRAVELER'S CHECKS

Traveler's checks are something of an anachronism from the days before the ATM made cash so easily accessible. Traveler's checks used to be the only sound alternative to traveling with large amounts of cash. They were as reliable as currency but unlike cash, they could be replaced if lost or stolen.

These days, traveler's checks are less necessary because most cities have 24-hour ATMs that allow withdrawals of small amounts of cash as needed. However, keep in mind that you will likely be charged an ATM withdrawal fee if the bank is not your own, so if you're withdrawing money every day, you might be better off with traveler's checks—provided that you don't mind showing identification every time you want to cash one.

You can get traveler's checks at almost any bank. **American Express** offers denominations of $20, $50, $100, $500, and (for cardholders only) $1,000. You'll pay a service charge ranging from 1% to 4%. You can also get American Express traveler's checks over the phone by calling ℭ **800/221-7282;** Amex gold and platinum cardholders who use this number are exempt from the 1% fee.

Visa offers traveler's checks at Citibank locations nationwide, as well as at several other banks. The service charge ranges between 1.5% and 2%; checks come in denominations of $20, $50, $100, $500, and $1,000. Call ℭ **800/732-1322** for information. American Automobile Association (AAA) members can obtain Visa checks for a $9.95 fee (for checks up to $1,500) at most AAA offices or by calling ℭ **866/339-3378. MasterCard** also offers traveler's checks. Call ℭ **800/223-9920** for a location near you.

Foreign currency traveler's checks are useful if you're traveling to one country, or to the euro zone; they're accepted at locations such as bed-and-breakfasts where dollar checks may not be, and they minimize the amount of math you have to do at your destination. **American Express, Thomas Cook, Visa,** and **MasterCard** offer foreign currency traveler's checks. You'll pay the rate of exchange at the time of your purchase (so it's a good idea to monitor the rate before you take the plunge), and most companies charge a transaction fee per check order (and a shipping fee if you order online).

If you choose to carry traveler's checks, be sure to keep a record of their serial numbers separate from your checks in the event that they are stolen or lost. You'll get a refund faster if you know the numbers.

Another option is the new prepaid traveler's check cards, reloadable cards that work much like debit cards but aren't linked to your checking account. The **American Express Travelers Cheque Card,** for example, requires a minimum deposit, sets a maximum balance, and has a one-time issuance fee of $14.95. You can withdraw money from an ATM (for a fee of $2.50 per transaction, not including bank fees), and the funds can be purchased in dollars, euros, or pounds. If you lose the card, your available funds will be refunded within 24 hours.

CREDIT CARDS

Credit cards are a safe way to carry money: They provide a convenient record of all your expenses, and they generally offer relatively good exchange rates. In Croatia, credit cards are accepted by most hotels and restaurants in larger cities, but they generally are not accepted for private accommodations or in rural areas. In addition, some establishments that accept credit cards will offer a discount if you pay in cash. You can withdraw cash advances from your credit cards at banks or ATMs, provided you know your PIN. If you've forgotten your PIN, or didn't even know you had one, call the number on the back of your credit card and ask the bank to send it to you. It usually takes 5 to 7 business days, though some banks will provide the number over the phone if you tell them your mother's maiden name or some other personal information. Keep in mind that when you use your credit card abroad, most banks assess a 2% fee above the 1% fee charged by Visa or MasterCard or American Express for currency conversion on credit charges. But credit cards still may be the smart way to go when you factor in things like exorbitant ATM fees and higher traveler's-check exchange rates (and service fees).

Visa, MasterCard, Diners Club, and American Express credit cards are accepted in most Croatian establishments that accept plastic. The Maestro debit card is also widely accepted.

The Croatian Kuna

For American readers At this writing, $1 = 5.4kn (or 1kn = approximately 19¢), and this was the rate of exchange used to calculate the dollar values given in this guidebook.

For British readers At this writing, 1kn = approximately 0.09 British pounds and £1 = 10.71kn. This was the rate of exchange used to calculate the pound values in the chart below.

Regarding the euro At this writing, 1€ = $1.40 or 7.3kn. Many Croatian establishments express their prices in both euros and kunas for the convenience of European tourists.

For the latest on exchange rates, you can go online to **www.xe.com**.

kn	US$	UK£	euro
1	0.19	0.10	0.14
2	0.37	0.19	0.27
3	0.56	0.29	0.41
4	0.74	0.38	0.55
5	0.93	0.48	0.68
6	1.11	0.57	0.82
7	1.30	0.67	0.96
8	1.48	0.76	1.10
9	1.67	0.86	1.23
10	1.85	0.95	1.37
15	2.78	1.43	2.05
20	3.70	1.90	2.74
25	4.63	2.38	3.42
50	9.26	4.76	6.85
75	13.89	7.14	10.27
100	18.52	9.52	13.72
125	23.15	11.90	17.12
150	27.78	14.29	20.55
175	32.41	16.67	23.97
200	37.04	19.05	27.40
225	41.67	21.43	30.82
250	46.30	23.81	34.25
275	50.93	26.19	37.67
300	55.56	28.57	41.10
350	64.81	33.33	47.95
400	74.07	38.10	54.79
500	92.59	47.62	68.49
1,000	185.19	95.24	136.99

7 Travel Insurance

Check your existing insurance policies and credit card coverage before you buy travel insurance. You already may be covered for lost luggage, canceled tickets, or medical expenses. Be sure to examine limitations in the coverage carefully to be sure it covers international travel.

The cost of travel insurance varies widely, depending on the destination, the cost and length of your trip, your age and health, and the type of trip you're taking, but expect to pay between 5% and 8% of the vacation itself. You can get estimates from various providers through **Insure-MyTrip.com.** Enter your trip cost and dates, your age, and other information, for prices from more than a dozen companies.

U.K. citizens and their families who make more than one trip abroad per year may find an annual travel insurance policy works out cheaper. Check **www.money supermarket.com,** which compares prices across numerous providers for single- and multi-trip policies.

Most big travel agents offer their own insurance and will probably try to sell you their package when you book a holiday. Think before you sign. **Britain's Consumers' Association** recommends that you insist on seeing the policy and reading the fine print before buying travel insurance. **The Association of British Insurers** (© 020/7600-3333; www.abi.org.uk) gives advice by phone and publishes *Holiday Insurance,* a free guide to policy provisions and prices. You can

shop around for better deals: Try **Columbus Direct** (© 0870/033-9988; www.columbusdirect.net).

MEDICAL INSURANCE

For travel overseas, most U.S. health plans (including Medicare and Medicaid) do not provide coverage, and the ones that do often require you to pay for services upfront and reimburse you only after you return home. British passport holders are entitled to free hospital treatment in Croatia, but sometimes that includes a lot of hassle. While the standard of medical care in Croatia is good, you should opt for private, not public, hospitals and medical care if you have a choice.

As a safety net, you may want to buy travel medical insurance, particularly if you're traveling to a remote or high-risk area where emergency evacuation might be necessary. If you require additional medical insurance, try **MEDEX Assistance** (© 410/453-6300; www.medex assist.com) or **Travel Assistance International** (© 800/821-2828; www.travel assistance.com; for general information on services, call the company's **Worldwide Assistance Services, Inc.,** at © 800/ 777-8710).

Canadians should check with their provincial health plan offices or call **Health Canada** (© 866/225-0709; www. hc-sc.gc.ca) to find out the extent of their coverage and what documentation and receipts they must take home in case they are treated overseas.

8 Health

STAYING HEALTHY
GENERAL AVAILABILITY OF HEALTH CARE

Croatia provides its citizens with excellent, all-inclusive healthcare. Foreign tourists do not have to pay for medical services if there is a signed health insurance convention between Croatia and

their home country. Healthcare costs for tourists from a country that does not have a signed convention with Croatia are paid directly by the user at the time of service.

Before you go: No special vaccinations are required to enter Croatia.

Contact the **International Association for Medical Assistance to Travelers**

(IAMAT) (📞 716/754-4883 or, in Canada, 📞 416/652-0137; www.iamat.org) for tips on travel and health concerns in the countries you're visiting, and for lists of local, English-speaking doctors. The United States **Centers for Disease Control and Prevention** (📞 800/311-3435; www.cdc.gov) provides up-to-date information on health hazards by region or country and offers tips on food safety. **Travel Health Online** (www.tripprep.com), sponsored by a consortium of travel medicine practitioners, also may offer helpful advice on traveling abroad. You can find listings of reliable medical clinics overseas at the **International Society of Travel Medicine** (www.istm.org).

COMMON AILMENTS

INSECT BITES AND STINGS Mosquitoes found in most parts of Croatia generally do not carry malaria. Use an insect repellent containing DEET. Bees and wasps are commonplace, especially on some islands and where beekeeping is an industry. Be especially aware of this if you are allergic to bee venom, and always carry an Epi-pen for emergencies.

DIETARY RED FLAGS Croatian food is generally not spicy, so gastric sensitivities are rarely triggered by the national cuisine. However, if you have fish or shellfish allergies, be sure to ask about ingredients, especially when dining on the coast. Restaurants serving vegetarian choices are becoming more commonplace, especially in larger cities, but you can feed on cheese *burek* or plain pasta almost anywhere.

SEA URCHINS & OTHER WILD-LIFE CONCERNS Sea urchin needles and sharp rocks pose the greatest health hazards to swimmers, especially around Croatia's rockier beaches. It is best to wear rubber swim shoes both on the beach and in the water. These are available in most resort areas and in towns near the sea. Snake sightings are rare but can occur in heavily wooded areas. If you are bitten, immobilize the site and get medical help as quickly as possible.

SUN/ELEMENTS/EXTREME WEATHER EXPOSURE Visitors should be aware that summer in Croatia can be very hot, especially in the southern regions. Air-conditioning is not prevalent in private accommodations or outside of the larger cities. Sunstroke and heat exhaustion can overtake the unwary quickly. Be sure to drink lots of water and get to a shady area or into air-conditioning if you feel dizzy and tired or if you develop a severe headache. These may be signs of heat exhaustion. Sunstroke is more serious and may require emergency medical attention. Symptoms can include fainting and/or agitation. Always carry enough sunscreen with an SPF of at least 15 for all members of your party.

WHAT TO DO IF YOU GET SICK AWAY FROM HOME

For travel abroad, you may have to pay all medical costs upfront and be reimbursed later. Medicare and Medicaid do not provide coverage for medical costs outside the U.S. Before leaving home, find out what medical services your health insurance covers. To protect yourself, consider buying medical travel insurance (see "Medical Insurance," under "Travel Insurance," above).

Very few health insurance plans pay for medical evacuation back to the U.S. (which can cost $10,000 and up). A number of companies offer medical evacuation services anywhere in the world. If you're ever hospitalized more than 150 miles from home, **MedjetAssist** (📞 800/527-7478; www.medjetassistance.com) will pick you up and fly you to the hospital of your choice virtually anywhere in the world in a medically equipped and staffed aircraft 24 hours day, 7 days a week. Annual memberships are $225 individual, $350 family; you can also purchase short-term memberships.

U.K. nationals will need a **European Health Insurance Card (EHIC)** to receive free or reduced-costs health benefits during a visit to a European Economic Area (EEA) country (European Union countries plus Iceland, Liechtenstein and Norway) or Switzerland. The European Health Insurance Card replaces the E111 form, which is no longer valid. For advice, ask at your local post office or see www.dh.gov.uk/travellers.

We list **hospitals** and **emergency numbers** under "Fast Facts," p. 37.

9 Safety

STAYING SAFE

Croatia is generally very safe for travelers. Theft and crimes against persons are not commonplace. However, you should exercise caution anytime you're out and about in an unfamiliar area after dark wherever you are.

In some areas, land mines left over from the 1991 war can pose hazards to unsuspecting travelers. According to www.land mines.org, more than 700,000 land mines were buried in Croatia, mostly in eastern Slavonia, around Zadar in northern Dalmatia, and some near Dubrovnik in southern Dalmatia. The government has been de-mining the country since the end of the Homeland War in 1995, but finding and destroying the ordnance is a slow process. Usually, suspected land-mine areas are marked with red-and-white skull-and-crossbones signs (in Croatian), but you shouldn't tramp around any part of the countryside unless you have a local guide, especially in the above areas. Land mines kill a few Croatians every year. These are mostly hunters who disregard posted signs, or farmers who are impatient to till unswept fields.

10 Specialized Travel Resources

TRAVELERS WITH DISABILITIES

Most disabilities shouldn't stop anyone from traveling. There are more options and resources out there than ever before.

In Croatia, as in other parts of Europe, many hotels, restaurants, and sites are not equipped to provide easy access for visitors with disabilities. However, public restroom facilities in train and bus stations, airports, and some hotels usually have been modified to accommodate wheelchairs. In general, museums, churches, private accommodations, ferries, shuttle boats, and local trams have not. There are a few exceptions and those are noted throughout this book.

Organizations that offer a vast range of resources and assistance to travelers with disabilities include **MossRehab** (© 800/ CALL-MOSS; www.mossresourcenet. org); the **American Foundation for the Blind (AFB)** (© 800/232-5463; www. afb.org); and **SATH (Society for Accessible Travel & Hospitality)** (© 212/447-7284; www.sath.org). **AirAmbulanceCard.com** is now partnered with SATH and allows you to preselect top-notch hospitals in case of an emergency.

Access-Able Travel Source (© 303/232-2979; www.access-able.com) offers a comprehensive database on travel agents from around the world with experience in accessible travel; destination-specific access information; and links to such resources as service animals, equipment rentals, and access guides.

Many travel agencies offer customized tours and itineraries for travelers with disabilities. Among them are **Flying Wheels Travel** (© 507/451-5005; www.flying wheelstravel.com); and **Accessible Journeys** (© 800/846-4537 or © 610/521-0339; www.disabilitytravel.com).

Flying with Disability (www.flying-with-disability.org) is a comprehensive information source on airplane travel. **Avis Rent a Car** (℃ **888/879-4273**) has an "Avis Access" program that offers services for customers with special travel needs. These include specially outfitted vehicles with swivel seats, spinner knobs, and hand controls; mobility scooter rentals; and accessible bus service. Be sure to reserve well in advance.

GAY & LESBIAN TRAVELERS

In Roman Catholic Croatia, gays are tolerated but not celebrated. The country legalized homosexuality in 1977, but overt homosexual behavior is frowned upon in general and may be met with hostility in rural areas. Except for a few places in Zagreb, gay clubs are almost nonexistent, though some nightclubs and discos are patronized almost exclusively by homosexuals. During the summer, many gays frequent FKK (nudist) beaches (p. 142), the larger cities (Dubrovnik, Split), and the island of Hvar. As in many other cities worldwide, the last Saturday in June is Gay Pride Day in Zagreb.

Many agencies offer tours and travel itineraries specifically for gay and lesbian travelers. **The International Gay and Lesbian Travel Association (IGLTA)** (℃ **800/448-8550** or 954/776-2626; www.iglta.org) is the trade association for the gay and lesbian travel industry, and it offers an online directory of gay- and lesbian-friendly travel businesses and tour operators. For Croatia-specific tips, check out http://travel.gay.hr/en which posts a real-time special interest guide for gays. If you are traveling to Zagreb, you can find arts and entertainment information geared to gays at www.queerzagreb.org.

Many agencies offer tours and travel itineraries specifically for gay and lesbian travelers. **Above and Beyond Tours** (℃ **800/397-2681**; www.abovebeyond tours.com) are gay Australia tour specialists. San Francisco–based **Now, Voyager**

(℃ **800/255-6951**; www.nowvoyager. com) offers worldwide trips and cruises, and **Olivia** (℃ **800/631-6277**; www. olivia.com) offers lesbian cruises and resort vacations.

Gay.com Travel (℃ **800/929-2268** or 415/644-8044; www.gay.com/travel or www.outandabout.com) is an excellent online successor to the popular *Out & About* print magazine. It provides regularly updated information about gay-owned, gay-oriented, and gay-friendly lodging, dining, sightseeing, nightlife, and shopping establishments in every important destination worldwide. British travelers should click on the "Travel" link at **www.uk.gay.com** for advice and gay-friendly trip ideas.

The Canadian website **GayTraveler** (**gaytraveler.ca**) offers ideas and advice for gay travel all over the world.

The following travel guides are available at many bookstores, or you can order them from any online bookseller: *Spartacus International Gay Guide, 35th Edition* (Bruno Gmünder Verlag; www. spartacusworld.com/gayguide/) and *Odysseus: The International Gay Travel Planner, 17th Edition* (www.ody usa.com); and the *Damron* guides (www. damron.com), with separate, annual books for gay men and lesbians.

SENIOR TRAVEL

In most Croatian cities, reduced-price admission to theaters, museums, and other attractions is available for "retired persons," though no age requirement usually is given. Otherwise, there are no breaks for seniors, perhaps because Croatia's senior population is so active and vibrant.

Members of **AARP,** 601 E St. NW, Washington, DC 20049 (℃ **888/687-2277**; www.aarp.org), get discounts on hotels, airfares, and car rentals. AARP offers members a wide range of benefits, including *AARP: The Magazine* and a monthly newsletter. Anyone over 50 can join.

Many reliable agencies and organizations target the 50-plus market. **Elderhostel** (© **800/454-5768;** www.elder hostel.org) arranges worldwide study programs for those aged 55 and over. **ElderTreks** (© **800/741-7956** or 416/ 558-5000 outside North America; www. eldertreks.com) offers small-group tours to off-the-beaten-path or adventure-travel locations, restricted to travelers 50 and older.

WOMEN TRAVELERS

Women do not face any particular travel difficulties in Croatia They are treated with courtesy and respect in both big cities and small towns. However, female visitors who go out in public looking unkempt might earn a few disapproving looks because Croatian women take great pride in how they look and what they wear. Women should leave the sloppy PJ bottoms and flip-flops at home and opt for a put-together look to fit in. If any church visits are planned, keep in mind that women are expected to wear tops with sleeves and bottoms that fall beneath the knees. Churches and some museums post their dress codes and they will turn you away if you are not in compliance.

11 Sustainable Tourism/Ecotourism

Each time you take a flight or drive a car CO_2 is released into the atmosphere. You can help neutralize this danger to our planet through "carbon offsetting"—paying someone to reduce your CO_2 emissions by the same amount you've added. Carbon offsets can be purchased in the U.S. from companies such as **Carbonfund.org** (www.carbonfund.org) and **TerraPass** (www.terrapass.org), and from **Climate Care** (www.climatecare.org) in the U.K.

Although one could argue that any vacation that includes an airplane flight can't be truly "green," you can go on holiday and still contribute positively to the environment. You can offset carbon emissions from your flight in other ways. Choose forward-looking companies that embrace responsible development practices, helping preserve destinations for the future by working alongside local people. An increasing number of sustainable tourism initiatives can help you plan a family trip and leave as small a "footprint" as possible on the places you visit.

Responsible Travel (www.responsible travel.com) contains a great source of sustainable travel ideas run by a spokesperson for responsible tourism in the travel industry. **Sustainable Travel International** (www.sustainabletravelinterna tional.org) promotes responsible tourism practices and issues an annual Green Gear & Gift Guide.

You can find eco-friendly travel tips, statistics, and touring companies and associations—listed by destination under "Travel Choice"—at the TIES website, www.ecotourism.org. Also check out **Conservation International** (www. conservation.org)—which, with *National Geographic Traveler,* annually presents **World Legacy Awards** (www.wlaward. org) to those travel tour operators, businesses, organizations, and places that have made a significant contribution to sustainable tourism. **Ecotravel.com** is part online magazine and part eco-directory that lets you search for touring companies in several categories (water-based, land-based, spiritually oriented, and so on).

In the U.K., **Tourism Concern** (www. tourismconcern.org.uk) works to reduce social and environmental problems connected to tourism and find ways of improving tourism so that local benefits are increased.

Frommers.com: The Complete Travel Resource

It should go without saying, but we highly recommend **Frommers.com**, voted Best Travel Site by *PC Magazine*. We think you'll find our expert advice and tips; independent reviews of hotels, restaurants, attractions, and preferred shopping and nightlife venues; vacation giveaways; and an online booking tool indispensable before, during, and after your travels. We publish the complete contents of over 128 travel guides in our **Destinations** section covering nearly 3,800 places worldwide to help you plan your trip. Each weekday, we publish original articles reporting on **Deals and News** via our free **Frommers.com Newsletter** to help you save time and money and travel smarter. We're betting you'll find our new **Events** listings (http://events.frommers.com) an invaluable resource; it's an up-to-the-minute roster of what's happening in cities everywhere—including concerts, festivals, lectures, and more. We've also added weekly **Podcasts, interactive maps,** and hundreds of new images across the site. Check out our **Travel Talk** area featuring **Message Boards** where you can join in conversations with thousands of fellow Frommer's travelers and post your trip report once you return.

The **Association of British Travel Agents (ABTA)** (www.abtamembers.org/responsibletourism) acts as a focal point for the U.K. travel industry and is one of the leading groups spearheading responsible tourism.

The **Association of Independent Tour Operators (AITO)** (www.aito.co.uk) is a group of interesting specialist operators leading the field in making holidays sustainable.

12 Staying Connected

TELEPHONES

To call Croatia from another country:

1. Dial the international access code: 011 from the U.S.; 00 from the U.K., Ireland, or New Zealand; or 0011 from Australia.
2. Dial Croatia's country code 385.
3. Dial the city code. For Zagreb, for example, that is 1.
4. Dial the number.

To make international calls from Croatia:

1. Dial the access code 00.
2. Dial the country code (U.S. or Canada 1, U.K. 44, Ireland 353, Australia 61, New Zealand 64).
3. Dial the area code.

4. Dial the number.

For example, if you wanted to call the British Embassy in Washington, D.C., from Croatia you would dial 00-1-202-588-7800.

To call from one city code to another within Croatia: Dial the Croatian city code, including the zero, followed by the phone number.

To make a local call within a Croatian city: Dial the phone number. No codes necessary. Local calls cost about 5kn ($1) per minute.

For directory assistance: Dial 988 if you're looking for a number inside Croatia country, and dial 902 for numbers to all other countries.

For operator assistance: If you need operator assistance in making a call, dial 901 if you're trying to make either an international call or if you want to call a number in Croatia.

Toll-free numbers: Toll-free numbers in Croatia start with 0800. *Warning:* Calling a 1-800 number in the United States from Croatia is **not** toll-free. In fact, it costs the same as an overseas call.

Prepaid Phone Cards: To use a prepaid phone card, call the service, key in the code on the back of the card, and call the number. It's a good idea to have a prepaid phone card for emergencies because Croatian pay phones don't take coins and you'll need a card to use them. You can buy prepaid cards in denominations of 50, 100, 200, and 500 units at most newspaper kiosks, at post offices, and at some tobacconists. Calls are based on unit-per-minute rates, and the farther away you call, the more each unit costs and the faster you use up your units.

In Zagreb, you can buy prepaid cards at **Nexcom,** Zavrtnica 17 (② **01/606-03-33**); or at **Voicecom,** Ilica 109 (② **01/376-01-23;** www.voicecom.hr). Free 0800 access.

CELLPHONES

The three letters that define much of the world's wireless capabilities are **GSM (Global System for Mobile Communications),** a big, seamless network that makes for easy cross-border cellphone use throughout Europe and dozens of other countries worldwide. In the U.S., T-Mobile, AT&T Wireless, and Cingular use this quasi-universal system; in Canada, Microcell and some Rogers customers are GSM, and all Europeans and most Australians use GSM. GSM phones function with a removable plastic SIM card, encoded with your phone number and account information. If your cellphone is on a GSM system, and you have a world-capable multiband phone such as many Sony Ericsson, Motorola, or Samsung

models, you can make and receive calls across civilized areas around much of the globe. Just call your wireless operator and ask for "international roaming" to be activated on your account. Unfortunately, per-minute charges can be high—usually $1 to $1.50 in Western Europe and up to $5 in places like Russia and Indonesia.

Note: If you have a GSM-equipped phone with an activated roaming feature, your phone will adjust to the city's prevailing carrier automatically.

For many, **renting** a phone is a good option. If this is your choice, we suggest renting a phone before you leave home because there are no phone rental opportunities in Croatia. Be sure your rental works with Croatian providers. North Americans can rent a phone before leaving home from **InTouch USA** (② **800/872-7626;** www.intouchglobal.com) or **RoadPost** (② **888/290-1606** or 905/272-5665; www.roadpost.com). InTouch will give complimentary advice on whether your existing phone will work overseas; simply call ② **703/222-7161** between 9am and 4pm EST, or go to http://intouchglobal.com/travel.htm.

Buying a phone for overseas use can be economically attractive, as many nations have cheap prepaid phone systems. Once you arrive at your destination, stop by a local cellphone shop and get the cheapest *uncoded/unlocked* phone you can find. You'll probably pay less than $100 for a phone, a starter calling card, and a SIM card. Local calls may be as low as 10¢ per minute, and in Croatia, incoming calls are free to you. You can replenish your calling card at news kiosks and at some convenience stores in Croatia.

Croatia has 4 mobile phone providers: **T-Com** (www.t-mobile.hr/eng/1/10-00-00-00.asp) and **VIP:** (www.vipnet.hr/cw/show?idc=8748940) have the biggest networks. Their SIM cards start at 150kn ($28), but just 100kn ($20) of that applies to minutes. *Note:* If you buy a phone package from one of Croatia's providers, you also must buy its service and you get a coded or "locked" phone that does not work with other providers' SIM cards.

INTERNET/E-MAIL WITHOUT YOUR OWN COMPUTER

Croatia is a "wired" country. Cybercafes have been a fixture in larger cities and most resorts for a long time, and now many smaller towns have them, too. In addition, hotels increasingly make at least one computer available for guest use, even if it is the computer at the front desk. We have even seen stand-alone coin-operated computers that allow connection to the Web. To find cybercafes in Croatia, check **www.cybercaptive.com** and **www.cybercafe.com**.

Most major airports have **Internet kiosks** that provide basic Web access for a per-minute fee that's usually higher than cybercafe prices. Check out tourist offices, some of which offer computer stations with fully loaded software (as well as Wi-Fi).

WITH YOUR OWN COMPUTER

More and more hotels, resorts, airports, cafes, and retailers are going **Wi-Fi** (wireless fidelity), becoming "hotspots" that offer free high-speed Wi-Fi access or that charge a small fee for usage. Most laptops sold today have built-in wireless capability. To find public Wi-Fi hotspots at your destination, go to **www.jiwire.com**; its Hotspot Finder holds the world's largest directory of public wireless hotspots.

For dial-up access, most business-class hotels throughout the world offer dataports for laptop modems, and a few thousand hotels in Europe now offer free high-speed Internet access.

Wherever you go, bring a **connection kit** of the right power and phone adapters, a spare phone cord, and a spare Ethernet network cable—or find out whether your hotel supplies them to guests. *Tip:* If you expect to charge your laptop, be sure to carry a converter and a two-pronged Continental plug. Croatian electrical current is 220V 50Hz voltage.

13 Packages for the Independent Traveler

Package tours are simply a way to buy the airfare, accommodations, and other elements of your trip (such as car rentals, airport transfers, and sometimes even activities) at the same time and often at discounted prices.

One good source of package deals is the airlines themselves. Most major airlines offer air/land packages, including **American Airlines Vacations** (© 800/ 321-2121; www.aavacations.com), **Delta Vacations** (© 800/654-6559; www.delta vacations.com), **Continental Airlines**

Vacations (© 800/301-3800; www.co vacations.com), and **United Vacations** (© 888/854-3899; www.unitedvacations. com). Several big **online travel agencies**— Expedia, Travelocity, Orbitz, Site59, and Lastminute.com—also do a brisk business in packages.

Travel packages are also listed in the travel section of your local Sunday newspaper. Or check ads in national travel magazines such as *Arthur Frommer's Budget Travel Magazine, Travel & Leisure, National Geographic Traveler,* and *Condé Nast Traveler.*

14 Escorted General-Interest Tours

Escorted tours are structured group tours, with a group leader. The price usually includes everything from airfare to hotels,

meals, tours, admission costs, and local transportation.

Despite the fact that escorted tours require big deposits and they predetermine hotels, restaurants, and itineraries, many travelers derive security and peace of mind from the structure they offer. Escorted tours—whether they're navigated by bus, motor coach, train, or boat—let travelers sit back and enjoy the trip without having to drive or worry about details. They take you to the maximum number of sights in the minimum amount of time with the least amount of hassle. They're particularly convenient for people with limited mobility, and they can be a great way to make new friends.

On the downside, you'll have little opportunity for serendipitous interactions with locals. The tours can be jam-packed with activities, leaving little room for individual sightseeing, whim, or adventure. They often focus on the heavily traveled sites, so you miss out on many a lesser-known gem.

More than 50 U.S. tour operators offer packages to Croatia. Try **Adriatic Tours,** 777 W. 9th St., San Pedro, CA 90731 (© 800/262-1718; fax 310/831-8382; www.adriatictours.com) or **Homeric Tours,** 55 E. 59th St., New York, NY 10022 (© 800/223-5570; fax 212/753-0319; www.homerictours.com).

Adriatic specializes in Croatia and offers both escorted and hosted tours to almost all regions of the country. Adriatic also puts together religious tours and cruises. **Homeric** offers one hosted tour with a Croatian component and a "Dalmatian Sunshine" escorted tour that visits Dubrovnik, Split, Plitvice Lakes, Zagreb, and more. The New York-based **Croatia Travel Agency** (© 1-**800-554-7016;** ww.croatiatravel.com) offers a full complement of itineraries for Croatia.

Private guides: If you have the resources, consider booking a private English-speaking guide who not only can plan a custom itinerary for you but also can arrange transport, transfers, and admittance to otherwise inaccessible sites. **Jelena Delić** (© **91-531-8782;** damale 3@hotmail.com) is one of the best. **Nada Kozul** (© **098/373-167;** OS571643@ yahoo.com) is another accomplished English speaking guide who can take you "behind the scenes" at vineyards, kulen and cheese factories, national parks, and other venues where tourists rarely venture on their own. She will customize your Croatia tour to fit your specifications as well as accompany you along the route.

15 Special-Interest Trips

There is a wide variety of special-interest tours available in Croatia. Tour operators in and outside the country can arrange tours to suit almost any specification.

CULTURAL TOURS

Classic Journeys, 7855 Ivanhoe Avenue, Suite 220 La Jolla, CA 92037 (© **800/ 200-3887;** www.classicjourneys.com.) is a California-based operator that specializes in customized itineraries for small groups. The focus is culinary, family, and cultural walking tours. Accommodations, meals, and transport are first-rate and each tour is led by a local English-speaking guide,

who accompanies you through the entire trip. Currently, Classic Journeys offers two Croatian itineraries, one to Dubrovnik and Hvar and another through Istria.

Smithsonian Journeys (© 1-877-338-8687; www.smithsonianjourneys. org) runs a 12-day Mediterranean boat adventure down the Dalmatian coast from Venice, Italy. The tour includes lectures on the culture and history of the area.

Adriatica.net (www.adriatica.net) is a general tour operator based in Zagreb that puts together stays in many of Croatia's lighthouses and farmhouses and arranges sailing vacations.

SAILING AND DIVING TOURS

With 1185 islands and miles of coastline, Croatia attracts a huge number of boating and water sports enthusiasts. Croatia has a large number of charter companies that can put sailors in the captain's chair.

Sunsail, www.sunsail.com, offers charters with (skippered) or without (bareboat) crews that let you set your own course. If you have the proper boating certifications, you can captain your own ship. If you don't, you can rent a fully crewed ship and kick back and assume the role of pampered passenger. Sunsail has offices in Dubrovnik, Biograd (Kornati), and Kremik near Primošten.

Sail Croatia, www.sailcroatia.net, puts together customized floating holidays for experienced sailors and novices alike. Its offices are in Split, Pula, and Dubrovnik.

Dalmatia Charter, www.dalmatia charter.com, operates boating holidays out of Trogir and Kremik. It is family-run.

The remains of the passenger ferry Baron Gautsch, off Rovinj, is one of the most popular diving sites in Croatia. **Diving Petra** (✆ 052/812-880; www.divingpetra.hr) in Rovinj organizes excursions to the 1914 wreck.

Check out the **Issa Diving Center** on the island of Vis (✆ 021/713-651; www.scubadiving.hr), to book a dive to the WWII US B17G bomber off the island's coast. Issa can arrange dives to other wrecks and it can put beginners through an elementary diving course, too.

Diving at Kornati National Park is strictly regulated. Most excursions to Kornati originate at Murter. Check with the **Murter Tourist Office** (✆ 022/434-995; www.tzo-murter.hr) for advice on diving trips to Kornati.

FOOD AND WINE TOURS

Increasingly, Croatian entrepreneurs are marketing local products by developing wine and olive roads as well as special excursions for truffle hunting and wine dinners. Istria, Međimurje, and Slavonia all have mapped out winery routes where you can stop and taste and even get a meal in some instances. For maps and information on Istria's wine roads go to www.istra.com/zupan/eng/v1.html. For Međimurje wine tours, check out the **Tourist Board of Međimurje County** in Cakovec at R. Boskovica 3, (✆ 040/390-191; www.tzm.hr). They can provide you with a well-done map tracing Međa imurje's wine road and wineries where you can stop to taste or buy local vintages. You can get similar information at the **Cakovec Tourist Office** at Trg Kralja Tomislava 2, (✆ 040/313-319; www.tourism-cakovec.hr). Slavonia/Baranja wine road information can be found at www.tzosbarzup.hr. General information on Croatian wine is at www.vino croatia.com.

16 Getting Around Croatia

BY PLANE

Croatia Air has a near monopoly on flights that travel among Croatia's seven airports (Zagreb, Split, Dubrovnik, Rijeka, Pula, Zadar, and Brač), and unless one of these locations is your final destination, you'll have to transfer to some other mode of transportation to finish your trip. Domestic flights booked on Croatia Air from outside the country cost nearly twice as much as flights booked at a Croatia Air office in the country unless they are part of a multi-city international ticket.

BY BUS

Almost every town in Croatia has a bus station, and the country's network of bus routes makes this an excellent, economical option for travel within Croatia.

Express routes on updated highways facilitate travel among major cities. Buses also travel to almost every town and village in the country, though schedules might be inconvenient.

BY BOAT

Ferries and catamarans are a way of life on Croatia's coast. There is no other way to get to the islands (except Pag and Krk, which are linked to the mainland via bridges). For some, ferries are the transport of choice between mainland cities such as Rijeka and Dubrovnik. Croatia's ferries vary in size and type: Some are huge ships that carry people, cargo, and vehicles. Others are small taxi boats, and still others are speedy catamarans. Jadrolinija, Semmarina, and SNAV are the major operators (see "Getting There," earlier in this chapter). In summer, ferry schedules are beefed up to handle increased traffic, but in winter some lines cancel certain runs altogether and reduce the rest of their schedules. When there is a *bura*, ferries can be sidelined.

BY CAR

Except for transport around Zagreb and Dubrovnik, driving is far and away the best method for seeing the real Croatia—even the islands. However, renting a car and paying for fuel can be extremely expensive, with rentals for a subcompact starting at about $50 a day and gas selling at unprecedented high prices.

Croatia's main highways (autocestas) are modern, well-marked, and well-maintained. Secondary roads vary in quality and can range from well marked, paved, multi-lane expanses to unmarked, one-lane dirt roads.

Gas stations are readily available near larger cities. They usually are open from 7am to 7pm every day and until 10pm in the summer. Some gas stations in larger cities and on major international routes are open 24 hours. It's a good idea to fill the tank and pick up a Croatia road map

that locates gas stations across the country before you start a long trip. These are usually available at the stations themselves. See www.ina.hr, www.hak.hr, and www.omvistrabenz.hr for details.

If you plan to rent a car during July and August, it is critical that you reserve a vehicle before you arrive at the rental agency. If you have car trouble on the road, call the rental agency or the Croatian Automobile Club at ℂ 987; or check the auto club's website at www.hak.hr. Croatia road maps are available at any tourism office, gas station, or supermarket, and they are fine for charting the main roads. However, sometimes maps are moot because signage off the main roads is not the best.

Parking in Zagreb and other population centers can be difficult. It is easier to find a space in smaller towns, but in all cases you'll pay. Croatia allows payment for parking via cellphone. The cellphone owner loads money on account, calls a pre-set number, indicates the city where the car is parked and the number of minutes desired, and the amount is deducted from the owner's account. The service calls the driver's cellphone 5 minutes before the parking time is up to give him/her the opportunity to buy more time. If you don't have a local cellphone, most parking lots have machines that take coins or they employ attendants to take the fees.

CAR RENTALS   There are numerous car rental companies in Croatia, and almost all have offices at the airports and major cities. **Budget** (ℂ 800/472-3325; www.budget.com) has outlets at the Split, Dubrovnik, Pula, and Zagreb airports, and in other major population centers. **Hertz** (ℂ 800/654-3131; www.hertz.com) has branches at all of Croatia's airports, including Pula, Rijeka, and Zadar, as well as rental outlets on Hvar and Mali Losinj. **Uni rent** (ℂ 021/317-297; www.uni-rent.net) is a local independent vendor that has an office in Split near the Hotel Marjan. All offer a broad spectrum of auto choices, ranging from small economy models such as the Opel Corsa to luxury rides like the Volvo S80 to SUV 4×4s. To rent a car in Croatia, you must be 21 years old, have a valid driver's license and proof of insurance. *Note:* Almost all cars rented in Croatia have manual transmissions. If you need an automatic, reserve well in advance and be prepared to pay a premium for it.

BY TRAIN

Croatian Railways (www.hznet.hr) is an efficient way to travel between Zagreb and the northern and inland parts of the country. There is also train service to Rijeka and Pula in Istria and south to Split. However, the trains do not run along the coast south of Split. Croatian trains are not part of the Eurail system, and international travel usually requires train changes because the rail gauge in Croatia is different from that used on Eurail track.

17 Tips on Accommodations

Hotel room prices in Croatia vary considerably with location and time of year. Generally, hotel prices in larger inland cities and towns are the most stable, while hotels in major tourist areas along the coast sometimes publish as many as seven rate schedules based on time of year, as well as price variations based on amenities. Croatian hotel rates almost always include breakfast, while private accommodations almost always do not. Private accommodations rented through individuals are the least expensive and can cost as little as $10 per night. In one word: BARGAIN.

For example, one night in a double room at a hotel in central Zagreb (Sheraton) costs $100 to $150 with breakfast, while a similar room in New York would go for $180 to $200 or more without breakfast. In London, the same Sheraton room without breakfast costs $265. These are Internet rates, which tend to be lower than rack rates.

Croatia has more than 400 star-rated hotels that are a combination of '60s and '70s high-rises; stately, ornate, turn-of-the-20th-century buildings; and, more recently, family-run boutique hotels. Currently, the country seems to be in a "renovate and rebuild" mode, and many establishments have completed or are undergoing updating.

HOTELS Most hotels in Croatia carry international star ratings from one star to five stars, which seem to relate to amenities only and don't consider service, atmosphere, or quality of accommodations. In addition, the star ratings can seem arbitrary: In some cases a room in a one-star hotel might offer rooms with private bathroom, TV, and restaurant, while another one-star hotel might sell rooms with the bathroom down the hall, no TV, and breakfast in the lobby. In general, a one-star hotel offers a bare-bones room with a bathroom down the hall; a two-star hotel room has a private bathroom and usually a TV. A three-star room has a private bathroom (usually with a shower, not a tub), TV, and perhaps other amenities, though this category is unpredictable and can be a value or a rip-off depending on management. Four-star hotels will offer a room with a larger bathroom, possibly with tub; good quality furnishings; little extras like toiletries; and other facilities like a fitness center, several restaurants, and a pool. Five-star hotels are few and far between and mostly in larger cities, though increasingly some of the smaller hotels are earning their fifth star by adding a swimming pool, an elevator, or some other amenity to meet the requirement. They offer the highest level of luxury and in some cases rival the best the U.S. has to offer.

Croatian chains tend to be local: Arenaturist in Pula, Liburnia in Opatija,

Tips bb

The initials "bb" stand for *bez broja* (without number). This is quite common in Croatia, particularly if the place is a well-known church or restaurant. If you see an address listed with a street name followed by bb, and you are having trouble finding it, ask a local for directions.

Hoteli Borik in Zadar. These generally manage either package hotels in resort areas or former grande dames in various stages of repair from crumbling to completely refurbished. Many establishments are single-site houses, usually owned by a family or group of friends who live on-site or nearby.

PRIVATE ACCOMMODATIONS Private rooms and apartments are by far the most common accommodations (and the best deals) in Croatia. These are divided into three categories: An A-level room has a private bathroom, perhaps a TV, and good quality furnishings. A B-level room has a private bathroom. A C-level room will have a bed, a place to hang clothes, and a shared bathroom. What you get in any given category can vary wildly, so it is always a good idea to inspect the rooms before you plunk down any money. Private accommodations are often unused apartments or rooms that generate extra income for the owner. Frequently proprietors will refuse to rent their extra space for fewer than 4 nights, and if they do, they will charge extra. Licensed private accommodations are best booked through local tourist agencies but you can find and book private villas and rooms via www.adriatica.net, too.

SOBES Another tier of accommodations in Croatia is the sobe, or room in a private home. These are generally cheaper than those procured through agencies, but they are unregulated and thus can be anything from a suite of rooms with private bathroom to a bed in an attic. Sobe signs are often found outside houses in smaller towns, but sometimes they are "advertised," usually by older men and women who whisper, "Need a room?" to new arrivals at ferry, bus, and train stations.

CAMPGROUNDS Camping is very popular in Croatia, especially on the coast. Most autocamps are minicities with campsites, markets, restaurants, laundries, and sports facilities. Frequently, campgrounds will be located on prime real estate close to the beach or near a large resort facility.

FKK Campgrounds: Croatia has more FKK campgrounds (naturist camps) than any other European country. Many regular campgrounds have sections set aside for naturist campers. Most of these camps are outside cities in the northern Adriatic resort areas (Vrsar, Rovinj, Pag, Poreč, Krk) and are similar in size and scope to the larger regular autocamps.

YOUTH HOSTELS Croatia doesn't have a strong network of youth hostels, but these establishments do exist in Zagreb, Zadar, Dubrovnik, Pula, and a few other locations. Most of the time they are quite reasonable, though they usually have check-in and checkout times and rules similar to those enforced in college dorms.

18 Tips on Dining

Croatian cuisine, like the country itself, is regional in character and divided into coastal and interior styles, with fish and pasta the prevalent offerings in Dalmatia and Istria, grilled meat the entree of choice in the interior, and anything laced with paprika the specialty in Slavonia, the country's easternmost region.

Meals at most Croatian restaurants are excellent values, but the smaller, family-run establishments known as *konobas* generally are the best buy because much of the food and wine is family produced, prepared, and reasonably priced.

Whether you choose a restaurant that aspires to be "gourmet," an intimate ma-and-pa place, or a meal cobbled from the town market and corner *pekara* (bakery), you should try local specialties like *čevapčići* (spicy grilled beef or pork meatballs), *blitva* (Swiss chard boiled and served with potatoes, olive oil and garlic),

and *burek* (a heavy pastry filled with cheese, meat, or fruit). Fish is often sold by the kilogram in restaurants and the average portion is about 250 grams (9 oz.). Service is sometimes included in the menu prices, and even if it is, leaving loose change as a tip is appreciated. Credit cards are accepted at many upscale restaurants, but even some of the fancier dining rooms offer a discount for cash.

In Dubrovnik and elsewhere, many restaurants no longer build gratuities into the cost of a meal, though almost all charge a *couvert*, which is a cover charge attached to the bread basket. If you don't want bread, refuse it before it lands on your table and you'll avoid the couvert.

FAST FACTS: Croatia

American Express Atlas Travel is the agent for American Express in Croatia. It has agencies in most major cities and tourist areas.

Area Codes Croatia's country code is +385.

ATM Networks See "Money & Costs," p. 21.

Business Hours Banks and post offices generally are open from 7am to 7pm Monday through Friday without midday breaks. Public offices are open Monday through Friday from 8am to 4pm. During the tourist season, post offices generally are open until 9pm, including Saturday. Shops and department stores stay open from 8am to 8pm and to 2pm Saturday without a midday break. Note: Hours in some new urban shopping malls are from 9am to 9pm daily.

Car Rentals See "Getting Around Croatia," p. 33.

Cashpoints See "ATM Networks," above.

Currency See "Money & Costs," p. 21.

Customs **What You Can Bring Into Croatia:** Visitors can bring in foreign currency in any amount, but anything above 40,000kn ($7,400) must be declared in writing. One liter of spirits, 2 liters of wine, 2 liters of liqueur and 1 carton of cigarettes can be brought in duty free.

What You Can Take Home from Croatia: Returning U.S. citizens who have been away for at least 48 hours can bring back $800 worth of merchandise duty free once every 30 days. Canada allows its citizens a C$750 exemption; Australia sets a A$400 limit; New Zealand allows NZ$700 in duty free items.

U.S. Citizens: For detailed information on what you can bring back and the corresponding fees, download the invaluable free pamphlet *Know Before You Go* online at www.cbp.gov. (Click on "Travel," and then click on "Know Before

You Go! Online Brochure.") Or contact the U.S. Customs & Border Protection (CBP), 1300 Pennsylvania Ave., NW, Washington, DC 20229 (© **877/287-8667**) and request the pamphlet.

Canadian Citizens: For a clear summary of Canadian rules, write for the booklet *I Declare,* issued by the Canada Border Services Agency (© **800/461-9999** in Canada, or 204/983-3500; www.cbsa-asfc.gc.ca).

U.K. Citizens: For information, contact HM Customs & Excise at © **0845/010-9000** (from outside the U.K., 020/8929-0152), or consult their website at www.hmce.gov.uk.

Australian Citizens: A helpful brochure available from Australian consulates or Customs offices is *Know Before You Go.* For more information, call the Australian Customs Service at © **1300/363-263,** or log on to www.customs.gov.au.

New Zealand Citizens: Most questions are answered in a free pamphlet available at New Zealand consulates and Customs offices: *New Zealand Customs Guide for Travellers, Notice no. 4.* For more information, contact **New Zealand Customs,** The Customhouse, 17–21 Whitmore St., Box 2218, Wellington (© **04/473-6099** or 0800/428-786; www.customs.govt.nz).

Driving Rules See "Getting Around Croatia," p. 33.

Drugstores Croatian drugstores are called *Ljekarna.* They are open from 8am to 7pm weekdays and until 2pm on Saturday. In larger cities, at least one ljekarna stays open 24 hours.

Electricity Croatian electricity is 220V, 50Hz; the two-prong Continental plug is standard.

Embassies & Consulates **U.S.:** Andrije Hebranga 2, Zagreb; © 01-66-12-200. **Australia:** Krsnjavoga 1, Zagreb; © 01-48-36-6000. **United Kingdom:** Vlaska 121, Zagreb; © 01-45-55-310. Also Obala Hrvatskog Narodnog Preporoda 10, 21000, Split; © 021/341-464.

Emergencies 911 equivalent: © **112.** Police: © **92.** Fire: © **93.** Ambulance: © **94.** Roadside assistance: © **987.** (When calling from abroad or by cellphone, call +385-1-987.) General information about international numbers, © **902.** Weather forecast and road conditions: © 060/520-520.

Etiquette & Customs **Appropriate Attire:** Croatians, especially Croatian women, take pride in their appearance. In cities, both men and women usually dress in business casual while on the coast and countryside, the "dress code" is more relaxed. You will never see Croatians wearing immodest or sloppy clothes in public places. If you plan to visit museums or churches anywhere, plan to wear tops with sleeves and pants that go to at least the knee.

Gestures: Dobar dan (good day) is the way Croatians generally greet each other. Handshakes are appropriate for first meetings and between business associates. Good friends will kiss on both cheeks in the European style.

Avoiding Offense: Religion and politics are topics to avoid universally. In Croatia, stay away from discussing Croat-Serb relations or anything related to the Homeland War unless you know what you're talking about and have lots of time for debate.

Holidays Croatian shops and banks are closed on public holidays, which are: January 1, New Year; January 6, Epiphany; March or April, Easter Monday; May 1, Labor Day; May, Corpus Christi; June 22, Anti-Fascist Day; June 25, Croatian Statehood; August 5, Thanksgiving; August 15, Assumption; October 8, Independence Day; November 1, All Saints Day; December 25 and 26, Christmas. For more information on holidays, see "Calendar of Events," earlier in this chapter.

Hospitals **Zagreb:** Sisters of Mercy Hospital Clinic (Klinička Bolnica "Sestre Milosrdnice), Vinogradska cesta 29 ⓒ **01-37-87-111. Split:** Split Hospital Clinic (Klinička Bolnica Split), Spinčićeva 1, ⓒ **021/556-111. Dubrovnik:** Dubrovnik General Hospital (Opća Bolnica Dubrovnik), Toka Mišetića bb, ⓒ **020/431-777.**

Language Most residents of major Croatian cities speak English. Most movie houses and programs on Croatian TV are in English with Croatian subtitles. Check out the glossary in the back of this book for basic phrases and words. For more specific vocabulary, see the Langenscheidt Universal Croatian Dictionary.

Laundromats Self-service laundromats are few and far between in Croatia, though many hotels have laundry service and most family-run establishments will wash and iron your clothes for a price. In larger cities, you can take your clothes to a *kemijska Čistionica* (dry cleaner) or use one of very few *praonica rublja* (self-service) laundromat. In Zagreb, you can find Lahor at Stupnička Ulica 16, ⓒ **01/6061-483.** Mon-Sat 9am-8pm.

Legal Aid Consult your embassy if you get into legal trouble in Croatia. See p. 38 for contact information.

Liquor Laws The minimum age for purchasing liquor is 18, but there is no minimum age for consuming it. Croatia has a zero tolerance law regarding drinking and driving; the legal limit is 0.0% blood alcohol. Package liquor (wine, beer, spirits) can be purchased in markets, wine stores, and some souvenir shops, and at almost every gas station in Croatia.

Lost & Found Be sure to tell all of your credit card companies the minute you discover your wallet has been lost or stolen and file a report at the nearest police precinct. Your credit card company or insurer may require a police report number or record of the loss. Most credit card companies have an emergency toll-free number to call if your card is lost or stolen; they may be able to wire you a cash advance immediately or deliver an emergency credit card in a day or two. Keep a copy of this number separate from your credit cards. International collect phone numbers for credit card companies are: Visa and Master-Card: ⓒ **605/335-2222;** American Express: ⓒ **336/393-1111.**

If you need emergency cash over the weekend when all banks and American Express offices are closed, you can have money wired to you via **Western Union** (ⓒ **800/325-6000;** www.westernunion.com).

Mail It costs 3.50kn (65¢) to send a postcard to the U.S. and 5kn ($1) to send a letter weighing up to 20 grams (¾ oz.). The post office is fairly reliable, but very slow. It takes about 10 days to 2 weeks for postcards to arrive in the U.S. from Croatia and up to a month for regular mail and packages. Other carriers are available (DHL, Fedex, UPS) in major population centers, but the cost is prohibitive (about $50 per pound).

Measurements Weights and measures are metric. See the chart on the inside front cover of this book for details on converting metric measurements to non-metric equivalents.

Newspapers & Magazines English-language newspapers and magazines are a rarity at Croatian newsstands, even in Zagreb. Some of the better hotels supply faxed copies of various U.S. publications. Algorithm bookstores in major population centers are the only common outlets for English-language publications. Look for the **International Herald Tribune** and **USA Today** if you crave English-language news.

Passports See "Entry Requirements," earlier in this chapter.

Police Call ⓒ **92.**

Restrooms There are no free-standing public restrooms in Croatia, but most restaurants and public buildings have them. But keep in mind that it's considered impolite to use a restroom in a restaurant if you're not eating or drinking there.

Safety See "Health & Safety," earlier in this chapter.

Smoking There are no restrictions on smoking in restaurants or public places in Croatia, though many hotels offer nonsmoking guest rooms and a few restaurants have nonsmoking areas.

Taxes Croatia's VAT is 22%. Refunds of VAT are made to foreign nationals when they leave the country for goods purchased in Croatia for amounts over 500kn ($93) with a tax check form. Salespeople will provide this form when you make a purchase over 500kn. There is a 10% nonrefundable tax on excursions and tax on hotel rooms, too. For further information, go to www.carina.hr.

Time Zone Croatia is 1 hour ahead of Greenwich Mean Time, 6 hours ahead of New York (Eastern Standard Time), and 9 hours ahead of Los Angeles (Pacific Standard Time). Daylight Saving Time is observed from late March to late September, when clocks are advanced 1 hour.

Tipping A 10% to 15% gratuity is expected in upscale restaurants. Otherwise, it is considered polite to leave any coins from your change on the table in cafes and restaurants. A 10% tip for other service providers (taxi drivers, hotel personnel, and others) is the norm, as is a tip for anyone who helps you carry your luggage or conducts a tour.

Useful Phone Numbers U.S. Dept. of State Travel Advisory ⓒ **202/647-5225** (manned 24 hrs.). U.S. Passport Agency ⓒ **202/647-0518.**

Water Tap water is potable throughout Croatia—feel free to order tap water at restaurants.

3

Suggested Croatia Itineraries

Croatia is such a diverse country that it is difficult to standardize any touring plan of action that will cover all its important places without leaving out many "must-sees." Consequently, we've divided our itineraries into two parts: routes for those who enter the country at Zagreb, and routes for those who start in Dubrovnik. These include our favorite places and allow for a variety of time frames.

Note: If you plan to spend 2 weeks in Croatia, simply follow both 1-week itineraries, in whichever order you prefer.

1 Zagreb & Beyond in 1 Week

If you are flying to Croatia directly from North America, chances are you will land in Zagreb. That means that even if your plan is to move on to somewhere else, you will likely have at least half a day to explore the Croatian capital—just enough time to scratch the surface. You may want to consider giving yourself more time to explore.

Day ❶: Zagreb
Pick up your rental car or catch the shuttle to town at the Zagreb airport. Settle into your hotel and then catch the tram to Jelačića Trg, the central square at the foot of Old Town. Explore Zagreb's historic Old Town—discover trendy bars, a rustic *klet* (a restaurant serving local cuisine), a jeweler's atelier, and a museum full of sculpted masterpieces.

Days ❷ & ❸: Opatija Riviera & Pula
Drive to **Samobor,** where you can stop for a midmorning *kremešnite* (the custard-filled pastry this town is famous for) and explore Samobor's quaint town square. Get back on the highway and take the exit to **Karlovac,** where **Karlovačko Brewery,** historic buildings, and a lovely riverwalk await you. Spend the night at the **Hotel Korana** in Karlovac (p. 291). Continue on toward Rijeka, where you'll cross into Istria. Follow the road that goes south along Istria's eastern coast to **Pula.** If you haven't reserved a room at **Valsabbion,** stop at any tourist agency to book private accommodations—preferably one that advertises agri-tourism. Or, if you want to sample a tiny, family-run hotel, arrange to stay at the **Scaletta,** just a few blocks from Pula's magnificent **amphitheater** and the sea.

On **Day 3,** spend the morning exploring the amphitheater and the rest of Pula's cache of Roman ruins. Then head toward **Rovinj** (p. 219) around 2pm. That should give you plenty of time to stop in **Vodnjan** to see its mummies (p. 217) and still get to Rovinj for dinner. If you haven't booked a room at **Angelo d'Oro,** stop at any tourist agency and book private accommodations. Spend the evening walking up to **St. Euphemia Church** and down **Grisia Street.**

Suggested Croatia Itineraries

Days ④ & ⑤: Poreč

Take a morning walk to Rovinj's market near the dock and stop at any cafe for coffee and a roll. Be sure to photograph this part of town in the morning light. Collect your things and head north to **Poreč** (p. 225). Once you settle into **Villa Filipini** just outside Poreč or in the private accommodations that you booked on the way into town, head back to Poreč and park in the big public lot just outside the city center. Once in Poreč, you'll first want to head for the city's walled Old Town, which is laid out in a geometric design popular with the Romans. Poreč is very attuned to tourists' needs; you'll notice multilingual signs and captions in front of every important building. **Trg Marafor** used to be the site of the town's

Forum and a temple dedicated to Jupiter, Juno, and Minerva. You can still see the ruins of that ancient house of worship. You'll want to reserve a couple of hours to explore the **Basilica of Euphrasius,** its art, and its fabulous mosaics. Once you're finished, take a pre-dinner promenade through Old Town, which probably has more jewelry shops per capita than any other place in Croatia, followed closely by the number of ice-cream shops. You'll have to resist their siren's song if you want to see anything historic.

Plan to spend **Day 5** out of town. Poreč is an excellent jumping-off point for a trip to **Pazin** and its wonderful **castle-museum and chasm.** From there, you can see the frescoes at **St. Mary's in Beram** as well as the **Church of St. Nicholas.** If you didn't catch Vodnjan on the way into Poreč, now is the time. Head back to Poreč to spend the night.

Days ❻ & ❼: Motovun & Opatija

Leave Poreč after breakfast and head for Istria's medieval hilltop towns. These are fairly close together, but the roads are narrow, steep, and winding, so the trip through this part of Istria takes longer than you might think. You'll start by going north toward **Pazin,** but about halfway there you'll veer north on the road to the town of **Motovun,** which is about 16km (10 miles) northwest of Pazin. You'll have to leave your car at the bottom of the hill that leads to Motovun and walk. You'll find that walking around this little walled enclave is like lurching on a cobbled roller-coaster framework, but the effort is worth it because the views of the valley are stunning. From Motovun, go north a few miles through seemingly endless vineyards to **Livade,** and stop for lunch at **Zigante** (p. 242), one of Croatia's best restaurants. Lunch will be pricey, but you'll be sure to find out what all the hoopla over truffles is

about. From Livade, head a few more miles north to **Grožnjan** and take time to soak up the atmosphere here. If you're lucky, there will be music in the air. Finally, head back toward Zagreb via **Glagolitic Alley** and its sculpture garden displaying ancient Croatian symbols; Roč and its very low fortification wall; and **Hum,** supposedly the world's smallest town. You can stop at any agri-hotel displaying a sign or get back on the main road and drive through the **Učka Tunnel** toward **Opatija** (p. 178) and spend the night there.

Start **Day 7** with a swim off Opatija's concrete beach and then drive to **Lovran** to inspect the countryside and **Mount Učka. You'll want to head back** to Opatija for a mile-and-a-half walk along the waterfront promenade to **Volosko,** where **Amfora** restaurant serves a fabulous lunch (you can also drive there). You'll know at this point that you haven't had enough time in Opatija, but to keep to your schedule, you must now head toward Zagreb.

2 Dubrovnik & Beyond in 1 Week

If you are visiting Dubrovnik, chances are you changed planes in Zagreb and landed in Dubrovnik; deplaned in Zagreb, took the overnight train to Split, and drove to Dubrovnik; or took a ferry from Rijeka or Italy. Whichever way you arrived at this spectacular city in southern Dalmatia, you'll want to make the most of every moment inside—and outside—its walls.

Days ❶ & ❷: Dubrovnik

Settle into your hotel, take a swim, and catch the bus to the **Pile Gate** (or walk there if you happen to be staying at the **Hilton Imperial** (p. 62). Before you get to the gate, however, stop at the tourist office across the street from the Hilton and pick up a map of Dubrovnik's Old Town and any other publications available. You can sign onto one of their computers and let everyone at home know that you've arrived safely. Next, check the

time. If it is between 11am and 5pm, kill time by strolling the Stradun: Explore the Old Town's churches and museums; stop for lunch, perhaps at **Rozarij;** and wait until the sun is low in the sky before you start your walk on the walls. Then grab a bottle of water and head for the Pile Gate entrance to the stairs leading to the top of the stone fortification. Doing the entire 2km (1¼-mile) circuit atop the walls is a non-negotiable must-do if you are physically able. After all, you've traveled all the way to Dubrovnik and this is the ultimate Dubrovnik experience. Allow a minimum of an hour for this trek, more if you are prone to ooh-ing and ahh-ing at spectacular scenery or if you decide to join other intrepid tourists in the sea off the walls before or after you start your trek. When you've come back down to earth, you'll be ready for a break, a swim, or a glass of wine, and by this time, the promenade on the Stradun will have begun.

Spend **Day 2** in Dubrovnik exploring everything Old Town has to offer, including all the places up and down the streets that radiate from the **Stradun.** You'll find some interesting surprises there, including the second-oldest synagogue in Europe, galleries, restaurants, and a shop or two. This is the day to "do" the churches, museums, and palaces in Old Town. Perhaps check out **Lokrum** via the water taxis; or swim in the Adriatic off the rocks next to the wall. Have dinner in **Lapad** or at any place overlooking the sea, but make it an early night because Day 3 will be busy.

Day ❸ & ❹: A Day Trip from Dubrovnik

An ideal side trip will take you to the **Pelješac Peninsula** (p. 127). You can take a self-guided tour or sign up at Atlas or another agency for an escorted tour of the Pelješac vineyards and wineries. If you drive yourself, take the coastal highway north.

The next stop is **Ston** (p. 129), the Pelješac town closest to the mainland. Ston's obvious draw is the 5km (3-mile) **14th-century defensive wall** that stretches above the town from both sides and forms a horseshoe above it in the hills. You'll want to climb this mini–Great Wall of China with a friend just so he or she can take your picture with the wall behind you. This is not an easy climb (think climbing the stairs in a skyscraper), and not all of the wall is navigable, though renovation is under way. Ston and

its twin city **Mali Ston** up the road are both known for their oyster and mussel beds, and both have restaurants that serve fabulous versions of these shellfish. You can tour the salt pans outside town to see how this ancient salt collection method works.

The Pelješac Peninsula runs for about 64km (40 miles) from Ston to Lovišće and measures from 2.4km to 6.8km (1½–4¼ miles) wide at various points. However, those parameters are deceptive because Pelješac is quite mountainous, and the end-to-end drive usually takes more than 2 hours. It will be mid-afternoon by the time you finish with Ston, and you'll have time to visit some of Pelješac's wineries, which are scattered all over the peninsula.

Day ❺: Orebić

From Ston, you'll head to lovely **Orebić** (p. 127) toward the far end of the peninsula, where you'll spend the night in private accommodations you arranged in Dubrovnik.

Orebić is a lively town from dawn to dusk; you find people on the beach and in the sea at all hours. At night the promenade along the waterfront is alive with families walking to and from restaurants, the sound of live entertainment pouring out of tavernas, and glowing lights from little galleries where art shows are in progress.

Days ❻ & ❼: Korčula

From Orebić, it is a half-hour's boat ride to the island of **Korčula** (p. 118) and the walled city of **Korčula Town** where Marco Polo supposedly was born. You can book Atlas-led excursions to Korčula at the main tourist office on the promenade and through other agencies in Orebić. Korčula Town is a nice, relaxing day trip, and while its beach isn't the best, there are plenty of museums, restaurants, and other sites to explore here. Or you can venture farther afield and see more of the island. You'll return to Orebić to spend the night and prepare for the trip back to Dubrovnik.

The trip back to Dubrovnik will take about 3 hours if you drive straight through, but you'll undoubtedly see more wineries along the road worth a look, more quaint towns to investigate, and lots of places to take photos or go for a swim. Once back in Dubrovnik, you can reprise your favorite experiences or see the things you missed when you arrived.

3 Istria with Kids in 1 Week

Croatia is a destination with something for everyone, but many of the country's most popular pastimes, such as swimming off secluded coves, diving around offshore islands, and rock climbing on nearly vertical limestone walls, are geared to older kids and adults. Certainly, Croatia is one of the best countries in Europe for extreme sports and outdoor adventure, but along with its many adult activities, almost every city in Croatia offers options that the entire family can enjoy and many that are supervised and designed to appeal specifically to kids' interests.

Days ❶ & ❷: Pula ✸✸✸

On **Day 1,** arrive at Pula 113km (70 miles from Rijeka) and settle in at your hotel; hotels near the center are close to Pula's showcase Roman ruins and those in the resort complexes outside town have lots of amenities that will appeal to kids.

Explore Pula's fabulous Roman ruins. Start at the spectacular 2nd-century **Roman Amphitheater** (p. 212) and be sure to rent at least one audio tour apparatus to use as you explore the arena. Kids will be able to actually walk on the former "stage" where gladiator contests were held and explore the area underneath the arena where animal and human competitors were kept before battles. After the amphitheater, head to the **Temple of Augustus** (p. 210) on Trg Republike in the center of town. Consider hopping on **Tram Tina,** a little green and yellow "train" that stops at the amphitheater and main square and that will take you on a whirlwind tour of Pula's major sites. End the day with pizza or spaghetti at one of Pula's many restaurants.

On **Day 2,** you'll hop on a boat to the lovely and historic **Brijuni Islands** (p. 216). Be sure your booking includes an actual stop on the islands and not just a ride around them.

There's just enough variety on **Veliki Brijuni** (where all tours go) to keep kids entranced for the entire 4-hour land tour. You'll see a fine collection of rare taxidermed animals that once roamed **Josip Broz Tito's Safari Park,** and you'll see a few live wild animals in the park, too. On the island's **Verige Bay,** you'll see alleged **dinosaur footprints.**

Days ❸ & ❹: Rovinj & the Limski Fjord ✸✸✸

Start **Day 3** by picking up your rental car and heading north to **Rovinj** (p. 219). Check into the **Park Hotel** with its swimming pools and kid options, then stop for a snack on the hotel's terrace spend the hottest hours of the day at the pool or on the beach near the hotel. The kids will then be ready to explore the fairy-tale town visible from the hotel.

Start with a walk up Rovinj's hilly streets to its highest point and **St. Euphemia Church.** Explain that St. Euphemia is not just another boring European church, but rather the resting place of the saint and her stone coffin, which mysteriously washed up on Rovinj's shore in A.D. 800. Be prepared to answer a lot of "how" questions after the kids see the mammoth stone container.

Slowly head back down to the dock via **Grisia Street** and stop at any of the restaurants along the quay for dinner. They *are* touristy, but the food is consistently good and the kids will enjoy the sea spray during the meal.

On **Day 4,** take a tour and fish picnic on an excursion to **Limska Draga Fjord** (p. 220) north of Rovinj. This is an all-day trip through the flooded karstic canyon, which has been declared "a special maritime reserve" and "an area of outstanding natural beauty." The inland village of **Mrgani,** founded by the legendary Captain Morgan, is also here. You won't get back until 6 or 7pm so plan to have dinner in Rovinj when you return.

Days ❺, ❻, & ❼: Poreč and Green Istria 🐸🐸🐸

Drive to **Poreč,** your base for the rest of the week. Check into your hotel and catch an excursion to **Baredine Cave.** The kids will be entranced by the stalactites, subterranean fauna, and other wonders, and if you're in Croatia in summer, you'll welcome sightseeing in the cave's chilly chambers.

Return to Poreč and wander around the **Basilica of Euphrasius** and its adjacent buildings and take a look at the amazing **Byzantine mosaics** preserved there. Have dinner and then spend some time poking around Old Town's many shops with an ice-cream cone in hand from one of Poreč's many ice-cream parlors before you call it a night.

Day 6 will be spent exploring Green Istria's medieval hilltop towns. Head to **Livade** where kids can see a model of the world's largest truffle at **Zigante's deli** or where the family can splurge on a gourmet lunch at **Zigante's restaurant** if so inclined. If you're there in September or October, you can book a truffle hunt before you hit Livade at the tourist office in Pula or you can call ahead to Zigante, which arranges the tours. Kids will love watching the dogs sniff out the elusive fungi, though they might not love the truffle taste.

From Livade, go west to the artsy medieval town of **Grožnjan,** then east to **Oprtalj,** a town perched on a hill that is even higher than Motovun's. If you have time, stop at **Roč** and its 16th-century walls. The last stop is **Hum,** the smallest town in the world. Outside Hum, you'll see **Glagolitic Alley,** a small park with large Stonehenge-type rocks inscribed with the ancient script.

Day 7 is departure day, but you'll want to leave early so you can stop at **Pažin,** where kids will love one of the best castle museums in Croatia and gape at the scary chasm that is just outside its door. If you have time, you can make the short drive 5.5km (3½ miles) from Pažin to **Beram** and ask one of the local women who take care of the Church of St. Mary outside Beram to take you there so you can see the *real* **"Dance of the Dead"** fresco. It then will be time to get on the road and head out of town through the **Učka Tunnel** and to **Rijeka** and the airport.

Dubrovnik

It would take a legion of Hollywood's most creative architects to design a set as perfect as Dubrovnik. Yet this "city made of stone and light" is as enchanting as the shimmering sunsets that ricochet off its 14th-century ramparts. In short: The Dalmatian UNESCO World Heritage city is stunning.

Even though Serb shells devastated the city during the 1991–92 siege, today's Dubrovnik is remarkably whole. In fact, a shade of red is one of the few telltale reminders of those violent days: New terra-cotta roof tiles on buildings blasted in the war are a little brighter and a little more orange than older roof tiles missed by Serb mortars. You might find a tiny bullet scar if you are looking for such reminders, but by and large the "Pearl of the Adriatic" is as lustrous as it was 5 centuries ago, when Dubrovnik was a major sea power bustling with prosperous merchants, and dripping with Renaissance grandeur.

Dubrovnik (nee Ragusa) began as a Roman settlement. From the Middle Ages on it was a prize sought by Venice, Hungary, Turkey, and others who recognized the city's logistical value as a maritime port. But *Libertas* (Liberty) has always been uppermost in the minds of Dubrovnik's citizens, and through the ages their thirst for independence repeatedly trumped other nations' plans to conquer their city.

In 1667, another kind of assault leveled Dubrovnik when an earthquake destroyed almost everything except a few palaces and church buildings in Old Town. The city was quickly rebuilt in the baroque style of the time, only to be shattered again during the 1991–92 siege. Croatia's war with Serbia destroyed the tourism industry throughout Croatia, but Dubrovnik was especially hard-hit. Not only was the city physically scarred from the war, but it was also economically crushed. Happily crowds are now once again flocking to this charming city nestled between the Adriatic and the Dinaric Alps, and Dubrovnik has regained its status as a vacation destination par excellence.

Inside protective walls, the pedestrian-only Old Town is again bustling with an international crowd. Here you will find almost all the area's sights worth seeing—historic churches and public buildings; designer shops and homey restaurants; ancient sculptures and modern galleries; fountains and bell towers; monasteries and gardens; and the most famous of all, the ancient city wall and its towers. Today's Dubrovnik attracts visitors from all socio-economic levels and corners of the world, from student backpackers to celebrities.

Outside the walls of Old Town, Dubrovnik's suburban districts are packed with hotels, restaurants, parks, campgrounds, and other services, all for the hordes of tourists clamoring to bask in the city's Mediterranean magic and revel in its citizens' exuberant devotion to Libertas.

1 Orientation

Accessing Dubrovnik by any means except air can be inconvenient and expensive. Even driving there from elsewhere in Croatia is challenging because of the city's position between the mountains and sea and the lack of modern roads in the area. Ferry routes to Dubrovnik often include multiple stops at various islands, and train service is nonexistent. It's wise to build in extra travel time when you visit Dubrovnik.

ARRIVING BY PLANE   Croatia Airlines (www.croatiaairlines.hr) operates daily flights to and from Zagreb and select European cities. Planes land at Dubrovnik International Airport (Zračna Luka), located at Čilipi, 18km (11 miles) from the city center (www.airport-dubrovnik.hr).

Croatia Airlines operates shuttle buses to and from Dubrovnik Airport and they are coordinated with incoming flights, even the late ones. Buses supposedly leave the main terminal in Dubrovnik at Gruž Port 90 minutes before each Croatia Airlines flight, but there is no posted schedule. You don't have to be a Croatia Airlines passenger to ride, however. The fare is 30kn ($5.50) one-way; it takes about 25 minutes.

There is also taxi service to and from the airport. Taxi cost is metered at 25kn ($4.50) plus 8kn ($1.50) per kilometer. Twenty-four kilometers (15 miles) from the airport to Dubrovnik costs about 250kn ($46), and it could be more if you don't settle on the price and terms before you get in the cab. The taxi company's website (www.taxiservicedubrovnik.com) tells you not to pay if the driver doesn't turn on the meter, but that could get ugly.

BY BUS   Daily buses operate between the Dubrovnik ferry port at Gruž and Zagreb, Zadar, Split, Šibenik, Rijeka, Orebić, and Korčula in Croatia, as well as Mostar and Sarajevo in Bosnia and Međugorje in Hercegovina. The main Dubrovnik bus terminal is at Put Republike 19 (© **020/357-020**).

BY FERRY   Jadrolinija operates ferries that connect Dubrovnik with the islands and cities up the coast, including the island of Hvar and the cities of Split and Zadar. There are also local ferries that run to the Elafiti Islands and Mljet. Buy tickets and obtain schedule information at the Dubrovnik Jadrolinija office in Gruž (© **020/418-000**) or at Jadroagent at Radića 32 (© **020/419-000**).

BY CAR   The A1 autocesta between Zagreb and Split opened in June 2005 and was extended another 27km (16 miles) to Omiš in 2007, reducing travel time between the two cities to about 3 hours. The leg of highway that continues on to Dubrovnik still is in the planning phase and not expected to open until 2010. Consequently, if you travel by car down the coast from Omiš to Dubrovnik, you still have to take the much slower E-65 for the entire 190km (115-mile) trip, which can take as long as 4 hours. If you drive straight from Zagreb to Dubrovnik, it will take approximately 7 hours—more during summer gridlock—so plan to take your time for this trip. *Warning:* Do not try to drive into Dubrovnik at night. Besides narrow roads and tight turns on hilly roads leading into town, the city's streets can be confusing. There are few street signs in the city and even those are impossible to see in the dark.

VISITOR INFORMATION

You'll find a **Dubrovnik Tourist Office** across the street from the Hilton Imperial on the road leading to the Pile Gate, Starčevića 7 (© **020/427-591**) as well as at several other locations around town. The Pile Gate location is also an Internet center where you can check your e-mail or connect with home. For a complete list of tourist offices, contact the **Dubrovnik Tourist Board** at Cvijete Zuzorić 1/11 (℃ **020/323-887;** fax 020/323-725; www.tzdubrovnik.hr).

The **Tourist Information Center** at Placa 1, across from the Franciscan monastery in Old Town (℃ **020/323-350;** fax 020/323-351), can help with maps, brochures, and information on local concerts, events, and some excursions. Private tourist agencies can be helpful, too—the following represents a partial list that can help. **Atlas Travel Agency** has several locations in Dubrovnik: at the Pile Gate, in Old Town, and at the harbor. Atlas operates almost all excursions out of Dubrovnik and can help you find private accommodations and general information. **Elite Travel** at Vukovarska 17 (℃ **020/358-200**) runs specialized tours such as the UNESCO World Heritage Croatia Tour, which visits the country's protected cultural and natural sites, a horseback tour of Konavale, and a canoe safari on the Trebezit River, among others. **Generalturist** can book sailboat and car rentals as well as excursions and accommodations (Obala Stjepana Radića 24; ℃ **020/432-974;** www.generalturist.com). **Gulliver Travel** offers a broad range of excursions to Dubrovnik's offshore islands and towns up and down the southern Adriatic coast (Obala Stjepana Radića 32; ℃ **020/313-313;** www. gulliver.hr). **Huck Finn** is Croatia's premier adventure travel source. Even though it is based in Zagreb, Huck Finn offers an extensive slate of active Dubrovnik excursions, including sea kayaking around Koločep Island, bicycling across Šipan Island, rafting the Neretva River, and much more (Vukovarska 270, 10000 Zagreb; ℃ **01/618-3333** www.huck-finn.hr). **Metro Tours** at Šetalište Kralja Zvonimira 40A (℃ **020/437-320**) offers excursions to various locations each day. You can choose Mostar in Bosnia on Monday for 290kn ($54), Cavtat on Tuesday for 125kn ($23), and Korčula and the Pelješac wine country on Friday for 320kn ($56), for example. Prices include transfers, guides, bus, and boat, depending on the destination.

If you have the resources, consider booking an English-speaking private guide who not only can plan a custom itinerary for you, but also can arrange transport, transfers, and admittance to otherwise inaccessible sites. **Jelena Delić** (℃ **91/531-8782;** damale3@hotmail.com) is one of the best.

FAST FACTS: Dubrovnik

American Express **Atlas Travel's** main office at Ćira Carića 3 (℃ **020/419-119;** fax 020/442-645; www.atlas-croatia.com) is the American Express agent in Dubrovnik. Atlas-Amex also has an office at Brsalje 17 (℃ **020/442-574**), open from 8am to 7pm Monday through Saturday.

ATMs Dubrovačka Bank operates eight Bankomats (ATMs) in Dubrovnik; Privredna Bank operates four. Other Croatian banks operate Bankomats throughout Dubrovnik. These are centrally located at the Stradun, Lapad, and Pile Gate (at the cafe bar Dubrava), in Gruž and in Cavtat.

Banks Banks are generally open from 7:30am to 7pm Monday through Friday and from 7:30 to 11:30am Saturday. Some banks close for lunch.

Business Hours Most grocery stores and department stores are open from 7:30am to 8pm. Non-government offices generally work 8:30am to 5pm Monday through Friday.

Credit Cards Credit cards are generally accepted at hotels and larger restaurants, but be sure to ask before you order.

Emergencies Dial © **94.**

Fire Dial © **93.**

Holidays See "When to Go," p. 15.

Hospital Go to the **Dubrovnik General Hospital** (© **020/431-777**).

Information You can reach the **Dubrovnik Tourist Board** at © **020/323-887;** the **Dubrovnik Neretva County Tourist Board** can be reached at © **020/413-301.** Also see "Visitor Information," p. 12.

Internet Cafe Try the cozy **Netcafe Internet Bar** (no. 21 in the middle of Prijeko St.'s restaurant block). Connections are fast, the coffee is excellent, and the place is air-conditioned. Open 9am to 11pm daily.

Pharmacy Pharmacies in Dubrovnik have varied working hours: They're open mornings and afternoons Monday through Friday, but only in the morning Saturday. Almost all accept credit cards.

Police Dial © **92.**

Telephone Public telephone boxes accept only phone cards available from newspaper stands and post offices.

Time Zone Dubrovnik is on Central European Time (GMT plus 1 hr.). Daylight saving time starts at the end of March and ends on the last day of September.

Tipping Tipping is generally not expected, though it is appreciated.

Weather The climate in Dubrovnik is typical Mediterranean, with mild, rainy winters and hot, dry summers. Daily forecasts are available at www.dubrovnik-online.com/english/weather.php.

DUBROVNIK NEIGHBORHOODS

Old Town   The area within Dubrovnik's walls is known as Old Town, and most of the city's main attractions are there. Besides historic buildings, Old Town is home to restaurants, cafes, shops, and services that line the Stradun—a long (just under a quarter of a mile) and wide street that runs from the Western Gate (Pile) to the Eastern Gate (Ploče)—and its backstreets.

Ploče   Ploče is the neighborhood just outside Old Town's Eastern Gate. Most of the city's upscale hotels are located on beachfront property in this area, as is the city's main public beach, Banje.

Lapad   There are no big-time historic sites in Lapad, which is just a long, leafy promenade lined with hotels and restaurants, backed by a residential area on this peninsula west of Old Town. Lapad abuts Lapad Bay, so it has some beachfront, but the neighborhood's main attraction is several moderately priced hotels—moderate in comparison with the luxury hotels in Ploče and Old Town. The no. 6 bus connects Lapad with Old Town at the Pile Gate; the ride takes about 15 minutes.

Babin Kuk   On the Lapad Peninsula, at some indeterminable point less than 6.4km (4 miles) from Dubrovnik's center and bordered on three sides by the sea and pebble beaches, the Lapad neighborhood ends and the Babin Kuk neighborhood begins. Babin Kuk has several hotels in various price ranges. It also has access to rocky coves with what optimists call beaches (read: major pebbles/rocks, no sand), as well as to scores of restaurants, shops, and services. Babin Kuk is connected to Dubrovnik by the city's bus system. Camp Solitudo, Dubrovnik's only close-in campground, is here.

GETTING AROUND

There are no trains or trams in Dubrovnik, but the Libertas city bus system is fairly efficient (www.libertasdubrovnik.hr). If you are staying within comfortable walking distance of Old Town, everything important is accessible on foot.

BY BUS Buy one-way tickets from a news kiosk or at your hotel for 8kn ($1.40) and save 2kn (35¢). All buses stop at the Pile Gate and continue on to outlying hotels, the ferry port, and beyond. Schedules and route maps are available at the Tourist Information Center in Old Town across from the Franciscan Monastery.

BY TAXI Taxi stands are at the airport, bus station, and at the Pile Gate. Taxis can be called locally ℂ 020/424-343 (Pile Gate), ℂ 020/423-164 (Ploče), ℂ 020/418-112 (ferry port), ℂ 020/357 044 (bus station; and ℂ 020/435-715 (Lapad). Rides start with 25kn ($5) on the meter and go up 8kn ($1.50) per kilometer. If you agree to a meterless ride, negotiate a price beforehand to avoid rip-offs and unwanted excursions.

ON FOOT Negotiating the busy streets outside the walls can be confusing, especially at night. But once you are in the vicinity of Old Town, you can devise your own walking tour using the suggestions in this book. You also can employ a private guide to accompany you on a walk, or you can book a guided Old Town walking tour through the tourist office or through a private tourist agency.

BY CAR Congestion and parking make driving in Dubrovnik stressful, and Old Town is pedestrianized anyway, but if you rent a car for excursions to nearby Pelješac or Ston, car rental companies at the airport include: **Hertz** (ℂ 01/484-6777; www.hertz.hr), **Budget** (ℂ 020/773-290; www.budget.hr), and **Thrifty** (ℂ 020/773-3588; www.thrifty.com). Be sure to reserve a car in advance to insure availability.

BY BICYCLE No companies currently rent bikes in Dubrovnik.

WHAT TO SEE & DO

Dubrovnik sprawls well beyond the city walls, to Ploče in the east and the Lapad and Babin Kuk peninsulas in the west, but just about everything worth seeing is within the walled Old Town.

City Wall ✫✫✫ No visit to Dubrovnik is complete without at least a partial walk around the top of its wall. The wall and its fortresses and towers are works of art built in medieval times; they undulate around Old Town in a protective embrace, creating an architectural frame for the historic city like none other. As you make the 2km (1¼-mile) circuit atop the wall, which is 25m (82 ft.) high and 6m (20 ft.) thick at some points, you'll see greater Dubrovnik and its landmark rooftops from every conceivable angle. You'll be able to see tourists and residents below going about their lives, swimming in the Adriatic off the wall's rocky base, or dining at restaurants set on outcroppings. It takes about an hour to complete the walk around the wall.

You can access the wall at three points: just inside the Pile Gate, near the Maritime Museum/John's Fortress, and near the Dominican Monastery at the Ploče Gate. From this point, you can choose a route around the wall's entire perimeter or half that distance. If you start at the **Pile Gate** entrance, you'll walk up a steep flight of stairs through an arch topped by a statue of St. Blaise. If you want to do the entire 360-degree stroll, continue straight up toward the **Minčeta Tower,** which is recognizable by its distinctive "crown." If you decide on the partial walk, halfway up the stairs you'll have to do a 180 from the stairs via a small landing to reach the wall, and you'll exit near **St. John's Fortress** on the south side. The 16th century **Revelin Fort** is on the eastern side of the wall above the Ploče Gate; and the 15th-century **Bokar Fortress,** which guarded against sea incursions, is at the southwestern corner across from the 12th-century **Lovrijenac Fortress.**

Old Town. Daily 9am–7:30pm July-Aug. Hours vary other times. 50kn ($8.60) adults; 20kn ($3.45); audio rental 40kn ($7).

Dominican Monastery and Museum ✹✹✹

Dubrovnik's Dominican Monastery is off a narrow passageway behind the Sponza Palace leading to the Ploče Gate. The monastery was built in the 14th century with the help of the Ragusa government and many local and foreign craftsmen, who positioned it against the city wall to strengthen the ramparts' northeastern flank. An impressive stairway leads to the Dominican's church doorway, decorated with a statue of St. Dominic; the door opens to the 15th-century Gothic cloister designed by Maso di Bartolomeo. The monastery's rooms circle the cloister, whose graceful triple arches frame a garden heady with Mediterranean plantings; an ancient well lies in the center. But architecture aside, the real reason to visit is the museum, which holds some fine religious art from Dubrovnik and elsewhere. Paintings, triptychs, silver church vessels, and a reliquary purportedly containing the skull of King Stephen I of Hungary are part of the museum's rich collection.

Sv. Dominika 4. Museum admission 10kn ($1.75). Daily 9am–6pm.

Dubrovnik Aquarium and Maritime Museum ✹✹ (Kids)

For a change of pace, follow the street opposite the cathedral's main door past several down-in-the-mouth side streets to St. John's Fortress and the aquarium and maritime museum. Instead of jumping into the sea, you can step back and take a close look at the ocean. Located in Tvrđava Sv. Ivana (St. John's Fortress) next to the old port, the Dubrovnik Aquarium has a large array of indigenous fish and ocean dwellers on display in its 27 tanks. Stingrays, conger eels, scorpion fish, and spotted dogfish are alongside spiny lobster, grouper, and other specimens from the deep. There are also delightful displays of colorful sea anemones, corals, shells, sea urchins, and sea horses. The tanks are fed by a constant stream of fresh sea water. The maritime museum has charts, documents, boat models, and artifacts related to Ragusa's sea industry.

Damjana Jude 2, St. John's Fortress. ✆ 021/427-937. Admission to both museum and aquarium 20kn ($3.50) adults, 10kn ($1.75) children. Aquarium summer daily 9am–9pm; winter Mon–Sat 9am–1pm. Maritime Museum summer daily 9am–6pm; winter Tues–Sun 9am–6pm.

Dubrovnik Cathedral (Church of the Assumption) ✹✹✹

The original Church of the Assumption was built between the 12th and 14th centuries atop the ruins of a 6th- or 7th-century Byzantine basilica. According to legend, it was financed by King Richard the Lionhearted, who was shipwrecked and rescued in Dubrovnik and made the donation to build a church to give thanks for his rescue. The legend probably isn't

Old Town Attractions

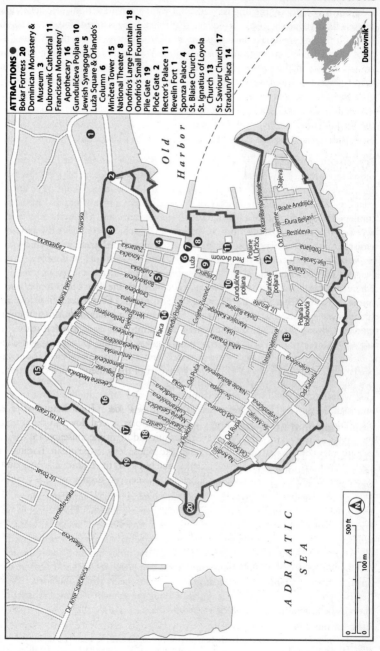

ATTRACTIONS ●

Bokar Fortress **20**
Dominican Monastery & Museum **3**
Dubrovnik Cathedral **11**
Franciscan Monastery/ Apothecary **16**
Gundulićeva Poljana **10**
Jewish Synagogue **5**
Luža Square & Orlando's Column **6**
Minčeta Tower **15**
National Theater **8**
Onofrio's Large Fountain **18**
Onofrio's Small Fountain **7**
Pile Gate **19**
Ploče Gate **2**
Rector's Palace **11**
Revelin Fort **1**
Sponza Palace **4**
St. Blaise Church **9**
St. Ignatius of Loyola Church **13**
St. Saviour Church **17**
Stradun/Placa **14**

Dubrovnik

true, but historians say the original cathedral was an elaborate Romanesque affair so severely damaged in the 1667 earthquake that it had to be restored. The cathedral was rebuilt following the quake in the *au courant* baroque style and it thus became the third church to be constructed on that site. In fact, remnants of both earlier churches are still visible in the present-day cathedral, which is a three-nave structure in the shape of a cross. The cathedral also has a rich treasury that includes many valuable gold and silver reliquaries and the *pièces de résistance,* the skull, arm, and leg of St. Blaise, all plated with gold. *Tip:* Don't miss Titian's polyptych "The Assumption of the Virgin" (1552) in the church's apse.

Poljana Marina Držica. Treasury 10kn ($1.75). Mon–Sat 9am–5:30pm; Sun 11am–5:30pm.

Franciscan Monastery 🎬🎬 A small **apothecary** inside the 14th-century monastery complex has been in business in 1317 and claims to be the oldest working pharmacy in Europe (it still seals herbal lotions and tonic made according to ancient recipes). It has a fascinating display of ancient lab equipment, mortars, measuring implements, and decorative containers used over the centuries. The monastery itself is accessed via a narrow passage from **St. Saviour's Church;** the complex's **Romanesque cloister** is the monastery's most compelling feature (the post-quake Renaissance cloister is open to Franciscans only). The lower cloister's open wall of double columns (topped with human, animal, and plant carvings) frame a tranquil open garden area where you can imagine monks enjoying the contemplative life. The complex also is home to a **15th-century well,** the single-nave **St. Francis Church,** a **bell tower,** and the **monastery museum,** whose library contains ancient writings, music manuscripts, gold and silver objets d'art, and other items that illuminate Dubrovnik's history.

Monastery museum 20kn ($3.50) adults; 10kn ($1.75) kids. Summer 9am–6pm. Erratic hours other times of the year.

Gundulićeva Poljana 🎬 West of St. John's Fortress and behind the Rector's Palace is a raucous morning market where fruits, vegetables, cheeses, homemade wine, recycled water bottles filled with *rakija* (fruit brandy), and other produce from the area and islands are sold. The market is near the exclusive **Pučic Palace Hotel** 🎬🎬.

Jesuit Church of St. Ignatius of Loyola 🎬🎬🎬 If you make a right turn from Gundulićeva Poljana, you'll run into a long set of baroque stairs designed by Pietro Passalacqua and reminiscent of Rome's Spanish Steps. The stairs lead up from Uz Jezuite to the Jesuit Church of St. Ignatius of Loyola, Dubrovnik's largest house of worship. The stairs were severely damaged in the 1991–92 siege of the city, but they have been restored. They end at the 1658 Jesuit College (Collegium Ragusinum), the school where many of Ragusa's greatest scholars were educated. The college is next door to the baroque church, which was modeled after Rome's Chiesa del Gesu, the mother church of the Jesuit order. Dubrovnik's single-nave structure was designed by Jesuit architect Andrea Pozzo, who worked for the order building Jesuit churches throughout Europe. The Dubrovnik church was completed in 1725 and decorated by Spanish artist Gaetano Garcia according to Pozzo's plan, which included frescoes depicting scenes from the life of St. Ignatius along the semicircular divided apse. The church's bell is said to be the oldest in Dubrovnik.

Poljana R. Boškovića. Daily 9am–noon and 3–7pm.

Jewish Synagogue 🎬🎬 You'll have to leave the Stradun and veer north up a steep street and staircase to find Dubrovnik's only synagogue on Žudioska Ulica (Jews' St.).

This is Europe's second-oldest Judaic house of worship. The synagogue is on the second floor of a town house given by the city government to the Jewish community: first, those who fled persecution in Spain during the late 15th century; and later, in the early 16th century, Jews from Italy. A small museum chronicles the Jewish community in Dubrovnik and holds an ancient Torah brought to Dubrovnik by the city's first Jewish residents.

Žudioska Ulica 5. Summer daily 10am–8pm; winter Mon–Fri 10am–1pm.

Luža Square ✶✶✶   The eastern end of the Stradun opens into a busy square that is a kind of crossroads in the Old Town where tourists stop to cool off with water from **Onofrio's Little Fountain,** explore an exhibit in **Sponza Palace,** meet friends at the **city bell tower,** take a *bijela* kava break at the **Gradska Kavana,** or sit down for a few minutes on the steps of **St. Blaise Church.** Luža Square is also where Dubrovnik's Summer Festival kicks off and where the big February 3 St. Blaise procession ends.

Onofrio's Fountains ✶✶✶   When you enter through either the Pile Gate or the Ploče Gate at the western and eastern ends of the Stradun respectively, the first thing that you will see is one of two Onofrio fountains in Old Town, which were constructed beginning in 1438 so that visitors could wash away the possibility of carrying plague into the city before they entered. The fountains, designed by Italian hydro-engineer Onofrio della Cava and architect Pietro di Martino, provide clean, cold water via an aqueduct from the Dubrovnik River (Rijeka Dubrovačka), 11km (7 miles) away, but the fountains' efficacy as germ killers is questionable. The larger fountain at the Pile Gate looks like a giant sectioned vat with a dome; it delivers cold water from 16 carved stone heads that ring the structure's lower third. The 16 heads are all that is left of the fountain's stone ornamentation after the 1667 quake and the 1991–92 siege. Water from the Luža Square fountain flows through a more ornate device with detailed sculpture work. Many people fill their water bottles and soak their bandannas in the fountains' cold water, especially in summer when Dubrovnik is steamy.

Orlando's Column ✶✶   This statue, chiseled into a stone column in the center of Luža Square, represents the legendary knight from Ludovico Ariosto's "Orlando Furioso," an Italian poem immortalizing the warrior, who reputedly was Charlemagne's nephew (and also the subject of the French epic poem, the "Chanson de Roland;" Roland is the French form of Orlando). The column was erected in 1419 and once served as the city's forum for public proclamations, notices, rallies, and punishments. According to legend, Orlando helped the people of Ragusa fight off a Saracen attack in the 9th century. Since the Orlando of poetic lore died in battle in 778, the legend defies plausibility. Other free cities also erected statues of Orlando, with the knight's image representing a city's status as a free-trade city-state. It is likely Dubrovnik's Orlando statue had a similar purpose. In 1990 a flag with the city's LIBERTAS motto was flown above the column, which became a rallying point for Dubrovnik's freedom fighters. Today the Libertas banner is flown here each year to herald Dubrovnik's annual summer festival.

Pile Gate ✶✶✶   The gate on the western end of the Old City was built on the site of the former Pile fortress and it is Old Town's busiest port of entry, largely because buses from the city and ferry terminals deposit their passengers there. A stone bridge leads to the outer gate, which is decorated by a statue of St. Blaise, the city's patron saint. The outer Pile Gate was guarded from 1537 on, so the city could monitor trade in and out of the city. The wooden drawbridge leading to it was pulled up at night in an elaborate ceremony. During summer, honorary guards in period costume stand guard mornings as tourists shuffle in for a day of sightseeing. However, the moat was drained long ago and is now just a green space. The interior gate was built in the 15th century and it, too, has its statue of St. Blaise—this one done by the prolific 20th-century Croatian sculptor Ivan Meštrović.

Entrance at the Pile Gate 30kn ($5.25). Summer daily 9am–7:30pm; winter daily 9am–3pm.

Ploče Gate ★★★   The Ploče Gate is similar to the Pile Gate, but at the eastern end of the Old City. Like the Pile Gate, this 15th century portal has inner and outer sections and the approach is via a stone bridge. The Revelin Fortress is built into the Ploče's outer section and was used as a lookout point. The gate is adorned with a statue of St. Blaise and the words, "Keep away, men of violence. For centuries, war has not affrighted this fortress, cherished by the spirit of the aged Saint."

Rector's Palace ★★   The first Rector's Palace once was more a forbidding stone heap than the graceful mansion it is today, but the original 13th-century building was destroyed in 1435 when gunpowder stored inside exploded. The palace was rebuilt in a Venetian-Gothic style based on a design by architect Onofrio della Cava (p. 55), only to explode again just 28 years later. The current Rector's Palace is on the same site just south of Luža Square, but it is more of a rehab than a redo; its Florentine designer Michelozzo Michelozzi merely grafted his work onto what was left of della Cava's. Functionally, the Rector's Palace was Ragusa's governmental nerve center and housed state offices as well as a dungeon and quarters for the rector, who was required to live in the palace for the duration of his term. Today, the palace's upstairs rooms house the City Museum (Gradski Muzej), filled with exhibits depicting how people lived in Ragusa. Classical music concerts are held in the palace courtyard during Dubrovnik's Summer Festival.

Pred Dvorom 3. ☎ 020/321-497. Admission 15kn ($3). Summer daily 9am–7pm; winter Mon–Sat 9am–2pm.

St. Blaise Church ★★★   St. Blaise is Dubrovnik's patron saint and protector. It seems as though the original city fathers had his image engraved on everything possible—public buildings, walls, city seals, fortresses and, of course, the magnificently baroque St. Blaise Church. The present church was built between 1706 and 1714 on the site of a 14th-century Romanesque church that was damaged in the 1667 earthquake, but after the quake the church still was usable until a 1706 fire put an end to that. Today's St. Blaise footprint is that of a Greek cross; the domed church has a wide staircase and terrace that attracts weary tourists from Luža Square, many of whom sit on its steps for a break, much the same as flocks of pigeons settle on the square itself. Inside you'll find many works of art that were saved from the old church; the most notable is a silver-plated statue of the saint on the main altar. The statue depicts St. Blaise holding a 15th-century model of the city as it was before the great earthquake.

Luža Trg (Sq.). Daily 8am–7pm.

Sponza Palace ★★   As you approach Luža Square from the Stradun, you'll see the arches of the 15th-century Sponza Palace on your left. Today the palace courtyard is a bright venue for art exhibits and concerts. There are several rooms off the courtyard. Two of the rooms hold artifacts significant to Dubrovnik. One contains copies of documents that chronicle Dubrovnik's history. The other is called the Memorial Room of

Who is St. Blaise?

St. Blaise once saved a child from choking on a fish bone. For this reason, Roman Catholics everywhere know the Armenian physician and martyr of the faith as the patron saint of people with throat problems. However, the people of Dubrovnik revere St. Blaise (Sv. Vlaho) as the hero who saved their city from a sneak attack by Venetian galleys in the 10th century. According to legend, the Venetian ships dropped anchor off Lokrum, supposedly to pick up fresh water for their journey, but the fleet was actually surveying the city in preparation for an attack. However, St. Blaise (later put to death by the Roman Emperor Diocletian in 316 B.C.) appeared to the city cathedral's priest in a dream wearing a long beard with a miter and staff. He told the priest about the nefarious plot, thus thwarting the attack. Ever since then, St. Blaise has been immortalized in sculpture, art, and other media in Dubrovnik as the city's protector and biggest hero. To show their appreciation for his help, the citizens of Dubrovnik go all out to honor St. Blaise on his feast day, February 3, which the city celebrates with food and festivities. The reliquaries purportedly containing several of the saint's body parts are carried through the city in a parade; and people line up to have their throats blessed by the local priests.

the Defenders of Dubrovnik; it contains photos and short biographies of the Croatian patriots who died during the 1991–92 siege of Dubrovnik. There is also a small souvenir shop. A 30m (100-ft.) bell tower to the left of the palace tolls the hour.

Luža. © 020/321-032. Free admission, except for some exhibitions. Daily 9am–2pm, though times vary during exhibitions.

St. Saviour Church ⊕ The Renaissance-Gothic facade of St. Saviour Church faces the larger Onofrio fountain inside the Pile Gate. St. Saviour was built in the early 16th century by Petar Andrijić of Korčula and it is one of the few structures not damaged in the 1667 quake. Some say it was influenced by Šibenik's UNESCO World Heritage cathedral (p. 165). It is certain, however, that St. Saviour influenced several Dalmatian churches, most notably the cathedral of Hvar. St. Saviour's is no longer used for Mass. The church's interior appears to have been recently restored, as the marble and ceiling paintings are quite bright and clean looking.

Between the Pile Gate and the Franciscan Monastery at Stradun 2. Daily 9am–7pm.

Stradun ⊕⊕⊕ The Stradun (aka Placa) is Dubrovnik's main thoroughfare. It runs from the Pile Gate straight through the city to the Ploče Gate on land that once was a marshy and dividing line between Ragusa and Dubrava on the mainland. Today's Stradun is paved with limestone buffed to a smooth, shiny surface by the hordes of tourists who pass through every day. It is lined with neat, uniform buildings housing shops, restaurants, and entryways radiating to the alley-sized side streets. Historic pictures show that the street and its buildings along the Stradun were far more ornate and acquired their present subtle style after the 1667 earthquake. To aid tourists, the city of Dubrovnik has hung banners at the entrance to each of these narrow streets to let people know what they'll find if they veer off the main drag. Almost everyone who visits explores Dubrovnik's side streets, but inevitably, they rejoin the seemingly never-ending promenade of humanity on the Stradun to window-shop or wander.

WALKING TOUR	DUBROVNIK'S STRADUN

Start:	Brsalje Square outside the Pile Gate, the west entrance to Old Town.
Finish:	St. Blaise Church/Luža Square.
Time:	Anywhere from 30 minutes to 3 hours, depending on how much time you spend exploring side streets, in churches and museums, shopping, or dining.
Best Times:	Mornings from 8am–noon before the sun is overhead; evenings after 6pm and until the last bar closes. This when the promenade starts and segues into a fashion show for the young and beautiful.
Worst Times:	Noon to sundown or whenever the temperature rises above 30C.

Walking around the top of Dubrovnik's wall is a stroll no visitor should miss, but once you've made the circuit, you'll realize that there's much more to Dubrovnik than the red-tile roofs visible from the ramparts. A walk up and down both sides of the Stradun is an ideal way to become acquainted with the city's charms. Old Town's smooth limestone path originally was a canal separating Old Ragusa from the mainland and walking its length is a good way to get your bearings and become familiar with the attractions between the Pile Gate and the Ploče Gate. There is a high concentration of important sites on and just off the Stradun, and the pedestrian thoroughfare is always crowded. Lots of narrow side streets radiate up and out from the Stradun and intersect with cobbled streets that are packed with religious sites, historic architectural spots, shops, restaurants, a few courtyards, and even some residences.

Start your tour outside the Pile Gate in Brsalje Square next door to the Atlas Travel Agency and between the Nautika restaurant and Dubravka Kavana café

① Brsalje Square

Rendezvous in this leafy park, but before you enter Old Town, walk away from the street to the low balustrade. You'll have an unobstructed view of the sea and **Fort Lovrijenac** to the right and the 16th-century **Bokar Fortress** to the left. Lovrijenac is built on a high, rocky peninsula that juts into the sea and it is Dubrovnik's oldest defensive structure. These days it is used as a theater for Shakespearean productions and for performances during **Dubrovnik's Summer Festival.** Croatian native and television star Goran Višjić of "ER" fame is a frequent performer there. Bokar was used as a prison in the 19th century.

Return to the street, turn right, and approach the:

② Pile Gate

This is the busiest portal to Old Town, and it is really two gates you approach across a wooden drawbridge that once was pulled up each night to protect the city. Note the statue of St. Blaise carved into a niche above the opening of the 16th century outer gate and another statue of the city's patron (by **Ivan Meštrović**) inside the even older (15th-century) inner gate. Occasionally musicians and vendors hang out in the courtyard between the gates to catch people on their way out.

Step through the inner gate and stop a moment to orient. Walk through and note:

③ Onofrio's Large Fountain and the Wall Walk Entrance

Walk inside the Pile Gate and to the left you'll see a steep stairway that leads up to the **Minčeta Tower** at the top of the wall (see p. 52 for details). This is one of three access points to the wall. To the right is **Onofrio's Large Fountain,** a tall concrete dome that during the Middle Ages was a collection point for water that flowed into the city from the **Dubrovnik River** 12km (7½mi) away via an aqueduct. The fountain was more ornate when it was completed in 1444, but the iron embellishments were destroyed in the 1667 earthquake.

Stay left. The first building on your left is:

❹ Church of Our Saviour

This tiny church was built as a memorial to the victims of a 1520 earthquake, but it became a symbol of strength when it became one of the few buildings to survive the 1667 quake that destroyed most of the city. Today it is used for concerts and exhibits.

Walk on a few steps to:

❺ The Franciscan Monastery/Museum

Before you explore this building with its columned cloister and ancient pharmacy, note the small stone protruding from the bottom left of the church's front and the people who keep jumping on it. This building, with its garden, architectural features, pharmacy, and museum exhibits is worth a visit (p. 54).

Exit the monastery and begin your Stradun stroll in earnest to investigate the:

❻ Stradun Shops and Side Streets

The Stradun (aka Placa) runs to the clock tower and the **Ploče Gate.** All the buildings along the way are almost identical in style, a result of post quake construction in the 17th century. Note the arches that frame a combo door and window. The sill was used as a counter over which business was conducted. If you are up for a detour, head up **Žudioska Street** to visit the second-oldest synagogue in Europe and its original 17th century furnishings (p. 54).

Continue along the Stradun past Zlatarska Street to the:

❼ Sponza Palace

As you approach Luža Square, note the graceful Renaissance arches of the **Sponza Palace** (p. 56), which used to be Dubrovnik's Customs House. Today it houses the **Memorial Room of the Dubrovnik Defenders,** a visual tribute to the more than 300 people who were killed from Oct. 1, 1991 to Oct. 26, 1992 while defending Dubrovnik against Serb attacks. Multi-media images of the destruction and photos of the young people who died in the conflict are moving reminders of the devastation that swept Croatia at that time.

Exit the palace and walk up to Orlando's Column in the center of Luža Square and pause at:

❽ Orlando's Column and Onofrio's Small Fountain

Orlando's Column (p. 55) will be in front of you as you exit the Palace, and the **Clock Tower** will be to your left. Note the statue's forearm, which was Old Ragusa's standard of measurement (512mm/20 inches). The **Clock Tower** features a pair of bronze men who move up to strike the bell on the hour. The **Town Hall** is to the right of the Clock Tower and **Onofrio's Small Fountain** is in front of that.

Turn left from the front of Orlando's Column and walk through the passageway between the Sponza Palace and the Town Hall. Turn left and head to the Dominican Monastery:

❾ Dominican Monastery, the Old Port, and the Ploče Gate

The Dominican Monastery is a complex that includes a large church, cloisters, and a museum. The original 14th century church was destroyed in the 1667 quake, and this one was rebuilt in the 17th century. There are some interesting paintings inside and the church also doubles as a concert venue during the Summer Festival. The cloisters are a must-see with courtyard gardens and interesting stonework (p. 52).

Exit the monastery and left onto Svetoga Dominika. Continue on to explore the Old Harbor, Ploče Gate, and Revelin Fortress, and/or retrace your steps and return to Luža Square:

⑩ Gradska Kavana and the Rector's Palace

As you return from the Dominican Monastery, the Town Hall and **Gradska Kavana** (Town Café) will be on your left. You can break for a cold drink or coffee and sit at tables facing the square or go inside and grab a spot on the terrace overlooking the Old Harbor. The **Town Theater** is also in this building. The Venetian-Gothic **Rector's Palace** (p. 56) is adjacent to the Gradska Kavana complex fronted by pillars made of marble from Korčula and topped with interesting carvings. The interior is used for summer concerts.

Exit the Rector's Palace and turn left:

⑪ Dubrovnik Cathedral

Note the minimalist gray marble altar that was installed when Roman Catholicism ruled that the priest should face the people during Mass—its block style is incongruent the church's baroque design. Don't miss the **treasury,** which is loaded with priceless relics, including the skull of St. Blaise and a piece of the True Cross (p. 52).

Exit the cathedral and walk around to the rear and walk up Androvićeva to the Jesuit Steps and Church of St. Ignatius Loyola (p. 54) or turn left and walk past the Rector's Palace to return to Luža Square.

⑫ St. Blaise Church

This 18th century baroque church (p. 56) is a tribute to Dubrovnik's patron saint. Inside, the altar is the main draw with its statue of the saint holding a model of the city of Dubrovnik as it was before the 1667 quake. Outside, the church's wide steps are a popular resting/meeting place for tourists.

From St. Blaise you either can return to the Pile Gate and inspect the shops along the south side of the Stradun, explore what you've just seen in greater depth, or venture up the steep side streets to discover more sights between the Stradun and the walls.

ESCORTED WALKING TOURS

Mediterranean Experience Ltd., Ćira Carića 3 (ⓒ 020/442-201), offers daily 1-hour "Discover Dubrovnik" walks from the Large Onofrio Fountain at 10am and 7pm. The itinerary introduces Dubrovnik's major sights for 90kn ($15.50) per person.

BEACHES

Croatians loosely define beaches as any place the sea meets the land, and while some beaches may have names, they are little more than rocks you can use to jump into the water. One such place is a must-see, if not a must-swim area in Dubrovnik. Just around the corner from the old port you'll find a **rocky indentation** 🕌🕌🕌 where those who are confident in their swimming skills routinely take a dip.

There is no such thing as a privately owned beach in Croatia. Nonetheless, several of the hotels east of the port have staked out *access routes* to sections of the beach for their guests, making it hard for others to get there. Dubrovnik's main public beach, **Banje,** exists as a beach club (below).

Bobin Kuk's **Copacabana Beach** is another choice. Copacabana is a pebble-and-concrete beach with a view of the graceful Dubrovnik bridge and part of the Elafiti Islands. It is one of the few beaches in Dubrovnik with facilities for kids, sports enthusiasts, and swimmers with disabilities. Here you can ride a jet ski, get whipped around on a banana-boat ride, or go parasailing. There are also sea slides for kids. A lift on the concrete part of the beach gives seniors and people with disabilities easy access to the water. Grown-ups can relax in a beach bar or a beach restaurant. At night, the beach bar becomes a cocktail bar and disco.

Day or night, the **Eastwest Beach Club** is Dubrovnik's answer for people who want to experience the luxury of a beach hotel without paying beach-hotel prices. Situated on Banje, about 46m (150 ft.) from the entrance to the Ploče (Eastern) Gate, Eastwest is also in the shadow of the upscale Excelsior and Villa Argentina hotels. The club has a restaurant with a view and a sophisticated Dalmatian menu, a cocktail bar with space for dancing, watersports galore, a beach with crystal-clear water, beach attendants, and the unique baldachin. This "bed" on the beach looks like a raised four-poster hung with gauzy curtains that blow in the breeze. You can rent the baldachin for 200kn ($37) per day and enjoy privacy on the beach.

Frana Supila bb. ⓒ 020/412-220. www.ew-dubrovnik.com.

WHERE TO STAY

There is a conspicuous lack of budget accommodations in Dubrovnik. Even moderately priced rooms are difficult to find unless you opt for private accommodations in Lapad or Gruž. Try the tourist office or look for signs in windows that say SOBE (room available). If you arrive at the ferry or bus terminal, you'll be greeted (or accosted) by men and women waving photos of lodging options—mainly rooms in private homes. In general, the cheapest are from the seated old ladies asking you if you need a place to sleep. *Warning:* If you choose this option, be sure to inspect the room before you hand over any money. You never know what you'll get—perhaps a dirt-cheap find in the center, or a tiny bed (sharing a bathroom with the owner) on the outskirts of town. If you want to be more certain of what you're getting into, go to a tourist office.

VERY EXPENSIVE

Rixos Libertas ⭐⭐⭐ The opening of this exclusive property was delayed several times since 2004, when the Turkish hotelier bought the crumbling landmark Libertas Hotel and its real estate 15 minutes from Old Town's north gate. Nearly 4 years and 70 million euros ($98 million) later, Rixos unveiled the result of its Pygmalion project, which has transformed the former refugee shelter into a 14-story temple of glass, steel, and stone. The new Libertas is terraced into a cliff overlooking the Adriatic and it is loaded with every conceivable amenity. From stylish rooms outfitted with high-grade furnishings, large, upscale bathrooms, and enough technology to run computers and plasma TVs to a long menu of water sports, gourmet restaurants, and a two-story, full service spa, Dubrovnik's newest luxury address has it all.

Liechtensteinov Put 3. ⓒ 020/333-720. Fax 020/333-723. www.rixos.com. 315 units. Doubles from 390€ ($545); suites from 750€ ($1,050). AE, DC, MC, V. Rates include breakfast. **Amenities:** 3 restaurants; 5 bars; patisserie; cigar bar; night club; casino; spa; indoor and outdoor pools; designer retail outlets; room service; valet parking; kids' program; laundry; rooms for those w/limited mobility; nonsmoking rooms. *In room:* AC, SAT TV, minibar, hair dryer, safe, Wi-Fi and broadband Internet access.

Hotel Dubrovnik Palace ⭐ *Overrated* The Palace has reigned over Dubrovnik's hotel scene for years, winning awards as the best hotel in Croatia for two years running (2005 and 2006) from the World Travel Market Association following an ongoing 45-million€ ($63 million) renovation that was spread over more than a decade. Today, the hotel in the woods at the southern end of the Lapad Peninsula has positioned itself as an elite facility catering to business travelers with expense accounts and others with deep pockets, but as a luxury tourist destination, the Palace deserves no more than a mixed review. The hotel's public areas and facilities are gorgeous and views are knock-outs. All rooms have sea views, private balconies, and flatscreen TVs, but they (especially bathrooms) are a bit cramped and chintzy for the price. In addition, food in the

Palace's restaurants is mediocre at best; and perhaps the most egregious lapse—service and the friendliness of the staff leave lots of room for improvement.

Masarykov Put 20. ℂ 020/430-000. Fax 020/430-100. www.dubrovnikpalace.hr. 308 units. Doubles from 348€ ($490). Suites from 495€ ($695). AE, DC, MC, V. Rates include buffet breakfast. **Amenities:** 3 restaurants; 4 bars; night club; 3 outdoor and 1 indoor pool; spa; tennis courts; diving center; children's program; room service; Wi-Fi access; laundry; parking; 1 room for those w/limited mobility; VIP wing w/private entrance. *In room:* AC, SAT TV, Wi-Fi access, minibar, hair dryer, safe.

Bellevue ★★★

The Bellevue closed late in 2005 to undergo an extensive renovation and the result is a clifftop beauty with jaw-dropping views of Dubrovnik and the sea. Parent Adriatic Luxury Hotels chose Feb. 3, 2007, the feast of St. Blaise (Dubrovnik's protector), to reopen for business, but no saintly miracle is necessary to recognize that Croatian race car driver Goran Štrok's 20-million euro ($28 million) investment in the 5-story hotel has transformed it into an upscale destination. Natural materials that include Dalmatian stone and olive wood are featured in the decor throughout the hotel and there's even a palm tree growing up from the restaurant to the reception area. Guest rooms are done in a sailboat motif and walls are hung with original works by Croatian artists. All rooms also have a view of the Adriatic and 88 of them have balconies, too. The hotel also has a full complement of amenities that includes a private theater room for movie screenings.

Pera Cingrije 7. ℂ 020/330-000. Fax 020/330-100. www.hotel-bellevue.hr. 93 units. Doubles from 250€ ($350); suites from 545€ ($765). AE, DC, MC, V. Rates include breakfast. **Amenities:** 2 restaurants; 2 bars; indoor pool; spa; valet service; retail shops; car rental; business center; Wi-Fi/Lan access; private beach; screening room; garage. *In room:* AC, SAT TV, minibar, hair dryer, safe. Suites have Jacuzzis.

Importanne Resort ★★

Two hotels, the Neptun/Importanne Suites and the Ariston, and the upscale Villa Elita now comprise Importanne Resort, a cluster complex that opened in spring 2007 on the Lapad Peninsula 10 minutes from Dubrovnik's Old Town. The facilities are mostly renovated and offer accommodations to suit a wide demographic that includes both families and tycoons. Villa Elita, which opened in July 2007, is the poshest (and most expensive) of the lot, with a stratospheric tariff that *does* include the use of one of several luxury cars, use of a speedboat, and valet service.

Kardinala Alojzija Stepinca 31. ℂ 020/440-100. Fax 020/440-200. www.hotel-neptun.hr. 158 units (Neptun/Importanne Suites), 116 units (Ariston), 6 units (Villa Elita). Doubles from 95€ ($135) for standard room in the Neptun to 12,000€ ($16,800) for Villa Elita. AE, DC, MC, V. **Amenities:** 3 restaurants; beach bar; 2 seawater pools; spa; parking. *In room:* AC, SAT TV, Internet access, minibar, hair dryer, safe, balconies in most rooms, room service.

Grand Hotel Park Dubrovnik ★ *Overrated*

All guest rooms in this Lapad hotel have balconies overlooking either the sea or Lapad's park area. All are spacious, with middle-of-the-road furnishings that could use a major freshening. Room prices at the Grand Hotel Park are high for what you're getting, even if the hotel is in the middle of Lapad's restaurant and nightlife districts and a short distance from Uvala beach.

Šetalište Kralja Zvonimira 39, Lapad. ℂ 020/434-444. www.grandhotel-park.hr. 162 units including 6 suites. July 1–Sept 30: from 1,500kn ($259) seaside double; from 3,000kn ($520) suite. Other times: from 810kn ($140) seaside double; from 2,400kn ($415) suite. Rates include breakfast. **Amenities:** Restaurant; bar; indoor and outdoor pools; sauna; elevator; parking; Internet access. *In room:* A/C, TV, minibar.

Hilton Imperial ★★★

Hilton's first hotel in Croatia isn't within the walls of the Old Town, but with a location just steps outside the Pile Gate, it's as good as it gets. The 1897 Imperial (and its guesthouse across the street), which sheltered refugees from Croatia's civil war and took a direct mortar hit on the upper floors, has emerged

Where to Stay & Dine in Dubrovnik

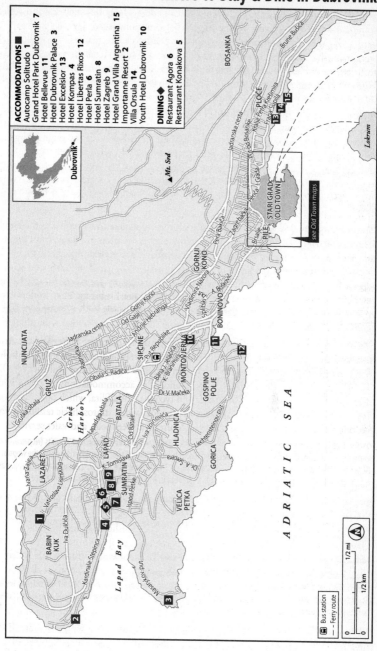

ACCOMMODATIONS ■
Autocamp Solitudo 1
Grand Hotel Park Dubrovnik 7
Hotel Bellevue 11
Hotel Dubrovnik Palace 3
Hotel Excelsior 13
Hotel Kompas 4
Hotel Libertas Rixos 12
Hotel Perla 6
Hotel Sumratin 8
Hotel Zagreb 9
Hotel Grand Villa Argentina 15
Importanne Resort 2
Villa Orsula 14
Youth Hotel Dubrovnik 10

DINING ◆
Restaurant Agora 6
Restaurant Konakova 5

▲ Mt. Srd

BOSANKA

Brune Bušića

PLOČE

Kralja Petra Krešimira

Frana Supila

13 14 15

Jadranska cesta

Put Bosanke

Iza Grada

Put od Bosanke

Zagrebačka

Perla

Peračka

Branitelja

Bruašė

Bilale

PILE

STARI GRAD
(OLD TOWN)

see Old Town maps

Lokrum

Perå Bakića

GORNJI
KONO

Od Gornji Kono

Andrije Hebranga

Put Republike

Vladimira Nazora

Splitski

A. Boškovic

BONINOVO

10
11
12

Jadranska cesta

NUNCIATA

Radnička

GRUŽ

Obala S. Radica

Gruška obala

Gruška obala

ŠIPČINE

Bana J. Jelačića

K. Branimira

MONTOVJERNA

Dr.V. Mačeka

GOSPINO
POLJE

BATALA

Lapadska obala

Lapadska obala

Dr. A. Starčeva

Liechtensteinov put

Od Batale

Iva Vojnovića

HLADNICA

GORICA

_Gruž
Harbor_

LAPAD

K. Tomislava

Isnod Petke

SUMRATIN

7 8 9

6

5

4

Kardinala Stepinca

Iva Dulčića

BABIN
KUK

Ivana Zajca

Vatroslava Lisinskog

LAZARET

1

2

Lapad Bay

Mašanikov put

3

VELIKA
PETKA

_A D R I A T I C   S E A_

1/2 mi

1/2 km

0

0

N

■ Bus station
— Ferry route

Dubrovnik

63

as an undisputed jewel of the Dubrovnik hotel market. The hotel's redbrick-and-white stone facade and Hapsburg yellow filigree balcony railings are Hilton's face to the world, but the hotel personnel are its link to guests. Unlike many Dubrovnik hotel workers, Hilton staff members are usually a class act and extend the same courtesies to Brioni-suited businesspeople and backpackers alike, an anomaly in Croatia. While Hilton was changing worker attitudes, it kept whatever it could of the old Imperial—its stone staircases, the lobby footprint—but everything else is brand-new. Rooms are spacious and done in the similar earth/sun color schemes. All are loaded with amenities, whether you stay in a single room or a suite. It's easy to get comfy in your room with room service from the hotel's Porat Restaurant ⭐⭐⭐ or in the huge lobby bar where you can read a newspaper or get a snack with your coffee frappe.

Marijana Blažića 2, at the Pile Gate. ☎ 020/320-320. Fax 020/320-220. www.hilton.com. 147 units, including 8 junior suites. From 232€ ($276) double; from 340€ ($405) suite. **Amenities:** Restaurant; piano bar; pool; sauna; steam bath; elevator; garage; nonsmoking rooms; room for those w/limited mobility. *In room:* A/C, TV, Wi-Fi, minibar, hair dryer, safe.

Hotel Excelsior ⭐⭐⭐
The Excelsior is on the same piece of real estate as the Hotel Grand Villa Argentina (below); thus it enjoys a great location just steps from the sea and within close walking distance of Old Town. The Excelsior was built in 1913, expanded in the 1960s, completely renovated in 1998, updated in 2006, and scheduled for a complete overhaul in time for the 2008 season. Guest rooms, whether in the old or new parts of the hotel, are well appointed. Rooms in the older section have gentle touches of yesteryear but they are also fresh and modern: The Excelsior's latest renovation focused on the old part of the hotel. Book one of the rooms overlooking the sea. They have stunning views of Dubrovnik's wall and lookout towers.

Frana supila 12, Ploče. ☎ 020/353-300. Fax 020/414-214. www.hotel-excelsior.hr. 152 units. From 515€ ($720) double with sea view and balcony; from 735€ ($1,030) suite. Rates include breakfast and remain the same all year. Half-board available. **Amenities:** 2 restaurants; piano bar; indoor pool; elevator; sauna; access for those w/disabilities; garage; Internet access. *In room:* A/C, TV, fax, dial-up Internet connection, minibar, hair dryer, safe.

Hotel Grand Villa Argentina ⭐⭐⭐
Grand Villa Argentina is really a complex of five buildings—one hotel and four smaller (but just as elegant) villas, all with the same aura of refined luxury. Personalized service is the Grand Villa Argentina's mission, and it shows. Guest rooms in this hotel within walking distance of Old Town are comfortable and decorated with the highest quality furnishings. While the sea views are spectacular, the guest rooms are not as large as those in Villa Orsula.

Frana Supila 14, Ploče). ☎ 020/440-555. Fax 020/432-524. www.hoteli-argentina.hr. 151 units. July 1–Sept 30: from 320€ ($380) double with sea view and balcony; from 500€ ($595) suite. Other times: from 250€ ($298) double with sea view and balcony; from 420€ ($500) suite. Rates include breakfast. **Amenities:** 3 restaurants; bar; indoor and outdoor pools; sauna; spa; elevator; Internet access; casino. *In room:* A/C, TV, minibar, hair dryer.

Villa Orsula ⭐⭐⭐
One of the best addresses in Dubrovnik, Villa Orsula is everything you would expect of an opulent 1930s Mediterranean villa. In fact, Villa Orsula was built in the 1930s and was converted into a hotel in 1989. Orsula is adjacent to the Grand Villa Argentina; the two buildings share a pool and other facilities as well as a garden leading to the sea. Villa Orsula is graced with areas like the gorgeous **Victoria Terrace Restaurant,** which is shaded by fragrant flowers and lush vegetation. The restaurant and most of the guest rooms both have incredible sweeping views of Old Town and the sea, and both are sumptuously decorated. Open from April to November only.

Frana Supila 14, Ploče. ✆ **020/440-555.** Fax 020/432-524. www.gva.hr. 15 units, including 3 suites. July 1–Sept 30: from 340€ ($405) double with sea view and balcony; from 520€ ($619) suite. Other months: from 254€ ($303) double with sea view and balcony; from 420€ ($500) suite. Rates include breakfast. **Amenities:** Restaurant; bar; indoor and outdoor pools; sauna; spa; elevator; garage; Internet access. *In room:* A/C, TV, minibar, hair dryer.

Pucić Palace 🟊🟊 *(Overrated)* The Pucić Palace is already a legend and *the* favorite Dubrovnik accommodations for the well-heeled. Formerly the home of a Dubrovnik nobleman, the hotel combines the cachet of a Renaissance palace with contemporary creature comforts, but it falls short of what you'd expect for the prices Pucič charges for its guest rooms. Guest room furnishings are first-rate and bathrooms are loaded with toiletries and lined with non-skid tiles and tasteful mosaics, but we're talking showers here. The hotel maintains a yacht in the harbor for its guests to use; the terrace has a great view of the city; and you *are* staying in a historic monument. Service is impeccable; but you'll have to decide for yourself if those things justify the hotel's sky-high tariffs.

Ulica Od Puča 1, Old Town. ✆ **020/326-200.** Reservations 020/326-222. Fax 020/326-223. www.thepucicpalace. com. 19 units, including 2 suites. June–Sept: from 479€ ($570) double; from 721€ ($858) suite. Other times of year: from 273€ ($325) double; from 515€ ($613) suite. Rates include breakfast. **Amenities:** Restaurant; bar; concierge; 24-hr. room service. *In room:* A/C, TV, minibar, safe.

EXPENSIVE

Hotel Kompas 🟊 The Kompas is a package hotel at the end of Lapad's promenade street where it meets the marina. Guest rooms overlook either Lapad Bay or Lapad's park area, and some have balconies. Bathrooms are adequate in size, but those with bathtubs are a little larger than those with showers. The Kompas has an Internet cafe on the lower level. The stop for the no. 6 bus to Old Town (4km/2½ miles away) is just around the corner.

Šetalište Kralja Zvonimira 56, Lapad. ✆ **020/352-113.** www.hotel-kompas.hr. 115 units. Doubles from 192€ ($230). **Amenities:** Restaurant; bar; outdoor pool; elevator. *In room:* A/C, TV, minibar.

Hotel Perla 🟊 The Perla opened in 2005 on the Lapad promenade and it is still evolving. However, the tiny hotel and its **Agora restaurant** 🟊🟊 are on the right track. Guest rooms are spacious and quiet; most have balconies that look onto the hotel's landscaping. Bathrooms are good-size and well equipped, but there is no elevator, which makes the trek to rooms on upper floors a pain. Once you check in, your location is excellent, but you cannot drive up to the Perla to unload your luggage because of its position on the promenade: You need to park a couple of blocks away and schlep.

Lapad Mali Stradun bb, Lapad. ✆ **020/438-244.** www.perla-dubrovnik.com/index.htm. 15 rooms and 5 apts. From 120€ ($142) double. Rates include breakfast. **Amenities:** Restaurant; bar. *In room:* A/C, TV, hair dryer, balcony.

Hotel Stari Grad 🟊 The aristocratic home that has been the tiny Stari Grad since 2002 is also a cultural monument and just one of two hotels within Dubrovnik's walls. Each room is elegantly furnished, comfortable, cozy, and augmented by bathrooms equipped with hydromassage showers. The view of Lokrum and Cavtat from the fifth-floor terrace is dynamite.

Od Sigurate br. 4, Old Town. ✆ **020/322-244.** Fax 020/321-256. www.hotelstarigrad.com. 8 units. From 994kn ($172) double. Rates stay the same all year and include breakfast. **Amenities:** Restaurant; valet; safe-deposit box; babysitting options. *In room:* A/C, TV, dataport, minibar, hair dryer.

Domino Apartments 🟊 These luxury apartments tucked into a tiny courtyard at the end of Siroko St. are the equivalent of condo rentals: The "larger" apartments have a tiny living room while the smaller ones are really studios with kitchenettes. Furniture and appliances are new; window views are of neighboring buildings; and the apartments can get noisy when the ✪ **Steak House Domino** in the courtyard is busy. Rental office is in the Fendi store at ground level.

Hlidina 4. Old Town. ✆ **020/324-940.** Fax 020/324-824. www.dominoapartments.com. 6 units. July 1-Sept. 30 studio units from 1470kn ($272); 1-bedroom units from 1875kn ($325). Rates vary other times. In room: A/C, TV, kitchen facilities.

MODERATE

Sesame Inn ✪✪   The Sesame Inn is really a very small boutique hotel attached to a ✪✪ restaurant. The entire package blends convenience, history, and gourmet dining for anyone who is lucky enough to book one of the Inn's 4 modern rooms. The 200-year-old Dalmatian stone house has been updated with handsome white bathrooms, stylish furniture, and windows that overlook a fragrant garden and sunny terrace. Add to that reasonable (for Dubrovnik) rates, the hosts' (Ercegović family) cordiality, the ✪✪ Sesame Taverna, and the Inn's position 175 yards (150m) from the Pile Gate, and you have a perfect base from which to explore Old Town Dubrovnik.

Don Frane Bulića 4. ✆ **020/412-910.** www.sesame.hr. 4 units. Doubles from 440kn ($82) July and Aug. Other times: doubles from 320kn ($60). No credit cards. Rates do not include breakfast, which is available for 25kn ($5) per person and there is a 20% surcharge for stays of less than 3 days. **Amenities:** Restaurant; terrace.

Hotel Zagreb ✪✪ *Finds*   A fabulous restoration has turned this salmon-colored 19th-century mansion with white trim into a showplace hotel on the Lapad promenade. Each guest room is unique, and staying here is like staying in a grand Hapsburg home complete with shaded garden and sprawling lawn. Some of the staff speak English; all of them are very helpful.

Šetalište Kralja Zvonimira 27, Lapad. ✆ **020/436-146.** Fax 020/436-006. 24 units. From 1,060kn ($186) double July 1 to mid-Sept; from 700kn ($123) double at other times. **Amenities:** Restaurant; bar. *In room:* TV, hair dryer.

INEXPENSIVE

Autocamp Solitudo ✪✪   The bathrooms at this campground outside Dubrovnik are like new, and there's a laundry area. It is the only campground near Dubrovnik, but a private room is a better choice.

Vatroslava Lisinskog 17, Babin Kuk. ✆ **020/448-686.** Fax 020/448-688. www.babinkuk.com. 166 campsites. Site with electricity and 2 persons 16€ ($19). Apr 1–Oct 15. **Amenities:** Restaurant; market; pool; excursions; laundry.

Youth Hostel Dubrovnik   Unlike some of Dubrovnik's hotels and inns, this hostel stays open all year long. It is just a 10-minute walk from the Dubrovnik bus station and a 15 minute walk to Old Town. Dubrovnik's hostel has a fine reputation and some say it is the best in Croatia. You must be a member of a hostelling association to stay in these dorm-style accommodations (4- to 6-person rooms), which are in high demand. Guests can use the communal kitchen and dining room, too. *Note:* The hostel is near one of Dubrovnik's hottest nightlife areas and there is a 2am curfew.

Vinka Sagrestana 3, near Old Town. ✆ **020/423-241.** Fax 020/412-592. www.hfhs.hr. 19 units with 82 beds. Bed only: 120kn ($22) per person July–Aug. Other times, bed-and-breakfast from 80kn ($15) per person. Extra charge for breakfast. **Amenities:** Restaurant; TV room; membership kitchen.

Villa San ✪✪   Private apartments and rooms are Dubrovnik's best moderately priced accommodations options and Villa San can't be beat for convenience: Villa San is situated above a bank behind the Pile Gate bus stop, 300 feet from the beach and steps from the water taxi to Lokrum. The property is managed by the Ahmić family and it comprises four apartments ranging in size from "mini" to "penthouse." The latter is on

The Siege of Dubrovnik

In October 1991, during the first year of the Serb-Croat war, Dubrovnik came under attack by Serb forces, who tried to take control of the city by cutting it off from supplies and services while shelling its UNESCO-protected monuments. For 3 months, the city was cut off from electric, water, and telephone services, which effectively isolated the people but did not leave them helpless.

Rather than surrender, Dubrovnik dug in and survived the Serb blockade without water service largely because of water supplied by the 15th-century Onofrio Fountains, which do not have to rely on outside water pumps. Instead, the Fountains draw drinking water directly from the Dubrovnik River via an ancient hydro system.

When Serb forces realized that taking Dubrovnik was not going to be easy, they shelled the city indiscriminately, causing extensive damage and the loss of more than 100 lives. Churches and monuments marked with UNESCO flags were shelled; private houses were destroyed; the city's airport was reduced to rubble and looted; and many people fled the city for safer ground.

The siege lasted for 10 months, and the city lost more than its buildings: Even after it was declared safe, this vacation destination remained a ghost town as tourists stayed away in droves, a situation that decimated the region's economy.

Dubrovnik's infrastructure and buildings have been restored and tourism has recovered, but not all the people who left during the siege have returned. Some of the issues related to the city's liberation are still open in the World Court.

the top floor and can sleep 8 in three bedrooms, kitchen, living room, and two baths, one with a Jacuzzi.

Tiha 2, near Old Town. ☎ 020/411-884. www.villa-san.com. 4 apartments. Doubles from 60€ ($72)July-Sept, 50€ ($60) May-June, and 40€ ($48) Oct-Apr. Penthouse from 180€ ($215) July-Aug and New Year's; from 120€ ($143) other times. 20% deposit required; cash only. **Amenities:** Parking. *In room:* A/C, SAT TV, some balconies.

WHERE TO DINE

You definitely won't have to search very long for a restaurant no matter where you are in the Dubrovnik region. In some areas, like Prijeko Street in Old Town, restaurants are so close together you can't tell where one ends and another begins. Competition is so stiff that some even pitch passersby on the glories of their food. Whether you are looking for a table with a spectacular view of the sea or just a decent meal, you'll find it in Dubrovnik.

INEXPENSIVE

Café Festival ⋆ SANDWICHES   It can get rather warm in the afternoon sun at tables under the nautical blue awning outside this smart cafe near the Pile Gate, so go inside to try the salads, pastas, fancy drinks, and homemade pastries. Café Festival is the ideal place for a light lunch or a cool drink.

Stradun bb, Old Town. ☎ 020/420-888. www.cafefestival.com. Entrees 15kn–45kn ($3–$8). AE, DC, MC, V. Daily 8am–11pm.

The Gaffe Pub _Value_ BURGERS   If you hanker for a taste of home but you're determined to stay away from the golden arches, try a burger at the Gaffe. Known locally as "The English Pub," the Gaffe serves a mixture of burgers, salads, and omelets on its covered terrace. Inside, patrons can watch horse racing or live sports on SKY TV while they lift a few pints.

Miha Pracata 4 (5th street on the left from St. Blaise Church), Old Town. ☎ 020/324-841. Entrees 30kn–40kn ($5.25–$7). No credit cards. 10am–3am during Dubrovnik's festival; till 11pm other times.

Kavana Dubravka ⭑⭑ SANDWICHES   The view of the fortresses and the sea is the same from Dubravka as it is from the pricey Atlas Nautika next door, but at a fraction of the cost. The food isn't bad, either. Order a prsut-and-cheese sandwich or a pastry, sit back, and congratulate yourself on finding a bargain.

Brsalje. ☎ 020/426-319. Sandwiches from 15kn–25kn ($2.75–$5). No credit cards. Summer 10am–midnight daily and 10am–8:30pm daily in winter.

Konoba Lokanda Peskarija ⭑ _Value_ FISH/RISOTTO   Entertainment is all around you at Konoba: Watch walkers atop the wall; see boats dock; and observe chefs working in an open kitchen that looks like a beach bar. Prices are low, main courses are limited to a few fish dishes and risottos, but portions are huge. The octopus salad and black risotto are standouts.

Gorica Svetog Vlaha 77. Old Town. ☎ 020/324-750. Entrees 40kn–65kn ($7–$11). No credit cards. 8am–2am. Kitchen noon–midnight.

Konoba/Spaghetteria Toni ⭑ _Value_ PASTA/PIZZA   This colorful sidewalk konoba next to Baracuda serves up pasta more ways than you thought possible under massive umbrellas that keep the place cool. Try the _macaroni arrabiata_ with tomatoes and peppers as a pasta choice with a little kick to it, or dig into the tagliatelle with salmon, cream, and garlic for something more serene.

Nikole Božidarevića 14, Old Town. ☎ 020/323-134. Entrees 30kn–59kn ($5.50–$10). No credit cards. Daily noon–11pm.

Pizzeria/Spaghetteria Baracuda PIZZA   Baracuda may look like an everyday pizza place tucked into a narrow side street, but the super-thin pizza crust sets it apart. Tables are picnic-style with umbrellas that line the tiny street. Space is so tight that there's barely room for a waiter carrying a large pizza to get in the serving aisle between the tables and the building. But the pizza is worth taking a chance: Each has a crispy upturned rim that is a perfect counterpoint to the bubbling ingredients on top.

Božidarevićeva 10, Old Town. ☎ 020/323-160. Pizza 25kn–50kn ($4.50–$9). No credit cards. Daily 10:30am–12:30am.

Restaurant Jadran DALMATIAN   Jadran is a touristy but solid restaurant with both a garden setting and an indoor dining room. The restaurant is in the former Convent of the Poor Clares and it doesn't fool with tradition. The menu doesn't have any surprises and you will find all the usual Dalmatian entrees—squid, risotto, mixed grill, and the occasional omelet and salad. But the food is competently prepared, making the Jadran a good place for a quick bite before or after you tackle the walk around the city wall.

Paska Miličevića 1, Old Town. ☎ 020/323-403. Fax 020/323-403. Entrees 19kn–49kn ($3.50–$8.50). AE, DC, MC, V. 10am–midnight.

Where to Stay & Dine in Old Town

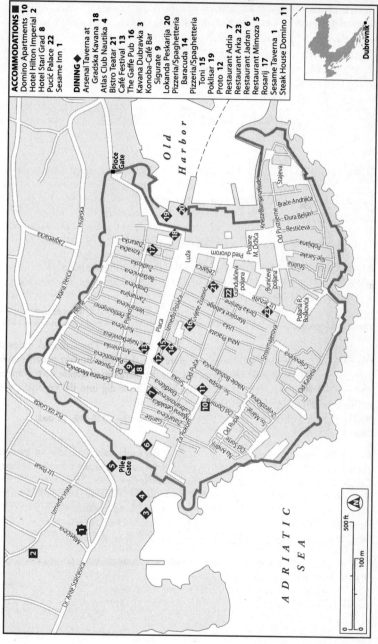

ACCOMMODATIONS ■
Domino Apartments 10
Hotel Hilton Imperial 2
Hotel Stari Grad 8
Pucić Palace 22
Sesame Inn 1

DINING ◆
Arsenal Taverna at
  Gradska Kavana 18
Atlas Club Nautika 4
Bistro Teatar 21
Café Festival 13
The Gaffe Pub 16
Kavana Dubravka 3
Konoba–Café Bar
  Sigurate 9
Lokanda Peskarija 20
Pizzeria/Spaghetteria
  Baracuda 14
Pizzeria/Spaghetteria
  Toni 15
Poklisar 19
Proto 12
Restaurant Adria 7
Restaurant Arka 23
Restaurant Jadran 6
Restaurant Mimoza 5
Rosarij 17
Sesame Taverna 1
Steak House Domino 11

Dubrovnik

Old Harbor

Ploče Gate

Pile Gate

ADRIATIC SEA

MODERATE

Arsenal Taverna at Gradska Kavana ✦ CROATIAN   This upscale terrace spot became a delightful addition to Dubrovnik's restaurant scene when it reopened in November 2005 on the Old Harbor near the Ploče Gate. The menu is typical of Dubrovnik with lots of fish dishes, but it also has a better-than-average selection of grilled meats and an extensive but pricey selection of Croatian wines. Appetizers include Paški sir, a specialty sheep's milk cheese from the island of Pag, and kulen, a spicy sausage from Slavonia in Eastern Croatia. Service can be slow, but who wants to hurry through a meal when the twinkling lights of Dubrovnik are the backdrop?

Pred Dvorom 1. Old Town. ☎ 020/321-065. Entrees 70kn–140kn ($12–$24). AE, DC, MC, V. 9am–2am. Kitchen closes 11:30pm.

Bistro Teatar ✦ DALMATIAN   This strictly sidewalk restaurant across from the National Theater expands and contracts with the crowds: Tables are added to or subtracted from the space depending on the number of diners. Either way, you won't be disappointed by the food. Seafood, steaks, and pasta are touted here, but you can't go wrong with the grilled fish dishes, which are prepared in traditional Dalmatian style.

C. Zuzorić 1, Old Town. ☎ 020/323-977. Entrees 40kn–150kn ($7–$26). DC, MC, V. Daily 10am–2am.

Konoba-Café Bar Sigurata DALMATIAN   Order any fish dish at this secluded side-street spot and you'll be happy. If you're not in the mood for that, Sigurata offers a vegetarian platter, spaghetti, and fried calamari. Tables are covered with awnings to keep things cool on hot afternoons.

Sigurate 2, Old Town next to the Stari Grad Hotel. ☎ 098/358-818. Entrees 40kn–90kn ($7–$16). AE, DC, MC, V. Daily 11am–1am.

Poklisar ✦✦ SEAFOOD/PIZZA   Poklisar has unabashedly been catering to tourists for 10 years and its extensive menu, friendly waitstaff, and crowded seaside tables are testament to that. The cuisine ranges from pizza to lobster and everything is well-prepared and attractively presented. Try the house specialty, skewers of grilled shrimp resting atop blue cheese risotto, or savor one of the super-thin-crust pizzas while you breathe in the scent of the sea.

Ribarnica 1, Old Town. ☎ 020/322-176. www.poklisar.com. Entrees 41kn ($7) pizza; 590kn ($102) kilo (2.2 lbs.) lobster. AE, DC, MC, V. Daily 9am–midnight.

Proto ✦✦ SEAFOOD   There is some sidewalk seating here, but opt for the gorgeous upstairs terrace or the sublime winter garden, which features lots of glass, stone walls, and dark wood. According to the menu, food is prepared "according to our grandparents' recipes" using local ingredients. Try any of the grilled meats—or even the Dalmatian ham appetizer—to see if either conjures up childhood memories. The wine list is full of reds from Pelješac and whites from Korčula.

Široka 1, Old Town. ☎ 020/323-234. www.esculap-teo.hr. Reservations recommended. Entrees 74kn–110kn ($13–$19). AE, DC, MC, V. Daily 11am–11pm.

Restaurant Agora ✦✦ DALMATIAN   Located inside the Hotel Perla, the terrace in front is shielded from Lapad's promenade by greenery, which helps muffle traffic noise and affords some privacy. When you walk in, it at first looks as if you've stumbled into another ordinary konoba because the menu lists the usual grilled fish and meats, but look again. Entree preparations are strictly straightforward here, which plays up Agora's fresh ingredients, including an unusually large number of steak cuts. If you need a meat fix, the filet mignon with a baked potato is an excellent choice.

Mali Stradun bb, Lapad. © 020/438-244. Entrees 50kn–150kn ($9–$26) except fish portions in kilos. AE, DC, MC, V. Daily 7am–midnight.

Restaurant Arka ★ *Value* DALMATIAN/ITALIAN   Lasagna any way you like it is the specialty of this busy dining spot in the shadow of St. Ignatius of Loyola Church. The seafood platter is piled high with various types of crustaceans, while the Plata Arka overflows with vegetables and fish. There are several vegetarian choices, too.

Uz Jezuite bb, Old Town. No phone. Entrees 45kn–150kn ($8–$26). No credit cards. Daily 11am–midnight.

Restaurant Konakova ★ *Value* DALMATIAN   You'll probably have to stand in line to get a table at this second-floor terrace restaurant, which packs them in every night. Like most other Dubrovnik dining spots, specialties are seafood, grilled meat, pizza, and pasta, but equal care is given to all dishes. Little touches like complimentary fish pâtés served with bread make this bargain choice even better.

Šetalište Kralja Zvonimira 38, Lapad. © 020/435-105. Entrees 45kn–120kn ($8–$21). AE, DC, MC, V. Daily noon–midnight.

Rozarij ★★ *Finds* DALMATIAN/SEAFOOD   Rattan tables outside this tiny dining room are arranged on steps around Rozarij's entrance, set on a hard-to-find corner of Prijeko (corner of Prijeko and Zlatarska). But Rozarij and its impeccable seafood are worth searching out. Try the shrimp with white risotto or the mixed *buzzara*, a combination of mussels and scampi cooked in a fragrant court bouillon.

Prijeko 2, Old Town. © 020/321-257. Entrees 50kn–120kn ($9–$21). No credit cards. Daily 11am–midnight.

Sesame Taverna ★★ DALMATIAN   This dining room doesn't have a seaside location, but it does have stone walls, a vaulted ceiling bathed flickering candlelight, and a menu of beautifully presented dishes. Sesame Taverna is as romantic as it gets, especially on the upstairs terrace. Try the chicken Elafiti with rosemary and olives or any of the dishes with truffles accompanied by a reasonably priced bottle of wine.

Din Frane Bulića 7, west of the Pile Gate. © 020/412-910. www.sesame.hr. Entrees 65kn–150kn ($12–$28), more for seafood sold by the kilo. AE. Daily 8am–11pm.

Steak House Domino ★ CROATIAN   Meat, meat, and more meat dominates the menu at Domino, a restaurant up a narrow street off the Stradun. In summer, waiters in white shirts tend to diners seated under a canvas canopy at bench-style tables on the restaurant's charming terrace; in winter the action moves inside to Domino's white tablecloth dining room. Portions are generous and grilling seems to be the preferred method of cooking—a good thing since steak is a specialty of the house. Try that, or the grilled calamari with blitva. Service can be slow when all the tables are full, and they often are as Domino is a favorite stop for tour groups.

Od Domina 6. © 020/323-103. Fax 020/323-101. Entrees 80kn–160kn ($15–$30). AE, DC, MC, V. Daily 10am–midnight. Closed Dec 1–Jan 20.

EXPENSIVE

Porat ★★★ CONTINENTAL/DALMATIAN   Porat's elegant second-floor dining room offers a menu laden with local foods, but with creative twists and sauces. Try crispy skinned sea bass filet with sea salt and candied lemon from the lava-stone grill, or beef tenderloin and tomato-shallot marmalade. You can also find duck breast on the menu, which is unusual in Dalmatia. The Porat's version is served with apricot/pancetta rolls and veggies.

In the Hilton Imperial. Marijana Blažića 2. ℂ 020/320-320. Fax 020/320-220. www.hilton.com. Reservations required for dinner. Dinner entrees 140kn–190kn ($25–$33); lunch and breakfast entrees 70kn–120kn ($12–$22). AE, DC, MC, V. 7–10:30am for breakfast; 12:30–2:30pm for lunch; 7–11pm for dinner.

VERY EXPENSIVE

Atlas Club Nautika ⚔ *Overrated* GOURMET DALMATIAN   Nautika has the best location of any restaurant in Dubrovnik; it boasts an unobstructed view of the sea and the Bokar and Lovrijenac fortresses. Less impressive is the light lunch menu offered from noon to 4pm at 60kn to 120kn ($11–$21) for one of six uninspired choices. *Tip:* You can skip lunch and get the view for free in the space along the rail next to the restaurant. Dinner is a different story: Diners can choose elegant cuisine from an extravagant dinner/degustation menu with choices such as sea bass with cuttlefish-ink sauce, stuffed snails Pelješac style, and excellent vintages from an impressive wine list, including international choices from nearby Bosnia to far-flung California. *Note:* The restaurant accepts credit cards for dinner but not lunch.

Brsalje 3, Old Town. ℂ 020/442-526. www.esculap-teo.hr. Dinner entrees 148kn–380kn ($26–$66). 7-course degustation menu 99€ ($118) per person without wine. AE, DC, MC, V at dinner only. Noon–midnight (light lunch served noon–4pm).

BARS & NIGHTLIFE

Once the sun goes down, Dubrovnik is a hive of humanity, with crowds walking in waves to one restaurant or another and then moving to the Stradun or the Lapad promenade. From about 8–11pm the crowd is a diverse mix of families and couples strolling with ice cream cones. But at 11pm, there's a changing of the crowd as the early birds file out and 18-to-20-somethings flow in dressed in outfits that rival the costumes in a Busby Berkeley musical. Follow the throbbing music blaring from jam-packed side streets where nightly block parties convene after the restaurants close and you'll experience Dubrovnik cafe society's second shift.

Buža I ⚔⚔⚔   People sitting at tables stuck in a rocky indentation and jumping from there into the sea are visible to anyone walking the wall, and the inevitable question is, "How do I get there?" Wonder no more. This alfresco bar is accessible from the ground via a doorway marked "8-20" opposite the terrace of the Ekvinocijo restaurant on Ilije Sarake. Open daily in summer 8am to whenever. Buža II is open from 10am to whenever. Ilije Sarake access. No phone. No credit cards.

Capitano ⚔   Deejay dance music is the norm at this sprawling bar near the Pile Gate, but occasionally a live band comes to jam. Capitano seems to lure a mostly young and restless crowd, as everyone in the place seems to be on the prowl. Open daily 6pm to 4am Wednesday through Saturday. Izmedju vrta 2. No phone. No credit cards.

Casablanca ⚔   The decor and size of this popular bar almost makes it seem sedate, but Casablanca can rock. There is a big TV screen playing everything from soccer reruns to music videos; drinks range from straight up to complicated, and DJs spin a good mix of music. Open daily 5:30pm to 1am. Zamanjina 7. No phone. No credit cards.

East-West ⚔⚔⚔   East-West has a dual personality as a restaurant for families and bikini-clad sun worshipers when the sun is up and a bar full of fashionistas when the sun goes down. However, East-West's location on the city's public beach (Banje) ensures that it's crowded no matter the time of day. There is music, but it takes a back seat to East-West's spectacular location and clientele. Open daily in summer only from 5pm to 3am. Banje Beach, Frana Supila. ℂ 020/412-220. www.ewdubrovnik.com. MC, V.

Latino Club Fuego 🍸   For a disco experience, try **Latino Club Fuego** outside the Pile Gate. Don't expect nonstop salsa here despite the name: There is nothing vaguely Latino about this club, but it's a popular after-hours spot just the same. Open in summer 10pm to 4am daily; open in winter 10pm to 4am Thursday to Sunday only. Pile Brsalje 11. ✆ 020/312-871. No credit cards. Admission charge is nominal and covers the cost of a drink.

Night Club Revelin 🍸🍸🍸   This club in the Revelin Fortress at the wall attracts a younger crowd and it's always packed. Revelin's location in the 16th century fortress affords views of the old harbor and even the sunrise if you stay that long. There is a terrace where you can catch a breather from the always-jammed dance floor. Open 9pm to 2am Wednesday through Thursday and 9am to 3am Friday through Saturday. Reveling Fort, Sveti Dominika. ✆ 020/322-164. www.revelinclub.com. No credit cards.

Sunset Lounge 🍸🍸 (Hotel Dubrovnik Palace)   Everything is chic in this high-end lounge with a killer view of the sea. From the hip piano player to designer drinks to the panoramic views out the floor-to-ceiling glass walls, Sunset reeks of money and style. Even if cocktails aren't your cup of tea, spend an hour or two just for the views. Open daily noon to 1am. Masarykov Put 20. ✆ 020/430-000. www.dubrovnikpalace.hr. AE, DC, MC, V.

Trubadur 🍸🍸🍸   You can jam to the music inside or sit back on comfy chairs outside and let the music wash over you at this venerated jazz club. Performing groups change almost nightly. Inside is cramped and tiny, but you can sit at one of the T-mobile umbrella tables on the terrace and tap away at your laptop in the Hotspot zone with a drink and sandwich. Open daily 9am to 3am in summer and 5 to 11pm in winter. Bunićeva Poljana 2. ✆ 020/323-476. No credit cards.

2 Around Dubrovnik

ELAFITI ISLANDS

This group of 14 islands and islets between Dubrovnik and the Pelješac Peninsula is one of the most popular excursions from Dubrovnik. Only the largest of the "deer islands" (from the Greek *elfos*)—Koločep, Lopud, and Šipan—are populated. They have a long history and are believed to have been inhabited since prehistoric times. During the 10th century, the islands became Dubrovnik territories, liberally strewn with chapels, churches, and crumbling villas designed in a riot of pre-Romanesque, Gothic, and Renaissance styles. Today, the few residents of these islands are indifferent to tourists, and visitors are mostly left alone to poke around in the pine forests and ruins that cover much of the islands. If you have the time, visit the islands one at a time instead of with the popular "overview" excursion that hits all three (it is a bit of a whirlwind, and you don't get to embrace any island fully). However, if time is short, **Vivado Travel Agency** (✆ 020/486-471; www.dubrovnik-online.com/vivado) and many others operate ticket kiosks at the Old Harbor near the Ploče Gate. They sell daily fish picnic excursions for about 250kn ($46) per person.

TOURIST INFORMATION   Information offices for the islands are on Lopud and at Šipanska Luka. Both are open June to September, Monday through Saturday from 8am to 1pm and from 5 to 8pm, on Sunday 9am to noon. Lopud's office can be reached at ✆ 020/759-086 and Šipanska Luka's at ✆ 020/758-084.

GETTING THERE   Besides the fish picnic tours mentioned above, you can get to the Elafitis via daily Jadrolinija ferries, which serve the islands all year long. The trip to Koločep takes about half an hour and costs around 25kn ($4.50); the ride to Lopud is just under an hour and costs around 25kn ($4.50); and transport to Šipanska Luka takes about an hour and 20 minutes and costs 30kn ($5).

GETTING AROUND   These islands are small, and cars and motorcycles aren't allowed, so walking is the primary way to explore them.

WHAT TO SEE & DO

Koločep: Koločep is the island in this group and it is closest to Dubrovnik; at less than a square mile, it is also the smallest. Less than 3.2km (2 miles) from Dubrovnik, Koločep is scattered with a number of sacral buildings worth visiting. Its fewer than 200 residents live in tiny villages of stone houses like Donje Čelo on the northwest side and Gornje Čelo on the island's southwest side. You can cover the distance between the two villages in less than an hour on foot unless you are lured off the path between them to explore Koločep's olive groves and church ruins.

Lopud: Lopud is the midsize island of the three and covers just under twice the territory that Koločep does. It attracts more visitors than its sister islands because it is the most tourism-oriented and has the most attractions–the shell of a Franciscan monastery, a small ethnographic museum, the ruins of a small fortress, ancient churches in various stages of decay, and a wonderful sandy beach with a restaurant and bar. Fewer than 100 families live on Lopud and they are mostly involved in farming or in providing food and services to visitors.

Šipan: Šipan is the largest of the Elafitis, but it is also the least developed. Ferries deposit passengers at Šipanska Luka (Šipan Harbor) every hour and a half or so. You are then free to explore what's left of the island's 15th-century manor homes, and to relax on the island's tiny sand beach. There is a pleasant valley (Šipansko Polje) between Šipanska Luka and Sudurad, another village at the opposite end of the island, as well as assorted towers, houses, and a little church.

WHERE TO STAY & DINE

Each of the Elafitis has places where you can get cool drinks and light snacks. Lopud has two restaurants that offer more elaborate meals.

Obala ⭑ SEAFOOD   The sea is a backdrop for your just-caught lunch. Waiters in semi-formal dress and piped-in music add a touch of elegance to your meal at this seafood place, which serves grilled fish that is well-prepared and beautifully presented.

Obala Ivana Kuljevan 18. ☎ **020/759-108**. Entrees 30kn–75kn ($5–$13). No credit cards. Hours vary.

Perčin ⭑⭑ SEAFOOD   Grilled fish and a few meat choices are on the menu at this family-run konoba on Lopud. Nothing fancy here, just delicious food.

Obala Ivana Kuljevan[a] 27. ☎ **020/759-028**. Entrees 40kn–80kn ($7–$14). No credit cards. Daily 8am–midnight.

Villas Koločep ⭑   If you decide to stay on Koločep, the renovated (2006) **Villas Koločep** is your best bet. The quiet hotel is on the water and actually is composed of 8 villas with 151 rooms.

Donje Celo, 20221 Koločep. ☎ **020/757-925**. 151 units. Doubles in July and Aug start at 149€ ($208). Off-season rates start at 89€ ($125) for the same double. **Amenities:** Restaurant; pool; beach. *In room:* AC, SAT TV, balcony, hair dryer, free Wi-Fi

LOKRUM

Lokrum is the island closest to Dubrovnik and water taxis leave from the old harbor every 30 minutes daily in summer from 9am–6pm. The journey takes about 15 minutes

and costs 35kn ($6.50) round-trip. Once there, you have your choice of relaxing on the beach or exploring the woods and the vestiges of an 11th century Benedictine monastery purchased in 1859 by Hapsburg Archduke Maximillian Ferdinand and his wife Charlotte as a vacation home. Maximillian didn't have much chance to enjoy his Lokrum digs: He was dispatched to Mexico to be its emperor three years after acquiring the property, and never returned to Lokrum—he was assassinated in Mexico in 1867. But before Maximillian left, he put in a botanic garden at the monastery. The garden still is open to the public, but is a mess. But you can follow his walking path to Fort Royal, a French fortification built on Lokrum's highest hill in 1806.

MLJET

Mljet's background is laced with legends, but its present is a real-life experience of nature and history at their best. There is proof that ancient Greeks were familiar with Mljet, an island they called Melita, or "honey," for the swarms of bees they found there. But except for amphorae in the sea off Mljet, there is no tangible evidence that the Greeks ever settled there. However, later settlers—Romans, Byzantines, Avars, Slavs—did leave traces of their time on Mljet; the area around Polače boasts several sites with ruins from the 1st through the 6th centuries, including a 5th-century Roman palace and some fortifications.

Today the western side of Mljet is a national park known as a "green island" because Mljet is heavily wooded (more than 70% of the island is covered with forests). Its centerpieces are the two saltwater lakes. Water in these lakes is warm: 77°F (25°C) for Malo Jezero and 82° to 86°F (28°–30°C) for Veliko Jezero. The lakes' high saline concentration is said to have healing properties, especially for skin diseases and rheumatism. The smaller lake actually was a swamp until the 12th century, when Benedictine monks who built a monastery on St. Mary's Islet on Veliko Jezero dug a channel between Malo Jezero and the larger lake, which is connected to the sea by a canal.

The 12th-century monastery and its Church of St. Mary have gone through several incarnations since they were built, including a stint as a hotel during Tito's administration. The 1991 war ended that phase, leaving the monastery and church vacant and neglected. However, there are signs that the church and monastery are being renovated; according to a Mljet tour guide, the Benedictines plan to once again use its monastery and church by 2008.

The monastery is closed to visitors, but the tiny Church of St. Mary is open, though there isn't much to see. St. Mary is single nave and mostly empty. Small engraved stones in the foyer floor mark graves where the monks were buried standing up.

Mljet and Mljet National Park are easily reached from Dubrovnik and other nearby islands and points on the mainland. Excursion and car ferries run here from Trstenik on the Pelješac Peninsula. Atlas (8am–6pm) runs excursions from Orebić that depart via water taxi from the dock across from the tourist office on Trg Mimballa; the boat also picks up people at the Orsan hotel farther up the beach. The daylong excursion costs 270kn ($47) per person. The fee includes admission to the park.

The water taxi takes you to Korčula, where you pick up the boat to Mljet. The ride to Mljet from Korčula takes an hour and 40 minutes, so you spend half a day just getting there and back. The excursion boat, which is like a crowded bus on water, disgorges passengers at Pomena, Mljet's center of tourism. Mljet is a very low-key island with just the one hotel and several apartments for rent. It only seems crowded when you dock at Pomena because everyone congregates around the Odisej hotel, which is on the marina.

You can pick up a cold drink at the Odisej Hotel and then walk just short of a mile to boats that will take you to St. Mary's Island on Veliko Jezero. There you can poke around in the 12th-century Benedictine monastery or swim in the saltwater lakes, which are very warm. Malo Jezero, the smaller of the two lakes, has a small beach, but access to Veliko Jezero is off a small rock ledge. Boats between St. Mary's and Pomena leave every hour.

WHERE TO STAY

Hotel Odisej ⚐   The Atlas Odisej is Mljet's only hotel and it is the stepping-off point for visits to the national park. The hotel isn't anything special, but guest rooms are comfy and a good place to relax after negotiating the woods. The hotel is managed by Atlas, the tour operator who brings groups to the island on day trips.

Pomena bb, 20226 Pomena. ℭ 020/744-062. Fax 020/424-383. www.hotelodisej.hr. 155 units, 2 suites. In Aug, from 139€ ($165) double with balcony and sea view. Other times from 80€ ($95). Rates include breakfast. Closed mid-Oct to mid-Apr. **Amenities:** Restaurant; bar; excursions; Internet access; bike, car and scooter rental; diving school. *In room:* A/C, TV, minibar, hair dryer.

WHERE TO DINE

Galija ⚐⚐ DALMATIAN   Seafood is the specialty at this waterfront restaurant cum rooms across from the Hotel Odisej. Try the cold platter, which includes prsut, octopus, and olives.

Pomena. ℭ 020/744-029. Entrees 45kn–100kn ($8–$18). More for fish sold by the kilo. No credit cards. Hours vary.

Magical Mljet

Mljet is awash in legends and folklore. The most oft-told story is the legend of Homer's hero Odysseus, whose ship supposedly was blown ashore at Mljet, where he was enchanted by the nymph Calypso and kept in her cave for 7 years.

Another legend says that St. Paul stayed on Mljet during one of his trips spreading Christianity. As with many legends, this one is based on a kernel of truth. According to historians, St. Paul was shipwrecked off the island of Melita and there is a debate as to whether Melita refers to Mljet or Malta. Nonetheless, St. Paul is held in high esteem by the residents of Mljet.

Part reality, and perhaps part exaggeration, is the story of Mljet's relationship with snakes and boars. According to records, Mljet once was overpopulated with poisonous snakes, and in 1911 experts brought in mongooses to get rid of them. The little critters eliminated the snakes but created another problem by killing the island's rabbits and chickens, too. Currently, the island has a problem with wild boars, which prowl the forests. The boars supposedly swam 8km (5 miles) across the sea to Mljet years ago during a fire in their former habitat.

Pomena Pansion CROATIAN   You can grab lunch here before you head for the saltwater lakes of Mljet. This family restaurant at the trail head has a solid menu of Dalmatian specialties. Pomena has a few rooms to rent, too.

Pomena. Just past the Hotel Odisej on the way to the national park trail head in Pomena. (℃ 020/744-075. Entrees 30kn–65kn ($5.50–$12). No credit cards. Days and hours vary.

CAVTAT

Cavtat is just 19km (12 miles) southeast of Dubrovnik and it originally was founded by Greeks from Vis as a settlement called Epidaurum. In the 1st century B.C., the Romans under the Emperor Augustus took over, and eventually the town became known as Cavtat. Existing archaeological finds from those times include underwater ruins in the bay, foundation remains, tombs, and vestiges of a Roman road above the present town. The ancient town was destroyed at the beginning of the 7th century, during the invasions of the Avars and the Slavs, and it was then that the founders of Dubrovnik fled to the north and established their new city. Cavtat shared Dubrovnik's destiny in the years that followed.

Today, Cavtat (pronounced Sahvtaht) is a sleepy fishing town loved by tourists for its beaches and its beautiful horseshoe-shaped harbor as well as several sights worth investigating. The town's proximity to Dubrovnik makes it an acceptable alternative place to stay when Dubrovnik is full. **Cavtat** is half an hour south of Dubrovnik and reachable by bus, water taxi, or organized excursion. Cavtat is an easy day trip from Dubrovnik and a relaxing respite from its crowds. Go there for a leisurely lunch at **Restoran Leut** at Trumbićev Put 11 (℃ 020/479-050), then browse the art at the **Pinakoteka-Galerija** (10am–1pm Mon–Sat in summer). Stop at the parish church of **St. Nicholas,** but don't miss the spectacular sculpture work inside the Račić mausoleum (10am–noon daily plus 5–7pm in summer) in the town cemetery.

ESSENTIALS

VISITOR INFORMATION The **Cavtat Tourist Office** is at Tiha 3 (© 020/479-025; www.tzcavtat-konavle.hr) and can supply you with maps and information on the town's attractions. During July and August it's open from 8am to 6pm daily. September through June, it's open from 8am to 3pm Monday through Friday, and 9am to noon Saturday and Sunday.

GETTING THERE Cavtat is an easy drive from Dubrovnik, but if you don't have your own transport, a bus (no. 10) runs from Dubrovnik's main station hourly and takes less than an hour. You can also hop a shuttle boat from Lokrum Island harbor three times a day.

GETTING AROUND As with most towns in Croatia, walking is the best way to see the area's attractions.

WHAT TO SEE & DO

Franciscan Monastery and Our Lady of the Snows Church ⍟
The church and monastery are at the north end of Cavtat harbor at the bottom of the hill on which Ivan Mestrovic's Račić Mausoleum stands. The monastery recently was converted to an 8-room bed-and-breakfast, and guests can explore the adjoining church at their leisure. Look for the church's medieval altarpieces and the remains of what may be an ancient Roman amphitheater nearby. Inside, you'll find a 16th-century triptych by artist Vicko Lovrin. The most popular event on Cavtat is the festival of Our Lady of the Snows on August 5, and the church plays a pivotal role in that.

Put Od Rata 2. 20210 Cavtat. No phone, no website. 8 units. Apr 1–Oct 15. Doubles from 52€ ($90). **Amenities:** Breakfast served in the restaurant next door. *In room:* TV.

Rector's Palace and St. Nicholas Church ⍟
This Renaissance mansion is located near the bus station and was renovated in 1958 to make it a suitable home for the Baltazar Bogišic Collection, documents and volumes that belonged to one of Cavtat's native sons and 19th-century lawyer. The baroque building next door houses St. Nicholas Church and its unusual wooden altars.

Obala Ante Starčevića 18. © 020/478-556. Rector's Palace 10kn ($1.75) adults, 5kn ($1) children. Mon–Fri 9am–1pm. St. Nicholas Church 5kn ($1). Daily 10am–1pm.

Town Cemetery ⍟⍟
A path from the monastery leads to this cemetery, which contains the beautiful white stone mausoleum made by Croatia's preeminent sculptor, Ivan Meštrović, for the prominent Račić family in the 1920s.

Admission 5kn ($1). Daily 10am–noon; summer Mon–Sat 5–7pm also.

WHERE TO STAY

If you choose to stay in Cavtat, there are plenty of private rooms. You can get leads on available accommodations at the tourist office (above). Cavtat also has several hotels. The Croatia is one of the country's largest, with nearly 500 rooms.

Hotel Croatia ⍟⍟
You'll find comfort and convenience at this huge package hotel which has its own beach. Guest rooms are well-appointed and spacious; suites are especially fancy. Since the hotel has its own beach, you needn't root around to find an outlet to the sea as you must in some Dubrovnik hotels.

20210 Cavtat. © 020/475-555. Fax 020/478-213. www.hoteli-croatia.hr. 487 units, including 7 suites. Mid-July to Aug: from 220€ ($262) double with sea view; from 460€ ($548) suite. Other times: from 144€ ($172) double with sea view; from 252€ ($300) suite. Rates include buffet breakfast. **Amenities:** 2 restaurants; tavern; coffee bar; 3 bars; terrace; 2 pools; tennis courts; sports programs; children's program; salon; art gallery; parking. *In room:* A/C, TV, hair dryer, safe.

Hotel Supetar ⊛   Much smaller than Hotel Croatia, this value-priced hotel on the harbor is managed by the same company. Guest rooms are smaller and more modestly furnished than the Croatia's but they are comfortable and near the beach.

Obala Anton Starčevića 27. (Ĉ) **020/479-833.** Fax 020/479-858. www.hoteli-croatia.hr/supetar. 28 units. Mid-July to Aug from 96€ ($115) double; other times, from 56€ ($67) double. **Amenities:** Restaurant; limited access to Hotel Croatia facilities. *In room:* TV.

WHERE TO DINE

Food is plentiful and easy to find in Cavtat. Menu choices are usually exclusively Dalmatian and the only differences are restaurant location and view. Wander around the tiny town, letting your nose lead the way.

3 Međugorje

Međugorje isn't in Croatia, but it might as well be because almost everyone who visits this Catholic pilgrimage site passes through and spends time in Croatia on the way. Roman Catholics in the United States and elsewhere know that Međugore is the site of purported appearances of the Blessed Virgin Mary, but many people are unclear about where Međugorje is or how this tiny village in the middle of Hercegovina came to be the second-largest Roman Catholic pilgrimage site in the world. It is a popular day trip from Dubrovnik for independent travelers, and it is also a popular pilgrimage package tour organized by hundreds of Catholic parishes across the United States and other parts of the world.

The parish of Međugorje is just 25km (16 miles) southwest of Mostar in Bosnia-Herzegovina; and about 137km (85 miles) from Dubrovnik. It has about 4,000 permanent residents who reap the benefits of the village's popularity as a religious site and the revenue generated by the 2,000 or more people who visit there every day. Before the apparition, Međugorje was just another poor, rural village in an area full of poor, rural villages, but the economic surge it is now experiencing has changed both the village's economy and its character. Streets are lined with souvenir vendors, restaurants, and shops; new, modern hotels and pensions are proliferating; and residential areas are burgeoning with large, just-built homes or additions to existing structures. This is truly a town whose success has been fueled by religious fervor.

The actual site of the apparition is several hundred feet above the Bijakovići hamlet called Podbrdo at a place called Apparition Hill. Access is via a steep path leading to the exact spot where the Virgin Mary supposedly appeared to the teens in 1981. In 1989 the path was framed with bronze reliefs representing the joyful and sorrowful mysteries of the rosary; reliefs depicting the glorious mysteries can be seen on the way down. A blue cross marks the foot of the hill and it is here that the now-adult children who witnessed the apparition gather regularly to pray. It is also the place that thousands of pilgrims travel thousands of miles to see.

In town, a small, humble church stands in the shadow of the new, modern St. James Church, which has twin towers and an outdoor dais/altar for large celebrations and Masses. Neither is ever empty.

What Happened at Međugorje?

Međugorje is considered a holy place thanks to the testimony of six children who say the Virgin appeared to them for the first time on June 24, 1981, in Podbrdo, a hamlet of the village of Bijakovići.

Today, the group, most of whom are now in their 40s, say the Virgin continues to appear daily, inviting all people to embrace peace and conversion. During the apparitions, Mary conveys the message that "Peace, peace, peace—and only peace must reign between man and God and between men." This statement is particularly resonant for the people of this war-torn area. The Catholic Church has not formally recognized Međugorje as a pilgrimage site, but more than 20 million people have visited the shrine since the first vision, many claiming they experienced miracles thanks to their visits.

ESSENTIALS

VISITOR INFORMATION   For information on tours, hotels, and anything Međugorje-related, contact Information Centre "Mir" Medjugorje, Fr. Mario Knezović OFM (Gospin Trg 1 88266 Međugorje, Bosnia &Hercegovina; © **036/651-999;** www.medjugorje.hr.). You find excellent private accommodations in Međugorje and the surrounding area at any house with a SOBE (rooms available) sign out front; or contact G-tour Međugorje (© **036/650-126;** fax 036/650-156; www.globtour-medjugorje.com) for help. G-tour also books guides who speak a variety of languages.

GETTING THERE   Once you head north toward Hercegovina from the E65 highway, you can literally follow any bus on the road to Međugorje (although some continue past the turnoff toward Mostar) because there is a constant line of traffic to Međugorje from early morning to dark. Buses travel there regularly to and from Dubrovnik and Split and from Mostar in Bosnia-Hercegovina. Most carry people on organized tours, but there are public buses to Međugorje, too. Makarska and Zagreb also run regular buses to the Bosnia-Hercegovina pilgrimage site.

GETTING AROUND   Everyone walks in Međugorje. In fact, many buses leave and pick up their passengers half a mile outside of town, though St. James Church in the center has a huge, free, paved lot where cars and some buses park.

WHERE TO STAY

Most of the lodging in Međugorje and Bijakovići is modern and brand-new. If you are with an organized tour, you probably will stay in one of the larger hotels in the area. Otherwise, any of the SOBE (rooms available) offerings can be a good, economical choice.

Hotel Annamaria   Guest rooms in this 10-year old hotel are a little more luxurious than convent cells but not by much—they were clearly designed for pilgrims. Each room has a phone, a shower, and a crucifix on the wall, but beyond that, each is simply a place to spend the night.

Bijakovići bb. ⒸÐ **036/615-512.** Fax 036/651-023. www.tel.net.ba/hotel.am. 44 units, including 3 apts. From 56€ ($67) double; from 82€ ($98) apt. Rates include breakfast. Half- and full-board are available for stays longer than 2 days. Group rates available. **Amenities:** Restaurant; bar; terrace; elevator; exchange; prayer room; clinic. *In room:* TV.

WHERE TO DINE

Most of the hotels in Međugorje and Bijakovići have restaurants with multilingual menus and tasty choices, but you needn't go upscale to find a good meal. Pizzerias, bakeries, cafes, and ice-cream shops abound in Međugorje's center and its outlying areas.

5

Lower Dalmatia

The Dalmatian coastal region from Split to Dubrovnik is the inspiration behind Croatia tourism's "The Mediterranean As It Used To Be" mantra, and with good reason. With the imprint of Greek, Roman, and Venetian cultures on its cities, the bustle of maritime commerce and modern tourism on its shores, and the Dinaric Alps and Adriatic as a backdrop, the skinny strip of land stretching north to south between Bosnia-Herzegovina and the sea is the source of one breathtaking experience after another.

It's almost impossible to zip through lower Dalmatia on a scattershot tour these days, even though driving from Zagreb to Omiš (13 miles south of Split) is now a high-speed breeze on the country's new toll road. However, once you run out of divided highway, traffic—and life—slow to a languid tempo and visitors to this Mediterranean rat-race-free zone are forced to go with the flow. There's so much to see and process in 436km (260

miles) of old road between Omiš and Dubrovnik that at least one pit stop to smell the lavender is necessary if you want to understand the Dalmatian way of life. Split is Croatia's second-largest city and it is home to some of the best-preserved Roman ruins around. Sparsely populated Pelješac boasts some of the country's best vineyards and beaches while Hvar surrounds visitors in a cloud of glamour and herbal fragrance. Brač puts wind in the sails of board bums off its Golden Cape and Korčula draws people in with the white stone of its medieval walls. Farther out on the Adriatic, Vis and nearby Biševo islet beckon travelers to bask in the blue glow of an underwater cave. In between, multiple towns and islands and their beaches, historic sites, architectural gems, natural wonders, and age-old traditions are the key that unlocks the door to some of the treasures waiting to be explored by anyone savvy enough to meander this stretch of the Dalmatian coast.

1 Orientation

ARRIVING

How you get to the country's coast and its playgrounds depends on your wallet, time, and whether you are heading for one destination to settle in or whether you plan to move from one place to another to see as much as possible. In this part of Croatia, Split is the northern starting point for any trip along the southern coast unless you are traveling by boat and can pick your ports of call without worrying about traffic, bus schedules, or flight plans. You'll see the most and have the best flexibility if you have your own wheels, but you can also travel by bus or ferry or a combination of the two. We have charted possibilities from Split (p. 83), which is the logical place to start any tour of southern Dalmatia.

2 Split

Split celebrated its 1,700th birthday in 2005, an anniversary that marked the dual event of the city's founding and the completion of Diocletian's magnificent palace in A.D. 305. Diocletian deliberately chose this tract of land near ancient Salona, thereby securing a location that could provide the best of both country and city pleasures for his retirement years. As emperor emeritus in Split, Diocletian might not have had the power of a sitting Roman emperor, but he still had some clout. (It didn't hurt that he claimed to be a descendant of the god Jupiter and that he still had many loyal followers in the area.)

When in Split, Diocletian was just 6km (4 miles) from Salona, close enough so that he could easily visit Dalmatia's provincial center of power and stick his finger in affairs of state. Off duty, Diocletian retreated to the Split palace where he maintained the illusion of imperial position by receiving heads of state and other important visitors, who paid lavish homage to the former emperor.

ESSENTIALS

Split is a transportation hub for the Dalmatian coast, which makes it a busy crossroads. Despite Split's spectacular Old Town, whose borders are defined by the walls of

Diocletian's 3rd-century palace, the city has never had the exotic cachet of other Dalmatian destinations, though most travelers who head for Dubrovnik or Croatia's islands pass through Split or make connections there. Today, Split is the source of an extensive transportation network and it is one of the most accessible cities in Croatia.

VISITOR INFORMATION   Finding the official **Tourist Information Center** in Split can be confusing. The main bureau is near the Silver Gate or Peristil (© 021/342-666; www.visitsplit.com) just behind the cathedral and in the former chapel of St. Rocco, which still looks like a church. The tourism center is not easy to spot if you are looking for a typical office, so ask any shopkeeper to direct you. There is also a private **tourist agency** at Obala Hrvatskog Narodnog Preporoda 7 (Riva; © 021/348-600; fax 021/348-604), across the street toward the ferry port. It is a good place to locate private accommodations. Signs direct you from there across the Riva to the Old Town and the official tourist center.

GETTING THERE

BY CAR   Before May 2005, it took 5 hours or more to drive from Zagreb to Split. But that changed when Croatian officials cut the ribbon to open the new Zagreb-Split autocesta that flows through mountains and bypasses country roads running through smaller villages and towns. The new route isn't quite as scenic as the old, but this toll way has cut about an hour from the trip. Except for weekends in July and August, the 364km (226-mile) drive from Zagreb to Split now takes less time than the 217km (135-mile), south-to-north drive from Dubrovnik to Split on the Adriatic Coastal Highway. In 2007, another 27km (16 miles) of highway opened between Split and Omiš but the Sveti Rock tunnel just north of Split is still just one lane in each direction and bottlenecks can be miles long on summer weekends.

BY PLANE   Split's **airport** (© 021/203-171; www.split-airport.tel.hr) is 26km (16 miles) northwest of the city center between Kaštela and Trogir. Flights from all over Croatia as well as from many European cities fly in and out on regular routes. Service is more frequent in the summer months than in the winter, and an airport bus shuttles passengers between the airport and Split's main bus station for 30kn ($5.50) each way. Contact the **main bus station,** next to the train station at Obala Kneza Domogoja 12 (© 021/203-305), for schedule information.

BY BOAT   Except for its historic core, Split's ferry port is the busiest part of town. It is directly across the street from the Riva and palace.and international, local, and island ferries move in and out of the area almost constantly. The port also accommodates daily fast catamarans to the islands of Brač, Hvar, Vis, Korčula, Lastovo, and Šolta, as well as huge car/passenger ferries that make overnight runs to Ancona, Italy. Contact the local Jadrolinija office (© 021/338-333), Semmarina (© 021/338-292), or Adriatica (© 021/338-335) for schedule and price information. In summer from June to September, a high-speed catamaran runs between Split and Ancona, Italy, on a daily basis. **SNAV,** an Italy-based transit company, can be reached locally at © 021/322-252. SNAV also runs high-speed ferries (4 hr. or less) to Ancona from early June to mid-September.

BY BUS   Split is well-served by local, national, and international buses and the station is conveniently located next to the ferry port. Local bus lines run through Split and its suburbs, including Salona, Klis, Omiš, and Trogir, while others travel many times a day to Zagreb, Zadar, Rijeka, Dubrovnik, and destinations beyond. International buses

Split

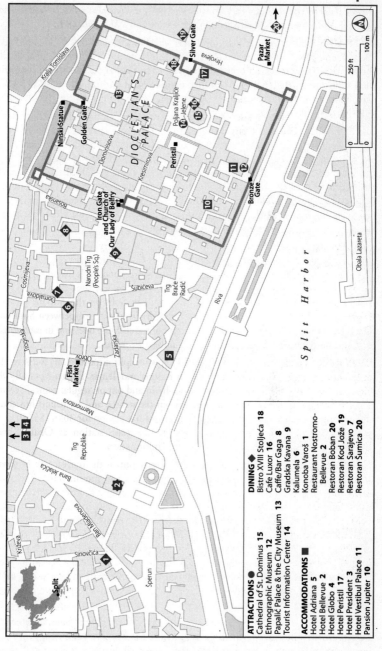

ATTRACTIONS ●
Cathedral of St. Dominus **15**
Ethnographic Museum **12**
Papalić Palace & the City Museum **13**
Tourist Information Center **14**

ACCOMMODATIONS ■
Hotel Adriana **5**
Hotel Bellevue **2**
Hotel Globo **4**
Hotel Peristil **17**
Hotel President **3**
Hotel Vestibul Palace **11**
Pansion Jupiter **10**

DINING ◆
Bistro XVIII Stoljeća **18**
Cafe Luxor **16**
Caffe/Bar Gaga **8**
Gradska Kavana **9**
Kalumela **6**
Konoba Varoš **1**
Restaurant Nostromo-Bellevue **2**
Restoran Boban **20**
Restoran Kod Jože **19**
Restoran Sarajevo **7**
Restoran Šumica **20**

provide daily service to Slovenia, Germany, and Italy, and weekly service to Austria and England. Schedule and fare information is available at ℂ **021/338-483.**

BY TRAIN Split's main train station is next door to the main bus station at Obala Kneza Domogoja 10 near the town center. It runs between Split and Zagreb, Knin, and Šibenik. There is also an overnight train between Split and Zagreb. Call the **Split train station** (ℂ **021/338-535**) or the **national train office** (ℂ **060/333-444;** www.hznet.hr) for schedule and fare information.

GETTING AROUND   Most of Split's best sights are within the walls of Diocletian's Palace or nearby. The walled city is limited to pedestrians; even the street skirting the Riva immediately outside the palace walls is closed to motorized vehicles. There are a few sights worth taking in outside the historic core—the **Meštrović Gallery** in Marjan, the public beach at **Bačvice**—and you can reach those via bus or taxi. The main taxi stands are at each end of the Riva (in front of the town market and in front of the Bellevue Hotel). If you don't see a cab, call ℂ **970.** Be sure to negotiate your taxi fare before getting in the vehicle. Prices for the same ride can vary wildly and cabbies will compete for your business if more than one is available.

CITY LAYOUT

Split's historic core is bounded by Obala Hrvatskog Preporoda (Riva) in the south, Marmontova Street in the west, Kralja Tomislava in the north, and Hrvojeva in the east; Old Town's main square, Narodni Trg, is almost in the center of the rectangle.

FAST FACTS: Split

Ambulance Call ℂ **94.**

American Express/Atlas Travel Atlas is the official American Express agent in Croatia. You can buy maps, arrange accommodations, and book excursions at this office at Nepotova 4 (ℂ **021/343-055**). To get to Atlas from the Silver Gate, head west on Poljana Kraljice Jelene; then north on Nepotova.

ATMs Available all over Split, with several on the Riva.

Banks Many of Croatia's banks have branches in Split. Zagrebačka Bank has an office on the Riva at Obala Hrvatskog Narodnog Preporoda 10. It is open from 7:30am to 12:30pm and 2:30 to 7pm Monday through Friday.

Fire Call ℂ **93.**

Holidays Split Summer Festival is from mid-July through mid-August. The Split Melodies of the Adriatic Festival is in August.

Hospitals Firule hospital is located at Spinciceva 1 (ℂ **021/556-111**); it is open 24/7.

Pharmacy There is a pharmacy at Guduliceva 52 (ℂ **021/341-190**), and one at Pupačićeva 4 (ℂ **021/533-188**).

Police Split's main police station is at Trg Hrvatske Bratske Zajednice 9 (ℂ **021/307-281**).

Post Office Split's main post office is at Kralja Tomislava 9. Hours are 7am to 8pm Monday through Friday, 7am to 3pm Saturday.

WHAT TO SEE & DO

Be sure to stroll down Split's spiffed up **Riva**, one of Croatia's busiest promenades. In the early morning hours, people linger over coffee at the Riva's sidewalk tables before work, after the market, or before a day of sightseeing. From then on the tables aren't empty until closing time. Never deserted, the Riva is at its busiest in the evening when people dine, stroll the concrete length with their ice cream cones, and arrive or depart on the late ferries.

Another must is **Marmontova Street,** a broad, brick-paved pedestrian street that forms Old Town's western border. You won't find too many quaint shops here, but you will find some international retail outlets (Tommy Hilfiger, Benetton) and a set of McDonald's golden arches. There are smaller shops, too, and some stalls selling Croatian crafts and handiwork at the northern end of the street. Just south of the walls at Marmontova's, you'll run into the Bellevue Hotel and the **Prokurative,** a horseshoe-shaped set of neoclassical government buildings on **Trg Republike.**

Diocletian's Palace ★★★ Some say the Roman Emperor Diocletian (A.D. 245–316) began building his imperial complex as a retirement home while he was still in power so he could live out his golden years near Salona. Historians say Diocletian was born in a village near Salona, which at the time was the nerve center of the Roman government in Dalmatia and the emperor's headquarters when he was in power and later when he took up residence in the grandiose palace that is now Old Town Split. Whatever Diocletian's intention in building a mega-mansion, this project was no pre-fab getaway cottage on the beach, but rather a heavily protected enclave that included a military installation with a footprint covering nearly 3 hectares (10 acres). It included the emperor's apartments, several temples, and housing for soldiers and servants.

Diocletian lived in the palace built of local limestone (mostly from the island of Brač) after abdicating his throne in A.D. 305 following a reign of 21 years. According to some historians, he actually commissioned construction of the palace in A.D. 293 from the architects Filotas and Zotikos, whose names are engraved on palace foundation stones found during recent excavations.

In the years immediately following Diocletian's death in A.D. 316, the immense palace was used as government office space, but it inadvertently became a city of refugees in the early 7th century when the Avars and Slavs attacked and destroyed Salona. Salona's residents first fled to nearby islands and later sought the security of the palace walls, which were 2m (6 ft.) thick and nearly 30m (100 ft.) high at points, and which provided protection against invaders.

This huge influx of refugees overcrowded the palace compound, and the new settlement spread outside its walls. Successive rulers, including the Byzantine emperors, the Croatian kings, the Hungarian-Croatian kings, and the Venetians, later built structures within and outside the complex, changing it so much that its Roman character has all but disappeared.

After the fall of Venice in 1797, the Austrians took over, ceded control of the city to France for a short time in the early 19th century, then took over again until World War I, when control reverted to the Yugoslav government and ultimately Croatia.

Today greater Split is mostly a working-class city of 250,000 and one of Croatia's busiest ports. It has a population of rabid sports fans; it functions as a transportation hub; and it is home to some of the most spectacular Roman ruins in the world.

Because of its size and because it has undergone so much change, imagining what Split's UNESCO World Cultural Heritage gem must have looked like in its prime is

Exploring the Palace

There are several access points for entering Split's historic core, but perhaps the best place to start your exploration is the **Bronze Gate** where the sea once came right up to the palace's back walls. Today the Bronze Gate opens outward from the palace's southern flank to Split's Riva and the ferry port beyond; and inward toward the **podrum** or basement area that meanders under the place. The podrum was the palace's "plant" where support staff cooked meals for Diocletian and his guests, fixed palace equipment, and took care of day-to-day maintenance. The underground space was sadly neglected until the mid-1950s, and parts of it have yet to be restored and cleared of centuries of debris. The **cryptoporticus** (gallery) that runs east and west from the Bronze Gate was an open promenade and probably the site where Diocletian went to catch a sea breeze and take his daily constitutional. Today the outdoor promenade can only be imagined from the form of the long corridor beneath it. The part of the podrum that extends from the Bronze Gate toward the steps to the Peristil above is a brick-lined minimall filled with merchants and craftspeople selling jewelry, maps, and other souvenirs of Split.

At the far end of the aisle that runs through this section of the podrum, you'll find a staircase that leads up to the **Peristil,** which was the palace's main courtyard and the place where Diocletian received important visitors. Today, the Peristil is one of the busiest spots in the historic city and home to cafes, **boutique hotels,** the cathedral, and passages leading to the heart of Old Town. It also functions as a stage during the Split Summer Festival, and on May 7 when the city celebrates the feast of St. Domnius.

Note the black granite sphinx standing guard outside the cathedral. It was one of 11 acquired by Diocletian during battle in Egypt and it is the only one still standing.

If you are approaching the palace from the Riva and entering through the **Silver Gate** on the eastern wall, you first must walk through the jumble

difficult. You can, however, get a feel for the original floor plan by exploring the palace's lower level or podrum, which provides a mirror image of the layout of the upper floors.

Cathedral of St. Domnius ⟨⟨⟨   In its former life, the Cathedral of St. Domnius was Diocletian's mausoleum, an elaborate domed structure that local Christians converted to a church in the 7th century. The original structure was built from massive stone blocks and framed by 28 granite and marble columns that Diocletian supposedly brought to the palace after looting them from Greek and Egyptian temples during one of his campaigns. Because of its proximity to the Silver Gate, which leads to Hrvojeva Street and access to the Riva, the cathedral is a popular meeting place and its courtyard is the site of performances during the **Split's Summer Festival** in July and August.

Diocletian, who is known for his brutal persecution of Christians, was laid to rest in the mausoleum in A.D. 316, following a focused campaign to eradicate Christianity. His body was removed from the mausoleum in the 7th century while the building of stalls that is the **city fruit and vegetable market (Pazar).** Making this walk is fine during the day, but it can be a little dicey at night, even though the market often stays open until 10pm or later during the summer despite the posted signs that say it closes at 2pm. The Silver Gate leads directly to **Decumanus,** the original east-west street that intersects with **Cardo,** the original north-south artery, at the Peristil. These former thoroughfares sectioned the palace into quadrants, which in turn became districts. The medieval **Church of St. Dominic** outside the Silver Gate was completely rebuilt in the 17th century and is home to several good pieces of sacral art.

The **Golden Gate** at the north end of the wall was the portal to Salona and was the most ornate gate into the palace. It has a guardhouse that contains the 9th-century **Church of St. Martin.** Ivan Meštrović's largest **statue of Bishop Grgur (Gregorius of Nin) Ninski,** a 9th-century bishop who defended church use of the Glagolitic script and Slav language, towers over visitors approaching the gate. The sculpture is entirely black except for one toe, which is shining bronze because visitors inevitably touch it for good luck as they pass. To the west, the **Iron Gate**'s guardhouse is the site of the oldest Romanesque belfry in Croatia and the 10th-century **Church of Our Lady of Belfry.**

The **Cathedral of St. Domnius** (below) is on the eastern side of the Peristil. The **Temple of Jupiter** (now the cathedral's baptistry) and what's left of the small, round **temples of Venus and Cybele** are on the Peristil's western side. *Tip:* To gain perspective on the palace's footprint, take a walk through the subterranean halls that run beneath it. The vaulted halls were built to support Diocletian's living quarters, but they mirrior the original palace layout before development infringed. For 15kn ($3/2€) you get a helpful guidebook with map. The halls are open from 9am–9pm Mon–Sat and from 9am–6pm Sun from June–September.

was being converted into a church, and the emperor's mortal coil was replaced with a shrine to St. Domnius (Sv. Duje). There is no record of who took Diocletian's body or where his remains are today. Ironically, part of the cathedral/mausoleum is now used as a huge reliquary for the bones of the same Christian martyrs slaughtered by Diocletian in an effort to destroy their religion.

The **cathedral treasury** above the sacristy contains valuable church documents and artifacts. Enter through the cathedral's magnificently carved wooden doors leading to the interior, which has been purged of its pagan decoration but still sports reliefs of Diocletian and his wife Priscia around the dome. The doors are protected by glass, but you can see its magnificent carvings depicting scenes from the life of Christ done by Croatian sculptor Andrija Buvina in the early 13th century. You should also note the 15th-century altar of St. Anastasius on the left as you enter. It was created by Croatian architect Juraj Dalmatinac, who also designed the UNESCO protected Šibenik Cathedral (p. 165).

After viewing the church's cache of gold and silver in the treasury, you can climb the bell tower for 10kn ($1.75) from 8am to 8pm in summer and whenever it is open in winter. You can also explore the cathedral crypt, though it has no posted hours and was closed whenever we tried to visit during the height of the 2007 summer season.

Kraj Sv. Duje 5. ℂ 021/342-589. Admission 5kn ($1). July–Aug daily 8am–8pm; other times daily 7am–noon and 5–7pm. You can see the cathedral treasure for an extra 5kn ($1): saints' heads done in silver, body-part reliquaries, plus body relics displayed behind glass. When you're finished in the treasury, you can climb the adjacent campanile for another 5kn ($1) 8am–noon and 4–7:30pm daily.

Temple of Jupiter (Baptistry) 𝕽𝕽 This small structure directly facing the mausoleum probably was a temple dedicated to Jupiter in Diocletian's time. During the Middle Ages, the building was converted into a baptistry; now only the enclosed part of the temple and its richly decorated portal remain. The baptistry also contains a Meštrović statue of John the Baptist and the 7th-century sarcophagus of Ivan Ravenjanin, the first archbishop of Split who had the martyrs' relics taken to the cathedral. In the 19th century, the baptismal font was decorated with stone carvings that portray a Croatian ruler (possibly the Croatian King Zvonimir) on his throne.

Papalić Palace & the City Museum 𝕽 Croatian designer Juraj Dalmatinac designed the 15th-century Gothic town house that is the Papalić Palace on Papalićeva Street north of the Peristil. Note the star-and-feather coat of arms over the portal leading to the building's charming courtyard: It represents the Papalić family's symbol. Split's City Museum is on the town house's first floor; it contains a hodgepodge of artifacts from Split's past. Sculptures, documents, medieval weaponry, and coins stamped with Diocletian's image form the crux of the exhibit.

Papalićeva 1. ℂ 021/344-917. www.mgst.net/eng/indexEFrameset.htm. Admission 10kn ($1.75) adults, 5kn ($1) children. Summer Tues–Fri 9am–9pm; Sat–Sun 9am–1pm. Winter Tues–Fri 10am–5pm; Sat 10am–noon; closed Sun–Mon.

Narodni Trg (People's Square) 𝕽𝕽 If you walk west along Krešimirova (formerly the Decumanus) through the Silver Gate, you will come out on Narodni Trg, Old Town's current main square. West of Narodni Trg you'll find the indoor fish market (Ribarnica) at Kraj Sv. Marije. It is open from 7am to 1pm Monday through Saturday, and from 7 to 11am Sunday. You'll smell it before you see it.

In the center of town.

Ethnographic Museum This small museum founded in 1910 has limited collections of Dalmatian folk costumes, jewelry, and arms, but its setting in Diocletian's former apartment in the south part of the palace adds an extra dimension to the displays. The museum also houses the church of St. Andrew de Fenestris and the former convent of St. Clare. Of special note are the collection of chests that were used for storing valuables and the collection of 20th century art, from mostly Split artists.

Severova 1. ℂ 021/343-108. Admission 10kn ($2) adults; 5kn ($1) children. Mon–Fri 9am–9pm, Sat 9am–1pm. Closed Sun and holidays.

Split Summer Festival 𝕽𝕽𝕽 This homage to culture takes place in Split from mid-July to mid-August. During this time, the arts take center stage, usually in the beautiful Croatian National Theater, in the Peristil, at other Old Town squares, and at other venues around town. Theatrical performances, classical musical concerts, operas, puppet shows, dance performances, and other arts performances attract thousands of visitors to the city, so if you go, be sure you have hotel reservations and tickets to the events you want to see. Contact the Croatian National Theater for information and tickets to various performances.

Gaje Bulata 1. ✆ 021/585-999. www.hnk-split.hr.

Braće Radić Trg (Voćni Trg or Fruit Square) ⊛   Smaller than Narodni Trg, this medieval square is dominated by Ivan Meštrović's sculpture of Croatian author **Marko Marulić,** who wrote "Judita," the first narrative poem in Croatian. Marulić (1450–1524) is revered as the father of Croatian literature and his statue shows him with—what else?—a book.

Croatian National Theater ⊛⊛   The theater is outside the walls directly north of the intersection of Marmontova and **Kralja Tomislava.** Once a nondescript mousy brown, the exterior of this beautiful 19th-century building has been restored to Hapsburg yellow splendor. The cool, dark interior is no less impressive than the exterior. The theater is the setting for assorted performances during Split's summer festival and periodically during the rest of the year.

Trg Gaje Bulata 1. ✆ 021/585-999.

Split Archaeological Museum ⊛⊛   This museum is a repository for artifacts— jewelry, coins, and pottery—mostly unearthed at Salona in the hills above Split. The collection includes many religious objects used by the people who fled to the palace from Salona during the Avar-Slav invasion in the 7th century. It also displays heavier stone objects such as sarcophagi outdoors. Founded in 1820, this is Croatia's oldest museum and is a 10-minute walk north of the historic core.

Zrinjsko-Frankopanska 25. ✆ 021/318-714. www.st.carnet.hr./split/arheol.html. Admission 20kn ($4). Summer Tues–Sat 9am–1pm and 4–7pm; Sun 10am–noon. Rest of year Tues–Sat 9am–1pm. Closed Mon.

Museum of Croatian Archaeological Monuments (Marjan) ⊛⊛   Take a bus (no. 12) or a taxi to this block-style multistory building with a view of the sea at Marjan just west of the center. Like many museums in Croatia that display artifacts from ancient cities, exhibits are both inside galleries and outside on the museum grounds. Early Croatian sacral art from the 7th to the 12th centuries and other medieval pieces are the focus here, but the most interesting pieces are those reminiscent of Celtic art.

Stjepana Gunjace bb. ✆ 021/343-983. Fax 021/345-255. http://mdc.hr/hrv-arh-split/en/1-opci.html. Admission 20kn ($4). Tues–Sat 9am–4pm; Sun 9am–noon. Closed Mon and holidays.

Meštrović Gallery (Marjan) ⊛⊛⊛   The Meštrović Gallery is housed in the magnificent mansion built from 1937-1939 as a home/atelier for Croatian sculptor Ivan Meštrović and his family. Meštrović lived there for just two years before emigrating from Croatia, but he left behind a magnificent artistic legacy. The house and garden hold some of the artist's best work, including a pair of huge walnut Adam and Eve figures and the powerful bronze Cyclops. Meštrović's religious art comprises much of the gallery's permanent exhibits, but traveling exhibitions from Croatia and other locations are periodically on display. Walk up the road to Šetalište Ivana Meštrovića 39 to visit the 16th-century **Kaštelet,** a Renaissance-style summer house on the gallery property purchased and remodeled by Meštrović in 1939 as a showcase for his "Life of Christ Cycle" reliefs. The carvings were completed over the course of Meštrović' lifetime between 1916 and 1950 and they line Kaštelet's Holy Cross Chapel. **Note:** During the Tito era, Meštrovic obtained an unusual signed decree from the Yugoslav leader that gave priests permission to say mass whenever they wished at Holy Cross Chapel and at Holy Redeemer, the chapel above Meštrović' crypt at Otavice.

Split Walking Tours

Even if your time in Split is limited to a layover between ferries, you can hit the city's highlights via an organized walking tour that starts out a few hundred yards from the ferry port at the tourist office outside the Peristil, just inside the Silver Gate. You'll see the Riva, the palace basement halls, all four palace gates, Narodni Trg (Peoples Square), Vočni Trg (Fruit Square), the iconic statue of Gregory of Nin, and Marmontova Street. Tours last 60–90 minutes and leave 3 times daily at 10am, 11:45am, and 7pm and cost between 70kn–90kn ($13–$17) per person, depending on the agency. *Note:* **Split Walks**, which meets under a red umbrella at the Peristil, conducts all tours in English from June 15-October 31. For more information call ✆ **091/537-9538** or go to www.mediterranean-experience.hr.

There is no extra charge to enter Kaštelet if you have a ticket to the main gallery. Šetalište Ivana Meštrovića 46. ✆ 021/358-450. Admission 15kn ($3) adults, 10kn ($1.75) children. Summer Tues–Sat 9am–9pm, Sun 9am–6pm; winter Tues–Sat 9am–4pm; Sun 10am–3pm. Closed Mon and holidays.

WHERE TO STAY

Hotel rooms in Split are scarce in general, and reasonably priced hotel rooms are almost nonexistent, though private accommodations are fairly easy to secure. Split has never been known as a vacation destination in Croatia. Rather, its reputation has been that of a gateway to points south along the Dalmatian coast, and as the birthplace of such sports stars as Tony Kukoc (Chicago Bulls), Goran Ivanisevic (tennis), and the headquarters of the Hajduk soccer club. Consequently, until recently not much attention was paid to tourist lodging in Split. But that attitude is changing. Existing hotels are renovating, small boutique hotels are entering the market, and one large luxury chain (Le Meridien) has opened an integrated resort complex on the site of a historic landmark hotel (Nov 2006).

VERY EXPENSIVE

Le Meridien 🏨🏨   Starwood kept the basic footprint of the former Hotel Lav when it turned the block-style 4-building complex into the only internationally affiliated hotel in the Split area. Le Meridien Lav was unveiled in fall 2006 and the facility's metamorphosis from package hotel to exclusive resort is a mixed success. The 381-unit hotel has been positioned as a seafront destination and it certainly has the real estate for that boast. Inside however, vestiges of the Lav's socialist roots live on and detract from the ambience. For example, the Restaurant Spalatum 🏨 has an ambitious menu executed by a talented chef, but the room is a brightly lit cavern more suited to a workplace cafeteria than an elegant dining experience. The Art Café across from reception is more successful—its comfy seating arrangements are tastefully broken up by local works of art displayed in 7-foot-high glass panels. For the most part, the Lav's staff is courteous and helpful, but we did encounter some serious service lapses that should not occur at this pricing level. Le Meridien has the potential to become a true first-class resort, but it still is a little rough around the edges. The hotel is in Podstrana, 6km (4 miles) from Split's Old Town (20 min.) and 40 minutes from Split-Kastela International Airport.

Grljevač 2a, 21312 Podstrana. ☏ **021/500-500**. Fax 021/500-705. www.lemeridien.com/split. 381 units, including 15 suites. Doubles from 1,650kn ($315); suites from 462€ ($647) Rates include VAT but not breakfast, which is 30€ ($42) per person. **Amenities:** 2 restaurants; cafe; pub; 2 bars; indoor and outdoor pools; private beach; marina; tennis courts; spa; casino; nightclub; children's program; laundry service; valet parking; shops; nonsmoking rooms; Wi-Fi in public areas (charge); rooms for those w/limited mobility and access. *In room:* A/C, SAT TV, minibar, broadband Internet access (45kn ($8) per hr./145kn ($27) per day), safe.

Hotel Vestibul Palace ✸✸✸

Clever 21st-century architects carved this intimate boutique hotel into the space next to what was Diocletian's boudoir. The hotel opened in 2006 and the interior uses high design to meld glass with the ancient stone palace walls. The result is spectacular. Most of the bathrooms have tubs, but those without have high-tech showers and black marble fixtures. Each room is different but each incorporates some detail of the palace with modern comforts like flatscreen TVs.

Vestibula 4. ☏ **021/329-329**. www.vestibulpalace.com. 7 units. Doubles July–Aug from 240€ ($240); suites from 300€ ($510) Other times doubles from 210€ ($360); suites from 285€ ($485). Rates include breakfast and VAT. AE, MC, V. **Amenities:** Restaurant; excursions. *In room:* A/C, SAT TV w/LCD screen, minibar, hair dryer, Wi-Fi.

Atrium Hotel ✸✸

Dark reflective glass, marble, black and white leather, and artifacts on loan from a local museum exude sophistication in the lobby of this 101-room beauty that opened in July 2007. Guest rooms are light and airy, oversize, and lavishly outfitted with ultramodern baths, desks, and high-speed Internet access. The hotel also had the foresight to put in an underground garage that comes in handy in parking-challenged Split. Add to that pieces of Diocletian's aqueduct out back, a spa pool with a panoramic view of the city, and a restaurant ✸✸ that is a stand-alone dining destination, and you have the makings of a fine hotel. However, the Atrium's setting in the shadow of a cluster of brand-new, garishly painted apartment high-rises in Brodarica, 15 minutes from the Old Town, could be a turn-off for some.

Domovinskog Rata 49a. ☏ **021/200-000**. Fax 021/200-100. www.hotel-atrium.hr. 101 units, including 2 suites. Doubles from 1,425kn ($270); suites from 1,800kn ($340). Rates include breakfast and VAT. AE, DC, MC, V. **Amenities:** Restaurant; bar; indoor pool; spa; garage. *In room:* A/C, SAT TV, minibar, hair dryer, high-speed Internet, safe.

Art Hotel ✸

The guest rooms in this converted Bobiš Bakery building are comfortable and better equipped than rooms in most of Split's hotels, but the Art Hotel's location in a nondescript neighborhood a good 15-minute walk from the Old Town might be off-putting to some. The bland rectangular structure got its name because the designer's vision was that of a hotel cum showcase for local artists, but that didn't materialize. You might think the designer then used the hotel as a canvas for splashes of primary colors because the exterior walls and interior public spaces are liberally doused with ribbons of red, yellow, and blue paint, a decorating scheme that makes the Art Hotel feel like a graffiti showcase. Guest rooms are more sedate with soft gold and green spreads and drapes and decent-size bathrooms with white enamel and stainless fixtures, including cigar-shaped showerheads from Italy. A big plus—the whole hotel is wired for Internet use and both Wi-Fi and broadband are free to guests.

Ulica Slobode 41. ☏ **021/302-302**. Fax 021/302-300. www.arthotel.hr. 36 units. Doubles from 1,330kn ($250). Rates include breakfast and taxes. AE, DC, MC, V. **Amenities:** Restaurant; bar; fitness center; parking for 50kn ($10) per day. *In room:* A/C, SAT/TV, minibar, free broadband Internet access, hair dryer, safe.

EXPENSIVE

Hotel Peristil ✸✸ *Finds*

The Peristil opened in 2005, giving guests a place to sleep smack in the middle of Diocletian's former living room and next door to the Cathedral of St. Domnius. The Peristil is just inside the Silver Gate and shares walls with the palace, which puts guests in literal touch with history. The Peristil's owners worked with conservators for 6 years to come up with a design that respects the surrounding ancient architecture before they were able to build and open their hotel, and they have done an excellent job. Guests can eat breakfast on the limestone terrace surrounded by the hotel and palace walls; inside, they can listen to the annual Split Summer Festival performance of *Aïda* (and other musical masterpieces) from any of the rooms when the windows are open. All guest rooms are comfortably sized and have original artwork on the walls. Most have showers rather than tubs. The rooms are equipped with Internet access via the phones, though this service can be pricey. **Restoran Tifani** ☆☆ downstairs is a delight.

Poljana Kraljice Jelene 5. ① 021/329/070. Fax 021/329-088. www.hotelperistil.com. 12 units. July–Aug: from 1,200kn ($230) double; other times doubles from 900kn ($170). AE, MC, V. Rates include breakfast. **Amenities:** Restaurant; bar. *In room:* A/C, TV, dial-up Internet access, hair dryer.

MODERATE
Hotel Adriana ☆☆   The Adriana's accommodations are really rooms over its popular **Adriana Restaurant** ☆☆ (see below for review) right on the Riva. If you can snag one of these rooms, you will be in an ideal location for sightseeing and close to the sea. Guest rooms are plain but comfortable, especially those with a sea view.

Preporoda 8. ① 021/340-000. www.hotel-adriana.hr. 5 units; 2 apts. Mid-Apr to mid-Oct: from 850kn ($147); 1,200kn ($222) apt. Mid-Oct to mid-Apr: Doubles from 750kn ($140); apt from 1,000kn ($185). AE, DC, MC, V. **Amenities:** Restaurant. *In room:* A/C, TV, minibar.

Hotel Park (Bačvice) ☆☆   Even though it was modernized in 2004, old-world formality is a hallmark of this elegant hotel, which was quite exclusive during its heyday in the 1920s and 1930s. Guest rooms are a departure from the grand atmosphere of the public areas, however, as they have been outfitted with modern furniture and bathrooms. The rooms can be noisy, especially those in the front of the house, so book accordingly. At this time, the Park is one of the nicer hotels in Split, partially because of its excellent Restaurant Bruna and partially because of its proximity to Bačvice beach and park. But be warned that the short walk from the hotel to the city center is rather convoluted and takes longer than it should.

Hatzeov Perivoj 3. ① 021/406-400. Fax 021/406-400. www.hotelpark-split.hr. 54 units; 3 apts. From 465kn ($80) double; from 700kn ($120) apt. AE, DC, MC, V. **Amenities:** Restaurant; bar; sauna; solarium; money exchange; room service; laundry. *In room:* A/C, TV, minibar, Internet.

Hotel Globo   The Globo was constructed in 2001 in a residential area 10 minutes southeast of the city center, an area that has nothing to recommend it. Guest rooms are pleasant and comfortable, but besides the breakfast buffet, the hotel has no real amenities. It is a good choice if all you need is a room.

Lovretska 18. ① 021/481-111. Fax 021/481-118. www.hotelglobo.com. 25 units. From 1,100kn–1,350kn ($129–$243) double. AE, DC, MC, V. Limited free parking. **Amenities:** Breakfast room; elevator. *In room:* A/C, TV, minibar, Internet access.

Hotel President ☆☆   The President is one of the most conveniently located hotels in Split and very close to the Croatian National Theater at Trg Gaje Bulata just north of the walled center. The President isn't a lavish hotel, but guest rooms are tastefully done in soothing earth tones with good quality furnishings. Regular doubles are smallish, but the next grade up is more than adequate.

Starčevićeva 1. ① 021/305-222. Fax 021/305-222. www.hotelpresident.hr. 44 units. From 975kn ($168) standard double; from 1,125kn ($195) superior double; from 1,575kn ($272) suite. AE, DC, MC, V. Rates include breakfast.

Garage 75kn ($13) per night. **Amenities:** Restaurant; bar; car rental; laundry; nonsmoking rooms. *In room:* A/C, TV, minibar, safe, hydromassage bath (some rooms).

Hotel Consul ⟨★⟩ The Consul is a bit of a hike northeast of the center of town, but with Split's dearth of hotel rooms, it's an option worth considering if you can't book anywhere else. The Consul has the aura of a business hotel with large, bright guest rooms, traditional comfy furnishings, and bathrooms with Jacuzzis. The hotel's Consul Restaurant is quite good, and its semi-covered terrace restaurant is surprisingly stylish, with a menu to match.

Tršćanska 34. ✆ **021/340-130.** Fax 021/340-133. www.hotel-consul.net. 19 units. From 820kn ($142) double; from 1,100kn ($190) suite. Rates include breakfast. Half- and full board available. Limited free parking. AE, DC, MC, V. **Amenities:** Restaurant; bar. *In room:* A/C, TV, high-speed Internet, fax, minibar, hair dryer, safe.

INEXPENSIVE

Hotel Jupiter ⟨★⟩ ⟨*Value*⟩ Accommodations in Split's Old Town are few, and those in greater Split are expensive, so when you find clean, attractive rooms at bargain prices, you have found a treasure. The Jupiter is located next to the 1,700-year-old Temple of Jupiter near Narodni Trg and in the midst of Split's nightlife action. The hotel is really a guesthouse that rents rooms with shared bathrooms, but it is an excellent place to bunk if you don't mind not having a private bathroom. Jupiter had an overhaul for the 2005 season and the spartan rooms and bathrooms now gleam, though they are light on luxuries.

Grabovčeva Širina 1. ✆ **021/344-801.** www.hotel-jupiter.info. 25 units (3 singles, 10 doubles, 12 triples). 250kn ($48/34€) per person. Rates do not include breakfast. No credit cards. **Amenities:** Cafe/bar; TV room. *In room:* A/C double and triple rooms; fans in singles. Towels supplied but bring soap.

Hotel Kaštel ⟨★★⟩ ⟨*Value*⟩ One of a handful of accommodations within the palace walls, the Kaštel is really a well-placed pension and the least expensive of the 3 hotels built into the palace walls. Rooms are clean but modest and the place is a family enterprise. Unless you need absolute quiet, choose a room overlooking the Riva. Rooms are outfitted with sound-reducing windows, but they aren't perfect.

Mihovilova Širina 5. ✆ **098/973-8601.** www.kastelsplit.com. 12 units, including 2 suites. Doubles from 80€ ($112) in June–Sept; doubles from 50€ ($70) other times. Rates do not include breakfast or taxes. *In room:* A/C, SAT/TV.

Hotel Bellevue This 115-year-old hotel saw its last upgrade in 1979, and it shows. Situated on lovely but nearly deserted Prokurative Square outside Old Town's western wall, the Bellevue is waiting for liberation from its drab decor. The hotel is spitting distance from Old Town and its attractions and close to the water. It is also one of the few accommodations options so close to Split's Old Town besides private rooms.

Bana Josipa Jelačića 2. ✆ **021/345-644** or 021/347-499. Fax 021/362-382. www.hotel-bellevue-split.hr. 50 units. From 682kn ($118) double; from 986kn ($170) suite. Rates include breakfast. Limited free parking. AE, DC, MC, V. **Amenities:** Restaurant/bar; concierge; money exchange; room service; laundry. *In room:* TV, minibar (suites only), hair dryer.

WHERE TO DINE

It isn't difficult to find a place to eat in Split, but it is difficult to find a restaurant that is more than a pizzeria or konoba. However, Split's restaurant scene is improving as new hotels open and bring more tourist traffic to town.

VERY EXPENSIVE

Restoran Boban ⟨★★★⟩ DALMATIAN Boban is one of the finest restaurants in Split with a reputation that goes back to its founding in 1973. Both the indoor dining room and outdoor terrace are beautiful settings for the consistently excellent food prepared in Boban's kitchens. From seafood preparations to grilled meat to traditional Croatian fare, this place does it all, and does it very well. Boban also offers a few select dishes that use Istrian truffles. Its quality wine list includes such labels as Grgić, Zlatanotok, and Dingač.

Hektorovićeva 49. © **098/205-575** or 021/543-300. www.restaurant-boban.com. Entrees 70kn–330kn ($12–$63/10€–45€). AE, DC, MC, V. Mon–Sat 10am–midnight; Sun noon–midnight.

Spalatum 🌟🌟 DALMATIAN (Le Meridien Lav)   Its name is Latin for "Split" and its cuisine is creatively prepared to showcase local products. Spalatum tries to be a glitzy hotel restaurant and family friendly buffet at the same time and the result is that neither effort is spectacular. There is potential: One wall of the restaurant showcases the city of Split and an outdoor dining terrace through floor-to-ceiling glass and the chef has talent. However, the overall ambience of the place is too institutional, even for a hotel as large as the **Lav** 🌟🌟. Don't let that deter you from trying dishes such as the trio of Dalmatian lamb or olive oil poached tuna. Bigger appetites can choose the "all-you-can-eat" option from the mind-boggling choices offered at the nightly buffet for 220kn ($42). The trio of chocolate crème brulees is a standout for dessert, service for the a la carte menu is topnotch, and the breakfast buffet is full of options.

Grljevačka 2a. 21312 Podstrana. © **021/500-500.** Fax 021/500-705. www.lemeridien.com/split. Entrees 85kn–350kn ($16–$68). AE, DC, MC, V. Daily 6:30–10:30am for breakfast, 12:30–3:30pm for lunch, and 6:30–10:30pm for dinner.

EXPENSIVE

Bistro XVII Stoljeća 🌟 PIZZA/PASTA   There are lots of noodles and risottos on the menu of this restaurant, which shares a courtyard with three others. This is one of the few places in Split with waitresses, and their very presence makes the restaurant diner-friendly for families and for women dining alone. Besides pizza, inventive pasta entrees on the menu include noodles Matriciana, which is wide pasta dressed with tomatoes, bacon, and chili. The Diocletian salad is a lighter dish with veggies, squid, and anchovies sprinkled among the greens.

Poljana Grgura Ninskog 7. © **021/314-519.** XVII stoljeca@st.t-com.hr. Entrees 30kn–175kn ($6–$34). No credit cards. Mon–Sat 10am–midnight; Sun noon–midnight.

Caffe Restaurant Vestibul 🌟🌟   It is open for breakfast and dinner only, but the restaurant in the **Hotel Vestibul** 🌟🌟🌟 is worth putting on your schedule if only to dine surrounded by history. The food here is Dalmatian in tone and prepared with elegant simplicity to match the hotel's mood. Try the excellent grilled fish at dinner.

Iza Vestibula 4. © **021/320-329.** Fax 021/329-333. www.vestibulpalace.com. Breakfast 40kn–110kn ($8–$21) and dinner entrees 80kn–150kn ($15–$30). AE, DC, MC, V. Daily 7–10am for breakfast and 7–10pm for dinner.

Restaurant Noštromo-Bellevue 🌟🌟 SEAFOOD   Noštromo has a respectable menu, but it has the disadvantage of being on the first floor of the Hotel Bellevue, which has seen better days. Noštromo's outdoor tables are set on what looks like a miniature St. Mark's Square (minus St. Mark's) under the Venetian balustrades of the Bellevue (minus crowds and pigeons). The menu lists lots of fresh fish entrees, and the tux-clad waiters lend a formal air, but you may be the only patron in the place on any given evening.

Kraj Sv. Marije 10. © **091/405-666.** Entrees 45kn–200kn ($9–$38). MC, V. Daily noon–11pm.

Restoran Šumica 🌟🌟🌟 SEAFOOD   Šumica is an upscale restaurant with one of the most romantic atmospheres of any restaurant in Split and serves some of the most pristinely fresh seafood in town. Choose the house specialty of tagliatelle with scampi and salmon, and pair it with a bottle from Šumica's excellent cellar. You can dine under pines on the outdoor terrace or in the slightly formal but airy dining room. Either way, Šumica is a good but pricey choice if you want something special.

Put Firula 6. ✆ **021/389-897.** Fax 021/389-894. Entrees 80kn–300kn ($14–$52), more for seafood sold by the kg. AE, DC, MC, V. Daily 10am–midnight.

MODERATE

Adriana ✿✿ DALMATIAN   This sprawling restaurant on the Riva near Old Town is always crowded. Perhaps that's because the excellent food is fairly priced or perhaps it's because of the Adriana's prime location for people-watching. Try the seafood risotto or any grilled meat or fish dish. There is live music on weekends and sometimes on weekdays during the summer, which is great for patrons but which can be annoying if you're staying in one of the Adriana's rooms upstairs. Service can be slow when the restaurant is crowded.

Obala Hrvatskog Preporoda. ✆ **021/344-079.** www.dalmatianet.com/adriana/indexhrv.htm. Entrees 45kn–160kn ($8–$32). AE, DC, MC, V. Daily 8am-11pm.

Gradska Kavana ✿ PASTRY/DALMATIAN   This staid cafe and restaurant across from Narodni Trg is obviously geared toward tourists. Most of the fare here is traditional Dalmatian and a bit overpriced, but there are a few surprises. If you're feeling adventuresome, try the special lasagna, which includes prawns, Dalmatian smoked ham, veggies, cheese, tomato sauce, eggs, and cream. There is a designated smoking section.

Narodni Trg 1. ✆ **021/317-835.** Entrees 40kn–90kn ($8–$17). Lobster (per kg) up to 650kn ($125). AE, DC, MC, V in the restaurant, but not the cafe. Daily 7am–midnight.

Restoran Sarajevo ✿✿ CROATIAN   Grilled meat dominates the menu at this old-style dining room housed in a space supported by vaulted arches constructed at the beginning of the last millennium. Try the *ražnjići*, chunks of grilled meat skewered on tiny swords. The mixed-grill plate is excellent, too, but be warned that one of the grilled meats is liver. Pasta also appears on the menu. There's a nice wine list. Service can be slow and impersonal.

Domaldova 6. ✆ **021/347-454.** Entrees 62kn–150kn ($12–$29). AE, DC, MC, V. Daily 9am–midnight.

Restoran Tifani ✿✿ *Finds* DALMATIAN   Tifani (in Hotel Peristil) is a welcome departure from the same old, same old, that characterizes most of the Split's restaurants. Grilled meats and fish are menu staples, but Tifani's young chef also tries to cook out of the box. House-made noodles with mussels, mortadella, and peppers come together in a creamy sauce laced with cheese. Sautéed stroganoff is a happy mix of beef, Madeira sauce, mushrooms, gherkins, and cream. Tifani has a nice wine list and even nicer servers.

Poljana Kraljice Jelene 5. ✆ **021/329/070.** Fax 021/329-088. www.hotelperistil.com. Entrees 45kn–160kn ($9–$31). AE, DC, MC, V. Daily 7am–midnight.

INEXPENSIVE

Black Cat ✿ SALADS/SANDWICHES   This addition to Split's dining scene is a five-minute walk from the Riva and easy on the pocketbook. Black Cat also offers food that is a little different from the usual Croatian grills and pizzas. Croissant sandwiches, wraps, curry concoctions, and wonderful home-style desserts star here. Full English breakfasts are available, too.

Segviceva 1. ✆ **021/490-284.** Entrees 20kn–60kn ($4–$12). AE, DC, MC, V. Mon–Sat 8am–11pm; closed Sun.

Kalumela ✺ HEALTH FOOD   If you get the munchies and you're tired of pizza and grilled meat, Kalumela can supply organic whole-grain sandwiches and pastries as well as the usual health-food-store staples.

Domaldova 7. ☎ **021/348-132**. Entrees 40kn–70kn ($7–$12). AE, DC, MC, V. Mon–Fri 8:30am–1pm and 5:30–8:30pm; Sat 9am–1pm; closed Sun.

Konoba Varoš ✺✺ DALMATIAN   A little off the beaten path, this place not too far from the town center is creatively draped with fishnets, creating a cozy, comfortable atmosphere in a restaurant that charges decent prices. You'll see lots of locals here, which is usually a sign of a good restaurant in Croatia. Tuck into a big plate of lamb or veal hot from the *peka* (grill); or try the blue fish or octopus. Varos has an unusually long and varied wine list for a simple konoba, which translates to very fair bottle prices.

Ban Mladenova 7. ☎ **021/396-138**. Entrees 60kn–80kn ($11–$14). AE, DC, MC, V. Daily 11am–midnight.

Luxor ✺✺ SANDWICHES   You can't get much closer to the palace walls than this cafe in the Peristil, across from the cathedral. In fact, the place shares a wall with the ancient structure and the waitstaff will bring your biela kava to you while you take in the sights sitting on the steps outside. If you do that, be sure to poke your head inside to see the dining room, which recently has been restored.

Kraj Sv. Ivana 11. No phone. Sandwiches 35kn–65kn ($6–$12). AE, DC, MC, V. Daily 9am–midnight.

Pizzeria Galija ✺ ⓥ*alue*   This tiny place serves some of the best pizza in Split and it is one of the best bargains, too. Galija is a little off the tourist track on the western edge of town, but it is a worthwhile detour if you just want a relaxing beer and pizza. *Note:* You have to buy pizza whole here, so take a friend.

Kamila Tončića 12. ☎ **021/347-932**. Pizza from 26kn–100kn ($5–$18). AE, DC, MC, V. Daily 10am–11pm.

Restaurant Kod Joze ✺ DALMATIAN   This atmospheric restaurant just outside the Silver Gate is that of a genuine Dalmatian konoba with a brick-and-wood interior, lots of candlelight and camaraderie, and a menu with traditional Dalmatian choices whose expert preparation makes them stand out above other restaurants' fare. Any fish choice or pasta dish is a winner here.

Sredmanuška 4. ☎ **021/347-397**. Entrees 45kn–100kn ($8–$17). AE, DC, MC, V. Mon–Fri 9am–midnight; Sat–Sun noon–midnight.

Skipper Club Grill ✺ CROATIAN/PIZZA   The view from this informal dining spot above the ACI Marina is nothing short of spectacular. Whether you are at an umbrella table on the deck or at a table next to the windows in the air-conditioned dining room, you can see all the activity in the harbor below, the Split skyline, and everything in between. Skipper specializes in pizza (there are 34 kinds and it is also sold by the slice) but the huge, freshly made salads and pasta dishes are satisfying, too. Be sure to ask for bread. Skipper's variety is a cross between pita and nan and it comes to the table hot and freshly baked.

Uvala Baluni bb. ☎ **021/398-222**. Entrees 35kn–60kn ($6–$11). AE, DC, V. Daily 7am–midnight.

NIGHTLIFE

Finding something to do in Split after 11pm isn't too difficult if you know where to look. Or you can just follow the music and the dressed-to-party pedestrians. After dark, the beach and the warren of streets that honeycombs the palace become singles bar central. Many places get going around 10pm and stay open until the last patron goes home. Bars within the palace boundaries must close at 1am.

Tips **Split Card**

> *Tips* **Split Card**
>
> Consider picking up a Split Card, which entitles you to discounts at more than 40 hotels, restaurants, museums, and merchants. The card is free and available from hotel reception desks and at the Tourist Info Center at the Peristil if you are staying in Split for at least 3 days. If you are staying fewer than 3 days, you still can save by purchasing a card for 5€ ($7).

Academia Ghetto Club ★★   Art and drinking combine in this multilevel gallery cum bar near Trg Brać Radića (Fruit Square) just off the Riva. When both are busy, the place rocks. Academia is one of a triad of hot spots in the area (Fluid, Puls) perfect for bar-hopping within the palace confines. Daily 10am to 1am. Dosud 10. ☎ 021/346-879.

Caffe/bar Gaga ★   This coffeehouse/bar is lively all the time, but especially after 11pm when everything else closes down. Crammed into a narrow street junction, Gaga by day is a crowded coffee stop, and by night is a collection of tables on the street where wall-to-wall people try to hold conversations over throbbing disco music. Daily 7am to whenever (officially 1am). Iza Loža 5. ☎ 021/342-257. Entrees 20kn–40kn ($3.50–$7). No credit cards.

Club Vanilla ★   Vanilla overlooks the pool in the sports complex on the beach near the Poljud soccer stadium. It is more upscale than most Split bars in that it attracts an affluent clientele and serves complicated mixed drinks. Open 9am to 3am Monday to Thursday and 9am to 4am Friday through Saturday. Closed on Sunday. Baženi Poljud Put bb, Poljudsko Šetalište. ☎ 021/381-283.

Žbirac ★★   The beach is part of Žbirac's charm but so are the scenic photos and the self-deprecating humor that are incorporated in the decor. Žbirac is really just an open-air bar set on a terrace on Bačvice Beach, but it draws a more sophisticated crowd than neighboring establishments. Open 7am to midnight Monday through Friday and 7am to 1am Friday and Saturday. Closed Sunday. Bačvice. No phone.

3 Salona

Anyone wandering around the remains of deserted, windswept Salona in the hills above Split will inevitably wonder what it was like to live in the provincial Roman settlement during its prime. The archaeological leavings are so spread out and so vast that the city's former status in the empire is unmistakable. There is just enough left of the original ancient structures to give even the casual observer a good picture of what the ancient city of 60,000 must have looked like, but a depressed economy has left Salona sadly neglected and overgrown.

When you arrive and buy your ticket, you will be given a map to follow as you explore the vast ruined city, but the gravel paths meander—and sometimes disappear—without many signs to direct you to various places on the tract, which seems to blend into patches of working farmland. Oddly, none of these "flaws" detracts from Salona's mantle of history, and even if you get lost, it is clear that Salona is an integral cog in Split's—and Croatia's—heritage.

Salona originally was a sheltered town on the Jadro River that was settled primarily by Illyrians and Greeks from Vis (Issa) who were trading partners with each other. In the 2nd century B.C., the Romans began to infiltrate the city, and eventually Salona was named Colonia Martia Julia Salona and transformed into Rome's administrative center for the province of Dalmatia. It subsequently became the largest city on the eastern Adriatic coast.

During Diocletian's reign, Salona prospered and the Romans undertook extensive building projects there, most notably a huge gate on the eastern boundary (Porta Caesarea); a theater; a forum with a temple consecrated to Jupiter, Juno, and Minerva; and a magnificent three-story amphitheater that could seat more than 15,000 spectators and which served as the city's primary sports and entertainment venue.

At the same time, Salona became a magnet for adherents of various spiritual movements of the times. According to scholars examining archaeological finds at Salona, these immigrants brought their customs and beliefs with them from such far-flung places as Egypt, Asia Minor, and Persia.

The new Christian faith was also in the mix of emergent religions sprouting in Salona, a situation that particularly vexed Diocletian, who was devoted to his pagan gods and claimed to be a descendant of Jupiter. In A.D. 303, toward the end of his reign, Diocletian solidified his reputation as one of Christianity's most zealous persecutors. He attempted to purge his corner of the empire of the new religion by ". . . ordering the churches to be razed to the ground and the Scriptures destroyed by fire, and giving notice that those in places of honor would lose their places, and domestic staff, if they continued to profess Christianity, would be deprived of their liberty. Such was the first edict against us." Soon after, other decrees arrived in rapid succession, ordering that "the presidents of the churches in every place should all be first committed to prison and then coerced by every possible means into offering sacrifice."

Bishops Domnius and Anastasius of Aquileia were among the Christian proselytizers of the times and both probably were among those martyred in Salona's amphitheater for their beliefs during Diocletian's campaign against Christianity. Ironically, the bodies of both these martyrs replaced Diocletian's in the Cathedral of St. Domnius in Old Town Split after Christianity was legalized and after it became the religion of the majority in the realm.

At the beginning of the 7th century, the Avars and Slavs invaded Salona, driving the city's residents to nearby islands from which they fled to Diocletian's palace.

Today Salona is a ghost city of ruins, and little of its former glory remains, though it still affords a panoramic view of Split and the surrounding area. The amphitheater's foundation is breathtaking in its scope and size and historians say the arena was still standing in the 17th century when it was deliberately destroyed by Venetian generals who decided it was better to level the structure than leave it for encroaching Turks. After that Salona was ignored until a Split priest and well-regarded archaeologist, the Rev. Frane Bulić, began an excavation in the late 19th century. He sent most of his significant finds to Split's archaeological museum, where they currently are on display.

ESSENTIALS

Salona is an area to be explored on a day trip rather than a place for an extended stay, so you will likely approach Salona from Split or Trogir and move on the same day. If you brush up on the place's history and know what you are looking at when you get there, your visit will be more meaningful.

VISITOR INFORMATION   Before going to Salona, check with the tourist office of the Town of Solin at Ulica Kralja Zvonimira 69 (© **021/210-048;** fax 021/269-900; www.solin.info.com) for directions and information. When you arrive at Salona, you will encounter an information booth at Tusculum, the entrance to the ancient city, that sells tickets for 10kn ($1.75), maps, and other printed material related to the site. The Salona site is open from 7am to 7pm Monday through Friday, from 10am to 7pm Saturday, and from 4 to 7pm Sunday.

GETTING THERE & GETTING AROUND Salona occupies 156 hectares (385 acres) about 6km (4 miles) from Split. If you are driving, take the Trogir-Split road (D8) directly to the parking lot. If you are using public transportation, buses to Salona leave Split every 20 minutes from the stop across the street from the Croatian National Theater from 7am to 10pm, and the trip takes about half an hour.

WHAT TO SEE & DO

Salona is one of Croatia's most important archaeological sites and it is navigable on foot only. You should wear sturdy shoes to tramp around the overgrown fields and gravel paths, and if you are visiting during the heat of the day, be sure to take ample water and wear a hat and sunscreen. Except for the arbor near the entrance, there is no shade.

Tusculum ✰✰✰ This structure just outside the entrance was built in 1898 by Rev. Frane Bulić at Manastirine next to the ruins of an early Christian basilica. Rev. Bulić is responsible for saving Salona from disappearing into the Earth: He started excavating the site in the late 1800s after decades of neglect had left it a mess. His purpose in building a house at Tusculum was to provide the archaeologists who were excavating Salona with an on-site place to stay. Today the house is a memorial museum for Rev. Bulić and a regional branch of the Split Archaeological Museum. Inside, on the first floor you will find a display of furniture from Rev. Bulić's time, his personal belongings, and photographs documenting his work. Outside, the building is decorated with capitals, inscriptions, and statues; a garden has a walkway framed by a variety of columns from old Salona.

Put Starina bb, Manastirine. ✆ 021/212-900. Mon–Fri 7am–7pm; Sat 10am–7pm; Sun 4–7pm.

Manastirine Necropolis ✰✰✰ From the 4th century on, early Christians from Salona and Split buried their martyrs outside the walls of this site south of Tusculum. The sarcophagus of Salona Bishop (and later Saint) Domnius was buried here, as were countless other Christian martyrs. As with many Christian burial sites of the times, the Manastirine evolved into a place of worship where Christians gathered to pray for and to their dead, and in the 5th century, a basilica was built over the graves. Rev. Bulić is buried near the Manastirine. He died in 1934.

South of Tusculum.

Caesarea Gate ✰✰✰ The Caesarea Gate is a good example of imperial Roman architecture. It lies just past Tusculum in an area where the foundations of two basilicas have been unearthed. The gate's arches are no longer discernible, but you can still make out the octagonal shape of the two towers that flanked it.

Near Tusculum.

Salona Amphitheater ✰✰✰ The amphitheater is a good 20-minute walk from the Tusculum entrance at the easternmost part of the ancient city, but it is a walk worth taking. The ruins of the 2nd-century amphitheater are very impressive as they lie in their huge circular footprint above chambers that are still hidden underneath the ruins. The site has not yet been excavated completely and archaeologists say there is much more to unearth.

4 Kaštel Klis & Sinj

Both Klis and Sinj are nice day trips outside Split and Salona. Neither is a destination, but each has at least one feature worth seeking out.

Kaštel Klis   About 10km (6 miles) inland from Split, Klis is a modest-looking village that spills down the hill beneath **Kaštel Klis,** a fortress (Tvrđava) that has a long history as one of Croatia's most important defensive positions. Records first mention the fortress in the 7th century and go on to enumerate its long list of occupiers, starting with the invading medieval Avars and ending with Italian and German Axis forces in World War II. Today the once-imposing fortress still affords a spectacular view of the three roads that lead into Klis, but the interior, while impressive in scope and design, is essentially devoid of artifacts.

Admission 10kn ($1.75). Summer Tues–Sun 9am–7pm; rest of year Tues–Sun 10am–4pm. Closed Mon and holidays.

Sinj's claim to fame is a 16th-century painting of the Virgin Mary **(Sinjska Gospa)** that is reputed to have miraculous properties. The painting by an unknown artist is in **Our Lady of Sinj Church (Crkva Sinjska Gospa)** at Šetalište Alojzije Stepanica 1, which is attached to the local Franciscan monastery. The friars brought the painting to Sinj from Bosnia in the late 17th century because even then it was said to channel miracles. The painting has particular meaning to the people of Sinj, who say the town was saved from the Turks in 1715 after the locals prayed to the icon to help them repel the invaders. Every August 15 on the feast of the Assumption of Mary, the town celebrates the miracle with a festival, during which the painting is paraded through town.

Sinj has a secondary celebration, **Sinjska Alka,** the first weekend in August to commemorate the above victory over the Turks. Sinjska Alka is more of a big block party than a commemoration and it is marked by medieval games that include jousting, costumes, and of course lots of food, drink, and music. For information, contact the Sinj Tourist Office in town at Vrlička 41 (© **021/826-352;** fax 021/660-360; www.dalmacija.net). Hours are 9am to 3pm Monday through Friday.

5 Makarska Riviera

This stretch of waterfront property from Omiš south to Gradac is dedicated to sea and surf aficionados. Pebbles cover every semi-gentle slope that leads into the sea; and in July and August, well-oiled bodies cover the pebbles from sunup to sundown almost the entire length of the 58km (36-mile) strip of coastline. There are six recognized resort towns along the Riviera and the Cetina Gorge; Brela and Makarska are the most notable, but the two towns couldn't be more different.

Brela, at the top of the chain of pebble beaches that punctuate the coast south to Gradac, is a two-level town. Most of the town's motor traffic, commercial enterprises, and private accommodations are on the road that continues down the coast. The major hotels and the town's nearly 6km (4 miles) of beach are at the bottom of a terraced, pine-forested slope. Near the bottom, a lovely walkway wends its way along the coast and the many secluded coves.

ESSENTIALS
VISITOR INFORMATION   The **Brela city tourist office** at Trg Alojzija Stepinca bb (© **021/618-455;** fax 021/618337; www.brela.hr) and the private agencies in town are very helpful and courteous. Through them you can secure accommodations and pick up maps and brochures. **Berulia Travel** (© **021/618-519**), one of the most helpful private

Biokovo Nature Park

The majestic peaks of the Biokovo Mountain Range rise about 3km (2 miles) northeast of Makarska and beckon those who want to supplement beach time with aerobic activity. The range is home to the Biokovo Nature Park, which is honeycombed with karst caves and landscapes, botanical gardens (at Kotosina), and some challenging hiking and climbing trails. More experienced mountaineers can tackle the peaks of Sveti Jure, Vošac, or any of 10 other peaks. The rewards are breathtaking views and a sense of accomplishment. You can also drive the 4.5 miles (7km) to the summit in the summer, but that can be scarier than climbing thanks to lots of sharp hairpin turns. As with any climbing adventure, you should pack emergency gear, check the weather, carry an accurate map and water, and wear good climbing boots.

agencies in the area, has a huge inventory of private accommodations. **Bonavia Travel Agency** at Obala Kneza Domagoja 18 (© **021/619-019;** www.bonavia-agency.hr) also finds private rooms and books excursions as well. The **Makarska city tourist office** is at Obala Kralja Tomislava 16 (© **021/612-002;** www.makarska.com), open daily June through September, 7am to 9pm; and Monday through Friday, October through May, 7am to 2pm.

GETTING THERE   The bus line that runs up and down the coast and through the Makarska Riviera stops at Brela behind the **Hotel Soline** and goes on to Makarska, where it stops at Ante Starčevića 30. Makarska also has a Jadronlinija office on Obala Kralja Tomislava (© **021/338-333**). It's about a 2-hour or longer drive to Brela from Split along the Adriatic Coastal Highway, but that time could be cut in half if you didn't have to drive through Omiš, an overcrowded resort town north of Brela that is clogged with pedestrian and auto traffic all summer.

GETTING AROUND   With most traffic relegated to the part of town above the beach, Brela is a wonderful walking town (though some of the paths are vertical). In fact, it is possible to navigate the 14km (8½-mile) path along the water all the way to Makarska, though you will pass through the town of Baška Voda 5km (3 miles) into it. Makarska's waterfront has the usual pedestrian promenade, but the town can turn into a massive traffic jam on any weekend day or night during July and August.

WHAT TO SEE & DO

The centerpieces of each of these towns are the beach and the sea, with a lot of watersports and spectacular scenery; but several historic churches and a monastery are sprinkled here and there, too. Brela is also home to several sports centers.

Aquanaut Diving at Bartola Kašića 50 (© **021/618-664;** GSM 098/371-651; ines.medic@st.htnet.hr) outfits novice and experienced divers and conducts excursions off Brela. **Mountaineering Club Pozjata,** Sv. Juja 1 (© **021/618-337**), conducts hikes and climbs in the area.

WHERE TO STAY

There are lots of big, impersonal package hotels up and down the Makarska Riviera, but there are also many charming private accommodations and a few small hotels, too.

During July and August it is difficult to find a parking place at Makarska or Brela, much less a room. If you do choose to visit then, you will have to book for at least 7 days in most places.

Biokovo 𝒜𝒜 This medium-size hotel is on the city promenade and close to the city center—a superb location, especially if you decide to leave the beach for lunch. Rooms are large and bright. The **Biokovo Dining Room** is quite elegant. There is a pretty outdoor terrace cafe.

Obala Kralja Tomislava bb,Makarska ⓒ 021/615-244. Fax 021/615-081. www.hotelbiokovo.hr. 60 units. July–Aug from 122€ ($145) double; from 136€ ($162) suite. Rest of year: from 86€ ($103) double; from 122€ ($145) suite. 20% surcharge for stays fewer than 4 days. AE, DC, MC, V. Rates include breakfast. Half- and full board available. **Amenities:** Restaurant; cafe; pizzeria; Internet access, room service. *In room:* A/C, TV, minibar.

Hotel Berulia 𝒜𝒜 Pine trees provide scent and privacy for this large white structure set back from Brela's magnificent pebble beach. Though the Berulia is a fairly large and well-equipped facility, its layout and landscaping create an illusion of intimacy. Rooms are average but with decent appointments; most have balconies that overlook the sea, the park, or the mountains. Bathrooms are immaculate but nothing special, and almost all have showers only.

Trg Gospe od Karmela 1, Brela. ⓒ 021/603-599. Fax 021/619-005. www.brelahotels.com; www.brela.hr. 199 units. July–Aug: from 916kn ($158) double with sea view. Rest of year: from 400kn ($70) double with sea view. Rates include breakfast. Limited free parking. Closed Nov–Mar. AE, DC, MC, V. Parking. **Amenities:** Restaurant; terrace cafe; beach restaurant; bar; pool; minigolf; tennis courts, sauna; solarium; bocce. *In room:* A/C, TV, minibar, hair dryer.

Hotel Dalmacija 𝒜𝒜 The Meteor's sister hotel overlooks the beach and sea and, like its more luxurious sibling, it, too, had a recent makeover. Rooms are a little smaller than those at the Meteor but there is a casino where you can stretch your legs and empty your wallet. The Dalmacija is a nice compromise if you need something a little more economical. Dalmacija is next to Makarska's biggest diving center.

Put Cvitačke bb, Makarska ⓒ 021/615-777. Fax 021/612-211. www.hoteli-makarska.hr. 190 units. From 60€ ($72) double. Rates include breakfast. Half- and full board available. Closed Nov–Easter. AE, DC, MC, V. **Amenities:** 2 restaurants; bar; 2 pools; casino. *In room:* A/C, TV, minibar.

Hotel Makarska 𝒜 It's not on the beach, but if the promenade is crowded, that could be a plus. The Makarska is located in the old part of town, a 5-minute walk from the water. Rooms have all the essentials, but not a lot of extras. Despite the drab decor, all rooms have balconies. Bathrooms have showers.

Potok 17, Makarska. ⓒ 021/616-622. www.makarska-hotel.com. 20 units. July–Aug: from 78€ ($93) double. Rest of year: from 68€ ($81) double. Closed Nov–Apr. AE, DC, MC, V. **Amenities:** Restaurant. *In room:* TV, minibar, safe.

Hotel Meteor 𝒜𝒜 The Meteor is the largest and the best of the three major hotels at Makarska. The property has the most amenities of the Hoteli Makarska's major properties along the beach. It is the only one of the three that is open year-round. There are seven tiers of rates through four seasons here. The best accommodations are the terrace rooms that face the pool, though the decor tends to be bland at every level.

Kralja P. Krešimira IV bb, Makarska. ⓒ 021/615-344. Fax 021/611-419. www.hoteli-makarska.hr. 275 units. July–Aug: from 130€ ($155) double; from 140€ ($167) suite. Rest of year: from 84€ ($100) double; from 110€ ($131) suite. AE, DC, MC, V. Rates include breakfast. Half- and full board extra. **Amenities:** Restaurant; tavern; disco; snack bar; 2 pools; whirlpool; sauna. *In room:* A/C, TV, minibar.

WHERE TO DINE

Makarska is a resort area that lives or dies depending on tourism. Thus, almost all of its restaurants serve decent food, but few venture into new territory with menu choices or preparation. Brela's eateries are even more casual and predictable, perhaps because of board arrangements at the hotels and because many people prepare meals in their private accommodations. Several restaurants in both towns, however, try a little harder than the rest, and they're noted below.

Grma ☆ DALMATIAN   This sprawling place next to the beach serves up traditional specialties and a nice selection of quality wines. As at most Dalmatian restaurants, seafood and meat are the menu mainstays, but there is some variety, too.

Šetalište Donja Luka 1, Makarska. ✆ 021/612-143. Entrees 45kn–150kn ($8–$26). AE, DC, MC, V. Daily 11am–midnight.

Jež ☆☆ DALMATIAN   Another perennial on the "100 best restaurants in Croatia" list, Jež richly deserves the honor. Located near the beach, Jež is a great choice for a special occasion or just to celebrate vacation. Whether you sit inside or on the terrace, be sure to try the pineapple torte for dessert. The restaurant also offers an excellent list of Croatian wines.

Petra Krešimira IV 90, Makarska. ✆ 021/611-741. Reservations recommended. Entrees 60kn–130kn ($5.50–$23). MC. Daily 11am–midnight.

Konoba Decima ☆☆ DALMATIAN   It's in the city center rather than on the beach, but the energy at this family konoba makes up for its location. The menu offerings are well-prepared though the choices are run-of-the-mill Dalmatian with lots of grilled fish and meat. But the grapevine-arbor covered terrace and the live traditional Dalmatian music performed by *klap* musicians make dining here memorable.

Trg Tina Ujevića, Makarska. ✆ 021/611-374. Entrees 50kn–110kn ($9–$19). No credit cards. Daily 8am–1am.

Riva ☆ DALMATIAN   This restaurant near the harbor routinely shows up on "best restaurant" lists in Croatia, and with good reason. Enjoy fish and meat specialties and a great wine list in a white-tablecloth dining room or on the terrace under palm and pine trees. Specialties include grilled seafood and filet mignon.

Obala Kralja Tomislava 6, Makarska. ✆ 021/616-829. Fax 021/615-422. restoran.riva@htnet.hr. Entrees 75kn–180kn ($13–$31). AE, DC, MC, V. Daily 11am–midnight.

Stari Mlin ☆☆ DALMATIAN   Dalmatia meets Thailand on the interesting menu in this restaurant set in an old stone mill. The patio is an oasis of green—the perfect setting for savoring steamed mussels, shrimp curry, or grilled fish with Thai sweet-hot sauce. Mlin also has a solid wine list and a children's menu.

Ulica Prvosvibanjska 43, Makarska. ✆ 021/611-509. Entrees 68kn–150kn ($13–$28). AE, DC, MC. Mon –Sat 10am–3pm and 6pm–1am; closed Sun.

6 Brač

Brač is known in Croatia both as a windsurfer's paradise and as one of the country's least-developed populated islands, but it is much more than that. This rugged land mass is about an hour's ferry ride from Split and it also is famous as the source of the stone that built Diocletian's palace on the mainland, the White House in Washington, D.C., and the Reichstag in Berlin. Brač also has a reputation as the source of Bolski Plavac and other highly regarded, locally produced wines. It is the third-largest island off Croatia (Krk is the largest and Cres the second-largest) and the site of Zlatni Rat (Golden Cape), Croatia's most famous beach.

Despite its size, Brač is really just a two-town island. That's because only Supetar on Brač's northern shore and Bol on its southern shore are easily accessible or frequently visited by those who love Brač's Mediterranean climate and unspoiled countryside. Tourism currently supplies most of Brač's revenue.

ESSENTIALS

VISITOR INFORMATION **Turistička Zajednica Grada Supetar** is at Porat 1 (© 021/630-551; www.supetar.hr). Hours are 8am to 10pm daily from June to the end of September. At other times, it's open 8am to 4pm Monday through Friday. Bol's tourist office is at Porat Bolskih Pomoraca bb (© 021/635-638; www.bol.hr). Both offices can help you locate private accommodations, provide you with maps, and even suggest excursions and walking routes.

GETTING THERE In the summer, more than a dozen car ferries make the daily hour-long journey from Split to Supetar on Brač's northern shore; and high-speed catamarans travel to Bol on the southern shore. Car ferries from the resort area of Makarska, south of Split, run to Sumartin on Brač's eastern shore. Several independent ferry services run between Brač and Hvar.

GETTING AROUND Buses run from Supetar to Bol six times a day and to several other towns and villages on Brač three times daily, but making connections can be limiting. The best way to explore more than one town per visit is to rent a car, a motor scooter, or even a bike (in Supetar) and explore the island independently. If you plan to stay in one place on Brač, walking is the preferred mode of travel. There are a limited number of bikes and mopeds for rent in Supetar, but there are no cars for rent unless you arrange to have one available before you arrive.

WHAT TO SEE & DO

Supetar and Bol are the locations most frequently visited by tourists to Brač. Supetar is by far the closer landing point from Split, but its **horseshoe-shaped beach** ⚲ is quite ordinary and not as interesting or as attractive as the famous **Zlati Rat (Golden Cape)** ⚲⚲ at Bol. Supetar does have a resort hotel complex and a decent-size pebble beach, but it doesn't have the cachet of its glamorous counterpart on the other side of the island. However, both towns are ideal locations for diving and other watersports thanks to their clear water and prevailing winds.

SUPETAR

With 3,500 inhabitants, Supetar is the largest town on Brač and an easy ferry ride from Split, with several boats running every day. The ferries landing at Supetar deposit passengers on a dock that sits just outside the town's quaint center at the business end of the beach. The beach starts south of the dock and curves away from the town toward the west up to the island's main hotel complex, which is home to three large package hotels and several smaller establishments.

Supetar's tourism revolves around its beach, which arcs away from the ferry port and is the center of almost all activity. The town does have a few other sites that can keep anyone busy for an afternoon. The best of these is the baroque **Church of the Annunciation,** which is a short uphill walk from the port toward the city center. Next to the church on the left, you'll find remnants of a **mosaic floor** that was part of an early (6th c.) church dedicated to St. Peter and built on this site. The present church was built on top of its predecessor; what's left of the original church's floor is in sections *in situ* on the ground, open to the elements and foot traffic. The courtyard entrance is graced by a very modern bust depicting **Mother Teresa.**

As you explore the church grounds, you should note the church's beautiful bronze doors and the Stations of the Cross chiseled in stone and hung on the rock wall that leads to a bell tower to the right of the church.

Supetar's **cemetery** and its ornate **Petrinović Mausoleum** are other attractions worthy of a stop. The cemetery is at the far end of the beach on a small, eerie-looking peninsula draped with cypress trees. Supetar native Ivan Rendić (1839–1932) is responsible for creating many of the unique grave markers there and for the huge Petrinović tomb built for shipping tycoon Francisco Petrinović, who was born in Croatia. The cemetery is also home to two stone Christian sarcophagi and the ruins of a Roman *villa rustica.* Sculpture styles in the cemetery range from classical to Byzantine, and if you enjoy necropolis art, you'll love poking around this collection.

After you've investigated the two sites above, you'll find that the allure of Supetar's attractions falls off sharply. However, you can take quick bus trips from Supetar to **Škrip,** the oldest settlement on Brač; or to **Milna,** birthplace of tennis ace Goran Ivanisevic. Or you can take the ferry back to Split or hop a bus to Bol.

BOL

Bol is home to what may be Croatia's most publicized beach. Almost every photo touting the country's unspoiled landscapes uses an aerial shot of **Zlatni Rat (Golden Cape)** ★★ beach in its promotions. From the air, Zlatni Rat does look like a long, inviting tendril of white sand lazily stretching into the sparkling azure sea. Add a gorgeous sunbather lounging here and there and the shape-shifting strip of land appears to be the perfect place for an idyllic sojourn. In reality, Zlatni Rat is a sun-washed finger of land that juts into the sea west of town. The Golden Cape is anything but a good choice for a dreamy vacation; and it isn't made of sand. Rather, Zlatni Rat is a mini-peninsula topped with chicken-egg-size pebbles and packed with people during the summer months. You can rent a beach chair and umbrella for 60kn ($10) if baking on hot rocks under a relentless sun doesn't appeal to you. If you don't enjoy sharing a beach and bathing area with a cast of thousands, you may wonder what all the Zlatni Rat fuss is about. On the bright side, the water off Zlatni Rat deepens gradually from the shore, and it is interesting to hear the cacophony of languages and pickup lines tossed about on the beach and to see the various sunbathing "styles" present there. If you just want to see the place but don't want to invest in the 20-minute walk each way to get from town to the beach, a water taxi shuttles passengers between the dock at the west end of town and the beach for 5kn ($1).

To be sure, Zlatni Rat is more upscale and tourist-savvy than the beach at Supetar, its sister to the north, and there is a certain satisfaction in setting foot on this super-hyped playground, but if sun worship isn't your cup of tea, you can stay in town and duck into **Branislav-Dešković Modern Art Gallery** at Porat Bolskih Pomoraca bb near the tourist office in Bol. It is open only in July and August (6pm–midnight). It has a fine collection of Brač landscapes from such renowned Croatian artists as Ivan Rendić, the man who created much of the sepulchral art in Supetar's lovely cemetery.

WATERSPORTS

Bol has a worldwide reputation as a windsurfer's paradise. It's not unusual to see "schools" of boarders riding the waves around the island, especially near Potočine beach west of Bol.

Big Blue   Big Blue is the big kahuna of watersports in Bol, a thriving operation that caters to all levels of athletes. You can rent a board for an hour for 15€ ($18) or for a week for 150€ ($180). Big Blue also rents equipment for mountain biking, diving, and sea kayaking. Or you can take a 6-day (2 hr. per day) certification course for 139€ ($165), certificate fee not included.

Podan Glavice 2 (near the Hotel Borak between Zlani Rat and town). ℂ 021/635-614. www.big-blue-sport.hr.

WHERE TO STAY

In Supetar, most accommodations consist of package hotels at the west end of town, though you can secure private accommodations at the tourist office near the dock (p. 106). You also can inquire wherever you see a SOBE sign. Bol has its share of rooms in well-equipped resort hotels, too, but it also has some charming private accommodations.

In Bol, you can book private accommodations at Boltours at Vladimira Nazora 18 (ℂ **021/635-693;** fax 021/635-695; www.boltours.com).

Hotel Riu Borak 🏖🏖   This all-inclusive Blue Sun hotel, just a 10-minute walk from either Zlatni Rat or town, is set back in the trees so you are away from the constant stream of people heading to the beach. Guest rooms in this newly renovated hotel are spacious and equipped with all the comforts of home. In addition, most rooms have balconies that overlook the pool or even the beach.

Bračka Cesta 13. 21420 t, Bol. ℂ 021/306-202, 021/635-210. Fax 021/306-215. www.riu.com. 234 units, including 48 suites. July–Aug: from 185€ ($260) double; from 210€ ($295) suite. Rest of year: from 145€ ($205) double; suite 117€ ($165). Rates include breakfast and dinner. AE, MC, V. **Amenities:** Restaurant; 2 bars; pool; solarium; Internet; live music, kids' program; tennis center. *In room:* A/C, TV, dataport, minibar, hair dryer, safe.

Hotel Elaphusa 🏖🏖   Another package hotel, the Elaphusa originally was built in the 1970s, renovated in 1999, and recently taken over by the Blue Sun Hotel chain, which in 2006 doubled the hotel's capacity and upgraded everything, including the prices. Guest rooms are newly renovated or rebuilt, large, and all have bathtubs (suites have Jacuzzis, too). The hotel now boasts a huge, full service spa center and scores of activities like excursions, disco bowling, and themed dinners. Like most of the hotels on Bol, this one is a 10-minute walk from Zlatni Rat and the town center.

Bračka Cesta 13, 21420 Bol ℂ 021/306-200, 021/635-210. Fax 021/635-477. www.zlatni-rat.hr. 306 units, including 6 suites. July–Aug: from 336€ ($470) double with half-board; rest of year: from 154€ ($215) double with half-board. July–Aug: from 490€ ($685) suite with breakfast only; rest of year: 350€ ($490) suite with breakfast only. AE, DC, MC, V. **Amenities:** Restaurant; bar; multiple pools; tennis courts; watersports; massage; infirmary. *In room:* A/C, SAT/TV, minibar, hair dryer, Internet access.

Hotel Kaštil 🏖🏖🏖   Hotel Kaštil is loaded with personality thanks to its location in an old baroque fortress on the water in the town center. It is the most interesting place to stay in Bol. Each of the Kaštil's 32 guest rooms is unique, modern, and cheery, in keeping with the welcoming atmosphere of the hotel's public spaces. The partially covered pizzeria on a terrace overlooking the water is an especially nice place to dine.

Frane Radića 1, Bol. ℂ 021/635-995. Fax 021/635-997. www.kastil.hr. 32 units. July–Aug: from 140€ ($170) double. Rest of year: from 64€ ($76) double. Rates include breakfast. MC, V. **Amenities:** 2 restaurants; pizzeria; bar. *In room:* A/C, TV.

Hotel Kaktus 🏖🏖   This Supetar hotel is one of several managed by the same company (Waterman Resorts) in a gated compound on the west side of the city and beach. Kaktus is the epitome of a resort hotel, a white multilevel building with services galore. Guest rooms are smallish but immaculate, and most have balconies that overlook the pool or the sea. In reality, the facilities here outshine the town's offerings, but be warned that if you make a reservation for a single night (if you can get one), you'll pay considerably more than the going rate for multiday stays, a practice that is all too common in Croatia.

Put Vela Luke 4, Supetar. © 021/640-155. Fax 021/631-344. www.watermanresorts.com. 120 units. Mid-July to mid-Aug: from 100€ ($120) double with half-board. Rest of year: from 46€ ($55) double with half-board. **Amenities:** 3 restaurants; bar; 2 pools; tennis courts; diving school; spa; sauna. *In room:* A/C, TV, minibar, Internet access.

Hotel Pastura ★★ *Finds* This blue and white hotel is right on the water in Postira, 10km (6 miles) from the Supetar ferry port, making the hotel close enough for convenience and remote enough for a holiday that makes rat-race stress disappear. The architecture and interior design are reminiscent of an Art Deco ocean liner and guest rooms in the hotel are furnished accordingly. All have barrier-free views of the sea, too. There is a gorgeous, oval fresh water pool, a pretty restaurant whose glass walls showcase the scenery, and bike rentals if you decide you want to commune with nature at close range.

21410 Postira. © 021/740-000, 021/632-100. Fax 021/632-109. www.hotelpastura.hr. 50 units, including 15 suites and 4 apt. Open early April to mid-Oct. Doubles from 110€ ($154). **Amenities:** Restaurant; bar; pool; sauna; fitness center; elevator; parking. *In room:* A/C, SAT/TV, minibar, safe.

Palača Dešković ★★ Rooms in this 15th-century former mansion are filled with art, antiques, and other beautiful accoutrements; Countess Ružica Dešković is the hotel's lovely and charming hostess. Palača Dešković is on Brač's north coast, 21km (12 miles) east of Supetar, and out of the center of the island's tourism flow, but that's part of its allure. You can pretend that you are as royal as the Countess herself in the hotel's elegant restaurant, on a yacht in its private harbor, or even in your room surrounded by period furniture and the Countess's artwork. Modern touches like heated bathroom floors, Jacuzzis, and Internet connectivity add to, rather than detract from, the hotel's Renaissance ambience.

21412 Pučišć, Brač. © 021/778-240. Fax 021/778-247. www.palaca-deskovic.com. 15 units, including 2 suites. Doubles from 206€ ($290) and suites from 248€ ($350) July and Aug. Other times, doubles from 124€ ($175); suites from 148€ ($210). Closed Jan to mid-Feb. DC, MC, V. **Amenities:** Restaurant; bar; marina; parking. *In room:* A/C, SAT/TV, Internet, minibar, Jacuzzi.

Hotel Villa Adriatica ★ This small hotel is more intimate than the neighboring resort hotels. If you are looking for a more personal experience, this is the place. Guest rooms are spare, but each is decorated with quality furniture and lively colors, and each has a balcony. The tiled bathrooms are adequate; most have showers. The individual attention you'll get from the staff makes up for any shortcomings. *Tip:* Proprietors Zlatan and Nevenka Jelovac are walking encyclopedias when it comes to Brač's history and little-known treasures. Ask them for suggestions about hiking trails, secluded coves, and other "discoveries."

Put Vele Luke 31, Supetar. © 021/343-806. Fax 021/755-015. www.villaadriatica.com. 22 units. Late July to late Aug: from 108€ ($130) double. Rest of year: from 66€ ($80) double. Closed Nov–Mar. Rates include buffet breakfast. MC, V. **Amenities:** Restaurant; cafe; bar; pool; minigolf; tennis courts; bike rental; volleyball; watersports; massage; excursions. *In room:* A/C, TV w/cable.

Dominikanski Samostan Campground (Dominican Monastery) ★★★ *Finds* This campground east of town near the Dominican Monastery has limited space (70 sites) and is run by the monks. Exceptionally popular because of its location near the sea and its well-kept facilities, it is always full. However, if you are inclined to walk around in a state of skimpy dishabille, this is not the place for you. The site is posted with dress-code signs.

Šetalište Andeleka Rabadana. ⓒ 021/635-132. May–Oct: 105kn ($18) 2 adults and campsite. No credit cards.

WHERE TO DINE

Restaurants in both Bol and Supetar are pretty predictable, though Bol has a better selection. Most of the people who book rooms on Brač stay in the resort complexes and take advantage of all-inclusive deals or at least half-board, so the restaurants in both towns are few and far between except for cafes and pizzerias.

Bistro/Pizzeria Riva *☞ DALMATIAN/PIZZA* Riva's menu has a respectable selection of grilled fish, but lots of grilled meat is available here, too. In addition, Riva offers pizza, a staple among Supetar's restaurants.

Riva bb, Supetar. ⓒ 021/631-155 or 091/580-195. Entrees 40kn–60kn ($7–$10). AE, DC, MC, V. Daily 7am–midnight.

Bistro Palute *☞ (Value)* DALMATIAN You can watch locals demolish huge plates of fish at this local hangout with tables inside and out. *Janjetina* (roasted or grilled lamb) is one of the specialties. Palute also operates a bed-and-breakfast.

Put Pašike 16, Supetar. ⓒ 021/631-730. palute@st.htnet.hr. Entrees 35kn–49kn ($6–$9.50). AE, MC, V. Daily 8am–3am.

Restaurant Dolac *☞☞ DALMATIAN* You can't really call Dolac a fancy restaurant, but it is a little more upscale than most of the places in Supetar. Dolac sits behind a stone wall and has lots of courtyard tables shaded by trees and a tiled canopy. The menu lists the usual assortment of grilled fish and pasta, but there are some very nice steaks to be had here, too.

Ulica Petra Jakšića 6, Supetar. ⓒ 021/630-446, 021/630-445. Entrees 40kn–80kn ($7–$14). AE, DC, MC, V. Daily 3pm–midnight.

Bistro Pumparela *☞ DALMATIAN* This little place on the harbor serves breakfast, lunch, and dinner. You can eat indoors or outdoors in little wooden booths. Well-prepared fish and pasta are the menu mainstays for dinner.

Porat Bolskih Pomoraca bb, Bol. ⓒ 021/635-886. Entrees 50kn–140kn ($9–$24). No credit cards. Daily 6am–2am.

Konoba Gušt *☞☞ DALMATIAN* This taverna near the Hotel Kaštil and just behind the Riva has a limited menu (a chalkboard list) of the fish and pasta dishes that you would expect at an island restaurant in Dalmatia. It also has a few traditional beef preparations and a dynamite lobster salad. The dining room is air-conditioned and decorated with agri-art (farming implements). The terrace has just half a dozen tables and a great breeze. Regardless of where you choose to sit, start your meal with a bottle of local wine and end with herb-infused *rakija* (a strong brandy), if you dare.

Frane Radića 14, Bol. ⓒ 021/635-911. www.bol.hr/index.php?ukljuci=taverna%20gust. Entrees 122kn–175kn ($21–$30). No credit cards. Daily noon–2am.

Terasa Dva Ferala/Papaya *☞☞☞ FUSION* If you are looking for something out of the ordinary, step through the marble entryway into this multilevel terrace restaurant punctuated with a huge peka, pine trees, and a tiki-hut bar. It looks as though the owners spent time in America's Southwest and tried to bring some of that ambience to Croatia. Try the beefsteak *al tonno* (stuffed with tuna) or the meatball beignets (grilled ground meat with bacon and cheese) for a break from Dalmatia's ubiquitous grilled fish and pizza. Dva Ferala also prepares standard Dalmatian fare, if you want to play it safe.

Fran Radića 18, Bol. Entrees 75kn–280kn ($13–$48). No credit cards. Daily 5pm–midnight.

Taverna Riva ★★★ DALMATIAN   Riva is across the street from Dva Ferala and next door to the Hotel Kaštil. It is also right at the edge of the sea, which makes dining at its outdoor terrace tables an invigorating and romantic experience. Try a creative fish dish like squid Pandora (cylinders of tender calamari stuffed with Dalmatian ham and cheese) or one of the steaks. If you make reservations 48 hours ahead and can muster a party of four, Riva will prepare lamb or veal on the peka. One server unabashedly said that Riva is the best restaurant in Bol, bar none; he recommended the Vrhunsko vino Bol, the area's best wine. Riva is much pricier than any other restaurant in town, but it is also Bol's finest dining experience.

Frane Radica 5, Bol. ℂ 021/635-236. www.bolnabracu.com/eng/taverna.htm. Reservations required. Entrees 58kn–200kn ($10–$35). AE, DC, MC, V. Daily noon–2pm and 6pm–midnight.

7 Hvar

St. Tropez, Majorca, Aspen, and other glamor destinations don't have anything on Hvar, the glitzy Croatian playground patronized by celebrities, the idle rich, and the average Joe tourist who wants to find out what the Hvar hoopla is about.

Hvar is indeed a lush, sunny Shangri-la with more hours of sunshine (2,724) than any other place in Croatia, according to the literature. But when you're talking just 24 more hours of rays than Brač (2,700) and only 124 hours (4 days) more than most of Croatia's other islands, you're splitting hairs. Nonetheless, some Hvar hotels will discount the price of your room if it rains continuously for 4 hours on any given day and give you a free night if it snows (fat chance).

Ultraviolet rays aside, Hvar is a lovely piece of real estate with vineyards, fields of lavender and other aromatic herbs, a few interesting sites, a lot of good restaurants, and some rather expensive—but historic—places to stay.

Hvar's principal towns are Hvar Town, Stari Grad, Vrboska, Jelsa, and Sucuraj, though Hvar Town seems to be the center of current interest in the island.

ESSENTIALS

VISITOR INFORMATION   Hvar Town's principal **tourist office** is at Trg Sv. Stjepana bb, Hvar's main square (ℂ 021/741-059; fax 021/742-977; www.tzhvar.hr). Stari Grad's is at Nova Riva 2 (ℂ 021/765-763; www.hvar.hr). Both can provide literature and maps, but if you want accommodations in Hvar Town, go to **Pelegrini Travel,** steps from the boat landing (ℂ 021/742-743; pelegrini@inet.hr), open 8am to 10pm Monday through Saturday and 6 to 8pm on Sunday. Pelegrini handles most of the private accommodations in Hvar Town and books rooms through travel agencies in Split and other towns. **Atlas Travel,** on the west side of the harbor (ℂ 021/741-670), is an excellent place to book excursions. During July and August, there is the potential for a reservation snafu, so be sure you have confirmed—and preferably paid for—accommodations before you arrive.

GETTING THERE   Jadrolinija operates car ferry service between Split and Stari Grad, and some also stop at Korčula and Dubrovnik. Buses connect from the ferry port in Stari Grad and go across the island to Hvar Town and Jelsa. Jadrolinija has an office on the Riva in Stari Grad (ℂ 021/741-132) and can provide prices and schedules. In summer, there usually are half a dozen or so buses that ply the route between Stari Grad and Hvar Town, but Sundays, holidays, and other times, service is spotty. Catamarans that carry only foot passengers also serve the island and they are faster than the car ferries. Most pick up and drop off passengers at the Hvar Town marina. It is possible to spend the day in Korčula and go on to Hvar in the afternoon; however, you'll have to overnight on Hvar because the last boat arrives there about 6:15pm, and nothing leaves late at night. In addition, it is very difficult to see much on Hvar if you only have a day.

GETTING AROUND   Hvar Town is closed to motorized traffic from the bus station to the Riva, which is also the busiest thoroughfare until after nightfall, when the long, rectangular main square, Trg Sveti Stjepana, becomes a circus. If you want to see anything besides Hvar Town and Stari Grad, a car is a time saver, but Hvar Town is best covered on foot.

WHAT TO SEE & DO

Hvar Town is St. Moritz with surf instead of snow. It's Hollywood meets Nice, Milan sophistication melded with Mediterranean relaxation, and the Las Vegas Strip transported to Tuscany. Hvar Town is a celebrity magnet for rock stars, tycoons, and the hip beautiful people drawn to their blazing orbits.

The uniqueness of the place is that everyone looks rich and famous. It's difficult to recognize even a well-known face, because in Hvar Town a nom de guerre, a pair of Maui Jim's sunglasses, designer jeans, and a look of ennui are enough for anyone to blend into the sculpted, perfumed crowd.

Make no mistake, Hvar Town has a nice cachet of lazy, sensual countryside and 13th-century attractions. However, it's really the sun, the sea, and the 21st-century social scene that pull in visitors, who make their entrances on everything from sleek yachts to ferries packed sardine-style. But even if you're here primarily for the beach scene, be sure to check out **St. Stephen's Square (Trg Sveti Stjepan)** 𝆑𝆑𝆑. Dating to the 13th century, this square is Hvar Town's center of activity. It is book ended by St. Stephen's Cathedral at its east and by a small harbor on the west. The square's borders are lined with restaurants, cafes, and galleries. A 16th-century well sits in the center of the paved space, which was redone in the late 18th century.

St. Stephen's Cathedral 𝆑   St. Stephen's is a rather unremarkable triple-aisled church with a nice 17th-century bell tower. The inside has quite a few late Renaissance paintings and a nice wooden 16th-century choir area.

Trg Sv. Stjepana bb. Daily 7am–noon and 5–7pm. Hours sometimes extended during tourist season.

Venetian Loggia & Clock Tower 𝆑𝆑𝆑   The Loggia and Clock Tower are part of the Hotel Palace's face to the world. The Loggia is a magnificent example of Renaissance architecture, but it was damaged by the Turks in 1571, repaired, and then used as a cafe from the late 19th century to as recently as the early 1970s. Today it frames an elegant salon in the Hotel Palace, complete with a grand piano. The clock tower was built in the 19th century on the site of the ducal palace. The palace was destroyed in the same assault that damaged the Loggia.

Trg Sv. Stjepana bb.

Franciscan Monastery 𝆑𝆑   Walk along the sea to the 15th-century monastery south of the center and enter through a lovely cloister, where concerts are held every 2 days during the season. Inside you'll find a nice museum with a collection of sacral art. The museum opens to an idyllic garden with a view of the sea. The adjacent church, Our Lady of Mercy, also dates from the 15th century and it is home to three polyptychs and many other pieces of religious art.

Hvar Town. © 021/741-123. 10kn ($1.75). Summer daily 10am–noon and 5–7pm; winter daily 10am–noon. Performance times and prices vary.

Hvar & Korčula

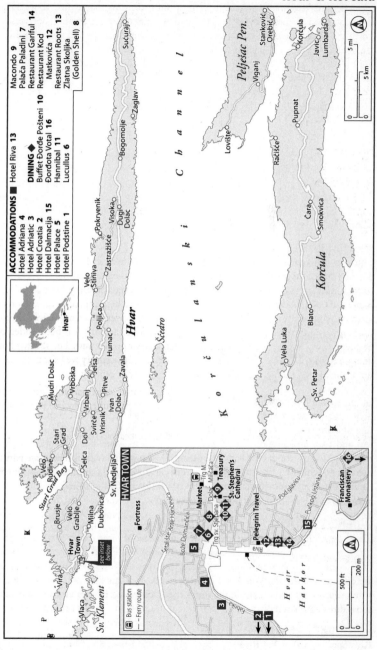

ACCOMMODATIONS ■
Hotel Adriana **4**
Hotel Adriatic **3**
Hotel Croatia **2**
Hotel Dalmacija **15**
Hotel Palace **5**
Hotel Podstine **1**

Hotel Riva **13**

DINING ◆
Buffet Đorđe Pošteni **10**
Đordota Votal **16**
Hannibal **11**
Lucullus **6**

Macondo **9**
Palača Paladini **7**
Restaurant Gariful **14**
Restaurant Kod Matkovića **12**
Restaurant Roots **13**
Zlatna Školjka (Golden Shell) **8**

Fortress (Fortica) 𝒜𝒜   The large 16th-century fortress that stands above Hvar Town once was a medieval castle. The current structure, built by the Venetians, is worth the climb to see spectacular views of Hvar Town's rooftops and its harbor from the ramparts. Inside the fortress you'll find displays of amphorae found offshore; and you can visit a spooky dungeon. There is a small cafe atop the castle. The walk up to the fortress is a nice but challenging trek during the day, but at night the climb can be treacherous because the steps/path leading up to the site are not lighted.

North of Hvar Town center. ✆ 021/741-816. Admission: 10kn ($1.75). Summer daily 8am–midnight; by appointment only in winter.

BEACHES
Hvar Town has a public beach west of the center. It is a pebble beach and, like most of the patches of Croatian land that have either been turned into paved strips or covered with pebbles and proclaimed a beach, this one is usually crowded with sunbathers from the nearby package Hotel Amfora. However, for a mere 10kn ($1.75), you can hop a taxi boat to nearby **Pakleni Otoci,** a cluster of pine-forested, uninhabited islands whose coastlines are alternately rimmed with rocks and little pebble beaches.

WATERSPORTS
This part of Croatia is home to some of the best conditions in Europe for windsurfing, kite boarding, jet-skiing, sailing, diving, and swimming.

Viking Diving Center   The Petrinovic family runs this establishment right next to the Podstine Hotel, and it can furnish equipment, instruction, and even rooms. Many of Viking's diving excursions go to the waters off Pakleni Otoci. Viking offers a wide range of options: You can buy almost any service, from a single dive at 220kn ($38), to a package of 5 days and 10 dives for 1,720kn ($300), to a full-day trip with cave diving for 490kn ($85), to everything in between. Equipment rental is extra.

Podstine bb. 21450 Hvar. ✆ 021/742-529. www.viking-diving.com.

Dive Center Hvar   This large professional dive center near the Hotel Amfora runs diving trips between Hvar and the island of Vis, which recently has become the darling of extreme sports enthusiasts. The Dive Center offers a long menu of dive services and trips and supports other watersports such as water-skiing, snorkeling, kite boarding, windsurfing, and banana boating. It also rents boats, kayaks, and equipment to go with all its sports. Dives run from 250kn ($43) for a single dive including equipment to an all-inclusive certification course for 2,360kn ($405).

At the Hotel Amfora. ✆ 021/741-503. www.divecenter-hvar.com.

WHERE TO STAY
There are no hotel bargains in Hvar Town, and most of the accommodations in Stari Grad are huge, impersonal package resorts. Since the island became all the rage, innkeepers have been scrambling to expand and renovate, and the result is that prices are escalating faster than the hotel improvements. You can still find modestly priced private accommodations, but in the summer especially you have to book for 4 days or more just to get a reservation.

VERY EXPENSIVE
Riva (aka Slavija) 𝒜𝒜   Riva wins the ugly-duckling-to-swan award and it's still all about location. Anyone who stays at this hotel about 30 feet from the pier where passengers disembark has a bird's-eye view of the waterfront action and since 2006, they

also have plush surroundings: A 6-month-long renovation turned this historic building into a chic, hip place to stay, dine, and socialize. Rooms are still small because of the building's protected status, but now they have ultramodern bathrooms, flatscreen TVs, slick designer colors, and walk-out patios. The hotel's terrace is home to a Mediterranean restaurant ★ that serves nouveau interpretations of Dalmatian cuisine and a cocktail space ★★ where you can schmooze the night away.

Riva bb, Hvar Town. ⓒ 021/741-820. Fax 021/741-147. www.suncanihvar.com/riva. 54 units including 8 suites and 1 twin. Mid-July to Aug: Doubles from 275€ ($350); suites from 325€ ($390); Riva suite from 370€ ($475). Rest of year: Doubles from 214€ ($275); suites from 238€ ($305); Riva suite from 295€ ($378). Rates include breakfast. AE, DC, MC, V. **Amenities:** Restaurant; bar; spa access; Wi-Fi in public areas; terrace dancing. *In room:* A/C, SAT/TV, hair dryer, free Wi-Fi, safe patios (some).

Adriana ★★★   After a 2-year renovation, the Adriana emerged in 2007 as Croatia's first and only member of the Leading Small Hotels of the World. Adriana deserves the recognition. Its rooftop terrace has a heated indoor/outdoor seawater pool plus bar and lounge area. Guest rooms are done in soft neutral colors and natural materials with wood floors and touches of rattan. They are spacious and full of light, which makes for a relaxing ambience. Bathrooms are big and ergonomic and stocked with plenty of toiletries. Adriana's Sensori Spa is its showpiece. Besides the usual beauty and massage services, the spa offers boutique services like a VIP suite for couples, an olive leaf and salt scrub, and a sea mud wrap.

Fabrika bb. ⓒ 021/750-200. Fax 021/750-201. www.suncanihvar.com. 59 units including 9 suites. Doubles from 350€ (490); suites from 380€ ($535). Rates include breakfast. **Amenities:** Restaurant, cafe; 2 bars; pool; spa. *In room:* A/C, SAT/TV, minibar, hair dryer, free Wi-Fi, LAN connection (charge), safe.

Hotel Palace ★ *Overrated*   This grande dame is situated behind the 16th-century loggia that once graced the town's ducal palace. The Palace was built in the early 20th century and has many elegant features that haven't changed much over the years. Despite its soaring ceilings and architectural appointments, the Palace's guest rooms are small, dated, and without air-conditioning. Oddly, the color scheme on the guest floors is peach and Miami aqua, which only ages this lady more. If you open the window in your room, you'll hear the noise on the square or beyond, and that can last until sunrise. As of press time, the Palace was scheduled for a late 2007 makeover that will transform it into a luxury accommodation.

Trg Sveti Stjepana bb. ⓒ **021/741-966.** Fax 021/742-240. www.suncanihvar.hr. 73 units. Mid-July to Aug: from 916kn ($158) double. Rest of year: from 420kn ($73) double. AE, DC, MC, V. Rates include breakfast. **Amenities:** Restaurant; bar; pool. *In room:* TV.

Hotel Adriatic ★   The all-inclusive (June–Sept) Adriatic has basic guest rooms and a decent location overlooking the harbor and the Old Town. Despite its "recent renovation," the hotel could use some updating to make it worth the cost of its guest rooms, which have been freshened but not transformed.

Harbor bb. ⓒ **021/741-024.** Fax 021/742-866. www.suncanihvar.hr. 63 units. June–Sept: from 170€ ($203) all-inclusive double. Rest of year: from 66€ ($52) bed-and-breakfast double. AE, DC, MC, V. **Amenities:** Restaurant; bar; pool. *In room:* A/C, TV.

Hotel Dalmacija   You'll have to walk up the stairs from the Riva behind the wall to find this hotel, which originally was built in the 1940s and expanded in the 1960s. The hotel is a true throwback and looks like something out of an old movie, though a renovation may be in its future. The 1940s building is a typical stone Dalmatian structure. There is no air-conditioning in the hotel, and guest rooms are very basic.

Fun Fact   Lavender Blues

Hvar is sometimes known as "Lavender Island" because the graceful plant with silver-green foliage and a hypnotic fragrance grows in profusion all over the place. Lavendula, as the plant is known in botanical circles, is a native of the dry Mediterranean climate and is the subject of many legends and superstitions. It is also thought to have medicinal properties.

One legend claims that lavender acquired its soothing fragrance when Mary hung baby Jesus's swaddling clothes on a bush and transformed it. A popular superstition says that lavender flowers scattered between the mattress and sheet of the conjugal bed will prevent spousal arguments. Today dried lavender flowers are used as sachets to add a pleasant scent to closets and drawers, and lavender oil is used to promote relaxation.

On Hvar, lavender is an industry and you'll pick up the lavender scent as soon as you disembark from the boat that brought you there, because it is sold in kiosks up and down the dock at Hvar Town. It is said that the whole island is enveloped in a cloud of lavender scent in the spring, and that may be so. But even after hiking in the Hvar hills, the only lavender we saw or smelled originated at the kiosks on the dock.

Amenities are almost nonexistent and nothing in the hotel has been refurbished in recent memory, according to the staff.

Riva bb. ✆ **021/741-120.** Fax 021/742-014. 21 units in the 1940s building, 37 in the other. Mid-July to Aug: from 110€ ($131) seaside double. Rest of year: from 38€ ($45) seaside double. Rates include breakfast. Half-board available. AE, DC, MC, V. **Amenities:** Restaurant; bar; TV room; salon.

Hotel Podstine ✦✦✦   The Podstine is set in the middle of palm and citrus trees next to its own beach, which is actually a concrete strip with a view of the Pakleni Islands. The hotel is a good 20-minute walk from the hotel to the center of town but it has its own shuttle, which will take you to the ferry landing or pick you up when you arrive. Guest rooms, while not anything special, are clean and the rooms on the upper floors have nice views. The shaded dining terrace is a wonderful place to kick back with a glass of wine.

Pod Stine. ✆ **021/740-400.** Fax 021/740-499. www.podstine.com. 40 units. Mid-July to late Aug: from 1,860kn ($321) seaside double. Rest of year: from 1,085kn ($187) seaside double. AE, DC, MC, V. Guarded parking. **Amenities:** Restaurant; bar; diving center; excursions; bike, scooter, and car rental; room service 11am–11pm. *In room:* A/C, TV, minibar.

Hotel Croatia   From the outside, Hotel Croatia looks like an upscale mansion nestled in a woodsy flower garden. Inside, it's evident that the hotel was built during the Tito regime and caught in a time warp. Rooms are tiny, dark, and cooled by a table fan, while the bathrooms are closet-size and dimly lit. While the hotel's location a few yards from the sea is a plus, its value-for-dollar is very low.

Majerovica bb, Hvar Town. ✆ **021/741-707.** Fax 021/742-400. www.hotelcroatia.net. 28 units, including 6 family units joined by a bath. Mid-July to Aug: Seaside doubles from 140€ ($180); family units (4 persons) from 252€ ($323). Other times seaside doubles from 58€ ($75); family units (4 persons) from 154€ ($198). Rates include breakfast. **Amenities:** Restaurant; bar; Internet; excursions. *In room:* SAT/TV, fan, hair dryer.

WHERE TO DINE

The restaurants up and down the Hvar Town harbor all serve pretty much the same dishes—pizza, pasta, and grilled fish. However, some restaurants in the narrow, unnamed streets off the main square and Riva offer distinctive cuisine.

VERY EXPENSIVE

Roots ⭐ NOUVEAU MEDITERRANEAN   Roots gets points for its casual-chic terrace setting and creative menu, which is unique in a region of cookie cutter menus. However, as beautiful as the food and surroundings may be, this brand new dining room sometimes pushes the envelope a little too far, especially with its designer pizzas topped with bizarre ingredient combos like the shrimp and goat cheese with raspberry vinaigrette spread. Stay on the safe side and order seared tuna with balsamic vinaigrette and cucumber casserole or grilled langoustines with olive oil, garlic, and fried parsley. For dessert, the crème brulee trio (orange, mint, vanilla) is a cooling surprise. Roots also offers weekly theme menus with Tex-Mex offerings and it has a long list of wines and exotic cocktails, both grossly overpriced.

Riva bb, Hvar Town. ℭ **021/750-101.** Entrees 140kn–420kn ($27–$80/19€–57€); pizzas 60kn–95kn ($12–$18/ 8€–13€). AE, DC, MC, V. Daily 7am–midnight.

EXPENSIVE

Lucullus ⭐⭐ SLOW FOOD   Light-slow food is how the chef describes his menu. That translates to a leisurely meal of well-prepared seafood and Dalmatian specialties served in a convivial atmosphere. Wood-grilled pizza is on the menu, but try the island lobster *brodeto* in Lucullus's cozy dining room or at home—the chef shares his recipe for *brodeto* and for lobster stew with tomatoes and onions *(gregada)* on restaurant flyers. Peka-grilled meat is available if ordered 3 hours in advance.

Off the main square. ℭ **021/742-498.** Reservations recommended. Entrees 60kn–175kn ($11–$26). AE, DC, V. Daily noon–1am. Closed Nov–Apr.

Đorđota Vartal ⭐⭐ DALMATIAN   This terrace restaurant on an elevated stone porch is a world all its own, with a vine-covered canopy and potted lavender plants. The menu is typical Dalmatian with pasta and grilled meat and fish. There is also a great *brujet* (spicy fish stew) and, of course, lobster.

Križna Luka 8. ℭ **021/743-077.** djordje.tudor@st.t-com.hr. Reservations recommended. Entrees 45kn–160kn ($8–$28), more for lobster and fish sold by the kilo. AE, MC, V. Daily noon–midnight. Closed Oct 15–Apr 1.

Palača Paladini ⭐⭐⭐ SLOW FOOD   A beautiful garden setting with stone walls and orange trees is the setting for this attractive bi-level restaurant specializing in slow food. Try anything grilled from the huge seafood menu, or go vegetarian with an amazing creation called "vegetarian pleasure."

Petra Hektorovića 4. ℭ **021/742-104.** www.tihi-hvar.com. Reservations recommended. Entrees 70kn–160kn ($12–$28). AE, DC, MC, V. Daily noon–3pm and 6pm–midnight. Closed Jan 15–May 15.

Zlatna Skoljka ⭐⭐ SLOW FOOD   The affable owner says that slow food is the opposite of fast food, which doesn't begin to explain this Croatian style of dining. It's really a leisurely presentation of courses, leaving time for diners to savor their meals. Start with Dalmatian ham and goat cheese in olive oil, and follow that with steak stuffed with goat cheese and capers, the excellent lamb stew, or grilled fish. This is a place where food is an art form.

Petra Hektorovica 8. ℭ **098/168-797.** Entrees 75kn–175kn ($13–$30). AE, DC, MC, V. Daily noon–3pm and 7pm–midnight. Closed Jan 5–Mar 31.

Hanibal 🎇🎇 DALMATIAN   Hanibal has been a fixture on Hvar since 1997 and it's a good choice no matter what you're in the mood for. The tables outside are usually crammed until midnight, so you might have to settle for a spot in the spiffy polished wood interior, where model ships are mounted on Plexiglas. Try the stuffed squid, the scampi risotto, or the grilled lamb, and you can be sure it will be prepared to your liking. Service is exceptionally cordial and attentive.

Trg Sv. Stjepana 12. 🕐 **021/742-760.** Reservations recommended. Entrees 70kn–140kn ($12–$24). AE, DC, MC, V. Daily 10am–midnight.

Restaurant Gariful 🎇🎇 DALMATIAN   Seafood and pasta are on the menu at this restaurant next to Carpe Diem (at the end of the harbor overlooking the sea). There are lots of meat entrees, too, including *janjatina* (lamb grilled on a spit), available daily for 90kn ($16). Specialties include green tagliatelle with scampi, chicken in Gorgonzola sauce, and anything crustacean. You know the lobster is fresh because you can choose your own from the restaurant's aquarium.

Obala bb. 🕐 **021/742-999.** Fax 021/741-587. Entrees 50kn–120kn ($9–$21); more for fish sold by the kilo. AE, DC, MC, V. Daily 10am–1am. Closed Jan 1–Apr 1.

Gostiona Kod Matkovića 🎇 (Value DALMATIAN   This courtyard restaurant off the Riva isn't anything unusual in fish-crazy Dalmatia, but besides its well-rounded seafood/shellfish offerings, Matkovića also has a nice selection of meats, including spit-roasted lamb. Wine selections are limited to the house white or red. Service can be very slow when all the tables are taken.

55 Godina Tradicije. Hvar Town. 🕐 **021/741-854.** Entrees 35kn–150kn ($6–$25), more for fish sold by the kilo. AE, DC, MC, V. Daily noon–2pm and 6pm–midnight.

Macondo 🎇🎇   Macondo is a seafood restaurant off St. Stephen's Square that spills into a nameless alley. Portions are huge, prices are moderate, and the waitstaff is young and friendly. You won't be able to resist the *gregada*, a garlicky seafood stew.

Groda bb. 🕐 **021/742-850.** Entrees 45kn–110kn ($9–$23). AE, DC, MC, V. Daily 11am–midnight.

INEXPENSIVE

Buffet Đorđe Pošteni 🎇 PIZZA   One of the many pizza/grill restaurants on the square, the outdoor tables are almost always full. Pošteni is as much a place to see and be seen as it is a restaurant. The pizza is nonetheless quite good. Service can get bogged down on busy nights.

Trg Sv Stjepana 13. 🕐 **021/741-138.** posteni-hvar@hi.htnet.hr. Entrees 50kn–95kn ($9–$16). No credit cards. Daily 10am–midnight. Closed Oct 15–May 15.

8 Korčula

No matter what time your boat arrives at the walled city of Korčula Town on this close-in Adriatic island, you'll encounter crowds of people mobbing the Marco Polo Tours office on the dock. They are there looking for accommodations, maps, directions, and other information about the island before they disappear through the Land Gate and into Korčula Town's historic walled core. That's probably due to the island's status as one of the most popular day trips available from Split, Dubrovnik, and Orebić on the Pelješac Peninsula.

Korčula Town is the focus of most tourist activity on the island as well as the main transportation hub. Its ferry landing is full of shops, kiosks, cafes, and tourism-related offices that give a disconcerting Grand Central Station feel to the area. Your first

CLOSED
due to
accidental demolition

WEGEN BISSIGEN
EICHHÖRNCHEN GESCHLOSSEN

CERRADO

CABRAS

Κλειστό
Μετεωρίτες

POOL CLOSED

ELECTRIC EELS

Hotel
closed for
facelifting

FERMÉ POUR
RAISON
DE GRÈVE
DES BONNES

FECHADO!
POR CAUSA DE
ATAQUES DOS CROCODILOS

I don't speak
sign language.

A hotel can close for all kinds of reasons.

Our Guarantee ensures that if your hotel's undergoing construction, we'll
let you know in advance. In fact, we cover your entire travel experience.
See www.travelocity.com/guarantee for details.

travelocity®
You'll never roam alone.

instinct might be to get back on the boat and go someplace else, but don't. Once you climb the 19th-century Grand Staircase with its 15th-century Revelin tower and walk through the 14th-century Land Gate, Korčula Town becomes a medieval cocoon that wraps you in a sense of how life was lived here centuries ago.

Behind the wall that's visible when you approach the island (the south wall is the only one left standing), Korčula Town is crisscrossed with picturesque structures built with materials from local islands' stone quarries. These house restaurants, museums, families, and offices. Hilly, dark, narrow streets branch off from the enclave's major north-south thoroughfare (Korčulaskog Statuta) in a pattern that resembles a trout skeleton. The street grid creates the illusion of a central boulevard with a lot of short side streets radiating from it. You can spend hours walking up and down these narrow offshoots and never know exactly where you are in relation to the walled town's exit. The approach to Korčula Town from the sea in the morning makes for one of the best vacation pictures ever.

Korčula, which is just a little over a mile from the mainland across the Pelješac Channel, once was covered with so many pine trees that the sight led the Greeks who settled here around 400 B.C. to dub the island Kerkyra Malaina (Black Corfu). As with many of the islands in the southern Adriatic, there is evidence that Korčula was the site of Neolithic settlements. Records show that it also experienced much the same historic string of takeovers and fortunes as the rest of Dalmatia's coastal settlements, including long stretches of Venetian rule.

Today, tourists are drawn by Korčula Town's well-preserved walled city and its medieval attractions, plus the city's claim that it is the birthplace of legendary explorer Marco Polo. Tourists also travel to Korčula to see the traditional **Moreška Sword Dance,** an annual spectacle that recalls a battle between Christians and "infidels" that was fought over a woman. And finally, the island is the source of excellent olive oil and wine, most notably white wines (Pošip, Grk) produced from grapes grown in the island's interior.

ESSENTIALS

VISITOR INFORMATION   The folks in Korčula Town's tourist office are very courteous and helpful. With a little notice, they will gladly help bewildered tourists and will sometimes even arrange for guides. Their office is next door to the Hotel Korčula at Obala Dr. Franje Tuđmana bb (© 020/715-701; www.korcula.net). **Marco Polo Tours** (© 020/715-400; www.korcula.net) is the main agent for excursions on and from Korčula and for accommodations on the island. You can buy books and maps on Korčula there. Their office right on the dock opens at 8am and closes from 1:30 to 2pm. It opens again until 8pm. You can rent a scooter or jet ski next door to Marco Polo at **Rent-a-Scooter** (© 091/787-754), open from 8am to 8pm daily. **Kantun Tours** (© 020/715-622; www.kantun-tours.com) across the street from Marco Polo offers Internet access and luggage storage, and arranges tours. **Atlas Travel** (see "Fast Facts: Split," earlier in this chapter) also rents cars, but it is a good idea to reserve ahead.

GETTING THERE   Korčula is linked to Split by speedy catamarans and ferries, each of which makes the round-trip at least once per day. A few ferries serve Korčula from nearby Orebić, with pedestrians landing at Korčula Town and car ferries landing at Vela Luka more than a mile from there. There is also daily bus service from Dubrovnik via the car ferry. For ferry information, contact the Jadrolinija office in Korčula Town at © 020/715-410. It is open from 8am to 8pm Tuesday through Thursday; and from 8am to 9pm Monday, from 8am to 1pm Saturday, and from 6am to 2pm Sunday. Ferry service runs from Orebić through **Mediteranska Plovidba** in Orebić at ℂ **020/711-156.** Bus schedule and fare information can be obtained at the Korčula Town bus station (ℂ **020/711-216**).

GETTING AROUND   Local buses make five runs daily from one end of the island to the other. You can also rent a bike and easily pedal the 6km (4 miles) between Korčula Town and Lumbarda (where the best beaches are). At its widest point, Korčula is about 8km (5 miles) wide and less than 32km (20 miles) long.

WHAT TO SEE & DO

Korčula's main attraction is the medieval Korčula Town and its walls, where you will find several historic churches and other buildings. Korčula Town likes to promote a once-nondescript stone edifice as the birthplace of Marco Polo, but there is no credible documentation that the great explorer ever set foot on the island.

Land Gate ✿✿✿   This 14th-century portal and its 15th-century Revelin tower frame the only land access to the walled Old Town. The gate (Kopnena Vrata) is embellished on the inside with a sculpture of St. Mark's lion over its arch. It leads to the core's main square, Trg Braće Radića, which is home to a 16th-century column, the town hall, and the 17th-century Church of St. Michael.

At Trg Bracé Radića.

Cathedral of St. Mark (Katedrala Sv. Marka) ✿✿   One of the main points of interest on the facade of this Gothic Renaissance building is the curious collection of sculpture at the entrance. You'll see statues of Adam and Eve carved from Korčula limestone at the main door, and above it a statue of St. Mark. Add to that sculptures of a mermaid and an elephant, and the result is a weird mix of imagery. Inside, the sculpture is more modern and more classic, too. Note the Pieta by renowned Croatian sculptor Ivan Meštrović in the baptistry. There is also a Meštrović sculpture of St. Blaise near the altar, and an altar painting allegedly done by Tintoretto.

Strossmayer Trg. Summer daily 7am–9pm; winter daily 7am–7pm.

Town Treasury/Abbey Treasury ✿✿   The collection of 15th- and 16th-century paintings, religious art, jewelry, furniture, and ancient documents from Korčula's past may not have great monetary value, but they are precious vestiges that help put today's Korčula in historical perspective.

Trg Sv. Marka Statuta. Admission 15kn ($3). Daily May 1–Oct 31 9am–8pm.

Town Museum ✿✿   Situated in the 16th-century Gabriellis Palace (across from the treasury), this three-story museum is a repository of Korčula culture and history. Here you will see a lovely collection of amphorae and stone remnants. The second-floor displays concentrate on furniture, textiles, and glassware. An exhibit features wall remnants still decorated with old frescoes. Most captions have English translations.

Trg Sv. Marka Statuta. ℂ 020/711-420. 10kn ($2). Daily June–Aug 9am–1:30pm.

St. Peter's Church ✿   This modest 14th-century church is on its own square north of the cathedral. You'll notice it because of the rope gate and ticket-takers outside. In the summer of 2005, an 18th-century statue of St. Peter made by an anonymous Venetian artist was sharing the holy space with a bizarre Marco Polo exhibition. Displays of model ships and statues make for a garage-sale atmosphere for exhibits that include tacky cardboard standup figures dressed in period garb representing Korčula's

---

(*Fun Fact* **The Legend of Marco Polo**

Legend, but not documentation, says that explorer Marco Polo was born in 1254 in Korčula Town in a modest stone house to the right of the cathedral's bell tower. Korčula Town's city fathers have not hesitated to capitalize on the city's supposed link to greatness; there is at least one restaurant, hotel, boat, and sandwich in this town named after the legendary navigator. However, according to a tour guide, there is no concrete evidence that Marco Polo ever set foot in Korčula Town even though as a captain of the Venetian navy he was involved in a sea battle with the Genoese navy off Korčula in 1298. Marco Polo was taken prisoner, and sent to a jail in Genoa, not Korčula. The alleged birth house at Put Sv. Nikol bb (10kn/$1.75; 9am–1pm and 5–7pm daily in summer, closed in winter) post-dates Marco Polo's death by a couple of centuries and the claim that Marco Polo was born there actually grew from the fact that someone with the surname "DePolo" once lived in the house.

---

favorite son and his contemporaries. The exhibit's centerpiece is a board that lights up as it traces Marco Polo's trips on a poster-size map.

Admission 15kn ($3). Summer daily 10am–2pm and 6pm–10pm.

WHERE TO STAY

Hotels on Korčula tend to be large out-of-date package-type places that haven't been improved much since they were built, but they have raised their prices as if they had refurbished early and often. These hotels also charge a premium if your stay is less than 4 days, so unless you intend to make Korčula your base, you are better off looking for private accommodations.

Hotel Park   From a distance, the Park looks like a sparkling luxury hotel, but it's really just a big 1960s-era block hotel set in the trees. The Park's last renovation was in 1996, but it was partial and the hotel still is short on amenities. Some rooms are two-star and some three. What that translates to is: Two-star rooms don't have TVs but some of the rooms have balconies. Each three-star room has a sea view, a balcony, and a TV. Room decor is straightforward and practical. A real downer: This four-story hotel is just steps from the beach, but it does *not* have an elevator or air-conditioning.

Korčula Town. (020/726-004. www.Korcula-croatia.com/hotel-park-Korcula-croatia.htm. 153 units. July–Aug: from 114€ ($160) 3-star double. Rest of year: from 60€ ($85) 3-star double. July–Aug: from 90€ ($126) 2-star double. Rest of year: from 52€ ($75) 2-star double. Rates include breakfast. Half-board available. AE, DC, MC, V. Closed mid-Oct to May. **Amenities:** Restaurant; bar; grill on beach; Internet in lobby; TV lounge. *In room:* TV in 3-star rooms.

Hotel Liburna   The Liburna's status as the epitome of Soviet drab is established in the lobby, which is dark and depressing. Guest rooms are worse but most have balconies and sea views. That doesn't make up for the fact that the hotel's last renovation was in the early 1980s. This is where you stay if you must overnight in Korčula and can't book anywhere else. The hotel does have redeeming features: Away from the lobby and guest rooms is a huge public area with taverna, couches, pool, and a lovely terrace. The beach is just steps away and Old Town is a 10-minute walk from the front door.

Hotel Liburna, Korčula. (**020/726-006**, or reservations 020/726-336. Fax 020/711-746. www.korcula-hotels.com. 83 units, 26 apts. 99 rooms have twin beds; 10 have doubles. July–Aug: from 176€ ($261) double. Rates include

Moreška Sword Dance

As a general rule, you'll be able to see people dancing in Korčula's streets every Monday and Thursday at 9pm in July and August; several times on July 29, the town's festival day; on Thursdays in June and September; and other times when tourist traffic is heavy.

The Moreška Sword Dance is a 15th-century narrative in motion that tells the story of two kings who compete for the love of a princess. As the story goes, the Black King kidnaps the young woman after she declares her love for the White King, who retaliates by initiating a battle. The kings and their armies then engage in an intricate "ballet" with swords drawn as they "fight" to musical accompaniment. The traditional dance is performed by townspeople, usually outside the town walls. The Moreška Sword Dance is thought to commemorate a real clash between Christians and Moors precipitated by the Moors' abduction of a young girl.

breakfast and dinner. AE, DC, MC, V. **Amenities:** 2 restaurants; 2 bars; taverna; minigolf; tennis courts; windsurfing school; sailing. *In room:* TV, minibar.

Hotel Marko Polo   The Marko Polo was built in 1972 and was completely renovated for the 2007 season. Both guest rooms and public areas have been modernized and spiffed up for looks and comfort, and prices have been hiked accordingly. However, Marko Polo is one of the best options on Korčula, if only because its rooms are air-conditioned.

Šetalište Frana Kršinića. ✆ **020/726-306.** www.korcula-hotels.com. 94 units. July–Aug: from 220€ ($310) for a superior double with a sea view. Other times sea view doubles from 143€ ($200). Rates include breakfast but not taxes. AE, DC, MC, V. **Amenities:** Restaurant; 2 bars; indoor/outdoor pools; money exchange. *In room:* A/C, SAT/TV, minibar, hair dryer.

Hotel Korčula ✦✦   Situated on the west side of town, the Hotel Korčula has a lovely veranda and an expansive terrace that lets you linger over breakfast with a view of the Riva. Built in 1912, the Korčula has the most personality of all the hotels on the island. Most of the rooms are small but nicely decorated; none has air-conditioning. Even though each room has a fan, try to book one of the rooms facing the sea.

Šetalište Frana Kršinića. ✆ **020/711-078,** or reservations 020/726-336. Fax 020/711-746. www.korcula-hotels.com. 24 units. From 160€ ($225) double. Rates include breakfast but not taxes. AE, DC, MC, V. **Amenities:** Restaurant. *In room:* TV, fan.

Hotel Bon Repos ✦   Just 3.2km (2 miles) from Old Town on the Bay of Shells, this big package hotel has the most creature comforts of any hotel in town, though they are distributed between two grades of rooms in four pavilions.

Šetalište Frana Kršinića. ✆ **020/726-306.** www.korcula-hotels.com. 278 units (2- and 3-star). Mid-July to mid-Aug: from 120€ ($170) double. Rates include breakfast but not taxes. Regular taxi boat to Old Town 5kn ($1). AE, DC, MC, V. **Amenities:** 3 restaurants; 2 bars; saltwater pool; minigolf; tennis; diving school.

Autocamp Kalac ✦   Kalac is near the Bon Repos on the Bay of Shells and has room for 600 guests. There are bathroom facilities, refrigerators, hookups, a snack bar, and a small market, but compared to most campgrounds in Croatia, Kalac is light on services. Right next to the water, it offers some shade.

Šetalište Frana Kršinića. ℂ 020/711-078. 162kn ($30) for site, car, and 2 people. Hookup and fridge extra. No credit cards. Closed June–Sept.

WHERE TO DINE

Dining tends to be a pretty informal affair in Korčula, and because most of the people who stay here take board at their hotels, the independent restaurants in town generally have varied menus to appeal to a diverse crowd. However, without much competition, the menus at most places are all about the same.

VERY EXPENSIVE

Konoba Mareta ⋆ DALMATIAN   This spot is a little pricier than most in its class, but its limited menu is a little better executed than some. Nice wooden bench tables are set up outside, where you can soak up the town's atmosphere while you dine. Try the salted fish appetizer if you haven't had the pleasure of sampling this Dalmatian specialty.

Plokata bb. No phone. Entrees 50kn–270kn ($9–$47). No credit cards. Daily 10am–2pm and 6–11:30pm.

Gradski Podrum ⋆ *Value* DALMATIAN   A 40kn ($7) daily plate is one of the draws at this Korčula institution. Any of the fish dishes done "Korčula-style"—with boiled potatoes and tomato sauce—are yummy. Try mixed meat and veggies (roasted in a closed pot covered with burning embers and ash); or savor the *pasticada* (marinated beef cooked with dumplings and gravy).

Put Sveti Antuna bb. ℂ 020/711-222. Entrees 40kn–280kn ($7–$48). The latter price is per kilo. AE, DC, MC, V. Daily 11am–2pm and 6-10:30pm. Closed mid-Oct to mid-Apr.

EXPENSIVE

Konoba/bar Adio Mare ⋆⋆ DALMATIAN   Local specialties and fish are the highlights of this atmospheric dining spot, whose rustic stone walls on the first floor of an old house make it resemble a fancy bunker. You'll be seated at long wooden tables with other patrons a la Japanese teppan-yaki style. Try some of the meat grilled right before your eyes while you and your tablemates make small talk with the restaurant's jovial chef. Adio Mare has a very nice selection of wines—including several versions of Korčula's famous whites—to accompany your food.

Sv. Roka 2. ℂ 020/711-253. Reservations recommended. Entrees 40kn–130kn ($7–$23). AE, DC, MC, V. Mon–Sat 5:30pm–midnight; Sun 6pm–midnight. Closed mid-Oct to mid-Apr.

MODERATE

Konoba Adriana   Fish and Dalmatian specialties crowd the menu here. Try the fish stew Adriana, something like bouillabaisse, but not as spicy. There is a very nice terrace for dining, but even with umbrellas, it can get extremely hot on a sunny day.

Near the Hotel Park. ℂ 020/715-661. Entrees 35kn–100kn ($6–$18). AE, DC, MC, V. Daily 11am–11pm.

Konoba Gajeta ⋆⋆ *Finds* DALMATIAN   Opened in 2005, this lovely spot under the trees along the Riva serves some of the best food in Korčula Town. Specialties are pancakes with cheese and scampi, as well as Žrnovski macaroni, handmade pasta lovingly produced by a local woman especially for the restaurant.

Setaliste Petra Kanavelića bb. ℂ 020/716-359 or 091/503-2829. Entrees 50kn–90kn ($9–$16). No credit cards. Daily 11am–11pm. Closed Nov–Apr.

Konoba Marco Polo ⌖ DALMATIAN   One of the nice thing about konobas is that each has its interpretation of traditional dishes. Marco Polo is no different. Tables here are set on tiered wide steps that descend onto the street. The menu is mostly grilled fish and meat. You can't go wrong with grilled octopus.

ACI Marina. ℭ 020/715-662. Entrees 50kn–95kn ($9–$17); more for fish by the kilo. AE, DC, MC, V. Year-round daily 11am–midnight.

INEXPENSIVE

Konoba Briskŭle ⌖⌖⌖ *(Finds* DALMATIAN   The food here isn't just good, it's *very* good, according to the restaurant's jovial owner Damir Plaziblat. Briskŭle is a fairly new entry in the Korčula dining scene, but since its opening in 2003, it is already gaining a following. This is because of its low prices, high quality, and, as Plaziblat says, because the cooking is "from the heart." The menu is flexible because he or chef Đuro Petrović buys whatever looks good that day at the fish market. The mussels, at 50kn ($9) for a huge portion, are a steal.

Setaliste Frana Kršinića bb. ℭ 091/242-245. Entrees 35kn–65kn ($6–$11). No credit cards. Daily 10am–midnight. Closed Nov 1–May 1.

9 Vis

Vis, the inhabited island farthest from Croatia's mainland, has only recently become a hot destination. Vis's location is not the only factor that kept it off the tourist track: Vis was closed to visitors until 1989 because of its status as a military base. Almost as soon as the island was able to open its shores to the world, the 1991 Homeland War threw a wet blanket over tourism in Croatia and Vis's debut was delayed.

But now Vis is a perfect poster child for the country's "Croatia: The Mediterranean As It Used To Be" promotion. It is developing into the next must-see Croatian vacation spot precisely because the country's previous tourism booms bypassed the formerly forbidden island and it is in pristine condition.

The downside is that Vis is short on accommodations and tourism infrastructure, but it is beginning to catch up. Its two main towns, **Vis Town** and **Komiža** on the coast, are seeing increased tourist days thanks to the island's unspoiled interior, its deserted beaches and clear-as-glass water, and its fine authentic restaurants. Travel between the island and the mainland has increased thanks to new fast-boat routes blessed by Croatia's government.

Vis's recorded history goes back to the 4th century B.C. when Dionysius of Syracuse founded Issa, presumably as a strategic base for Greek enterprises in the Adriatic. Issa became a city-state and eventually was taken over by the Romans, the Byzantines, and the Venetians. Vis attained its greatest notoriety during World War II, when Marshal Tito used a cave on the island as his base for masterminding Partisan strategies. Called **Tito's Cave,** the chamber on the south side of Mount Hum is still a place of interest.

There are lots of secluded bays on Vis, particularly on the island's southern side (Rukavac, Stiniva, Milna, Srebarna), where most of the time you'll have the rocks and sea to yourself.

ESSENTIALS

VISITOR INFORMATION   The **tourist office** in Vis Town is the best place to get information and maps. It is at Šetalište Stare Isse 5 (ℭ 021/717-017; fax 021/717-018; www.tz-vis.hr). In Vis Town you can book private accommodations through the

Ionios Agency at Obala Svetog Jurja 36 (© **021/711-352;** fax 021/711-356). Ionios also rents scooters and bikes and arranges excursions. Komiža's tourist office, at Riva bb (© **021/713-455**), provides the usual services. Jadrolinija's local office is in Vis Town at Šetalište Stare Isse (© **021/711-032**).

GETTING THERE   Besides private excursions offered by Atlas and other tourist agencies in various cities on the mainland, travel to Vis is possible on "public" transportation thanks to catamaran service between the island and the mainland. Both Jadrolinija and Semmarina operate routes from Split (p. 84 for details).

GETTING AROUND   Vis Town is the island's main port. Bus service shuttles passengers between the ferry port and Komiža, currently the island's most visited population center. However, if you want to see the inland villages or anything besides Vis Town and Komiža, you'll need your own transport.

WHAT TO SEE & DO

Vis Town ✦✦ has a permanent population of less than 2,000 but it is the island's largest town and its major center of commerce. Like Zagreb, Vis Town, which is on the island's north coast, is a combination of two separate settlements: Kut on the east side of town and Luka to the west. Kut is a prosperous-looking residential neighborhood and the location of the town's best restaurants. A seaside promenade connects the two neighborhoods; most of the town's beaches are along this path. One of the most interesting sites on the island is located near the Kut neighborhood: Just west of Kut, there is a British naval cemetery that is walled and locked. It dates to the War of 1812 and is the resting place of fallen British soldiers who fought in battles from the Napoleonic Wars through World War II. Luka is where you will find the ferry port, the tourist office, and a string of modest stone houses. This is also where the Franciscan Monastery stands. Vis Town has a pleasant beach in front of the Hotel Issa on a lovely stretch north of the promenade on Vis Bay, about a quarter of a mile from the center. Here you will find "snack" huts where you can get lunch or a cool drink.

A wharf, a castle built by the Venetians, a 17th-century church, and several beaches are the main attractions in **Komiža** ✦. One of the beaches is in front of the Hotel Biševo, but the water there is not as clear as it is at other parts of the island. Another beach a short distance northwest of Komiža at Uvala Srebrena has clearer water, but less hospitable rocks to lie on and little black "beasts" in the water that latch onto human flesh.

Biševo ✦✦✦ is a tiny piece of land 5km (3 miles) southwest of Vis. This is the site of the spectacular **Blue Cave (Modra Špilja),** a sea cave that "lights up" in shades of blue and silver for an hour each day between 11am and noon. Boats leave Komiža at 9am to make it to the cave in time for the light show. The Blue Cave is one of 26 underwater caves on Biševo. All are made of limestone, whose whiteness is perfect for reflecting color. For centuries the only way to enter the Blue Cave was by diving into the sea and swimming in, but more than 100 years ago the cave was altered so visitors could enter by boat, a setup similar to the one at the Blue Cave near Capri off southern Italy. If you visit the Cave earlier or later than the optimal hour, you'll be disappointed because the blue color will not be visible. To get there, you can either book an excursion or take your own boat to the Cave. Almost every agency in Komiža offers Blue Cave "picnic" tours for about 90kn ($17) per person. *Warning:* Crowds and the unpredictable *Jugo* (south wind) can be deterrents to investigating the underwater cave.

WHERE TO STAY

Vis is short on hotels and campgrounds, but private accommodations are plentiful. Check with Ionios Agency (above) for bookings. One nice place is **Apartments Marinković** at Mihovila Pavlinovica 9 in Komiža (© **021/713-821**). For 35€ ($42) per night for two, you get a room on the top floor with a balcony and a great view of the harbor.

Hotel Biševo   This place in Komiža has a decent beach and a nice view of the water. Guest rooms are smallish and a few of them have been renovated, so ask for one of those.

Ribarska 72, Komiža. © **021/713-008**. 135 units. From 610kn ($105) double. Rate includes breakfast. AE, DC, MC, V. Parking. **Amenities:** Restaurant. *In room:* TV, minibar.

Hotel Tamaris 🏖   Tamaris, the nicest hotel on the island, is walking distance to the ferry port. The 19th-century building itself is a squarish red structure adorned with brick gingerbread. It is in the center of town and convenient to everything. Its seafront terrace is a delight.

Svetog Jurja 30, Vis Town. © **021/711-350**. 26 units. From 650kn ($112) double. AE, DC, MC, V. **Amenities:** Restaurant; bar. *In room:* A/C, TV.

Villa Nonna and Casa Nonno 🏖🏖   Wood floors, stone accents, and lots of light were incorporated into the 2003 renovation plan for Villa Nonna, a 400-year-old Komiža town house that once was a tavern. The result is 7 studios with personality and plenty of elbow room. If self-catering doesn't appeal and you don't need that much space, book a room at Casa Nonno, a 4-room sister facility located in the parallel street behind and up from Villa Nonna. Casa Nonno was restored in 2005 and it has a central kitchen guests can use if they want to store or prepare snacks. Restaurants are steps away from both for those who don't want to be bothered with cooking. Both facilities require week-long bookings from Saturday through Saturday (except in the off season, which is Jan1–Apr 28).

Ribarska 50, 21485 Komiža. © **098/380-046**. Fax 021/713-500. www.villa-nonna.com. Villa Nonna: 7 units. From 476€ ($665) per week. Casa Nonno: Doubles from 310€ ($430) per week. No credit cards. **Amenities:** Garden; excursions; use of private yacht. *In room:* A/C, full kitchen in Villa Nonna units.

WHERE TO DINE

The restaurants on Vis are exceptional. Their proximity to the source of the catch makes any fish dish you order a sublime dining experience. Traditional dishes are also made with fresh local ingredients.

Kantun 🏖🏖   A recent renovation has made Kantun a destination restaurant that is at once urban and homey in feel: The place looks like a laid-back konoba, but the food is laced with subtle sophistication. Try the smoked tuna carpaccio appetizer and the sublime fish soup. There is a great selection of local wines.

Biskupa Mihe Pusića 17, Vis Town. © **021/711-306**. Entrees 60kn–160kn ($11–$30). No credit cards. Daily 8am–midnight.

Pojoda 🏖🏖🏖 *Value* SEAFOOD   Pojoda is famous for its creative cuisine and its starters, and once you see the menu you might not get to the main course. Try the tuna in caper sauce or the pasta and beans. If you do have room for an entree, any of the barbecued fish dishes are luscious, as is the fish cooked in wine. The garden is fringed with orange and lemon trees. Reserve a table on the upper floor for the view.

Don Cvjetka Marasović 8, Kut. © **021/711-575**. Fax 021/718-031. Entrees 40kn–125kn ($7–$22). AE, DC, MC, V. Daily in summer noon–3pm and 5pm–1am. In winter, 5pm–midnight daily.

Villa Kaliopa ✿✿✿ CROATIAN   Situated in the garden of the Garibaldi Palace midway between Old Town and Kut, this stylish place set among palm trees and sculptures is a favorite of the yacht set that ties up in the harbor. Besides serving exquisite local fare and seafood, Kaliopa serves Vis wine, which has been made on the island since the time the Greeks called the island Issa. This restaurant is as romantic (and expensive) as it gets.

Vladimira Nazora 32, Kut. ℂ 021/711-755, 099/529-667. Entrees 250kn–600kn ($45–$100). AE, DC, MC, V. Daily in summer 5:30pm–12:30am.

10 Pelješac Peninsula

OREBIĆ

This town in the southwestern part of the Pelješac Peninsula boasts that it has one of the sunniest climates in Croatia thanks to the town's position at the foot of the 961m (3,153-ft.) Mount St. Ilija. Beachgoers take advantage of this in droves and it isn't unusual to see moms carting picnic baskets there for breakfast, lunch, and dinner. Orebić's atmosphere is upscale but not intimidating; laid-back but not laissez-faire. This is where you will find some of Croatia's best beaches and one of the most interesting and congenial promenades anywhere. Orebić is a place where you can settle in and let your mood take you to the beach, on a day trip to Korčula, or out to sea on a sailing excursion. Orebić owes much of its cachet to its history as a town of sea captains, who in the 18th and 19th centuries built many fine houses inland. Some of these structures are still standing and in use as inns and private residences.

ESSENTIALS

VISITOR INFORMATION   The **Orebić Tourist Information Office** is on the beach at Trg Mimbeli (ℂ **020/713-718;** www.tz-Orebić.com). The staff double as Atlas agents and book excursions from Orebić to Dubrovnik, Mljet, and other southern islands. **Orebić Tours** at Bana Josipa Jelačića 84a (ℂ **020/714-054;** fax 020/713-616; www.orebic-tours.hr) does an excellent job of booking private accommodations and arranging excursions, too.

GETTING THERE   Orebić is on the southern coast of the Pelješac Peninsula, which is a strip of hilly, fertile land noted for its vineyards. The town is about an hour by car from the peninsula's eastern border and makes a nice base for day trips to Korčula or to explore the peninsula.

GETTING AROUND   Everybody walks everywhere in Orebić, especially in the evening. The Riva, of course, is pedestrians-only.

WHAT TO SEE & DO

Orebić is the quintessential resort town. The beach and the sea are its primary attractions, and all watersports are very popular there. The surrounding area is excellent for hiking, too. Don't miss the walk along the seaside promenade, which is so close to the water you could fall in.

Franciscan Monastery ✿✿   This stately 15th-century structure sits on a plateau above the beach and water with a grove of pine trees as its backdrop. It once was used as a lookout point for invasions from the sea. Inside, the walls are hung with a series of paintings done on wood, mostly donated by seafaring men. Each commemorates its donor's escape from death during a storm.

Admission 5kn ($1). Daily 8am–noon and 5–7pm.

Maritime Museum   You really have to be into boating to appreciate this shrine to things nautical. The place is filled with models of boats, paintings of boats, pieces of boats, and boating equipment. Captions have English translations.

Obala Pomoraca. ℂ 020/713-009. Admission 10kn ($1.75). Mon–Fri 10am–noon and 6–9pm; Sat 6–9pm.

WHERE TO STAY

Hotel Orsan ⊛   Located on a sandy bay steps from the sea and backed by thick forest, the Orsan is a lovely way to spend a few days enjoying the shimmering waters of Orebić. Each room's balcony offers sea or park views.

Obala Pomoraca 36. ℂ 020/713-026. Fax 020/713-267. www.tz-Orebić.com. 94 units. July–Aug: from 100€ ($120) half-board double. Subtract 7€ ($8.50 per person) for rooms with breakfast only. AE, MC, V. **Amenities:** Restaurant; bar; pool. In room: TV, minibar.

Hotel Castello Antonio ⊛⊛⊛ (Finds   If you want to know what it's like to stay in the home of an aristocrat from yesteryear, book a room at this gracious mansion surrounded by some of Pelješac's best vineyards. Tall windows and open balconies afford unsurpassed views of the grapes and the sea, and attention to detail and rich decor make the interior worthy of a home-and-garden magazine. Guest rooms, though modest in size, continue the theme with comfy beds, functional bathrooms, and balconies that overlook the sea. The hotel is just under 3.2km (2 miles) from Orebić's center, but it's a stone's throw from the sea.

Postup 48. ℂ 020/713-464. Direct line to owner ℂ 098/230-607. Anto.bezek@du.htnet.hr. 25 units. From 84€ ($100) double. Rates include breakfast. MC, V. **Amenities:** Restaurant. In room: A/C, TV.

Apartment Rental ⊛⊛   To rent an apartment, try **Orebič Tours,** Bana Josipa Jelačića 84a (ℂ **020/714-054;** fax 020/713-606; www.Orebić-tours.hr). The company also arranges excursions and hotel accommodations.

WHERE TO DINE

The most difficult task in finding a good restaurant in Orebić is deciding which tempting aromas to follow: There are many places along the beachfront in full cooking mode simultaneously, a situation that can set off olfactory overload and salivation. Menus are posted outside most places, and the greatest danger is finding a restaurant you can't resist trying *after* your post-dinner promenade along the shore.

Bistro/Caffe/bar Coco ⊛⊛⊛ (Value DALMATIAN   Everything on the menu at this ma-and-pa spot set between greystone walls and shade trees is prepared with care. Squid dishes are done to perfection, whether fried or grilled, and the mussels Bouzzara are among the best in Croatia. Fifteen kinds of pizza round out the offerings. You don't have to dress up to feel at home here: You'll be given a dish towel to protect your clothes if you order something messy.

Obala Pomoraca 8. ℂ 020/713-640. Entrees 40kn–220kn ($7–$38). No credit cards. Daily 5pm–1am.

Café/Bar Jadran ⊛⊛ (Value   This restaurant on a raised terrace above the beach uses the sea as a backdrop for its competently prepared offerings. Think beach fast food prepared with pizazz. You have to put your faith in the chef when you order an item that simply reads "fish," but arriving at table is the real deal, perfectly grilled and served with just a sprinkling of herbs. Jadran has excellent pizza and grilled meat, too. It's the kind of place where you can wear your grubbies and still feel like a gourmet.

Trg Mimbeli 11. ℂ 020/713-243. Entrees 38kn–180kn ($7–$31). No credit cards. Daily 9am–1am. Closed Oct–May.

⟨Finds⟩ Wine Road Detour

East of Orebić, about 32km (20 miles) along the main road to Ston, you'll come across a turnoff for Trstenik, an out-of-the-way town with a couple of small, uncrowded beaches, a few restaurants, and a concrete pier for diving. But that's not all.

From the road to Trstenik, you can also make a side trip to the Croatian branch of Grgich Hills, one of America's greatest wineries. Here, Grgić Vina is very modest compared to its American counterpart. This operation is just a concrete bunker on a spur off the switchback road that leads to Trstenik, but it produces some of Croatia's most sought-after wines. After Croatia gained its independence in 1991, Miljenko Grgić, who had emigrated from Croatia to the U.S. in 1954, returned to his homeland and started the tiny winery. Grgić, who was already famous worldwide for the fine vintages produced by his Grgich Hills Winery in Napa, California, started the winery in his homeland with his daughter Violet and two others. The winery produces white Pošip and red Plavac Mali, a relative of zinfandel.

The winery hidden in the trees above Trstenik is not a slick commercial enterprise, nor is it as polished as the vicinity's other wineries. In fact, behind the tall wooden doors leading to Grgić Vina, the place looks like a bare-bones field office with a lot of wine boxes and shipping materials. However, you'll be offered a taste of the latest vintage of both wines produced here, and you can save a significant amount of money over retail if you buy a few bottles. The winery is open from 10am to 5pm daily and takes credit cards. You can contact Grgić at **Grgić Vina** d.o.o., 20245 Trstenik, Poluotok Pelješac (✆ **020/748-090**; grgic-vina@du.htnet.hr).

Note: From June 15 to September 15, you can hop a daily **Semmarina ferry** (✆ **021/352-533**; www.sem-maria.hr) at Trstenik and head to Polače on the island of Mljet.

STON & MALI STON

Ston and Mali Ston are adjacent "blink-and-you'll-miss-them" towns at the isthmus where the Pelješac Peninsula meets the Croatian mainland about an hour northwest of Dubrovnik (58km/36 miles). However, both low-key Mali Ston and its more working-class sister Ston were important strategic locations for the Republic of Dubrovnik, which acquired them in the 14th century. The city-state's officials then built an amazing system of fortified walls and fortresses that runs straight up the southern slope of Sveti Mihaljo (St. Michael) Hill behind the town and that served to limit enemy access to the rest of the Pelješac Peninsula in medieval times.

Several sets of brick stairs—some overgrown—appear to lead from various streets in town to the top of the wall. These are dead ends, but not until you climb a good third of the way up. Approach from the right.

The town of Ston is a small area scored with a number of very narrow streets designed to flummox intruders. In addition to the walls, the towns prize their salt pans and oyster beds, which are still active today. Stay for dinner at one of the town's good restaurants to feast on oysters taken directly from nearby oyster beds and to drink one of the Pelješac's fine wines.

ESSENTIALS

VISITOR INFORMATION Ston's **tourist office** is at Pelješka cesta bb (© **020/ 754-453** or 098/296-192; www.tzo-ston.hr). It is on the road leading into and out of town across the street from the daily market. Maps, brochures, and information about the town and its treasures are freely dispensed here.

GETTING THERE The bus stops on the road outside Ston, but public transportation for Ston and the whole Pelješac Peninsula is not regular or very efficient. If you want to see the exceptional but hidden gems in the hills and valleys of this rarely visited part of Croatia, you'll need a car.

GETTING AROUND The roads through Pelješac are generally narrow and winding, especially the coastal roads as you approach Mali Ston and Ston. The pavement varies from flats through the valleys to heart-stopping hairpin turns in steeper areas. Walking is the best way to explore Mali Ston and Ston, however. There is a free parking lot outside Ston near the market.

WHAT TO SEE & DO

Mali Ston and Ston are the gateways to the long and rugged Pelješac Peninsula, which is home to some of the most awe-inspiring landscapes in the country. Even if your objective is to follow Pelješac's wine road to sample its well-respected wines or to head to one of the peninsula's quiet beaches, Mali Ston and Ston should be one of your stops. The monumental Ston Wall and its fortifications are the obvious draw, but if you linger awhile, you'll be able to explore the towns' charming historic buildings and their still-working ancient salt pans, then stop for a sublime meal of oysters or mussels fresh from nearby Malostonski Bay.

Ston Wall and Fortifications From afar, the 5.6km (3½ miles) of walls and their positioning resemble the Great Wall of China running straight up and across Sv. Mihaljo behind the town. St. Michael's Church is just up the hill via steps leading from the center of town. The steps do not lead up to the fortress; both the wall and the city of Ston were devastated by a 1996 earthquake, and the path leading up to the fortress at the top sustained damage that has not been completely repaired. However, restoration is in progress. The climb to the top of the wall is a steep one, so be sure to ascend on the right side of the fortress as you face it because there is a metal handrail there. The view of the town and peninsula is magnificent from the top. There is no fee to climb the walls and they are open 24/7, according to the town's tourism office, but climbing the stairs to the top is not recommended after dark.

WHERE TO STAY

The Ston region is an ideal place to stay if you want to explore the Pelješac Peninsula or if you simply want to tour the peninsula's wineries.

Ostrea Hotel Ostrea is the Latin word for oyster, and this tiny hotel in Mali Ston is a wonderful place to stay. In Mali Ston, oysters are a backbone of the economy. The hotel, which opened in 1998, is managed by the Kralj family, whose ancestors have lived in the vicinity of Ston since the 16th century. The stone house was renovated to accommodate guests comfortably in rooms that are individualized and

Perusing Pelješac

You'll never feel crowded in Pelješac because it is overlooked by most visitors to southern Dalmatia. Perhaps because most tourists make a beeline for the glitzier Dubrovnik and bypass this gorgeous region. Their loss, your gain. Pelješac is low-key in every respect, but that doesn't mean it is low on worthwhile attractions: It is dotted with vineyards, beaches, out-of-the-way konobas, and glorious scenery. Make a stop at Podobuče, a little fishing village that also has a small beach and a thriving wine-making enterprise. Stop at Konoba Molovran for a lunch of fresh-caught fish with homegrown veggies, olive oil, and wine. If you like the place, you can stay in one of Molovran's rooms for 25€ ($35) per person and enjoy a breakfast fit for a king. Call ahead for reservations for either the restaurant or accommodations. Molovran is open June-October. Podobuče. (℃ **020/713-569**; www. molovran.com).

modern, with slick bathrooms and Internet access. Staying here is like staying with a sophisticated friend in the country.

Mali Ston bb, Mali Ston ℃ **020/754-555.** Fax 020/754-575. www.ostrea.hr. 10 units, including presidential suite. From 140€ ($170) double; 165€ ($195) suite. AE, DC, MC, V. Parking available. **Amenities:** Restaurant; bar. *In room:* Hot water heat, cold water, TV, minibar, Internet access.

WHERE TO DINE

Kapetenova Kuća ✩✩✩ DALMATIAN   You don't have to be a seafood lover to enjoy this excellent restaurant on the minisquare in front of the harbor in Mali Ston. Like the Ostrea Hotel, Kapetenova Kuća is owned by the Kralj family. It specializes in products from the twin towns, which translates to oysters and mussels. Other treats from the sea appear on the menu, too, like octopus burgers with tartar sauce, baked veal with cheese and potatoes, and scampi flambé. Try a bottle or two of fine Pelješac wine with your meal, and the Ston *makarula* cake for dessert.

Mali Ston bb. ℃ **020/754-264.** Fax 020/754-4369. www.ostrea.hr. Reservations required. Entrees 65kn–220kn ($11–$38), more for lobster. AE, DC, MC, V. Daily 9am–midnight.

Taverna Bota ✩✩ DALMATIAN   Taverna Bota has become a haven for foodies from Dubrovnik and others into munching on Dalmatian delights taken to the next level. Try the black risotto or one of the fish soups. The menu has grilled-meat entrees, too. Everything goes with the restaurant's sublime homemade bread. Be sure to check out the wine list, which is full of local labels like Dingac and Grgić. Bota can get very crowded, especially on weekends when people are traveling to and from nearby Dubrovnik.

Mali Ston bb. ℃ **020/437-099.** Reservations recommended. Entrees 70kn–200kn ($12–$35). AE, DC, MC, V. Daily 8am–3am.

Upper Dalmatia

The area from Senj to Trogir, a region known as Upper Dalmatia, is a collection of contradictions. The cities and sites are among some of Croatia's most accessible and enchanting; but the region also is home to what is arguably among the most forbidding and barren terrains in the world. Still, there is something for everyone in this gateway to Croatia's coastal playground, whether your interests tend toward poking around ancient ruins, getting an adrenaline rush rock climbing the challenging Velebit range, feeding your cultural appetite with classical music at the Church of St. Donat in Zadar, or taking the night air from the top of Trogir's Kamerlengo fortress.

All roads to and from Upper Dalmatia seem to go through Zadar, the largest city on the region's coastal highway. In many ways Zadar's mix of monuments and commerce, of ancient history and proactive civic vision make it one of Croatia's most cosmopolitan centers. Senj, the Velebit, and Pag Island make up the Velebit Coastal Area in the northern part of Upper Dalmatia, while Paklenica National Park, Nin, and Zadar and the Kornati Archipelago offshore to the west are its center. Krka National Park, Primošten, Sibenik, and Trogir extend to the south just above Split, which is the trail head for Lower Dalmatia.

1 Orientation

EXPLORING THE REGION

Transportation vagaries in Upper Dalmatia make travel logistics difficult for people who want to see a lot in a short time. But covering the maximum amount of territory during a trip to the coast north of Split can be accomplished with careful planning.

For example, most visitors to Pag spend a weekend or more on the beach or on the water, while visitors to Zadar might make that city a base for a week or more for excursions to nearby Paklenica National Park and Nin. Others might spend their whole stay in Zadar, investigating its imposing churches and monuments, and then venture out of the city for half- or full-day trips with local cruise lines to see some of the area's numerous offshore islands. The latter is a strategy that makes good sense for those who don't like roughing it, but do want to see Dugi Otok and Pašman in the Zadar Archipelago. Those two island destinations and several others have few accommodations options and making day trips is the pragmatic way to see them.

Senj, Nin, and Primošten each can be thoroughly explored in a few hours, but you'll need at least a day each to explore Zadar, Šibenik, or Trogir; a day to see each of the national parks (more if you want to do some hiking or camping); and a day or more for each of the islands you choose to visit (mostly because of ferry timetables).

It's fairly simple to access all the major coastal sites in Upper Dalmatia by driving from Senj down, but it's much trickier to coordinate ferry connections from the mainland to the islands or to travel between islands.

ESSENTIALS

VISITOR INFORMATION Coastal Dalmatia is Croatia's most celebrated region, so it is not surprising that tourism services are fairly well organized and developed. For tourist office contact information in Upper Dalmatia, see "Visitor Information" for individual cities; or contact the Croatia National Tourist Office (p. 12).

GETTING THERE **Bus** travel is the most popular mode of public transportation in Croatia and many other European countries, because it is the most efficient and economical. Croatian buses are air-conditioned and can not only get you from one mainland destination to another, but they also can get you to islands served by larger ferries. See contact details for the Jadrolinija ferries (p. 146).

GETTING AROUND Private **auto** is the most efficient and comfortable way to visit the Upper (or Lower) Dalmatian coast because you'll be able to set your own schedule, linger where you find something you like, and move on when you don't without worrying about bus or ferry schedules. For those who don't have their own transportation, **buses** are the next best way to get around because they are frequent and serve almost all coastal towns. **Ferries** link coastal towns with major Croatian islands and with each other or, if you have the means, you can rent a **yacht** and map out a sea tour of your own. Split and Dubrovnik have major airports, and Zadar has a small one. All are connected by **air** with Rijeka and Zagreb. **Rail** travel is the least desirable way to travel up and down the coast because not all towns have train service and connections are often difficult.

2 Senj & the Velebit

Senj, dubbed "the fortress city," has two dubious distinctions: First, it has a reputation as the coldest, windiest town in Croatia; and second, it is the site of an infamous 16th-century pirates' haven for the flamboyant Uskoks, who lived in Senj in the 16th century and preyed on passing merchant ships.

In 1535, the Uskoks were a community of controversial anti-Turk fighters who helped fend off Ottoman assaults on the city and later channeled their aggression toward more lucrative pursuits until they were driven out in the early 17th century.

Today's Senj is worth a stop to see **Nehaj Fortress,** which was built by the Uskoks and which makes a great photo op from the sea or highway and a great photo perch from its position above the sea at the edge of the harbor. The **town museum** is also worth a quick look to get a sense of Senj's history, but neither is worth a lot of time.

South of Senj, you can catch the ferry to Pag Island at Prizna or a ferry to Rab from Jablanac, but on land there aren't many settlements of note between Senj and Zadar—and the ones that are there don't have much to recommend them. In fact, Zadar is the next major population center on the coast south of Senj.

Those who prefer uninhabited, unspoiled, rugged terrain to city development can veer off the coastal highway to the Velebit Range, which includes Paklenica National Park south of Senj and which extends almost the entire length of the coast from Senj to Zadar.

ESSENTIALS

VISITOR INFORMATION   The **Senj tourist office** is at Stara Cesta 2 on the waterfront (© **053/881-068;** fax 053/881-219; www.senj.hr). The staff there can provide a city map and information about the town. It is open from 7am to 8pm daily in July and August and from 7am to 2pm Monday through Friday the rest of the year.

GETTING THERE   Senj, just 69 km (43 miles) from Rijeka and a little over 161km (100 miles) from Zagreb, is easily reached from the newly opened (2005) Rijeka-Split highway. In addition, most buses routed through coastal cities stop at Senj on their way somewhere else. See "Getting There" under "Essentials" in "Orientation," above, for transport contact information.

GETTING AROUND   Senj is a very walkable city, and you don't even have to walk too far, because except for the fortress on the harbor and the town's quaint center, there isn't that much to see.

WHAT TO SEE & DO

Nehaj Fortress 🏰🏰   Senj's biggest (and some say only) attraction is the Nehaj Fortress, which was built in the mid–16th century by Uskok Captain Ivan Lenković. He tore down unprotected buildings outside the fortifications to get materials to construct the fortress because he reasoned that they would be sitting targets anyway. The

Uskoks

For most of the 16th century the Uskoks, who are thought to have been Hercegovinan refugees driven from their land by the Turks, owned the minds and hearts of the people of Senj almost as soon as they arrived to save them from attack. At the time, Senj was under Austrian control, and frequent assaults by the Ottoman Turks were common.

The Uskoks had a reputation for daring exploits, bravery, and a bit of larceny, and with tacit approval from Senj's Austrian occupiers, they fortified the city against Ottoman invaders from land and sea and saved the Christian townspeople from being conquered by the Muslim army.

In the process, the Uskoks expanded their acquisitive activities to Venetian merchant ships carrying Turkish goods and expanded their targeted victims to any other vessel that was a potential source of booty. The Austrians looked the other way from the Uskoks' extracurricular activity because Uskok sea raids kept the Venetians at bay and because the people in the region considered the Uskoks heroes for protecting them against the Turks.

Besides their propensity for raiding passing ships, the Uskoks had a soft side: They were good neighbors to people outside Senj and, in Robin Hood fashion, they shared their pillaged prizes with Krk, Cres, Rab, Pag, and others whenever possible, a practice that earned them goodwill and security. Consequently, they were able to use Senj as a headquarters and safe harbor from which to launch their attacks without fear of internal sanctions.

The Uskoks controlled this part of northern Dalmatia from the 1530s to the Uskok War of 1615–17. Some say that the war began because the Venetians were tired of being plundered, and in retaliation they provoked a confrontation with Austria. The Uskok War lasted 2 years and ended in agreement by the Austrians to expel the Uskoks from Senj and drive them inland. The pirates have not been heard from since.

exhibits inside the three-story fortress trace the history of the Uskoks and display weapons, clothing, and other artifacts related to the times. Captions are in Croatian and English. The fortress was rehabbed in 1977 and now serves as the city's symbol. You can climb to the top for unparalleled views of the sea and Senj.

Above the harbor. 15kn ($2.75). July–Aug daily 10am–9pm; daily May, June, and Sept 10am–6pm. Closed Oct–Apr.

Senj Town Museum ✿   The 15th-century Gothic-Renaissance Vukasović Palace in the town center is the site of the town's museum, which has a good collection of local architecture and botanical specimens. There is also a collection of modern artifacts (1914–45) and another showing the development of Glagolitic writing and printing.

Ogrizovićeva 7. ✆ **053/881-141.** Admission 15kn ($3) adults, 10kn ($1.75) children. July 15–Sept 1 Mon–Fri 7am–3pm and 6–8pm; Sat 10am–noon and 6–8pm; Sun 10am–noon. Rest of year Mon–Fri 7am–3pm; closed Sat–Sun.

WHERE TO STAY

Private accommodations are the way to go if you intend to spend any time in Senj. Inquire at the tourist office (above).

WHERE TO DINE

Dining is casual in Senj. Most places have the same menu—grilled fish, meat, and pastas/pizza—and all are at about the same quality level, i.e., quite good.

Lavlji Dvor ✿ CROATIAN   This cute konoba in a former 16th-century farmhouse has a shaded terrace with an old well as centerpiece and a dining room loaded with Croatian antiques. The predictable menu offers pizza and grilled meat and fish, but the atmosphere provides a nice respite from sightseeing.

P. Preradovića 2. ✆ 053/881-738. www.lickosenjska.com/turizam/52.htm. Entrees 35kn–180kn ($7–$33). No credit cards. Daily 10am–11pm.

Konoba Stari Grad ✿ CROATIAN   A stone interior and shaded tables outside make this small dining spot a good place to get a break from the heat. The fare is simple and the prices low, with soups, pastas, and risottos taking center stage. Try the risotto with truffles for 55kn ($10) or the tagliatelle Montarana (pasta with smoked ham, cream, and mushrooms) for 50kn ($9). They're a steal.

Uskočka 12. ✆ 053/885-242. Entrees 40kn–100kn ($8–$19). No credit cards. Daily 7am–1am.

3 Pag Island

60km (36 miles) N of Zadar; 240km (150 miles) W of Zagreb

When you approach the island of Pag on the ferry from mainland Prizna south of Senj you'd never guess that Pag is home to one of the biggest party beaches in Europe. At first glance it looks as if you're headed for a landing on Mars rather than a sojourn on an island awash with nouveau riche villas, condominiums, and a pedigree that goes back to the Roman Empire.

It's difficult to imagine that anything could survive for long on Pag's barren terrain, which appears to be either entirely karst (limestone) or dry dust, but the island once was covered with lush forests. Agriculture thrived on Pag when the Romans settled here in the 1st century, and during the next 1,300 years or so, not much disturbed Pag's flora, not even the Slav invasion in the 7th century or Pag's fights over its prized salt fields with Rab and Zadar in the 13th and 14th centuries.

In the 15th century, however, the rulers of Venice and Zadar were in competition for the island and its natural resources. Venice won in the end when it took control of much of Dalmatia in 1409, including Pag and Zadar. Some might say that Pag lost because once the Venetians had control, they used the island's vast tracts of timber as their exclusive lumberyard and indiscriminately stripped the island of its trees to build ships. The triple whammy of Venetian deforestation, grazing sheep, and fierce northwestern wind (bura) that frequently hammers the Kvarner and northern Dalmatian coast so traumatized the environment that it has never recovered.

Even though the Venetians showed little concern for ecology, they were engrossed in building and by the mid–15th century, their salt trade on Pag had grown so much that the island's Old Town could no longer handle the population or the business. Consequently, the Venetian administrators hired Juraj Dalmatinac to design a new city, which became Pag Town.

Sheep breeding and salt production have always been and still are mainstays of Pag's economy, but it is tourism that now contributes the biggest chunk of revenue to the island. Thanks to that trend, Pag recently has been the site of a building boom that is driving development of other commerce on the island. Thus, Pag is beginning to catch up with nearby vacation venues in terms of tourism days, but the island still is mostly undiscovered and underrated, leaving it an incredible vacation opportunity for the knowledgeable traveler.

Pag Island is 60km (36 miles) long and 10km (6 miles) wide at its broadest point. Most of the island's eastern side is barren or covered with a grid of rock walls that delineate property lines and keep sheep from wandering from one patch of scrub grass to another. However, on the northwest end of the island, from Šimuni to Lun, olive trees and other vegetation have taken root in large fertile sections.

Several small islands surround Pag. Some are inhabited only by sheep (Škrda) and others aren't inhabited at all, but they offer secluded pristine pebble beaches for anyone who arrives from the sea. Most of Pag's irregular coastline is indented with countless coves sparkling with water so clear you can see the sandy bottom 6m (20 ft.) down, a siren's song for swimmers, snorkelers, and scuba divers who have discovered Pag's charms.

Pag Island is not densely populated—yet. In fact, most of the time, visitor numbers for Pag's waters and beaches are thin, and FOR RENT signs are numerous—except from July 15 to August 15, when it seems as if half of Italy descends on the island, fills its rooms and apartments, and takes over its party beaches and restaurants. That short window of time often finds Pag on the 10pm news throughout Europe as a video clip with sound bite showing scantily clad women and men engaging in wild, nonstop partying, though those images don't accurately reflect the true Pag.

Most of the year, Pag is a quiet island whose permanent residents produce and promote four products for which the island has become famous—cheese, lamb, lace, and salt. The cheese is known as Paški sir, and it is reminiscent of Parmesan, though a bit saltier. It is sold throughout the island by both commercial and home-based producers and usually served sliced and drizzled with olive oil. Paški sir is exported to Croatia's larger population centers, where it goes for a much higher price than it does on Pag.

The second is Paški lamb. Pag is home to many herds of sheep, and meat from the island's lamb is prized because of its high quality and unique flavor, which is a result of the lamb's diet of scrub grass and local herbs that grow wild in the rocky soil and the lot of salt-infused air they breathe. The combination creates lamb that has an indefinable taste, but one that is sought after by Croatian gourmets.

The third Pag product worth noting is Paški lace. The art of lace making is a tradition that has been preserved in Pag, which makes it possible to buy handmade rounds of exquisite lace. Authentic Pag lace can be very expensive even if you buy some straight from the woman who tatted it. A 6-inch round can sell for 750kn ($140) or more, but it makes a beautiful souvenir that will last indefinitely. Look for elderly ladies dressed in black sitting in Pag Town's center square or near Novalja's market for the best examples of this art. Usually these are the lacemakers themselves, who will bargain with you on the price of their wares. Once you see real Pag lace, which is incredibly intricate, you'll be able to tell imitations from the genuine article.

Finally, there is the salt once fought over by would-be conquerors. Today, Pag's salt pans are still in production, mostly in the island's central valley. Pag salt is commonplace in Croatian supermarkets, and is exported as well. Many of the island's souvenir shops sell decorative bottles of pebble-size Pag salt as an inexpensive souvenir.

It's a shame that "the season" on Pag isn't longer than the traditional mid-July to mid-August rush because the climate is still warm in spring and fall, and the island offers lively nightlife, crystal-clear azure water for swimming, plenty of first-class accommodations, historic sites, and quaint attractions.

> **Tips** *Bura* **Winds**
>
> Check the weather reports before you head out for a weekend on Pag. Ferry traffic, and sometimes bridge traffic, is halted altogether when the *bura* winds are strong.

ESSENTIALS

VISITOR INFORMATION The **Pag Tourist Board (Turistička Zajednica)** can provide helpful maps, brochures, ferry schedules, and information on excursions from and around Pag. The board's office is at Ulica Od Spitala 2 in Pag Town (© **023/ 622-301;** fax 023/611-311; www.pag-tourism.hr). Novalja's **tourist office** can be reached at P.O. Box 20, 53291 Novalja (© **053/661-404;** www.tz-novalja.hr). It is open from 7am to midnight mid-June to mid-September, and from 7am to noon and 6pm to midnight during most of May and October. Hours and opening days vary the rest of the year.

Various private tourism agencies on the island are helpful for finding private accommodations and for directing you to diving centers where you can arrange dives at some of the marked sites in the sea around the island. **Meridijan 15** and **Mediteran** are two of the better agencies. Both are located in Pag Town, with Meridijan 15 at Ante Starčevića 1 (© **023/612-162;** fax 023/612-121; www.meridijan15.hr); and Mediteran at V. Nazora bb (© **023/600-042;** fax 023/611-238; www.mediteran-pag.com). These private agencies are open from 8am to 8pm daily May through September, but their hours and open days vary the rest of the year. In Novalja, try **Sunturist** at S.S. Kranjčevića (© **053/611-611;** www.islandpag.com) or **Novalja Kompass** at Slatinska (© **053/661-211;** www.navalija-kompas.hr) for private accommodations.

GETTING THERE If you are traveling to Pag Island from Zadar and points south, the island is reachable from Posedarje on the mainland via **Pag Bridge,** which takes visitors to the island's south end. Jadrolinija ferries (p. 146) make hourly runs from mainland Prizna to Žigljen on the island's north end, depositing visitors about 4.8km (3 miles) from Novalja. When demand is high during peak season, the ferries often throw out their schedules and leave port as soon as they are full. Nonetheless, waits to board can approach several hours during July and August. A one-way ferry ride for a car with two people costs about 100kn ($19). Backups at the Pag Bridge are rarely more than half an hour, except for weekends during July and August. Unless you are coming from Zadar and points south, getting to the bridge involves a few extra driving hours. During the summer, a fast boat (catamaran) runs between Novalja and Rijeka with stops at Rab Island three times a week. Eight daily buses from Rijeka stop in Pag Town and Novalja and go on to other stops along the Dalmatian coast. See "Getting There" under "Essentials" in "Orientation," above, for transportation contact information.

Getting Around Except for private taxis and intercity buses that run from the mainland and between Pag Town and Novalja, there is little public transportation on Pag. Luckily, both Pag Town and Novalja are compact enough to explore on foot, as are their waterfronts—but travel between the two towns can be time-consuming unless you have your own car. Most visitors spend just a few hours touring the town and head directly for the beach. Thus, cars are the transportation mode of choice on Pag, and you'll want a rental car or motor scooter here if you intend to explore more than one area of the island or if you want to go beach-hopping. Rental agencies, including Budget, Dollar, Hertz, and Avis, have kiosks at the Zagreb airport and in other major Croatian cities. *Note:* When navigating the Pag's streets and outlying roads, it is a good idea to call ahead to your destination to get detailed directions, because street signs are sparse and road signs are few and far between.

WHAT TO SEE & DO

Besides hauntingly beautiful landscapes, pristine waters, and deserted beaches in isolated coves, Pag has a nice collection of Roman ruins, medieval walls, churches, and cultural icons. Most of the attractions worth seeing are concentrated in Pag Town and Novalja, which are separated by about 19km (12 miles) and a big socio-economic gap. **Pag Town** has a partial **15th-century wall** and an Old Town complete with the last of four standing **watchtowers** that once rose from the town fortifications. The town center is home to two original Juraj Dalmatinac (a prominent Renaissance stonemason) buildings: the **Rector's Palace (Knez[az]ev dvor),** which is now a cafe; and the **Parish Church of St. Mary** opposite **Trg Kralja Krešimira IV,** Pag Town's center of social activity. Pag Town is nearly a mile south of the original 14th-century settlement that preceded it, and a few crumbling remnants of the ancient town are still visible and can be visited. There is also a small **lace museum** near the square where you can see what genuine Pag lace looks like before you consider a purchase. Pag Town is where most of the island's locals live and where its nearby salt fields are situated, but it is not as populous as Novalja. You can also see the town's "wall" of windmills on the hills above Pag, an energy-generating project that takes advantage of *bura* wind power.

If Pag Town is the island's historic center, then Novalja is its New World colony, because **Novalja** is oceans away from Pag Town in atmosphere. Novalja is about 19km (12 miles) north of Pag Town and far trendier. Its charming square, **Trg Bazilike,** is on the same waterfront spot where the Romans used to hang out when Novalja was one of their ports. Now it seems as if everyone in town stops at Bazilike for morning coffee before picking up a few *buhtle* (rolls filled with cheese or jam) to take back to their plush multistory vacation homes. Novalja is also home to a very active party beach **(Zrče),** a huge auto campsite with its own fine beaches **(Straško),** numerous konobas and cafes, and countless private rooms and rental condos. There is also a **hotel/winery/restaurant** ⟨★★★ set in the middle of a vineyard (Boš-ki-nac) outside Novalja, and more **secluded coves** ⟨★★★ (that double as Adriatic swimming holes) than there are tourists to splash around in them.

Zrće Beach is a nice pebble beach a little over a mile south of Novalja and the epicenter of Pag's swinging nightlife. Almost every bar in town (and some from Zagreb like Papaya and Aquarius) has set up shop on this stretch of real estate, which in summer vibrates with nonstop rock music and gyrating bodies during the day but doesn't *really* get going until about 10pm. Zrće draws hordes of the 18- to 29-year-old demographic and has become Croatia's answer to "Where the Boys Are" in the Balkans. In a nod to Croatia's zero tolerance policy on drinking and driving, minivans run partygoers from Zrće to Novalja's harbor through the night, but action on the beach usually continues until dawn.

Church of St. Mary ⟨★ This Gothic-looking church was built by Pag Town's civil architect Juraj Dalmatinac, and today it is an amalgam of styles that reflect its history. The church was begun in the 15th century, completed in the 16th, and renovated in

Pag Patterns

Pag is best known for its forbidding naked terrain, its salty sheep's-milk cheese (Paški *sir*), its herb-infused lamb, and its wild party beaches. But Pag also has a reputation as the source of the incredibly intricate lace produced by local women who can spend days creating a single 6-inch round. Pag lace is quite expensive and used as trim on clothing and tablecloths, as home decorating accents, and sometimes as framed art. You'll find older women dressed in black from head to toe hawking large and small pieces of lace in other cities besides Pag, but once you've seen genuine Pag lace, you won't have trouble recognizing inferior imitations. Pag lace is as complex and unique as snowflakes and a wonderful souvenir from this diverse island.

the 18th. Inside, you'll find sculptures and sacral art from other eras, including a Gothic wooden crucifix from the 12th century.

Trg Kralja Krešimira IV. ✆ 023/611-576. May–Sept 9am–noon and 5–7pm. Other times for Mass only.

Pag Carnival 𝒶𝒶 This joyous celebration is held mostly in Pag Town's main square on July 31 at the height of the tourist season. Activities include Slavic dancing *(kolo)* by performers wearing traditional Pag costumes, as well as the folk play *Paška Roninja (The Slave Girl of Pag)*.

Pag Lace Museum 𝒶 Information on the history of lace making and examples of this intricate craft are the focus here. The museum also houses a school that insures there will be new lace makers trained to carry on this delicate tradition.

Kralja Zvonimira. Free admission. Mid-June to mid-Sept daily 8am–11pm.

WATERSPORTS

Pag is a favorite of snorkelers and scuba enthusiasts because of its crystal-clear water and the underwater cliffs, caves, and wrecks where remnants of Rome and other eras rest. Stara Novalja across the Novalja inlet is a haven for diving schools and suppliers.

Connex Diving 𝒶𝒶 Besides excursions for accomplished divers, Connex offers a "Discovery" program that combines 30 minutes of instruction with a 30-minute dive in fairly shallow 6m (20-ft.) water. The package includes all necessary equipment. Connex also rents Zodiac craft.

Kunera bb, Stara Novalja. ✆ 091/721-3234. www.connex.diving.cz. Discovery Program 30€ ($36). May–Oct.

WHERE TO STAY

Pag has become a popular weekend getaway for people who live in north-central Croatia or within a 4-hour drive of the island. Rather than build single-family dwellings as second homes, in the last 5 years most new construction consists of multi-unit buildings or even multi-building complexes to accommodate extended family and renters during the high season. Consequently, in addition to a few hotels, there is an abundance of reasonably priced, modern, private accommodations on Pag.

Hotel Boškinac 𝒶𝒶𝒶 Boškinac is one of the finest hotels on the northern Adriatic coast, and its surrounding pine forest and vineyard in a secluded location near Stara Novalja 3.2km (2 miles) north of Novalja add to the hotel's exclusivity. Guest rooms and suites in this family-owned establishment, which opened in 2003, are named after local plants and decorated in chic Mediterranean style and colors that reflect the seasons. Every unit includes a sitting area and a bathroom luxuriously appointed with every convenience imaginable, including a Jacuzzi tub, making the whole effect one of warmth and tranquillity. Add to this the exquisite meals in the hotel's restaurant **Restoran Boškinac,** excursions such as grape or olive picking, horseback riding, or gourmet cooking classes, and you have the makings of a memorable getaway.

Novaljsko Polje, 53291 Novalja. ✆ **053/663-500.** Fax 053/663-501. www.boskinac.com. 11 units, including 3 apts. Doubles from 200€ ($240). AE, DC, MC, V. Rates include breakfast. **Amenities:** Restaurant; konoba/wine cellar; terrace; horseback riding; cooking classes; wine study, complimentary bicycles for guests. *In room:* A/C, TV, Internet access.

Hotel Luna ★★   The newest hotel (2007) on Pag is a modern 3-story north of Novalija. It incorporates comfort and a fabulous seaside location and eliminates the crowds that flock to Pag in summer. Guest rooms are spacious and 70% of them have seaside views. Hotel Luna is in Jakišnica, 14km (8.5 miles) north of Novalija, a bit of a hike from the island's larger population centers, but if you want to get away from it all, this is the place.

Jakišnica bb. ✆ **053/654-700.** Fax 053/654-754. www.luna-hotel.hr. 93 units. Doubles with a sea view from 136€ ($190) in high season. **Amenities:** 2 restaurants; 2 bars; indoor and outdoor pools; Internet access; tennis, basketball, handball, and soccer courts. *In room:* A/C, SAT TV, minibar, hair dryer, safe.

Vila Nacional ★★★ *(Value*   This beautiful three-plex with two condo-type units and the owner's apartment is walking distance from Novalja's center and the harbor. Built in 2004, Nacional resembles a sleek Mediterranean mansion, but one with units that have air-conditioning, balconies, and modern kitchen conveniences. Nacional's affable, English-speaking owner and Bjelovar businessman, Zeljko Maletić, is usually on-site and always eager to talk about Pag's highlights. He'll even take guests for a ride around the island on his speedboat if coaxed.

Orišići bb. Novalja. ✆ **091/532-9878.** nacional1@bj.htnet.hr. 2 units. 75€ ($105) per night. AE, DC, MC, V. Private parking. *In room:* A/C, full kitchen (including dishwasher), laundry facilities.

Hotel Loža ★   The Loža's location just steps from Novalja's waterfront can't be beat for convenience. Most of the Loža's rooms face the sea and have balconies, but the hotel's guest rooms are as basic as they come. The hotel itself hasn't caught up with Novalja's tourism demands. In light of the plethora of newer, more modern accommodations available on Pag, the Loža's rates seem a bit steep.

Trg Loža 1, Novalja. ✆ **053/663-381.** Fax 053/663-430. www.turno.hr. 35 units. From 514kn ($90) double with balcony and sea view. AE, DC, MC, V. Rate includes breakfast. Half-board available. **Amenities:** Restaurant; bar; Internet access in lobby. *In room:* TV.

⟮*Fun Fact* **Honey Buns**

Paški *sir* may be synonymous with Pag, but *baškotini,* a hard roll made only in the kitchens of the island's Benedictine convent of St. Margarita from a secret recipe, is another of Pag's trademarks. These crunchy biscuits usually are eaten plain or dipped in *bijela kava* (literally, white coffee), but they also are good drizzled with the honey produced at the convent. *Tip:* The sweet golden nectar is rumored to have healing properties.

Hotel Tony 🐾🐾 This little hotel on Paški Bay is a little apart from the fray about three-quarters of a mile from Pag Town's center, but the large rooms, the long list of services, and the hotel's proximity to the beach more than make up for the inconvenience. Hotel Tony even has its own cinema with movies in English.

Dubrovačka 39, Pag Town. ✆ 023/611-370. www.hotel-tony.com. 12 units, 1 apt. From 300kn ($52) double. AE, DC, MC, V. Rates include breakfast. Half- and full board available. **Amenities:** Restaurant; bar; disco; tennis courts; boat rental; diving center; excursions; transfer to and from the hotel; room for those w/limited mobility. *In room:* TV, Internet access.

Hotel Biser 🐾🐾 This sun-washed hotel at water's edge is an excellent place to chill or to use as a base while exploring Pag's charms. Most guest rooms have balconies and sweeping views of the bay plus plain but pleasing furnishings. Hotel Biser also has a sister location, Vila Bisera, next door with similar accommodations in six more rooms and six apartments.

A. G. Matosa 46, Pag Town. ✆ 023/611-333. Fax 023/611-444. www.hotel-biser.com. 20 units. From 54€ ($65) double. DC, MC, V. **Amenities:** Restaurant; tennis courts. *In room:* A/C, TV.

Camping Straško & FKK 🐾🐾 As campsites go, Straškois big enough for 4,000 campers and loaded with amenities. It's also less than a mile from the center of Novalja on the 2.4km (1½-mile) beach of the same name. Besides being able to pitch your tent or park your camper in the shade of pine and olive groves on a site near the water, you can take advantage of Straško's restaurants, markets, bars, an Internet cafe, sports facilities, a gas station, and a boat launch, all there for the use of its guests. For those who like more permanence, Straško also has well-equipped, air-conditioned bungalows for rent on the premises. As is customary in much of Croatia, about one-third of the camp is FKK (i.e., a nudist camp) and reserved for naturists, but that part of the camp is well-marked and partitioned, and has separate dining and recreation facilities.

Pag Island. ✆ 053/661-226. Fax 053/661-225. www.turno.hr. Accommodates 4,000 people. From 29€ ($35) site plus 2 adults; from 85€ ($102) bungalow. AE, DC, MC, V. Closed May–Sept. **Amenities:** Restaurants; bars; market; tennis; golf; fitness classes; rock climbing; hiking; biking; bowling; scuba diving; excursions; children's programs.

WHERE TO DINE

There are plenty of family-style konobas and pizzerias on Pag, as well as a few places where cuisine is an art form.

Restoran Boškinac 🐾🐾🐾 CREATIVE CROATIAN You can dine in Boškinac's richly appointed second-floor dining room agleam with crystal and silver, or move outside to a table on the adjacent balcony overlooking the Boškinac vineyard. Either way, superbly prepared Mediterranean cuisine will be yours. Boškinac prides itself on its creative use of fresh, local ingredients, and you won't be disappointed in any of the dishes served here or in its more informal taverna/wine cellar. Try the veal roasted with domestic herbs, any of the fresh Adriatic fish dishes and, of course, wine produced on the premises. The Boškinac Taverna on the lower level serves more casual fare but with the same attention to quality.

Novaljsko Polje, 53291 Novalja. ✆ 053/663-500. Fax 053/663-501. www.boskinac.com. Entrees 70kn–220kn ($12–$38). AE, DC, MC, V. Reservations required. Tues–Sun 10am–1am. Closed Mon. Closed for vacation Jan 3–Feb 10.

Konoba Kormil 🐾🐾 CROATIAN Kormil isn't much more than a few bench-seat tables tucked into an alley-size side street off Novalja's main square, but the local hangout is definitely worth seeking out for its atmosphere and its food. The menu is limited to a few dishes served family style, and each is enough for a very large family. Don't miss the fried calamari, which is among the best-prepared in Dalmatia. Not far behind are the pan-fried sardellen and local pršut, each of which can be ordered separately or as part of a variety platter that lets you taste everything.

Zrinsko-Frankopanska bb, Novalja. © **053/662-332.** Entrees 23kn–45kn ($4–$8). No credit cards. Daily 8am–11pm.

4 Zadar

Zadar has had its ups and downs through the ages, and over time this beautiful city by the sea suffered grave wounds at the hands of the same factions that aspired to control it. However, today's Zadar seems to have shaken off most of its injuries, though the healing process is ongoing.

Despite frequent reconstruction, Zadar remains an ancient city brimming with more than 3,000 years of history and culture. Like most cities on the Dalmatian coast, Zadar evolved from a prehistoric settlement to an Illyrian village to a Roman municipality, and to many other incarnations involving administrative changes and foreign assaults that finally ended with the city's liberation and reunion with Croatia in 1993.

Zadar is first mentioned in 9th-century writings as the residence of Bishop Donat, the cleric who built the Church of the Holy Trinity in the former Roman Forum, remains of which lie next to the cathedral. Today that 9th-century church is known as St. Donatus to honor Bishop Donat, and it has become the city's symbol. After the construction of St. Donatus, many other churches were built in Zadar, making it a center of Roman Catholicism.

When Venice tried to capture every city on the Dalmatian coast starting in the late 10th century (it finally succeeded in the 15th), Zadar fought back harder than any other municipality under attack. From 1096 to 1346, Zadar was conquered and liberated an incredible seven times and taken over six times until it was sold in 1409 to Venice by King Ladislav of Naples, who was Zadar's ruler *du jour.* Following the sale, Venice had authority over Zadar for almost 4 centuries until 1797. During that time, the Venetians developed the city and its economy, but only to the extent that those efforts benefited Venice.

Eventually, the Venetians were driven out, and for 120 years or so after that Zadar was governed by Austria (with a short stint of French rule), a regime that ended with World War I but did not end Zadar's occupation. From 1920 to 1944 Zadar was governed by Italy and forced to accept Italian acculturation, though many citizens left during this time rather than become "Italianized."

During World War II, Zadar was almost destroyed by Allied forces, though it was mostly rebuilt during the postwar Yugoslavia era. Then, during the 1991 war, the city

Cherries in a Glass

Before you leave Zadar, try the local drink that has become one of the city's specialties. Maraschino is a drink made from a unique variety of maraska cherry grown in the region, and it can be had in alcoholic or nonalcoholic forms. According to legend, alcoholic Maraschino, usually a treacly sweet cherry liqueur, was first made by monks in the 16th century and was thought to improve the disposition. Today the liqueur is made in Zadar in a factory near the footbridge.

Tips **Weekend Traffic**

Avoid driving to Zadar or anywhere on the coast Friday morning through Sunday afternoon during July and August. The sheer volume of traffic that descends on Croatia from outside its borders combined with local traffic heading to the same destinations on the coast can create backups 32km (20 miles) or longer, especially at border crossings and at tunnels.

took another devastating hit when Serb forces cut the city off from Zagreb and reduced it to rubble once again. The Croatian army at last liberated Zadar in 1993 and the outlying areas in 1995.

Today's Zadar is an exceptional mix of new and old architecture and a diverse mix of cultures. It is also fiercely nationalistic, a characteristic that took hold while the city was isolated from the rest of Croatia by the Serbs.

ESSENTIALS

VISITOR INFORMATION   Zadar is a tourist-friendly town with well-marked streets and addresses and large, illustrated, explanatory posters installed in front of almost every notable building. For more detailed information, maps, and brochures, you can check with the local **Tourist Information Center** at Narodni Trg 5 (✆ 023/316-166). Or try the **Zadar Tourism Board** at Ilije Smiljanića bb (✆ 023/212-412; tzg-zadar@zd.htnet.hr; 8am–4pm Mon–Sat). For information on Zadar and the surrounding region, contact the **Zadar County Tourist Board** at Sv. Leopolda B. Mandića 1 (✆ 023/315-107; www.zadar.hr).

Most accommodations near the city center are private and can be secured through **Aquarius Travel Agency** at Nova Vrata bb (✆ 023/212-919), which can get you a room or book an excursion to regional sites, too. **Atlas Agency** at Branimirova 12 near the footbridge (✆ 023/235-850), one of Croatia's largest, offers lodging and excursion bookings plus access to some transportation services.

GETTING THERE   Almost every mode of transportation flows through Zadar, but some methods of getting there are better than others.

By Car   Driving is one of the easiest ways to reach Zadar since the new A1 superhighway along the coast opened in June 2005, reducing the drive time between Zagreb and Zadar from 6 or more hours to 3.

By Bus   Bus service to Zadar from Zagreb is convenient and inexpensive at about 100kn ($18) each way. The Zadar bus station, just northeast of Old Town, is as busy and bright as any suburban shopping mall, perhaps because it has so much traffic. There is a place to leave your luggage for 1.20kn (25¢) per hour; it's open from 6am to 10pm. You'll also find cafes, bakeries, and a market open the same hours. There are two ATMs and a couple of travel agencies for those who need local money, plus public phones for those who want to call home. For schedule and ticket information, contact the **Zadar Coach Station** at Ante Starčevića 2 (✆ 023/211-555; www.liburnija-zadar.hr).

By Boat   Ferry travel is common up and down the Dalmatian coast, whether the route originates in Rijeka or Italy, and Zadar is a major stop for most lines during the

Zadar

0 — 250 ft
0 — 100 m

Zadar

Harbor Gate

St. Chrysogonus

St. Anastasia

Trg sv. Stošije

Sea Organ

Forum

St. Donatus

Archaeological Museum

St. Mary's

The Gold & Silver of Zadar

Zeleni trg

Narodni trg

Footbridge

St. Simeon

5 Wells Square

Land Gate

Zadarski Channel

Perivoj Vladimira Nazora

- - - Ferry route

ACCOMMODATIONS ■
Hotel Kolovare **12**

DINING ◆
Corso **10**
Forum Café **4**
In Time **9**
Konoba Stipe **5**
Konoba Stomorica **6**
Kornat **1**
Kult **7**
Restaurant Zadar na Rivi **8**
Ribiji Restaurant Foša **11**
Slastičarna Donat **3**
Trata **2**
Trattoria Canzona **7**

summer months. Jadrolinija runs ferries between Ancona and Bari (Italy) and Zadar, and between Zadar and just about all coastal Croatian cities. See "Getting There" under "Essentials" in the "Orientation" section, above, for Jadrolinija contact information.

By Plane   Zadar Airport, about 8km (5 miles) south of the city, handles an average of four domestic and international scheduled flights per day (more on weekends)—from Croatia Airlines shuttles to flights on private planes, international carriers, and commercial airlines. Contact the airport at P.O. 367, 23000 Zadar (© **023/313-311**, or flight information 023/205-800; fax 023/205-805; www.zadar-airport.hr).

Croatia Airlines in Zadar, Poljana Natka Nodila 7 (© **023/250-094;** fax 023/250-109; Zadto@croatiaairlines.hr), is open 8am to 4pm Monday to Friday, 9am to noon Saturday, closed Sunday.

By Train   Train travel in Croatia improved in 2005, including travel to Zadar. That said, it should be noted that it still takes about 7 hours to get to Zadar from Zagreb via train because rail travelers must change trains at Knin on that route. Thus it takes roughly twice as long to get to Zadar from Zagreb by train than it does by car. The Zadar train station (Ante Starčevića 4; © **060/333-444;** www.htnet.hr) is adjacent to the bus station.

GETTING AROUND Croatia Airlines provides shuttle service between the airport and Zadar's center every hour for 15kn ($2.50). Zadar's Old Town is closed to vehicular traffic and thus is only navigable on foot. However, most of the hotels are outside the center and reachable by city bus or by car.

FAST FACTS: Zadar

Airport **Airport Zadar** (⊘ **023/313-311**; www.zadar-airport.hr).

ATMs **Privredna Banka**, Stjepana Radića 3; **Raiffeisen Bank**, Široka Ulica bb; **Zagrebačka Banka**, Brne Krnarutića 13.

Banks **Hypo Alpe-Adria Bank**, Jurja Barakovića 4 (⊘ **023/200-999**; www.hypo-alpe-adria.hr). Hours 8am to 8pm Monday to Friday; 8am to noon Saturday; closed Sunday.

Bus Station **Zadar Bus Station**, Ante Starčevića 1 (⊘ **023/211-555**; www.liburnija-zadar.hr). Ticket office open 6am to 10pm.

City Buses **Liburnija**, N. Jurišiśa (⊘ **023/343-730**).

Emergency **Emergency 94**, Ivana Mažuranića 28 (⊘ **023/239-800**). 24 hours.

Exchange **Aquarius**, Nova Vrata bb (⊘ **023/212-919**). Hours 7am–11pm daily. **Croatia Express**, Široka Ulica 12 (⊘ **023/250-502**). Hours 7:30am to 8pm Monday to Friday; 8:30am to 1pm Saturday; closed Sunday.

Express Mail **DHL**, Franje Tudmana 2 (⊘ **023/224-444**). Hours 8am to 4pm Monday to Friday; closed Saturday and Sunday.

Ferry Office **Jadrolinija**, Liburnska Obala 7 (⊘ **023/254-800**; www.jadrolinija.hr). Hours 6am to 4pm and 6 to 10pm Monday to Saturday; 7am to 1:30pm and 3 to 10pm Sunday. **Jadroagent**, Poljana Natka Nodila 4 (⊘ **023/251-447**).

Hospital **Hospital Zadar**, Bože Peričića 5 (⊘ **023/315-677**). Open 24 hours.

Laundry **Lotos**, Miroslava Krieže 19a (⊘ **023/335-140**).

Pharmacy **Ljekarna Centar**, Jurja Barakovićca 2 (⊘ **023/302-931**). Hours 7am to 8:30pm Monday to Friday; 8am to 1:30pm Saturday; closed Sunday. **Ljekarna Donat**, Braće Vranjanin bb (⊘ **023/251-342**). Hours 7am to 8:30pm Monday to Friday; 7am to 1:30pm Saturday; closed Sunday.

Photocopying **Pharos**, Široka Ulica 6 (⊘ **023/317-054**). Hours 8am to 1pm and 6 to 8:30pm Monday to Friday; 9am to 1pm Saturday; closed Sunday.

Police Police Station, Zore Dalmatinske 1 (⊘ **023/345-141**; www.mup.hr).

Post Office Central Post Office, Kralja S. Državlava 1 (⊘ **023/316-552**). Hours 7am to 9pm Monday to Saturday; closed Sunday.

Taxi Call ⊘ **023/251-400**.

WHAT TO SEE & DO

Zadar is full of dichotomies that juxtapose modern construction with ancient architecture, laissez-faire living with fiercely patriotic conviction, and bustling commerce with laid-back Mediterranean attitude. You can visit the city's historic sites and countless churches, stop for an ice-cream cone in Old Town, then go on to browse in the glitzy shops that line the narrow streets, but it's much more interesting to seek out Zadar's less obvious charms.

For example, one of Zadar's best features is its sounds, which emanate from the city's busy ferry port and other points on its open-air stage. At one end of the Riva you can watch one of the world's most beautiful sunsets accompanied by a fanfare of ferry horns, while at the other you can sit on steps leading into the sea with scores of people who fall silent to listen to the eerie melody created by the waves and the city's ingenious sea organ. Whatever your interests, you'll find something to pique them in Zadar, a city of surprises and never-ending fortitude.

Archaeological Museum ✿   This museum on Forum Square holds many artifacts that chronicle Zadar's development and history as well as items that represent the evolution of northern Dalmatia. This is a well-designed, well-captioned collection of exhibits, but watching kids skateboard or couples picnic among the Roman ruins out in front is much more interesting.

Trg Opatice Čike 1. ✆ 023/250-542; 023/250-516. arheoloski-muzej-zadar@zd.htnet.hr. Admission 10kn ($1.75) adults, 5kn ($1) children. Mon–Fri 9am–1pm and 6–9pm; Sat 9am–1pm; closed Sun.

Church of St. Mary ✿✿   The Romanesque Church of St. Mary dates to the early 11th century, but its present look is a result of a 16th-century renovation. The bell tower, sometimes called Koloman's Tower in honor of the 12th-century Hungarian king of Croatia, was built around 1110. St. Mary's and its bell tower were severely damaged during World War II and it took almost 30 years to rebuild them. The church is open for Mass only, but glass doors in the vestibule allow you to peek inside when the church is closed.

Masses daily 7:30 and 8:30am.

Church of St. Simeon ✿✿   Visit this 17th-century church to see what's inside—an incredible 14th-century silver casket containing the remains of St. Simeon, one of Zadar's patron saints. The casket sits on the church's altar supported by four bronze angels and its intricate detail shows scenes from the saint's life. Created by Zadar silversmiths in 1381 at the request of the wife of King Ludwig I of Anjou, one of Croatia's Hungarian rulers, it is hailed as one of the finest examples of silverwork ever produced in Zadar. If you happen to be in Zadar on October 8, the saint's feast day, you will be able to view the saint's mummified body *in situ* during the annual opening of the casket.

Trg Šime Budinića. During Mass only.

City Walls and Gates ✿✿✿   At one time, Zadar was the largest fortified city in Venice's portfolio. Today the walls and military facilities once devoted to defense are used as parks and backdrops for walking paths, especially near the city walls. Some sections of the walls were built by the Romans, and some were built by the Venetians much later as fortification against the Turks, who mounted relentless attacks on the city during the Middle Ages. Today only portions of the walls and four gates remain. The most impressive of these is the **Land Gate** on Foša Harbor, built by the Venetians in 1543 and decorated with sculptures that include the winged lion of St. Mark and the city's coat of arms. The **Sea Gate** is behind the Church of St. Chrysogonus between the ferry port and the market. It contains part of a Roman arch, but it was redone by the Venetians in 1573 to celebrate a Christian victory over the Turks. The gate is adorned with a relief of St. Mark's lion on the side facing the sea and is dedicated to Pope

Alexander III, who visited Zadar in 1171. It also has a plaque noting the visit on the gate's land-facing side, and the street leading up to it is named Alexander. The **Bridge Gate** is the newest opening in the wall, cut through to Narodni Trg by the Italians in the 1930s. The last and smallest gate is **St. Rocco Gate.** It connects Three Wells Square with the harbor.

Five Wells Square (Trg 5 Bunara) 🐾🐾 Zadar survived Turkish attacks during the 16th century in part by building a huge water tank and five ornate wells. After the Turks retreated, the city built a park over the fortifications and it includes a concrete square built around the wells. The wells no longer provide drinking water, but they do serve as "gates" for skateboarders, who like to practice their technique on the span.

Forum 🐾🐾🐾 Zadar's Roman Forum was constructed sometime between the 1st century B.C. and the 3rd century A.D. but was dedicated during the reign of the Emperor Augustus, as evidenced by one of its cornerstones. The Forum included a temple consecrated to Jupiter, Juno, and Minerva, and it had meeting rooms and other "offices" that sat above subterranean shops and workshops. The Forum's paving stones are still there, as is a stairway leading inside, some walls, and one of a pair of huge columns. The tall stone stand-alone column is known as the "Pillar of Shame," and was used to punish and humiliate transgressors during the Middle Ages. The Forum ruins weren't discovered until the 1930s, and the site was damaged during World War II when Allied troops bombed the city.

In front of the Church of St. Donatus and the Archbishop's Palace.

The Gold and Silver of Zadar 🐾🐾🐾 The Benedictine Convent next to the Church of St. Mary doesn't look like much from the street, but inside you'll find one of the most breathtaking museums in Croatia. The church dates from the 11th century, and its amazing collection of precious sacral art and even more precious relics is in the convent next door, where the church treasures have been guarded by Benedictine nuns since the end of World War II. The collection includes elaborate reliquaries for various saints' remains, many in the shape of an upraised arm or hand done in gold or silver. Paintings, crucifixes, vestments, and other examples of religious art from Croatia are also installed in the museum's well-designed rooms, where nuns in flowing black robes keep an eye on visitors and explain the exhibits. Before you leave the building, stop in at the ground-floor chapel of St. Nediljica behind the ticket office at the main entrance and take a peek at the tranquil convent garden that is visible only from inside the building. This is a fitting home for one of the most important cultural collections in Croatia. *Tip:* The ticket office/entrance to the museum is staffed by a nun in full-length black habit who will enforce the museum's dress code, which is similar to the dress code in many Croatian churches: You will be turned away if you are wearing revealing or skimpy clothing.

Trg Opatice Čike 1. ✆ 023/211-545. Admission 20kn ($3.50). Mon–Sat 10am–1pm and 6–8pm; Sun 10am–1pm.

The Riva 🐾🐾🐾 In most Croatian cities that face the sea, the Riva is usually a public "runway" where people go to see and be seen dressed in their trendiest outfits, always accessorized with an ice-cream cone. In Zadar, the Riva is a path called Petra Krešimira IV through a sort of waterfront park between Old Town and the sea, more garden walk than sidewalk. At night Zadar's beautifully landscaped Riva is a hive of activity, with a few vendors' stalls, traditional a cappella groups singing as they stroll, and folks getting exercise. By day, the Riva is a park and beach where people aren't shy

Riva Review

Zadar's Riva was undergoing extensive renovation when we visited in the summer of 2007. What we saw was convincing evidence that it should be a contender for one of the best in Croatia when it's finished—some time in 2008. White stone walkways, new lighting, the existing Sea Organ, the planned Column of Light, vendors, musicians, the throng of pedestrians who walk there nightly, and the sea itself will be the draw.

about stripping down and taking a dip. The Riva also goes past Zadar's knockout university, which overlooks the sea. Founded in 1396, it is the oldest university in the region and the oldest in Croatia.

Midway along the Riva, you'll come across **The Sea Organ** ✰✰✰, a one-of-a-kind pipe organ that employs air and water movement rather than an organist. It is difficult to classify the Morske *orgulje* (sea organ) as anything but an art installation with its smooth, wide, white-stone steps and ever-changing audience of passersby who come to marvel at the sea's musical talent. The exhibit is a source of constantly changing sound created by the organ's 35 pipes, which have underwater whistles. Sea motion drives air and water through the whistles' openings, producing an endless string of sounds that vary according to the force and speed of the waves and that is best described as a mellow whale-cello duet. The organ was designed by architect Nikola Bašić and built by experts from Zagreb and Murter Island. It was installed in spring 2005 and won the European Prize for Urban Space shortly thereafter.

On the south end of the Old Town.

St. Anastasia Cathedral and Bell Tower ✰✰   This Romanesque cathedral built during the 12th and 13th centuries is the biggest in Dalmatia. The cathedral's facade is interesting because of its three doors, arches, and rose windows. Inside it are an understated simple stone main altar and a smaller altar off to the side that contains the remains of its namesake saint. But it is the cathedral's detached 15th-century bell tower that attracts the most attention because you can climb to the top to take in a great view of the city.

Trg Sveti Stošije 1. ✆ 023/251-708. Admission 15kn ($3). Daily 6pm.

St. Chrysogonus Church ✰✰   This 12th-century Romanesque church is notable for its frescoes, high altar, and exterior stonework. The church's facade is very plain, but the sides are adorned with elaborate columns whose shapes resemble red licorice Twizzler sticks. The exterior walls of three apses at the back of the church have several graceful blind arches. The altar was built in 1701 by grateful Zadar citizens who had escaped the plague, and it is adorned by statues of Zadar's four patron saints—Chrysogonus, Zoilus, Simeon, and Anastasia. The church is almost never open, but in July and August a few evening concerts are held there.

North of the Forum on Pape Aleksandra St.

St. Donatus ✰✰✰   This unusual 9th-century church and the buildings around it were erected on the ruins of the city's Roman Forum. Some of the Forum's foundations lie exposed outside like an ancient sculpture garden. Kids play on them, people sit on them, and sellers display their wares on them all day and far into the night,

Fun Fact   **Full Moon Festival**

Every year on the night of July's full moon, Zadar's electric lights are turned off for *Noć Punog Miseca* (Night of the Full Moon), and the Riva glows under the lights of the moon, torches, and candles. It is on this night that Zadar celebrates regional Croatian culture and customs with floating markets, impromptu restaurants, singing, dancing, and plenty of food. Local specialties from towns and islands in Zadar's vicinity are available up and down the waterfront from boats and kiosks, where people sample them and listen to traditional music all without benefit of electricity. On this night you can really get to know the region's culture through the sounds, tastes, and aromas of enthusiastic Mediterranean merrymaking.

oblivious to their history. St. Donatus originally was called the Church of the Holy Trinity, but eventually it was re-christened with its present name in honor of the bishop who founded it. The church's interior has a circular center and three apses; the narthex lies between the principal entrance and the rotunda. A circular stairway leads to the first floor. The church grew into a complex of ecclesiastical buildings over the years, and the cathedral itself is very plain inside with walls and altars devoid of statues, paintings, and other ornamentation. Mass has not been said in St. Donatus for more than 2 centuries, but the church is used for classical and sacral concerts because of its superior acoustics.

Forum. Daily 9am–1pm and 5–7:30pm.

WATERSPORTS

Anyplace you can touch the water on the Dalmatian coast is a potential swimming hole, but diving opportunities are fewer and require much more planning. If you are in Zadar, you can access diving operations on offshore islands and up and down the coast.

Zlatna Luka Diving Center 🐟🐟   Half-day excursion includes two dives, full tanks, and weights. Zlatna Luka offers weekend tours to Kornati National Park and other Adriatic locations. The center is about 7km (4½ miles) south of Zadar, at Marina Dalmacija, Bibinje-Sukošan (© **023/263-121;** www.diving-zlatnaluka.net).

WHERE TO STAY

There are no hotels in Zadar's Old Town. Most accommodations are more than 3.2km (2 miles) away in Borik, a suburb on the sea northwest of town. However, there is good public transportation between the central city and the surrounding resort areas.

Hotel Kolovare 🐟🐟   The Kolovare is a 15-minute walk along the Zadar Channel from the Land Gate and Old Town in the Kolovare district, which makes it the closest hotel to the central city. It is also one of the largest hotels in Zadar and you'll run into lots of tour groups here. However, thanks to a 2004 renovation, the Kolovare's guest rooms are brighter, more spacious, and more comfortable than those in most package hotels, especially guest rooms with balconies facing the pool and the sea beyond. All major car rental agencies—Thrifty, National, Budget, and Dollar—have offices in the lobby.

Bože Peričića 14, Kolovare. ℂ **023/211-017.** Fax 023/213-079. www.hotel-kolovare-zadar.htnet.hr. 237 units. July–Aug: from 140€ ($170) double. Rest of year: 130€ ($160) double. AE, DC, MC, V. Rates include breakfast. Half- and full board available. **Amenities:** Restaurant; bar; pool; valet service. *In room:* A/C, TV, dataport, minibar, hair dryer, safe.

Hotel Niko ✦✦✦ *Value*

The Niko is a bit of a hike from Old Town, but it is one of the nicest hotels in the area and definitely worth the extra effort. The huge guest rooms have balconies large enough for a table and chairs, and half the rooms face the sea. Decor throughout is high quality and extends to the bathrooms, where the gleaming modern appointments reflect the fact that the all-season hotel was built in 2003. Add to that the hotel's magnificent **Restoran Niko** ✦✦✦ and you have a recipe for success.

Obala Kneza Domagoja 9, Puntamika. ℂ **023/337-880.** Fax 023/337-890. www.hotel-niko.hr. 12 units. From 780kn ($145) double. AE, DC, MC, V. Rates include breakfast. Parking. **Amenities:** Restaurant; bar. *In room:* A/C, TV, minibar, hair dryer.

Club Funimation ✦✦✦

Funimation is an all-inclusive package hotel that delivers a lot of bang for the buck, especially if you have kids. It's also the Croatian version of a Disney World hotel with countless amenities, lots of activities for the younger set, and plenty of services for the adults, too. Funimation's big draws are its water park, terraced pool, pleasant beach, and long list of kids' activities that include Falky Land, a structured babysitting service. There are talent shows, dance and art classes, diving classes at the hotel's diving center, and lots of chaise longues with green and yellow umbrellas where parents can relax while keeping an eye on the kids. Guest rooms are beautiful but secondary because everyone is outdoors almost all the time. However, all of Funimation's guest rooms are done in modern Mediterranean decor and range from singles to penthouse suites.

Majstora Radovana 7, Borik. ℂ **023/206-637.** Fax 023/332-065. www.media.falkensteiner.com. 258 units. From 214€ ($300) double; from 278€ ($390) suite. Rates include breakfast, lunch, and dinner; babysitting; use of all sports facilities; and some instruction programs. They are based on a stay of 3 or more nights during the high season. AE, DC, MC, V. **Amenities:** Restaurant; bar; live entertainment; 2 pools; water center; children's programs. *In room:* A/C, TV, hair dryer, safe.

Garden Wing Adriana ✦✦✦

Think of the Adriana as the adult branch of Funimation. These accommodations adjacent to Funimation appeal to grown-ups, though anyone can get in touch with his or her own kid side at Adriana, which shares Funimation's Acquapura water park (included in the price of accommodations). Thanks to a recent renovation, the Garden Wing Adriana now exudes quiet luxury with bright, modern furnishings; balconies; and big bathrooms complete with high-style fixtures. Outside, a romantic English-style garden and tranquil pool are protected from the fray by vegetation. Most guests take advantage of the hotel's **Adriana Mediterranean a la carte restaurant** ✦✦✦ by booking full-board packages, but you also can book suites with half-board or breakfast only. Details such as a welcome drink and fruit basket, and deck chairs and towels are nice touches included in the price.

Majstora Radovana 7, Borik. ℂ **023/206-637.** www.media.falkensteiner.com. 48 junior suites. July–Aug: from 260€ ($365) double with full board. Rest of year: from 180€ ($252) double. Rates are based on a stay of 3 or more days. AE, DC, MC, V. **Amenities:** Restaurant; bar; pool; sports/fitness programs; spa/salon; access to Acquapura Borik swimming complex; concierge services; child care at Funimation. *In room:* A/C, TV, hair dryer, safe.

President Hotel ✦✦ *Overrated*

Privacy and pampering are the President's strategy for making guests feel at home. There are no doo-dads like a pool or spa here, just an award-winning **gourmet restaurant,** Vivaldi ✦✦, quietly elegant rooms and suites, and attentive service that drips with class. Guest rooms and suites are outfitted with Biedermeier-style furniture and have balconies. The large granite bathrooms, outfitted with shower only, are filled with a generous array of toiletries, though a bubble bath is impossible. Each room has individual temperature controls within 3° of the default, which can be overridden by the front desk. There is 24-hour room service from the Vivaldi.

Vladana Desnice 16, north of Borik. © **023/333-696.** Fax 023/333-595. www.hotel-president.hr. 27 units. July–Aug: from 222€ ($310) double; from 394€ ($552) suite. Rest of year: from 125€ ($175) double; from 262€ ($367) suite. AE, DC, MC, V. Parking. **Amenities:** Restaurant; 24-hr. staff. *In room:* A/C, TV, Internet access, minibar, hair dryer, safe.

Mediteran ⌓

This pale-peach building houses a delightful family-run hotel with a good restaurant. It's not on the beach but is within walking distance of the water; some rooms even have sea views and balconies. Only a few rooms have air-conditioning and a minibar. Book these if you have a choice, especially in summer.

Matije Gupca 19, near Borik. © **023/337-500.** Fax 023/337-528. www.hotelmediteran-zd.hr. 30 units. From 540kn ($100) double. Rates include breakfast. AE, DC, MC, V. Parking. **Amenities:** Restaurant; bar. *In room:* A/C (select rooms), TV, minibar (select rooms).

Hotel Donat ⌓

Situated a short walk from the sea near Funimation, this all-inclusive hotel was redone in 2004 and a new pool was added in 2005. The Donat, a large hotel in the Borik group, provides an economical alternative and has almost all the same amenities as Funimation.

Majstora Radovana 7, Borik. © **023/206-637.** Fax 023/332-065. www.media.falkensteiner.com. 107 units. Aug: from 118€ ($165) double; from 126€ ($177) suite. Rest of year: from 46€ ($65) double; from 54€ ($76) suite. Rates include breakfast, lunch, dinner, and snack. AE, DC, MC, V. **Amenities:** Restaurant; bar; pool; organized sports and children's programs; babysitting; live entertainment. *In room:* A/C, TV.

Borik Youth Hostel

A recent re-do of the pavilion has spiffed-up this budget stop near the beach. Rooms are dorm-style and well-kept. You can get a bed with breakfast or half-board, but don't expect gourmet chow or many creature comforts here.

Obala Kneza Trpimira 76, Borik. © **023/331-145.** www.hfhs.hr. B&B from 90kn ($17). AE, DC, MC, V.

Camping Borik ⌓⌓

Woods and access to sand and pebble beaches are two of the amenities that make this campground tucked in the midst of road, houses, hotels, and sports facilities a desirable location. In addition, washroom facilities are clean and well-equipped. The campground is a short ride from Zadar's center if you use public transportation.

Majstora Radovana 7, Borik. © **023/332-074.** Fax 023/332-065. www.hoteliborik.hr. Capacity 1,800 people. Tent sites with 2 people 120kn ($22). AE, DC, MC, V. **Amenities:** Restaurant; bar; market; sports facilities.

WHERE TO DINE

Zadar offers a wide range of dining choices. Hole-in-the-wall konobas serve everything from tasty stew to pizza to continental cuisine. Modest establishments offer a large repertoire of Croatian and Italian fare, while classy, expensive gourmet restaurants feature menus with blow-out prices.

Kornat ⌓⌓ *(Finds* NOUVEAU CROATIAN This chic restaurant doesn't look like much when you see it from the ferry port across the street, but it is a hidden oasis of imaginative Croatian cuisine served in a refined atmosphere. Kornat is cleverly protected from street noise, fumes, and ferry horns by glass baffles that make it possible to enjoy a tranquil meal while sitting outside on the wooden deck or inside, where the dining room is all high style. After you finish the complimentary *amuse bouche,* try the

Zadar's Neighborhoods

Zadar's Old Town peninsula is unquestionably the city's core, but there are several areas outside the walled center that visitors should note.

Kolovare: This residential area is directly east of Old Town and home to the hotel that is closest to the city center. Kolovare's personality is quite civilized and full of shady paths, cafes, and private villas. It is also home to Zadar's public beach and a long coastal promenade.

Arbanasi: This older, non-touristy older district north of Kolovare is home to a nice assortment of Neolithic and Roman archaeological remains. It is a quiet neighborhood much like an upscale suburb in the U.S. or Great Britain.

Borik: This large hotel-resort complex is one of the Zadar area's most popular because of its position on the sea and its proximity to town. Parts of Borik already resemble a Disney community, and Croatia's exploding tourism industry is spurring development of more facilities, restaurants, and other attractions.

Puntamika: The city lighthouse resides in this district on the sea, which once was guardian to Zadar's shipping port in Old Town.

Relja: Zadar's biggest and newest indoor shopping mall is here, though it pales in comparison to Zagreb's Jankomir Center. The rest of the area is made up of older residential buildings and a few restaurants and cafes.

Voštarnica: This could be classified as Zadar's blue-collar neighborhood with commercial enterprises and residences dominating. It is west of the footbridge.

Old Town Peninsula: Old Town is Zadar's undisputed main attraction, with its gaggle of churches and monasteries; its mishmash of preserved and rebuilt historical sites and Roman ruins; its ferry port and its burgeoning collection of shops and boutiques; and its galleries, restaurants, and cafes—all crammed into the fortified peninsula.

octopus fish balls with potatoes and rosemary—two fish patties covered with arugula and large slices of shaved Parmesan with escalloped potatoes. Any grilled fish—sea bass with scampi sauce and tiny shrimp—is done to perfection. For meat eaters, the lamb with rosemary and red wine can't be beat, especially if you pair it with a selection from Kornat's excellent wine list. Top off your meal with one of the menu's light but sophisticated desserts such as melon in champagne, or go all out and choose a richer treat.

Liburnska Obala 6. ℂ **023/254-501.** Reservations recommended. Entrees 45kn–100kn ($8–$18), more for fish or lobster served by the kilo. AE, DC, MC, V. Daily 11am–midnight.

Riblji Restaurant Foša 🌟🌟🌟 SEAFOOD   Named after the harbor that flows next to the city's east wall, which is just outside its front door, Foša has the best location of any restaurant in Zadar. When you enter, skip the inside dining room and go straight to the terrace, which opens to the sea. By day your table is the best place to catch a cool breeze, and by night you'll have an unobstructed view of the water and the city lights. Foša is a local favorite for its well-prepared fish dishes. There are other choices, too, like the omelet with smoked ham.

Kralja Dmitra Zvonimira 2. ⓒ **023/314-421**. Reservations recommended. Entrees 40kn–80kn ($7–$14). AE, DC, MC, V. Daily noon–11pm.

Restaurant Zadar na Rivi ⭐ PIZZA & FISH   It's a shame that Zadar's Hotel Zagreb is closed for renovationsbecause it faces the sea and it is just steps from the door to the water. However, you still can take the sea air from the hotel's terrace if you grab a table at Zadar na Rivi, a casual dining spot set on the hotel's ground floor. The food is mostly so-so pizza and a few Dalmatian specialties, but you can sip coffee, have a snack, listen to live Dalmatian music, or enjoy the expansive view of the sea at a table here. Stop at Zadar na Rivi for the atmosphere, not the food, then walk around to the back of the shuttered hotel to see the ruins of the 10th-century St. Stomorica Church *in situ.*

Obala Kralja P. Krešimira IV. ⓒ **023/212-182**. Entrees 40kn–80kn ($7–$14). More for lobster and specialty. No credit cards. Daily 7am–midnight.

Konoba Stomorica ⭐ *Value* DALMATIAN   It might have been the sound of locals belting out off-key renditions of Croatian songs that drew us to this place where tables are filled from morning to night. This traditional Dalmatian konoba serves up huge portions of good food at reasonable prices. Seating is indoors or out. The black risotto is probably the biggest and cheapest portion around, at 30kn ($5).

Stomorica 12. ⓒ **023/315-946**. Entrees 25kn–35kn ($4.50–$5). No credit cards. Daily 9am–midnight.

Trattoria Canzona ⭐⭐ ITALIAN   Just down the street from Konoba Stomorica, this traditional pizzeria is all Italian all the time. The menu has a huge array of pastas and pizzas and a Chicago tribute called Al Capone steak that comes topped with ham, cheese, peppers, and tomatoes. Canzona, a spin off of a pizzeria with the same name in Zagreb, has both indoor and outdoor seating.

Stomorica 8. ⓒ **023/212-081** or 023/212-080. Entrees 33kn–60kn ($6–$10). No credit cards. Mon–Sat 10am–11pm; Sun noon–11pm.

Konoba Stipe ⭐ CROATIAN   Konoba Stipe isn't an ordinary pizzeria/grill restaurant, though the food is pretty predictable. This konoba also has a pretty garden setting done in dark green and white, though you have to walk through a mall passageway to get there.

Plemića Borelli 5a. ⓒ **023/213-275**. Entrees 30kn–70kn ($6–$12). AE, DC, MC, V. Mon–Sat 7am–midnight; Sun 11am–midnight.

Konoba Ankora CROATIAN   Enjoy traditional cuisine in the heart of Zadar in this park setting where you can feast on roasted meat, fish *brudet* (stew with hard corn mush), or just simple grilled fish.

Oko Vrulja 10. ⓒ **023/236-688**. Fax 023/333-150. ankora@interieur.hr. Entrees 30kn–65kn ($5–$11). AE, DC, MC, V. Daily 10am–midnight. Closed Jan.

Niko ⭐⭐⭐ CROATIAN   With a track record that dates to 1963, Niko qualifies as an institution in the Zadar area and it is also one of the best restaurants around, hands-down. Casual elegance, a great sea breeze on the awning-covered terrace, and a view of the harbor combined with a congenial waitstaff make this restaurant in the Niko hotel a great place for a leisurely lunch or a special night out. Any grilled fish dish is worth a try, but those with smaller appetites should try the scampi salad, a plate

Outdoor Ed

It's a mystery how students at Zadar's University concentrate on their work: This white stone classroom building surrounded by lush vegetation on Zadar's Riva faces the sea and is a stone's throw from Old Town action. The Dominican monks who founded the institution of higher learning in 1396 must have known what they were doing, however—Zadar University is Croatia's oldest and has been attracting students for more than 600 years.

of little shrimp and cold potato salad. The Dalmatian plate is a generous sampling of pršut, sardellen, and Paški cheese; wash it all down with a bottle of local white wine. A bonus: Real Maraska (cherry juice) is served here.

Obala Kneza Domagoja 9, Punamika. © 023/337-888. Reservations recommended. Entrees 38kn–150kn ($7–$26). AE, DC, MC, V. Daily noon–midnight.

Vivaldi ⭐⭐ *Overrated* MEDITERRANEAN/CONTINENTAL   Vivaldi has a reputation for haute cuisine and even "hauter" prices. The decor of this restaurant in the lower level of the exclusive **Hotel President** ⭐⭐ in the Borik area outside of town doesn't contradict that. The entryway is covered by a canopy and flanked by high hedges that would protect the identity of any celeb on a night out. Once inside the almost painfully formal dining room, you'll encounter lots of silver and crystal, a Continental menu, and a small but well-chosen list of high-end Croatian wines with prices to match. The menu seems a bit pretentious, with a mix of classic and contrived dishes such as duck in orange sauce, *pescano* Mexicano (mixed fish with Tabasco), fish rolled in citrus fruits and bread crumbs, and lots of big steaks as entrees. Save room for Vivaldi's version of cherries jubilee, made with local fruit.

Vladana Desnice 16. © 023/333-696. Reservations required. Entrees 115kn–250kn ($20–$43). AE, DC, MC, V. Daily 7am–1am.

Trata ⭐ DALMATIAN   The word "trata" refers to an ancient dance performed by Greek women to ensure a good catch for their fisherman husbands before the fleet went out to sea. You won't see any costumed dancers in this konoba set in a garden littered with 2nd-century Roman foundations, but you will find a menu filled with mouthwatering fish dishes and a few Dalmatian specialties, which also feature fish.

Jerolima Vidulića 5. © 098/532-057. Entrees 40kn–100kn ($7–$17). No credit cards. Daily 11am–midnight.

COFFEE, PASTRIES, & ICE CREAM

A visit to Zadar is not complete without doing a bit of cafe hopping. It's fun, it's cheap (around $1 to $2 for a coffee, pastry, or ice cream), and you'll get a chance to relax with the locals.

Forum Café ⭐ PASTRY   This cafe's location couldn't be better. Set on a shaded terrace on the Kalelarga between St. Donatus and the Forum, the cafe is a natural stopping point for a cappuccino or a *bijela kava* for anyone exploring Old Town Zadar. However, despite the table umbrellas, the Forum can get uncomfortably warm in the afternoon.

Široka Ulica bb. © 023/205-554. No credit cards. Daily 7:30am–1am.

Kult ⭐ COFFEE   This is the shadiest cafe in town, which is important during Zadar's blazing heat in July and August. Kult has the usual umbrella-protected tables, but they are double-insulated by their position under leafy trees. Kult is a popular gathering place for locals, who know how to keep cool.

Stomorica 6 at the junction of Stomorica and Svete Nediljice. ✆ **091/392-2595**. No credit cards. Daily 7:30am–1am.

Café Gallery Gina ✿✿ If you're over 30, this is the place for you. Gina attracts a crowd that's more "mature" than most, perhaps because it also has a little art gallery and more mellow music.

Varoška 2. No phone. No credit cards. Daily 7am–1am.

In Time ✿ COFFEE In Time is one of those local hangouts where cruisin' and schmoozin' are de rigueur. It's in the path of Riva walkers, so it's also an excellent spot for people-watching.

Mihovila Pavlinovića 6. ✆ **091/536-8840**. No credit cards. Daily 7am–1am.

Corso ✿ COFFEE If you want to try cafe-hopping, Corso is right next door to In Time. However, Corso is a little more upscale with a polished modern interior and almost nonstop DJ music on weekends.

Milhovila Pavlinovića 4. ✆ **098/182-7741**. No credit cards. Daily 7am–2am.

Slastičarna Danica ✿✿ ICE CREAM Ice cream plays second fiddle to excellent cakes and pastries at this modern cafe across from the National Theater.

Široka Ulica 3. ✆ **023/211-016**. No credit cards. Daily 7am–11pm.

Slastičarna Donat ✿✿✿ ICE CREAM Even people from out of town have heard of Donat, reputed to have the best ice cream in Zadar due to its creative flavors and funny, congenial scoopers. This is no small feat in ice-cream-mad Dalmatia, where competition among *slastičarnama* is fierce and people aren't properly accessorized without a cone. There is always a long line waiting to place orders. The tables outside are full for good reason. The ice cream is superb and available in an endless array of concoctions.

Trg sv Stošija. ✆ **023/250-829**. No credit cards. Daily 7am–midnight.

BARS AND CLUBS

Much of Zadar's nighttime action is outdoors on the Riva or at other seaside locations. However, there are a few rockin' indoor spots worth a mention.

The Garden ✿✿✿ There is nothing closer to nightclub Nirvana than The Garden, a cool, understated club on an expansive terrace high up in the city's walls. During the day, The Garden is parklike with people playing outdoor chess, reading, or daydreaming on its terrace. As the sun sets, The Garden becomes a glowing red planet; then as darkness takes over, it roars to life as a sophisticated alfresco dance club. This is a don't-miss experience no matter the time of day.

Liburnska Obala 6. ✆ **023/364-739**. www.thegardenzadar.com. Daily 10am–1:30am May–Sept.

Mango ✿ As waterfront bars go, Mango is a cut above. It has an energized atmosphere, an interesting drink menu, and it is a vantage point for Zadar's magnificent sunsets.

Krešimirova Obala. Diklo. No phone. No credit cards. Daily 8am–1am.

Barbara Bar (Funimation Hotel, Borik) ✿✿ Funimation's decor is tropical/Afro and Barbara carries out that theme, too. Barbara's wicker chairs and chaises with cool white upholstery, lots of plants, and a languid vibe are make for a relaxing break.

Majstora Radovana 7. Borik. ✆ **023/206-100**. AE, DC, MC, V. Daily 8am–1am.

Sun Spot

If you happen to be on Zadar's Riva at sunset, you'll be bathed in the reddest glow imaginable, a phenomenon that is the result of Zadar's setting in the middle of several islands and the Velebit range. You'll also see a large poster of Alfred Hitchcock under glass on the south end of Obala Kralja Petra Krešimira IV. It is captioned in 5 languages and tells the story of how he strolled the Riva during a visit and proclaimed that "Zadar has the most beautiful sunset in the world." It's a statement that can withstand any challenge.

City Club Forum ★★   Togas are optional and you won't hear strains from Nero's fiddle at this trio of bars designed to conjure the fall of Rome. Music is mostly pop and rock and the ambience is all Roman excess.

Marka Marulića bb. © 023/214-556. No credit cards. Daily 11pm–4am in summer and 11pm–4am Thurs–Sat in winter.

5 Zadar Environs

Zadar is truly the center of activity for northern Dalmatia and also a point of departure for many other destinations worth visiting. The medieval city of Nin is just a short drive north of Zadar. It is a town with funky charisma, the smallest cathedral in the world, and a lot of spirit legends. Zadar is also a ferry port for the decidedly undeveloped northern Dalmatian islands of Silba, Ugljan, Pašman, and Dugi Otok. Sometimes known as "the islands of the Zadar Archipelago," Ugljan, Pašman, and Dugi Otok are the three most visited of the offshore islands, but none is overrun by tourists. From Zadar, it's an easy drive to Paklenica National Park, a challenging environment for hikers, rock climbers, and spelunkers. And Zadar is also a major departure point for tours to the Kornati National Park, which is really a portion of the southern islands of the Zadar Archipelago. South of Zadar on the way to Sibenik, you'll hit Biograd, once a medieval metropolis and now a crowded package resort. Each of these locations has its own charms, and each is a reasonable distance from Zadar—accessible either by private or public transport.

6 Paklenica National Park & Nin

ESSENTIALS

VISITOR INFORMATION   Paklenica information can be had at the Starigrad **tourism office** at Trg Tome Marašovića 1 (© **023/369-255;** www.rivijera-paklenica.hr), which is open from June 6 to September 15. Nin's **tourist office** is at Trg Brače Radića 3 (© **023/265-247;** www.nin.hr). The tourist office can provide maps, brochures, and information about Paklenica and private accommodations in the area.

GETTING THERE   Paklenica is a little less than 3 hours from Zagreb on the new Zagreb-Split highway. Exit at a sign for the park before you get to Zadar and continue on the old road that skirts the sea. You'll pass lots of SOBE signs before you get to Starigrad; a sign leading to the park turns into a one-lane road that appears to go through a residential area. The road leads to park reception, where you can leave your car, buy a ticket, fill your water bottle, and enter the park on foot. There is no direct public transportation to the park.

Nin is easy to get to by car or bus. Buses run between Zadar and Nin frequently; and the 16km (10-mile) ride takes less than half an hour.

GETTING AROUND   Paklenica is all about walking and climbing. No motorized vehicles are allowed inside the park boundaries, though they do stop at Starigrad, a little over a mile away. Nin is very compact, and walking is necessary to take in the sites.

WHAT TO SEE & DO

There is a beautiful karst landscape between Paklenica National Park and Nin, but there are quite a few land-mine warning signs, too. Those are alarmingly near weekend homes and all along the way to Zadar, but the people staying there seem pretty blasé about them; you'll see houses and people precariously close to the signs as you drive through. Paklenica is the Velebit's best hiking territory and has many gorges, mountains, and caves to tempt adventurous explorers. Nin is a quaint medieval town with lots of ancient churches and a dynamite restaurant.

Paklenica National Park ଈଈଈ   Once you get to the entrance of Paklenica National Park, you'll think you know what to expect because you will have been looking at the Velebit's breathtaking rock walls and vertical landscapes for miles along the highway. However, when you stop at the reception kiosk at Starigrad, you'll be amazed at the park's softer side—the sound of locusts, the caress of the wind, the colors of wildflowers, and the scent of pine in the air.

Paklenica, which was proclaimed a national park in 1949, is truly a do-it-yourself experience: The only drinking water source is at reception, and you have to carry everything in yourself. There is no overnight camping at the park, either, but if you can't bear to get off the trail, you can book a bed at either of two communal huts on the mountain. Paklenica offers a huge choice of rock-climbing experiences, from beginner to expert, and there are more than 40km (60 miles) of hiking trails that can be charted for treks of a couple of hours or a couple of days.

Starigrad Reception Office: Admission 30kn ($5) adults, 20kn ($3.50) ages 7–18. Daily 6:30am–8pm. Cave 10am–1pm for 10kn ($1.75) surcharge. **Paklenica Park Office:** F. Tudmana 14a, 23244 Starigrad-Paklenica. ℂ 023/ 369-202. Fax 023/359-133. www.paklenica.hr. Apr–Oct Mon–Fri 8am–3pm.

NIN ଈଈଈ

Most people who explore this little town on an island don't stay overnight, but visit as part of a day excursion. Nin is connected to the mainland by a couple of stone pedestrian bridges (*Gornji most* and *Donji most*) and there aren't many facilities for housing tourists in town. In addition, there isn't a lot to do in Nin except explore the historic churches and a few shops, and rub the toe of yet another Meštrović statue of Gregorius of Nin for luck. Nonetheless, the little town that once was an important center of Catholicism in medieval times is alluring.

Nin was a thriving town during the Roman Empire and became a municipality at the end of the 1st century under the Emperor Augustus. As with most Roman settlements, Nin had its own Forum, an amphitheater, and a temple that is the largest discovered in Croatia so far.

The Romans kept control of Nin until the 7th century, when the Avars and Slavs appeared on the scene, but the invaders didn't completely destroy the town, and it managed to maintain its way of life to a degree. From then on, Nin developed culturally and politically and became a center of church activity and a headquarters for some of Croatia's kings and bishops. When the Venetians conquered most of the Dalmatian coast in 1409, Nin was included in the takeover. A century later, Nin became the

Gregorius of Nin

Gregorius of Nin was a Croatian bishop from the end of the 9th century to the beginning of the 10th who was chancellor of the Croatian court and who is known for his defense of Croatian culture, specifically the Glagolitic language. Gregorius was a Glagolitic scholar, a high-ranking cleric, and an adviser to the Croatian royalty who became Bishop of Nin in A.D. 867, the third priest to hold that office. Gregorius became known as a courageous fighter when he stood up against attempts to abolish the Glagolitic Mass. However, he lost that battle in a political struggle with the Archbishop of Split when the Church Synods of A.D. 925 and A.D. 928 forbid priests from using Glagolitic language in their liturgies and ordered them to use Latin instead. The Synod subsequently gave control of Dalmatia to the Archbishop of Split, and Gregorius of Nin was transferred to Skradin, a city that is now one of the main entrances to Krka National Park.

target of Turkish attacks, and in 1570, Venice destroyed most of the city rather than let it become an enemy stronghold. Nin was rebuilt at the start of the 18th century, but it has not regained its former glory.

Holy Cross Church ✿✿✿   At first glance, the 9th-century Holy Cross Church is reminiscent of any pueblo church in America's Southwest. The church's whitewashed exterior is all shadow and angle in the direct Mediterranean sun, thanks to the cathedral's shape in the form of a cross. In any case, this tiny church, which bills itself as the world's smallest cathedral, is a showstopper and a mystery. According to Mladen Pejaković, a Dubrovnik artist, besides being a place of worship, Holy Cross is also a giant sun dial and calendar. Pejaković posits that the church is situated and constructed according to exact mathematical calculations that allow the sun's rays to fall on the floor and walls in such a way that they can be used to tell time and graph the summer and winter solstices.
In the center of town, Nin.

Bishop Grgur Ninski (Gregorius of Nin) Memorial ✿✿   Ivan Meštrović's sculpture of the famous cleric is sometimes mistaken for a statue of Merlin the magician from Arthurian times, and versions of it can be viewed in many locations and in many sizes in Croatia. This one in Nin is larger than all except the truly mammoth version in Split. It is surrounded by a small garden.
In the center of town, Nin.

Church of St. Anselmo and Treasury ✿   The plaque outside identifies this parish church as the town's former cathedral with a construction/renovation history spanning the 6th to the 18th centuries. It is dedicated to St. Anselm who, according to legend, was Nin's first bishop and also one of Christ's early disciples. The church's side chapel is the only remaining part of the original church. The treasury next to the church has just over two dozen exhibits, most of which are gold. The treasury also contains a gold reliquary in the shape of a hand that is said to contain St. Anselm's shoulder bone.
Trg Sv. Marcele 1 XV Anselma, Nin. Admission 10kn ($1.75) adults, 5kn ($1) kids. The church is rarely open but the treasury hours are Mon–Sat 9:30–noon and 5:30–9:30pm; closed Sun and holidays.

The Zadar Archipelago

Ugljan, Pašman, Murter, and Dugi Otok all are part of what is sometimes called the Zadar Archipelago, a group of islands numbering over 300. Three of the most popular with tourists are detailed below. Each has a distinct personality. All the inhabited islands in the archipelago can be reached by ferry only, with the exception of Murter, which is connected to the mainland by a bridge.

Ugljan is the Archipelago island closest to Zadar and one of the most populous, though it is never very crowded. Ugljan has been inhabited since prehistoric times. It was once the site of Roman habitation, as indicated by the *villa rustica* still found there. Today nearly 8,000 people call it home, including some who work on the mainland but live on Ugljan. Ugljan's main industries are farming, animal husbandry, and fishing, though tourism is becoming a growing source of revenue for the island.

Pašman, like Pag, has barren areas and fertile ones, which are used for farming and grazing. Most of the sites on Pašman date from medieval times. The only occupied Benedictine monastery in Croatia (Sts. Cosmos and Damian) is behind walls and atop a hilltop near Tkon. That and the island's Franciscan monastery in Kraj are worth a stop.

Murter is south of Pašman and actually closer to Šibenik than it is to Zadar. However, it is mostly under Zadar's jurisdiction. Murter doesn't have much to recommend it except that it can be accessed from the mainland by a short bridge and it is also just south of the islands that make up Kornati National Park, making it a good staging area for visits to Kornati. Murter's largest and most interesting town, Murter Town, is the site of the Kornati National Park's office. Murter is also the best place to book an excursion to Kornati National Park, as its citizens own 90% of the park (p. 163).

Dugi Otok is the biggest island (117 sq. km/45 sq. miles) in the Zadar Archipelago, the farthest from the mainland. It also boasts the most irregular and "wild" coastline, which makes it particularly appealing to those who like adventure and who want to avoid the usual tourist haunts. Eleven villages are strung out along the northeastern side; on the western side, Dugi Otok's cliffs rise almost vertically from the sea. Dugi Otok also offers the remains of several medieval churches worth seeing, as well as a gorgeous beach on Sakarun Bay at the island's north end. A nature park at Telašćica Bay, once used as a port by the Venetian fleet, is protected on one side from the sea winds by a sheer cliff and on the other by pine forests.

Ferry service exists to Dugi Otok from Zadar, but there is little transportation on the island itself, so if you want to thoroughly explore it, you will need a car. The extreme southern portion of Dugi Otok is part of Kornati National Park (below). *Note:* The lighthouse at Veli Rat is one of the best attractions on Dugi Otok. It is at the extreme western tip of the island and is surrounded by pines, bays, and beaches. The lighthouse is an unusual shade of yellow, said to be the result of the inclusion of 1,000 eggs in the paint.

WHERE TO STAY

Most of the accommodations near Paklenica are private or at campsites, though there is one high-rise hotel in Starigrad and several small, family-run hotels in town. Contact the Starigrad tourist office (above) for accommodations information. You can also check out the ubiquitous SOBE signs around the park. Prices for sobe doubles start at 100kn ($18) without breakfast. For hard-core hikers, there is overnight shelter in a bare-bones mountain hut available in the park. In Nin, private rooms are the only options; the tourist office (above) can help you locate those.

Hotel Vicko/Villa Vicko 🐟🐟   The luxury you'll find at this small family-run hotel near the tourist office seems almost incongruous against the rugged wildness of Paklenica, but the Vicko is a nice place to stay whether you're seeing the park or not. Hotel guest rooms are roomy and bathrooms are up-to-date thanks to a 2004 renovation. Accommodations in the Villa Vicko annex on the beach, which opened in 2004, are even more plush.

Jose Dokoze 20, 23244 Starigrad Paklenica. 📞 023/369-304. Fax 023/359-191. www.hotel-vicko.hr. In the hotel: from 73€ ($87) double with balcony; in villa: 75€ ($89). AE, DC, MC, V. Rates include breakfast. Half- and full board available with 7-day stay. Parking. **Amenities:** Restaurant; cafe/bar; room for those w/limited mobility. In room: A/C, TV, Internet access.

Hotel Alan 🐟   This hotel is a regular stop for organized tours, but the guest rooms are better than adequate after a 2003 renovation, and they are less than a mile from the park entrance. The hotel also has a surprising array of amenities like tennis courts, an outdoor pool, and children's programs, and it is just half a football field away from the Starigrad town beach.

Franje Tuđmana 14, 23244 Starigrad Paklenica. 📞 023/369-236. Fax 023/369-203. www.hotel-alan.hr. 115 units. From 89€ ($106) double; from 134€ ($160) apt. Rates include breakfast. Half-board available. AE, DC, MC, V. Parking. **Amenities:** Restaurant; pizzeria; bistro; bar; outdoor pool; sauna; elevator; room for those w/limited mobility. In room: A/C, TV, minibar (fee), hair dryer.

WHERE TO DINE

The Alan and Vicko hotels above both have good restaurants and there are lots of pizzerias and grill places throughout Starigrad and along the road leading to it. In addition, there are several markets and bakeries where you can stock up on sandwich makings and bottled water. In Nin, there are several cafes and grill restaurants near Donji Most and a few others on the main square, but the restaurant below is the best place in town.

Konoba Branimir 🐟🐟 CROATIAN   This ambitious restaurant is right behind the Holy Cross Church. The restaurant's architecture was cleverly designed to blend right in with the 9th-century church and the ruins in front, so its rustic look is an illusion. There are a bar and a huge peka in back of the restaurant for roasting lambs and suckling pigs; if you happen along when a roast is in progress, you won't be able to resist taking a table on the lovely stone terrace. Besides the usual grilled meat, the menu lists chicken breasts stuffed with bitter lettuce and bits of melon, and several special dishes like grilled lamb or *tingul* (turkey stew with prunes and potatoes) that have to be ordered 24 hours ahead. Luckily, the restaurant will prepare the roasted specials for even just one person, so it's worth a call if you can plan that far ahead.

Viseslavov Trg 2, Nin. 📞 023/264-866. Entrees 50kn–300kn ($9–$52). MC. Daily 8am–1am.

7 Biograd na moru

Biograd na moru translates to "Biograd on the sea." Located about half an hour's drive southeast of Zadar, it's a huge resort town catering to families. In medieval times, Biograd was home to many aristocrats, but in the early 12th century (1115-1125), the city was taken over and destroyed by the Venetians and again by the Turks in the mid–17th century. There isn't much left that's older than 18th century except its magnificent waterfront location. In the summer of 2007 Biograd na moru was a real garden spot thanks to its entry in the "Golden Flower of Europe" competition, which rewards towns for their use of flowers and landscaping. The town's efforts were not in vain: Biograd placed second and the gorgeous plantings will be around for years to come.

WHAT TO SEE & DO

As a seaside resort, Biograd has impeccable credentials. And Biograd's position near the **Kornati Island,** the **Velebit Paklenica, Krka National Park,** and the historical cities of **Zadar, Šibenik,** and **Nin** makes it a good choice as a base for exploring the immediate area. Kornati excursions can be booked on the waterfront from several providers. Most excursions go from 8:30am to 5:30pm and cost 150kn ($30) per person. For those who want to stay put in Biograd, the Riva offers nightly possibilities ranging from kiosks selling souvenirs, ice cream, and candy to electric go-carts to entertainment to seaside tables meant for conversation. There is a tram that takes visitors on a quick tour and to hotels along the waterfront. Cost is 10kn ($4) for adults and 10kn ($2) for children.

WHERE TO STAY AND DINE

Hotel Villa Donat 🏵🏵 *Finds* Donat, formerly the Hotel Mayica, is actually a hotel and an adjacent dependence. It was newly renovated and landscaped for the 2007 summer and the result is a couple of long 3-story (no elevator) buildings painted deep salmon to show off the masses of lavender and greenery planted all around them. Donat is walking distance to the beach but it is in Sv. Filip I Jakov, 4km (2.5 miles) from Biograd proper, so if you stay at the Donat, you have the best of two resort towns at your disposal. Rooms are nice size and showers are outfitted with sleek Italian fixtures.

Liburnska 1. Sv. Filip I Jakov. ✆ 023/383-556. Fax 023/383-008. www.ilirijabiograd.com. 72 units. Doubles in the Villa from 150€ ($210); doubles in the dependence from 100€ ($140). Rates include buffet breakfast. Half-board available. **Amenities:** Restaurant; bar; volleyball court; pets allowed for 10€ ($14) per day. *In room:* A/C, SAT/TV, minibar, hair dryer. May-Sept.

Ilirija Hotels 🏵 The Donat (above) is part of the Ilirija d.d hotel group, which includes several larger, package hotels in Biograd proper. The Adriatic, Ilirija, and Kornati hotels have different exterior looks, but rooms, prices, and facilities are exactly the same. These hotels have been updated in the last 5 years, but their renovations can't disguise that they were built and designed for family getaways during Croatia's socialist era. The Adriatic is open all year, while the Kornati is open from April to October, and the Ilirija from mid-March to December.

Tina Ulevića 7. ✆ 023/358-333. Fax 023/383-008. www.ilirijabiograd.com. 364 total units. Doubles with sea view from 130€ ($182). Rates include breakfast. AE, DC, MC, V. **Amenities:** Restaurants; bars; indoor pool; outdoor pool; parking; pets allowed. *In room:* A/C, SAT/TV, minibar, hair dryer.

Restaurant Marina Kornati 🏵🏵 CROATIAN The contemporary design and sophisticated ambience of this lovely restaurant at the Biograd marina are the perfect setting for a special meal whether you are a yacht owner or day-tripper. Dark wood floors, subdued lighting, and a menu that features Croatian cuisine with an emphasis on Dalmatian specialties.

Marina Kornati, Šetalište Kneza Branimira 1. Biograd. (C) 023/384-505. Entrees 60kn–140kn ($11–$26). More for fish sold by the kilo. AE, DC, MC, V. Daily 7am–midnight.

Restaurant Aquarium 𝒢 DALMATIAN   Watch the evening promenade and boats docking in the harbor from your table at this waterfront terrace restaurant. Fish fresh from the Adriatic is the specialty of the house and it's wonderful with a side of grilled veggies. Menus are printed in 4 languages in this tourist restaurant with very casual, family friendly ambience.

Krešemira IV 10. (C) 023/383-883. Entrees 50kn–110kn ($10–$21), more for fish sold by the kilo. No credit cards. Daily 8am–11pm Apr-Oct.

Lavender Bed Bar 𝒢𝒢 COCKTAILS   This bar on the terrace of the color coordinated Adriatic Hotel really does use beds as seats and they really are lavender. You can pretend you're in ancient Rome while sipping cocktails and listening to music among the trees at night or you can visit during the day and use the beds as a base for gazing at the sea.

Tina Ujevića 7. (C) 023/290-700. Fax 023/383-008. www.ilirijbiograd.com. Daily 8am–1am.

8 Kornati National Park

Kornati National Park is part of a group of nearly 150 mostly uninhabited islands south of Pašman and Dugi Otok. The park's 89 islands, islets, and reefs are scattered across an area of about 78 sq. km (30 sq. miles) of land and 207 sq. km (80 sq. miles) of sea. Kornati's unusual landscape of mostly barren, irregular karst terrain is a submerged mountain range; the visible parts actually are ancient mountaintops and valleys that now are islands and channels. Less than a quarter of the Kornati area is land, while the rest of the park is under the sea, and the park's underwater landscape is perhaps its most fascinating feature. Kornati's undersea world is renowned as a diver's paradise with unusual rock formations where many species of fish and plant life thrive. Both scuba divers and snorkelers will enjoy Kornati, but scuba enthusiasts must be part of a group approved by the National Park if they want to explore any of the seven zones set aside for diving visits.

If you'd rather stay on land, don't miss the Kornati "crowns," steep island cliffs that face the sea, a result of a rift caused by a continental collision millions of years ago.

The island of Kornat is the largest of the park's islands and the site of the 6th-century fortress of Toreta, an excellent example of Byzantine architecture. The precise history of Toreta is not known, but it's probably safe to assume that the fortress was built to protect navigation on the Adriatic. Near the fortress, you can also see the remains of an early Christian three-nave church from the same period.

The islands were sold in the 19th century to the people of Murter by the Zadar aristocrats who owned them. Today the inhabitants of Murter own 90% of the land, and use it to raise sheep or to grow olives and other crops suited to its rocky soil.

There are no permanent residents on the Kornati islands, but some do have houses that they use when tending sheep or taking care of their crops. It is possible to stay on Kornati if you stay with one of the families who have cottages there. To stay with a Kornati family, make arrangements with any tourist agency in Murter. Kornati also has 16 bays with mooring areas designated for boaters who want to drop anchor overnight.

ESSENTIALS

VISITOR INFORMATION For information on visiting Kornati National Park, contact the Kornati National Park office at Butina 2, Murter (℗ **022/434-662;** www. kornati.hr). The park office can direct you to approved dive escorts. The tourist office can direct you to private agencies approved to run individual tours and accommodations on Kornati.

GETTING THERE There is no ferry service between the Kornati Islands and the mainland, and the only way to get there is by boat. You'll have more travel flexibility if you have your own boat, but you can't dive unless you are with an approved dive group. You can book excursions to the islands from Zadar, Šibenik, or Split. You can arrange for private boat tours and accommodations at the travel agencies on Murter.

9 Šibenik

Šibenik is a former industrial port town that has fallen on hard times since the 1991 war and still is suffering from the subsequent economic woes. However, as coastal towns go, Šibenik offers a change of pace from Dalmatia's strong Italianate influences since its origins are pure Croatian rather than Roman.

Situated on a broad bay at the mouth of the Krka River, Šibenik's footprint is sometimes likened to an amphitheater as it hugs the slopes that emanate from St. Anne's Fortress, a sprawl that began shortly after the city was first mentioned in Croatian historical writings in 1066. Today, much of Šibenik's charm comes from the warren of steep, winding streets and passages, the many sets of stone steps leading up to the center, and the ruins of city fortifications that fan out from St. Anne's to the water. Above the harbor, Šibenik's center is crowded with churches and monasteries as well as stone dwellings on narrow, covered streets that open to a series of interior town squares.

The Cathedral of St. Jacob, the city's most prominent attraction, was added to the UNESCO World Heritage List in 2000. St. Jacob is a must-see for anyone who comes to town, including a large number of upscale tourists who berth their yachts overnight in Šibenik's harbor. Indeed, the city is a favorite port of call for yachts touring the eastern Adriatic and the Kornati National Park. The city also is within easy access of Krka National Park, a region in the Dinaric Alps with karst and waterfalls similar to those of Plitvice, though Krka has the bonus of ruins from medieval fortified cities.

Immediately offshore, Šibenik has an archipelago of its own, a group of small islands with picturesque coves, blue Croatian sea, idyllic beaches, and few inhabitants. Two of them, Zlarin and Prvić, once were summer havens for Croatian writers, who retreated there to find their muses. Zlarin is known for its coral, while Kaprije and Žirje are centers for grape growers, olive growers, and fishermen. The islands are linked to Šibenik by ferries on regular runs to the Vodice resort area north of town.

ESSENTIALS

VISITOR INFORMATION The city's tourist information bureau is at Fausta Vrančića 18 (℗ **022/212-075**). It can provide maps, brochures, and basic information about Šibenik and neighboring sites. However, excursions to Kornati and nearby islands are booked through private agencies such as Atlas Travel on Trg Hrvatske 2 near the cathedral (℗ **022/330-232;** www.atlassibenik.com); or by Mag Tours at Franje Tuđmana 2a (℗ **022/201-150**). It's a good idea to call ahead to find out which tours are offered, and when. For example, Atlas's Kornati tours leave just three times a week (Sun, Mon, and Thurs) and if you aren't in town that day, you miss the tour.

Rest in Peace

The tiny farming village of Otavice west of Šibenik in the Dalmatian interior is the site of a magnificent church/mausoleum designed and built by Croatian sculptor Ivan Meštrović to serve as his family crypt.The road to Otavice from Šibenik is clearly marked, but this is land that was occupied by Serb forces during the Homeland War. If you venture here, you will pass through the town of Drniš where there is a museum displaying several Meštrovic works. You also will see quiet, pastoral landscapes, some marred by crumblng homes that sustained war damage. Occasionally, you may spot a "Go no farther" land mine warning off-road. The Meštrović family mausoleum sits on a high hill overlooking the valley and the home the artist built for his mother in the 1930s-era town. At the moment it is in ruins. During the Homeland War, Serb forces desecrated the crypt beneath the little chapel in the mausoleum on the hill and stole Meštrović reliefs of his wife and children that served as decorative panels on the mausoleum door. Today a lone caretaker keeps the mausoleum presentable—and open—for tourists.

Atlas also runs bus tours to Krka National Park (Tues, Wed, Fri) and other regional sites.

GETTING THERE   There is decent bus and train service to Šibenik from larger cities in Croatia as well as from select international locations. The bus station is on the seafront at Draga bb. The train station is south of the bus station at Milete bb. They are just 5- and 10-minute walks from the Jadran Hotel, respectively.

GETTING AROUND   Driving in Šibenik is a nightmare. There is street parking on the waterfront, and the Jadran has a private lot, but the tangle of narrow streets that serve the outer town is almost always jammed with cars. In addition, the town core is pedestrian-only. You must climb long, fairly steep staircase steps to get there, and the streets themselves can be difficult to navigate because of their incline.

WHAT TO SEE & DO

Šibenik isn't positioned as a vacation destination, but it can provide a nice sojourn from the rigors of a trip through Croatia. Its marquee attraction is the Cathedral of St. Jacob and the quirky town center, but there are several beaches and two national parks within easy reach, too.

Cathedral of St. Jacob 🐸🐸🐸   This Gothic-Renaissance church took more than a century to build between 1431 and 1536 because of its complex design and emphasis on craftsmanship. The Venetians initiated the project, but architect Juraj Dalmatinac (who designed Pag Town on Pag Island) is recognized as the principal designer. Dalmatinac worked on the project for more than 30 years, but died in 1473 before it was finished. In the end, one of Dalmatinac's protégés, Nikola Fiorentinac, supervised the rest of the project, including construction of the exterior's unique stone masonry, which consists of interlocking stone slabs and bricks custom-fit without mortar. Inside, the cathedral's walls and furnishings are richly embellished with intricate carvings and sculpture, as is the baptistry. The cathedral is a blend of styles and features

Krka National Park ✦✦✦

Waterfalls, gorges, and traces of ancient settlements along the Krka River are some of the attractions at this national park less than 16km (10 miles) outside of Šibenik. Krka was proclaimed a national park in 1985. You can tour as much or as little of the park as you like via boat, car, or shoe leather. All public roads marked on the park map are open to cars, except for pedestrian areas of Skradinski buk and Visovac Island and its monastery, which are accessible only by bus and the Krka National Park boats.

Like the falls at Plitvice, the falls at Krka were formed from deposits of limestone sediment (travertine). But Krka's are considered more dramatic. In fact, Skradinski Buk is considered one of the best falls in Europe as it tumbles from 46m (150 ft.) over 17 distinct travertine deposits.

Krka National Park begins at the Šibenik bridge and continues to Knin. Road signs along the way are numerous and clear, marking all the park entrances. Each entry point has a parking lot (free), an information office, and a ticket office (60kn/$11 adults, 45kn/$8 children in July and Aug). Like Plitvice, boats connect several parts of the park (Skradin and the Skradinski buk waterfalls, for example). Boats also take visitors to the 15th-century Franciscan monastery on an island in the middle of Visovac Lake.

Krka National Park Tourism Office is at Trg Ivana Pavla II, b.r. 5, p.p. 154, 22001 Šibenik ((© **022/217-730**; fax 022/336-836; www.npkrka.hr). Hours are 8am to 8pm all year.

incorporated into the design by each of the architects who worked on the project. Dalmatinac, however, is credited as the plan's visionary. Among St. Jacob's best features is a whimsical frieze of 74 faces that festoons the outer walls. Legend says that these sculptures—which are almost caricatures set in stone—were created to take a jab at penurious citizens who refused to give their fair share toward the building of the cathedral, which is now on the UNESCO World Heritage List.

Trg Republike Hrvatske. Daily 9am–7pm.

Bunari Secrets of Šibenik ✦✦✦   This award-winning exhibit is built around four 15th-century *bunara* water storage tanks about 46m (150 ft.) from magnificent St. Jacob's Cathedral. Inside, two floors of sequentially arranged exhibits trace the city's history in words, photos, and even film. All are numbered so visitors can follow the displays in a specific order using a timeline that traces the city's evolution from its origins to the present day. The self-guided tour of explaining Šibenik's culture, development, and famous native sons ends at a coffeehouse on the bottom level, where you can ruminate about what you've just seen.

Palih Omladinaca 2. (© **098/341-175**. Admission 30kn ($5) adults, 20kn ($3.50) children 7–14. Daily 10am–11pm. June–Sept, entrance through main door. Other times, entrance through cafe downstairs.

St. Anne's Fortress ✦   As castles go, this one is all show and little substance. St. Anne's is more impressive from afar than it is close up, but it is a great place to get a view of the city, the remains of Šibenik's walls, and the sea beyond. However, its interior has fallen to ruin, and there isn't much to see inside.

Note: This is a quite a hike, and it is really only worth it for the panoramic view of the Old Town.

Above (northeast of) the Old Town.

WHERE TO STAY

Accommodations in the Šibenik area are mostly in big resort settlements north and south of the city with a few small hotels and lots of private accommodations in between. There is just one hotel in Šibenik itself.

Hotel Jadran   The marina near St. Jacob's Cathedral is its front yard; it's convenient to most of the city's attractions; and it's the only game in the town core. This old-style package hotel is dowdy and overpriced. If you do stay here, ask for a room on the sea to take advantage of the breeze. The guest rooms are not air-conditioned. If you get one of the small rooms at the hotel's back, you'll be close enough to neighboring buildings to see what's for dinner, and you won't get any air even if the window is wide-open. However, if you're at the front of the hotel and keep your window open, you'll be an accidental audience for the live music on the terrace, and you'll be able to keep an eye on the folks in their luxury yachts moored out front.

Obala Dr. Franje Tuđmana 52. Šibenik. ℭ 022/212-644. Fax 022/212-480. www.rivijera.hr. 57 units. July–Aug: from 93€ ($130) double; from 132€ ($185) suite. Rest of year: from 77€ ($108) double; from 106€ ($150) suite. Rates include breakfast. AE, DC, MC, V. Half- and full-board rates available. **Amenities:** Restaurant; terrace; bar. *In room:* TV, minibar (some rooms).

Solaris Holiday Resort 𝒜𝒜   Five separate hotels comprise this huge development 4km (2½ miles) southwest of Šibenik that collectively can accommodate more that 3,000 guests at once. To be sure, the hotels are designed for families and tour groups who need value for their kunas, but they also are an ideal base for exploring Šibenik and nearby Krka National Park. The complex also has a spa where you can de-stress tired feet after hiking around the Krka waterfalls. Most rooms are the same compact, no-nonsense dorm style, but the Ivan and Niko were updated most recently (2005) and are the freshest.

Hotel Ivan: Hotelsko naselje Solaris bb, 22000 Šibenik. ℭ 022/361-001. Fax 022/361-801. www.solaris.hr. 335 units, 12 apts. Aug: from 113€ ($158) double; 104€ ($145) apt. Rest of year: from 56€ ($78) double; from 62€ ($87) suite. AE, DC, MC, V. Rates include breakfast and are based on stays of 4 days or more. Free parking. **Amenities:** 2 restaurants; pizzeria; bar; 2 pools; 2 tennis courts; bowling alley; minigolf; ATM. *In room:* A/C, TV, minibar, hair dryer. **Hotel Niko:** Hotelsko naselje Solaris bb, 22000 Šibenik. ℭ 022/361-001. Fax 022/361-801. www.solaris.hr. 218 units, 2 apts, all with shower only. Aug: from 82€ ($115) double; from 88€ ($123) suite. Rest of year: from 46€ ($65) double; from 37€ ($52) suite. All rooms have balconies. Rates include breakfast. Half- and full board available. Rates based on stays of 4 days or longer. AE, DC, MC, V. Free parking. **Amenities:** Restaurant; bar; seawater pool. *In room:* A/C, TV, hair dryer.

Hotel Imperial 𝒜   The Imperial is a huge hotel complex with a pebble beach in the resort town of Vodice, less than 16km (10 miles) north of Šibenik. It is within easy reach of Krka National Park and the Kornati Islands. Only 170 rooms and 15 suites of its more than 400 units are in the main building, so if convenience is a concern, ask for one of these. The others are in annexes/villas. Only some of the rooms are air-conditioned; you should request one when booking.

Vladimira Nazora 53, Vodice. ℭ 022/454-437. Fax 022/442-611. www.rivijera.hr. 423 units, 12 apts. Aug: from 140€ ($196) double with A/C; 20% supplement for suite. Rest of year: from 70€ ($84) double; 10% supplement for suite. AE, DC, MC, V. **Amenities:** Restaurant; bar; indoor heated seawater pool; access to outdoor pool; diving school; children's program; excursions. *In room:* TV, phone.

Hotel Miran Pirovac ⚐ The Miran is a medium-size hotel in the cute seaside village of Pirovac about 6km (4 miles) north of Vodice and 23km (14 miles) from Šibenik. It is at the center of a complex that includes an autocamp and villas done in traditional Dalmatian architecture.

Zagregačka bb, Pirovac. ⓒ 022/466-803. Fax 022/467-022. www.rivijera.hr. 99 units. High season: from 124€ ($174) seaside double with balcony. Rest of year: from 70€ ($98) seaside double with balcony. Rates include breakfast. AE, MC, V. Half- and full board available. Rates are based on stays of 4 days or more. **Amenities:** Restaurant; snack bar; wine cellar; excursions. *In room:* TV, phone.

WHERE TO DINE

Like most of Dalmatia, Šibenik and the surrounding area are full of pizzerias and simple grill restaurants where you can get excellent grilled fish and pastas. If you want a dramatic setting, walk north from the ferry terminal to the Dolac area, which has become a kind of neighborhood food/entertainment court with numerous restaurants, cafes, and bars, many with live music.

Gradska Vijećnica ⚐⚐ DALMATIAN Its name means "City Hall" and it has made Croatia's largest newspaper's "100 Best Restaurants" list. The "best restaurant in Šibenik" is situated in the loggia (first floor of the old town hall) on the north side of Trg Republike Hrvatska, across from St. Jacob's Cathedral. Vijećnica is the picture of elegance thanks to its loggia setting and an abundance of woodwork inside. The menu is pure Dalmatia, with lots of grilled fish and a few Italian-inspired pasta dishes. Try the peppers stuffed with cheese or the very generous portion of super-big scampi while you enjoy the pure, languid, Venetian ambience at tables that spill onto the square.

Trg Republike Hrvatska 1. ⓒ 022/213-605. Entrees 40kn–110kn ($7–$19). AE, DC, MC, V. Daily 9am–1am.

Hotel Restaurant Jadran ⚐ DALMATIAN The menu appears to be geared to tourists and is filled with the usual grilled meat and fish typical of coastal restaurants (though some pastas and omelets are available), but the expansive terrace that overlooks Šibenik's busy marina is a delight. *Note:* Jadran can be noisy when live music plays on the terrace.

Obala Dr. Franje Tuđmana 52. ⓒ 022/212-644. Fax 022/212-480. www.rivijera.hr. Entrees 30kn–80kn ($5–$14). AE, DC, MC, V. Traditional Croatian menu of meat and grilled fish. Some pasta and omelets available. Daily 7am–11pm.

Tinel ⚐⚐ SEAFOOD This unusual multistory restaurant stresses whimsy and originality in the decor, but the ingredients—and many preparations—are unadulterated Dalmatia. Fish dominates, but options include lamb and baked dishes. Try the *brodet* (fish stew) and match it with a local wine from the restaurant's nicely balanced cellar.

Trg Pučkih Kapetana 1. ⓒ 022/331-815. Entrees 65kn–120kn ($11–$22). AE, DC, MC, V. Daily 10am–11pm.

10 Primošten

Primošten is actually an island, but you hardly notice that because it is linked to the mainland by a tiny causeway built in the 16th century. What you do notice about this island shaped like a fish is the laid-back atmosphere, impossibly clear turquoise water, and excellent beaches backed by pine trees. Primošten truly has something for everyone, with its block of clay tennis courts, watersports, and 15th-century church (rebuilt in the 18th c.) overlooking the sea from its hilltop perch. Primošten is just 19km (12 miles) south of Šibenik and 29km (18 miles) west of Trogir, a kind of middle ground for tourists who want to take a beach break from tracing Croatian history, if only for a day.

ESSENTIALS

VISITOR INFORMATION   Primošten's **tourist office** is at Rudina biskupa Josipa Arnerića 2 (© **022/571-111;** www.summernet.hr/primosten). It's open from 8am to 10pm daily during July and August; from 8am to 9pm during June, September, and October; and from 8am to 2pm Monday to Friday other times of the year. The office (which has the town's only Internet connection) can provide maps and information about Primošten and the surrounding area. For private accommodations, visit tourist agencies like **Nik Agency** at Raduča 2 (© **022/571-200**). Nik is open daily from 8am to 10pm and can link you with available rooms and apartments in the area.

GETTING THERE   Intra-city buses (from Split and Šibenik) serve Primošten. The bus station is just a short walk from the tourist office at the entrance to the Old Town. For schedules and fares, contact the local torist office listed above.

GETTING AROUND   The beach area is bordered by a long walkway that has restaurants and shops on one side, and tables and chairs on the other. It's not far to the town center, where walking is the most efficient way to get around and the only way to get to the top of the hill to see St. George's (Sv. Juraj) Church. *Note:* The climb to this church is a steep, terraced one, though it is lined with restaurants and other stopping points.

WHAT TO SEE & DO

Watersports rule in Primošten, and the long pebble beach is well served by food kiosks and lots of activities like swimming, water-skiing, parasailing, jet-skiing, and banana-boat rides. On shore, you can play soccer or reserve time on the red clay tennis courts for a fee (© **091/761-247**).

Up from the beach you'll find lots of jewelry stores and restaurants, but you can also hike up Ulica Svetog Jurja to Sv. Juraj Church at the top of the hill. The aromas floating from the restaurants along the way up to the church will make you salivate, so by the time you walk down, you'll be ready for a meal. There is nothing notable about the church, but it does have an interesting little graveyard with elaborate tombstones and shrines and a fabulous view of the sea and coast.

These days Primošten is known for its Babić wine, a nice red made from grapes grown in nearby vineyards, which are visible as you drive along the coast. There are a couple of places in town where you can buy Babić by the liter straight from the vat; the women selling it will offer you a taste and fill an empty water bottle with the deep red liquid for about 30kn ($5).

WHERE TO STAY & DINE

Unless you fall in love with Primošten's beach, there is not much of interest that will keep you in town overnight. However, if you want to spend more than a few hours, there are plenty of private rooms, a huge hotel, and lots of restaurants.

Hotel Zora 🛋   Almost every single room in this 800-bed behemoth has a balcony view of the sea and beach, which is lovely, and the hotel stretches the length of the peninsula followed by a pine forest. Guest rooms are standard issue and could use freshening even though most of the hotel was renovated in 1996 and others even more recently. Some guest rooms are air-conditioned, but only from 5pm to 1am in July and August.

Raduča bb. ✆ 022/581-111. Fax 022/571-161. www.primosten-hoteli.hr. 360 units. Late July to late Aug: from 700kn ($130) double. Rest of year: from 400kn ($74) double. Rates include breakfast. A 20% surcharge is added for stays of less than 4 days. Half- and full board available. AE, DC, MC, V. **Amenities:** Restaurant; bar; tavern; cake shop; pizzeria; bowling alley. *In room:* A/C (see above), TV, hair dryer.

Konoba Antonija ★★ SEAFOOD   Antonija's menu is basic, with the expected Italian influence and a large complement of seafood dishes. The restaurant has a nice dining room and tables in a walled garden setting, but during the day almost everyone sits at the big umbrella tables under the trees so he or she can have a view of the water. Try the famous Primošten spiny lobster, the town's signature dish.

Mala Raduča 2. ✆ 022/570-371. Entrees 40kn–140kn ($8–$26). No credit cards. Daily 8am–midnight.

Restaurant Kamenar ★★   This restaurant opposite the tourist office has a menu translated in four languages as well as a nice terrace that has a good view of the city's foot traffic. Inside, the walls are stone and the tablecloths real linen, which might signal stuffy formality, but the atmosphere is quite the opposite. While from the outside Kamenar appears to be the typical tourist trap, inside the offerings go way beyond the ordinary. There is grilled tuna, but there is also tuna in green-pepper sauce. Kamenar doubles as a pension for those who want breakfast.

Rudina bis J. Američa 5. ✆ 022/570-889. www.crodirect.com/kamenar. Entrees 45kn–100kn ($8–$19). AE, DC, MC, V. Daily 8am–midnight.

11 Trogir

Trogir is the stuff of fairy tales and one of the most enchanting towns on the Adriatic coast, bar none. It was founded in the 3rd century B.C. by the Greeks of Issa (Vis), occupied by the Romans, and escaped destruction by invading Slavs in the 7th century. Trogir prospered and eventually became part of the Venetian fold, where it remained until Austria took over in 1797. Today's Trogir is a jewel in Croatia's crown with its postcard-perfect profile, its well-preserved stonework, and its excellent tourism infrastructure. In fact, Trogir's unique architecture, decorative stonework, and the medieval character of Old Town prompted UNESCO to add the entire town to its World Heritage List in 1997.

Trogir's **historic center** ★★★ is actually on an islet on part of Kaštela Bay that flows between the mainland and the island of Čiovo, which was a settlement in prehistoric times, a place of political exile in Roman times, a pariah in the Middle Ages when it served as a leper colony, and now home to a cluster of communities best described as suburbs. Čiovo is connected to Trogir by a bridge and resembles a series of bedroom communities in the middle of a housing boom with closely packed pensions, summer homes, and permanent residences in various stages of construction scattered along the shoreline and in the hills.

But it is Old Town Trogir itself that is the area's most intriguing site and also the source of Trogir's greatest treasures. Almost all houses and other structures in the Old Town are emblazoned with stonework that hint at the past by depicting a coat of arms or some other family symbol over doorways or windows on the buildings, some of which are more than 700 years old. Ambling through the town's narrow streets or promenading along the waterfront is almost like walking back in time. And at night, the Riva comes alive with vendors selling everything from candy by the kilo to laven-der oil. There is also street entertainment in the forms of fire-baton twirlers, mimes, and impromptu singing groups. On the mainland, the city market and other sellers stay open until midnight to give you one more chance to buy something before you leave.

ESSENTIALS

VISITOR INFORMATION   Trogir's **tourist office** on the main square at Trg Ivana Pavla II/I (✆ **021/885-628;** fax 021/881-412; www.dalmacija.net/trogir.htm; 8am–9pm June–Sept and 8am–2pm other times) is a gold mine of information. The office can provide you with maps, brochures, and even restaurant recommendations. The staff will give you a short course on the city if they aren't too busy. **Vila Sikaa Travel Agency,** across the strait on Čiovo at Obala Kralja Zvonimira 13 (✆ **021/881-223;** fax 021/885-149; www.sikaa-travel.com), is a full-service agency on the first floor of the Vila Sikaa Hotel. This agency does it all—excursions, private accommodations, boats, cars, and scooters—and it even serves breakfast. **Atlas Travel Agency** at Obala Kralja Zvonimira 10 (✆ **021/881-374;** fax 021/884-744) is the place to go for raft-ing excursions, fish picnics, and trips to Brač and Hvar and beyond.

GETTING THERE   The bus station is just outside the city gate next to the outdoor market and across the street from the local Konzum supermarket. Buses between Split and Trogir run about every half-hour; others that travel between Split and Šibenik stop here as well. In addition, at a little over a mile from Trogir, Split's airport is closer to the island city than it is to Split. See "Getting There" in the section on Split (p. 83).

GETTING AROUND   Trogir's core is a pedestrian zone, so walking is the only option. If you stay outside town, there is a local bus system and a few taxis.

WHAT TO SEE & DO

Trogir can best be characterized as a happy city. Walking along the water, you'll feel positive energy flowing through this delightful town, which has just about every-thing—beaches, harbor, historic town, nice restaurants, comfortable accommoda-tions—that any tourist could want.

Kamerlengo Castle & St. Mark's Tower 🕀🕀🕀   The Kula fortress of Kamerlengo (Fortress Sv. Marko) was built in the mid–15th century by Marin Radoj as part of an expansion of the Veriga Tower, built on the site in the late 14th century. As part of the defense system, the fortress was surrounded by a ditch filled with sand; inside the walls were a well and other structures for withstanding long sieges. St. Mark's Tower on the north end of the fortress was built shortly after the castle in typical Renaissance style and its roof once was ringed with guns at the ready to repel invaders. Kamerlengo began to deteriorate at the end of the 19th century and was renovated after World War II. Today the castle's interior courtyard is used as a summer stage and open-air cinema. Tourists can climb to the top of the tower and enjoy the view during the day and also at night when no movie is showing.

Kaštel Kamerlengo. Admission 10kn ($2). Daily 9am–10pm.

Land Gate 🕀🕀   This city gate is adorned with St. Mark's lion and a statue of the town's patron saint, John of Trogir. The Renaissance-style portal was built after the city walls (15th c.) and renovated in the 17th. It is one of the ancient city's busiest points of entry.

Southwest corner of the islet on the Riva.

Cathedral of St. Lawrence 🌟🌟🌟   Like many churches in Dalmatia, the Cathedral of St. Lawrence is built on the site of an earlier church that was destroyed by medieval invaders. Construction on the current church building began in the late 12th century, but it wasn't completed for decades and it is done in a variety of styles (Romanesque, Gothic, Mannerist) that reflect the ages. The triple-nave St. Lawrence is one of Trogir's singular buildings and one of its best examples of medieval architecture. Inside, the Chapel of St. John is the cathedral's principal feature; numerous statues in a tableau-like scene include the coffin of St. John of Trogir. The chapel was built by Nikola Fiorentinac, the same architect who continued the work on Šibenik's Cathedral of St. Jacob after the death of its principal designer and his patron, Juraj Dalmatinac.

Trg Ivana Pavla II. ☎ 021/881-426. Daily 8am–noon and 4:30–7pm.

Clock Tower & Loggia 🌟🌟   The 15th-century Loggia on Trg Ivana Pavla II probably was used as a courtroom where town trials were held in Renaissance times. The walls behind the judge's table are decorated with a 1471 relief portraying Justice done by the prolific Nikola Fiorentinac; another has a 1950s relief by the equally prolific Ivan Meštrović. The clock tower once was part of the Church of St. Sebastian.

Trg Ivana Pavla II.

Čipiko Palace 🌟   During the 15th century, Čipiko Palace was home to Trogir's most prominent family. Today its architecture and furnishings are what draw visitors, who also marvel at an intricately carved Venetian-Gothic triple window here.

Trg Ivana Pavla II.

Church of St. Dominic 🌟   Nikola Fiorentinac was a busy man in Trogir: Besides working on the Cathedral of St. Lawrence, he updated the single-nave 14th-century Romanesque-Gothic church and monastery in Renaissance style in the 15th century.

Obala Bana Berislavića. Summer only; daily 8am–noon and 4–7pm.

WHERE TO STAY

There is no shortage of accommodations in the Trogir "metro" area, though there are few rooms on the island itself. You may need to cross the bridge to Čiovo to find a place to stay.

Villa Meri 🌟🌟 *Finds*   Statues and pictures of St. Anthony abound in this tiny, comfy inn in Trogir's center because its owner, who also runs the Don Dino restaurant 🌟🌟, is a woman who reveres the saint. Meri even opened on the saint's feast day (June 15) in 2006 for good luck. So far, the luck is working. The inn is a family operation run by the owner's daughter and her husband. The couple has effected a transformation on the 7-room structure—from an elderly woman's home into a charming B&B with Old World charm and modern comforts like flatscreen TV. Staying at Villa Meri is like being an honored guest staying in a friend's home.

Splitska 1. ☎ 021/882-555. Fax 021/882-533. www.villa-meri.com. 7 units. Doubles from 120€ ($170). Rates include breakfast. AE, DC, MC, V. Closed Jan. **Amenities:** Restaurant. *In room:* A/C, SAT/TV, minibar, dial-up broadband, hair dryer.

Tragos 🌟🌟   Tragos was a palace in the 18th century, and there has been a Tragos restaurant 🌟🌟 at this location about 20 yards off Trogir's main square since 1972. In 2004, the nobleman's residence above it morphed into a cute hotel with an entrance on a narrow cobblestone street. Inside the hotel is cheery and bright with interior stone walls, lots of pine furniture, and brightly colored fabrics throughout. Each of Tragos's rooms is named after a Dalmatian town, and the staff of the family-run hotel couldn't be friendlier. *Tip:* Tragos gets a lot of repeat business and rooms are often booked a year in advance, so plan accordingly.

Budislavićeva 3. (C) **021/884-729.** www.tragos.hr. 12 units. Doubles from 110€ ($155). Rates include breakfast. AE, DC, MC, V. **Amenities:** Restaurant; room service; excursions; pets allowed. *In room:* A/C, minibar, Internet access, hair dryer.

Hotel Fontana 🐸   This waterfront hotel on Trogir Channel was renovated in 1999 to house a classy pension that has 13 rooms and one apartment. Three of the rooms and the apartment have Jacuzzis, and the rest have showers, so ask for the former for a real treat. Some of the guest rooms are a little tight, but each is different because of the building's historic status. The Fontana's location on the Riva is unbeatable.

Obrov 1. (C) **021/885-744.** Fax 021/885-755. www.Fontana-commerce.htnet.hr. 14 units. From 700kn ($121) double; from 1,000kn ($173) suite. Rates include breakfast. AE, MC, V. **Amenities:** Restaurant; bar; excursions. *In room:* A/C, TV, minibar, Jacuzzi. Suite has living room and kitchenette.

Vila Sikaa 🐸🐸   This tiny hotel in a renovated medieval house has a view of Trogir across the channel. It's only a short walk across the bridge to the UNESCO-protected city. The Sikaa is above the Vila Sikaa travel agency, which also rents scooters, so it can be noisy, but another tiny hotel is on the floor between them. Ask for a room with a view of the Old Town.

Obala Kralja Zvonimira 13, Čiovo. (C) **021/881-223.** Fax 021/885-149. www.vila-sikaa-r.com. 7 units. June 1–Sept 1: from 81€ ($97) double; from 108€ ($130) suite. Rest of year: from 68€ ($81) double; from 95€ ($113) suite. AE, DC, MC, V. **Amenities:** Restaurant; bar; room service; valet service; excursions. *In room:* A/C, TV, Internet access.

Vila Liza 🐸 *Value*   This budget entry into the Trogir hotel market has four rooms, a tiny terraced dining area, and a veranda. It's in the same building as the Vila Sikaa, sandwiched between the Sikaa and its travel agency. Rooms are surprisingly large, though furnishings are plain. Bathrooms have showers only, but they are adequate.

Kralja Zvonimira 1. (C) **021/884-690.** www.vila-liza.hr. 4 units. From 550kn ($95) double. Rate includes breakfast. AE, DC, MC, V. *In room:* A/C, TV, Internet access.

Hotel Concordia   The facade of this hotel in Trogir's core on the Riva is 300 years old and fits right in with the neighboring Kamerlengo fortress. The terraced hotel opened in 1995, however, and guest rooms, though simple, are much more contemporary than the outer walls. Most have a sea view and fit the needs of today's tourists better than the rooms of other hotels in Trogir. Because of its great location and modern facilities, the Concordia's guest rooms are in high demand, so reserve early.

Obala Bana Berislavića 22. (C) **021/885-400.** Fax 021/885-401. www.Concordia-hotel.htnet.hr. 14 units. From 600kn ($104) double. Rate includes breakfast. AE, MC, V. Parking. **Amenities:** Restaurant. *In room:* A/C, TV.

ApartHotel Bavaria 🐸🐸   Just 92m (300 ft.) from the beach in Donji Seget, 5 minutes by car from Trogir, and 29km (18 miles) from Split, the ApartHotel Bavaria is a good choice for those who want to be close to everything, but not on top of it. Rooms at the Bavaria range from singles to mini-suites with kitchenettes, but it's the sea views from the rooms with balconies decked with flower boxes that make this place special. Bathrooms are a decent size and well-appointed. The only drawback is the lack of an elevator for those with rooms on the third floor.

Hrvatskih Žrtava 133. 21220 Trogir-Seget Donji. ℂ **021/880-601.** Fax 021/880-553. www.hotel-bavaria.hr. 18 units. Late July through late Aug: from 100€ ($119) double with balcony; from 162€ ($193) suite. Rest of year: from 68€ ($81) double; from 104€ ($124) suite. Rates include breakfast. AE, DC, MC, V. Free parking. **Amenities:** Restaurant; bar. *In room:* A/C, TV.

WHERE TO DINE

Restaurants are plentiful in the Trogir area, though during the July-to-August tourist season, they can be crowded. Occasionally, area restaurants that usually take credit cards refuse to take them during this time, according to one waiter. Nonetheless, you won't go hungry here. *Tip:* For dessert or a sweet treat, head to the area around Gradska 16 in the center of town. It features a large block of tables surrounded by ice-cream shops.

Mirakul Pizzeria/Spaghetteria ⭐ *(Value* PIZZA   Pizzerias and Italian restaurants are easy to find in Trogir, which caters to Mediterranean tastes. This establishment in a narrow passage that cuts through the town's stone buildings is better than most. Enjoy scampi risotto or a thin, crusty pizza in this open-air spot off the Riva.

Gradska 7. ℂ **021/885-614.** Entrees 21kn–220kn ($4–$38). No credit cards. Daily 8am–midnight.

Fontana ⭐⭐ CROATIAN   The Fontana Hotel's restaurant in the shadow of St. Dominic Church is a classy, mostly alfresco watering hole on the Riva that offers rather pricey but excellent grilled fish, some pizzas, and a bit of attitude toward tourists. Outdoor tables are scattered among three terraces separated by potted palms and rosemary hedges; you can watch the Riva action while you dine. Black-suited waiters provide competent, slightly formal service but tell obvious foreigners (us) they must pay in cash during the season.

Trogir Obrov 1. ℂ **021/885-744.** Fax 021/885-755. www.htnet.hr/Fontana-commerce. Entrees 30kn–240kn ($5.50–$42). No credit cards in summer. Daily 7am–midnight.

Restaurant Kamerlengo ⭐⭐⭐ CROATIAN   Like a lot of Trogir's restaurants, Kamerlengo does most of its tourist business from an open-air site wedged between the walls of the city's ancient stone buildings. Kamerlengo has a nice inside dining room, too, and it is dominated by a huge wood-burning oven in the center of the room. Order grilled fish or meat here and you can't go wrong.

Vukovarska 2. ℂ **021/884-772.** www.trogir.com. Entrees 30kn–150kn ($5.50–$26). AE, DC, MC, V. Daily 10am–midnight or 1am from early July to end of Aug.

Don Dino ⭐⭐ DALMATIAN   Dalmatian specialties are the emphasis at this beautiful little restaurant in Trogir's center. The terrace is an especially nice setting for feasting on excellent grilled specialties and deftly prepared Italian choices such as seafood risotto and spaghetti carbonara. For a special treat, try Don Dino for breakfast, and order the ham omelet made with local pršut. Yummy. *Tip:* Try to book a room at the Villa Meri ⭐⭐ across the street. It's run by the restaurant owner's daughter and son-in-law.

Augustina Kažotica 8. ℂ **021/882-656.** www.dondino.hr. Entrees 60kn–170kn ($11–$30). AE, DC, MC, V. Daily 9am–1am.

Top Baloon Grill and Pizzeria ⭐ PIZZA   It's just another courtyard pizza joint, but this restaurant and its neighbor (below) really pack them in. Pizza, pasta, meat, fish, and salads offer diners a hefty list of choices. Try the Top Baloon pizza made with tomatoes, ham, mushrooms, bacon, pepperoni, and cream.

Obrov 7. ℂ **021/884-869.** Entrees 38kn–100kn ($6.50–$17). No credit cards. Daily 10am–midnight.

Jambo Bistro Pizzeria 🌟 *Value* PIZZA   At first glance there doesn't seem to be much difference between Jambo and its courtyard neighbors—until you look at the menu and see the prices. *Risotto con funghi* and pizza picante are among its offerings. Jambo's fare is similar to that of the restaurants that flank it, but it is a better bargain— one of the best in Trogir, in fact.

Obrov 6, 21220 Trogir. ✆ **021/885-630**. Mobile: 091/510-4924. Entrees 33kn–60kn ($6–$10). No credit cards. Daily 4pm–midnight.

7

The Kvarner Gulf

Experiencing the all the diverse charms of the Kvarner Gulf region requires a strategically orchestrated campaign. For example, some visitors to Opatija ensconce themselves in 19th-century villas, emerging to luxuriate in the sun and surf by day and then to promenade in their best resort wear or to dine and dance by moonlight. Others hop-scotch among Kvarner's many islands, where yachts from all over Europe dock in marinas that lie in the shadow of ancient buildings and reminders of Croatia's multicultural roots. Ecologically savvy tourists can explore Mount Učka, which looms over the Opatija Riviera and offers hikers the opportunity to wander among its wonders for hours. Others prefer the rocky hills of Cres Island, where rugged paths dotted with grazing sheep run a dizzying course to deserted azure coves.

It's fairly simple to visit all the major mainland towns that dot the Kvarner coast by driving the coastal highway from Opatija to Senj, but it's much trickier to coordinate ferry connections to, from, and between the islands. Indeed, except for the facilities along the Opatija Riviera, the region's tourism infrastructure is uneven at best though tourism services on the offshore islands are improving. Visitors to the mainland can expect a huge range of accommodations and services, while visitors to the islands will find large package-hotel complexes, a respectable variety of campgrounds (including many naturist colonies) and modest-size, family-run hotels, usually within old homes or simple villas.

1 Crikvenica

Croatians sometimes refer to Crikvenica as the "poor man's Opatija." Like the glitzy strip of real estate that skirts Kvarner Bay, Crikvenica is a resort town and has been since the late 19th century when the town was developed. Since then, Crikvenica has become a comfortable weekend getaway for folks who live in Rijeka and central Croatia. They stay in the town's post WWII hotels and apartment complexes or at weekend homes, and take advantage of Crikvenica's long waterfront promenade, lined with shops and cafes, and its acres of pebble beach.

GETTING THERE AND GETTING AROUND

Crikvenica is a 2-hour drive from Zagreb an half an hour or so from Rijeka. Hourly buses travel the 30km (18 miles) between Rijeka and Crikvenica and deposit passengers a block from the city's tourist office at Trg Stjepan Radića 1c at the south end of the promenade (© 051/241-051). Open every day from 8am to 10pm July to August and from 8am to 2pm Monday through Friday the rest of the year. The Crikvenica Tourist agency (© 051/241-249), which is open 8am to 10pm daily June to September and from 8am to 3pm October to May, books rooms and apartments from the

same office, which simplifies reserving a room. The office is stocked with maps, brochures, and books on the area and the rest of Croatia.

WHAT TO SEE AND DO

Crikvenica is a resort town that seems to cater to families and an older clientele seeking a beach vacation. The entire town is arranged around that concept. However, if you're a history buff and want to take a break from the sun, a trip to the nearby town of **Novi Vinodolski** just 9km (5.5 miles) south of Crikvenica is doable. The Vinodol Statute recognizing the rights of local citizens and Frankopan rule was signed in Novi Vinodolski in 1288. You can also explore the remains of a 13th-century Frankopan castle in the hills above the town.

WHERE TO STAY AND DINE

Hotels in Crikvenica are, for the most part, bland, and restaurants seem to use the same template for their menus. However, there are a couple of notable exceptions.

Palace Hotel Therapia ★★★ *Finds* When Archduke Josef, brother of Hapsburg Emperor Franz Josef, built Crikvenica's first hotel in 1895, he was so proud of the effort that he named it "Nadvojvoda Josip," after himself. The hotel became *the* place to be for the aristocracy and during the 1930s, the hotel became part of the same luxury chain as the Georg V in Paris. Fast forward through several wars and economic catastrophes to May, 2006, the date that the hotel reopened as the Palace Hotel Therapia after a long and painstaking renovation. From its newly painted Hapsburg yellow facade to its gorgeous full-service spa and handsomely refurbished rooms, the Therapia is now a destination all by itself. The hotel's designers wisely incorporated features like the building's original stone stairways and ironwork into their plan while adding all the conveniences expected of a first-class hotel so guests could soak up history along with the hotel's thermal indulgences.

Braće Buchoffer 12. 51260 Crikvenica. ℂ 051/209-700. Fax 051/785-072. www.therapia.hr. 123 units, including 13 suites. Doubles with balcony and sea view in July-Aug from 190€ ($265); suites from 306€ ($428). Other times doubles from 120€ ($168); suites from 194€ ($272). Rates include breakfast and use of the pool. **Amenities:** Restaurant; bar; pool; full-service spa; tennis courts; elevator; free parking. *In room:* A/C, SAT/TV, minibar, safe, broadband Internet, some tubs, hair dryer.

Hotel Villa Ružica ⓖ *Value* Ružica was built in 1912 as a getaway hotel for Rijeka's workers. It is one of the few Crikvenica hotels with personality, even after a 2001 renovation that updated its guest rooms (on a budget). *Tip:* One-third of Ružica's 36 rooms are affordable suites, which makes it a good place for families.

Bana Jelačića 1, PP: 22, 51260 Crikvenica. ℂ 051/241-959. Fax 051/784-378. www.vila-ruzica.hr. 36 units including 12 suites. Doubles in July-Aug from 126€ ($176); suites from 144€ ($202). Other times doubles from 66€ ($93); suites from 80€ ($112). **Amenities:** Restaurant; bar; Internet cafe; excursions. *In room:* A/C, SAT/TV, minibar, hair dryer, safe.

Amor ⓖ SEAFOOD Amor stands out as the best—and most expensive—restaurant in town based on its selection of pristinely fresh seafood. Even if the interior appears to have been decorated by a Hawaiian pirate, the black and gold palms on tall stands that are stuck behind and between tables in this otherwise pleasant dining room don't detract from the food.

Frankopanska 35. ℂ 051/242-017. Fax 051/242-017. Entrees 110kn–160kn ($20–$30). More for fish sold by the kilo. AE, DC, MC, V. Daily 8am–11pm.

2 The Opatija Riviera

OPATIJA

Opatija and its adjacent villages have something for everyone—vibrant, welcoming, clean, and full of facilities offering clear-water beaches, breathtaking views, comfortable rooms, and excellent restaurants.

Opatija started as a tiny, nondescript fishing village with a church and a population in the low double digits. But in the mid–19th century, the mild climate and spectacular seashore caught the fancy of **Iginio Scarpa,** a wealthy Italian businessman who built the lavish **Villa Angiolina** (named after his dead wife), surrounded it with a jungle of exotic flora from around the world, and invited all his aristocratic friends for a visit. Privileged Europeans were so taken with Villa Angiolina and Opatija that they erected villas of their own, each bigger and more ornate than the next, thus cementing Opatija's reputation as a winter playground for the wealthy.

It didn't hurt that in 1873 the railroad built a spur to connect Opatija to Ljubljana and beyond, and that the town was given a medical imprimatur as a healthy environment. In fact, Opatija originally was a health resort for Austrian snowbirds; its season ran from October to May. Thanks to word-of-mouth from the railroad and from prominent folks who visited Opatija, the city became wildly popular. Regal hotels such as the **Kvarner** (Opatija's first hotel), **Imperial** (formerly Kronprinzessin Stephanie), and **Palace-Bellevue** were built to accommodate the fancy new tourists.

From the mid-1880s to the start of World War I, Opatija was the place to see and be seen for such notables as dance maven **Isadora Duncan,** author **Anton Chekhov,** and a horde of Hapsburg aristocrats. World War I put a crimp on European vacations and Opatija was not immune to the downturn, but tourists never really abandoned it, either. Today, after two subsequent wars, Opatija still is popular with European tourists, who flock to the resort all year long, especially from mid-July to mid-August.

GETTING THERE

BY CAR   If you've driven to Rijeka, it's only another 20 minutes to Opatija via the coastal highway.

BY BUS   The bus (no. 32) stops in front of the Rijeka train station and travels the length of the Riviera from there to Lovran every 20 minutes for 10kn ($2) one-way.

WHAT TO SEE

Šetalište Franza Josefa (aka Lungomare) ✶✶✶   Promenading in the evening
is an art form in Croatia in general and in Opatija in particular, and this 12km (7.2 mile) flagstone walkway along the shore from **Volosko** ✶✶ (2km/1¼ miles north of Opatija) to **Lovran** ✶✶ (5.6km/3½ miles south of Opatija) is the granddaddy of them all. Along the way you can observe street theater, check out what people are having for dinner in the seaside restaurants that flank the path, take a dip from a rocky outcrop, or simply enjoy the stroll along the shore.

Villa Angiolina ✶✶   This is the villa that started it all, and thanks to careful
restoration, it's easy to see why. Neoclassical design, mosaics, frescoes, and lush landscaping combine to illustrate why every rich 19th-century aristocrat wanted a place like this. The villa was built in 1844 and was renovated completely in 2000. Today Villa Angiolina is a popular venue for weddings when it isn't being used for art exhibits and other cultural events. The surrounding **Park Angiolina** ✶ is a monument to horticulture with colorful formal gardens as well as many tropical species that include the camellia, Opatija's official flower.

Park Angiolina. Daily June–Sept 10am–9pm.

Operetta ✶   To some it's just a shopping mall in a fixed-up old building, but the
Operetta is worth visiting because this cleverly restored and partitioned 19th-century villa at Sv. Florijana 1, next to the Bristol Hotel, houses several upscale stores including Benetton as well as a pizza-by-the-slice fast-food emporium. If nothing else, you'll be able to marvel at the clever interior architecture. *Tip:* The mall is open for browsing until 11pm, but the stores inside set their own hours.

Volosko ✶✶   This Mediterranean fishing village is just a 20-minute walk north of
Opatija along the promenade, but it is free of the Hapsburg bling that characterizes its sprawling neighbor. Volosko is also known for outstanding restaurants, which include **Amfora** ✶✶✶ and **Le Mandrać** ✶✶✶, two of the area's best. There aren't any important monuments or museums here, but Volosko's winding streets, modest vintage buildings, and decent beach are good places to explore when you are in the mood for some quiet time or a fabulous meal.

WHERE TO STAY

EXPENSIVE

Millennium ✶✶ *Overrated*   If your idea of the perfect hotel is one so loaded with fea-
tures that you never have to leave the property, you can't beat the pricey Millennium.

The question is, how much of this stuff do you really need and what are you going to use on vacation? Sure, the spa offers 10 kinds of facials, but standard guest rooms are typical hotel-chain, even the ones with tiny balconies with views of the water. The over-size bathrooms are better than average, with double marble sinks and conveniences like retractable clotheslines, and the windows have remote-control awnings, but the pillows are flat as pancakes, and the towels are skimpy. The buffet breakfast in the hotel's Restaurant Argonauti is the best in Opatija; tables on the columned terrace make morning coffee an event. Guests have pool and gym privileges, and the staff will make dinner reservations or send your faxes, but except for those and a piece of chocolate on your pillow at night, most services outside the basic room tab require an extra fee.

Maršala Tita 109, 51410 Opatija. ☎ 051/202-000. Fax 051/202-020. www.ugohoteli.hr. 91 units, 3 with kitchenettes. High season: from 1,160kn ($215) double; from 2,375kn ($440) suite; from 3,100kn ($575) kitchenette unit. Rest of year: from 1,015kn ($190) standard double; from 1,660kn ($307) suite; from 2,650kn ($490) kitchenette unit. Rates include breakfast. AE, DC, MC, V. Limited free parking. **Amenities:** 2 restaurants; bar; tennis courts; spa; concierge; travel agency; car rental; excursions; currency exchange; 24-hr. room service; babysitting; nonsmoking rooms; valet services; jeweler; newsstand; shoeshine machine in lobby. *In room:* A/C, TV w/pay stations, minibar, hair dryer, safe.

Bristol ⭐⭐   Don't confuse this *fin de siècle* gem with the creaky Bristol in Lovran, and don't be put off by the lemon-drop yellow of its newly painted facade. This hotel reopened in late June 2005 nearly 2 decades of being closed to the public, during which time it served as a shelter for Slavoninan Croats who were displaced by the 1991 war. Happily, an extensive renovation turned the Bristol into a sophisticated, tastefully dec-orated showpiece. Guest rooms are spacious and done in soothing earth tones, and most have at least partial sea views. The Bristol is more buttoned-down than its avant-garde sister Hotel Astoria, but its traditional atmosphere exudes comfort and confi-dence. The Bristol's exceptional English-speaking staff will help guests find a restaurant, book a bike tour/countryside picnic, and everything in between. Guests have access to the saltwater swimming pool at the regal **Opatija Hotel** down the block.

Maršala Tita 108, 51410 Opatija. ☎ **051/706-300.** Fax 051/706-301. www.hotel-bristol.hr. 78 units. High season: from 145€ ($203) double; from 215€ ($300) suite. Rest of year: from 100€ ($140) double; from 200€ ($280) suite. Rates include breakfast. AE, DC, MC, V. Parking 30kn ($6) per day. **Amenities:** Restaurant; cafe; pool (at Hotel Opatija); elevator; excursions; room for those w/limited mobility. *In room:* A/C, TV w/pay stations, Internet access, minibar, hair dryer.

Design Hotel Astoria ⭐⭐ *(Finds)*   High design is the guiding principle behind the new look of the Hotel Astoria, which opened in July 2005 after a year of renovation. When it was built in 1904 as Villa Louise, the hotel was an excellent example of stately Austrian–Mediterranean style. Today the hotel's new look is more Guggenheim Museum with touches of whimsy. Guest rooms are sleek and comfortable with bath-rooms fitted with sophisticated fixtures that make use of every inch of space. Lots of details such as artwork on the walls and vases filled with lucky bamboo make the spaces feel homey, but it is the generous-size flatscreen TV that makes each room feel like home. If you can swing it, ask for a suite on the sixth floor, which was built atop the old hotel and is completely new, including balconies with louvered awnings and wood plank floors on three of the floor's six units.

Maršala Tita 174, 51410 Opatija. ☎ **051/706-350.** Fax 051/706-351. www.hotel-astoria.hr. 51 units including 6 penthouse suites. High season: from 130€ ($182) double; from 190€ ($266) suite. Rest of year: from 90€ ($126) double; from 210€ ($295) suite. Rates include breakfast. Children 6 and under free in parent's room. AE, DC, MC, V. Parking 60kn ($11) per day. **Amenities:** Restaurant; pool (at Opatija Hotel); elevator; excursions. *In room:* A/C, flatscreen TV w/pay stations, Internet access, minibar, hair dryer.

W.A. Mozart ☆   Spending a night in this pink confection on Opatija's "Hotel Row" is like being a guest in a regal 19th-century home. In fact, that's what the Mozart was when it was built in 1895. Since then, the building has undergone renovation (1995) and has added modern conveniences such as air-conditioning and an elevator without changing its original character. Features include a stone-walled terrace enhanced with flowers that serves as a backdrop for dining, polished wood floors strewn with Oriental rugs, guest rooms decked out in period furniture that include canopied beds, and modern bathrooms. The liveried staff will jump in the gulf to make guests comfortable. Wolfgang Amadeus Mozart memorabilia is everywhere.

Maršala Tita 138, 51410 Opatia. ☎ 051/718-260. Fax 051/271-739. www.hotel-mozart.hr. 25 units, 1 with kitchenette. High season: from 1,289kn ($239) double; from 2,062kn ($382) suite. Rest of year: from 1,031kn ($190) double, from 2,580kn ($478) suite. AE, DC, MC, V. Parking 40kn ($8) per day. **Amenities:** Restaurant; cafe/piano bar; elevator; excursions. *In room:* A/C, TV w/pay stations, minibar.

Miramar ☆☆☆   The Miramar is a spa hotel in the heart of the Opatija. The Miramar was built in 1876, and it once again is vying to be the top choice of discriminating travelers. The hotel's rooms now sparkle in soft colors. Bathrooms, outfitted with the latest fixtures and toiletries, are large enough to accommodate two. Some rooms have sea views. Everyone has easy access to the hotel's new spa, which includes a seawater pool, sauna, and salon.

Kaline 11. ☎ **051/280-000.** www.hotel-miramar.info. 85 units, including 3 with kitchenettes. Summer: from 1,450kn ($269) double; from 2,264kn ($420) suite/kitchenette unit. Rest of year: from 1,112kn ($206) double; from 1,540kn ($285) suite/kitchenette unit. Limited free parking. **Amenities:** Restaurant; cafe; bar; pool; spa. *In room:* A/C, TV w/pay stations, Internet access, minibar, hair dryer, safe.

MODERATE

Admiral ☆   A member of the Liburnia Riviera chain, which operates 14 hotels on the Opatija Riviera, this refurbished hotel (May 2005) is a favorite destination for tour groups. The rooms are serviceable but small for the price, and not all amenities work all the time. However, every single room has a balcony that overlooks the Kvarner Gulf and the huge outdoor swimming pool. The Admiral doesn't have much history or atmosphere, but it is well placed, with Maršala Tita at its front door and the sea and marina at its rear. If you just want a comfortable place to sleep with a pool and easy access to shopping and the water, and if you don't mind staying in a large, generic hotel that caters to tour groups, this is one of the best choices in town.

Maršala Tita 139, 51410 Opatija. ☎ 051/271-533. Fax 051/271-708. www.liburnia.hr. 180 units. High season: from 1,075kn ($200) double; from 1,160kn ($215) suite. Rest of year: from 800kn ($148) double; from 930kn ($172) suite. Rates include breakfast buffet. AE, DC, MC, V. **Amenities:** 2 restaurants; cafe; bar; outdoor pool; indoor pool w/heated seawater; marina; garage. *In room:* TV w/pay stations, Internet access, minibar, valet service.

Villa Ariston ☆   The terraced gardens behind this 19th-century villa are the setting for its renowned **Villa Ariston restaurant** ☆☆, which is a knockout, as are the views of the sea. But despite Viennese architect Carl Seidl's artful 1924 reconstruction of the villa, the guest rooms—especially the doubles on the top floor—are disappointingly cramped, dim, and in need of updating. The presidential suite, however, has a fabulous balcony and an unsurpassed view of the garden and water; it is even equipped with period furniture that includes a fainting couch. It is said that Coco Chanel and JFK slept here, but no one on staff knows which rooms they used. Could it be?

Maršala Tita 179, 41310 Opatija. ☎ 051/271-379. Fax 051/271-494. www.villa-ariston.hr. 10 units including presidential suite. High season: from 110€ ($154) double; from 169€ ($237) suite. Rest of year: from 82€ ($115) double;

from 123€ ($172) suite. Rates include breakfast. AE, DC, MC, V. Limited free parking. **Amenities:** Restaurant; wine cellar; garden. *In room:* TV, minibar, hair dryer, period decor.

Kvarner-Amalia (★)   The oldest Croatian hotel on the Adriatic has a prime location on the sea and an exquisite terrace that abuts the Lungomare. The Kvarner's park setting and Austro–Hungarian pedigree create an old-world atmosphere that makes you feel as if you've just hit a time warp. Antique furniture, high ceilings, and lots of sparkling crystal and gleaming wood enhance the effect. Be sure to take a peek at the Crystal Ballroom, which looks poised for a formal Viennese ball. The indoor/outdoor swimming pool that opens to the sea is another draw, as is the Villa Amalia Annex, which once was an official Hapsburg hangout. Rooms are anything but cookie-cutter, but those on the sea are head and shoulders above the rest (in price, too).

P. Tomašića 1–4, 51410 Opatija. (℃ **051/271-233.** Fax 051/271-202. www.liburnia.hr. 83 units, 30 in Villa Amalia. From 550kn ($102) double; from 655kn ($121) suite. Rates include breakfast. AE, DC, MC, V. Limited free parking. **Amenities:** Restaurant; bar; 2 swimming pools; sauna; massage. *In room:* TV, minibar.

INEXPENSIVE

Hotel Imperial (*Value*)   Walking up the long, wide staircase to the Imperial's front door makes you feel like you're approaching a monument, and once inside, the impression sticks. Staying in the hotel, which was built in 1885, is like staying in a fine old opera house—crystal chandeliers, soaring ceilings, long corridors, heavy velvet curtains, etched glass doors, and a dining room fit for a royal banquet. Guest rooms are generous spaces complete with updated bathrooms and period furniture, but they are dark and tired-looking even if they have balconies. Asking for a room that opens to the sea is a catch-22 because the sea is across busy Maršala Tito: You'll get a good breeze but the noise might keep you awake. Be sure to walk to the back of the hotel on the first floor and see the black-and-white photo exhibit made from negatives shot when the hotel was new.

Maršala Tita 124/3, 51410 Opatija. (℃ **051/271-577.** Fax 051/272-848. Imperial@liburnia.hr. 127 units. High season: from 585kn ($108) double. Rest of year: from 375kn ($70) double. AE, DC, MC, V. **Amenities:** Restaurant; cafe; bar. *In room:* TV.

Hotel Palace-Hotel Bellevue   These side-by-side hotels are showing signs of wear, but the historic grande dames in the center of Opatija still draw crowds. The large guest rooms are dingy and worn; bathrooms are small but serviceable. Both hotels are on prime real estate across the street from the central Opatija beach, and both are convenient to restaurants, shopping, and transportation. Don't miss dancing under the stars on the Palace's outdoor terrace, which overlooks Maršala Tita and the sea. There's live music every night from May to December—and there's no charge to claim a table and take a turn or two around the floor.

Maršala Tita 144, 51410 Opatija. (℃ **051/271-811.** Fax 051/271-964. palace@liburnia.hr. 219 units. High season: from 580kn ($108) double; from 765kn ($142) suite. Rest of year: from 340kn ($63) double; from 540kn ($100) suite. AE, DC, MC, V. **Amenities:** Restaurant; bar. *In room:* TV.

ROOMS & APARTMENTS

Accommodations in Opatija are expensive, especially during July and August, unless you stay in private rooms (sobes) and apartments available through private agencies. One of the most helpful agencies is **Da Riva,** which has an office at Maršala Tita 162 ((℃ **051/272-990,** 051/718-249, or 051/718-248; fax 051/272-482; www.da-riva. hr). The agency can find rooms from 145kn to 210kn ($27–$39) per night without breakfast, but you may have trouble securing one unless you book for at least 3 nights, especially during the summer. Besides rooms, Da Riva also books excursions.

CAMPING

There are no campgrounds within Opatija, but there are a few both north and south of the city. During peak season, the camps can be crowded, but they also may be your only chance for a place to sleep.

Preluk ★ About 4.8km (3 miles) north of Opatija near Volosko, Preluk is particularly well situated for those who love watersports.

Preluk bb. ℂ 051/622-249 or 051/621-913. Fax 051/622-381. tranzit@ri.htnet.hr. 32kn ($6) per person, 23kn ($4) per child; 45kn ($8) for car and tent site. Dogs allowed.

Ičići ★★ This camp has one of best beaches around, plus it throws a Saturday barbecue. It is 4.8km (3 miles) south of Opatija and is set into a hillside near the sea and Mount Ucka.

Liburnijska 46, Ičići. ℂ 051/704-387. Fax 051/704-046. 31kn ($5.75) per person per day; 105kn ($19) for 2 people, car, and tent site. Pets allowed. Closed May–Sept.

Medveja ★★★ This campsite is a little farther south of Ičići and can accommodate 1,200 people with its combination of sites, rooms, and a few bungalows. Private rooms are available in the village. Like Ičići, Medveja is on the water but its beach is *the* best in the area.

Medveja bb. ℂ 051/291-191. Fax 051/292-471. ac-medveja@liburnia.hr. From 455kn ($84) bungalow; from 235kn ($44) single room; 35kn ($7) campsite per person plus 47kn ($9) for car and tent site. Fido is welcome for an additional charge. May–Sept.

Autocamp "I" ★ Everything you need is in this resort/camp 12km (8 miles) south of Opatija. The grounds are well kept and the excellent beach is usually crowded.

A. Slatin bb, Mošćenička Draga. ℂ 051/737-523. Fax 051/737-460. www.croatia.net/autocamp-i. 45kn ($8) per person including tax, plus another 45kn ($8) for car and tent site. May–Sept.

WHERE TO DINE
EXPENSIVE

Bevanda ★★ SEAFOOD There are lots of fish restaurants to choose from in Opatija, but if you want a table with a view of Rijeka's shimmering lights at night, sound effects provided by the sea lapping at the shore, and the kiss of a gentle sea breeze on your face while you nibble on mussels *buzara*, then Bevanda is for you. Bevanda hugs Opatija's famous promenade, so strollers might pass within a few feet of your table in the middle of dinner, but it's all part of the atmosphere. The restaurant also has indoor seating in a handsome candlelit room with a personality all its own. Portions can be on the small side and service is quite formal and often a little slow, but that makes Bevanda a good place to linger over coffee and gaze at the sea.

G. Verdia 23, 51410 Opatija. ℂ 051/741-305. Fax 051/718-354. Reservations recommended. Entrees 52kn–305kn ($10–$57). MC, V. 11am–11pm.

Amfora ★★★ SEAFOOD If there is any doubt that Amfora is one of the best restaurants on the Opatija Riviera, there is no question that it has the most spectacular setting. Perched on a hill in the picturesque fishing village of Volosko a little more than a mile from Opatija's main drag, Amfora's ambience and menu are good enough to hold up anywhere in the world. After you order, you'll be served a complimentary taste of marinated and grilled sardella and shrimp or some other tasty *amuse bouche*. Try the savory black risotto done to creamy perfection and full of tender pieces of squid—it's an Adriatic specialty. The lobster tails are huge and attractively presented with melon, and salads are large and made with pristinely fresh ingredients. Service is exceptional. Parking is free, though timid drivers might want to park on the road above the restaurant and walk down instead of attempting the steep turns to the parking lot.

Črnikovica 4. ⓒ **051/701-222**. Fax 051/741-016. www.restaurant-amfora.com. Reservations recommended. Entrees 58kn–255kn ($11–$47). AE, DC, MC, V. 10% discount for paying cash. Daily 11am–midnight (until the last guest leaves).

Villa Ariston 𝄢𝄢 CROATIAN   There is no finer alfresco dining in Opatija than at the exquisite terraced garden of Villa Ariston. Tables set among trees on levels decorated with pots of lavender and other flowers form a private bower by the sea. The menu is a blend of traditional Croatian and unbridled adventure, so go for one of the fresh fish dishes, or try the chicken breasts stuffed with truffles and mushrooms. Service at Villa Ariston is efficient but not hovering.

Maršala Tita 179. ⓒ **051/271-379**. Fax 051/271-494. www.villa-arison.hr. Reservations recommended. Entrees 52kn–255kn ($10–$47). AE, DC, MC, V. Daily 8am–11pm.

Le Mandrać 𝄢𝄢𝄢 CREATIVE SEAFOOD   Le Mandrać bills itself as a "fish restaurant for the new millennium." Its ultramodern decor and stylized food presentations certainly follow that theme, but the restaurant is much more. The menu here is imaginative and changes frequently to take advantage of available fresh, seasonal ingredients, which the chef combines in unusual pairings. If you have the time (and the money), try the "tasting" menu, which allows diners to sample small servings of a wide range of dishes such as poached egg with Istrian ham and nettle, or fudge with pear ice cream and rosemary.

Obala Frana Supila 10, 51410 Volosko. ⓒ **051/701-357**. Fax 051/741-099. www.lemandrac.com. Reservations recommended. Entrees 70kn–290kn ($14–$54/10€–40€). Price of tasting menu varies. AE, DC, MC. V. Free limited parking. Daily 11am–midnight.

MODERATE
Plavi Podrum 𝄢𝄢 SEAFOOD   Crisp blue awnings and white tablecloths billow in the sea breeze on the waterfront terrace of this fine restaurant, which is just steps away from Mandrać in Volosko. Plavi Podrum offers creative cuisine like green tea tagliatelle with scampi, shrimp, wild asparagus and nettle without sky-high prices or formality. The wine list is solid, but the bar also pours a wide selection of Scotch and Irish whisky.

Obala F.Supila 4, 51410 Volosko. ⓒ **051/701-223**. Fax 051/741-195. Entrees 60kn–120kn ($12–$24/8€–16€). AE, DC, MC, V. Daily noon–midnight.

Slatina 𝄢 *Value* CROATIAN   This restaurant is a local hangout on an enclosed porch across the street from the promenade on Maršala Tita. It dishes up huge portions of Slav specialties. From your table next to large windows that overlook the street and sea, you can see all the action and hear the music from the nearby Palace Hotel, too. Try the *Šopse* salad, a mix of chopped cukes, tomatoes, onions, and peppers covered with shaved sheep cheese. The wild mushroom soup is a meal in itself, and the *tavće gravće* (beans in a paprika sauce) will make you turn up your nose at canned pork and beans forever. Heartier appetites will want to try any of the roast meats (lamb, veal, pork, chicken), which can also be had as *mućkalica* (meat with veggies on top).

Maršala Tita 206, 51410 Opatija. ⓒ **051/271-949**. Entrees 30kn–175kn ($6–$32). No credit cards. Daily 11am–1am.

INEXPENSIVE

Opatija is loaded with affordable pizza places and cafes, most of which are along Maršala Tita and the Lungomare.

NIGHTLIFE

Croatia's zero-tolerance law toned down Opatija's nightlife scene as would-be revelers from Rijeka figured that they could no longer go there to party and risk driving home if they had even a single drink. But even without Rijeka traffic, the town still rocks until around 11pm, which is closing hour for most Opatija restaurants and bars. Until then, you can sip a glass of wine, have a beer, or get rowdy at **Hemingway's** on the promenade or at any restaurant or cafe along the way.

However, the most nighttime action in Opatija is on the **Lungomare** and **Maršala Tita**—and it is alcohol-free. It seems that on any given evening all of Croatia is out taking a stroll, in-line skating, or pausing to watch break dancers and mimes. An ice-cream cone is the party treat of choice.

LOVRAN & ENVIRONS

Slower-paced and more casual than Opatija, the picturesque town of Lovran 6km (4 miles) to its north is the choice of tourists who want the Riviera's beaches and recreation opportunities, but not its upscale lifestyle. Lovran is where Opatija's Lungomare ends—or begins—depending on your point of view. Excitement in Lovran (named for its numerous laurel trees) is not limited to toasting on the beach. For 3 weekends every October there, the chestnut is king and you can feast on the celebrated nut in many forms at the annual **Chestnut Festival (Marunada).** There is also a **Wild Asparagus Festival** in April; and **Cherry Days** are in June.

There are reasons other than produce to consider a stay in Lovran, including stunning villas on the town's periphery; a quaint hilltop Old Town complete with a 12th-century church **(St. George's)** marked by lovely frescoes and Glagolitic inscriptions; a town gate known as Stubica; and two municipal beaches.

GETTING AROUND

Buses to and from Rijeka breeze through Lovran every 20 minutes or so, or if you have your own car, you can get to Lovran from Opatija in about 10 minutes. You can even walk there along the Lungomare from Opatija or any point north of town along the 12km (7.5-mile) promenade. The tourist office near the harbor can provide maps and other helpful information.

The Lovran Tourist Office's summer hours are 8am to 8pm Monday to Saturday; 8am to noon Sunday. Its winter hours are 9am to 4pm Monday to Friday. For more information, contact ② **051/291-740;** or check out www.tz-lovran.hr.

WHERE TO STAY

Hotel Park ★★ The Park is a blue and white confection of a hotel next to the historic East Gate that leads to Old Town Lovran. The Park has a long history as a hotel, but its new era began in July 2005 after an extensive makeover. Today the Park is a comfortable accommodations option with lots of amenities away from the hustle and bustle of Opatija's nightlife. Rooms are spacious and equipped with "smart" electricity that operates only when your room key is inserted in a slot at the door. Windows have automated shutters and open to a refreshing sea breeze. Bathrooms are spacious, too, and most have showers only that must have been installed by Paul Bunyan—the fixtures are a good 7 feet up the wall.

Šetabšte M. Tita 60, 51415 Lovran. ⓒ 051/706-200. Fax 051/293-791. www.hotelparklovran.hr. 49 units, including 6 suites. Doubles from 1,124kn ($208) and suites from 1,584kn ($293) July and Aug. Other times, doubles from 666kn ($123) and suites from 1,022kn ($189). Rates include breakfast. AE, DC, MC, V. **Amenities:** Restaurant; coffee shop; bar; pool; laundry service; free off-street parking. *In room:* A/C, SAT/TV, minibar, hair dryer, Internet access via free broadband, turbo showers.

Hotel Excelsior From the street, the Excelsior looks like a socialist-era attempt at modern architecture. Rooms are fairly small and plain, but most have balconies or terraces and are right across from the beach.

Maršala Tita 15, 51415 Lovran. ⓒ 051/292-233. Fax 051/291-989. www.liburnia.hr. 186 units. Summer: from 850kn ($146) double; from 1,095kn ($189) suite. Rest of year: from 515kn ($89) double; 800 ($138) suite. Rates include breakfast. AE, DC, MC, V. Free parking garage. **Amenities:** Restaurant; cafe; bar; 2 swimming pools; tennis courts; sauna; 24-hr. room service; massage. *In room:* A/C, TV, minibar, hair dryer.

Bristol *Value* This six-story Belle Epoque building is surrounded by greenery and has a nice view of the sea. Its exterior has recently been painted and repaired, and the tolerable interior seems geared to vacationers who just want a home base from which to get to the beach. Public areas retain touches of yesteryear such as brass sconces and marble staircases. Guest rooms are adequate. Almost all have balconies with views of the water or the Učka massif. If you can't find a sobe for a night, this will do.

Maršala Tita 27, 51415 Lovran. ⓒ 051/291-022. Fax 051/292-049. 102 units. Summer: from 570kn ($106) double. Rest of year: from 280kn ($52) double. Rates include breakfast. AE, DC, MC, V. Limited free parking. **Amenities:** Restaurant; bar; saloon; access to Excelsior's sports facilities. *In room:* TV, hair dryer. Closed mid-Nov to Mar except for holidays Dec 22–Jan 10 (varies).

WHERE TO DINE & DRINK

Bellavista *Finds* CROATIAN There has been a restaurant on this site for 40 years, but this iteration of the atmospheric space just past the historic East Gate entrance to Old Town Lovran opened in June 2007 with a new look and a new owner. Ask for one of the tables along the removable windows that look out to sea, but no matter where you sit, you will be rewarded with a fine meal and warm ambience. For a treat, try the salt baked fish, which is sold by the kilo. Or sample any of the homemade pastas like ravioli with spinach and truffles. Bellavista pays special attention to wines, too, and offers tasting plates of food that match select varietals.

Stari Grad 22, 51415 Lovran. ⓒ 051/292-123. www.bellavista.kvarnerinfo.net. Entrees 58kn–122kn ($10–$23/ 8€–17€). More for fish and meat sold by the kilo. AE, DC, MC, V. Daily 11:30am–11pm.

Najade SEAFOOD The menu at Najade is in 4 languages, which usually is code for "tourist trap," but the food at this seaside spot is competently prepared and quite fresh. Enjoy a great view of the water from a terrace table while you nibble on grilled squid or risotto Najade, and you'll forget that not many of the guests are locals. Prices are a little higher than they should be, but not high enough to be alarming.

Šetalište M. Tita 60, 51415 Lovran. ⓒ **051/291-866.** Fax 051/291-156. Entrees 40kn–90kn ($8–$17/6€–12€). More for fish and meat sold by the kilo. AE, DC, MC, V. Daily 11am–midnight.

Kvarner Grill SEAFOOD This covered seaside grill with an extensive fish menu is right on the water and puts its daily catch on display in a refrigerated case at the entrance. Try the calamari any way you like it—the Kvarner Grill serves squid five ways. There are pastas and meats on the menu, too. Finish with sour cherry sorbet made with cherries from the surrounding villages.

Šetalište Maršala Tita 68, 51415 Lovran. ℂ **051/291-118.** Entrees 40kn–255kn ($7–$43). AE, DC, MC, V. Daily 10am–11pm.

Lovranski Pub PIZZA   It's down a flight of stairs off M. Tita, but you can hear the merrymaking from the street. Good pizzas and some meat plates (prsut and cheese) are served here, but most stop by for the beverages and camaraderie.

M. Tita37, Lovran. ℂ **051/292-674.** Pizzas and plates 30kn–60kn ($6–$12/4€–8€). No credit cards. Daily 11am–midnight

Gradska Kavana ⊛ ICE CREAM/PASTRY/BREAKFAST   This fancy tearoom was restored and redecorated in 2006 and now it's all crystal and flowers in shades of lavender and white. Gradska Kavana is much more than a place to grab a cone: Cocktails, fancy pastries, and American-style breakfasts, including omelets and ham and eggs, are served here, too. Gradska Kavana shares the same real estate as Lovranski Pub, but the Kavana is at street level.

M. Tita 41, 51415 Lovran. No phone. Breakfast 25kn–75kn ($5–$15/4€–10€). AE, DC, MC, V. Daily 7am–midnight.

3 Krk Island

56km (35 miles) S of Rijeka

Croatia's largest island (pronounced "Kirk" with a strong Scottish burr) is also the country's most developed, especially in the north where the island is connected to the mainland via a mile-long toll bridge that sometimes is congested with commuters who live on Krk but work in Rijeka. Add Rijeka's airport, an oil storage facility, and an oil pipeline to the mix, and you have the ingredients for an industrial region.

Tourist facilities on "The Golden Island" (Krk's official nickname) are mostly on the island's coasts, and they run the gamut from huge modern package resorts such as **Omišalj, Njivice,** and **Malinska** on the northwest coast, to historic, partially walled **Krk Town** midway on the island, to the beach with promenade that is **Baška** in the south.

Krk Town's settlement followed the familiar Illyrian–Roman–Byzantium–Venetian–Hungarian chain of control that is characteristic of many coastal cities. In the 11th century the city became an important center for the country's Glagolitic script, which was used there until the beginning of the 19th century. At that time, Austria-Hungary took Krk from the Frankopans (the Dukes of Krk, a powerful feudal family), who had held it since the 12th century.

As with most of Croatia's islands, tourism is an economic mainstay for Krk, though there is some agriculture (wine and olive production) and industry (the Rijeka airport, pipeline, and a couple of shipyards). There also is an ongoing controversy about a proposal to connect the island's oil pipeline with Russia's.

GETTING THERE & GETTING AROUND

BY CAR   The Krk bridge connects the mainland with the island ($2.60 one-way). Ferries leave from **Valbiska** on the west side of the island for **Cres** and **Lošinj,** while another ferry line makes regular runs between **Lopar** on **Rab** and **Baška** on Krk's southern end during the summer months. There are several ferries each day from June through September, but ferry schedules are limited the rest of the year. Check the Jadrolinja website, www.jadrolinja.hr, for schedule and price details.

BY BUS   Krk Town is well-served by buses from Rijeka and so are the nearby towns of Omišalj, Njivice, Malinska, and **Punat,** which are stops on the same route. Eleven of the 14 daily buses from Rijeka to Krk also go on to Baška in the extreme southern part of the island. You can continue to Cres and Lošinj by bus, but schedules are not firm, so check with Jadrolinja to see what's what.

Even if you don't have your own car, you can see all of Krk's main sites. Buses run regular routes between major towns and connect with less frequent, local lines.

KRK TOWN

Krk Town, which is the island's largest population center and a tourism magnet, is also the island's economic, cultural, and religious fulcrum. It is situated in the middle of the Krk's western coast on Krčki Bay. Krk Town has an enchanting Old Town complete with sections of the settlement's original city wall; a 13th-century tower; and a narrow, busy shoreline walkway where restaurants, cafes, shops, and bars cater to beachgoers and promenading tourists. On summer nights, this route (**J.J. Strossmayera**) looks like a shopping mall the day after Thanksgiving: At night it seems as if every person on the island is out for a cone and a stroll.

Away from the center and the shore, the island's capital resembles a hilly suburban development that has expanded into every available vacant nook and cranny. In fact, finding your destination away from the center can be challenging as there are houses behind houses and hotels behind those. Krk Town is a popular weekend resort because it is so accessible to the mainland. If you're there just to see the important and interesting sites, you don't need to stay more than a couple of hours.

TOURIST AGENCIES

Krk Town Tourist Office You can get a map of the area and some brochures here, but private agencies have more info on rooms, excursions, and restaurants.

Vela Placa 1. © 051/221-414. tz@tz-krk.hr. Mon–Fri 8am–3pm. Closed weekends.

Aurea This private tourist office can book private rooms or hotel accommodations as well as arrange excursions.

Pupačića 1. © 051/222-277. www.aurea-krk.hr.

Krk-info Prices for private rooms are fixed by the tourist board at this city-run agency. They only deal in first-class properties, which means rooms with private bathrooms.

Nikolića 34. © 051/222-222. www.multilink.hr/quanarius. From 275kn ($47) double. Breakfast not included.

WHAT TO SEE

Katedrala Uznesenja (Cathedral of the Assumption) ∉∉ The architecture of this impressive house of worship on Trg Vela Placa is like a tangible timeline that spans 13 centuries, as it was built on the site of a 5th-century basilica during the 13th century and fitted with a bell tower in the 18th. The cathedral sits on the site of a 9th-century monastery, which in turn sits on the former site of the city's Roman baths. In fact, a unique feature of the cathedral's design is its utilization of pillars salvaged from a variety of Roman structures. The cathedral is usually open only when there is a Mass, but if you don't make the service, you can see a little of the interior through the vestibule doors. However, try to be there when the cathedral is open. You'll see the Roman columns, ancient mosaics, interesting paintings, and early stone carvings. The cathedral abuts a square with several examples of Frankopan architecture, where many concerts and cultural events are held.

A. Mahnica. Cathedral daily 9:30am–1pm.

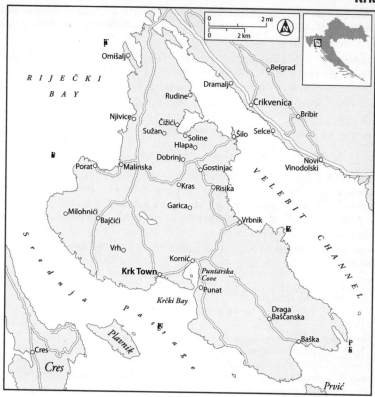

Sveti Kivrin (St. Quirinus) ✦

Krk Town's cathedral shares the square with the 11th-century Romanesque church of Sveti Kivrin (St. Quirinus), named after the city's patron saint. The church has an odd, four-section shape on both levels, and holds the town's collection of sacral art. The repository at St. Quirinus contains treasures from other churches in the area as well.

Mahnića. No phone. Admission 5kn ($1). Daily 9:30am–1pm.

WHERE TO STAY

Krk is a popular package destination for nearby European countries, which means that private rooms and accommodations are mostly generic and frequently overpriced. Still, despite the lack of cachet, the hotels in the town offer a wide range of services.

Koralj ✦   Located in a pine forest at the edge of a cove, this large hotel, which was renovated in 2003, is close to the water and about a quarter of a mile from the city center. The Koralj is not a luxury hotel, nor is it spartan, but there is no air-conditioning, which makes for a noisy night because if you keep the windows open, you can hear music from the town center as well as anyone walking into the hotel. Rooms are tight but functional. The restaurant terrace at treetop level is beautiful.

Vlade Tomašića bb, 51500 Krk. ☎ 051/221-063. www.valamar.hr. 172 units, 18 kitchenette units. Summer: from 132€ ($185) double; from 175€ ($245) suite. Rest of year: from 55€ ($77) double; from 80€ ($112) kitchenette unit. Rates for kitchenette units do not include breakfast. AE, DC, MC, V. **Amenities:** 2 restaurants; bar; tennis courts; sauna; excursions; children's program; massage. *In room:* TV, Internet access, minibar. Hair dryers available at reception desk.

Dražica *←*   Six floors of guest rooms make the Dražica a target for package tours and family vacations. A plus is that the hotel finished a 4-year renovation in 2003 when its guest rooms were retrofitted to accommodate elderly and people with limited mobility. The facility is close to, but not on, the water, and a 10-minute walk from the center.

Roužmarinska 6. ✆ **051/655-755; 051/221-022.** www.hotelikrk.hr. 127 units. Summer: from 128€ ($180) double; from 150€ ($210) suite. Rest of year: from 40€ ($56) double; from 50€ ($70) suite. MC, V. **Amenities:** Restaurant; bar; 2 pools; miniature golf; tennis courts; excursions; children's program; laundry service. *In room:* A/C, TV, minibar.

CAMPING

Autocamp Ježevac   There are no campgrounds in Krk Town, but this one is within a reasonable distance, about a quarter of a mile southwest of the town. It's on the coast and the ground is rocky, but if you have a decent air mattress, it's a good place to stay if you want to hit the water.

Plavinća bb. ✆ **051/221-081.** Fax 051/221-362. jezevac@zlatni-otok.hr. 5.50€ ($8) per person plus 7.50€ ($11) per tent site.

Politin FKK   If you want to try naturist camping (nude camping), this camp is just southwest of the Koralj Hotel.

Politin bb. 51500 Krk. ✆ **051/221-351.** Fax 051/221-246. www.zlatni-otok.hr. Closed Oct to mid-Apr.

WHERE TO DINE

There are fish restaurants and pizza places galore along Krk Town's shore. Most have the same offerings and prices. The restaurants listed below are representative of the city's dining options.

Konoba Šime *←←* SEAFOOD   With only the Riva between its varnished picnic tables and the water, this casual fish restaurant is always packed with tourists. Service is a bit indifferent, but local cats provide entertainment as they walk up to you and beg for food. There is also an attractive, medieval-looking dining room indoors. Try any of the grilled fish dishes or the local *cevapčicí.* The grilled scampi are served with their heads on and are both messy and pricey but delicious.

At the south town gate on the Riva. ✆ **051/220-042.** Entrees 40kn–150kn ($7–$28). No credit cards. Daily 10am–11pm.

Restaurant Nada *←←←* MEDITERRANEAN   It's 11km (7 miles) northeast of Krk Town in Vrbnik, and only two buses a day run there, but if you want a really special meal, this is the place to go. Set in a 100-year-old stone building near the sea, the tiny Nada has been open since 1974. It offers smoked ham, cheese made on Krk, salted fish, Krk lamb, scampi risotto, and Vrbnik's famous Žlahtina wine. You can tour the restaurant's wine cellar under the city walls if you make arrangements ahead of time. *Warning:* The only way to access the restaurant is uphill on foot, and it is a good idea to either stay overnight in Vrbnik after a meal with wine or have a designated driver: The roads leading to and from the town are winding and narrow.

Glavača 22, 51516 Vrbnik. ✆ **051/857-065.** Fax 051/857-205. www.nada-vrbnik.com. Reservations recommended. Entrees 52kn–256kn ($10–$49/7€–35€). AE, DC, MC, V. Mar 15–Nov 1 daily 11am–midnight.

4 Baška and Environs

70km (44 miles) S of Rijeka

When Croatians hear the word Baška, they immediately think about the 900-year-old tablet that is one of the nation's most important archaeological discoveries. The Baška Tablet is a large stone engraved with the oldest surviving text in Glagolitic script, and it is kept in Zagreb's Academy of Arts and Sciences. Besides its value as a cultural artifact, the Baška stone is also the first record of a Croatian king in that it commemorates a gift from the first Croat King, Zvonimir, to the church. The tablet was found in 1851 in the floor of a little church at Baš on Krk and thus its name, but on Krk, the word Baška is also synonymous with sun, surf, and beaches.

The town of Baška is a sun worshiper's paradise with 2,500 hours of rays a year and more than 30 beaches of various sizes. The people who settled here in Roman times wouldn't recognize what this former fishing village has become, partly because it was originally on a hilltop before being relocated closer to the sea following the 16th century Venetian Wars. Remnants of that era's structures still can be seen in the town's streets and tangled alleyways. Today's Baška retains much of the charm of bygone days, but it is also full of gleaming resorts and offers loads of activities for tourists.

GETTING THERE AND AROUND

Baška is about 72km (45 miles) from Rijeka and less than an hour from Krk Town but it's a world away from the Catskill atmosphere of Opatija. Buses originating in Rijeka stop at the edge of Baška between the harbor and the beach and it's a short walk to Zvonimirova, the town's main street and the site of the city tourist office, which can provide maps, brochures and directions. Information about the town and accommodations is also available at a number of private tourist agencies. In addition, summer ferries connect Baška with Lopar on the island of Rab to the south.

Baška Tourist Office   Maps, brochures, directions.

Zvonimirova 114. ✆ 051/856-817. Fax 051/856-544. www.tz-baska.hr. June–Sept 8am–8pm daily; Oct–May 8am–3pm Mon–Fri.

Hoteli Baška   All the big tourist hotels in Baška are managed by Hoteli Baška.

E. Geistlicha 34. ✆ 051/656-111. Fax 051/656-801. www.hotelibaska.hr.

Aventura   Finds private accommodations, changes money, arranges excursions.

Zvonimira 194. ✆ 051/856-774. www.aventura-baska.com.

Autocamp Zablać   Information about camping site, prices, availability, directions.

✆ 051/856-909. Fax 051/856-604.

WHAT TO SEE AND DO

Church of St. Lucy ☆   The floor of this church in Jurandvor, less than a mile north of Baška, is the place where Croatia's Baška Tablet was found in 1851. As with Egypt's Rosetta Stone, it took years to decipher the Glagolitic script that mentions Zvonimir, Croatia's first king. The church is impossible to miss—it's visible from all over this small town—and is always open.

Stara Baška ☆☆   It's just a tiny village on a bay to the west of Baška proper, but Stara Baška is a sight worth seeing if you can ignore the weekend homes nearby that seem to be multiplying like rabbits. There are no buses here, so you have to drive or devote a day to hiking in the hills. If you fall in love with the place, there are apartments and rooms available as well as three restaurants. In the summer, you can also catch a cruise to Rab, Cres, and Lošinj or just stay put and visit the remains of the medieval **St. Jerome Church.**

Baška beaches 🌟🌟 It goes without saying that anyone who visits Baška must see the beach, even if soaking up the sun isn't on the agenda. By day or night the city's beaches are a center of activity and a great place for people-watching. Baška's long expanse of beach once was a soft sandy strip, but the sand has been covered with pebbles.

Wellness Baška 🌟🌟🌟 As Croatian spas go, this is the most beautiful in the country. Situated near the Hotel Zvonimir Hotel, Wellness Baška opened in June 2005 and was designed to resemble a Mediterranean villa with all the soothing colors and scents associated with that part of the world. In addition to its beautiful environment, Wellness Baška has a list of facilities and holistic services second to none plus a huge, brand-new outdoor pool ringed with exotic plants and flowers.

Emila Geistlicha 38. ☎ 051/656-825. Fax 051/656-826. www.wellness-baska.info. Daily 9am–9pm.

WHERE TO STAY

Baška is full of hotels, villas, and private accommodations. Hotel rooms for July and August are usually booked well in advanced by German and Italian guests who have been coming to Baška for generations. If you must visit during these months, book your rooms by Easter.

EXPENSIVE

Hotel Zvonimir 🌟🌟 You'd never know that the Zvonimir was built in 1906 because the magnificent renovation completed in 2005 has turned the hotel into a comfortable contemporary showcase. Guest rooms are furnished in shades of the sea to complement the view out the window. The hotel is steps to the beach and the Wellness Baška spa 🌟🌟🌟.

Emila Geistlicha 34 51523 Baška. ☎ 051/656-111. Fax 051/656-880. www.hotelibaska.hr. 70 units, 15 suites. Summer: doubles from 960kn ($178); suites from 2,170kn ($403). Other times: doubles from 510kn ($94); suites from 1,270kn ($236). AE, DC, MC, V. Rates include breakfast. **Amenities:** Restaurant; cafe; bar; pool; spa; excursions. *In room:* AC, TV, minibar, Internet access, safe.

Villa Adria 🌟🌟 *Value* Another Hoteli Baška property, this apartment facility down the street from the Zvonimir is spacious and so close to the beach you could throw a rock into the water from your bedroom. The kitchenettes are fully equipped, which is a boon for families and anyone who doesn't want to bother going out for a meal. Guests at Villa Adria also have the option of using any of the Zvonimir facilities. And the 2-bedroom units can sleep 4 or more comfortably.

Emila Geistlicha 34. 51523 Baška. ☎ 051/656-111. Fax 051/856-880. www.hotelibaška.hr. 12 units. Summer: 1-bedroom from 1,120kn ($208); 2-bedroom from 950kn ($176). Other times: 1-bedroom from 360kn ($67); 2-bedroom from 410kn ($76). AE, DC, MC, V. **Amenities:** Privileges at all Zvonimir Hotel facilities. *In room:* A/C, TV, Internet access, safe.

Camping Zablać 🌟 You can wake up next to the sea at this camp by the water on the south end of the beach. Problem is that when the sun comes up there isn't any shade and everything bakes. But you can rent a refrigerator here and there's a surfing school with surfboards for rent about 300 ft. from the camp.

E. Geistlicha 38. ☎ 051/856-909. Fax 051/856-604. www.hotelibaska.hr. 220kn ($41) for 2 with car and tent site.

FKK Camp Bunculuka   This naturist campground has its own beach and is just over the hill east of the harbor. The camp has a restaurant, bar, and sports center, too. It also has washers and dryers so you can wash the clothes you aren't wearing anyway.

E. Geistlicha. ℂ **051/856-806.** Fax 051/856-595. www.hotelibaska.hr. 194kn ($36) for 2 with car and tent site.

WHERE TO DINE

Bistro Kvarner ⭐ CROATIAN/ITALIAN   Right on the promenade, this charming tile patio serves up some of the tastiest food around. The menu also has pastas, risottos, and the usual complement of grilled meats and fish. You can be adventuresome and order the steak with cherries, but it is the Italian-style pizza with ultrathin crust that stars here. Try the Pizza Pigalo, a concoction with prosciutto, tomatoes, mozzarella, and mushrooms. Service is quick and courteous.

Emila Geistlicha. ℂ **051/856-366.** Entrees 24kn–38kn ($4.50–$7) for a medium pizza and up to 125kn ($23) for a fish plate. AE, DC, MC, V. Daily 10am to midnight.

Restaurant Cicibela ⭐⭐ SEAFOOD   This cute fish restaurant near the tourist office serves well-prepared seafood and meat in a nautical atmosphere. The catch of the day is proudly displayed in an ice case as you enter so you can be sure your dinner is fresh. Try the Baška platter, a mixed grill for 2, or the grilled scampi. The blitva (potatoes mixed with Swiss chard) here is excellent.

Emila Geistlicha bb. ℂ **051/185-013.** Entrees 54kn–210kn ($10–$39). AE, DC, MC, V. Daily 10am to midnight.

Caffe Mateo ICE CREAM   At least one helping of ice cream is *de rigueur* for anyone on a beach vacation in Croatia. Some of the best frozen treats are served here along with pastries, coffees, and fancy fruit drinks with or without alcohol.

Emilia Geistlicha 22. ℂ **051/856-109.** Daily 10am to midnight.

5 Rab Island

Like an actor who insists on being photographed from his "better side," Rab's terrain has two halves that are quite different from each other. If seen from the mainland, Rab resembles a strip-mined mountainside devoid of vegetation and inhospitable to intelligent life. The southwestern side of the island, however, is a very different story. Tranquil beaches and coves, green spaces, and a beautifully kept medieval Old Town belie travelers' first impressions. Rab has been a haven for tourists since the 19th century, but its history goes back even further.

Like Pag to the south, Rab was settled by Liburnian Illyrians, who were succeeded by a series of conquerors: Romans, Byzantines, Croat-Hungarians, and finally the Venetians, who plundered the timber on Rab and other offshore Kvarner islands to build their ships. This wholesale environmental piracy left a vast swathe of ruined terrain. It wasn't until the late 19th century that tourism began to cross the forlorn-looking east side of the island to get to Rab's verdant southwest side, where hotels began to sprout for aristocrats intent on frolicking in the surf.

Italy and Germany dominated Rab around World War II, and the island finally reverted to Yugoslavia in the late 1940s when Tito took control. Tito converted the barren little island of Goli Otok (between Rab's east side and the mainland) into a prison camp where he detained Stalin supporters (though officially the place didn't exist and wasn't mentioned until Tito's death). It is said that men who wound up on **Goli Otok** spent their days carrying rocks from one site to another and back again.

Today Goli Otok is a tour-boat stop and Rab is a mecca for economical family vacations and for visitors who want to combine a beach vacation with a little history, The island's main tourist destinations are Rab Town with its medieval center and series of Venetian campaniles (bell towers); and Lopar Peninsula at the island's northern tip, with its sandy beach and shallow water. Rab is also becoming a popular overnight stop for luxury yachts, which become tourist attractions themselves when they tie up in Rab Town's horseshoe-shaped harbor.

GETTING THERE

BY CAR AND/OR BOAT   Getting to Rab can be tricky if you are anywhere but the mainland because of the vagaries of ferry connections between the islands. The ferry between Baška at the southern end of Krk runs to Lopar only between June and September, and then just five times per day. If you have a car, the efficient Rapska Plovidba car ferries zoom from **Jablanac** on the mainland south of Senj to **Mišnak** on the island's south end every half-hour (or more often) from 5am to 10:30pm during summer, but the schedule is reduced by half in winter. In the summer of 2007 the cost for a car and 2 people was 102kn ($19) one-way. Another Jadrolinja car ferry route runs from Rijeka to Rab and goes on to Mali Lošinj three times a week. At Mali Lošinj you can connect with the Mariner ferry that operates between **Kopar** and **Zadar** with stops at **Pula** and **Mali Lošinj.** Lines for the ferry at Jablanac can be excruciatingly long in July and August, but the once-a-day car ferry from Mali Lošinj to Pula or Zadar (depending on the direction) is frequently half-full, so plan accordingly.

BY BUS   There are two daily buses from Rijeka to Rab via the Jablanac ferry connection, and two others from Zadar. For other transit options, contact the Rab Tourist Office (p. 195), but in any case, be sure to book ahead. The buses fill up quickly during the summer months.

GETTING AROUND

Moving around the island is no problem as there is frequent bus service between Lopar and Rab Town, and between Rab Town and **Kampor, Barbat,** and **Suha Punta** on the island. A water taxi goes to the tourist complex at Suha Punta on the southwest side of the island four times a day from the Hotel Istra in Rab Town and another makes the same number of daily trips to the nearby Fraknj FKK compound (nudist camp).

RAB TOWN

Rab Town is a medieval wonder, rich with ancient churches and narrow, cobbled streets that seem to be vertical at points. There is also a wealth of stone buildings with red-tiled roofs, and 4 Venetian-inspired campaniles that stand sentry at the harbor.

ORIENTATION

Old Town is immediately behind the Riva and marina, and you have a choice of three narrow uphill paths, **Donja, Srednja,** and **Gornja** (lower, middle, upper), to get there. A Merkur store, the bus station, and a few tourist agencies are about a quarter of a mile north of the Old Town and, farther west, you'll find **Komrčar Park** and the **Franciscan Monastery and Cemetery,** with the town's beaches on its south end.

VISITOR INFORMATION

Numerous sources of information are available to visitors on Rab. Many arrange accommodations and excursions.

Turistička Zajednica   This is the official office of the city's tourist association.

Donja Ulica 2. ⓒ **051/771-111**. Fax 051/771-110. www.tzg-rab.hr. Daily June–Sept 8am–10pm; Oct–May 8am–noon and 7–9pm. There is a satellite tourist office behind the bus station.

Atlas Travel Agency   The agency can arrange for excursions and private accommodations as well as boat tours of the island.

Trg Municipium Arba. ⓒ **051/724-585**. www.atlas-rab.com. Daily June–Sept 8am–10pm; Oct–May Mon–Sat 8am–1pm; closed Sun.

Numero Uno   Numero Uno specializes in private rooms and apartments. Most charge 30% extra if you book for less than 3 days.

J. de Marisa 22, 51280 Rab. ⓒ **051/724-688**. www.dmmedia.com.

WHAT TO SEE & DO
CHURCHES & BELL TOWERS

Rab Town is a city of churches. Most of these are along the Gornja spur (upper road) that parallels the Riva. Some of the churches are open only for Mass, but most leave vestibule doors open all day so you can peek through a window or iron grate and get a glimpse of the inside. If you are heading uphill from the harbor, be sure to take a look at the **fountain** in **Trg Svetog Kristofora,** which is adorned with sculptures of the mythical figures of **Kalifont** and **Draga.** Between the fountain and the churches are a few 15th-century palaces built by highborn families. **Dominus Palace** and **Nimira Palace** are the most impressive, but both are closed to the public.

There are many strategies for seeing Rab Town's string of churches, but if you are coming from the Nimira Palace and continue on to the top of the hill, you'll run right into **St. Christopher's,** which once was part of the city's highest tower. A small **lapidarium** next door holds ancient tombstones and other artifacts. Turn down Gornja Ulica, and you'll come to **St. John the Evangelist Church (Sveti Ivan Evandelista),** which dates to the 6th or 7th century and is little more than a ruin. The church served as a monastery for various religious orders as well as a bishop's residence, but it was closed in the first third of the 19th century and many of its bricks were used to repair other churches in the city. The 13th-century bell tower next door can be climbed.

Next is **Holy Cross Church (Sveti Križ)** which, according to legend, has a crucifix with a Christ figure that wept because of the townspeople's immoral conduct. **St. Justine Church (Sveti Justina)** is next, with its 16th-century bell tower and collection of sacral items, including the reliquary that supposedly holds the skull of St. Christopher. Continue on past Trg Slobode and you'll come to a third bell tower at **St. Andrew Church (Sveti Andrije),** which dates from the 12th century.

Just beyond that is the Romanesque **Church of St. Mary the Great (Sveta Marija Velika),** which is not only on the highest hill in town, but has the biggest bell tower. Both the church and its bell tower were built in the 12th century. The *pieta* above the church door dates to the early 16th century. The church itself is full of centuries of history with its 11th-century altar canopy, its 15th-century choir stalls, and its 16th-century architecture. But it is the bell tower that draws the most attention. Situated on Roman ruins, the 23m-tall (75-ft.) tower has four floors and includes a balustraded pyramid on top. You can climb this one for about $1. If you look at the four bell towers from the sea, they clearly slope from tallest to shortest. The last church on the route is baroque **St. Anthony (Sveti Antun),** which has an impressively carved marble altar.

Church Hours

St. Christopher Church: July and August, 9am to noon and 7:30 to 10pm. June and September, 7:30 to 9pm.

St. Christopher Lapidarium: July and August, 9am to 1pm and 6 to 8pm. Admission $1.

Holy Cross Church: July and August, 9am to noon and 7:30 to 10pm. June and September, 7:30 to 9pm.

St. Justine: July and August, 9am to noon and 7:30 to 10pm. June and September, 7:30 to 9pm.

St. Mary the Great: ℂ 051/724-195. 10am to 1pm and 7:30 to 10pm daily. 5kn ($1) to climb the bell tower; kids can go to the first level if accompanied by a parent.

ACTIVITIES & CELEBRATIONS

Besides looking at churches and bell towers, Rab has a wide range of tourist attractions and activities that include watersports, tours, and festivals.

Tours   Most travel agencies in town offer boat tours of the island as well as day trips to nearby Lošinj or Pag. There are also excursions to Kampor, on the northwest part of the island; and to Barbat, on the south side of Rab.

Diving   Scuba-diving excursions can be arranged through **Mirko Diving Center** (Barbat 17, 51280 Rab; ℂ **051/721-154;** www.mirkodivingcenter.com); or through **Kron Diving Center** (413a Kampor, 51280 Rab; ℂ **051/776-620;** fax 051/776-630; www.dron-diving.com).

WHERE TO STAY
VERY EXPENSIVE

Arbiana Hotel 🐟🐟 *Finds*   The 1924 building that houses the Arbiana has never looked better. The Art Nouveau boutique hotel re-opened in June 2007 after decades of neglect and after an almost 4-year renovation. It has been making waves on Rab's waterfront ever since. The owners, who live in New York, took care to incorporate the original building's best features into their plans, and the result is a perfect combination of historic architecture and 21st-century luxury. Guest rooms differ in size and shape because of the building's construction, but all are done in deep jewel colors; and all have ample space, plush upholstered furniture, and several mirrors; and all bathrooms have tubs. At turndown time, Arbia's staff was leaving small, wrapped portions of Rabska torta on pillows instead of chocolate. The recipe for the delicious cakes is a secret, but they are made by local women and taste like dense pound cake with hints of orange and cherry and a ribbon of marzipan.

Obala Kralja Petra Kresimira 12. 51280 Rab. ℂ **051/775-900.** Fax 051/775-991. www.arbianahotel.com. 28 units, including 5 suites. Double deluxe from 310€ ($454); suites from 380€ ($552). AE, DC, MC, V. Rates include breakfast and VAT. **Amenities:** Restaurant; grill; 2 bars; room service; access for those w/disabilities; babysitting (extra charge); parking. *In room:* A/C, SAT/TV, minibar, hair dryer, wireless access, safe, robe and slippers.

EXPENSIVE

Hotel Ros Maris ✿   This hotel at the Riva's midpoint is all cool design and elegance that reeks of Euro-chic. A rooftop terrace overlooks the bay, and the renovated over-size guest rooms have views of either the sea or Old Town. Bathrooms are sleek; those in suites have their own Jacuzzis. This is a place to be pampered.

Obala Petra Krešimira IV, 51280 Rab. ℂ 051/778-899. Fax 051/724-206. www.rosmaris.com. 146 units. Summer and Christmas week: from 1,450kn ($270) double; from 2,610kn ($485) suite. Rest of year: from 550kn ($100) double; from 1,310kn ($262) suite. AE, DC, MC, V. **Amenities:** Restaurant; cafe; bar; pool bar; pool; spa; nightclub; room service, nonsmoking rooms available. *In room:* A/C, TV w/pay stations, minibar, hair dryer, safe.

MODERATE

Hotel Istra   "Cute" is the word that describes Hotel Istra. Guest rooms are done in sunny colors and have a family feel, even if they are a bit cramped. Bathrooms are clean and well kept. There are few amenities here, though each room has a phone.

M. de Dominisa bb, 51280 Rab. ℂ 051/724-050. Fax 051/724-134. www.hotel-istra.hr. 101 units. Summer: from 690kn ($128) double. Rest of year: from 565kn ($105) double. Rates include breakfast. AE, DC, MC, V. **Amenities:** Restaurant; cafe; bar; tennis court; parking. *In room:* SAT/TV.

Hotel Imperial   This sizeable hotel with the longest tradition on Rab is difficult to see from the Riva because it's set back in the woods at the end of the harbor. The hotel is a plain white box without the trees, but its location in Komrcar Park gives it a grand appearance. The terrace Taverna on the hotel's first level is lively, even in the middle of the day. Guest rooms were updated in 2006, but they still are small, and the bath-rooms could use better plumbing. The beach is only 5 minutes away. The hotel holds special programs at New Year's and Easter.

J. Baraković 2, 51280 Rab. ℂ 051/724-522. Fax 051/724-126. www.imperial.hr. 134 units. Summer: from 775kn ($144) double. Rest of year: from 435kn ($81) double. Rates include breakfast. AE, DC, MC, V. **Amenities:** Restaurant; bar. *In room:* A/C, SAT/TV, hair dryer.

Hotel Padova   This modern structure isn't much to look at from the outside, but a 2005 update has freshened 65% of the rooms and bathrooms. However, the hotel's public areas are still mired in its former dour socialist persona. The seawater pool is perfect for kids as it is no more than 3 feet deep; the indoor pool is out of commis-sion and the single computer in the "Internet Center" is coin operated. The hotel faces Old Town from across the bay, so the view from the small balconies on most rooms is of the skyline. *Warning:* Padova's parking lot is inadequate for the hotel's capacity and you'll often find lines of cars in throughways blocking legally parked vehicles.

Banjol bb. ℂ 051/724-444. padova@imperial.hr. 175 units. Summer seaside rooms: from 740kn ($127) double. Rest of year: from 500kn ($100) double. Rates include breakfast. AE, DC, MC, V. Limited free parking. **Amenities:** Restaurant; cafe; bar; pool; sun terrace; salon. *In room:* A/C, TV minibar, hair dryer.

WHERE TO EAT

Rab is the land of pizza restaurants and casual konobas that specialize in fresh fish. With a few exceptions, they all dish up roughly the same kind of fare.

San Marino (Arbiana Hotel) ✿✿ MEDITERRANEAN   San Marino may be the most romantic restaurant on Rab. On nice evenings diners sit at candlelit tables under trees in the park adjacent to the Arbiana with soft music and the sea as background noise. The restaurant's indoor space is also nicely appointed, but it is San Marino's menu that attracts diners. Start with beef and chicken minestrone accessorized with julienned crepes and move on to Kvarner risotto infused with scampi and garnished with zucchini. For dessert, the menu lists the usual Croatian suspects—pala činke, flan, ice cream—and the choices are a letdown after the chef's creative cuisine. Both the restaurant and the hotel are smoke-free, unusual in Croatia.

Obala Kralja Petra Kresimira 12. 51280 Rab. ℂ **051/775-900.** Fax 051/775-991. www.arbianahotel.com. Entrees 86kn–230kn ($16–$43). AE, DC, MC, V. Daily 7:30am–11pm.

Zeko Pizzeria PIZZA/BURGERS   "Zeko" refers to fast food in Croatian and this collection of bench seat tables along the waterfront sidewalk offers speedy service. Zeko appeals to families because of its reasonable prices and familiar offerings, but the food, though "fast" is well prepared and might even be nutritious. Try one of the pizzas—we liked the Neapolitan with tomatoes and olives—or even a burger and fries.

I Donja bb. No phone. Pizza 37kn–47kn ($7–$9); other choices 28kn–59kn ($5–$11). No credit cards. 11am–9pm June-Aug only.

Taverna Bistro ✿ PIZZA & PASTA   A beautiful park setting surrounds this terrace dining spot, which is full of red umbrella tables. Pizzas dominate the extensive menu; most are displayed outside on a board, there are lots to choose from. Try the plain Margherita or go for pizza with *frutti di mare* for an interesting change.

Jurja Barakovića bb (in the Imperial Hotel). ℂ **051/724-184.** Entrees 30kn–50kn ($6–$10). No credit cards. Daily 8am–10pm.

Konoba Riva SEAFOOD   Situated inside the Hotel Riva, the ambience of this casual fish restaurant is definitely rustic, with a decor employing lots of stone and wood. The food, however, is a little better than that of most restaurants in this class. Try any of the grilled fish dishes or the risotto with squid, which is outstanding. There is even something billed "American chicken" on the menu.

Biskupa Draga 3. ℂ **051/725-887.** www.konoba-riva.hr. Entrees 35kn–135kn ($6–$23). M, V. Daily 10am–11pm.

6 Cres & Lošinj Islands

Cres and Lošinj are really a single island, separated only by a 48m-wide (144-ft.) manmade channel that has been bridged by roadway. Despite their proximity and historical link, these islands couldn't be more different. Cres stretches 60km (40 miles) from tip to tip and is twice as long as Lošinj. Both islands are covered with biking and hiking trails, but it is Cres that is a haven for campers who like to rough it and for hikers who like a challenge. Lošinj, on the other hand, is the island of choice for yachters and tourists looking for relaxing cafes and beaches.

More than half of Cres is covered with rocks and scrub grass, a landscape interrupted only by intersecting rock fences and sheep shelters that create a crisscross pattern on the inhospitable terrain. Osor is home to the protected griffon vulture. Lošinj is blanketed with a thick tree cover, well-groomed pebble beaches, lots of shops and restaurants, and several large resort hotels.

Cres's tourist destinations are the island's main population centers—Cres Town, which could double as a fishing village in Italy; and Osor, where a tiny bridge spans the narrow canal separating Cres from Lošinj. Several minuscule, remote villages—**Beli, Lubenice,** and **Valun**—are worth a detour. Lošinj's main villages are **Mali Lošinj** and **Veli Lošinj.** Both attract a large number of tourists, but it is Mali Lošinj that is the more developed center, probably as a result of Lošinj's former status as a shipyard and winter vacation destination for wealthy Austrians. Today, both islands reap most of their revenue from tourism, while each retains its character.

Cres and Lošinj have been inhabited since the Stone Age and followed the familiar settlement pattern of the rest of Croatia's offshore islands. The islands were home to the Illyrians more than 3,000 years ago until the Romans came along in the 1st century, followed by the Byzantines and the Slavs. The Venetians, the Croat-Hungarians, the Austo-Hungarians, and the Yugoslavs followed until the islands finally came under Croatian control in 1991. Today Cres and Lošinj are thriving destinations that cater to a wide variety of tourism tastes.

GETTING THERE & GETTING AROUND

BY CAR AND/OR BOAT   Getting to Cres and Lošinj is easy if you are driving or taking the ferry; and a little more complicated if you are traveling some other way. The shortest ferry crossing is from **Brestova** on the mainland to **Porozina** at the northern end of Cres and costs about $20 for a car and two passengers. However, the wait to board there can be brutal in July and August, even though the ferries throw away their schedules and provide nonstop service by crossing as soon as they are full. Sometimes the wait to board is 2 hours long, and except for a small snack kiosk near the ticket booth, there isn't any shade. There is another crossing from **Valbiska** on Krk to **Merag** farther down on Cres. From June to September, a car ferry runs from **Zadar** and **Pula** to **Mali Lošinj,** continuing on to **Koper** across the border in Slovenia. Other routes stop in Mali Lošinj, and some go as far as Venice and Rijeka. Contact Jadrolinja or **Lošinjska Plovidba** (p. 199) for schedules and routes.

BY BUS   There are six daily buses from Veli Lošinj to Cres Town, and all stop at Mali Lošinj on the way. Buses also run to each of the islands' main ferry ports twice a day—Merag, Porozina, and Valbiska—and four buses per day go to Rijeka. In addition, two buses a day go to Zagreb. For details and schedules, contact any tourist agency on the island or the main bus station in Rijeka.

LOCAL BUSES   An hourly bus runs from the big hotels on **Čikat Bay** 5kn ($1) to Mali Lošinj, and nine buses a day run between Mali Lošinj and Veli Lošinj 10kn ($2).

VISITOR INFORMATION

Tourist offices are numerous in Mali Lošinj and difficult to find in Cres Town, but offices in either place can help you find accommodations and transport even if it is on another island.

CRES

Cresanka (www.cresanka.hr) provides links to private accommodations on Cres (© **051/571-161;** fax 051/571-16; July–Aug, daily 8am–8pm; Sept–June, 8am–4pm Mon–Fri). In summer, double private rooms with bathrooms cost from 280kn ($52), apartments from 715kn ($132). During the rest of the year, double private rooms with bathroom run from 140kn ($26), apartments from 340kn ($63).

MALI LOŠINJ

Mali Lošinj Tourist Office   Provides maps, information, and brochures.

Riva Lošinjskih Kapetana 29. © 051/231-884. www.tz-malilosinj.hr. Sept daily 8am–8pm; Oct–May Mon–Fri 8am–1pm.

Lošinjska Plovidba   This agency specializes in private accommodations on Lošinj. It also arranges sports excursions and sells tickets for the Marinas ferry that runs between Koper and Zadar. Hours here are flexible because the sales agents leave to sell tickets at the marina office half an hour before each sailing.

Riva Lošinjska Plovidba Kapetana 8. © 051/231-077. Fax 051/231-611. www.losinjplov.hr.

Manora　is a friendly agency that specializes in private accommodations, villas, hotels, and excursions. You can also rent a scooter here.

Priko 29, 51550 Mali Losinj. ℂ **051/520-100.** Fax 051/520-099. www.manora-losinj.hr.

WHAT TO SEE ON CRES
CRES TOWN

During the day, Cres Town resembles a deserted coastal village somewhere in southern Italy thanks to its complement of small fishing boats, Venetian-style architecture, and relentless sun. While the sun is high, patrons in the cafes are sparse; stores are closed by noon; and even the local dogs curl up in a shady spot to nap. When the sun goes down, however, families come out to walk around the little harbor with its backdrop of Venetian-style facades.

The sound of Cres's peculiar chatter in a mix of Croatian and Italian makes you forget that you're in Croatia. In fact, there is a strong Italian influence on Cres and its sister island Lošinj, both of which have been popular vacation destinations for Italian tourists for years, probably because of the islands' proximity to Venice and because both once were under Venetian rule. Everything here—street signs, menus, brochures—is bilingual in Croatian and Italian.

Cres's main square, **Trg F. Petrića,** extends to the harbor. It is home to a lovely 16th-century loggia where public announcements once were posted. It also has an impressive 16th-century clock. From Trg F. Petrića, go through the 16th-century gate to **Pod Urom,** another square where you will find the church of St. Mary of the Snow. This little church has a graceful 15th-century portal adorned with a relief of the Virgin and Child. It is open during services only, but it's worth trying to coordinate your visit with Mass so you can see the carved wooden Pieta inside.

At the south end of town, the **Franciscan Monastery** has a small museum. Much of the art inside depicts the order's clerics and it is rather boring, but there is a 15th-century Murano of the Virgin and Child that is worth a look if you are an art lover. It can be viewed 10am to noon and 4 to 6:30pm Monday to Saturday, at 10kn ($2) per adult.

BELI, VALUN, & LUBENICE

North of Cres Town, the island becomes steep and the road becomes a twisting, narrow ribbon more like a roller-coaster track than a thoroughfare. About 8km (5 miles) past Cres Town, the road forks into **Beli,** a captivatingly rustic village that is practically deserted. **Eco-Centre Caput Insulae** 🐦🐦 (Beli 4; ℂ **051/840-525;** www.caput-insulae.com; admission 20kn ($4) adults, 10kn ($2) children; daily 8am–9pm), which was established in 1993 to protect the island's griffon vultures, is here, and if you aren't lucky enough to spot one of these endangered birds in the wild, you can take in the center's exhibits.

Valun is just 14km (9 miles) southwest of Cres Town, and it can't be accessed reasonably without private transportation. Buses stop at the main road above the town three times a week, but you have to descend into town on foot from there (and walk back up), which takes nearly 2 hours down and longer for the trip back. Even with a car, you have to hoof it down a long flight of stairs to the harbor. Like Beli, Valun is anything but crowded. There are a few restaurants for those who are attracted by Valun's beaches. For history buffs, Valun is home to the **Valun Tablet,** which is really an 11th-century Glagolitic-inscribed tombstone. The Valun Tablet (with Latin translation in case you can read *that* dead language) can be viewed in the town's parish church. A Cresanka **tourist office** in town can arrange a booking in one of the town's few rooms, but it's better to have a reservation in hand before you go there with the expectation of staying the night. The Valun **tourist office** is near the harbor (© 051/525-050; www.cresanka.hr; July–Aug daily 8am–10pm). **Zdovice Camping** is a small campground (70 sites) with a restaurant and a bar near the beach at Valun. It has accommodations for tents only, and you have to leave your car outside. Its location is 51557 Valun 9 (© **051/571-161;** fax 051/571-163; www.cresanka.hr; 7€/$10).

Lubenice is 4.8km (3 miles) southwest of Valun atop a windy ridge high above a beautiful clear-water cove. You can get bottled water at a small snack bar at the top, and "remote" toilets are available, but that's about all. The **view** ✸✸✸ is breathtaking. You can get to the water below by picking your way down the gravel slope, but invest in a bottle of water and take it with you. Don't forget that you have to climb back up unless someone meets you with a boat in the bay.

There are buses to Valun and the neighboring towns of Lubenice and Beli, but they don't run every day, and schedules are more like suggestions. Buses from Cres Town hit Beli twice a week, for example, but it's best to arrange a tour with Cresenko in Cres Town or rent a car. *Warning:* This trip is not for anyone who is afraid of heights.

WHERE TO STAY

There are few hotel choices on Cres, but plenty of private accommodations. The Cresanka tourist agency in Cres Town is your best bet for these (p. 199).

Hotel Kimen   Until recently, this housing-development hotel in a wooded area was the only game in or near Cres Town. Kimen's rooms are basic bed-bathroom-balcony affairs without frills, but they are close to the beach and half a mile from the town center.

Melin I br. 16, 51557 Cres. © 051/571-161. Fax 051/571-163. www.hotel-kimen.com. 212 units. MC, V. Summer: from 70€ ($98) double. Rest of year: from 40€ ($56) double. Parking lot. **Amenities:** Restaurant; TV lounge; bar; children's program; salon.

Zlatni-Lav ✸   The tiny fishing village of MartinŠcica 27km (16 miles) southwest of Cres Town is home to 2 immaculate stucco buildings that comprise the Zlatni-Lav hotel and restaurant, an oasis of hospitality. You'll get a feel for Cres's unspoiled landscape while enjoying modern touches like satellite TV and air-conditioning in the hotel's cheery but utilitarian guest rooms, all of which have balconies and sea views.

MartinŠcica 18d. 51556 MartinŠcica, Cres. © 051/574-020. Fax 051/574-020. www.hotel-zlatni-lav.com. 30 units including 5 suites. Doubles mid-June to mid-Sept from 120€ ($168); suites from 225€ ($315) double occupancy. Other times, doubles from 63€ ($86); suites from 170€ ($258). Rates include breakfast. AE, DC, MC, V. **Amenities:** Restaurant; bar; bike and boat tours; hiking; diving; fishing. *In room:* A/C, SAT/TV, minibar, hair dryer.

Camping Bijar & Preko Mosta   These two campgrounds have 300 sites combined and are close to the tiny town of Osor. They have a playground for kids, a diving center, a boat ramp, and even some mobile homes for rent. Reservations are recommended.

Jazon d.o.o., 51542 Osor 76. © 051/237-027. Fax 051/237-115. booking@jazon.hr. 160kn (**$27/23€**) per day for 2 people, campsite, and car July–Aug; 105kn($21/18€) other times.

Autocamp Kovačine   You won't have to go far to get to the water at this campground half a mile from Cres Town. Autocamp Kovačine is steps away from the sea and backed by olive and pine trees. It has a restaurant, sports center, and even a diving school for the hearing-impaired. Part of this camp is reserved for naturists.

Melin 1/20, 51557 Cres. © 051/571-423. Fax 051/571-086. www.camp.kovacine.com. 175kn ($30) per day for 2 people, car, and site. Closed Nov–Mar.

WHERE TO DINE

The harbor in Cres Town is ringed with pizza places and a few grills. Most are pretty much the same and can be crowded on summer evenings.

Pizza Palada (Value) PIZZA   This pizza parlor on the marina serves decent food at reasonable prices. It is frequented by families, so tables can be difficult to find in the evening.

Palada 4. No phone. Medium pizzas 15kn–60kn ($3–$11). No credit cards. Daily 10am–midnight.

Pizza Luna Rosa PIZZA   Adjacent to Pizza Palada, the menu choices are the same, the ambience is the same, the prices are the same, but the decor differs slightly in that Pizza Luna Rosa has better shade during the day.

Palada 6. No phone. Medium pizzas 15kn–60kn ($3–$11). No credit cards. Daily 10am–midnight.

Restoran Cres ITALIAN   This bright yellow building at the end of the square near the harbor will catch your eye with its huge, bright awning. Restoran Cres serves breakfast, lunch, and dinner with a menu skewed toward Italian fare. Cres offers a kids' menu, vegetarian plates, and some nice-looking salads and tortellini, too.

Riva Creskih Kapetana 10, 51557 Cres. ✆ 051/571-163. Dinner entrees 27kn–140kn ($5–$26). AE, DC, MC, V. Daily 8am–midnight.

Gostionica Riva ✦ SEAFOOD   Fish is king at this local hangout, but you can also get omelets and pasta. Try the scampi with pasta or the grilled fish of the day. This place is a little classier than most of the cafes along the harbor.

Šetalište 24. ✆ 051/571-203. Entrees 20kn–60kn ($4–$11). No credit cards. Daily 10am–11pm.

WHAT TO SEE ON LOŠINJ
MALI LOŠINJ

Mali Lošinj started building its reputation as a tourist destination at about the same time it stopped building ships for the Austro–Hungarian Empire. When the shipbuilding industry declined in the 19th century, tourism came forward to take its place. Mali Lošinj prospered despite the economic downturn, because wealthy Austrians began to winter there much the same as they had in Opatija, though not to the same extent.

Some of the villas built in that era still exist, as does the shipyard, which is still working. Despite its annual influx of foreign tourists—from all around the globe—Mali Lošinj has retained its charm and character, mostly by keeping the big resort complexes outside of town on Čikat Bay, west of the center. On summer nights, the **Riva Lošinjskih Kapetana** along the harbor can resemble New Orleans at Mardi Gras, and getting a table at a restaurant or a room in a hotel can be impossible. But Mali Lošinj manages to handle the chaos without blinking an eye.

Art Collections ✦✦   Mali Lošinj isn't flush with vintage buildings and monuments, but it does have a collection of contemporary Croatian artworks and old masters accumulated by the Mihic[avić and Piperata families that is housed in the former House of Culture behind the harbor.

Vladimira Gortana 35. ✆ 051/231-173. Admission 9kn ($2). Daily 10am–noon, but hours are flexible.

Church of the Nativity of the Virgin   This 18th-century church off the main square is in the baroque style, and houses several religious paintings and sculptures of note.

Ulica Sveta Marija. Visit before or after Mass on Sun.

VELI LOŠINJ

Just 4km (2½ miles) southeast of busy Mali Lošinj, Veli Lošinj is still a sleepy fishing village, as yet largely undiscovered by the tourism machine that operates on Mali Lošảinj. However, like other coastal and island towns, it can be overrun in July and August. The island is also the hub for buses from and to Cres. It's also a nice hike along the sea from Mali Lošinj. Like Mali Lošinj, Veli Lošinj has few historical monuments but several villas are left over from the era of sea captains and industry tycoons.

St. Anthony's Church ★★   This is the most distinctive structure on the harbor, with its Venetian bell tower and collection of Italian art. St. Anthony's interior was lavishly outfitted with Italian marble altars by long-dead sea captains, who also contributed the rest of the church's art treasures.

Trg Sveti Antun. Sun before and after Mass.

Venetian Campanile ★   This 15th-century lookout tower behind the town has been recently restored and houses the city museum.

© 051/231-173. Admission 9kn ($2). June–Sept daily 10am–noon and 7–9pm.

WHERE TO STAY
EXPENSIVE

Hotel Apoksiomen ★★   Named after a 4th-century-B.C. bronze statue of a legendary Greek athlete found in the waters off Lošinj in 1999, the vintage building that was the Hotel Istra underwent a complete renovation in 2005 and emerged as a comfortable, gleaming hotel with pizazz. Done in sunny shades of yellow and blue, the Apoksiomen may be difficult to pronounce, but it's not hard on the eyes. Rooms are a bit larger than average, with soundproof windows that amazingly block out all noise from the Riva below when they are closed. The marble bathrooms are spacious and well-equipped.

Riva Lošinjskih Kapetana 1, 51550 Mali Lošinj. © 051/520-820. Fax 051/520-830. www.apoksiomen.com. 25 units. Summer: from 160€ ($224) double; from 210€ ($294) suite. Rest of year: from 120€ ($168) double; from 160€ ($224) suite. AE, DC, MC, V. **Amenities:** Restaurant; cafe; elevator; room for those w/limited mobility. *In room:* A/C, TV w/pay stations, Internet access, minibar, hair dryer, safe.

MODERATE

Hotel Villa Margarita ★ *Value*   Just steps from the town center, the Villa Margarita is an immaculate, friendly place convenient to everything. While the 19th-century villa exudes old-world charm, each of the unique guest rooms was updated in 1999, and each has a personality of its own. Bathrooms are generous, with separate rooms for tub and toilet; a few even have little balconies. The huge suites with privacy walls are perfect for family vacations. Be sure to check out the wine bar and garden terrace.

Bočac 64. © 051/233-837. Fax 051/231-940. www.vud.hr. 10 units. Summer: from 700kn ($130) double; from 1,010kn ($187) suite. Rest of year: from 440kn ($82) double; from 585kn ($108) suite. Suite rates do not include breakfast. 10% discount for stays over 7 days. 5% discount for cash payment. AE, DC, MC, V. **Amenities:** Restaurant; bar; wine bar; elevator. *In room:* A/C, TV w/pay stations, safe.

Villa Anna ★★   Tucked away along the bay on the opposite side of the promenade, Villa Anna reeks of exclusivity, but it really is a hotel for anyone who wants to be close to the marina and away from Riva madness. Built in 1999, Villa Anna's rooms have modern but minimalist furnishings with unobstructed views of the sea and the town. There are a lot of extras here, most notably the interesting menu in the hotel's **Villa Anna restaurant** ★★ that avoids the usual resort cuisine. Villa Anna is perfect for families and anyone wanting to stay away from Mali Lošinj's madding crowd but still close to the beach.

Velopin 31, 51550 Mali Lošinj. ℂ 051/233-223. Fax 051/233-224. www.vila-ana.hr. 13 units. Summer: from 730kn ($135) double; from 1,100kn ($204) suite. Rest of year: from 405kn ($75) double; from 655kn ($121) suite. Room rates include breakfast. AE, DC, MC, V. Limited free parking. **Amenities:** Restaurant; bar; pool; sauna; solarium. *In room:* A/C, TV w/cable, hair dryer, safe.

Hotel Vespera   Vespera is one of several large package hotels on Čikat Bay. If beach access and staying put are important to you, this is a perfect fit. Vespera and its twin sister Aurora both have pleasant though generic rooms, decent bathrooms, balconies, and a host of organized activities and kids' programs. Both also have the beach at their front door with umbrella attendants and a terrace cafe nearby.

Jadranka d.d. Dražica 1, 51550 Mali Lošinj. ℂ 051/661-101. Fax 051/231-904. Summer: from 580kn ($108) double; from 685kn ($127) suite. Rest of year: from 395kn ($73) double; from 580kn ($107) suite. Rates include breakfast. AE, DC, MC, V. Closed Nov–Apr. **Amenities:** Restaurant; bar; indoor pool; sauna; game room; children's program; Internet access; excursions; salon. *In room:* TV w/pay stations, minibar.

INEXPENSIVE

Camping Čikat   Set in a pine forest a little over a mile from Mali Lošinj, this campground is on a small bay and a small beach. The camp has a restaurant and a bar.

Dražica 1, 51550 Mali Lošinj. ℂ 051/232-125. Fax 051/231-708. www.camp-cikat.com.hr. 110kn ($20) for 2 people, car, and site. AE, DC, MC, V. Closed Oct 16–Mar 18.

WHERE TO DINE

The combination of a large number of Italian visitors and the availability of fresh fish makes restaurant menus look alike on Lošinj: Most restaurants serve pizza and pasta or fish, or a combination of the two, and prices don't vary much. However, some exceptions try to add surprises. As a general rule, the restaurants and cafes near the harbor are a little higher priced, and the ones inland offer more choices.

Restaurant Villa Margarita (Hotel Villa Margarita) ⚔ CROATIAN   As hotel restaurants go, Villa Margarita delivers tasty, well-prepared meals in a delightful setting, whether you choose the indoor dining room or the lovely terrace. The menu here is typical Mali Lošinj, so there aren't any surprises, but the fish is fresh, the pasta is al dente, and the price is right. Try the Villa Margarita salad with turkey for a change of pace; or splurge on fresh sea bass for a treat.

Bočac 64. ℂ 051/233-837. Fax 051/231-940. Entrees 40kn–122kn ($7–$23). AE, DC, MC, V. Daily 7am–11pm.

Gostonica Baracuda ⚔⚔ SEAFOOD   A nautical theme, fishnets, potted palms, and a menu that looks like that of every other fish restaurant in Mali Lošinj might make you think that Baracuda is just another seafood joint on the dock. You'd be wrong. Baracuda grills its fish over charcoal—and that makes all the difference. For a change of pace, try the tuna carpaccio as an appetizer and follow with grilled lobster.

Priko 31. ℂ 051/233-309. Entrees 70kn–250kn ($14–$46). No credit cards. Daily 10am–11pm.

Grill Konoba Odyssey *Value* CROATIAN   It's one of those little mom-and-pop grills with a few tables outside on the sidewalk, but this tiny restaurant really packs them in. Besides the usual spaghetti and scampi offerings, the chef mixes in a few Croatian specialties such as *pohani sir* (fried cheese) and goulash.

Velopin 14. ℂ 051/231-893. Entrees 30kn–116kn ($6–$22). No credit cards. Daily 11am–2pm and 6pm–2:30am.

Villa Anna (Hotel Villa Anna) ✸✸ CONTINENTAL   The classy Villa Anna has a restaurant to match, and that's what keeps tourists returning year after year. Just check the menu outside, and you'll know this is someplace special. But don't stop there. Try the chicken breast with wild berries and Camembert, an exquisite combination. Or go healthy and choose the eggplant stuffed with couscous. Of course Villa Anna serves fish and standards like roast lamb, but why limit yourself?

Velopin 31. ⓒ 051/233-223. Entrees 40kn–110kn ($7–$20). AE, DC, MC, V. Daily 6pm–midnight.

Restoran Dalmacija ✸✸ CROATIAN   Flowering trees, potted plants, and vines are part of the lovely terraced garden where this Dalmatian-style grill does a brisk business. The waiters are particularly cordial, and everything flows to make your meal an experience. Try the mixed grilled fish for two (which comes with potatoes and vegetables); it includes four whole fish and grilled calamari. It's fascinating to watch your waiter bone the fish with nothing but a spoon.

Mate Vidulića 19. ⓒ 051/232-400. Entrees 35kn–175kn ($6–$32). AE, DC, MC, V. Daily 10am–11pm.

8

Istria

Istria is a land of myth and magic, of glistening blue sea, vast green fields, and dark red earth. It is a triangle-shaped peninsula at the northwestern end of Croatia that protrudes just far enough into the Adriatic to catch the seductive Mediterranean climate. Most of Istria's pine- and rosemary-scented coastal landscape is lined with golden beaches and busy marinas framed by Venetian-style towns that look just as they must have when tall trading ships sailed in and out of their harbors.

Many nations have coveted and occupied Istria over the centuries, and it is remarkable that the peninsula has not become a cultural hodgepodge. Instead Istria has embraced the best of every country that contributed to its development through the ages. There you will find people with an easygoing attitude, tolerance for diversity, a love of fine food and wine, and above all, a passion for the land and sea.

Even the most transient tourist will recognize that Istrians have acquired Italian sensibilities without losing their Croatian souls. Many communicate with each other in a local dialect that is a lilting blend of Italian and Croatian, and most towns are known by both their Italian and Croatian names. Menus throughout the region read like a catalog of fusion cuisine and visitors often wonder if they've made an inadvertent border crossing.

Many Istrian coastal towns are dead ringers for Italian fishing villages, and much of the inland landscape's silvery olive groves and deep green vineyards could double as Tuscan. But when you get the bill for a meal or a hotel room, you'll know you're in Croatia and not Italy—the cost of a week in Istria is well below the cost of the same week just across the Adriatic.

Istria shares a border with Slovenia to the north, but its roots sink deeply into the Adriatic, connecting and separating it from Italy in a sometimes stormy relationship that is responsible for much of Istria's cachet.

All this and a well-developed tourist infrastructure make Istria a desirable destination for anyone looking for a vacation drenched in nature and history. Croatia's tourist bureau color-codes Istria into blue (coastal) and green (inland) sectors. Most travelers gravitate to blue Istria, which contributes big numbers to the more than 2.5 million people—mostly Europeans—who visit annually, a number that represents the largest single block of tourism in Croatia.

Istria's past is also rich with heroes, conquerors, states people, and myths, as well as agricultural and commercial tradition. This mélange gives every town and village a sense of drama smoothed with Mediterranean *joie de vivre* seasoned with mystery.

Those who believe in legends say the Greek hero Jason, his Argonauts, and their sailing ship *Argo* took shelter in the Bay of Pula during their quest for the Golden Fleece. Those who believe in miracles say St. Euphemia and her stone sarcophagus somehow washed up on the shores of Rovinj shortly after disappearing from Constantinople in A.D. 800. Historians say Bronze Age tribes built primitive settlements in Istria's verdant hills and that an Illyrian tribe known as Histri gave its name to the land. There is no question that ancient Rome prospered from the trade that flowed through Istria's ports, which were lucrative profit centers coveted by numerous nations. Venice, Austria-Hungary, Italy, and others all vied for Istria until Marshal Tito declared "game over" and made offshore Brijuni his home.

Istria has been through centuries of unrest, and its turbulent past could have resulted in a legacy of despair. Instead, hard times gave birth to tolerance and acceptance in an enchanting region that is geographically rich and historically significant, a can't-miss formula.

1 Orientation

VISITOR INFORMATION

Tourism is a $1.5-billion industry in Istria, accounting for more than 40% of all tourist overnight stays tourism traffic in Croatia. It's no wonder that Istria County has its own efficient tourist association with information offices in almost every town from Pula on the coast to Oprtalj in the interior highlands. The association maintains an exceptionally helpful and complete website (www.istra.com), where you can find information ranging from maps of the region's olive oil roads to an up-to-date schedule of festivals and events in cities throughout Istria. The county association also publishes a huge number of brochures, maps, CDs, and guides, some for special-interest travelers such as wine aficionados and spelunkers. Local tourist offices in most Istrian towns are staffed with knowledgeable people who will give you maps and brochures or even advice on where to go to dinner.

GETTING THERE

BY PLANE Istria's only major airport is at Pula, about 5km (3 miles) northwest of the center of town, and it is served by Croatia Airlines (www.croatiaairlines.hr). There is a smaller airport for private planes and charters near Vrsar in the middle of the coast. Shuttle buses and taxis (60kn–70kn/$11–$13) run between Pula's airport and the town center, where you can connect to other major Istrian towns via bus or train.

BY BOAT Venezia Lines runs regular catamarans from Venice to Umag, Poreč, Rovinj, Pula, and Rabac; and from Rimini to Pula. Check the website (www.venezialines.com) or call ✆ **041/24-24-000** from 9am to 6pm Venice time to book tickets or for detailed schedule information.

BY BUS Autotrans runs four daily buses from both Rijeka and Zagreb to Pula, and has other lines to major cities such as Umag and Rovinj on the coast. Most interior towns are connected to the coastal cities by at least one bus per day, but travel by bus to inland Istria can be inconvenient and time-consuming. For schedule information and prices, check the Autotrans website (www.autotrans.hr).

BY TRAIN There are train connections between Zagreb and Pula (7 hr.) and Rijeka and Pula (2½ hr.) as well as train connections to other coastal towns and to Pazin, the county seat in the middle of the peninsula. However, if you want to see the remote gems of inland Istria, a car is a necessity. See p. 35 for detail on Croatian Railways (www.hznet.hr).

Istria

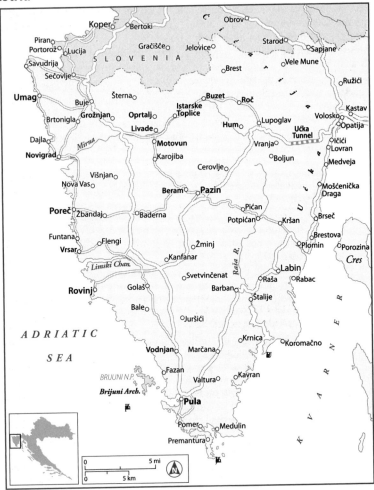

BY CAR Auto travel is by far the most flexible way to see Istria beyond the coast and the only sensible way to see the interior. There are car rental agencies in most of the major population centers (see p. 34 for contact information).

GETTING AROUND

BY CAR Gas prices and parking limitations in larger towns such as Pula notwithstanding, having access to your own car is the only way to explore side roads that lead to tiny wineries, picturesque villages, and hidden treasures (see p. 34 for car rental information).

BY BUS Regular and frequent bus service links Istria's coastal cities, but service to inland villages is much less convenient for travelers who want to see a lot in a limited amount of time or who are reluctant to walk a mile or more from the bus stop to get to the sites. For information on bus travel in Istria, the best bus company is **Autotrans** (© 052/741-817; www.autotrans.hr).

BY TRAIN   Croatian Railways (www.hznet.hr) does have trains that serve the major cities in Istria, and they are fine if you want to get to a destination where you will stay put for awhile, but there is no time-efficient way to explore the interior—or even the coast—by train because train schedules are not geared to touring (see p. 35 for more on Croatian Railways).

2 Pula (Pola)

This bustling city of 65,000 at the southern tip of Istria is a working port as well as a repository of some of the best Roman ruins in Europe, including a magnificent **amphitheater** ✫✫✫ from the 1st century that is Pula's biggest draw. Pula has other vestiges of Roman occupation (**Temple of Augustus, Forum, Arch of the Sergi** ✫✫✫) that are worth seeing, too. Besides its cache of Roman history, the city is home to a beautiful Gothic **Franciscan monastery** erected by the monks when they arrived at the end of the 13th century, as well as a 17th-century fortress built by the Venetians that now houses Istria's history museum.

ESSENTIALS

VISITOR INFORMATION   The **Tourist Information Office** is off Forum Square at Forum 2 (© **052/219-197;** fax 052/211-855; www.pulainfo.hr) opposite the Temple of Augustus. It provides maps, brochures, and lists of events in Pula and around Istria. The center is open from 9am to 8pm Monday through Saturday and from 10am to 6pm Sunday and holidays.

Private agencies like **Activatravel Istra** at Scalierova 1 (© **052/215-497;** fax 052/211-889; info@activa-istra.com) book special-interest tours, including a truffle-hunting excursion and dinner in Livade (in season). Several of the Pula area's hotels, as well as private accommodations, are operated by **Arena Turist;** its offices are in the Riviera Hotel at Splitska 1 (© **052/529-400;** www.arenaturist.hr). A short walk from the amphitheater, it is open from 7am to 8pm Monday through Saturday, 8am to 1pm Sunday. **Atlas Travel** at Starih Statuta 1 (© **052/393-040;** www.atlas-croatia.com) is open from 7am to 8pm Monday through Saturday; 8am to 1pm Sunday. Atlas books excursions, finds private accommodations, and is Pula's American Express agent. **Istra Sun-Way** at Kandlerova 34 (© **052/381-329;** www.istra-sunway.hr) is open from 8am to midnight and offers accommodations and excursions that range from island tours to land adventures. Istra books tours to the interior, so if you don't want to rent a car, you can see some of the smaller inland towns with them. You can surf online at **Enigma Computer Center,** one of the better Internet centers in Pula. Enigma, located at Kandlerova 19 (© **052/381-615**), is open daily from 10am to midnight June 1 to September; from 10am to 2pm and 5 to 8pm the rest of the year. The air-conditioned center sits between the cathedral and Augustus's Temple, providing users with free music, sweets, and drinks.

GETTING THERE   Pula's busy harbor enjoys healthy shipping and transportation traffic. Tourists can make both regional and international ferry connections between other towns in Croatia and Italy here. For more detailed information, see "Getting There" in "Orientation," earlier in this chapter.

(Fun Fact **Author, Author**

For almost a year (Oct 1904–Mar 1905), Irish author James Joyce lived in Pula where he taught English to Austro-Hungarian naval officers through the Berlitz School. Today, Joyce is immortalized in bronze in the coffee bar Uliks (Ulysses) just steps from the building where he taught. Passersby often do a double-take when they pass the statue of the author, who is portrayed seated at a table as if he were waiting for his afternoon biela kava.

GETTING AROUND   Pula is a very walkable city even outside its center, and its bus system can get you almost anywhere you need to go in town. Beyond that, a large number of bus routes emanates from Pula to Zagreb to Rijeka, and from the Istrian cities of Rovinj, Vrsar, and Poreč plus the gateway city of Trieste in Italy and coastal towns in Slovenia. If you want to explore the hills and valleys of the Istrian interior, you'll need a car.

WHAT TO SEE & DO

Pula's most interesting sites are its Roman ruins, and of those, the 1st-century amphitheater is the most impressive.

Temple of Augustus ✹✹✹   Built between 2 B.C. and A.D. 14, the Temple of Augustus is dedicated to Octavianus Augustus, the first emperor of Rome, and is situated on a square that once was the city's Forum. The temple was converted to a church after Christianity became the religion of choice in Croatia. It was also used for grain storage, but after being severely damaged during World War II, it was rebuilt. A small museum inside displays artifacts found near Pula, all captioned in English, Italian, and Croatian.

Trg Republike 3. No phone. Admission 4kn (70¢) adults, 2kn (35¢) children. Summer daily 10am–1:30pm and 6–9pm. Closed in winter.

Monastery and Church of St. Francis ✹   Just behind the tourist information center on Forum Square is the 14th-century complex that includes a single-nave basilica and a tranquil garden framed by Gothic triumphal arches. Quite a few stone pieces and mosaic fragments here date from the Roman period on, but they seem randomly strewn about and not well explained.

Castropola (west end of Sergijevaca). No phone. Admission 5kn ($1). June to mid-Sept daily 10am–1pm and 4–7pm.

Roman Floor Mosaic ✹✹   This floor mosaic from the 3rd century represents the mythological punishment of the original wicked stepmother, Circe, who was punished for her evil deeds by being tied to the horns of a bull.

Just past the Monastery and Church of St. Francis, off Sergijevaca.

Triumphal Arch of the Sergi ✹✹✹   Farther along Sergijevaca, you'll run right into the Sergi Arch, which opens to Trg Portarata and stands in the middle of a busy shopping area. The privately financed arch was built at the end of the 1st century by Salvia Postuma Sergi to honor three male family members who had fought in the Battle of Actium.

Pula

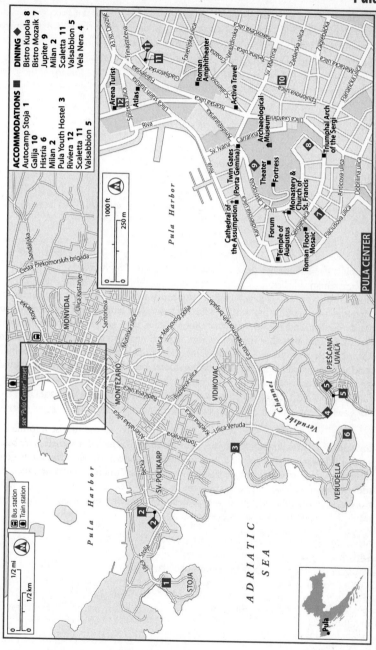

ACCOMMODATIONS ■
Autocamp Stoja 1
Galija 10
Histria 6
Milan 2
Pula Youth Hostel 3
Riviera 12
Scaletta 11
Valsabbion 5

DINING ◆
Bistro Kupola 8
Bistro Mozaik 7
Jupiter 9
Milan 2
Scaletta 11
Valsabbion 5
Vela Nera 4

Bus station
Train station

see "Pula Center" inset

PULA CENTER

Roman Amphitheater
Arena Turist
Atlas
Activa Travel
Archaeological Museum
Twin Gates (Porta Gemina)
Theater
Fortress
Cathedral of the Assumption
Forum
Temple of Augustus
Monastery & Church of St. Francis
Roman Floor Mosaic
Triumphal Arch of the Sergi

Pula Harbor

1000 ft
250 m

MONVIDAL
MONTEZARO
SV. POLIKARP
STOJA
VIDIKOVAC
VERUDELLA
PJEŠČANA UVALA

Pula Harbor

Verudski Channel

ADRIATIC SEA

1/2 mi
1/2 km

Pula

211

Hercules Gate 🐾🐾   Walk through the Sergi Arch and bear left until you get to Carrarina, where you will encounter Pula's oldest gate dating from the mid–1st century. It is decorated with a relief of its namesake mythical hero.

Twin Gates (Porta Gemina) 🐾🐾   This double arch is in front of the Archaeological Museum a little beyond the Hercules Gate. According to the literature, the gates date from the beginning of the 2nd century and lead to the amphitheater and beyond.

Archaeological Museum 🐾🐾   Archaeological finds from all over Istria are displayed in this museum that once was an Austrian secondary school. The emphasis is on artifacts from Old Histri and Roman times, but there are some nice medieval exhibits, too. Be sure to visit the outdoor sculpture garden casually decorated with scattered pieces of history. And note the Roman Twin Gates (above) at the entrance. There is also a Roman Theater in back of the garden **Tip:** You can access the garden and theater even when the museum is closed.

Carrarina 3. 🕐 **052/218-603.** Fax 052/212-415. Admission 12kn ($2.25) adults, 6kn ($1.10) children. Summer Mon–Sat 9am–8pm; Sun and holidays 10am–3pm. Winter Mon–Fri 9am–3pm; closed Sat–Sun.

Roman Amphitheater 🐾🐾🐾   The Emperor Augustus (31–14 B.C.) started construction of the amphitheater in 2 B.C.; it was finished in A.D. 14, during the rule of Vespasianus. Though smaller than the coliseum in Rome, the Arena, as it is known by locals, is remarkable because its outer wall is almost entirely intact. Inside, vestiges of the Arena's fittings are still visible, though its stone seats were removed in medieval times to complete other building projects. Designed to host gladiatorial contests and 20,000 people, the facility used a clever system of cloth canopies to shade spectators from the sun. The chambers under the Arena have been restored and now house a **museum** 🐾🐾🐾 whose permanent exhibit, "Olive and Winegrowing of Istria in Antiquity," is beautifully done and captioned in English. During the summer, the Arena is a concert site attracting such big-name stars as Andrea Bocelli. It is also the site of the prestigious Croatian Film Festival (July). **Tip:** Rent an audio tour the first time you visit the Arena.

Flavijevska bb. 🕐 **052/219-028.** Admission 20kn ($4) adults, 10kn ($2) students. Audioguide 30kn ($6). Daily 8am–9pm. Amphitheater closes early on concert days.

Cathedral of the Assumption 🐾   This cathedral has had many makeovers since it originally was converted from a Roman temple to a church in the 4th century. The current facade and bell tower date from the 17th century. Inside you can see a few 5th- and 6th-century mosaic fragments and the cathedral's unusual altar, which is actually a 3rd-century Roman sarcophagus that contains the relics of some 70 saints. The amphitheater's stone seats and other stones were used to build the bell tower.

Kandlerova bb. Daily 8:30am–2pm and 6–8pm.

WHERE TO STAY

There are very few hotels in the center of Pula, though there is a wealth of private accommodations. Inquire at the tourist office. Most hotel and beach options are south of the center in a large resort sector on the **Verudela Peninsula,** at **Pješčana Uvala,** or at **Stoja,** just a few miles from the center. These areas are reachable on the nos. 1, 3, and 7 buses.

Autocamp Stoja 🐾🐾   This campground about 3.2km (2 miles) southwest of the center in suburban Stoja is situated on a peninsula and has 670 spaces for tents plus a bank of mobile homes that sleep up to five people each. Guests have access to a beach, shops, a market, a restaurant, and sports equipment to use on the property or in the waters off the peninsula, which are some of the best around for swimming and watersports.

52110 Pula. ✆ **052/387-144**; 052/529-400. Fax 052/387-748. www.arenaturist.hr. Mobile home with A/C 114€ ($160) mid-July to mid-Aug with minimum 7-day stay starting on Sat; from 33€ ($46) other times with 3-day minimum stay. AE, DC, MC, V. Closed mid-Oct to mid-Mar.

Galija 🖈 You'll be within walking distance of the amphitheater and other Pula sites if you check in to this immaculate, family-owned hotel on a busy side street near the city center. Rooms in the main building are cheery and comfortable. The same tone continues in hues of peach and yellow in the Galija's annex, built in 2005 across the street (though doubles there are a squeeze). Parking can be challenging and rooms that face the street can get noisy. However, there are few hotels in Pula's center, so if convenience is important, you can't beat the Galija.

Epulonova 3, 52100 Pula. ✆ **052/383-802**. Fax 052/383-804. www.hotel-galija-pula.com. 21 units. July–Aug: from 63€ ($95) double and suite. Rest of year: 46€ ($69) double; 49€ ($74) suite. Rates include breakfast. AE, DC, MC, V. Limited free parking. **Amenities:** 2 restaurants; bar; sauna; massage. *In room:* A/C, TV, minibar, Internet access, hair dryer, safe.

Histria 🖈🖈 Situated in the Verudela resort area 4km (2½ miles) from the center of Pula, the Histria has the best position of all the strip's hotels: It's on a hill above the shore. Comfort and elegance are the Histria's watchwords. The hotel, managed by Arena Turist, has plenty of both. The spacious guest rooms are nicely appointed with sweeping balconies overlooking the sea. Plenty of activities keep kids and even blasé teenagers happy and occupied.

Verudela bb. ✆ **052/590-000**. Fax 052/214-175. www.arenaturist.hr. 248 units. Aug: from 160€ ($224) double. Rest of year: from 96€ ($135) double. Add 10% above the double-room price for suite. AE, DC, MC, V. Rates include breakfast. **Amenities:** Restaurant; cafe; bar; disco; casino; 2 pools; tennis courts; sauna; summer activity programs. *In room:* A/C, TV.

Milan 🖈🖈 Less than a quarter of a mile from the sea, this lovely 12-room hotel is both comfortable and classy. Rooms are furnished in Mediterranean style—soothing colors, smooth woods—and they are above the dynamite **Milan Restaurant** 🖈🖈🖈. The only disappointment is that most bathrooms have showers rather than tubs.

Stoja 4. ✆ **052/300-200**. www.milan1967.hr. 12 units. July–Aug: from 860kn ($160) double. Rest of year: from 620kn ($115) double. Rates include buffet breakfast. AE, DC, MC, V. Limited free parking. **Amenities:** Restaurant; bar; nonsmoking rooms; valet service. *In room:* A/C, TV, Internet connection.

Pula Youth Hostel 🖈 This hostel has a beautiful setting, but it is a bit of a hike from the town center. The hostel is 4km (2½ miles) south of Pula's center on Valsaline Bay and reachable via the no. 2 bus from Giardini near the Sergi Arch. The very plain hostel is located on a spectacular piece of real estate. It has its own beach and cafeteria, and a scuba-diving school is next door. Rooms are dorm-style with four to six beds each, and breakfast is included in the price.

Zaljev Valsaline 4. ✆ **052/391-133**. Fax 052/529-401. pula@hfhs.hr. MC, V. 98kn ($18) per bed per night. **Amenities:** Cafe/bar; bike rental; hiking trails; shopping center; laundry; luggage storage; free parking. *In room:* Sheets provided.

Riviera The fate of this 1907 Hapsburg-era gem could be in limbo since the hotel changed hands a few years ago, though the Riviera still is the choice for travelers who want to stay midway between the amphitheater and the train station. Graceful architecture gives the Riviera a regal street look, but inside it has been stripped of frills unless you count the amazing views of the amphitheater and harbor from room no. 406 and other corner units. Though guest rooms are huge and clean, and breakfast on the terrace is a delight, the tired condition of the furnishings and the dearth of facilities make the Riviera a bit overpriced.

Spliska 1. © **052/211-166.** Fax 052/219-117. www.arenaturist.hr. 76 units. June–Sept: from 85€ ($119) double. Rest of year: 64€ ($90) double. Rates include breakfast. AE, DC, MC, V. **Amenities:** Restaurant. *In room:* TV.

Scaletta 🌟 Book early because rooms go fast at this family-run hotel in central Pula, and it's no wonder: Following a recent renovation, the Scaletta is one of the most convenient hotels in town. Guest rooms are done in soft colors; bathrooms are roomy and gleaming. There aren't any magnificent views, but the Scaletta is within walking distance of the amphitheater and Pula's Old Town. Its **Scaletta Restaurant** 🌟🌟 has been recognized as one of the seven best in Istria. The only downside is that access to the reception area requires some stair-climbing and the breakfast room is a tight fit.

Flavijevska 26. © **052/541-025.** Fax 052/541-599. www.hotel-scaletta.com. 12 units (2 singles, 10 doubles). June 1–Sept 15: 750kn ($139) double. Rest of year: 518kn ($96) double. Rates include breakfast. AE, DC, MC, V. **Amenities:** Restaurant; wine cellar. *In room:* A/C, TV, minibar, hair dryer, safe.

Valsabbion 🌟🌟🌟 This chic boutique hotel 5.6km (3½ miles) south of the city center has been around since 1995, but Valsabbion still surprises with its avant-garde thinking. Set above Pješčana Uvala (Sandy Bay), Valsabbion is a stylish blend of comfortable rooms, beach, award-winning restaurant, and select spa services that help guests eliminate stress. Rooms are spacious and exude the same *joie de vivre* that extends throughout the hotel, its facilities, and its exceptionally helpful and personable staff. Room prices do not include breakfast, which can be added for 12€ ($17), and half-board is pricey, but you'll never forgive yourself if you miss the opportunity to eat as many meals as possible here.

Pješčana Uvala IX/26. © **052/218-033.** www.valsabbion.net. 10 units. July–Aug: from 104€ ($146) double; from 174€ ($244) suite. Rest of year: from 84€ ($118) double; from 119€ ($167) suite. Rates do not include breakfast, which is 12€ ($17) per person per day. Half-board available (includes welcome drink, fruit Valsabbion basket, buffet breakfast, 4-course dinner). AE, DC, MC, V. 10% discount for cash. **Amenities:** Restaurant; bar; pool; hydromassage pool; salon. *In room:* A/C, TV, minibar, hair dryer, safe.

Church of St. Fosca (Sveti Foška)

The only directional sign to this unremarkable 7th-century church is a hand-painted sign leading to a gravel strip off the main road to/from Fažana in the direction of Barbaringa. According to locals, the church, which has one interesting fresco, is built on a field of positive energy that allegedly is responsible for healing a wide range of ailments from headaches to arthritis. The first of these healings was noted in the late 17th century, but the Catholic Church has not acknowledged the validity of any claims of miracles at the site. Despite that, people from all over the world visit this tiny church in a meadow to seek their own miracles and to pray to the saint who was betrayed by her father and martyred at 15 because she wouldn't renounce Christianity.

WHERE TO DINE

There is no dearth of decent restaurants in central Pula, but most of the better (upscale) restaurants are in the suburbs south of the center.

Bistro Kupola 🎯 *Value* CROATIAN This touristy restaurant features a bird's-eye view of the imposing Sergi Arch from its terrace. Music from the street and from concerts at the nearby amphitheater float up to the outdoor tables above Pula's T-Mobile headquarters, adding a little extra to the dining experience. Service is polite and helpful, though food is a bit tourist-driven, but why not? This is the kind of spot that demands a look-see from anyone new to Pula. Try tagliatelle Alfredo, which is sprinkled with shaved truffles; or go for spaghetti with a generous helping of seafood. The house red is Plavac Zlatni, an excellent value.

Trg Portarata 6. ℂ **098/211-666.** Entrees 50kn–140kn ($9–$26). No credit cards. Daily 8am–midnight.

Bistro Mozaik 🎯🎯 *Finds* CROATIAN Set on a tiny side street near the town center, this delightful restaurant offers the usual assortment of grilled fish, meat dishes, and risottos found in most traditional Croatian places, but with a few touches that set them apart. Mozaik has a children's plate for 20kn ($4), and some very cute umbrella tables. It's just steps away from a wine store with an interesting selection of high-end Istrian wines.

Maksimilijanova 6. No phone. Entrees 50kn–130kn ($9–$24). No credit cards. Daily 10am–midnight.

Valsabbion 🎯🎯🎯 MEDITERRANEAN Unique, superb, a don't-miss experience: This is dining at Valsabbion, where Istrian specialties meet artistic sensibilities and expert preparation. Even a simple lunch can be spectacular with the "Petit Delice" or "Taste of Istria" samplers of Istrian cheeses, tapenades, or fish mousses and olives accompanied by house-made breads. Dinner is the *pièce de resistance* here, and if you can't make up your mind between the scampi rolled in Istrian ham or the chicken breast in vermouth sauce with grapes and artichokes, then try the degustation menu with 12 small portions of Valsabbion's best recipes. Don't miss the olive-oil aperitif— three cordial glasses filled with Istrian olive oil, olive tapenade, and olive butter, with crusty bread for dipping. With a bottle of fine wine from Valsabbion's well-chosen cellar, a gentle breeze wafting through the open terrace, and lighting provided by the reflection of the moon on the sea, a meal at Valsabbion is a sensory experience you won't soon forget. Our advice? Book a table on the VIP terrace, a breezy, canopied deck across the street from the hotel that has a view of the bay and a cachet of exclusivity. Splurge on the 12-course tasting menu. You'll feast on tasting portions of such innovative dishes as scallop wrapped in squid ink pasta or potato soup in a ring of spices. There is a 15% surcharge for the terrace and our tasting was 475kn ($88) per person (without wine.)

Pjescana Uvala IX/26. ℂ **052/218-033.** Fax 052/383-333. www.valsabbion.net. Reservations required. Entrees 90kn–120kn ($17–$22). AE, DC, MC, V. Daily 10am–midnight.

Vela Nera 🎯🎯 CREATIVE SEAFOOD You can watch your ship come in from Vela Nera's terrace or from the windows of its cozy dining room perched steps away from the Sandy Bay harbor. Either way, you'll be treated to knowledgeable service and inspired cuisine. Vela Nera is a little more casual than Valsabbion, but no less satisfying. Try the risotto Vela Nero for an unusual taste sensation. It's made with peaches, scampi, and sparkling wine. All of the truffle-enhanced entrees are tasty (beefsteak with truffles is especially good). Lighter appetites can try a mixed salad with bacon and freshly baked bread.

Pješčana Uvala bb. ⓒ 052/219-209. Fax 052/215-951. www.velanerahr. Reservations recommended. Entrees 50kn–150kn ($9–$28). AE, DC, MC, V. Daily 8am–midnight.

Jupiter ⭐⭐ PIZZA   Pizza is the specialty at this popular place near the Forum. Jupiter has several terrace levels of dining and a huge number of pizza toppings to choose from. Pretty good pasta, too.

Castropola 38. ⓒ 052/214-333. www.planetadria.com/Jupiter. Small pizza 15kn–40kn ($3–$8). No credit cards. Daily 9am–11pm.

Milan ⭐⭐⭐ SEAFOOD   This sleek, family-owned restaurant in the hotel of the same name is done in warm woods and has flattering soft lighting. It's in Stoja, less than 3.2km (2 miles) south of Pula. On offer are sublimely fresh fish and an extensive wine list. Try any of the shellfish entrees, which are a specialty. And save room for dessert: The pastry chef is a genius.

Stoja 4. ⓒ 052/300-200. www.milan1967.hr. Entrees 60kn–140kn ($11–$26). AE, DC, MC, V. Mon–Sat noon–11pm, closed Sun.

Scaletta ⭐⭐ *Value* CROATIAN   The lovely Scaletta is a gastronomic delight with surprisingly well-prepared cuisine that incorporates unusual combinations of ingredients. The dining room is warm and inviting, with soft lighting, a marble fireplace, and an attractive bar. The menu is the showstopper, however, and offers a long list of grilled meats and fish with a lot of twists.

Flavijevska 26. ⓒ 053/541-025. Fax 052/541-599. www.hotel-scaletta.com. Reservations recommended. Entrees 60kn–220kn ($11–$41). AE, DC, MC, V. Mon–Sat 10am–11pm; closed Sun.

3 Brijuni Archipelago (Brioni)

The Romans built summer villas on these islands northwest of Pula; the Austro-Hungarians spent their holidays there; and Marshal Tito chose them as the site for his private residence and official retreat. For 30 years Tito spent 6 months of the year receiving world leaders and celebrities amid Brijuni's natural wonders, but before that, the 14 islands and islets were swampland where malaria was rampant. It wasn't until Austrian steel magnate Paul Kupelweiser bought Brijuni in the late 19th century and cleaned it up to build a luxury health resort that the island group became a tourist destination. Today Brijuni is a national park and an official state residence. Consequently, only two of the islands—**Veliki** and **Mali Brijuni**—are open to visitors, who must arrive via organized tours unless they are staying at one of Brijuni's hotels.

ESSENTIALS

VISITOR INFORMATION   Almost all tourist agencies on Istria's west coast offer excursions to Brijuni. Once there, your itinerary is limited unless you plan to stay in one of Brijuni's hotels. It is a good idea to check with the national park office to see what's on and what's off-limits. The **Brijuni National Park Tourist Office** at Fažana (ⓒ 052/525-882; www.np-brijuni.hr) is open from 8am to 10pm daily in July and August; from 8am to 8pm daily in June and September; and from 8am to 3pm Monday through Saturday other times. Tickets sold at Fažana cost 190kn ($35) for adults and 95kn ($18) for children.

GETTING THERE & GETTING AROUND   You don't need more than a day to see the accessible parts of Brijuni, and it is easy to book an excursion. Tours to Brijuni leave from the dock at **Fažana,** which is a half-hour drive from Pula, three to five times per day, depending on the season. The trip to Brijuni from Fažana takes about 20 minutes and the guided land tour takes about 4 hours, including breaks and waits for the boat back to shore. (Fažana is also reachable by the no. 6 Pula bus.) *Tip:* Agencies in Pula sell tickets for Brijuni excursions, some of which include bus transportation between your hotel and Fažana. This can be a good choice if you must start and finish your tour at a specific time. But if you don't need that convenience, book at the Brijuni National Park office on the waterfront when you get to Fažana, which saves a considerable amount of money. If you are booking anywhere but the National Park office, be sure you are getting a tour that lets you off on the islands. Some tours merely cruise around Brijuni without docking there.

WHAT TO SEE & DO

Once you land on **Veliki Brijuni,** you'll be escorted by an English-speaking guide through the park both on foot and on an environment-friendly tram. The guided tour takes about 4 hours and hits the island's **safari park** (which is down to a few older animals), a 1st-century **Roman villa complex** at **Verige Bay,** the ruins of a **Byzantine fortress,** and the outskirts of Tito's **White Villa.** Other points of interest are the **"Old Lady,"** a 1,600-year-old olive tree in the running for oldest tree in Croatia; a small archaeological museum, **Church of St. Germaine,** with copies of the **Baška Tablet** and **Dance of the Dead Fresco** from Beram; and **Josip Broz Tito Memorial Museum** (✆ 052/525-883 or 052/525-822). The museum is open daily 8am to 7pm in summer; 8am to 2pm at other times, or when excursion boats come in. The Tito is a natural history museum with a collection of stuffed animals on the ground floor, and a photo exhibit titled **"Tito on Brijuni"** on the second floor. The guide will explain that the animals (some endangered species) either died on Brijuni's preserve or en route from exotic lands, and that the photos document Tito's activities on Brijuni. The photos should not be missed, as they give context to Tito and his style of leadership: Each image shows Tito shaking hands or dining with a different head of state or celebrity, indicative of his ability to use his strong personality to advantage for his country. There is a small concession outside the museum that serves baguette sandwiches, pastries, and beverages.

4 Vodnjan (Dignano)

Vodnjan, as with other Istrian towns, shows evidence of prehistoric settlements and of cultures from the Illyrians through the Italians, who ruled there before the Croatians took over thanks to its mild climate and the Venetians. Vodnjan eventually developed into the most important center of commerce in southern Istria and remained so until 1856, when Pula became Istria's chief port. Today Vodnjan is a sleepy collection of villages known primarily for a large Italian-speaking population and the **Vodnjan mummies,** a collection of remarkably preserved bodies that lie in state at **St. Blaise Church** on the main square.

ESSENTIALS

VISITOR INFORMATION   When you arrive at this small town just north of Pula, make your first stop the **tourist office** at Narodni Trg 3 (✆ **052/511-672;** fax

> **Fun Fact** **Kažuni**
>
> The fields of southwest Istria are dotted with small, dry-stone huts that look like giant gray beehives. Travelers often wonder what they are and what their purpose is. Usually, the huts were built in the corners of fields and served as shelters for shepherds and storage units for tools. Inside, small stone blocks often served as seats around an open hearth. Usually, the door and windows (if any) face away from prevailing winds and are the only openings in the structure. About 3,000 of these mostly intact folk buildings are in the vicinity of Vodnjan, and many are still in use. Today many kažuni have been restored and some are even used as summer cottages.

052/511-700; tz-vodnjan-dignano@pu.hinet.hr) on the main square. It is open from 8am to noon and from 5 to 8pm daily in the summer and has variable hours other times. You can pick up a map and brochures that will direct you to Vodnjan's surprisingly rich store of historical sites.

GETTING THERE See "Getting There," in "Orientation," earlier in this chapter.

GETTING AROUND You can drive on most main streets in Vodnjan, but if you do, you'll miss some of the more interesting tiny alleys that twist around the town center.

WHAT TO SEE & DO

When you walk through central Vodnjan, you'll find that the main street is cobblestone and uncharacteristically wide. As you get farther in, you'll notice that the town has a distinct medieval appearance with arched doorways; Gothic, Renaissance, and baroque architecture; offshoot streets the size of alleys; and a main square where **St. Blaise and its campanile**—the tallest in Istria—stand. Vodnjan is only 6km (4 miles) from the sea and 10km (6½ miles) from Pula. Today, it is not only a tourist stop between Pula and Rovinj, but also a town caught between Istria's agricultural and commercial traditions. Most visitors don't explore Vodnjan in depth, but go straight to St. Blaise Church and its mummies and then head out again.

Church of St. Blaise 🌟🌟 To get to St. Blaise, walk through the portal that once was the town gate and that still leads to Vodnjan's oldest sector **(Castelo),** which then opens to the main square and the 18th-century St. Blaise Church and its bell tower. St. Blaise is the largest church in Istria and its bell tower is reputed to be the highest, but the main attraction is behind the church's altar. Entrance to the church is free, but there is a charge to view the treasury of sacral art and the mummies. Both are worth a visit.

Trg Sveti Blaz. 🕾 052/511-420. Daily July–Sept 9am–7pm. Admission during Mass or when the priest is on the premises other times.

St. Blaise Treasury 🌟🌟🌟 St. Blaise's collection of sacral art and relics is in the sacristy off the sanctuary and rather fascinating in a macabre sort of way. It is filled with hundreds of the church's 370 relics (mostly bones) from about 200 saints, as well as vestments and other church objects. Most are displayed in glass reliquaries, one of which reputedly holds the tongue of St. Mary of Egypt. Even if viewing piles of bones is not your thing, consider visiting the treasury to see the **14th-century polyptych of Blessed Leon Bembo** 🌟🌟, who had a reputation for healing the sick before and after death, and whose preserved body is on view in the exhibit next door. The panel was painted by Paolo Veneziano in 1321 and was used as the lid to Blessed Leon's coffin. The exhibit is well marked, and both it and the mummies were brought to Vodnjan because they were in danger of being desecrated.

In St. Blaise Church.

The Vodnjan Mummies ⋆⋆⋆ The mummy exhibit is past the gated sanctuary to the rear of the altar in an area that is separated from view by heavy velvet drapes. Pew seats face the display cases, which are dimly lighted and roped off so you can't get too close to the cases. After you enter, the floor attendant will play a tape in English (or a dozen other languages) that gives the history of the exhibit and details about the lives and deaths of the three mummified bodies dressed in period clothing displayed in glass-fronted cases. The cases are topped with more glass cases that contain a foot-high jumble of bones and other body parts, including a bony form reputed to St. Sebastian's torso and a leg bone supposedly belonging to St. Barbara.

In St. Blaise Church at Trg Sveti Blaz. ℂ **052/511-420**. 38kn ($6.55) to view the sacral art and mummies; 28kn ($4.85) mummies only. Daily 9am–7pm.

5 Rovinj (Rovigno)

Rovinj is one of the most photographed cities in Croatia. From the air, its location on a promontory makes it look like a fairy-tale village suspended on a pillow of bright blue sea and at ground level, it looks like the quintessential Italian fishing village. Central Rovinj once was an islet, and it wasn't until the 18th century that the channel separating it from the mainland was filled in. Today, Rovinj's Old Town is a protected monument and one of Istria's most visited sites. Rovinj has preserved the best of its architectural and cultural legacy by allowing development but keeping industry on the mainland, where the Rovinj tobacco factory and cannery still play major roles in the town's economy. Central Rovinj is a tangle of steep pedestrian streets that are paved with sea-salt-polished cobblestones and marked with signs in Italian and Croatian. These narrow, winding streets are lined with galleries, quaint shops, and excellent restaurants. Most lead to the town's highest point, where **St. Euphemia Church** and its campanile, the tallest in Istria, dominate the skyline. Add to that Rovinj's strong Italian personality, which includes a thriving fleet of small fishing boats, a smattering of Venetian-style piazzas, numerous restaurants, cafes, and atmospheric rock walls set next to pounding waves, and you have a town that's both vibrant and historical.

ESSENTIALS

VISITOR INFORMATION The **Rovinj Tourist Information Office** is at Pino Budičin 12 (ℂ **052/811-566**; fax 052/816-007; www.tzgrovinj.hr). It is open from 8am to 9pm daily mid-June to mid-September; and from 8am to 3pm Monday to Saturday other times. Located just off the main square at the harbor, it has brochures, maps, and information on accommodations, the town, and Rovinj history.

GETTING THERE Rovinj is just half an hour or 16km (25 miles) north of Pula and linked by well-marked roads if you are traveling by car. There is frequent bus service to and from Pula; service to and from Croatian cities that range from Osijek to Dubrovnik; and international service to select cities in Italy, Germany, and Slovenia. The main bus station is at Trg Na Lokvi 6 (ℂ **052/811-453**; www.tzgrovinj.hr).

GETTING AROUND Rovinj is a wonderful walking city. To visit the Old Town, you'll have to leave your car in the city lot at the north end of town. Fees are a modest

6kn ($1.10) per hour. You can rent a bike at the lot's exit for 100kn ($19) per day or 5kn (85¢) per hour if you don't want to rely on walking or if you want to try Rovinj's picturesque bike trail. Local buses serve areas outside the Old Town area, as do taxis.

WHAT TO SEE & DO

Rovinj is a browser's paradise, with lots of places to explore on its narrow, winding streets. Most of the sites worth exploring are in the Old Town, but there are a few places outside the center. **Zlatni Rt-Punta Corrente Nature Park** 𝒜𝒜 is a fine reason to venture out: This densely forested park just steps from the Hotel Park is rimmed with rocky beaches and full of hiking paths. **Limska Draga Fjord** 𝒜𝒜𝒜 is a flooded karstic canyon less than 16km (10 miles) north of Rovinj. It looks like a ribbon of clear blue-green water framed with forested walls on two sides. At least two caves with evidence of prehistoric habitation have been discovered there, and several local legends say that pirates used the inlet as a base for surprising merchant ships. Mussels and oysters are farmed here and you can sample them at any of the restaurants along the road that skirts the area. Excursions to Limska Draga leave from Rovinj and Poreč daily and often can be booked directly at seaside or from any travel agency in town for about 190kn ($35) per person.

Balbi Arch 𝒜𝒜   You can enter Old Town from the main square through the 17th-century Balbi Arch, which leads up to Grisia, Rovinj's most interesting street. The arch is on the site where one of the town's seven gates once stood; it is carved with a Turk's head on one side and a Venetian's head on the other.

⎛Fun Fact Grisia Street Standouts

Rovinj's main street is really a steep, cobbled passageway that runs from the main square all the way up to St. Euphemia Church. It is lined with shops and galleries and buildings that still sport vestiges of the town's medieval roots. Galerija Peti-Božić at no. 22 is one of the most pleasant and most interesting. This tiny shop specializes in Croatian naive art created by Marija Peti-Božić, who has shown her work in galleries and museums in Zagreb and elsewhere in Europe. Most of Peti-Božić's work is oil on glass, typical of the Hlebine School. The shop is run by the artist's jovial husband, who will proudly rattle off his wife's accomplishments as well as wrap your purchases securely for packing.

Another Grisia Street shop worth a stop is no. 37, where award-winning artist Olga Vicel creates naive art in another medium—embroideries with silk thread on linen. Framed pieces run 50€–500€ ($70–$840). Galerija Peti-Božić, Grisia 22 (© **091/578-65-28**), is usually open Easter through October 8am to 10pm daily. (Call to confirm opening hours.)

Linens, embroidered fabrics, chess sets and gauzy skirts are the specialty of Boutique Maya, which occupies nos. 18 and 19, open 10am–9pm or later in summer.

August is officially the month of Grisia's art celebration; during this month, shops and restaurants remain open as long as there are people in the streets.

The Legend of St. Euphemia

St. Euphemia probably was just a teenager living in 4th-century Chalcedon near Constantinople when she fell victim to Diocletian's campaign to purge the Roman Empire of Christianity. St. Euphemia was the daughter of a prominent Chalcedon citizen and was imprisoned with 49 other Christians when they refused to worship the town idol and deny their faith. Because of her refusal to deny Christ, the young Euphemia was tortured with fire and snakes and by having her bones broken on a wheel before being thrown to the lions, which miraculously didn't devour her body after they killed her. Christians recovered Euphemia's body and buried it in Chalcedon, but in the 7th century they moved it to Constantinople because they feared the body would be defiled by Persian invaders. In Constantinople, the Christian Emperor Constantine ordered that a church be built in Euphemia's honor. Her sarcophagus remained there until A.D. 800, when the faithful again moved it because they feared that the Emperor Nicefor might remove it to parts unknown.

No one knows for sure how the coffin and its contents got to Rovinj, but one legend says that Christian fishermen probably put it on their boats in an attempt to get it to a safe place, and then somehow lost it in the sea. The legend goes on to attribute Euphemia's arrival on the shores of Rovinj to a miracle. One local legend further states that villagers who found the coffin couldn't budge the heavy stone container from the surf no matter how hard they tried. In the end it was a young boy with a pair of calves who was able to get the coffin out of the water after St. Euphemia appeared to him in a dream and told him what to do. The coffin is now a symbol of Rovinj and rests behind the altar in the right aisle of the church at the top of Rovinj's highest hill. Through the years, large numbers of worshipers come to pray at the site daily, especially on September 16, the day that St. Euphemia died in A.D. 304.

St. Euphemia Church ★★ The baroque church dedicated to Rovinj's co-patron saint is the third iteration of the shrine built in her honor. When the saint and her sarcophagus appeared in Rovinj early in the 9th century, they were housed in a chapel near the Church of St. George. A century and a half later, a larger church dedicated to both saints was built to accommodate pilgrims who steadily streamed into Rovinj to pray to Euphemia. Finally, the present church was built on the same site atop Rovinj's highest hill in the early 18th century. The adjacent **bell tower** was built 50 years earlier and is one of the highest campaniles in Istria. It is topped with a copper statue of St. Euphemia that includes a palm and a wheel, symbols of her martyrdom. The people of Rovinj made St. Euphemia a patron saint of the city along with St. George after the stone sarcophagus containing her body mysteriously showed up on their shores following its disappearance from Constantinople in A.D. 800.

Petro Stankovića. © 052/815-615. Daily summer 10am–3pm; only during Mass other times.

Rovinj Heritage Museum ✯   The museum was founded in 1954 to collect and exhibit works of art. Today its collections include old masters, contemporary works, a library, and a cache of local archaeological finds. The museum is situated in a baroque palace that once belonged to Italian aristocrats.

Trg Maršala Tita 11. ✆ 052/816-720. Fax 052/830-650. www.muzej-rovinj.com. Admission 15kn ($3) adults, 10kn ($2) children and students. Summer Tues–Sun 9am–noon and 7–10pm; closed Mon. Winter Tues–Sat 9am–1pm; closed Sun–Mon.

Rovinj Aquarium ✯   Founded in 1891, the Aquarium is Rovinj's oldest museum and also one of its best. It is in the same facility as the Ruđer Bošković Center for Maritime Research and has a nice collection of local marine life.

G. Paliaga 5. ✆ 052/804-702. http://more.cim.irb.hr. Admission 10kn ($2). Summer daily 9am–9pm; rest of year 10am–5pm.

WHERE TO STAY

Rovinj has very few hotels in the city center and not many in the surrounding area either, considering the number of tourists that visit each year. However, private accommodations are abundant and usually very nice. Stop at any tourist agency, some of which set up kiosks on the road into town so you can book a room on arrival. Not only will these agencies find you a place to sleep, they will also lead you to it so you can inspect the rooms before paying.

Hotel Adriatic ✯   Reserve your room in this waterfront hotel early because it fills up quickly, especially during July and August. Rooms in the renovated 1912 building are comfortable and spacious though not lavish, and the hotel's outdoor cafe is a popular place to enjoy a cup of kava. Several tour agencies are right next door.

Pino Budačin bb. ✆ 052/500-510. Fax 052/813-753. www.maistra.hr. 27 units. Aug: from 128€ ($180) double. Rest of year: from 72€ ($100) double. 50% reduction for children 2–12; children 1 and under free in parent's room. AE, DC, MC, V. **Amenities:** Restaurant; cafe. *In room:* A/C, SAT/TV, minibar, wireless Internet, hair dryer.

Villa Valdibora ✯✯   The four apartments in this 18th-century town house could not be more unique or more convenient to Old Town Rovinj. Oil paintings, antiques, and Old World service are juxtaposed with ultramodern bathrooms, electronics, and comforts. This is a perfect place to stay to explore Rovinj and environs.

Silvana Chiurca 8. ✆ 052/845-040. Fax 052/845-050. www.valdibora.com. 4 units. Apartments (2 persons) from 200€ ($280) July and Aug. From 130€ ($182) other times. AE, DC, MC, V. Rates include breakfast. **Amenities:** Room service; valet service; daily housekeeping; bike use; laptop rental; pets allowed. **In room:** A/C.

Villa Angelo d'Oro ✯✯✯   This 17th-century bishop's palace in the Old Town was renovated in 2001 and has been kept in superb condition ever since. Each room is unique in size and decor with plush period furniture and fresh colors. Bathrooms have modern fixtures, though most have showers rather than tubs. Guests can treat themselves to one of the best views in the city from the open-air balcony off the third-floor library before or after they dine in the hotel's **Angela d'Oro Restaurant** ✯✯✯. Parking is a quarter of a mile away from the hotel, but the staff will pick up and deliver guests and their luggage at their cars.

Via Svalba 38–42. ✆ 052/840-502. www.rovinj.at. 25 units. Mid-July to mid-Sept: from 220€ ($308) double. Rest of year: from 126€ ($177) double. 50% discount for children 3–11. Children 2 and under free. Rates include breakfast. Half-board available on request for 28€ ($40) per person per day. AE, DC, MC, V. Limited parking 5€ ($7) per day. **Amenities:** Restaurant; terrace dining; wine cellar; Jacuzzi; solarium; library. *In room:* A/C, TV, minibar, hair dryer.

Hotel Park 🛱🛱   From the front, this 1972 structure looks like another big package hotel. The Park might offer packages, but it is surprisingly user-friendly and personal. Rooms are done in yellows and blues in modest but comfortable style. The Park is conveniently located 2 minutes from **Zlatni Rt-Punta Corrente Nature Park** and 5 minutes from Old Town. Despite its size, the hotel fills up from May to October. Call no later than April for reservations during this time. *Tip:* The view of Rovinj and St. Catherine's Island from the balcony off the Park's lobby is spectacular.

IM Ronjigova. ✆ 052/811-077. Fax 052/816-977. www.maistra.hr. 237 units. Aug: from 182€ ($255). Rest of year: from 73€ ($102) double. 50% discount for children 2–11. Children 1 and under free. Rates include breakfast and are based on stays exceeding 3 days. 20% surcharge for stays of 3 or fewer days. Half-board available on request. AE, DC, MC, V. Closed 2 months each year, usually mid-Dec to mid-Feb. **Amenities:** Restaurant; bar; ice-cream parlor; 3 pools; excursions; kids' programs; Internet; exchange office; salon; babysitting. *In room:* A/C, SAT/TV, minibar, hair dryer.

Eden Hotel 🛱🛱   Every guest room has a couch and a balcony. The balconies overlook green space or lawn where guests can sunbathe or dine. The lunch buffet is set on a terrace under the hotel eaves where there is often live music at night. Bathrooms, balconies, and public spaces were renovated for the 2006 season and the Eden promptly won several "Best of" awards (best 4-star on the Adriatic best breakfast in Croatia). *Note:* The Eden offers more luxuries and sports options than any other hotel in Rovinj.

I Adamovića. ✆ 052/800-250. Fax 052/800-215. www.maistra.hr. 330 units. Aug: from 210€ ($294) double. Rest of year: from 90€ ($126) double. 50% reduction for children 2–11; children 1 and under free. Rates include breakfast and are based on stays exceeding 3 days. 20% surcharge for stays of 3 or fewer days. Half-board available on request. AE, DC, MC, V. **Amenities:** Restaurant; bar; 2 pools; Internet; babysitting 10am–5pm (included in room rate). *In room:* A/C, TV, minibar, wireless Internet, hair dryer, safe.

WHERE TO DINE

Restaurants that line the waterfront are touristy and predictable, and prices are a bit inflated. However, all serve respectable seafood and excellent pizza and pasta. Venture a little farther afield for menus that go beyond the expected.

Konoba Veli Jože 🛱 ISTRIAN   This rather dark dining room is so loaded with Croatian tchotchkes that they spill over to the outdoor tables, The food is first-rate and really representative of traditional Istrian cuisine. Try the *fuži* with truffles or fuži with goulash for a taste of the distinctive Istrian pasta and celebrated specialty. Or dig into one of Veli Jože's lamb or fish dishes, which are a bit expensive but worth the extra cost.

Svetog Križa 1. ✆ 052/816-337. Entrees 30kn–120kn ($6–$22). AE, DC, MC, V. Daily 10am–3am.

Gostonica Cisterna 🛱🛱 *Value* ITALIAN   Inside, stone walls and old farm implements create a rustic ambience. Outside, 12 tables with pink tablecloths beckon passersby to see what smells so good. The seductive aroma will usually be fish on the restaurant's grill or risottos simmering on the stove. Cisterna is in a small courtyard at the bottom of Grisia near the Balbi Arch—easy to miss if you're not looking for it.

Trg Matteotti 3. ✆ 052/811-334. Entrees 35kn–100kn ($7–$19). AE, DC, MC, V. Daily 8am–3pm and 6pm–midnight.

Stella di Mare 🛱🛱 *Value* PIZZERIA/SPAGHETTERIA   This laid-back restaurant is so close to the water that sea spray occasionally mists over outdoor tables when waves hit the rocky shoreline. Views of old Rovinj, boats in the harbor, gulls catching dinner, and the roiling sea are incomparable from the restaurant's blue-and-white umbrella tables. Besides pizza and pasta, the menu lists a few seafood dishes. For a local treat, try *koki sa jajem* pizza, a crispy crust topped with cheese, tomato, prosciutto, and an egg (added raw but baked into the mix). You can also get Hawaiian pizza or spaghetti *Sardonic* (anchovies, capers, olives, and tomatoes).

Croche 4. ℂ **091/528-88-83.** Pizzas run 28kn–45kn ($5–$8). Pasta from 35kn ($7). AE, DC, MC, V. Daily 8am–midnight.

Taverna da Baston ⭐⭐ ISTRIAN/SEAFOOD   A warm welcome will make you feel at home at this bustling place next door to Rovinj's fish market. Dark brick walls are hung with fishing nets, and local music provides background. Try any of the super-fresh fish dishes or the handmade gnocchi with truffles.

Svalba 3. ℂ **098/982-63-95.** Entrees 50kn–150kn ($9–$28). AE, DC, MC, V. Prices include tax, *couvert*, and service. Daily 6am–midnight or "All the time," as its owner says.

Amfora ⭐⭐⭐ SEAFOOD   The fish is fresh and the ambience cheerful in this beautiful restaurant that overlooks the marina and Old Town. Amfora is a cut above most Rovinj dining spots on the waterfront both in its cuisine and service—and that is also reflected in its prices. However, if you want first-class seafood, Amfora can't be beat. Try the salted sea bass or one of the risottos and wash it down with one of the restaurant's excellent wines. You won't be disappointed. Closed early January to early March.

A. Rismondo 23. ℂ **052/816-663.** Entrees 90kn–175kn ($17–$35). AE, DC, MC, V. Daily 11am–midnight.

Angelo d'Oro ⭐⭐⭐ ISTRIAN   During the summer, this restaurant is in the hotel's lovely walled garden, and during the winter it moves to an imaginatively styled room inside. Either way, the cuisine is creative yet traditional and beautifully presented. Try the cream of potato soup with truffles or any of the grilled fish dishes. Don't miss a tour of the stone wine cellar, where you can taste Istrian wines and gourmet specialties such as Istrian ham or cheese.

Via Svalba 38–42. ℂ **052/840-502.** www.rovinj.at. Reservations recommended. Entrees 90kn–165kn ($17–$30). AE, DC, MC. Daily 7pm–midnight.

6 Vrsar (Orsera) & Environs

Just north of the mouth of the Limska Draga Fjord you'll find Vrsar, a beautiful fishing village 10km (6¼ miles) south of Poreč and 25km (16 miles) north of Rovinj. Vrsar seems to begin at the hill that is home to the **Church of St. Martin,** its imposing bell tower, and a **12th-century castle,** then spill down the hill to the sea. The bell tower provides a 360-degree view of the sea and the undulating Istrian interior. Away from the harbor and all around its central hill, Vrsar is etched with steep, winding streets dotted with red-tile-roofed houses and restored town gates. The remains of Roman storehouses and a Roman cemetery also are there, as are several churches, some of which date from the 4th century.

VISITOR INFORMATION   The **Visitor Information Center** is at Rade Končara 46 (ℂ **052/441-187;** www.istra.com/vrsar) and can provide maps and directions as well as brochures on the town's sites and accommodations.

Vrsar is well known as a destination for campers or as a day trip from Rovinj or Poreč: It has four campgrounds that can accommodate nearly 20,000 people at sites near the sea. But Vrsar's contemporary claim to fame is its position as a gateway to **Koversada,** one of Croatia's largest naturist colonies. When this huge nudist resort was established on the Adriatic shore in 1960, it was the first in the region. Today, Koversada's villas and campground at 52450 Vrsar (ℂ **052/441-378;** fax 052/441-761; koversada-camp@ maistra.hr) are almost always filled to capacity. There are 72 units in the camp's villas.

July 30 to mid-August, doubles cost from 52€ ($73); during the rest of the year, from 30€ ($42). Rates include breakfast. Closed mid-September to May 1.

GETTING THERE   See "Getting There" in "Orientation," earlier in this chapter.

GETTING AROUND   It's easy to see everything Vrsar has to offer on foot, though some climbing is required. If you want to fully explore the nearby fjord, you'll need a car and a boat.

WHAT TO SEE & DO

Vrsar is a handy stop for those touring the Limska Draga Fjord, and it is noted for its nearby campgrounds, including the well-known Koversada naturist compound, but it isn't a destination. There are a few intriguing restaurants in the area, private accommodations, and some large package resorts. Poreč and Rovinj are better choices as bases for exploring.

Dušan Džamonja's Sculpture Park is another Vrsar site worth a look. Huge metal and stone sculptures scattered about the hills and meadows overlook the sea, creating a haunting open-air exhibit. Džamonja's works have been exhibited in the Museum of Modern Art in New York and at museums in London, Paris, Antwerp, and other cities in the world.

7 Poreč (Parenzo)

"There's something for everyone" could be Poreč's motto—the seaside resort offers a wide variety of attractions, from a UNESCO World Heritage basilica complex to endless shopping opportunities to slick resort hotels so crammed with activities and services that you think you're in Disney World. Poreč courts tourism, supports tourism, and profits from tourism, but the town and surrounding area still manage to intrigue, perhaps because they are a seamless blend of medieval heritage, a well-oiled service industry, idyllic vineyards and olive groves, and blatant commercialism. Old Town is the epicenter of this mecca, with immaculate cobblestone streets, precisely clipped plantings, multilingual signs explaining all points of interest, and enough jewelry stores and *gelaterias* for every tourist in Croatia.

Poreč is a lovely town with a plethora of leisure options, historical sites, and high comfort levels thanks to a sophisticated tourism infrastructure that lets visitors have a good time without feeling hassled. It is conveniently connected to transportation for anyone who wants to explore the Istrian Riviera. It's also a good staging area for venturing into the Istrian interior.

ESSENTIALS

VISITOR INFORMATION   Poreč knows how to make visitors feel at home and goes out of its way to lay out the welcome mat. People in the tourist offices are knowledgeable and accommodating, and merchants are welcoming. The **Poreč Tourist Information Office** can provide maps and brochures as well as leads on available accommodations and events. It can be found at Zagrebačka 11 (✆ **052/434-983;** www.istra.com/porec) and is open from 8am to 10pm Monday to Saturday all year. On Sunday during July and August, it is open 9am to 1pm and 6 to 10pm.

Istra Line Travel Agency, located on the outskirts of Old Town at Partizanska 4 (✆ **052/427-062;** fax 052/432-116; www.istraline.hr), is one of several agencies that can book private accommodations. Istra Line specializes in apartment rental but it also can direct you to individual rooms. **Atlas Travel Agency** at Eufrazijeva 63 (© **052/434-983;** www.atlas.hr) can arrange excursions, hotels, private accommodations, and airline reservations. It is also the local American Express agent.

Di Tours ✸✸ at Prvomajska 2 (© **052/432-100;** fax 052/431-300; www.di-tours.com) is just one of many private tourist agencies in town, but it has a huge inventory of rooms and apartments in Poreč and the vicinity. In August, it offers doubles with shower from 28€ ($40), apartments from 45€ ($63). During the rest of the year, doubles cost from 12€ ($17), apartments from 16€ ($23).

GETTING THERE   See "Getting There" in "Orientation," earlier in this chapter.

GETTING AROUND   Poreč's Old Town is easy to navigate on foot, though its end-to-end shopping opportunities might slow you down. Buses serve the Lanterna complex south of town (the bus station is a quarter of a mile from the town center) as well as nearby towns, but a car is necessary if you want to stay outside of town or if you want to explore the surrounding area.

WHAT TO SEE & DO

Poreč's Old Town is small, but it is packed with treasures, chief of which is the **Euphrasius Basilica** and its stunning **mosaics** ✸✸✸. The rest of Old Town's attractions pale in comparison but are interesting enough to warrant a walk-through.

Euphrasian Basilica Complex ✸✸   UNESCO has put this collection of early Christian and early Byzantine architecture on its World Heritage List, and you should put them on your "must-see" agenda, too. Situated near the town center off Eufrazijeva, the basilica is the last of four churches that were built between the 4th and 6th centuries, one on top of the other on this site. Evidence of those earlier churches is still visible, but the current complex originally built by Bishop Euphrasius in the 6th century is the focus. Besides the basilica itself, the complex is home to an atrium, a baptistry, a bell tower, and a bishop's palace. Visitors to the complex enter through the arches of the atrium. The bell tower was built in the 16th century, and the rest of the structures have undergone several renovations. Even if you aren't into visiting churches, make an effort to see the complex's spectacular **gem-studded mosaics** ✸✸✸ as well as its symbolic early Christian fish mosaic.

Eufrazijeva Ulica 22. Summer daily 7:30am–8pm. Other times during Mass only. Bell tower 10kn ($1.75). Daily 10am–7pm.

Regional Museum Poreč ✸   The 18th-century Sinčić palace is home to this showcase for archaeological finds that include carved Roman tombstones, amphorae from the bottom of the sea, and 17th-century portraits of Venetians. The exhibits chronicle Poreč's history from Paleolithic times to the present.

Dekumanska 9. © 052/431-585. www.culture-vision.com. Admission 10kn ($2) adults; 5kn ($1) children. Summer 10am–1pm and 6-9pm; winter 10am–1pm.

Trg Marafor ✸✸   The remains of Poreč's Roman Forum and two Roman temples (Mars and Neptune) are the highlight of Trg Marafor, which is on the tip of the peninsula. Today, Trg Marafor is the site of several sleek cocktail bars and jazz clubs such as **Lapidarium,** which is tucked into a courtyard strewn with stone carvings and artifacts. Lapidarium is located behind the Regional Museum and hosts jazz concerts in the courtyard nightly during the season.

Lapidarium Caffee/Bar/Gallery. © 052/432-374. www.poup.hr. Daily 9am–2pm and 6pm–2am.

Poreč Aquarium This is more coffee shop encircled with fish tanks than proper aquarium, though the specimens in those tanks are nice representatives of the area's indigenous marine life. You'll see huge signs and banners all over town advertising the Aquarium, but it is a little tricky to find in its home on a side street off Decumanus. Once there, it takes about 15 minutes to see everything that swims. The exhibit floor plan ends in the middle of the cafe/souvenir shop.

F. Glavinica 4. ✆ 052/428-720. www.aquarium-porec.com. Admission 10kn ($2). Daily 10am–5pm.

St. Nicholas Island 🐟🐟🐟 Porec's better beaches are off this close-in island, which is a short boat taxi ride away from the harbor.

Taxi boats leave the dock every half-hour.

Tar 🐟🐟 This quaint Istrian town just 10km (6½ miles) north of Poreč is perched on a plateau 104m (340 ft.) above sea level and the surrounding area. It is said that on a clear day you can see St. Mark's in Venice on one side and the Alps on the other from the town's bell tower. Tar is also known for its summer festival, which includes a donkey race, parades, Istrian music, and lots of food. Tar exudes old-world charm and reputedly produces the best olive oil in Istria.

Tar-Vabriga Tourist Association, Istarska 8/A. ✆ 052/443-250. istra.com/tar-vabriga. Summer daily 8am–9pm; Mon–Fri 8am–3pm other times.

Baredine Cave 🐟🐟🐟 Excursions to this collection of limestone caverns are among the most popular day trips out of Poreč. Just 7km (4½ miles) northeast of town on the road to Višjan, the caves are breathtaking chambers filled with stalactites and stalagmites. Entry fees cover the services of a guide, who takes you on a 40-minute tour of the underground halls and galleries and talks about the caves' flora, fauna, and minerals. Baredine's guides unfailingly relate the story of the legendary ill-fated lovers who died while looking for each other in the caves.

Nova Vas 52446. ✆ 052/421-333. www.istra.com/baredine. 45kn ($9). Daily. July–Aug 9:30am–6pm; May–June and Sept 10am–5pm; Apr and Oct 10am–4pm. Nov–Mar for pre-arranged groups only.

The Legend of Baredine Cave

Baredine's love story is a sad one that originated in the 13th century. According to the legend, a highborn young man named Gabriel fell in love with a beautiful shepherdess named Milka from Nova Vas. Gabriel's mother didn't approve of her son consorting with a mere farm girl and she couldn't dissuade him from the romance, so she hired bandits to kill the girl. Instead of killing her, the robbers took the mother's three pieces of gold and threw Milka into Baredine Cave. When Gabriel discovered the treachery, he supposedly tried to rescue his beloved and disappeared. (Gabriel's horse was found wandering near the cave, so it was presumed he had gone in to find Milka, but neither was heard from again.) The legend goes on to say that Milka's body eventually turned to stone in the cave and is slowly sinking to another chamber where Gabriel has been waiting for her for centuries.

WHERE TO STAY

Poreč is the most visited city in Istria, and as such it has a wide inventory of accommodations. Most hotels in Poreč are managed by a large Croatian chain, but there is a lot of variety available, especially if you opt for a small hotel outside the center. The Poreč area offers everything from luxurious all-inclusive hotels with sophisticated entertainment to rooms in rural homes surrounded by olive groves and vineyards. Nothing within a couple miles of the center can be classified inexpensive. No matter which option you choose, you'll have to book well in advance if you plan to stay any time during the "season," which runs through July and August.

Villa Filipini 🐸 *Value*   This family-run inn 10 minutes from Poreč opened in 2003 and has been going strong ever since. The charming inn is done in pine to resemble a rustic farmhouse and is adjacent to its own olive grove and vineyard. You can meet the family's world champion Istrian hunter in his home at the dog kennel behind the hotel or wander the olive grove next door. Mom serves breakfast and Dad is the accountant/handyman while their son manages the desk and waits on diners in the **Villa Filipini Restaurant** 🐸🐸 (when he isn't studying oenology in Poreč so the Uljančić family can begin to produce its own wines). Guest rooms are decorated in rustic Istrian style and are exceptionally clean and comfy, with French doors that open to the terrace or balconies. *Warning:* The rooms can get a bit toasty until the evening breeze cools them.

Filipini 1B. 🕐 052/463-200. www.istra.com/filipini. 8 units. From 62€ ($87) double. All rates are computed on a per-person basis and include breakfast. Half-board available. AE, DC, MC, V. Limited free parking. **Amenities:** Restaurant; bar; bicycle rental; laundry service. *In room:* TV, dial-up Internet access.

Neptun 🐸   Neptun has a great location facing the sea. It was built in 1968, renovated in 1995, and improved a little every year since. Some rooms have dynamite harbor views, as does the rooftop cafe, which is closed during very hot weather. Bathrooms are adequate but have showers and no tubs. Reception is very helpful and pleasant and also handles details for guests of the hotel's two dependances. The hotel sometimes closes in January and February or in November and December, depending on reservations.

Maršala Tita 17. 🕐 052/408-800. Fax 052/431-351. www.valamar.hr. 145 units. July 30 to mid-Aug: from 96€ ($135) double. Rest of year: from 68€ ($95) double. Rates include breakfast. AE, DC, MC, V. Half-board available. Discounts for children in parent's room. **Amenities:** Restaurant; bar. *In room:* TV. Suites have a minibar and hair dryer, but others must borrow a hair dryer from the desk.

Dependance Parentino *Value*   This former free-standing hotel on the water is now an annex to the Neptun and managed by Riviera hotels. That means the building has guest rooms but not a reception desk and other services, which currently are housed in the Neptun. The Parentino (and its sister hotel, the Jadran) appeals to economy-minded travelers who don't require a lot of frills. All of the Parentino's guest rooms face the sea, a good thing since none has air-conditioning. *Tip:* The Parentino's lobby and terrace have recently been remodeled in shades of gray and white to house a slick bar that is open from 8am–2pm and 6-11pm in summer and that attracts the beautiful people.

Marsala Tita 15. 🕐 052/408-800. Fax 052/451-440. www.valamar.hr. 14 units. July 30 to mid-Aug: from 84€ ($118) double. Rest of year: from 32€ ($45) double. Rates include breakfast. AE, DC, MC, V. Dependances Apr–Oct. **Amenities:** Hair dryer available at reception in Hotel Neptun. *In room:* TV.

Plava Laguna

The bulk of Poreč's hotels—more than a dozen—are in the huge Plava Laguna resort area that sprawls both north and south from Old Town. If you stay in a Plava Laguna property, you can choose from huge package hotels with every imaginable amenity and sports facility to a quiet villa in a residential setting. For information and a description of accommodations, contact Plava Laguna at Rae Končara 12. 52440 Poreč (© **052/410-210**; fax: 052/451-044; www.plava laguna.hr).

Diamant ✦✦✦ *Value*   From the outside, the Diamant looks like another 1970s package hotel, but the interior is a pleasant surprise. Guest rooms are huge and more like suites in this beautifully restored (2003) hotel less than a mile from the center of Poreč. Most guest accommodations have balconies and glass doors that are tinted and shaded, plus two bathrooms, one with a tub. The 10th floor is all suites and most have a refrigerator, dishwasher, and small stove. The Diamant offers every service imaginable, but it is most notable for its effort to make the entire hotel accessible to travelers with disabilities. The restaurant is cafeteria style, but there are so many food stations and selections that you won't notice. There is also a poolside grill. Service is personal and helpful, more typical of small boutique establishments than huge package hotels. The same is true of the hotel's special bike tour that you can book through Gulliver's Travel. It stops at local wineries, farms, olive groves, and monuments, and features a gourmet picnic.

Brulo. © **052/400-000.** Fax 052/451-206. www.riviera.hr. 244 units. End of July to mid-Aug: from 158€ ($221) double. Rest of year: from 70€ ($98) double. Rates include breakfast and are per person daily based on a stay of 4 or more days. 20% surcharge for stays of 3 days or fewer. AE, DC, MC, V. **Amenities:** 2 restaurants; bar; Internet cafe; juice bar; 2 pools; hot tub; whirlpool; kids' program; excursions; massage; solarium. *In room:* A/C, TV, minibar, hair dryer.

Hostin Poreč ✦✦   The Hostin reopened in March 2005 after a complete renovation. It is situated in the middle of a large park and is less than 91m (300 ft.) from the beach, which skirts fairly shallow water, making it perfect for children. However, you don't have to rely on the sea for swimming, thanks to the heated indoor pool. All guest rooms have balconies and all are spacious with bathrooms that are especially nice thanks to the recent renovation.

Rade Končara 4. © **052/432-112.** www.hostin.hr. 60 units. July–Aug: from 126€ ($177) double. Rest of year: from 56€ ($79). Rates include breakfast. Half-board available. 20% surcharge for stays fewer than 4 days. AE, DC, MC, V. **Amenities:** Restaurant; cafe; bar; pool; sauna; Turkish bath; elevator. *In room:* A/C, TV, Internet.

CAMPING

Lanternacamp ✦✦✦   If you must stay at a huge campground, Lanternacamp is one of the best. With more than 3,000 spaces for tents and/or campers, Lanterna wisely provides plenty of amenities such as electricity and water hookups, super-clean bathrooms, supermarkets, a laundry, a pool, and activities for kids. The camp is 13km (8 miles) from Poreč, but you won't mind because the beautifully landscaped, terraced property slopes toward the sea. There is an FKK section for naturists.

52440 Poreč. © **052/405-200.** Fax 052/451-440. www.valamar.com. AE, MC, V. Closed Nov–Mar.

Bijela Uvala ★★★   Located between Funtana and Poreč, this environment-friendly campground uses solar power and practices ecologically oriented camp management. The campground is partially wooded and blends with nature. Guests are encouraged to use ecologically sound products. The camp also offers a large pebble beach with paved sunning areas and lots of programs to amuse the kids.

52440 Poreč. ℂ **052/410-551**. Fax 052/410-600. www.plavalaguna.hr. July–Aug: campsite with tent, car, and 2 people 27€ ($38) per day. Rest of year: from 14€ ($20). AE, DC, MC. Closed Nov–Mar.

WHERE TO DINE

Dining in Old Town Poreč tends to be a one-note experience: Almost all the restaurants there rely on pizza, pasta, and grilled seafood for their menu mainstays. If you want to taste authentic grilled lamb or more unusual Istrian preparations, your best bet is to get out of (Old) Town.

Ulixes ★ ISTRIAN   Located in courtyard set off the main drag, the atmosphere at Ulixes is softened by indirect lighting on the brick walls of surrounding buildings, olive trees, soft background music, and cats that make the rounds looking for handouts. When you order, however, stick with fish dishes, which are competently prepared, or try a pasta like fuži with pršut or fuži with game. *Warning:* Grilled meat can be grisly and tough, and portions are on the small side, even for Croatia.

Decumanus 2. ℂ **052/451-132**. www.istra.com/ulixes. Entrees 40kn–110kn ($8–$20). DC, MC, V. Daily noon–midnight.

Restaurant Villa Filipini ★★ ISTRIAN   Pastas are handmade and the kitchen is imaginative in this tiny restaurant in one of Istria's delightful **rural small hotels** ★★. Seating on the outdoor terrace overlooks a small grove of trees and gives you the impression that you're dining in a forest. There is no written menu: The chef bases his dishes on what is fresh in the market. Choices can include green gnocchi with mixed cheese and walnut sauce, or ravioli filled with fresh cheese in herb butter. Fish dishes and sauces are particular strengths, as are the excellent wine list and gallant service. Sweet treats such as gelato on fresh cheese with sage honey and chocolate sauce are where the chef really gets creative.

Filipini 1B. ℂ **052/463-200**. www.istra.com/filipini. Entrees 40kn–150kn ($8–$28). AE, DC, MC, V. Daily noon–11pm.

Old Pub Cotton Club ★ PIZZA/PASTA   This handsome restaurant/cafe under burgundy awnings at the entrance to town looks like a tourist trap at first glance, but serious food is prepared here. Try the tortellini *mille voglie* (with clams); or the tortellini with pršut, pumpkin, cream, and truffles. Pasta and pizza are emphasized here, including nine kinds of tagliatelle that include tagliatelle all'Amatriciana (tomato, bacon, onion, olives, hot peppers), plus 20 kinds of pizza and risotto. There are good drink- and ice-cream menus and live music weekend evenings.

Trg Slobode 5. ℂ **052/453-293**. Fax 052/432-074. Entrees 40kn–110kn ($8–$20). No credit cards. Daily 9am–1am.

Cardo ★★ SEAFOOD   Fish is proudly displayed in an outdoor ice case in this classy terrace restaurant. A gnarled old olive tree and soft lights surrounding the terrace create a romantic mood for diners at the outdoor tables, which are always full. Try the salmon piquant or noodles with mussels, either of which is perfect with a glass of Istrian Malvasia. Cardo has the usual assortment of risottos and grilled dishes, too.

Cardo Maximus 6. ℂ **052/255-164**. Entrees 35kn–330kn ($7–$61). AE, DC, MC, V. Daily Apr 1–Nov 1 noon–midnight.

Stari Saloon/Bistro/Pizzeria 🔊🔊 *Value* PIZZA   It's plopped in a courtyard surrounded by brick buildings, but that doesn't stop people from jamming the place every night. Stari Saloon is primarily a pizza joint, and instead of the usual small, medium, or large designations on the menu, pizza sizes here are listed in centimeters. XXL pizzas a whopping 75 centimeters (29 in.) in diameter are served on a wooden disk the size of a small tabletop and start at 55kn ($10). Crusts are ultrathin and crispy. One of the unusual pizza combos is the Monte Carlo with tomatoes, cheese, salmon, crab, caviar, and scampi.

Ribarski Trg. 📞 052/453-228. Entrees 35kn–110kn ($7–$20). AE, DC, MC, V. Daily 10am–11pm.

Gostonica Istria 🔊🔊 SEAFOOD   Locals rave about the seafood at Gostonica Istria, a typical indoor/outdoor coastal place where people-watching from the terrace is a side dish. Istria's multi-language menu makes it easy to order. You'll get expertly prepared authentic Istrian cuisine along with lots of spaghetti options, such as Istrian minestrone, fuži, and spiny lobster with noodles. Service is accommodating even if the prices are a little high.

Msgr. Bože Milanovića 30. 📞 052/434-63. Fax 052/451-482. Entrees 65kn–190kn ($12–$35). AE, DC. Daily noon–midnight.

Sv Nikola 🔊🔊🔊   Nikola is one of the extremely chic dining spots on the "high style" segment of Poreč's waterfront where large private yachts like to congregate. Food is well prepared and beautifully presented, but pricey. Try the tagliatelle Altijež, ribbons of al dente pasta with scallops, langoustines, and a white wine reduction.

Obala Maršala Tita 23. 📞 052/423-018. Entrees 80kn–160kn ($15–$30), more for seafood sold by the kilo. AE, DC, MC, V. Daily 1–10pm.

Distinguished Guest 🔊🔊 MEDITERRANEAN   High fashion meets the waterfront at this stylish restaurant that is dressed up like a French salon with chandeliers and black and cream furniture. DG's broad selection of seafood and meat dishes is complemented by an outstanding wine list. Dine alfresco and enjoy the entertainment of the yacht lineup and the nightly promenade along the wharf. By day diners can gaze at St. Nicholas Island from DG's terrace tables.

Obala Maršala Tita 20. 📞 052/433-810. Entrees 70kn–140kn ($13–$26). AE, DC, MC, V. Daily noon–midnight May–Oct.

Restoran Marconi 🔊🔊 ISTRIAN   The delightful, shaded garden area of this bistro next to the cathedral is a great place to enjoy a light afternoon snack or early supper. And why not? Its palazzo setting was built by Italian nobles 500 years ago. Pizzas are flavorful, oozing with rich mozzarella; the seafood salad is loaded with squid, shrimp and mussels; and the seafood risotto is just as packed with the same ingredients. Save room for rich ice cream for dessert.

Eufrazijeva 24. 📞 052/431-922. Entrees 48kn–125kn ($9–$23). Pizzas 30kn–50kn ($6–$9). MC, V. Daily 7am–11pm May–Oct.

Peterokutna Kula 🔊🔊 SEAFOOD   Built into a pentagonal, 15th-century tower, this place has all the earmarks of another tourist trap—position on one of the highest traffic corners in town, old stone walls, steep steps—but it delivers first-rate food in a unique location. The spectacular view of the city from a rooftop 5 floors up (no elevator) is perfect garnish for PK's impeccably fresh food. The seafood assortment platter is a luscious collection of the shrimp, orada, mussels, and calamari at a very reasonable price. Service is friendly and prompt, a wonder since the kitchen is on the first floor. A word of caution: No credit cards are accepted and the occasional sea gull lands tableside to beg for leftovers.

Decumanus 1. ✆ **052/451-378.** Entrees 55kn–110kn ($10–$20). Daily noon–midnight. No credit cards.

8 Novigrad (Cittanova)

You might have a hard time keeping your eyes on the road if you drive the short stretch between Poreč and Novigrad in the early morning when the sun is hitting the water: During this time of day the landscape is bathed in a sheen of gold that gives it a mesmerizing, unearthly beauty. The scenic drive takes you just 18km (11 miles) north of Poreč. Once in Novigrad, you will immediately sense that this town is more relaxed than most coastal tourism destinations.

ESSENTIALS

VISITOR INFORMATION   The **Tourist Office** in Novigrad can provide maps, brochures, and information on area accommodations and events. It is located at Porporella 1 (✆ **052/757-075;** www.istra.com/novigrad) and is open from 9am to 9pm daily (8am–8pm daily in spring and summer; 8am–3pm Mon–Sat in winter).

GETTING THERE   See "Getting There" in "Orientation," earlier in this chapter.

GETTING AROUND   Novigrad is fairly compact and easy to negotiate on foot. It doesn't take more than an hour to see the entire town unless you can't resist trying out one of the many access points to the sea. Most of the action and attractions are at the waterfront, including Sts. Pelagia and Massima Church.

WHAT TO SEE & DO

Much of Novigrad's Old Town buildings have been replaced or redone, so there is little original architecture there, but the town has a comfortable feel and is a good place to wander around for a few hours, especially the rock walk around the city that takes the place of a beach. The town's breakwater creates a calm swimming area, but access areas for stronger swimmers also are built into the open-sea side.

Be sure to stop in at the **Sts. Pelagia and Massima Church** ⋆. Built in 1882, it has a beautiful ceiling and unusual elevated gallery behind the ornate marble tabernacle. There is also an intricately carved wooden pulpit inside the church and a soaring bell tower outside. When we visited in July 2007, there was a new hotel in town (Nautica) as well as a new harbor. Both opened in 2006. Photographers will want to use the **citi loggia** at the end of Belvedere Street as a frame for images of the sea.

WHERE TO STAY

Novigrad is an unabashed seaside resort and it is a relatively new town by Istrian standards—its medieval architecture was destroyed by the Turks in the 17th century and rebuilt in the prevailing Venetian style. However, there is something remarkable about accommodations options there. Novigrad does have its share of blah package hotels, but it also has a couple of places that are charmingly boutique and one that is downright decadent, a nice change from the monotonous in-your-face tourist-trap look of Umag to the north and the mind-boggling vacation options in Poreč to the south.

Nautica ⋆⋆⋆   Open since summer 2006, this is Novigrad's nod to luxury lodging—38 rooms and 4 suites dressed in mahogany and brass. Nautica is small enough to be exclusive and large enough to incorporate every conceivable amenity, all within a reddish-violet-hued building, a color that somehow works against the blue sea. The rooms have huge beds, tons of storage, and immense bathrooms that include tubs, bidets, and German-made toiletries. The hotel's **Restaurant Navigarre** and bar are sophisticated, spacious exercises in teak and brass with sprawling outdoor seating areas overlooking the marina. There is a free parking lot for guests' cars and 365 berths in the harbor for those who choose to arrive in their multi-million-dollar yachts.

Sv. Antona 15. ⓒ 052/600-400. Fax 052/600490. www.nauticahotels.com. 42 units, including 4 suites. Doubles with a sea view from 238€ ($333) in summer. Other times, doubles from 143€ ($102). Suites from 330€ ($466) in summer. Other times, suites from 270€ ($378). Rates include buffet breakfast, use of spa and pool, and parking. AE, DC, MC, V. **Amenities:** Restaurant; cafe; bar; indoor pool; sauna; room service; valet; yacht harbor; fitness center; shops; ATM. *In room:* A/C, SAT/TV, minibar, hair dryer, Wi-Fi or broadband Internet access, safe, balcony.

Cittar At first glance, the Cittar looks as if it's a castle protected by a high wall, but look again. The hotel was built in 1991 behind one of the few sections of the medieval city wall that still stands, and the wall out front was constructed at that time as a grand entryway. Behind it is the lovely Cittar with a gorgeous, leafy terrace and enclosed sunroom off the reception area that give the hotel the air of a Tuscan palazzo. The friendly staff and resident cocker spaniel add to the illusion. Guest rooms are a good size and beautifully decorated in earth tones and wood. They come with comfortably large bathrooms that make the Cittar a fine home away from home.

Prolaz Venecija 1. ⓒ 052/757-737. Fax 052/757-229. www.cittar.hr. 14 units. Aug: from 114€ ($160) double. Rest of year: from 78€ ($110). Rates include breakfast. Half-board available. There is a 30% discount for children 7–10; 50% discount for children 2–6; infants 1 and under free. AE, MC, V. Limited free parking. **Amenities:** Restaurant; elevator. *In room:* A/C, TV, minibar.

Rotonda Until the Nautica opened in 2006, the Rotonda was the only Novigrad hotel with a beach out front. It is situated in a renovated building on the waterfront. It offers standard guest rooms with plenty of elbow room, some seaside rooms with French balconies, and lots of great views of the water. There is a lovely rooftop terrace.

Rotonda 1. ⓒ 052/757-110. Fax 052/726-177. www.hotel-rotonda.hr. 37 units. Aug: from 124€ ($174) seaside double. Rest of year: from 70€ ($98) double. Rates include breakfast and are based on stays of 4 or more days. 20% surcharge for stays of 3 days or fewer. Half-board available. AE, DC, MC, V. Limited parking 3€ ($3.60) per day. Usually closed Jan–Feb. **Amenities:** Restaurant; terrace cafe; bar. *In room:* TV.

Torci 18 Torci 18's 12 rooms are simple, clean, and convenient. This is a good option that falls between the moderately priced Cittar and the private accommodations in Novigrad. The Cittar does not provide many luxuries, but you're not sharing a bathroom, either. Breakfast prepared in Torci 18's kitchen and served on the terrace is a big plus.

Torci 34. Outside Novigrad. ⓒ 052/757-799. Fax 052/757-174. www.torci18.hr. 12 units. Doubles from 60€ ($84) in July and Aug. Other times, doubles from 50€ ($70). AE, DC, MC, V. **Amenities:** Restaurant; bar; terrace. *In room:* SAT/TV.

Hotel San Rocco A haven for lovers of quiet, relaxation, and fine cuisine, complete with its own swimming pool, this 12-room boutique hotel in Brtonigla caters to guests who want to be near the sea, but not amid the hustle and bustle of the resort towns of Novigrad (5 min. away) or Porec (15 min.). The air-conditioned rooms in this 100-year-old, renovated stone house have sumptuous beds under wood-beamed ceilings, and big bathrooms, some with tubs and turbo-massage showers. In addition, the hotel restaurant has a way with local ingredients. *Tip:* If you can't get to Istria and the San Rocco, you still can get a feel for the hotel and its setting at **Istrian Charms,** a Zagreb boutique that sells San Rocco olive oil and other Istrian products. The store also offers a virtual tour of the hotel and restaurant on a flatscreen TV and you can book a room at the hotel on the spot. (See Shopping, chapter 9.)

Srednja Ulica 2, Brtonigla, 52474. ℂ 052/725-000. Fax 052/725-026. www.san-rocco.hr. 12 units. Doubles Apr 1–Oct 1 from 149€ ($205). Rest of year, doubles from 133€ ($186). Rates include breakfast. 35% discount for singles occupying a double room. **Amenities:** Restaurant; bar; pool; sauna; wine cellar; parking; Wi-Fi in bar area; elevator; access for those w/disabilities. *In room:* A/C, SAT/TV, minibar, hair dryer, safe.

Hotel St. Benedict ★★   Hotel St. Benedict is away from the fray in Dajla, a picturesque village, situated on the northwest coast of the Istrian peninsula, between Umag and Novigrad. Guest rooms are nicely decorated and they provide peace and quiet, plenty of elbow room, and a comfortable place to kick back after taking in the "bright lights" of Novigrad and Umag.

Dajla bb. Novigrad. ℂ 052/735-513. Fax 052/735-512. www.sv-benedikt.com/en/home. 27 units. Doubles with balcony and sea view in July and Aug from 119€ ($167). Other times, doubles from 83€ ($116). AE, DC, MC, V. **Amenities:** Restaurant; pool; beach. *In room:* A/C, SAT/TV.

WHERE TO EAT & DRINK

Novigrad has several excellent restaurants, but most are more expensive than the pizza/pasta places in Poreč. The best bars overlook the sea.

Mandrać ★ ISTRIAN   The street-level terrace with tables spilling onto the sidewalk is designed to look like it is located within ruined city walls. Inside, beamed ceilings and a blue-and-white color scheme create a pleasant marine ambience. Entrees are mostly variations on grilled fish and pasta dishes, and while preparations and presentation are very good, service can be haughty at times. If you can get past that, try some of Mandrać's specials like the mussels with cheese or the fish baked with potato, for a little twist on tried-and-true Istrian dishes.

Mandrać 6. ℂ **052/757-120.** Entrees 40kn–160kn ($8–$30). AE, DC, V. Daily 10am–midnight.

Restoran Torci 18 ★★ *Finds* ISTRIAN   It's hard to say if Torci 18 is a restaurant with pansion or a pansion with restaurant because the two are seamlessly blended into a solid building with dark wood beams, gardens, and glass under the old walls overlooking the sea. Menu choices are fairly predictable but well-prepared. (You know the fish is fresh as can be when you see women cleaning the morning's catch with clamshells on the restaurant's beach side.) Pastas require a 2-portion minimum and lobster is sold by the kilo. Atmosphere is gratis. Don't leave without buying a bottle of Torci 18's home grown olive oil.

Torci 18. ℂ **052/757-799.** Fax 052/757-174. www.torci18.hr. Entrees 50kn–85kn ($9–$16/7€–12€); more for fish sold by the kilo. AE, DC, MC, V. Daily noon–3pm and 6–10pm.

Restaurant Navigarre ★★★ ISTRIAN   The signature restaurant of the Hotel Nautica ★★★ opened in 2006 as a crisp, shipshape venue for serious food. Diners can choose either light meals or "slow" food both inside the brass and teak-fitted dining room and outside on the terrace under huge burgundy umbrellas. The menu, which is in 5 languages including Russian, features creative dishes based on local produce, including lamb, octopus, and veal prepared (with 3 hr. notice) under the peka. For a lighter meal, try homemade tagliatelle with prsut and peas, or the more complex gnocchi with scallops and truffles. For dessert, the Florentine cream cake is to die for.

Sv. Antona 15. 52466 Novigrad. ℂ **052/600-400.** Fax 052/600-490. www.NauticaHotels.com. Reservations recommended. Entrees 75kn–180kn ($14–$34). AE, DC, MC, V. Daily 7am–11pm.

Vitriol ★★ BEVERAGES   Novigrad's bar scene is decidedly low-key, but Vitriol is the center of it all from its seaside perch. The ambience could be classified as Croatian Starbucks in the morning when all the terrace tables are filled with people sipping coffee and reading the newspaper or catching up with e-mail on laptops via Vitriol's free Wi-Fi. Vitriol is behind the breakwater, so the breeze is soft and in tune with the jazz that is always playing softly in the background. In the afternoon, the crowd shifts to the ice cream and cake set and by night the music is hot and the beverages a lot stronger.

Podravska 31. ⓒ 052/758-270. MC, V. Mon–Fri 7:30am–midnight; until 1am Sat–Sun.

NEAR NOVIGRAD

Restoran San Rocco ★★★ *Finds* ISTRIAN   The chef at this restaurant in the San Rocco Hotel ★★★ in Brtonigla, 5 minutes from Novigrad, specializes in 3- to 5-course tasting menus that rely on local ingredients creatively presented. Typical offerings include octopus salad with olive oil foam and pork breast with pistachios. Pairings with local wines from San Rocco's well-stocked cellar are suggested for each course, but boost the tariff considerably. A la carte options are available, but prices are available only on request.

Srednja Ulica 2, Brtonigla 52474. ⓒ **052/725-000.** Fax 052/725-026. www.san-rocco.hr. Tasting menu 290kn–510kn ($54–$95/40€–70€). AE, DC, MC, V. Daily 1–10pm

9 Umag (Umago)

Umag hits visitors in the face with its huge modern hotels, concrete beach, and banners everywhere advertising the city's annual international ATP Croatia Open tennis tournament, festivals, concerts, and even restaurants. The crowded waterfront shops look more like bus station concessions than resort boutiques, and the atmosphere shouts "vacation package deal." However, Umag does have a few bright spots. Umag's Old Town is worth some time with its leafy squares and medieval streets. The spa in the renovated Sol Umag hotel is one of the best in Croatia. In fact, the Sol Umag is surprisingly nice for large tourist accommodations.

ESSENTIALS

VISITOR INFORMATION   Umag's **tourist information office** is at JB Tita 3/2 (ⓒ **052/741-363;** fax 052/741-649; www.istra.com/umag). They can give you brochures and maps as well as information on sports opportunities and excursions. Nearly two dozen tourist agencies broker thousands of privately owned rooms and apartments in Umag. Umag Renters' Association publishes an exhaustive catalog detailing them. Sol Melia, which manages many of Umag's big hotels and camping services, pumped a significant amount of money into its campgrounds in 2005. Brochures listing facilities and prices for both these types of accommodations are available at the tourist information office in town.

GETTING THERE   See "Getting There" in "Orientation," earlier in this chapter.

GETTING AROUND   Most of Umag's tourist activity is at the waterfront or in Old Town. If you are staying at one of the big hotels on the outskirts or if you want to access the **Stella Maris Sports Complex,** you probably will have to take one of the city buses or drive.

WHAT TO SEE & DO

Umag's beaches are more like concrete slabs in the water and not very appealing, but most of the big hotels have a full slate of activities and sports available as well as programs for children. If you are staying at one of these big hotels—or somewhere else—a few hours at Sol Umag's Istrian-style spa can be a rejuvenating interlude.

Sol Umag Wellness and Beauty ✿✿✿   It's tough to recommend what's essentially a fitness center and salon as a place to seek out on a vacation in a country with almost unlimited natural wonders, but this one is worth a few hours of your time. Designed to look like an Istrian village with arches, mosaics, flowers, waterfalls, and sculptures, the spa takes up three floors of the Sol Umag hotel and doesn't offer mere exercise opportunities and salon services: It offers imaginative exercise opportunities and salon services. Don't miss the amazing "Blue Cave" relaxation pool, the "Cleopatra" mud room, or the Istrian bio sauna. One- to 7-day beauty packages are available.

Jadranska bb. ✆ **052/714-000.** Fax 052/714-999. www.istra.com/istraturist. Daily 8am–9pm.

WHERE TO STAY

Accommodations at Umag range from several large Croatian chain hotels to a huge inventory of private accommodations and a string of camping facilities catering to a wide range of tastes.

Sol Umag ✿✿   Everything at Sol Umag is in place to fulfill almost any vacation need at this big hotel north of the city. Sol Umag underwent a partial renovation in 2004 and its facilities sparkle. Guest rooms are comfortably large and most have balconies that overlook the lovely outdoor pool or the sea. Premier features include a **spa** ✿✿✿ and access to world-class tennis facilities.

Jadranska bb. ✆ **052/714-000.** Fax 052/714-999. hotel.umag@istraturist.hr. 217 units. Aug: from 184€ ($258) double with balcony, sea view, and half-board. Rest of year: from 112€ ($157) double with balcony, sea view, and half-board. AE, DC, MC, V. Limited free parking. **Amenities:** Restaurant; poolside snack bar; bar; 3 pools; elevator; organized activity programs; salon; laundry service; wine shop. *In room:* A/C, TV, minibar.

WHERE TO DINE

As you might expect, Umag is full of pizzerias, spaghetterias, and other family-friendly dining spots. Most people who stay in the resort hotels take half-board and their meals there, but there is at least one upscale option for those who want to go a la carte.

Allegro ✿✿ CONTINENTAL   Allegro is a fancy hotel restaurant in a fancy hotel where you can choose the attractive dining room or the terrace, which is especially nice in moonlight. If you are tired of traditional Istrian cuisine, choose grilled venison, goat on a spit, or duck in basil sauce, though fish preparations can surprise you, too. Don't miss the huge seafood display on ice on the seaside terrace.

JB Tita 9. ✆ **052/700-000.** Fax 052/700-499. www.hotel-kristal.com. Reservations recommended. Entrees 70kn–180kn ($13–$34). AE, DC, MC, V. Daily 9am–midnight.

10 Inland Istria

It isn't easy being green in a country where blue is the dominant color, but the Istrian interior's countless hues of vegetation sparkling beneath the sun hint at the unspoiled nature and unique experiences that await those who venture into this often overlooked part of Croatia. It hits you as you exit the deep blackness of **Učka Tunnel** in the east or as you drive away from the golden brightness of the **Istrian Coast** in the west: This is territory that feeds the senses—all of them. In **Green Istria** you can take time to breathe the perfumed air, listen to the birds chatter, touch the rough stone of a medieval castle, or savor the taste of local wines.

Inland Istria is a land of discovery where you can climb a hill to listen to cool jazz at **Grožnjan,** travel the wine road through Momjan, watch films under a night sky in **Motovun,** or soak in hot spring waters at **Istarske Toplice.** Inland Istria is where you can marvel at still-vibrant 15th-century frescoes in a woodland church near tiny **Beram,** or tramp through the woods outside **Buzet** while following a couple of dogs hunting truffles.

Inland Istria is where you can feast on an elaborate dinner in an award-winning restaurant in **Livade** and wake up the next morning to a breakfast of home-smoked ham, homegrown fruit, and homemade cheese in the kitchen of the rural farmhouse where you spent the night. During the day, you can nose around Glagolitic artifacts in tiny **Hum** or explore the historic walled city of **Roč.** Inland Istria allows travelers to immerse themselves in the land and its people who reside there.

ESSENTIALS

VISITOR INFORMATION   Every town in Green Istria has its own tourist information center, though some offices in the smaller towns have very limited hours and are difficult to find. To help visitors get the most out of their trip, the **Istria County Tourist Association** has produced some exceptional materials. These include attractive publications on farmhouse stays, cultural itineraries, wine roads, olive-oil roads, and truffle-hunting opportunities. Information on those and many other topics is available through the association, whose main offices are in Poreč at Pionirska 1 (© **052/452-797;** fax 052/452-796; tzzi-po@pu.hinet.hr), and in Pula at Forum 3 (© **052/215-799;** fax 052/215-722). The association also maintains an excellent website with English-language links to almost every town: **www.istra.com.**

GETTING THERE   No matter how you get to Istria—by plane to Pula, by boat to one of the coastal cities, by bus to Pazin, or by any other method, unless you are on a guided excursion, you will need a car to thoroughly explore the inland area.

GETTING AROUND   Most towns in inland Istria are small; one of them, Hum, is known as the smallest town in the world. Thus, the main attractions in all of Istria's inland towns can be readily accessed on foot. However, many of these towns are extremely hilly and must be approached by walking over irregular cobblestone streets. To get to Motovun, for example, you have to leave your car at the bottom of a steep street and walk more than a quarter of a mile uphill. In addition, some of the smaller towns are remote, so driving your own car is the only practical way to cover the territory between them.

11 Pazin (Pisino)

Quiet Pazin in the center of Istria is the antithesis of the touristy coast: There are no glitzy resorts or hordes of tourists there, but there are some historic sites worth visiting. Pazin is not a huge transportation hub, but rail and bus service connect it to other parts of the country. While Pazin doesn't have Roman ruins like Pula or a gorgeous coastline like Rovinj, it does have a medieval castle with a long and interesting history and a deep chasm that inspired author Jules Verne while he was writing *Mathias Sandorf.* In reality, Pazin's personality is similar to that of any small town in middle America: It's in the middle of nowhere with a strong agricultural base, a little industry, and a neutral location that was a factor in its choice as a regional seat of government. Pazin's central position on the peninsula also makes it an excellent base from which to explore the rest of inland Istria, including the amazing frescoes at St. Mary of the Rock in nearby Beram.

ESSENTIALS

VISITOR INFORMATION   Pazin's **tourist office** is staffed with young, friendly people who speak English and are eager to help. Not only can they tell you about the town's most interesting sites and give you tips on how to find them, but they also can direct you to little-known points of interest in the surrounding area. The town's tourist office is at Franine I Jurine 14, P.O. Box 3, 52000 Pazin (© **052/622-460**). Pazin's website (www.tzpazin.hr) is exceptional.

GETTING THERE   Trains and buses serve Pazin from Zagreb, Rijeka, and cities in Istria. See "Getting There" in "Orientation," earlier in this chapter for information.

GETTING AROUND   Pazin is a small town, so its main attractions are best reached on foot.

WHAT TO SEE & DO

Pazin's notable sites can be seen in less than a day. Try to set aside a couple of hours to see the eye-popping frescoes in the tiny Church of St. Mary of the Rock outside the nearby village of Beram, 5.6km (3½ miles) to the west.

Istrian Ethnographic Museum ✶✶✶   The display of Istrian cultural artifacts in Pazin's Kaštel museum is one of the best in Croatia. The collection includes traditional Istrian costumes, farm and household items, a model of an old Istrian kitchen with its distinctive traditional hearth, looms, winemaking implements, and much more. Don't miss the display of 14th- through 20th-century bells on the ground floor. The bells were taken from village churches in all parts of Istria during World War II to save them from the fascists, who melted them down to make bullets. The oldest dates to the 15th century. The bells are displayed with photos or drawings that show how they looked in their churches. The bells in this museum are all that remain. The displays are well annotated in several languages. *Tip:* Entrance is through Pazin Kastle.

In Pazin Kaštel. Istarskog Razvoda 1. 052/625-040. www.tzpazin.hr. Admission 15kn ($3) adults, 8kn ($1.50) children. Summer Tues–Sun 10am–6pm. Winter Tues–Thurs 10am–3pm; Fri noon–5pm; Sat–Sun 11am–5pm. Closed Mon.

Pazin Kaštel ✶   The 9th-century castle is one of the best preserved in Istria thanks to numerous renovations, which altered its appearance somewhat. However, the view of the **Pazin Chasm** ✶✶✶ from the castle grounds and of the **Ethnographic Museum** ✶✶✶ inside are the biggest reasons to visit here.

Visitor information same as for the Istrian Ethnographic Museum, above.

Pazin Chasm ✶✶✶   The 91m-deep (300-ft.) gorge and sheer rock wall next to the Kaštel have inspired science fiction author Jules Verne (*Mathias Sandorf*) and many others to incorporate it into their work. It also apparently was the site of wartime horrors during World War II and the 1991 civil war. According to one historian, numerous skeletons still wearing military garb (including those of two women) were found at the bottom of the chasm after the last war.

Next to the Pazin Kaštel.

St. Nicholas Church This church next to the tourist office originally was built in the 13th century and rebuilt twice—in the 15th and again in the 18th centuries. The church is notable because of the 14th-century frescoes above the ornate altar depicting the Way of the Cross and scenes from the Old Testament. There are more frescoes under the plaster walls, but they probably won't be restored because it is likely that the process would destroy them. Until the 17th century, many of the church's frescoes were ruined by people who washed them repeatedly in the mistaken belief that the plague came out of the walls. The church priests are buried under the floor.

Eufrazijeva Ulica 22, across from the tourist office. Admission during Mass and for organized tours.

Frescoes at the Church of St. Mary of the Rock ⚔⚔⚔ Tiny Beram is a little more than 5.6km (3½ miles) west of Pazin. It's a one-street town with a nice church, but this isn't the church you're looking for. When you get to Beram, ask anyone in town to help you get in touch with the woman who has the key to St. Mary's where the famous frescoes reside. (Two women alternate key possession weekly and don't give out their phone numbers.) The townspeople will call her for you and let you know that you will have to drive her to the church and back to town, which is three-quarters of a mile northwest of the town limits. St. Mary's, a tiny, Gothic-style building in the forest, contains 15th-century frescoes stunning in their brightness and detail. There you will find the walls covered with scenes from the New Testament created by Croatian artist Vincent de Kastav. The main attraction is the almost cartoonish "Dance of the Dead" with skeletons carrying scythes and blowing horns as they lead townspeople to the netherworld. The original, though much older, is far more vibrant than the copy in the Church of St. Germaine on Veliki Brijuni. Explanations are printed in various languages, including English, though your guide probably will speak Croatian only. *Tip:* Your guide will tell you that three flash photos total are allowed per visit, so if you are with a large group, this could be a problem. There is no entry charge, but it is customary to offer the woman a gratuity for her time.

In the center of town, Beram.

WHERE TO STAY & DINE

There is only one hotel in Pazin and it is utilitarian at best. However, if you have your own transportation, private accommodations are the best option because private rooms are abundant, especially in rural farmhouses. Check with the tourist office (address above) for suggestions.

Lovac This generic hotel works for an overnight stay or if there are no other options. It's clean but it lacks personality. The a la carte **Restoran Lovac** ⚔ has a nice terrace and serves interesting fare such as game dishes and truffle pizza.

Šime Kurelića 4. ⓒ 052/624-324. Fax 052/624-384. 27 units. From 50€ ($30) double. AE, DC, MC, V. Limited free parking.

Laura ⚔ Private accommodations with two double rooms and four apartments afford a good view of the castle from this position on a rise with a beautiful garden in the town center. All units have balconies and access to fridges and stoves so you can buy and prepare local products from the Puris turkey outlet store in town.

Antuna Kalca 10A. ⓒ 052/621-312. 6 units. For stays of 3 days or fewer: from 28€ ($40) double; apts 17€ ($24) per person. For stays of more than 3 days: from 22€ ($31) double; 14€ ($20) apt. AE, DC, MC, V. Rates do not include breakfast. Limited free parking. *In room:* TV (apts only), access to kitchen facilities.

Boškarin ✦ ISTRIAN   The walls of this plain-looking dining room named after the protected Istrian ox display a few farm implements. Tables have bench seats and the menu covers all the traditional local food groups like fuži, smoked ham, and polenta. Dubravica 1. ℂ 052/621-327. Entrees 30kn–90kn ($6–$16). No credit cards. Mon–Sat 10am–11pm; closed Sun.

Restoran Lovac ✦ ISTRIAN   This restaurant in Pazin's only hotel gets points for variety on its menu. All dishes are prepared with local ingredients including venison and others incorporate truffles in unexpected dishes like pizza. Šime Kurelića 4. ℂ 052/624-324. Fax 052/624-384. Entrees 40kn–120kn ($8–$22). AE, DC, MC, V. Daily 7am–11pm.

12 Grožnjan (Grisignana), Buje (Buie) & Momjan (Momiano)

The roads that link **Grožnjan, Buje,** and **Momjan** are narrow, steep, and winding at times, but they snake through some of the most scenic real estate in Istria. Along the way you'll discover a ruined castle (Momjan), a WWII monument dedicated by Tito (Buje), and one of the prettiest hill towns anywhere in Croatia (Grožnjan).

Buje is a short hop from Novigrad and the town itself is fairly uninteresting, except for an 18th-century church (Sv. Servula Mučenika) and a monument and plaque commemorating Tito's 1954 visit to the town. At that time, Tito became an honorary citizen of Buje and dedicated a WWII monument to the freedom fighters from the area. The road out of Buje northeast toward **Momjan** is a jumping-off point for both the wine and olive oil roads of the region as it meanders through vineyards and olive groves past wineries, a restaurant ✦✦✦, and even the ruins of Momjan castle. The Momjan area is a good place to try the region's outstanding wines, especially those from the Kozlović winery, which has a dynamite tasting room built into the original 100-year-old winery building.

The tiny hilltop village of **Grožnjan** south of Momjan was almost deserted 40 years ago after most of its Italian population left for economic opportunity. In 1965, the town saw an influx of artists, who took over the town and saved it from extinction by renovating the Old Town core. Since then, Grožnjan has blossomed into a full-fledged artist's colony replete with galleries, shops, restaurants, and a summer jazz festival in July and August that attracts big-name talent and plenty of fans. If you can't get there for a performance, you can stop at one of the village's pleasant restaurants for a bite and listen to the mellow sounds emanating from all corners of the village during daytime practice sessions. It is also fun to poke around the maze of small cobbled streets, a loggia, gates, walls, and a church with good frescoes. In keeping with Grožnjan's title as a "town of artists," numerous shops and ateliers in town sell original paintings, pottery, and jewelry made by local craftspeople.

ESSENTIALS

VISITOR INFORMATION   Facts about this cluster of towns are available at the Istria County Tourist Offices in Pula and Poreč (above) and in each town's local bureau. Buje's visitor center is located at Istarska 2 (ℂ **052/773-353;** www.tzg-buje.hr). The staff there can provide you with maps and directions for the area's hiking trails. Grožnjan's tourist office is at Gorjan 3 (ℂ **052/776-131;** www.groznjan-grisignana.hr/tz). Any of the offices can provide you with a map of the wine and olive roads complete with the addresses of establishments open to the public for tastings.

GETTING THERE   See "Getting There" in "Orientation," earlier in this chapter.

On the (Wine and Olive Oil) Road

The best way to explore Istria's wine and olive oil roads is to pick up a map produced by the Istrian Tourist Board (www.istra.hr) that lists about 6 dozen winemakers and 2 dozen olive oil producers in the region. Most of Istria's wineries are in the country's north central region and you will need a car to get from one venue to the next. Roads do have directional signs marking the wine and oil routes and producers have marked the paths to their doors in some cases. Don't miss the cellars of **Kozlović, Kabola,** or **Matijašić,** all full-fledged wineries that have expanded their production into microclimate vintages. Kozlović is not set up for unannounced tasters, so call ahead, but Kabola welcomes drop-ins. Matijašić requires reservations for its accommodations. Below, a few more of our favorites.

Kozlović Winery at Vale 78 Momjan, (✆ **052/779-177**; www.kozlovic.hr) produces 100,000 bottles a year and is open from 8am to noon and 1 to 5pm Monday through Saturday. Closed Sunday.

Kabola Winery (✆ **052/779-033**) is in Kremenje between Buje and Momjan and includes a small winemaking museum and a knock-out restaurant 𝄪𝄪𝄪. (✆ **052/779-047**; fax: 052/779-047; www.kabola.hr). Open for tasting 10am to 5pm Tuesday through Saturday.

Matijašić Winery is a working vineyard near Motovun where you can spend the night and perhaps pick a few grapes, too. Pekasi, 52424 Motovun, Istria (✆ **052/682-126**).

Note: You can stop in at any of the olive oil producers on the map to purchase product, but if you want to see a pressing in action or pick a few olives, reservations are required. Consult Istria's Olive Oil Road Map for details and contact information.

GETTING AROUND   The important sites in all of these towns can be easily accessed on foot, but if you intend to visit wineries or sites in between, a car is a must.

WHAT TO SEE & DO

Besides the old buildings and beautiful views, each of the towns in this group has at least one marquee event during the year and all are worth a few hours of wandering any time. Grožnjan is probably the most accessible because of the large number of venues and restaurants concentrated in a central location.

Momjan Wine Festival 𝄪𝄪   Momjan is surrounded by wine country and the winemakers there are serious about their craft. Every November 9-11, the town celebrates the new vintage in honor of St. Martin, patron saint of winemakers and you can get a preview of the product just by walking around town. Like all Croatian celebrations, tons of food and nonstop music complete the picture. Go to www.momjan.com for more information.

Grožnjan Musical Summer and Jazz Festival 𝄪𝄪𝄪   If you walk through the streets of Grožnjan anytime during the summer you will be treated to the sounds of music—all kinds of music. On a random July day in 2007 our stroll through town

The Ruins of Momjan Castle

Momjan Castle was mentioned as early as 1102 as the property of the Counts Orlamund, in one of the only two existing transcripts of the oldest Glagolitic legal document in the Croatian language, "Survey of Istrian Land Boundaries" (Istarski razvod), which was found in the 19th century. The castle was destroyed in clashes between the Counts of Gorizia and the Republic of Venice and rebuilt in the 15th century. After the treaty of Madrid was signed between Venice and the Hapsburgs in 1617, the importance of the castle as a fortress diminished, so it was abandoned and gradually fell into ruins.

These ruins are located in north central Istria on a hillock just north of the village of Momjan. To get there, take the exit for Buje off the main north-south road, Istria highway, A-9. A secondary road leading northeast from Buje takes you to Momjan after about 7km (4.5 miles). The surrounding countryside is rugged and picturesque and the castle is situated spectacularly, with cliffs on the north side and a steep-sided ravine on the south. At one time there was a bridge across the ravine, but it, too, has fallen into ruin.

To reach the castle ruins you have to traverse the ravine and there is a rough trail that leads from the north side of Momjan into the ravine. The walk takes 10 to 15 minutes.

Courtesy of Tocher Mitchell

was accompanied by the sweet sounds of a violin concerto wafting from the practice rooms above our heads. Sometimes the sound is jammin' jazz and other times it's the voice of a choir—and that's just the free stuff. Grožnjan offers scheduled performances of all kinds almost every evening during July and August. Check www.hgm.hr for full schedules and information.

WHERE TO STAY AND DINE

Konoba Taverna Marino ☆☆☆ *(Finds* ISTRIAN   Marino's owner, Marino Markezić, also directs Kabola, his family's winery. The restaurant is in rural Istria, on the road between Buje and Momjan. Marino's peach-painted stucco terrace is a perfect setting for the kitchen's heavenly seasonal dishes: In summer it is heavy with hanging red geraniums and rattan furniture while the dining room is a study in wood, glass, and Istrian artifacts. If you have time to linger, order Marino's tasting menu, which matches Kabola vintages to the food. If not, the *sir sa tartufi* (fried cheese with truffles) is a delight, as is the tender gnocchi with mushrooms. Keep in mind, there are a few rooms for rent at Marino, which is handy if you sample all of Kabola's wines.

Kremenje 9. Momjan. ⓒ **052/779-047.** www.konoba-marino-kremenje.hr. Entrees 14kn–48kn ($9–$26). AE, DC, MC, V. Feb–Dec Wed–Mon noon–10pm. Closed Tues and Jan.

Zigante Enoteka ☆ *(Overrated* CHEESE & WINE   One of many Zigante franchises, this small room is a deli with tables that sells cheeses and other accompaniments to go with Zigante's wines, which are sold by the glass or bottle. You can take home truffle cheese, *pršut*, or truffle-infused olive oil; or you can order a variety plate to go with an overpriced glass of *vino* from the wine bar.

Gorjan 7, Grožnjan. ℂ **052/721-998.** Fax 052/721-999. www.zigantetartufi.com. Wines from 35kn ($7) per glass. No credit cards. Mon–Fri 10am–2pm and 5–11pm; 10am–11pm without a break on weekends. Store daily 9am–10pm.

Restoran Bastia ⭐⭐ ISTRIAN   Bastia is the fanciest restaurant in Grožnjan, and it also has the biggest menu in town, helpfully translated into four languages. The nice range of fish and meat dishes can be enjoyed outside or in the cozy dining room, which is done in cheery shades of blue and white and which has a wood-burning fireplace.

Svibnia 1, Grožnjan. ℂ **052/776-370.** Entrees 30kn–125kn ($6–$23). MC, V. Daily from 8am "until people leave."

Café Bar Arta ⭐ SANDWICHES   Arta is a sandwich and drink shop with a nice view of the valley from its balcony.

Trg Cornera 3, Grožnjan. ℂ **052/776-405.** No credit cards. Festival weekends 8am–midnight; 8am–2am other days. Closed Mon.

13 Motovun (Montona), Livade (Levade) & Oprtalj (Portole)

Motovun is one of Istria's better-known interior towns, perhaps because it hosts such events as the Motovun Film Festival, hot-air balloon competitions, and a festival celebrating truffles and wine. It doesn't hurt that this hilltop town is just over 14km (9 miles) north of Pazin or that it is home to the delightful **Kaštel Hotel** ⭐⭐.

The village of **Livade** is a short distance north of Motovun, and it is fast becoming a center for gastronomic delights, including the locally venerated truffle. In the countryside around Livade, you'll see huge tracts of vineyards and olive trees as well as workers toiling in the fields no matter what the season. Here there are new vineyards as well as old, along with lots of hand-painted signs on side roads advertising wine, olive oil, and grappa for sale.

If you continue on the same road a little farther, you'll reach **Oprtalj,** a charming town on a hill high above the Mirna river valley. Here you'll find the 15th-century **St. Mary's Church** and the 16th-century **Church of St. Rock,** both of which have a few lovely but minor frescoes. However, you'll probably have to be content with looking at these through the church windows, as they are rarely open.

Despite their remoteness and lack of efficient public transportation, all these tiny towns are quickly becoming centers of activity for lovers of film, music, fine dining, and other activities that feed the senses.

ESSENTIALS

VISITOR INFORMATION   Information on all three towns and their festivals is available at the Istria County Tourist Offices in Pula and Poreč (above) and in each town's local bureau. Motovun's tourist office is at Andrea Antico bb (ℂ **052/681-642**); and Oprtalj's is at M. Laginje 21 (ℂ **052/544-077;** tz@oprtalj.hr).

GETTING THERE   See "Getting There" in "Orientation," earlier in this chapter.

GETTING AROUND   The important sites in all of these towns can be easily accessed on foot.

WHAT TO SEE & DO

Besides the Motovun Film Festival in July and ballooning events in October, these towns are ideal places to wander about in search of medieval treasures. It doesn't hurt that they also have excellent restaurants, fine wines and, of course, truffles in abundance.

International Motovun Film Festival 🌟🌟   Less than a decade old, The Motovun Film Festival has established itself as a first-class showcase for European art-house films and other cinematic works. Like Aspen's Comedy Festival and Chicago's Film Festival and unlike Cannes, the Motovun event doesn't put barriers between the stars and the public. Instead, everyone throngs to the area for 5 days of nonstop partying.

International Motovun Film Festival. www.motovunfilmfestival.com. Early Aug, but dates are variable.

Truffle Hunting Excursions 🌟🌟🌟   You can arrange truffle-hunting excursions through Restaurant Zigante in Livade or through any of its franchise outlets across Croatia from September to December, though October is the height of truffle season. In addition, Activatravel in Pula arranges truffle excursions in season that include a 1½-hour hunt in the woods with dogs, followed by dinner in Livade.

Activatravel Istra. Scalierova 1, 52100 Pula. ℂ 052/215-497. Fax 052/211-889. info@activa-istra.com. Minimum 2, maximum 4 people per tour at 60€ ($84) per person. AE, DC, MC, V. Tours leave the Livade truffle center at 5pm daily in season only.

Zigante Tartufi 🌟   Livade is a town with one industry, and that is Zigante. There's nothing much here except a Zigante store selling truffle products and wine, and Restaurant Zigante, though several other restaurants are popping up along the town's main street. Besides selling truffle items and wines with the Zigante label, the store offers recipes in seven languages for using truffles, fresh cheese with truffles, and fresh truffles (at roughly $215 per lb.). Ask about the truffle that put Zigante in the *Guinness Book of World Records,* and the clerk will show you a plastic model of the giant underground fungus. It looks like a small cantaloupe (a normal truffle is the size of an egg).

Livade 7, Livade. ℂ 052/664-030. Fax 052/644-031. AE, DC, MC, V. Daily 9am–6pm.

WHERE TO STAY & DINE

Besides the Kaštel Hotel in Motovun, the only accommodations in these villages are in private establishments, making this an ideal opportunity to try a farmhouse stay and to savor the flavors of Istria at one of the area's fine-dining establishments.

Hotel Kaštel 🌟🌟 CREATIVE ISTRIAN   The Kaštel's perch at the highest point of the walled medieval town of Motovun provides panoramic views of the Mirna valley. Each room has a different view of the terrain, which includes the hotel's park. An excellent **Restoran Kaštel** 🌟🌟 serves Istrian home specialties and is adept at catering business meetings and other events. The sizeable guest rooms were refurbished in 2003 and are tastefully decorated with modern bathrooms that don't destroy the character of the 17th-century former palace. If you call ahead, the hotel will pick you up at the bottom of the street leading into Motovunso so you don't have to drag your luggage uphill.

Trg Andrea Antico 7, Motovun. ℂ 052/681-607. Fax 052/681-652. www.hotel-kastel-motovun.hr. 30 units. July–Aug and Christmas week: from 83€ ($116) double; from 113€ ($158) suite. Rest of year: from 67€ ($94) double; from 95€ ($133) suite. 50% surcharge for a single using a room with twin beds. AE, DC, MC, V. **Amenities:** Restaurant; excursions; pets (10€/$14 per day.). *In room:* TV, Internet connection.

Matijašić Agrotourism 🌟   This rustic cottage has been owned by the Matijašić family for four centuries. It is a typical Istrian stone house surrounded by nature in the middle of Istria's wine country. The cottage sleeps 6 and while no meals are provided, the owner runs a fine konoba 5km (3 miles) away. If you stay here, you also will have the opportunity to walk the vineyard with owner Darko Matijašić, tour his wine-making operation, and even pick a few grapes.

Pekasi, Motovun, 52424 Istria. © 052/682-126. Fax 052/682-012. www.matijasic.hr. 1 unit. 900kn ($167) per day. No credit cards. **Amenities:** Nearby konoba.

Zigante Restaurant 🎯🎯 *(Overrated)* GOURMET ISTRIAN
Two elegant, formal rooms designed in Istrian style are the setting for Giancarlo Zigante's celebrated cuisine. As expected, most of the dishes here (and even some of the desserts) incorporate truffles with spectacular results, but not as breathtaking as the prices. Try the medallions of lamb with goose liver and black truffles as an entree, or the homebred rabbit filled with—what else?—truffles. The wine list is loaded with Croatian wines, including some with the Zigante label, and service is impeccable. There is a cigar area plus another replica of that record-breaking truffle.

Livade 7, Livade. © 052/664-302. Fax 052/664-303. www.zigantetartufi.com. Reservations required. Entrees 135kn–205km ($25–$38). AE, DC, MC, V. Daily summer noon–11pm; winter 11am–10pm.

Barbacan Enoteque & Restaurant 🎯🎯🎯 ISTRIAN
This tiny restaurant on the main walkway into Motovun pays a lot of attention to detail, from its immaculate interior to its expertly prepared Istrian cuisine. A meal here is pricier than most, but it's also more interesting. Start with the pâté of veal sweetbreads with truffles or the truffled chicken broth. Entrees include filet of beef with black truffle butter; and risotto Montonese with saffron garlic and truffles. Service is delightful and the atmosphere is quite intimate.

Barbakan 1, Motovun. © 052/681-791. Entrees 85kn–145kn ($16–$27). AE, DC, MC, V. Wed–Sun 12:30–3:30pm and 6:30–10:30pm; Mon–Tues lunch only.

Restoran Kaštel 🎯🎯 ISTRIAN
The Kaštel's menu offers several unusual Istrian dishes as well as a signature dessert that's not on the menu. Try the *frkanci* with venison goulash, which is what the hotel calls a "forgotten" dish. Frkanci is a pasta that is a cross between gnocchi and noodle and usually only prepared in Istrian homes. In the Kaštel's case, the pasta is handmade by Istrian home cooks just for the hotel. Ask for the restaurant's special truffle for dessert: This one is chocolate, not tuber, and it is the size of an egg. You can dine under a 100-year-old mulberry tree or in the hotel's lovely dining room where service is not only efficient but friendly, too.

Trg Andrea Antico 7, Motovun. © 052/681-607. Fax 052/681-652. www.hotel-kastel-motovun.hr. Entrees 45kn–120kn ($9–$22). AE, DC, MC, V. Daily 10am–10pm.

Café-Bar Montana 🎯 PASTRIES & SANDWICHES
You'll see tables along the wall overlooking the valley immediately after you pass through the first gate that leads into Motovun proper. These belong to Montana, which is across the road and which also contains a nice art gallery. Be aware, this location can be very windy.

Motovun gateway. No phone. No credit cards. Daily 8am–midnight. Closed Jan 1–Easter.

14 Istarske Toplice, Roc (Rozzo), Hum (Colmo) & Buzet (Pinguente)

The stretch of road that connects **Istarske Toplice, Roc, Hum,** and **Buzet** is as rural as they come. Just below **Oprtalj,** and between **Buje** and Buzet, Istarske Toplice is a health resort nestled in a forested canyon with a spectacular, 91m-high (300-ft.) rock-climbing wall.

ESSENTIALS

VISITOR INFORMATION   The **Tourist Information Office** in Buzet serves Roč, Hum, and Istarske Toplice. It is at Trg Fontana 7/1 in Buzet (✆ 052/662-343; www.tzg-buje.hr) and can provide maps, brochures, and information on private accommodations, including farmhouse stays, camping, and events.

GETTING THERE   See "Getting There" in "Orientation," earlier in this chapter.

GETTING AROUND   Small towns in central Istria are best seen on foot, but travel between them requires a vehicle. Buses do serve the area, but not all routes are covered every day; and in some cases there is only one bus per day. Even then, you'll sometimes have to walk a mile or more to get to the center of town.

WHAT TO SEE & DO

Like many Croatian spas, **Istarske Toplice** *(Overrated)* was built, not as a playground where beautiful, healthy people came to be pampered, but as a place where crippled, infirm people came to be healed. The resort still seems to attract more of the latter than the former, and while you can enjoy a soak in the hot, sulphur-scented water or a rejuvenating mud pack, you could be sharing the pool with a physical therapy session. For those who like rock climbing, the almost vertical granite wall nearby is challenging.

Dubbed the "City of Truffles" because it and nearby **Livade** are prime truffle-hunting territory, **Buzet** is just 10km (6 miles) northeast of Istarske Toplice on top of a 137m (450-ft.) hill. It's worth a visit, especially during **Truffle Day,** usually the second Saturday in September. During this veneration of the earthy delicacy, the whole town throws a block party with music, food, and, of course, truffles. Cars are allowed up the narrow, twisting street into town, but don't try driving up there unless you're sure your brakes are good.

Approaching **Roč** by car or bus, you will see an unusually low **medieval wall** surrounding this fortified town. From that vantage point it doesn't seem as if the tiny town just under 8km (5 miles) southeast of Buzet could possibly have anything worth a detour. Sure, the medieval walls, **town gates,** and a **tower** are nice to see; and interesting **Roman tombstones** are displayed just inside the main gate arch. But one of the most compelling reasons to stop at Roč is its location at one end of the **Glagolitic Alley.** A string of 10 outdoor sculptures that dot the road between Roč and Hum was erected between 1977 and 1981 to celebrate and preserve Glagolitic script. Despite the fact that there aren't any explanations on most of them, the sculptures (dedicated to Glagolitic scholars) are interesting to look at. One of the sculptures, Razvoda, is an arrangement that looks like a Stonehenge garden. Today, Roč is primarily known as a center of Glagolitic literature, and every year the town puts on the **Small Glagolitic Academy** so that kids can keep the traditional writing alive. Private rooms are available in Roč (there are signs on the road), and there is a decent konoba.

The strip of road that links Roč and **Hum** is just 6.4km (4 miles) long, but it is a historic corridor because of the commemorative Glagolitic sculptures. Hum's biggest claim to fame, however, is its status as the world's smallest town. However, from the looks of the state of tourism in the present-day village, that could be changing. Tiny Hum has spiffed up in the last 3 years and is quite appealing. Only about 20 people live within Hum's well-preserved walls, which enclose two small streets and two churches (one dating from the 12th century).

Black (& White) Gold

Istria is fast becoming as famous as France and Italy for its wonderful truffles—pungent, underground tuberous fungi used in many traditional Istrian dishes and sauces. In Istria, specially trained dogs (Istrian hunters) are used to sniff out the malodorous treasures that grow a foot beneath the floor of the forests around Buzet (France and Italy traditionally use pigs, although dogs are becoming common there, too). True truffle madness takes over the area during Truffle Days, which occur at the start of the season in the area's villages. The most famous of these celebrations is the last Saturday in September in Buzet, where a Veli Jože-size omelet is cooked up with truffles and scarfed down by whomever happens to be merrymaking in town. Truffles' strong, distinctive flavor makes them an acquired taste, but their rarity and astronomical price make them a delicacy. Truffles are less expensive in Croatia than they are in other countries and thus are used more liberally in the cuisine.

WHERE TO STAY & DINE

Most accommodations in these small towns are in private apartments, rooms, or farmhouses, which makes this area a center of agro-tourism. Information on private accommodations is available at the tourist office in Buzet. Opportunities to sample authentic Istrian specialties abound in this rural area, which has a nice selection of excellent konobas.

Terme Mirna   The sheer granite wall called the **Iron Gate** that is a backdrop for this spa hotel is a spectacular feature of Istarske Toplice, but the facility itself is downright depressing. The Mirna still is primarily geared to those who need rehab or other medical therapies, though some people might want to stop for the thermal waters, which are rich in sulfur. In fact, sulfur's characteristic rotten-egg odor hits you as soon as you get out of the car in the parking lot. If you do stay, be sure to ask for a Type-A room, which is a little more expensive but which has been updated. Beauty treatments and multiday packages are available, including a 14-day "fit" (aka weight loss) package for 5,000kn ($926) that includes the services of a psychologist.

Sv. Stjepan 60, 52427 Livade. © 052/603-000. www.istarske-toplice.hr. 375 units, 4 suites. From 440kn ($82) double (A-type). Rate includes breakfast. AE, DC, MC, V. **Amenities:** Restaurant; coffee bar; 2 pools; spa services. *In room:* TV.

Fontana   Guest rooms in this Buzet establishment are quite worn and basic but larger than most and nicer than you'd expect from looking at the blighted exterior of this three-story hotel near the road into town. The staff is accommodating, however, and helpful in suggesting area sites and how to reach them.

Trg Fontana 1, Buzet. © 052/662-615. Fax 052/663-423. hotelfontana@pu.htnet.hr. 57 units. Half-board doubles from 60€ ($85). AE, DC, MC. Limited free parking. **Amenities:** Restaurant; bar; disco; laundry service; elevator. *In room:* TV.

Vrh ★★ ISTRIAN   Technically, Vrh is in Buzet, but it's really in the hills outside town. Get directions at the Buzet tourist office to this delightful spot on the road between Ponte Porton and Buzet. Vrh's menu is standard Istrian with dishes such as fužI with truffles or gnocchi with game. Sausages are house made, peka-baked meat is a specialty, and nettle pâté is a delicacy. Try Vrh's house label wine and if you're staying nearby, a glass of local grappa, which is renowned all over Croatia.

Vrh 2. Buzet. © **052/667-123**. Entrees 42kn–160kn ($8–$30), more for peka meat sold by the kilo. No credit cards. Tues–Sat 1–10pm and Sun 12:30–10pm.

Ročka Konoba 😺😺 ISTRIAN   You'll feel like you're in Mom's kitchen in this rustic dining room with a great view of the rolling countryside. The food is just like home cooking, too—if you live in Istria. Local specials such as fuži, spicy Istrian sausage, hearty soups, and fragrant homemade bread are on the menu here.

Roč Center. © **052/666-451**. Entrees 35kn–90kn ($7–$17). AE, DC, MC, V. Hours variable.

Humska Konoba 😺😺 ISTRIAN   The line was literally out the door when we visited this Hum institution in July 2007 and no wonder. Local flavors are in the food and in the decor and atmosphere, too, in this wood-and-stone building featuring a summer terrace that has a view of the countryside. If you dare, sip home-brewed *biska,* a grape brandy–based aperitif flavored with white mistletoe and other herbs. Nibble on locally produced smoked ham and sheep's cheese. Then dig into such Istrian specialties as fuži with goulash or truffles, and smoked meat and sauerkraut. Have *krostole* (doughnuts) for dessert.

Hum 2, 52425 Roč. © **052/660-005**. Fax 052/660-001. www.hum.hr. Entrees 9kn–35kn ($1.65–$6.50). No credit cards. Tues–Sun 11am–10pm. Closed Mon.

9

Zagreb

There is a new spirit in Zagreb, a city that was regarded as a stopover rather than a destination as far back as the days of the Orient Express. No more. To be sure, Zagreb's attractions aren't as famous as Paris's, or as numerous as Rome's, but it's nonetheless difficult to experience all the city's delights on an overnight stay. It takes patience to discover Zagreb, and its soul.

Zagreb has always played a pivotal role in the life of Croatia, mostly because of its location, at where Western and Eastern Europe meet. Today's Zagreb is far more tolerant and easygoing than it was when its forerunner settlements of Gradec and Kaptol were founded in medieval times, but it still is a dichotomy of old ways and new, of tradition and progress.

This is not a glitzy city, but rather a city of history, culture, and purpose informed by war and natural disasters. Zagreb is still finding itself after nearly a millennium of foreign domination, but it is changing, growing, and emerging as a destination in its own right. In the summer of 2007 there was scarcely a square block in central Zagreb that didn't have scaffolding or construction shrouds covering a renovation in progress. Squares were filled with people speaking a variety of languages, including English. New restaurants, attractions, and entrepreneurial ventures were sprouting everywhere. In some ways, contemporary Zagreb's personality is in transition from dour socialist to carefree socialite and it is subject to being misunderstood. On any rainy Sunday, Zagreb is deserted: Stores are closed, restaurants are empty, and museums are without patrons. If a visitor has just a day to see the city from under an umbrella, Zagreb can be interpreted as a sad, gray place. But if that same visitor is lucky enough to walk to the city center on a sunny Saturday, Zagreb is a city pulsating with color and buzzing with energy. On such a day Zagreb hums with chatter as *fashionistas* dressed to the nines haggle with wizened old ladies in babushkas at the colorful Dolac market. On such a day, Zagreb is a comfortable backdrop for friends sipping wine at sidewalk cafes, for curious tourists, and for anyone listening to street musicians who fill Trg Ban Jeličića with beautiful noise.

Weekdays, Zagreb is alive with serious hustle and bustle with what seems like endless hordes carrying briefcases or bags of bread and flowers past a perpetual gallery sipping coffee at sidewalk cafes. Evenings, Zagreb is all softness and laughter as diners linger over dessert in Gornji Grad, head for nightclubs to listen to jazz with friends, or stroll the cobblestone streets.

How visitors see Zagreb depends largely on the color of the sky and the day of the week, but the city's blend of old and new, of country and cosmopolitan, is somehow a yin-yang combo that works. This is not a city that instantly takes your breath away, but—given enough time—Zagreb will wiggle its way into your heart and tempt you to unpack your bags and stay awhile.

1 Essentials

ARRIVING

BY PLANE   There are no direct flights to Croatia from the U.S., Canada, or Australia, but Croatia Air, the national airline company, connects Zagreb with several major European hubs as well as with other cities in Croatia. **Pleso International Airport** (*©* **01/626-52-22**) is located about 16km (10 miles) south of the city center, and Zagreb is the entry point for most visitors to Croatia. Croatia Air's shuttle bus runs every 30 minutes from 5:30am to 7:30pm from the airport to and from Zagreb's main bus station for 25kn ($4); and the ride takes half an hour (*©* **01/615-79-92**). Taxi fares to the city center run between 150kn and 250kn ($28–$46). *Warning:* Croatia Air's weight limits for luggage differ from those of some other international carriers, so if you are not checking your bags directly through to Zagreb from the U.S., you should call Croatia Air for information on this policy, which is subject to seasonal changes. When returning to the U.S., be aware that Croatia Air does not allow any battery-operated devices in checked luggage, so be sure to remove your alarm clock before you get to the ticket counter.

BY BUS   Croatia Airlines runs frequent shuttle buses between the airport and Zagreb's main bus station (Autobusni Kolodvor) for 25kn ($5). The bus station is a bright, efficient hub with restaurants, shops, a post office, and connections to the city center. A 24-hour *garderoba* (luggage storage area) charges 1.20kn (20¢) per hour or $4 per day. ATMs are located near the ticket office as well as an exchange that is open from 6am to 10pm daily. Frequent bus connections link Zagreb and all of Croatia's main cities, which in turn hook up with local lines that run to virtually every village in the country. International connections link Zagreb to an increasing number of European nations.

BY TRAIN   The **Zagreb train station (Glavni Kolodvor)** facing Trg Kralja Tomislava on the city's Green Horseshoe was renovated in 2004 and the 19th-century exterior is now bubble-gum pink and adorned with angels and other statuary. It is close to bus and tram connections into the city center, which is a 10-minute walk past several hotels along the way. A 24-hour garderoba is available for 10kn per day ($2). A nice restaurant with a lovely terrace overlooks the park. There are ATMs, exchange facilities, and an information center (6–10am, 10:30am–6pm, and 6:30–10pm).

Catch the no. 5, 6, or 13 tram across the street in front of the Kralja Tomislav monument to get to Trg Bana Josip Jeličića. Bus routes may change for construction projects, and when that happens, a handwritten sign with changes is taped up at the bus stop.

BY CAR   Driving in Zagreb can be stressful. Most streets are marked (if they are marked) by small ornamental signs on plaques affixed to building walls at intersections so you can't see the sign until you're past it. Many buildings in Zagreb do not display street numbers at all, or if they do, they can't be read unless you are right next to them. There also is a tangled network of one-way and pedestrian streets, perpetual street construction, and a parking dearth, all of which add up to a driver's nightmare inside the city limits.

VISITOR INFORMATION

The **Zagreb Tourist Information Center** at Trg Bana Jelačića 11 (*©* **01/481-40-51;** www.zagreb-touristinfo) is open 8:30am to 8pm Monday to Friday; 9am to 5pm

Saturday; and 10am to 2pm Sunday and holidays. The information center provides maps, directions, and brochures, and it has a selection of books about Zagreb and Croatia as well as some souvenirs. It sells the **Zagreb Card** for 90kn ($17), which gives you 72 hours of unlimited city transportation (including the Sjleme cable car), a 50% discount at most museums and galleries, and assorted discounts at participating businesses, including theaters and concert halls. There is a second Tourist Information Center at Trg Nikole Šubića Zrinskog 14 (© **01/492-16-45**).

There is also a **Zagreb County Tourist Association** at Preradovićeva 42 (© **01/ 487-36-65; www.tzzz.hr**). It is invaluable for information about excursions from Zagreb to such places as Samobor and the Žumberak region. Hours are 8am to 4pm Monday to Friday.

Numerous travel agencies in town can book flights, packages, and hotels, but anyone flying out of Zagreb will eventually talk to **Croatia Airlines,** whose main office is at Trg Nikole Šubića Zrinskog 17 (© **01/481-96-33**). It is open 8am to 7pm Monday to Friday and 8am to 3pm Saturday.

Tours to sites and cities in Zagreb and all over Croatia can be arranged through various travel agencies. **Atlas Travel** (© **01/481-39-33**) at Zrinjevac 17 is Croatia's largest agency and has a huge menu of tours and travel packages. It is also the country's American Express agent. **Generalturist** at Praška 5 (© **01/480-55-55; www.generalturist. com**) books flights, excursions, cruises, and other trips.

CITY LAYOUT

The city of Zagreb is nestled between **Mount Medvednica** and the **Sava River.** It is a sprawling metropolis, but almost every attraction of note is within a mile and a half of **Trg Bana Jelačića,** the city's main square commonly known as Trg Jelačića. The area north of the Trg Jelačića includes **Gornji Grad (Upper Town)** and its Gradec and Kaptol neighborhoods, which are perhaps Zagreb's most picturesque areas. **Donji Grad (Lower Town)** south of Trg Jelačića includes Zagreb's famous Green Horseshoe and runs south to the main train station. You can walk to most points of interest from Trg Jelačića, or hop on the public tram system for 6.50kn ($1.20) per ride. After that, only a smattering of sights is worth seeking out. **Mount Medvednica Nature Park** and its **Sjleme Peak** in the hills north of town can be accessed from the square by taking tram no. 14 to the end of the line and then tram no. 15 to its terminus. From there you can get a cable car to Sjleme's top. **Mirogoj Cemetery** is also north of the center and can be reached via the no. 106 bus from the cathedral. **Novi Grad (New City)** is an area of bland apartment towers and industry south of the Sava; except for **Jarun Lake** just north of the river and the airport, there isn't much to see here. **Maksimir Park** is an elegant wooded zone east of the center. It can be reached via tram nos. 4, 7, 11, and 12.

THE NEIGHBORHOODS IN BRIEF

Zagreb is easy to navigate via public transportation if you have a good map and know a few key Croatian terms so you can decipher directional signs on the trams and buses, but you can walk to almost everything of note, too. Most of Zagreb's attractions are in the city center, which has three "neighborhoods," each with a distinct character and connected by the city's main square, Trg Jeličića. Gornji Grad (Upper City), the area north of the square, is Zagreb's heart. It is divided along historical lines into Kaptol and Gradec, territory that was halved by a stream that is now Tkalčićeva Street, home to the core of Zagreb's cafe society and increasingly to chic designer shops and artists' ateliers.

Kaptol is both a neighborhood and a street in modern Zagreb. In medieval times, Kaptol was a town and was dominated by the clergy, while neighboring Gradec was a lay settlement. Today, Zagreb's neo-Gothic cathedral and church buildings are still situated in Kaptol. North of the cathedral, Kaptol is quickly becoming a trendy enclave where well-heeled young professionals shop, drink, dine, and mingle. Parts of Kaptol have been converted to a pedestrian mall, though motor scooters rarely pay attention to that traffic law. Opatovina Street runs parallel to Kaptol north from the left of the Dolac market; its most interesting feature is the statue of Croatian comedian and social commentator Petrica Kerempuh at the bottom of the street.

Gradec, on the other hand, is a hilly residential area dotted with stately mansions and leafy squares as well as some of the city's best galleries and museums. There is a tennis center in the northern section of the neighborhood plus several embassies and consulates and a few upscale restaurants. Gradec is a good place to see ornate homes built by Zagreb's 19th-century aristocrats as well as the only surviving city gate.

Trg Bana Jelačića is Zagreb's fulcrum: It seems that everything begins and ends in this plaza dominated by a statue of Ban Josip Jelačić seated on a proud horse with its tail in the air. Ban Jelačić was a 19th-century governor of Croatia who was much beloved by the people for his bravery (p. 350). His statue is a focal point of the square and the space "under the tail" of the monument is a popular rendezvous spot for the Zagrebačka. The square is a wonderful place to start exploring the city because many tram routes crisscross there, and it is within easy walking distance of any of the sites in Kaptol or Gradec, the Dolac market, and Tkalčićeva Street.

Donji Grad (Lower Town) is south of Gradec, and it might seem like a solid block of buildings broken up by a few green spaces. Donji Grad begins at Trg Jelačić and includes Ilica Street, where designer shops are increasing in number every day. It ends at the main train station to the south. Draškovićeva is Donji Grad's eastern border, and Republika Austria the western border. In the middle of this section of the city, a U-shaped series of adjacent parks runs roughly from Trg Bana Jelačića south to the main train station, from there to the western end of the Botanical Gardens, then north to the end of Trg Marsala Tita. Known as the "Green Horseshoe" or Lenuci's Horseshoe, the public green spaces are edged with galleries, museums, and schools.

GETTING AROUND

BY TRAM OR BUS   Zagreb's electric tram system is quick, efficient, and reliable, and it runs 24/7 although the frequency is reduced in the wee hours. New, air-conditioned, Croatian-made cars were added in 2007 on most routes, and they make riding public transportation comfortable. Tram routes cover central Zagreb and connect to buses that run to outlying areas and suburbs. Most lines go to the main train station, Trg Ban Jelačića, or both.

Tickets for both can be purchased at Tisak news kiosks for 7kn ($1.30) or on board for 9kn ($1.65). Tickets are good for 90 minutes each way and must be validated with a time stamp at the orange machines on board. There are no conductors checking tickets, but there are random control checks. If you are caught without a ticket or with an nonvalidated ticket, the fine is 150kn ($28) on the spot, more if you don't have the money immediately.

There are maps of all tram and bus routes at stops and on most city maps, but if you aren't familiar with the city or the language, it can be difficult to figure out whether a given vehicle goes to your destination because only the final destination and a stop or two are listed on the tram or bus itself. *Tip:* Keep a map of the tram routes and one of Zagreb with you whenever using the system so you can locate the routes' end streets and determine if the tram is going in your direction. Almost none of the tram operators speaks English.

BY TAXI Taxis are expensive in Zagreb, even for short distances. Taxis charge a 25kn ($5) flat fee plus 7kn ($1.30) for every ⅗ of a mile. A 20% surcharge is added to that on Sunday and at night, which makes taxis a very expensive way to travel. However, if you must use a cab, you can call one at Ⓒ **01/668-25-05.** It's a good idea to try to negotiate a price for your trip before you hop in.

ON FOOT Walking is by far the best (and healthiest) way to see Zagreb. Crime in the city is low and on foot you can safely get to almost any museum or restaurant in the central town within half an hour.

FAST FACTS: Zagreb

American Express American Express services are available through **Atlas Travel Agency** at Zrinjevac 17, 10000 Zagreb (Ⓒ **01/481-39-33;** fax 01/487-30-49). There is also an American Express office at Lastovska 23, Ⓒ **01/612-44-22.**

ATMs & Currency Exchange There are numerous ATMs (Bankomats) in central Zagreb where you can withdraw cash using American Express, Diners Club, Maestro/MasterCard, Cirrus, and Visa. Just be sure the ATM you use is embedded in a building and not free-standing, as the latter have been the sites of recent fraud in some European cities. You can change money or traveler's checks at most banks, exchange offices, and travel agencies, but you'll be charged a 1.5% or greater fee. Bank hours vary, but most are open from 8am to 7pm weekdays and 8am to noon Saturday. The fee is even higher if you change money at a hotel. **A-Tours** at the main bus station (Ⓒ **01/600-86-66**) is the exchange office with the longest hours. It is open from 6am to 10pm every day.

Business Hours Most banks open at 9am and stay open until 7pm or later Monday to Saturday. The airport branch of Zagrebačka Bank is open on Sunday, too. Offices generally are open from 8am to 5pm; some have Saturday hours, usually until 1pm. Store hours vary, with many closing from 2 to 5pm or some other interval during the day, but as a general rule, smaller stores open at 9am, and close 8pm Monday to Saturday and are closed all day Sunday. Stores in larger malls are open 7 days a week but some don't reopen after the weekend until 2pm on Monday so employees can restock shelves.

Dentists & Doctors **Dental Emergency** at Perkovčeva 3 (Ⓒ **01/482-84-88**) is open 24/7 and takes walk-ins. For medical emergencies, try the **Emergency Center** at Draškovićeva 19 near the Sheraton. It's open 24 hours. **KB Dubrava** at Avenija Gojka Šuška 6 (Ⓒ **01/290-24-44**) makes house calls to most parts of town.

Embassies & Consulates The **U.S. Embassy** is at Thomasa Jeffersona ulica 2 (℃ **01/661-22-00**; www.usembassy.hr). See p. 38 for other embassies' contact information.

The **Canadian Embassy** is at Prilaz Gjure Deželića 4 (℃ **01/488-12-00**).

The **United Kingdom Embassy** is at I. Lučića 4 (℃ **01/600-91-00**; www.british embassy.gov.uk/croatia).

The **Irish Consulate** is at Turninina 3 (℃ **01/667-44-55**).

The **Australian Embassy** is at Centar Kaptol, Nova Ves 11/III (℃ **01/489-12-00**).

The **New Zealand Consulate** is at Trg S. Radića 3 (℃ **01/615-13-82**).

Emergencies For police dial ℃ **92**; for an ambulance, ℃ **94**; and to report a fire, ℃ **93**. For road assistance, dial ℃ **987**; for the **Croatian Auto Club**, dial ℃ **01/464-08-00**.

Internet Access Croatia has embraced computer technology in a big way, and Internet access is easy to find. Try **Ch@rlie's** in the shadow of the Hotel Dubrovnik at Ljudevita Gaja 4a (℃ **01/488-02-33**). The staff is helpful and you can catch up on e-mail for 10kn ($1.75) per hour while you sip an espresso. Hours are 8am to 10pm daily. **Sublink Cybercafe** is close to Trg Jelačića at Nikole Tesle 12 (℃ **01/481-13-29**). You can e-mail, print, copy, or scan for 14kn per hour ($2.60).

Mail You can mail letters at any yellow Posta box, but if you need to buy stamps or send a package, the Central Post Office is at Jurišićeva 13 near the Jadran Hotel (℃ **01/481-10-90**). Hours are 7am to 9pm Monday to Friday, 8am to 4pm Saturday. The post office will tell you that it takes roughly 2 weeks for regular mail to reach the U.S. from Croatia. Our experience is that mail to the U.S. takes 4 weeks or more—if it arrives at all.

Newspapers & Magazines Very few news kiosks sell English-language newspapers, and those that do sell out quickly. *The International Herald Tribune* is the easiest to find and costs 20kn ($3.75). Many hotels print faxed copies of U.S. and other English-language newspapers for their guests for a fee.

Algoritam at Gajeva 1 (℃ **01/481-86-72**), on the ground floor of the Hotel Dubrovnik has an extensive selection of English-language magazines and books. Hours are 8am to 9pm Monday to Friday; 8am to 3pm Saturday. Closed Sunday.

Pharmacies Need an aspirin? In Zagreb (and all of Croatia) you'll have to go to a pharmacy *(ljekarna)* to buy some. No drugs of any kind are sold anywhere except at a pharmacy. There are several 24-hour ljekarna in Zagreb. Two are at Trg Jelačića (℃ **01/481-61-54**) and at Ilica 301 (℃ **01/375-03-21**).

Safety Zagreb enjoys relatively low crime rates, though there have been some reports that car thefts are on the rise. It's perfectly safe to ride public transportation at night and to walk through high-traffic areas. The police presence on Zagreb streets is subtle and you'll rarely see a uniformed officer, but they're there. Exercise the same precautions you'd take in any big city.

Telephone To call Zagreb from the United States, dial the **international prefix 011**, then Croatia's country code, **385**; and then Zagreb's city code, **1**. Then dial the actual phone number.

To call the U.S. from Zagreb, dial the **international prefix 00,** then the U.S. country code, **1;** then the area code and number. Other country codes are as follows: Canada, **1;** the United Kingdom, **44;** Ireland, **353;** Australia, **61;** New Zealand, **64.**

To call from one city code to another within Croatia: Dial the Croatian city code, including the zero, followed by the phone number.

To make a local call, simply dial the phone number. No codes necessary. Local calls cost about 5kn ($1) per minute.

To use a prepaid phone card, call the service, key in the code on the back of the card, and call the number. It's a good idea to have a prepaid phone card with you for emergencies because most pay phones don't take money and you'll need a card to use them. You can buy prepaid cards in denominations of 50, 100, 200, and 500 units at most newspaper kiosks, at post offices, and at some tobacconists. Calls are based on unit-per-minute rates, and the farther away you call, the more each unit costs and the faster you use up your units. You can also buy prepaid cards at **Nexcom,** Zavrtnica 17 (✆ **01/606-03-33**); or at **Voicecom,** Ilica 109 (✆ **01/376-01-23**; www.voicecom.hr). Free 0800 access.

To use a mobile phone, you can buy a SIM card for 400kn to 600kn ($74–$111) from **VIP** (✆ **091**) or **T-Mobile** (✆ **098**). You can also buy pay-as-you-go SIM cards from news kiosks in smaller denominations. If you have a GSM-equipped phone, it will register and readjust to T-Mobile in Zagreb provided you have activated its international capabilities with your service provider in the U.S. To call the U.S., hold down the zero key until a plus sign appears in the display. Then dial 1 plus the area code and number. Be aware that you will pay for roaming charges besides the call, which are extremely expensive because the call has to bounce from Croatia to the U.S., and back to Croatia again.

Toilets There are no free-standing public toilets in Zagreb. On the other hand, most toilets in restaurants, hotels, and stores are well-kept and free, and you usually don't have to be a customer to use them.

2 Where to Stay

There are very few moderately priced or bargain hotels in Zagreb. In fact, unless you go with private accommodations, most options are at the extreme ends of the price—and quality—list. However, special rates at the better hotels are sometimes available on weekends, over the Internet, or for multiday stays, but you have to ask. For the most part, no matter where you stay, you will find clean, adequate rooms with private bathrooms, but except for top-end hotels, Zagreb accommodations are usually bland. Generally, accommodations prices in the city are not subject to seasonal changes or cash discounts, and most hotels include breakfast.

EXPENSIVE

Arcotel Allegra ★ *Overrated*   The Branimir Center encompasses not only the Allegra, but a multiplex cinema, offices, a fitness studio, and conference rooms. Everything hotel guests need is convenient, which is de rigueur for a hotel in Allegra's price range. But at the Allegra, the little nickel-and-dime things detract, as does the "so-what" attitude of the staff. For example, the hotel's **Radicchio Restaurant** advertises free parking for patrons, but hotel guests have to pay. The Allegra advertises wireless connections, but they work only at Joe's Bar in the sleekly modern but smoky lobby. To use the wireless, however, you have to go to the tobacconist next door to buy a code card with wireless minutes. Oddly, all hotel signs and instructions are in English and German only, no Croatian. Guest rooms look like Ikea ads with minimalist light-oak furniture, kitschy spreads, and curtains printed with the faces of famous celebrities. Bathrooms are designed for economy and fitted with one-soap-fits-all dispensers in the tub and at the sink; towels feel a bit like sandpaper. If you have kids, note that each room features a prominently displayed ad card (with explicit illustrations) that offers a selection of adult films.

Branimirova 29. 10000 Zagreb. ℂ **01/469-60-00.** Fax 01/469-60-96. www.arcotel.at/allegra.htm. 151 units. From 150€ ($180) double; from 320€ ($380) suite. Rates do not include breakfast. AE, DC, MC, V. Parking garage 4kn ($4.50) per day. **Amenities:** Restaurant; bar; sauna; room service; free lobby Internet (1 terminal). *In room:* A/C, TV/DVD player, minibar, hair dryer, safe, valet service.

The Regent Esplanade

Nixon slept here. So did Pierce Brosnan, Elizabeth Taylor, and a host of other notables. The elegant Esplanade has attracted well-heeled guests since its opening in 1925, and now a painstaking renovation has seamlessly added New World creature comforts to the historic hotel's old-world opulence. Add to that service that is second to none, and the result is one of the most beautiful and best-run hotels in Croatia. Guests are checked in over a glass of bubbly in the black-and-white marble lobby before being whisked to their richly appointed rooms where fresh berries, chocolates, and complimentary wireless connections await them. Amenities are first-class and augmented with little luxuries such as fresh flowers, twice-a-day housekeeping, and cushy slippers ideal for padding around on the bathroom's heated marble floor. Liberal use of wood and brass in both private and public areas, a chic Croatian fusion restaurant called **Zinfandel's**, a selection of spa services, and a staff ready to fulfill every need have brought back the landmark hotel's glory days as an indulgent interlude for well-heeled travelers on the Orient Express. This is how it feels to sit in the lap of luxury. *Tip:* The Esplanade has a menu of scented baths, ranging from a tub full of herbs and oils to a chocolate bath for kids. Staff members draw the bath upon request.

Mihanovićeva 1, 10000 Zagreb. ℂ **800/545-4000** U.S. toll-free. In Croatia: 01/456-66-66. Fax 01/45-60-50. www.regenthotels.com. 209 units. From 149€ ($180) double; from 300€ ($360) suite. AE, DC, MC, V. No pets. **Amenities:** 2 restaurants; terrace dining w/live music; bar; casino; sauna; salon; club floor; concierge; room service; valet service; nonsmoking rooms; 2 rooms for those w/limited mobility; pets welcome (20€ ($24) per day). *In room:* A/C, TV w/pay movies, wireless connection/dataport, minibar, hair dryer, safe, trouser press.

Sheraton Zagreb

The glass-and-metal front of this hotel not far from the train station makes it easy to spot among Zagreb's vintage architecture. With 306 air-conditioned rooms and suites furnished in tasteful shades of apricot, the Sheraton Zagreb reflects Croatia's shift from socialist drab to capitalist chic. Guest rooms and public spaces are bright and airy, and all bathrooms are generously endowed with bathtubs and a selection of toiletries. Most hotel services are available 24/7 and the Fontana Restaurant staff is remarkably adept and knowledgeable. There isn't a thing hotel management hasn't thought of, and everything in the Sheraton Zagreb is superbly executed.

Kneza Borne 2, 10000 Zagreb. ℂ **01/455-35-35.** Fax 01/455-30-35. www.sheraton.com/zagreb. 306 units. From 145€ ($175) double; from 250€ ($300) suite. Rates do not include breakfast. AE, DC, MC, V. Guarded parking lot.

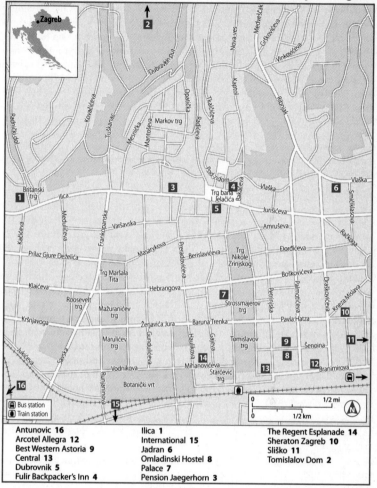

Amenities: 2 restaurants; pastry cafe; piano bar; pool; sauna; concierge; salon; room service; casino; valet service; nonsmoking rooms; rooms for those w/limited mobility. *In room:* A/C, TV, wireless/dataport, minibar, coffeemaker, hair dryer, iron/ironing board, safe, trouser press.

Hotel Antunovic ★★ Zagreb's newest hotel made a splashy entrance to the city's expanding lodging scene when it opened in September 2006, and it has been getting better with age. From sumptuous guest rooms, to a Zen-inspired spa to a glass-domed cocktail lounge that offers patrons a spectacular city panorama, the Antunovic has raised the bar for creature comforts in Zagreb's hotels. Guest rooms and public spaces are all glass and steel softened by lots of warm-toned wood. The comfort level is jazzed up with flatscreen TVs, free wireless access in every corner of the place, and strategically placed artwork. Bathrooms are generously endowed with gleaming fixtures, spacious tub-showers, a wide array of toiletries, and showerside phones. For a special treat, book one of the hotel's 9 suites: The Presidential suite has a lavish entertainment area, a powder room, and caterer's staging area, but even the junior suites are well-appointed. All suites are situated in the hotel's glass tower, which makes for dramatic floor plans and views. Antunovic seems to have thought of everything—in-house shopping mall, bank, casino, and on-premises gas station. The only drawback is its location, which is about 6km (3.6 miles) from Zagreb's center and 15km (9 miles) from Pleso Airport. To see the city's Old Town, you'll have to catch a cab or bus, which stops 300m (100 yards) from the front door and requires at least one transfer.

Zagrebačka Avenija 100A, Zagreb. © 01/204-1-121. Fax 01/20-41-119. www.hotelantunovic.com. 149 units including 9 suites. Doubles from 815kn ($190/150€); suites from 1,395kn ($235/195€). Rates include buffet breakfast, Internet, use of spa facilities. AE, DC, MC, V. **Amenities:** Restaurant; cafeteria; ice cream/pastry cafe; pizzeria; rooftop bar; pool; sauna; salon; room service; casino; concierge; valet service; nonsmoking rooms; rooms for those w/limited mobility; guarded parking lot. *In room:* AC, TV/SAT, minibar, coffeemaker, hair dryer, wireless/dataport, safe.

Hotel Dubrovnik ⭐⭐ "Rms w vu" should be the motto of this modern-looking glass-and-metal tower off Trg Jeličića where many of the hotel's comfortable rooms look directly down on the Croatian hero's statue in the main square. Opened in 1929 as the Hotel Milinov, the hotel changed its name to Dubrovnik, added more than 150 rooms in a new glass-and-aluminum wing in 1982, and completed a total renovation in 2003 to make rooms in the old and new sections equally plush and modern. The hotel is well-equipped to handle the needs of business travelers and tourists alike, convenient to just about everything in Zagreb, and staffed with an exceptionally helpful group of people. The business suite (210€/$250) is an eye-popper and includes a rooftop terrace. The indoor tables of the hotel's **Piccolo Mondo Restaurant** ⭐ outdoor tables of the hotel's ground-floor **Dubrovnik Kavana** comprise the undisputed "see and be seen" center of the city, especially on Saturday mornings.

Gajeva 1. P.P. 246. 10000 Zagreb. © 01/487-35-55. Fax 01/486-35-06. www.hotel-dubrovnik.hr. 280 units. From 160€ ($225) double; from 225€ ($315) suite. Rates include breakfast. Special 9-hr. "daily rest" rate 50% the regular room rate. AE, DC, MC, V. Limited free parking. **Amenities:** Restaurant; cafe; bar; business center; salon; room service; valet; nonsmoking rooms; rooms for those w/limited mobility. *In room:* A/C, TV, wireless/dataport, minibar, hair dryer, safe.

Palace ⭐⭐ Across the street from the Strossmayer Gallery and a section of Zagreb's Green Horseshoe, the Palace is just 5 minutes from Trg Jeličića. The Secessionist-style hotel was built as a private palace in 1891 and converted to a hotel in 1907, which makes it the oldest hotel in the city. So if you're looking for a comfortable, convenient place to stay that has character and a bit of history, then the Palace is the place for you. The restaurant has the ambience of a Viennese tearoom and guest rooms are in tune with the hotel's 19th-century charm. All but 30 of the 123 units have been updated for modern guests. *Tip:* Be sure to ask for one of the deluxe (updated) rooms, even though they cost 200kn (27€/$37) more than a standard room. Also, Wi-Fi Internet access is free in guest rooms, but dial-up can be quite costly.

Trg JJ Strossmayera 10, 10000 Zagreb. © 01/481-46-11, reservations 01/492-05-30. Fax 01/481-13-58. www.palace.hr. 123 units. From 980kn ($170) double; from 1,200kn ($210) junior suite; from 1,850kn ($320) suite. 20% discount on weekends. Rates include breakfast. AE, DC, MC, V. Limited free parking. **Amenities:** Restaurant; bar; room service; babysitting, nonsmoking rooms. *In room:* A/C, TV, Internet, minibar, hair dryer, safe.

Westin Zagreb ⭐ *Overrated* The former Opera Hotel has gone through several ownership changes in the last few years and is now positioned as a luxury property by its Starwood parent. Situated across the street from the Mimara Museum and its trove of objets d'art, it is too bad the Westin's rooms and amenities are so hotel-generic. Guests checking into a basic room (without breakfast) are offered the chain's Heavenly brand toiletries, bed, and other amenities. However, the room and bathroom are cramped and free of anything that would remind you that you are in Croatia. The Westin has everything you might expect at this level, but the overall impression is "impersonal chain." In addition, some amenities fall short: In-room Internet access is via non-broadband dial-up and very expensive, but there is free Wi-Fi in the business center. The property itself seems well-run and staff members seem well-trained in guest services. If you need a place for a night that has a full menu of on-site amenities, the Westin is fine, but if you want a place with a little charm and flavor of its home city, there are more convenient, less expensive choices in the city.

Kršnjavoga 1, 10000 Zagreb. ℭ 01/489-20-00. Fax 01/489-20-02. www.westin.com/Zagreb. 377 units. From 1,850kn ($343) double; from 2,700kn ($500) suite. Rates do not include breakfast. AE, DC, MC, V. Pets welcome with advance registration. **Amenities:** 2 restaurants; cafe; bar; business center; nonsmoking rooms; valet service. *In room:* A/C, TV, minibar, coffeemaker, hair dryer, iron/ironing board; safe.

MODERATE

Central ℛ   The Central's location across the street from Zagreb's main train station is a double-edged sword. On one hand, it's convenient to transportation; and on the other, rooms facing the street where trams rumble by day and night can be noisy, so you have to choose between a view and quiet. The quality of the Central's rooms' decor is Wal-Mart, but they are outfitted with a decent number of amenities following a 2002 renovation. Most rooms have showers rather than tubs. The lower-level dining room is bright and cheery. Room prices are moderate rather than bargain-priced (for Zagreb), but you're paying for location.

Branimirova 3, PP 97, 10000 Zagreb. ℭ 01/484-11-22. Fax 01/484-13-04. www.hotel-central.hr. 76 units. From 750kn ($140) double; from 1,360kn ($250) suite. AE, DC, MC, V. Rates stay the same all year and include breakfast. **Amenities:** Restaurant (breakfast only); adjacent casino. *In room:* A/C, TV, dataport and minibar in some rooms, hair dryer, Internet connection.

Best Western Astoria ℛℛ   This formerly frayed but now fabulous hotel is one of the most underrated in Zagreb. Besides being midway between the train station and Trg Ban Josip Jeličića, guest rooms are loaded with modern amenities like heated bathroom floors and French toiletries. Public spaces have a spiffy, polished look, and service is friendly and efficient.

Petrinjska Ulica 71, 10000 Zagreb. ℭ 01/484-12-22. www.bestwestern.com. 102 units. From 147€) ($205) double; from 298€ ($417) suite. AE, DC, MC, V. Rates include breakfast. **Amenities:** Restaurant; Internet; nonsmoking rooms; rooms for those w/limited mobility. *In room:* A/C, TV, minibar.

Pansion Jaegerhorn ℛ   Jaegerhorn gets points for its convenient location off Ilica, but demerits for being visitor-unfriendly. Getting luggage to your room can be difficult: You have to drag your bags through a mall courtyard mall and up a lot of stairs just to get to the lobby. Jaegerhorn was renovated in 1997, but rates are a little steep for what amounts to a small air-conditioned space furnished in army-surplus basics and a bed, shower, and TV. But if your objective is to roll out of bed and into the action, this is the place for you. Jaegerhorn is a quarter of a mile from the main square and opens onto Zagreb's main shopping street.

Ilica 14, 10000 Zagreb. ℭ 01/483-38-77. Fax 01/483-35-73. www.hotel-pansion-jaegerhorn.hr. 11 units. From 800kn ($148) double; from 950kn ($175) suite. Rates include breakfast. AE, DC, MC, V. Limited free parking. **Amenities:** Restaurant; terrace; bar. *In room:* A/C, TV.

Ilica   The Ilica, which is set back from the far end of Zagreb's main shopping street, has a great location going for it and is priced lower than almost all other hotels in the central city. Guest rooms are simple and adequate, but the suites are over-the-top kitsch that incorporates a lot of gilt and plastic. The staff is polite but reluctant to go beyond polite niceties without the boss present: The desk clerk refused to reveal the number of rooms in the hotel because his superior was out of the building. The no. 6 tram stops right in front of the hotel entrance, and Britanski Trg and its Sunday antique market are steps away, which makes the Ilica a convenient base for exploring the city.

Ilica 102, 10000 Zagreb. ✆ 01/377-76-22. Fax 01/377-77-22. www.hotel-ilica.hr. 24 units, including 1 junior suite, 1 suite, and 1 apt. From 599kn ($110) double; from 849kn ($157) suite and apt. Rates include breakfast. AE, DC, MC, V. Parking 50kn ($9) per day. **Amenities:** Restaurant; nonsmoking rooms; rooms for those w/limited mobility. *In room:* A/C, TV.

Jadran ✮   The Jadran is a pleasant, affordable choice just 5 minutes from the city center. Decor in guest rooms and public areas has been turned up a notch, and both are reasonably modern, though the rooms are not exactly spacious. The Jadran's main advantages are its location and easy access to public transportation.

Vlaška 50, 10000 Zagreb. ✆ 01/455-37-77. Fax 01/461-21-51. www.hup-zagreb.hr. 48 units. From 726kn ($125) double. AE, DC, MC, V. Rates stay the same all year and include breakfast. Limited free parking. **Amenities:** Restaurant. *In room:* A/C, TV, hair dryer.

Sliško ✮ *(Value)*   Located in back of the main bus station, the Sliško Hotel is a solid no-frills hotel a little off the beaten path. Opened in the mid-1990s, the Sliško has just enough amenities to make it comfortable and a pricing scale to prevent wallet welts, too. Rooms are furnished in utilitarian modern and some are a bit small, but all are clean and affordable. The restaurant is thoughtfully glassed off from the smoky bar on the first floor. Besides its proximity to the bus station, the hotel is an easy 10-minute walk from the main train station. Rooms are priced according to the number of beds used.

Supilova 13, 10000 Zagreb. ✆ 01/619-42-23. Fax 01/619-42-10. www.slisko.hr. 18 units. From 517kn ($96) double; from 748kn ($140) suite (4 beds). AE, DC, MC, V. 10% discount for cash. Rates include breakfast. **Amenities:** Restaurant; bar. *In room:* A/C, TV.

Tomislavov Dom ✮✮   You can't get any better view of Zagreb than from this property set on a rise among trees near the top of Zagreb's Sljeme peak on Mount Medvednica. In the summer it's an idyllic place to return to after a walk in the forest; in the winter, you can't get much closer to the slopes than the Tomislavov. After a 2006 renovation, most guest rooms have a view and simple but modern furniture and bathrooms with showers only. Tomislavov is just a couple of tram rides or a 20-minute drive from the center of town, but compared to most city commutes to the 'burbs, that's nothing.

Sljeme bb, 10000 Zagreb. ✆ 01/456-04-00. Fax 01/456-04-01. 41 units. From 860kn ($160) deluxe double. Rates include breakfast, VAT, and lift tickets during ski season. AE, DC, MC, V. **Amenities:** Restaurant; bar; pool; sauna; solarium; rooms for those w/limited mobility. *In room:* SAT/TV, minibar, Internet connection, hair dryer.

INEXPENSIVE

Fulir Backpackers' Inn ✮ *(Value)*   A couple of large, brightly painted second-floor rooms make up the entirety of the Fulir, but this hostel just off Trg Jelačića is loaded with personality. Its founders are college friends who opened Fulir in 2006 to mimic the kinds of places they like to stay in when they travel. It's clean, safe (someone is always on duty), affordable, and centrally located. The owners explained that Fulir once was owned by one of their grandmothers and that it is in a historic building. There is a kitchen for guests' use and lockers where they can keep their valuables when they are out and about. There is no age limit for guests and Fulir's doors are open from 8am-10pm. If you need to leave early or get back late, you can notify the person on duty to let you out or in.

Radiceva 3A. ☏ **01/483-08-82,** 098/193-05-52. www.fulir-hostel.com and www.myspace.com/fulirhostel. 2 rooms with 16 beds (1 with 12 and 1 with 4). 145kn ($27) per person. **Amenities:** Kitchen; TV room; lockers; bike storage.

Omladinski Hostel   The lobby looks like a homeless shelter intake area, and the scent of insecticide is in the air as you approach reception. However, Omladinski is one of the few bargain accommodations in Zagreb and, as such, its off-putting details can be overlooked. Accommodations range from six-bed, dorm-style rooms to doubles with private bathrooms. The only amenities are vending machines in the lobby, but the Omladinski is 5 minutes from both the city center and the train station, and the price is right.

Petrinjska 77, 10000 Zagreb. ☏ **01/484-12-61.** Fax 01/484-12-69. www.hfhs.hr. 215 beds, most in multibed dorm-style rooms with shared bathrooms. 120kn ($22) per person per night. Rates do not include breakfast. AE, DC, MC, V. Check-in is 2pm; checkout is 9pm.

PRIVATE ACCOMMODATIONS

Evistas ☏☏   This accommodations matchmaker is low profile but high on service. Evistas specializes in finding private apartments and sobes (rooms) in private homes for frugal travelers staying in Zagreb, but it also locates and books city youth hostels, rooms on the coast, and suites in posh hotels if that's your fancy. A couple from Albuquerque waiting in the office for a taxi couldn't hold back their effusive, unsolicited endorsement. "They let us store our luggage here and even found us a place in Dubrovnik. They were an enormous help."

Šenoina 28, 10000 Zagreb. ☏ **01/483-95-54.** evistas@zg.htnet.hr. Mon–Fri 9am–1:30pm and 3–8pm; Sat 9:30am–5pm. Closed Sun.

3 Where to Dine

Some say that eating is a Croatian sport and Zagreb is full of places to train, although the range of cuisine choices is narrow because most restaurants offer nearly identical bills of fare. Expect to find menus heavy with grilled meat and fish, Italian pastas and risottos, and a few traditional Croatian dishes. Other ethnic cuisines (except for Croatian and Italian) are thinly represented, but some of the better restaurants are adventuresome enough to experiment with unusual sauces and preparations. Pizzerias are the most common type of casual dining spot around the city center, and Croatian pizza is remarkably good and inexpensive. For snacks, many bakeries sell pizza by the slice as well as meat- and-cheese filled *burek* (filled phyllo "Hot Pockets"), baguette sandwiches, and other filled doughy treats that work as quick meals. For sweets, the city's ubiquitous cafes and *slastičarnicas* (ice-cream/pastry shops) provide indulgent treats in a dizzying array of types and flavors.

INEXPENSIVE

Restoran Ivica I Marica ☏☏ CROATIAN   This kitschy dining spot on busy Tkalčićeva has introduced a novel concept—Grandma's Croatian preparations made healthier with whole grains and seasonal local products. The restaurant has lots of wood and homey touches (servers wear traditional national dress) and what you can see of the kitchen reveals colorful tole-painted flowers on all the cabinets. The menu at this woodsy place named after Hansel and Gretel (in Croatian, of course), is no less fascinating. Begin with whole-grain flatbread accompanied by local fresh cheese or olives and tomatoes. Then move to *integral sujnudle* (boiled dumplings with hunter sauce or mushroom sauce). Fish is on the menu, as are moussaka with eggs and soya ham plus four varieties of *štrukli*.

Tkalčićeva 70, 10000 Zagreb. ⓒ **01/482-89-99**. Fax 098/317-092. ivicaimarica@adriazdravahrana.hr. Entrees 39kn–70kn ($7–$12). AE, DC, MC, V. Daily noon–11pm.

Slasterčarnica Ivica I Marica 🟊🟊 PASTRY & ICE CREAM   The ersatz ginger-bread house named after an errant brother and sister fairy-tale team serves some of the best desserts on Tkalčićeva, a hot address for Zagreb's cafe society. Stop here for a pastry or gelato after dining at Restoran Ivica I Marica next door; or grab a sandwich on whole-grain bread for a light supper or very late lunch.

Tkalčićeva 70, 10000 Zagreb. ⓒ **01/481-73-21**. Fax 098/317-092. ivicaimarica@adriazdravahrana.hr. Sandwiches 13kn–29kn ($2.25–$5). No credit cards. Daily 4–11pm.

Purger 🟊 (Value CROATIAN   It's easy to overlook Purger, a nondescript storefront near the Omladinski Hostel near Zagreb's center, but you shouldn't, especially if you're on a budget. The interior is "cute" but nothing fancy and the menu is loaded with tantalizing homemade dishes at a fair price.

Petrinjska 33. ⓒ **01/481-0713**. Entrees 30kn–920kn ($6–$17). AE, DC, MC, V. Mon–Sat 7am–11pm. Closed Sun.

Capuciner 🟊 (Value PIZZA/ITALIAN   Endless variations of spaghetti, pizza, and other Italian fare are on the menu at this noisy hangout across the street from the Zagreb Cathedral. Pizza is of the ultrathin-crusted European style, and toppings are mostly fresh ingredients, unless you opt for unusual varieties such as the (untried) Nutella version. Capuciner is a good place to stop if you want a filling meal instead of the coffee/ice cream/beer offerings common in the outdoor cafes in Old Town. The restaurant also has daily blackboard specials for 15kn to 30kn ($2.60–$5.20), including a horseburger.

Kaptol 6. ⓒ **01/481-48-40**. www.capuciner.hr. Entrees including pizza 15kn–60kn ($3–$11). AE, DC, MC, V. Mon–Sat 10am–1am; Sun noon–1am.

Pinguin Sandwich Bar 🟊🟊🟊 (Finds SANDWICHES   Get in line with the locals who mob this tiny made-to-order sandwich shack at all hours. The huge list of sandwiches is entirely in Croatian, but order-takers understand some English, and most sandwiches are illustrated with color photos. Try the Rustico, a tasty combo of mozzarella, pancetta, oregano, olives, tomatoes, herbed mayo, and any of half a dozen condiments between two fresh-made pitalike rectangles of olive bread. American hot dogs and hamburgers are also on the menu. Don't eat these Croatian subs while walking down the street or you'll wear them. Instead, polish them off with a beer at the high tables and stools provided.

Nikola Tesle 7. No phone. Sandwiches 13kn–20kn ($2.25–$3.45). No credit cards. Mon–Sat 9am–5am; Sun 9am–3am

Kod Žaca 🟊🟊 CROATIAN COUNTRY   This is a terrific place for meat dishes prepared in various tantalizing sauces. You won't find fish on the menu here—just meat and lots of it. Choose from veal, beef, ostrich, turkey, pork, horse, chicken, and ostrich.

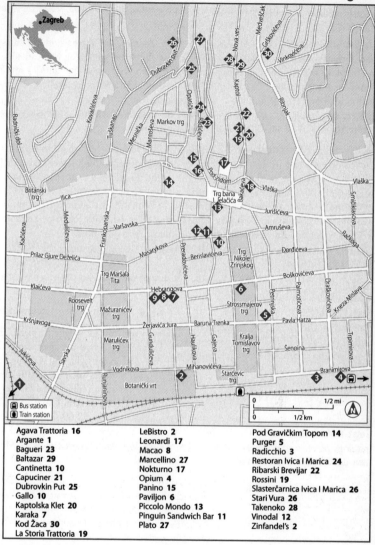

Agava Trattoria **16**	LeBistro **2**	Pod Gravičkim Topom **14**
Argante **1**	Leonardi **17**	Purger **5**
Bagueri **23**	Macao **8**	Radicchio **3**
Baltazar **29**	Marcellino **27**	Restoran Ivica I Marica **24**
Cantinetta **10**	Nokturno **17**	Ribarski Brevijar **22**
Capuciner **21**	Opium **4**	Rossini **19**
Dubrovkin Put **25**	Panino **15**	Slasterčarnica Ivica I Marica **26**
Gallo **10**	Paviljon **6**	Stari Vura **26**
Kaptolska Klet **20**	Piccolo Mondo **13**	Takenoko **28**
Karaka **7**	Pinguin Sandwich Bar **11**	Vinodal **12**
Kod Žaca **30**	Plato **27**	Zinfandel's **2**
La Storia Trattoria **19**		

For each, a selection of sauces is available. For example, beef is served in mushroom, truffle, pepper, or cheese sauce. The portions are generous and all meat dishes are accompanied by a choice of either homemade gnocchi or croquettes. If meat is not your fancy, then not to worry since the *fuži* (pasta) with truffle sauce is one of the best in the city. For starters, there is a selection of local meats and cheeses. The wine selection is quite adequate as well. With its old-country decor and only 10 small tables inside, Kod Žaca provides a cozy and very casual atmosphere in which to dine and feel relaxed.

Grškovićeva 4, just steps up from where Ribnjak changes to Medveščak. © **01/468-4178**. Reservations recommended. Entrees 60kn–120kn ($10–$20). No credit cards. Daily noon–2am.

La Storia Trattoria ⭐ ITALIAN   The name rhymes, but there's nothing cutesy about the food at this cellar restaurant (across the street from Zagreb's cathedral) where pasta and risotto rule. Eating here is like dining in your Italian aunt's rumpus room because the food is a ringer for homemade and almost as economical. Try the ravioli with porcini mushrooms or the green tagliatelle with shrimp.

Kaptol 4, 10000 Zagreb. © **01/481-32-79** or 098/926-83-53. www.delikatesa.hr. Reservations recommended. Entrees 28kn–46kn ($5–$8). AE, DC, MC, V. Mon–Sat 8am–11pm. Closed Sun.

Nokturno and **Leonardi** ⭐⭐ PIZZA/PASTA   At first glance it's hard to tell where Nokturno ends and its next-door neighbor Leonardi begins. Both are crammed in a space on the side of an alleyway (which was in the middle of a construction zone in summer of 2007); both have similar menus; and both have the same opening hours. Nokturno is always jammed with patrons, while Leonardi isn't quite so busy, but the pace there is slower, too. Nokturno's pizza attracts crowds with its crispy crust and fresh ingredients. Whichever restaurant you choose, you can't miss.

Nokturno: Skalinska 4. © **01/481-33-94**. Small pizzas 18kn–30kn ($3–$6); other dishes 20kn–45kn ($4–$8). AE, DC, MC, V. Daily 9am–1am.

Leonardi: Skalinska 6. © **01/487-30-05**. Small pizzas 15kn–35kn ($3–$6); other dishes 28kn–65kn ($5–$13). AE, DC, MC, V. Daily 9am–1am.

MODERATE

Vinodal ⭐ CROATIAN   Traditional local fare rules at this popular spot in the city center, with grilled meat taking center stage. Try the *janjetina* (lamb), which is grilled to perfection, traditional *sarma* (chopped meat and rice in marinated cabbage), or *vinski gulas* (wine goulash), which is boldly seasoned and melts in your mouth. Diners at Vinodol can enjoy their meals under the stars in the huge outdoor courtyard.

Nikola Tesle 10. © **01/481-13-41**. Fax 01/481-13-43. Main courses 50kn–95kn ($9–$17). AE, DC, MC, V. Daily 10am–11pm.

Cantinetta ⭐⭐ CONTINENTAL/ITALIAN   A warm Tuscan atmosphere envelops patrons who venture into this white-tablecloth spot, and the meal that follows doesn't disappoint. Grilled anything with an Italian accent is the specialty of the house, so try the calamari or the ostrich with veggies and apples. Pastas are cooked to al dente perfection, but there are very few on the menu. Service is notably professional and friendly, and the chef will prepare custom dishes if asked.

Nikola Tesle 14. © **01/481-13-15**. Main courses 45kn–120kn ($8–$21). AE, DC, MC, V. Daily 9am–midnight; kitchen closes at 11pm.

LeBistro ⭐⭐ FRENCH/CROATIAN   This glassed-in meet-and-eat place in the **Regent Esplanade** ⭐⭐⭐ specializes in classic French preparations such as baked escargot, but there is also a touch of nouveau in simple dishes such as bass with wilted Swiss chard and garlic confit. Le Bistro boasts that it serves the best *zagorski štrukli* (cheese baked in phyllo with cream sauce) in town and even offers a frozen version to take home, but we found the dish rather bland, even with sugar sprinkled on top. Order the crème brûlée with vanilla and ginger stem instead.

Mihanovićeva 1. © **01/456-66-66**. Main courses 40kn–100kn ($7–$18). AE, DC, MC, V. Daily 10am–11pm.

Piccolo Mondo 𝄘 CROATIAN/ITALIAN   It's kind of a super-storefront restaurant with a street-level view of the action in front of the Hotel Dubrovnik 𝄘𝄘—and there's a lot to see from this attractive dining room. The terrace cafe is always crowded and opens in time for breakfast, but it is the dinner hour that draws the big appetites. Most of the choices are predictable, though competently prepared, but there are a few creative surprises served in generous portions. For example, the risotto Bella Casa is a flavorful mix of scampi, tomatoes, wine, cream, cognac, Parmesan and, of course, *al dente arborio*, while *spaghetti aglio e olio ciro* combines anchovies, hot peppers, olive oil, herbs, and Parmesan. There is also a respectable wine list.

L. Gaja 1. ⓒ 01/481-86-13. Entrees 55kn–110kn ($10–$20). AE, DC, MC, V. Daily 6:30am–11pm.

Boban 𝄘 ITALIAN   This boisterous cellar restaurant named after a Croatian soccer star is two flights below Boban's kavana-bar and way below it in noise level. Food is straightforward Italian with a few Croatian-inspired dishes such as venison salami and vegetable-stuffed pancakes with béchamel. The food here isn't gourmet and you won't be wowed by creativity either, but the prices won't break your vacation budget. Service can be slow when all the tables are full—and that's usually all night, every night, as hungry patrons wander in from nearby Trg Josip Jelačića.

Gajeva 9. ⓒ 01/481-15-49. www.boban.hr. Entrees 30kn–80kn ($6–$14). AE, DC, MC, V. Daily 10am–midnight.

Macao CHINESE   When you think you can't bear another helping of *cevapči* (chopped spiced sausage), try this small cellar space accessed from the courtyard entrance of a standard 19th-century structure south of Trg Bana Jeličića. Offerings are standard Cantonese with a few Szechuan and Hunan dishes thrown in for variety.

Andrije Hebranga 30. ⓒ 01/485-26-76. Entrees 30kn–80kn ($6–$14). AE, DC, MC, V. Mon—Sat 11am–11pm; Sun 11am–5pm.

Agava Trattoria 𝄘𝄘 (Value) ITALIAN   Set above Tkalčićeva on a terraced hill, diners at this trendy spot have a bird's-eye view of the action whether they sit on the handsome outdoor deck or in the dining room behind tall glass windows. The food here tends to be Italian, but there are some Croatian specialties and salad and pasta choices, too. Try the Coquilles St. Jacques and cashe salad and end with the divine figs and plums in red wine sauce with vanilla ice cream. *Note:* There may be "reserved" signs on all the tables. Don't let that dissuade you. Our waiter quipped that the signs were there "for people who eat here."

Tkalčićeva 39. ⓒ 01/482-98-26. Entrees 46kn–125kn ($9–$23). AE, DC, MC, V. Daily noon–11pm.

Panino 𝄘 MEDITERRANEAN   Panino changed its address and concept in 2007, but it didn't lose any of its appeal. The menu now emphasizes huge, complicated salads, risottos, and pastas, with a few dishes thrown in for meat lovers. Diners get a tasty *amuse bouche* and three kinds of olive oil for bread-dipping in addition to the trendy fare. Try a salad of mixed greens topped with chicken or shrimp and a glass of white wine barrique (oaked) and finish with a plate of fresh fruits and chocolates. *Tip:* There is a 5% discount if you pay for your meal in cash.

Tkalčićeva 43. ⓒ 01/209-65-52. www.panino.hr. AE, DC, MC, V. Tues-Sun 11am–1am.

Kaptolska Klet 𝄘𝄘 CROATIAN   A huge array of steaks complements an amazing list of Croatian home recipes such as goulash and roasted lamb or pork at this attractive spot across from Zagreb's cathedral. There's a menu for dieters (including ostrich filet) and one for vegetarians, too. The folk-culture ambience on the terrace and inside seems more touristy than functional, but there's nothing ersatz about the food.

Kaptol 5. ⓒ **01/481-48-38.** Fax 01/481-43-30. www.mediacaffe.net/kaptolskaklet. Entrees 35kn–80kn ($6–$14). AE, DC, MC, V. Daily 11am–11pm.

Baltazar ⋆⋆ CROATIAN   Grilled meat is the focus of this pleasant dining spot with a nice terrace, north of the cathedral on Kaptol. It's in what may be the city's trendiest neighborhood, but the food here holds with tradition. This is the place to try Croatian schnitzel and any other national dish you've been curious about. Service is superb.

Nova Ves 4. ⓒ **01/466-69-99.** www.morsko-prase.hr. Entrees 55kn–125kn ($10–$22). AE, DC, MC, V. Mon–Sat noon–midnight. Closed Sun.

Opium ⋆ SOUTHEAST ASIAN   Dark as a den, this Asian restaurant/bar is on the lower level of Branimir Center, with tables spilling onto the mall. The menu lists mostly Thai and wok preparations, but there are also teriyaki and curry choices, too. You can't go wrong with Pad Thai, but Phat Wun Sen is more adventurous with glass noodles, seafood, cabbage, eggs, peppers, and onion.

Branimirova 29. ⓒ **01/461-56-79.** Fax 01/461-56-80. Entrees 55kn–95kn ($10–$17). AE, DC, MC, V. Mon–Fri 8am–1am; Sat 8am–1:30am; Sun 11am–1am.

EXPENSIVE

Gallo ⋆⋆⋆ ITALIAN   Food is art at this beautiful, unpretentious restaurant behind the facade of an unremarkable building a few blocks from the city center. Homemade pasta in countless shapes and a rainbow of colors dries behind glass near the restaurant entrance. The kitchen, too, is visible behind glass, so diners can watch the chef work his magic. Even the extensive wine cellar is artfully displayed in a corner of the house. The menu is mostly fish with several interesting recipes such as tuna with polenta and red-wine sauce, or beef soup with ravioli. There is a stylish white stone terrace, a cozy casual dining room, and more formal space where crystal and silver set the tone. The waitstaff is congenial and knowledgeable about both the food preparations and complementary wines.

Andrije Hebranga 34. ⓒ **01/481-40-14.** Fax 01/481-40-13. www.gallo.castellum.hr. Reservations recommended at dinner. Entrees 60kn–120kn ($11–$21). AE, DC, MC, V. Daily 11:30am–midnight.

Pod Gričkim Topom ⋆⋆⋆ CROATIAN   Location, location, location is one of the draws at this traditional-style restaurant on the Strossmayerovo Šetalište steps midway between Trg Bana Jelačića and Gornji Grad. The atmosphere is intimate and the food superb. Bread and tiny balls of Croatian pâté start the meal, which could be anything from grilled meat to pasta. Try the grilled monkfish, which comes with *blitva,* the Croatian version of chopped spinach; or shrimp risotto, generously laced with juicy, plump pieces of seafood. Desserts are decadent, but crepes with strawberries and ice cream is just right after the American-size main course. The wine list is loaded with fairly priced Croatian choices.

Zakmardijeve stube 5. ⓒ **01/483-36-07.** AE, DC, MC, V. Entrees 65kn–125kn ($12–$22). Daily in July and Aug 7am–11pm. From 11am–11pm Mon–Sat and 11am–5pm Sun Sept–June.

Plato ⋆ INTERNATIONAL   Ultrachic Plato opened in the spring of 2007 and it is a visually enchanting space that literally shines with wood, white decor and a bar that could double as a stage. However, dining is only part of Plato's offerings: It is also a nightclub, which is open to the wee hours (dawn on weekends). Plato takes its food seriously—the menu changes every two months and emphasizes fresh, seasonal ingredients. Try the salmon with bacon and potatoes or the chicken medallions with sesame seed and rice. Plato caters to those on the wildly popular (in Croatia) UN diet, which demands that dieters stick to one food group per day. That means it has menu offerings for "protein day," another for "fruit day," and even one for "dessert day."

Nova Ves 17, Kaptol Centar. © 01/481-34-21. Entrees 70kn–110kn ($13–$20). AE, DC, MC, V. Sun–Thurs 9am–1am; Fri–Sat 9am–4am.

Bagueri ✿✿✿ Value ITALIAN A small, understated stucco building painted in shades of cocoa and white and trimmed with gauzy white curtains and geranium window boxes is the setting for one of the best restaurants on Tkalčićeva Street. The dining room in this white-tablecloth spot is an intimate space with artsy vineyard photos on the wall and lots of crystal and silver. The menu is no less inviting, with entrees such as steak in balsamic sauce, and risotto with greens and prosciutto. Add to that a balanced wine list and a competent staff that smiles a lot, and you have the makings of a great meal.

Tkalčićeva 65. © 091/481-38-48. Reservations recommended. Entrees 45kn–120kn ($8–$21). AE, DC, MC, V. Daily 5pm–midnight.

Takenoko ✿✿✿ JAPANESE/SUSHI As beautiful as an origami swan, this restaurant at street level in the Kaptol Center is a no-brainer choice in a city that has access to some of the freshest seafood on the planet. The menu concentrates on sushi and wok preparations and painstakingly explains the ingredients of each in several languages. There are tables as well as a sushi bar, all done in cool dark wood, wicker, and white cloth upholstery. This is a very sophisticated-looking spot with food to match.

Nova Ves 17. © 01/486-05-30. Fax 01/486-05-31. Entrees 75kn–100kn ($15–$20). AE, DC, MC, V. Mon–Sat noon–1am; Sun noon–6pm.

Radicchio ✿ MEDITERRANEAN Radicchio is set in a large, modern-looking room that seems a little incongruous for a restaurant in an Austrian hotel (Arcotel Allegra ✿) in the heart of Croatia, but the food here is consistent with Allegra's Mediterranean decor. The menu is just as progressive as the interior, which continues the "famous faces" theme of the Allegra hotel's guest rooms. Try the grilled salmon in port-wine sauce, which is a surprisingly apt pairing. The risotto with pumpkin confit and Marchand de Vin sauce is creamy and complex, and the grilled prawns Provencale conjure visions of olive trees and the sea. However, the view outside the glass wall on the indoor mall is that of shoppers and a perfumeria.

Branimirova 29. © 01/469-60-40. Entrees 50kn–130kn ($10–$30). Daily 6:30am–3pm and 5:30–10:30pm.

Karaka ✿✿ SEAFOOD Anything that lives in the sea is a specialty of this easy-to-miss restaurant named after a medieval sailing ship. Watch for a small, white-sailed sculpture above the doorway of a large dark building on Hebranga. Inside, the nautical theme continues with a decor of sailcloth ceilings and lots of dark wood and fishnets. Preparations are well-seasoned classical Dalmatian, and the menu's fish varieties are based on the day's best available catch. The wine list is respectable.

Andrije Hebranga 12. 01/481-71-50. Entrees 50kn–150kn ($10–$30). AE, DC, MC, V. Daily noon–11pm. Usually closed first 3 weeks of Aug.

Ribarski Brevijar ✿ SEAFOOD Set back from the street in a courtyard across from the Komedija (Comedy Theater), this restaurant specializes in fish and seafood and offers a large number of choices. Fresh seafood rules, which makes sense because the restaurant is owned by fish merchants. Most preparations are Dalmatian, though there are a few gourmet surprises like scampi soup with saffron. Artisan touches such as house-made bread and pasta add a distinctive flair. The wine list is expensive, though the bottle prices seem a little high. The pleasant terrace is protected from street noise, as is the white-tablecloth dining room. The restaurant is convenient for theatergoers and for those who don't have their own wheels: There is a bus stop right outside the entrance.

Kaptol 27. ⓒ **01/482-99-99**. Fax 01/482-99-98. Entrees 65kn–100kn ($12–$20) or up to 450kn per kg ($40 per lb.) for lobster. Mon–Sat noon–1am. Closed Sun.

VERY EXPENSIVE

Zinfandel's ★★★ MEDITERRANEAN   By day, diners have a view of the ★★★ Esplanade's lovely Oleander Terrace through the window-walls of this sophisticated dining room, which is the source of the best breakfast buffet on the planet. A little later, Zinfandel serves a casual but wonderfully diverse lunch menu. However, it is at night that the menu gets really creative. Soft jazz, impeccable service, and lots of fresh flowers provide a wonderful setting for Zinfandel's creative menu. Dishes such as duck and venison casseroles served with a salad of walnuts, oyster mushrooms, and cranberries; or lamb filet wrapped in zucchini, are perfect companions for the breadth and depth of Zinfandel's wine list. For dessert try the praline terrine or the liquid chocolate cake.

Mihanovićeva 1. ⓒ **01/456-66-66**. Main courses 65kn–165kn ($15–$30). Barbecue 120kn ($21) per person. AE, DC, MC, V. Dinner 6–11pm daily.

Argante (Hotel Antunovic) ★★ REGIONAL CROATIAN   Argante's managers have been tweaking the restaurant's culinary profile since opening in 2006, but the emphasis has always been focused on innovation and local ingredients. That philosophy has developed into a menu defined by each dish's regional pedigree rather than its main ingredient, which makes for some interesting dining. Start with Konavale beef carpaccio or mountain trout caviar and move on to Mediterranean veal steak with mozzarella, veggies, and white wine sauce. Or, venture into the Zagorje region with grilled turkey fillet served with peas and savoy cabbage. Close with cheese from Pag or Livno accompanied by a dessert wine from Argante's competent wine list. The cellar is deep in Croatian bottles, punctuated with Slovenian, Italian, French, and a couple of token California and Australian labels.

Zagrebačka Avenija 100A. ⓒ **01/204-11-21**. AE, DC, MC, V. Entrees 80kn–170kn ($15–$31). Daily 6:30am–midnight.

Paviljon ★★ CROATIAN   Paviljon's setting on the Green Horseshoe flanked by some of Zagreb's best museums gives the restaurant a cultured aura and its formality and old school decor give it the patina of class. The terrace looks out over park area toward the main train station and Tomislav Trg and inside, the dining room is all elegance with a cherry wood floor and a fireplace. However, it is the restaurant's well-executed menu featuring Croatian interpretations of classic dishes that steals the show. Start with gooseliver in Cumberland sauce or smoked tuna carpaccio and follow with roast duck with red cabbage and figs for an unusual taste combination. Wines are on the high end, but when you're serving top Croatian names like Grgić, it's understandable.

Trg Kralja Tomislava 22. ⓒ **01/45-54-066**. Fax 01/484-10-73. www.restaurant-paviljon.com. Entrees 65kn–125kn ($12–$23). AE, DC, MC, V. Mon–Sat noon–midnight. Bar 10am–midnight. Closed Sun.

Dubrovkin Put ★★ SEAFOOD   Romantic ambience and pristinely fresh seafood are on the menu at this award-winning restaurant in the neighborhood behind

Gradec. Service is first-rate and attentive without being obtrusive, and the fish and shellfish preparations are flawless. A full meal is a little pricey but worth it, especially under the stars on the relaxing terrace.

Dubrovkin Put 2. ℂ **01/483-49-70.** Fax 01/482-81-49. Entrees 85kn–150kn ($15–$30). AE, DC, MC, V. Daily 10am–midnight.

Peperocino ♔ CROATIAN   Just outside the shrine at Kamenica Vrata, this small restaurant and wine bar caters to those interested in well-prepared food and fine vintages. The menu is limited to a few entrees, usually including one grilled meat dish and one grilled fish dish, but the wine list is extensive and there are lots of choices by the glass. Peperocino's owner lived in the U.S. for years, so Peperocino is English-language friendly.

Kamenica 5. ℂ **01/485-13-43.** Entrees 40kn–90kn ($7.50–$17). MC, V. Mon–Thurs 10am–midnight; Fri–Sat 10am; Sun 10am–6pm.

Marcellino ♔♔ INTERNATIONAL   Near the top of Jurjevska Street, which is home to embassies and diplomats, Marcellino turns out delicious Mediterranean cuisine. For lunch, the restaurant is a frequent choice of business folk who don't seem to care that service is a bit sloppy and that portions are beautifully presented but a bit small for the price. Try venison with chestnuts, blueberries and wine sauce or shrimp with orange-olive sauce. Bus no. 105 stops in right front of the restaurant. Be sure to ask for a table near the windows: In warm weather they open out into a forest that turns into a beautifully lighted woodland at night.

Jurjevska 65a. ℂ **01/467-71-11.** marcellinozg@yahoo.hr. Entrees 70kn–190kn ($13–$35). AE, DC, MC, V. Mon–Sat noon–midnight. Closed Sun.

Rossini ♔♔ ITALIAN   "Upscale" defines Rossini, which caters to a crowd that knows Italian food is more than red gravy and noodles. Risottos are especially good in this relatively formal dining room; some incorporate asparagus and pancetta, while others blend various kinds of seafood. The wine list is well-chosen, but prices seem a little high for Croatia: There aren't any bottles listed under 120kn ($25).

Vlaška 55. ℂ **01/455-10-60.** Fax 01/455-28-28. Rossini@open.hr. Entrees 60kn–130kn ($11–$23). AE, DC, MC, V. Mon–Fri 11am–midnight; Sat 11am–11pm. Closed Sun.

Stara Vura CROATIAN   This cute restaurant is set in the courtyard that also houses the Zagreb city museum (p. 273). The menu is typical Croatian with lots of roast meats. Stari Vura also has some pastas and game entrees, including boar and deer. The historic courtyard setting is a nice spot for lunch.

Opatička 20. ℂ **01/485-13-68.** www.stara-vura.hr. Entrees 65kn–180kn ($10–$26). AE, DC, MC, V. Mon–Sat noon–midnight. Closed Sun.

4 What to See & Do

The best—and in some cases the only—way to see Zagreb is on foot, with the occasional tram or bus ride. Almost everything in the city center is pedestrian-accessible and so are some of the sites farther afield. Gornji Grad (Upper Town) is flush with historical buildings and churches, restaurants, boutiques, monuments, and entertainment venues. Donji Grad (Lower Town) is strong on museums, parks, historic architecture, and shopping. Other attractions are a short ride from the center of town. Anton Dominik Fernkorn's statue of Ban Josip Jelačića is the centerpiece of **Trg Bana Jelačića (Jelačić Square)** ♔♔♔. It was created and installed on the square in 1866

Marija Jurić Zagorka

The bronze statue of a woman in 19th-century dress carrying an umbrella is a showstopper for pedestrians on busy Tkalčićeva Street. The sculpture was created by artist Stejepan Gračan and commemorates Zagorka, who was Croatia's first female journalist. Zagorka was born to a wealthy family in 1873 and was well-educated, but she still had a difficult time breaking into journalism. On the recommendation of Bishop J. J. Strossmayer, she was given a job on a local Zagreb paper, where she started on the editorial board and introduced the first Croatian publication exclusively for women. Zagorka also penned several well-received novels that are still read today. She died in 1957.

and it stood there until World War II, when the square was renamed Republic Square. The statue was removed and stored in pieces when the powers-that-be determined that the square and monument had become a rallying point for Croatian nationalists, who were seen as a threat to the ruling Communist Party. It wasn't until 1990 that the statue was returned to its original home, and the square to its original name. Today Jelačić Trg is ringed by shops and cafes; other, smaller plazas radiate from it.

KAPTOL

Dolac Market ★★★   Dolac is north of Jelačić Trg and every day starting around 5am, vendors pile their stalls with piles of colorful fruits, vegetables, baskets, and other Croatian products. Dolac opened in 1930 and ever since it has been Zagreb's most popular open-air market and some say one of the best in Europe. Fruits, vegetables, plants, and textiles are on the upper level, while meat, olives, and herbs are in the covered area below. Fish and cheese are in their own separate spaces to avoid olfactory overstimulation.

Dolac bb. Mon–Fri 6am–2pm; Sat 6am–3pm; Sun 6am–noon.

Tkalčićeva Ulica ★★★   This cobblestone street to the left of Dolac winds up a fairly steep incline into the belly of the upper city. It is lined with boutiques, bars, restaurants, galleries in rehabbed 19th-century mansions, and renovation projects. Tkalčićeva is also home to Zagreb's cafe society, and every evening the tables along this thoroughfare are full.

To left of the Dolac Market.

Cathedral of the Assumption of the Virgin Mary ★★★   The 105m (345-ft.) twin spires of this magnificent Gothic structure seem perpetually covered with scaffolding, and its entrance is hidden behind a tarp. Work began on the cathedral's exterior in 1990 and is ongoing. But despite the dust and mess, the grace and beauty of this Herman Bollé masterpiece shines as a symbol of Zagreb. Inside, the cathedral glows following a refurbishment that was completed in 1988. Note the 18th-century marble pulpit by Slovenian sculptor Mihael Cussal and the sarcophagus of the controversial Blessed Alojzije Stepinac behind the main altar. A beautiful Meštrović relief showing Stepanic kneeling before Christ nearby marks the Croatian priest's grave.

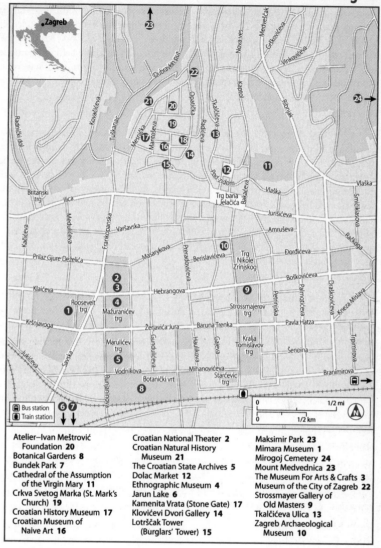

Legend
▣ Bus station
▣ Train station

Atelier–Ivan Meštrović
Foundation **20**
Botanical Gardens **8**
Bundek Park **7**
Cathedral of the Assumption
of the Virgin Mary **11**
Crkva Svetog Marka (St. Mark's
Church) **19**
Croatian History Museum **17**
Croatian Museum of
Naive Art **16**

Croatian National Theater **2**
Croatian Natural History
Museum **21**
The Croatian State Archives **5**
Dolac Market **12**
Ethnographic Museum **4**
Jarun Lake **6**
Kamenita Vrata (Stone Gate) **17**
Klovićevi Dvori Gallery **14**
Lotrščak Tower
(Burglars' Tower) **15**

Maksimir Park **23**
Mimara Museum **1**
Mirogoj Cemetery **24**
Mount Medvednica **23**
The Museum For Arts & Crafts **3**
Museum of the City of Zagreb **22**
Strossmayer Gallery of
Old Masters **9**
Tkalčićeva Ulica **13**
Zagreb Archaeological
Museum **10**

Kaptol 31, 10000 Zagreb. ⓒ **01/481-47-27**. Free admission. Mon–Sat 10am–5pm; Sun 1–5pm. Masses are at 7, 8, and 9am weekdays; and at 7, 8, 9, 10, and 11:30am Sun.

GRADEC

Gradec is the second arm of central Zagreb's civic triumvirate. Less commercial than Kaptol, Gradec is packed with some of the city's most interesting museums and monuments.

Kamenita Vrata ⭐⭐   It's a steep walk up a long flight of stairs to Radićeva from Tkalčićeva and a few minutes more up another steep cobblestone path to Kamenita

Vrata, which was one of four entrances to the walled city of Gradec. Kamenita Vrata is the only gate that survived a 1731 fire, which destroyed almost everything wooden in its path. Just inside the gate a small, dark area houses the **Chapel of God's Mother** 🌟🌟 where a **painting of the Virgin and Child** is ensconced in an alcove behind a baroque grid. According to legend, the painting incredibly survived the fire and it is revered as a miraculous sign. There are a few pews in the dark chapel, where people come to light candles and pray all through the day.

Kamenita bb.

Crkva Svetog Marka (St. Mark's Church)   The **tile mosaic** 🌟🌟🌟 depicting the

Croatian, Dalmatian, and Slavonian coats of arms is St. Mark's best-known feature. Inside, the church is rather ordinary except for some 20th-century frescoes depicting scenes from the Bible and a beautiful Meštrović crucifix. St. Mark's was covered with scaffolding and draped with construction plastic in the summer of 2007, but the newly cleaned bell tower is evidence that the renovation will be well worth any inconvenience. Hours are variable and posted on the door, but not always observed by the folks who have the key to the church. Call to be sure it's open. The church is always open for mass at 6pm Monday through Saturday, and for 7:30am, 11am, and 6pm mass on Sunday and holidays.

Trg Svetog Marka 5. ☎ 01/485-16-11.

The Croatian Museum of Naive Art 🌟🌟   Think Grandma Moses interprets

Croatia when you approach the baroque mansion that houses paintings and drawings by such Croatian masters as Ivan Generalić and Ivan Lacković. This enchanting museum focuses on the Hlebine School. Its 1,500 works are colorful, historical, political, and sometimes politically incorrect, but utterly charming. The imagery depicted by these artists can be a tad bizarre, but it often reflects local customs that still exist in the hinterlands—or in the mind of the artist.

Ćirilometodska 3. ☎ 01/485-19-11. www.hmnu.org. Admission 10kn ($2) adults, 5kn ($1) children and retirees. Tues–Fri 10am–6pm; Sat–Sun 10am–1pm.

Klovićevi Dvori Gallery 🌟🌟   Just down the street from The Croatian Museum of

Naive Art, this sister museum in a converted castle houses a huge exhibit of Hlebine (naive art) paintings on loan from galleries or private collections. At any given time, simultaneous exhibits on display here can include neon art, soft sculpture, and other "New European" art forms. There's also a cafe and a surprisingly good gift shop.

Jezuitski Trg 4. ☎ 01/485-19-26. www.galerijaklovic.hr. Tues–Sun 11am–7pm.

Atelier-Ivan Meštrović 🌟🌟🌟   The artist's studio and 17th-century house are the

setting for a vast array of his sculptures and models. Examples of Croatia's most famous sculptor's renderings of famous people, religious icons, and just plain folks are exhibited inside and outside in the garden. This is a fascinating museum where you

---

Fun Fact Let There Be Light

At night, Zagreb's Gradec neighborhood glows under the light of gas lamps. At promptly 7pm in the summertime, all 267 of the street fixtures are individually lighted by an old-fashioned lamp lighter.

Ivan Meštrović (1883-1962)

Ivan Meštrović is Croatia's most famous sculptor, and he is regarded as the greatest sculptor of religious art since the Renaissance. Meštrović was born in Vrpolje (Slavonia) August 15, 1883 to a peasant family but spent most of his childhood in Otavice, a tiny, impoverished village in the rocky, mountainous interior of Dalmatia west of Šibenik. When he was 16, Meštrović was apprenticed to a stonecutter in Split where he developed his skill by reproducing the city's Greek and Roman works of art. After just 9 months in Split, a wealthy Viennese patron sponsored him for a place at the Academy of Fine Arts in the Austrian capital. It was there that Meštrović's genius began to shine. In Vienna, Meštrović met the great French sculptor Auguste Rodin, who encouraged him to broaden his artistic vision through travel and who became a strong influence on the young artist. Meštrović took Rodin's advice and spent time working in Paris, Belgrade, and eventually Rome, where he won a first prize for sculpture at the World Exhibition of 1911. In the early 1920s, Meštrović settled in Zagreb, where he transformed a 17th-century house (Meštrović Atelier) into his home and studio. In 1942 he was imprisoned by the Ustashe for his political involvements and released thanks to intervention by Pope Pius XII. Meštrović then moved to Rome, and the next year he left for Switzerland. After World War II, he emigrated to New York where he became a professor of sculpture at Syracuse University. In 1955 he moved to a similar position at the University of Notre Dame in South Bend, Indiana, where he lived until his death in 1962. Throughout his career, Meštrović was a prolific artist. His works are on display in museums, public places (including Chicago's Grant Park), and at Notre Dame.

can imagine how the artist lived and worked during his years here (1924–42). Not only are finished works on display, but also sketches, models, and photographs, most notably a small study of the Grgur Ninski sculptures in Split and Nin in Dalmatia. Many other Meštrović sculptures are installed in public areas around Zagreb and other parts of Croatia, but currently there is no all-inclusive map that locates them. In his later life, Meštrović lived in the United States and worked as a professor of sculpture in South Bend, Indiana, at the University of Notre Dame, which also owns some of his works from that period. A wide array of Meštrović's books, catalogs, and CDs are available in the gallery's small bookstore.

Mletačka 8. (*) 01/485-11-23. www.mdc.hr/mestrovic. 20kn ($3.50) adults, 10kn ($1.75) children and seniors. Tues–Sat 10am–6pm; Sun 10am–2pm.

Museum of the City of Zagreb (*)   Displays in this museum situated in the renovated former convent of the Order of St. Clare illuminate life in Zagreb from medieval times to the present. Attractive presentations of weaponry, religious objects, furniture, ethnic costumes, and an incredible collection of photographs documenting the city through the years are augmented by scale models of Zagreb at various times in its history. Captions are multilingual. There is a nice restaurant (*) (p. 269) on the premises, too.

Heart of the Matter

The shiny red hearts on display in nearly every Zagreb souvenir shop are actually *licitar*, honey-dough similar to gingerbread that is shaped in wooden molds, hardened, and coated with edible red lacquer and decorated with flowers, swirls, and other trim. Young men traditionally gave the colorful hearts to their girlfriends as an expression of love. Today, the decorated cookies still are given as a sign of affection, but they also are given as special-occasion gifts or as remembrances. Personalized hearts sometimes are used as wedding favors, toys, and Christmas ornaments. Most recently, they have been used as hospitality tokens by some bureaus of Croatia's tourism board. The hearts have even been immortalized in a ballet, "Licitarsko Srce" ("Gingerbread Hearts"), by Croatian composer Krešimir Baranović, which has been performed all over Europe. Today, licitar is made in many shapes besides hearts and rarely eaten but rather saved or displayed as instantly recognizable symbols of Croatia.

Opatička 20. ✆ 01/485-13-64. www.mdc.hr/mgz. Admission 20kn ($4) adults; 10kn ($2) children, students, seniors, persons with disabilities, military; free for children 6 and under. Tues–Fri 10am–6pm; Sat–Sun 10am–1pm. Museum personnel will aid those with disabilities.

Croatian Natural History Museum This museum should be in a museum because the exhibits look like they haven't been touched since they were installed in the mid–19th century. Here, presentation is as much an artifact as the artifacts themselves. Nonetheless, it is fascinating to view the stuffed mammal collection as well as the endless cabinets filled with animal, vegetable, and mineral specimens. Don't miss the exhibit that showcases **Krapina Man** ⊛, the remains of a colony of Neanderthals found near Krapina in the Zagorje region north of Zagreb.

Demetrova 1. ✆ 01/485-17-00. www.hpm.hr. Admission 10kn ($2). Tues–Fri 10am–5pm; Sat–Sun 10am–1pm.

Kula Lotrščak (Burglars' Tower) ⊛⊛ A cannon is fired at this vestige of Gradec's fortifications every day at noon to commemorate a Croat victory against the Turks. You can climb the tower to get a fabulous view of the city or just to say you did.

Strossmayerovo Šetalište 9. ✆ 01/485-17-68. Admission 10kn ($2). Tues–Sun 11am–8pm for climbing. Closed Mon.

DONJI GRAD (LOWER TOWN)

Zagreb Archaeological Museum ⊛ A mixture of Greek, Macedonian, and Croatian artifacts fills glass cases throughout this monument to prehistoric times, but it is the mummies and funerary exhibits that draw the most oohs and ahs. Skeletal remains and the Bronze Age baubles they wore at interment are exhibited as they would have looked in situ. There is no museum map or audioguide available, but occasional English-language histories and titles are available in each exhibition room. The highlight of the collection is the "Zagreb mummy" and its bandages, which are actually a linen book inscribed with Etruscan script.

Trg Nikole Šubića Zrinskog 19. ✆ 01/487-31-01. www.amz.hr. Admission 20kn ($4) adults, 10kn ($2) children and retirees, 30kn ($6) family. Tues–Fri 10am–5pm; Sat–Sun 10am–1pm. 100kn ($20) English-speaking guide.

Strossmayer Gallery of Old Masters 🔭🔭   A huge sculpture of Bishop Josip Juraj Strossmayer dominates the park in front of the academy he founded as the Yugoslav Academy of Arts and Sciences in 1860 in the middle section of Zrinevac. The school occupies the building's ground floor and the gallery is spread out over the rest. Strossmayer began collecting art when he became bishop of Đakovo and made a mission of accumulating art. He secured funds to build the beige 19th-century building off Strossmayer Trg, where the gallery opened in 1884 to house his (mostly) religious art. Today it is also home to the fabled **Baška Tablet,** which is the oldest known example of Glagolitic script in existence and perhaps Croatia's most important artifact. The tablet is displayed under glass in the ground-floor lobby without any conspicuous sign or fanfare. Entry to the gallery is on the third floor of the building, though no signs direct you there. Fewer than 300 items from the Strossmayer's 4,000-item inventory are displayed at any given time. They include 14th- to 19th-century works from Italian and other European masters.

Trg Nikole Šubića Zrinskog 11. ✆ 01/489-51-17. www.mdc.hr/strossmayer. Admission 10kn ($2) adults, 5kn ($1) children. Wed–Sun 10am–1pm; Tues 10am–1pm and 5–7pm.

Botanical Gardens 🔭   Mihanovičeva Street runs west of Tomislavov Trg past Starčevic Trg and the 1925 landmark 🔭🔭🔭 **Esplanade Hotel,** one of the best examples of Secessionist architecture in Zagreb. Mihanovic also skirts Zagreb's Botanical Gardens, which opened in 1894 and were supposed to link the two legs of the Green Horseshoe. However, progress and several bland blocks of more modern architecture got in the way. The gardens feature an arboretum, ponds, and an ornamental bridge.

Trb Marka Marulića. ✆ 01/484-40-20. 9am–6pm. Closed Mon.

The Croatian State Archives 🔭   This Art Nouveau building is UNESCO-listed and one of Zagreb's finest—it's also home to Croatia's most important documents. The Archive's written holdings won't interest most English-speaking visitors because they are in Croatian, but architecture buffs from any country will be awed by the interior and exterior treasures concentrated in the stately building that opened in 1913. Both the lobby and atrium area one level up are adorned with brilliant mosaics, intricate ironwork, sparkling leaded glass, and lustrous marble. These spaces are also used for art exhibits, all secondary to their dazzling setting. Outside, the symmetrical park

Lenuci's Horseshoe

The U-shaped block of parks and gardens that runs from Trg Bana Josip Jelačića to the main train station and back is known as Lenuci's Green Horseshoe, a flowing, tree-lined series of grassy areas, fountains, flower beds, monuments, and pavilions dotted with museums and galleries. According to Lenuci's 19th-century plan, the green strips and stately cultural palaces are strategically placed to break up the visual monotony of blocks and blocks of gray apartments and office buildings that characterize this part of town. The horseshoe cuts a green pattern through Lower Town and is home to such landmarks as the neo-Renaissance Academy of Sciences and Art, the neo-baroque Croatian National Theater, and the Botanical Gardens.

landscape is home to an Ivan Meštrović masterpiece (unfortunately marred by graffiti taggers). Guided tours are required for admission.

Marulićev Trg 21, Zagreb. © 01/482-90-00. www.arhiv.hr. 20kn ($4) adults; 10kn ($2) children. Mon–Fri 8am–noon and 2–4pm (lobby viewing). Tours at noon, 1 and 2pm.

Croatian National Theater ★★   This neo-baroque building was designed by Ferdinand Helmer and Hermann Fellner of Vienna. The ostentatious temple to drama opened with lots of fanfare in 1890 when Emperor Franz Josef did the honors. Meštrović's celebrated 1905 ★★ **Well of Life** sculpture is in front of the entrance.

Trg maršala Tita 15. © 01/482-85-32. www.hnk.hr.

Ethnographic Museum ★★★ *(Finds)*   The Ethnographic Museum south of Trg Maršala Tita is perhaps one of Zagreb's most underrated museums. It is loaded with a dizzying array of traditional aprons and tunics from all parts of Croatia, as well as collections of agricultural artifacts such as olive- and grape-growing and winemaking implements. Most of the museum's items were acquired in the 19th and 20th centuries and cover the full spectrum of how people worked and lived in Croatia through the ages. There is even a gingerbread collection.

Mažuranićev Trg 14. © 01/482-62-20. www.etnografski-muzej.hr. Free admission Thurs. Other days: 20kn ($4) adults, 15kn ($3) children and students, free for seniors and Croatian military. Tues–Thurs 10am–6pm; Fri–Sun 10am–1pm.

Mimara Museum ★ *(Overrated)*   The incredible collection of art housed in this neo-Renaissance building west of the city center on Roosevelt Trg is the result of one man's donation: Croatian-born Ante Topić Mimara, an artist himself, was a lifelong collector who bequeathed his art inventory to his country. While there has been some controversy about the provenance of some of the works in the collection, the Mimara's vast portfolio is still impressive. Italian, Dutch, and Spanish artists dominate the painting collection, but Renoir and artists from other European schools are also represented. Glass, textiles, and Asian art dominate the ground-floor galleries; sculpture, archaeology, and applied art are in the galleries one flight up; and paintings fill the top floor. The entire collection numbers nearly 4,000 objets d'art, only half of which are on exhibit at any given time. The museum opened in 1987, but displays are surprisingly unsophisticated and the lighting design does not show the collections to advantage. Captions are in Croatian only.

Rooseveltov Trg 5. © 01/482-81-00. www.mimara.hr. Admission 20kn ($4) adults, 15kn ($3) children. Tues–Wed and Fri–Sat 10am–5pm; Thurs 10am–7pm; Sun 10am–2pm.

The Museum for Arts and Crafts ★★   The building housing the 160,000 exhibits that chronicle Croatian culture is all German Renaissance. Inside, the exhibits of furniture, textiles, photographs, sculptures, and other vestiges of traditional Croatian life are well done with legends, videos, and computer illustrations.

Trg Maršala Tita 10. © 01/482-69-22. www.muo.hr. Admission 15kn ($3). Tues–Fri 10am–6pm; Sat 10am–1pm.

Croatian History Museum   History buffs will love the 15 collections of 140,000 Croatian artifacts housed in this 18th-century mansion. The artifacts date from medieval times to the present. The sheer volume and minutiae represented here can be overwhelming to all but the most avid fans.

Matoševa 9. © 01/485-19-90. www.hismus.hr. Admission 10kn ($2) adults; 5kn ($1) children, students, retirees, military. Daily 10am-5pm.

FARTHER AFIELD

Maksimir Park ★★   This lush green oasis about 3.2km (2 miles) east of the center is Zagreb's biggest park and popular among families, dog walkers, and couples going for a stroll. Opened in the late 18th century, it has five lakes and a cafe, and it houses the **Zagreb City Zoo** ★. The park is easily accessible via tram (no. 11 or 12 from Trg Jelačić) and it's free (except for the zoo). Exit the tram at the Bukovacka stop, which is steps from the entrance.

Maksimirirski Perivoj bb. ✆ 01/230-21-98. Zoo: www.zoo.hr. Admission 20kn ($4) ages 7 and up, 10kn ($2) children 6 and under, and free for everyone on Mon. Daily summer 9am–8pm; winter 9am–4pm.

Bundek Park ★★   After decades of neglect, a renovated Bundek Park in Novi Zagreb reopened to the public in May 2007. The park's gravel-beach lakes, bike paths, gardens, and children's playground all were redone and the result is a serene urban greenspace that attracts families, joggers, and events such as flower and art shows. Bundek's transformation from overgrown eyesore to city showplace is just the first phase of "Zagreb on the Sava," the city's initiative to develop the banks of the Sava River for recreation and tourism. Bundek is less than a block from the city's new Museum of Contemporary Art on Avenija Dubrovnik and across from the Zagreb Fairgrounds. The new museum building was not completed in the summer of 2007 but it was scheduled to open at its new site later that year.

Free admission.

Jarun Lake ★★★   This man-made lake 4km (2½ miles) southwest of the center has something for everyone. There are cafes, bars, a white-tablecloth restaurant, a nude beach, sailing, jogging, bike paths, and much more. The beaches are pebble and the lakes are fed by the Sava and have pebble bottoms. In the summer, the city's bars and discos set up shop at Jarun and go well into the night, making it seem like Bourbon Street on the beach. You can get to the lake on tram no. 17 from Jelačić Trg and exit at Jarun. *Tip:* You can rent bikes at Jarun's entrance for 20kn ($4) per hour.

Entrance to Jarun is free, but there is a 15kn ($3) fee for 24 hours of parking.

Mount Medvednica ★★★   Skiing, hiking, biking . . . you can do it all on "Bear Mountain" north of the city. There are several cafes, as well as ski rental shops and warming huts. You can even explore the **medieval fortress** ★★ of **Medvedgrad**. By car, the top, Sljeme, is a 20-minute drive from Zagreb's center; and though the uphill turns are rather steep, you don't have to worry about oncoming traffic because the road up is one-way, as is the road down. Be sure you take the correct road down to Zagreb, however: There is another route that goes to the other side of the mountain and ends up in the Zagorje region. You can't go wrong by taking the cable car to the top and back.

Cable car: ✆ 01/458-03-94. www.zet.hr. 11kn ($2) up; 17kn ($3) down. Daily 8am–8pm. Leaves on the hour daily.

Mirogoj Cemetery ★★★   Think of Mirogoj as an open-air museum splashed with heavy doses of history and art. Many of Croatia's heroes and common folk are buried here, but this is no Arlington or Shady Lawn. Mirogoj is another Herman Bollé creation, and as such it is a fascinating mix of architecture that includes soaring domes; a neo-Renaissance arcade; and trees, flowers, and gravestones in all shapes, sizes, and colors imaginable, all enclosed by a protective wall. Even a short walk-through reveals that this is truly an egalitarian burial place: You'll see Christian crosses, Jewish six-pointed stars, socialist five-pointed stars, and slender five-sided Muslim headstones, indicating that people of all faiths and nationalities are interred here without segregation. Don't miss President Franjo Tuđman's tomb, a massive block of shiny black granite always adorned with a few tribute bouquets. To get to Mirogoj, take the no. 106 bus from Kaptol opposite the cathedral for 8kn ($1.40) or the no. 14 tram from Jelačić Trg toward Mihaljevac, and exit at the fourth stop.

Mirogoj bb, about 2.4km (1½ miles) northeast of the city center. Daily 8am–8pm.

ORGANIZED TOURS

There isn't any compelling reason to take a formal tour of Zagreb because almost everything worth seeing is within walking distance of the main square or a short tram or bus ride away. However, if you want to inject some whimsy into your sightseeing, try one of the city's 2-hour-long costumed walking tours. A guide dressed like a famous person from Zagreb history will show you around and perhaps throw in a few little-known facts about the city and its sites. You can buy tickets at the Tourist Information Center on Jelačić Trg.

Andrijevićeva 12. © 01/370-35-53; 01/370-30-88. www.event.hr. 95kn ($16) per person. Tours leave from the Tourist Information Center on the square daily at 10am and 4pm.

ESPECIALLY FOR KIDS

Exploring Zagreb with children in tow can be challenging on a number of fronts. Ushering little ones across the open tram tracks, up and down steep cobbled streets, and through churches and museums that appeal mainly to interested adults and large groups of students can put a strain on parents and kids alike. Most of Zagreb's hotels and sights don't have any special extras for kids, though most offer a rate reduction for the younger set. Unlike hotels in Croatia's resort towns, Zagreb hotels have no all-day programs to keep younger kids amused, and no special facilities like arcades or Internet rooms for older ones. Very few restaurants have children's menus or highchairs, though most will do what they can for customers with children.

Some of the best bets for keeping kids amused in Zagreb are **Maksimir Park** and the **Zagreb City Zoo** (p. 277). There are a couple of playgrounds with equipment in Maksimir, so kids can let off a little steam before heading back to the hotel. Bundek Park (p. 277) is a draw because of its river-fed lakes and a rather elaborate playground set up for kids. **Jarun Lake** (p. 277) south of the center is another option. Besides a beach, Jarun has paddle boats, playground equipment, and often some sports competitions like beach volleyball to keep kids entertained. Children might also enjoy **Zagreb's cinemas.** Most run American movies with English soundtracks and Croatian subtitles, so kids won't have any trouble understanding what's going on.

5 Shopping

Zagreb's economy is quickly recovering after years of being in the dumps following occupation by foreign governments and the 1991 war. The country has not yet been admitted to the European Union, so E.U. countries have not yet made many investments in retail in Zagreb or elsewhere in the country, though that is slowly changing. Except for the action at Dolac Market, shopping isn't very exciting in Zagreb, and serious bargain hunters will be disappointed in the prices and what's available, especially in clothing. The number of stores that sell good quality or even designer garb is increasing, but as a rule, clothing here is either imported and very expensive, or very cheap, depending on its country of origin. However, shopping malls anchored by huge stores that resemble Super K-Marts are popping up all over town and attracting big crowds. There are also a few places that sell apparel and other items worth checking out.

ACCESSORIES

Cerovečki   You're likely to need one of their handmade umbrellas if you stay in Zagreb more than a couple of days. Open 8:30am to 8pm Monday to Friday; 8:30am to 3pm Saturday. Closed Sunday. Ilica 50. ✆ 01/484-74-17.

BOOKS

Algoritam   The store has a large selection of English-language books and magazines as well as reading materials in other languages. Barnes & Noble it's not, but you can find what you need here. Hours are 8am to 9pm Monday to Friday; 8am to 3pm Saturday; closed Sunday. Gajeva 1. ✆ 01/481-86-72.

CLOTHING

Escada   This shop sells the designer's elegant wear at prices that match the high style. Open 8am to 8pm Monday to Friday; 8am to 3pm Saturday. Closed Sunday. Gundulićeva 15. ✆ 01/487-55-77.

Marks and Spencer   This English retailer in Kaptol Center specializes in traditional style and conservative casual wear. Also at King Cross shopping mall in Jankomir. Hours are 9am to 9pm daily; closed Sunday. Nova Ves 11 (Kaptol Center). ✆ 01/468-61-99.

COSMETICS

Muller   Muller just opened a new outlet in Zagreb's flashy City Center Mall (below) and there are rumors this central store with two floors of everything from high-end French perfume to German-made rubbing liniment (Diana brand) will be closing. Tax-free option for purchases over 300kn ($60). Hours are 8am to 8pm Monday to Friday; 8am to 3pm Saturday. Closed Sunday. Trg Jelačaća 8. ✆ 01/489-31-50.

CROATIAN SPECIALTIES

Natura Croatica   This shop sells a wide selection of Croatian delicacies and some crafts. Hours are 9am to 9pm Monday to Friday; 10am to 4pm Saturday. Closed Sunday. Petra Preradovića 8. ✆ 01/485-50-76.

Pršut Galerija   Here you'll find a selection of Dalmatian ham, prosciutto, *paški sir* (a distinctive cheese made on the island of Pag), and olive oil and wine from Istria and other parts of Croatia. Hours are 8am to 8pm Monday to Friday; 8am to 2pm Saturday. Closed Sunday. Vlaška 7. ✆ 01/481-61-29.

Zigante Tartufi   Truffles are the specialty of this ubiquitous food specialty retailer whose owner holds the Guinness record for finding the world's largest truffle. Zigante's elegant **gourmet restaurant** ✰✰ is in the tiny town of Livade in Istria (p. 243), but his products are widely distributed in supermarkets and free-standing stores all over Croatia. You can even shop for his truffles, oils, and wines in the duty-free catalog on board the plane on your way home. Hours are 8am to 8pm daily; 8am to 3pm Saturday. Closed Sunday. Jurišićeva 19 (Rotonda Center). ✆ 01/481-77-94. www.zigantetartufi.com.

JEWELRY

Lazer Rok Lumezi *Finds*   This atelier-cum-retail shop is unique in that Mr. Lumezi likes to collaborate with his customers on designs so he can match his creations to the personality of the person who will wear them. His work has been shown in museums and galleries throughout Croatia. Hours are 9am to 8pm Monday to Friday; 9am to 3pm Saturday. Closed Sunday. Tkalčićeva 53. ℂ **01/481-40-30**. ilumezi@inet.hr.

TOYS

Turbo Limač   Though there are several branches in Croatia, this one in Zagreb is fine for picking up something with which to amuse the kids. Think Toys "R" Us, only smaller. Hours are 8am to 8pm Monday to Friday; 8am to 3pm Saturday. Closed Sunday. Ljudevita Gaja 9a. ℂ **01/481-15-48**.

SHOPPING MALLS

Croatians love to shop, and large, Western-style malls are springing up all over Zagreb. **Kaptol Center** on Nova Ves in Gornji Grad houses upscale retailers; a multiplex cinema; and an excellent assortment of cafes, restaurants, and bars. **Importanne** runs two malls, one under the park across the street from the main train station, and another at Iblerov Trg just west of the city center. **Branimir Center** on Branimir just east of the train station also has a multiplex plus several decent restaurants, in addition to shops and the Arcotel Allegra Hotel ⚐. **King Cross** at Jankomir and City Center southwest of Zagreb are the closest things to an American mall. Each has nearly 100 stores that include brand-name retailers like Benetton, Sisley, and Esprit, plus electronics, sporting goods, and home stores. There are also lots of cafes and a couple of huge supermarkets there. *Tip:* King Cross Mall doesn't open until 2pm on Monday. It opens at 9am Tuesday to Saturday and stays open until 9pm Sunday.

6 Zagreb After Dark

Nightlife in Zagreb is varied but not obvious: You have to look for the action. Besides the usual complement of bars and cafes, there are casinos, jazz clubs, discos, cinemas, and comedy clubs to occupy even die-hard night owls. Lately, Jarun Lake has become hot year-round with "branches" of almost all of Zagreb's popular bars setting up shop there.

CASINOS

Casino City   This comfortable casino beneath the elegant Regent Esplanade hotel has roulette tables, card tables, slot machines, and a VIP area for serious gamblers. Free entrance for Esplanade guests. Open daily 8pm to 4am. Mihanovićeva 1. ℂ **01/450-10-00**.

Club Casino Vega   The stars come out (and dress up) to play at this high-powered casino in the Sheraton Hotel where the games include blackjack, roulette, slot machines, and poker. Open daily 8pm to 7am. Draškovićeva 43. ℂ **01/461-18-6**. Fax 01/461-19-25. casinovega@post.htnet.hr.

COCKTAIL BARS

Apartman ⚐   Apartman is a new hip club near Flower Square in Zagreb's center. It is frequented by a younger crowd both day and night. Open 9am to midnight Monday through Wednesday and Sunday. Open 9am to 1am Thursday through Saturday. Preradovićeva 7. ℂ **01/487-2168**.

Boban ⚐⚐   This bar/restaurant, owned by one of Croatia's top soccer players, is always packed to the max with a noise level to match. There is also outside seating where promenading in resplendent finery is a sport for both sexes. Hours are daily 7am to midnight. Ljudevita Gaja 9. ℂ **01/481-15-49**. www.boban.hr. AE, DC, MC, V.

Hemingway's ⚐⚐   This Hemingway opposite the Croatian National Theater is part of a chain of bars that has a presence all over Croatia. This location is one of the chain's busiest, perhaps because it is in the center of Zagreb's culture district or perhaps because of its long work hours. Open 7am to 3am daily. Trg Marsala Tiga.© 098/980-50-00. www.hemingway.hr.

Jackie Brown 👫 This cocktail bar at Kaptol Centar is aimed at a sophisticated crowd that enjoys the finer things in life—cool jazz, vintage Armagnac, and classic cars. Open daily 8am to 1am. Nova Ves 17 (Kaptol Center). © 01/486-0241.

Joe's Bar (Allegra Arcotel) The open-design concept of this slick lounge in the lobby of the **Allegra Arcotel** 👫 lets you watch traffic on Branimirova while you keep tabs on who's checking in. The hotel's lone Internet computer is here and the whole area is wireless, too, so you can use your laptop if you buy wireless minutes from a local provider at the desk or the tobacco shop next door. However, the ventilation system doesn't clear the smoke well despite the room's high ceilings. Open daily 7am to 2am. Branimirova 29. © 01/484-69-48. AE, DC, MC, V.

Khala 👫👫 This hip lounge tends toward Far Eastern harem style, with jeweled lights covered with gauzy fabric and sheer tiebacks hanging from every portal. The effect screams "extremely chic and wealthy," and the clientele does, too: Brown wicker chairs and couches fitted with white linen cushions are always filled with beautiful people sipping exotic drinks while murmuring into cellphones and keeping an eye on their Porsches parked at the curb. Open daily 10am to 2am. Nova Ves 11 (Kaptol Center). © 01/486-02-41.

Maraschino 👫 Named after the famous cherry juice from the coast that is also available in a potent fermented version, Maraschino carries the fruit theme to its drink menu. The crowd here is young and casual, and the music is loud, funky, and occasionally live. Open 8am to 1am Monday through Saturday; 9am to 1am Sunday. Margaretska 1. © 01/481-26-12.

NIGHTCLUBS
Aquarius This hoppin' club specializes in theme nights. Live music. In summer, Aquarius opens a waterside franchise at Zrče Beach on the island of Pag. Cafe open from 9am to 9pm daily. Nightclub from 10pm to 6am daily. Matije Ljubeka bb. © 01/364-02-31. www.aquarius.hr.

B.P. Club B.P. is Zagreb's premiere jazz club. It's managed by internationally acclaimed vibraphonist Boško Petrović and it attracts notables to both play and listen to the cool sounds emanating from this basement space. Pinguin sandwich shop (p. 262) is just outside the entrance to B.P. It's open 24 hours and a good place to grab a bite after the show. Open 10am to 2am Monday through Saturday and 5pm to 2am Sunday. Nikole Tesle 7. © 01/481-44-44. www.bpclub.hr. Cover charge depends on performer but averages 25kn–120kn ($5–$20).

GAY & LESBIAN
Global Club The most popular gay club/bar in Zagreb, Global has a split personality. By day it is an Internet cafe, but Wednesday, Thursday, and Friday nights it's a dance club for which you need a special club card. The club sponsors boys' nights and girls' nights, and has three bars and a dance floor. Open 11am to 4am Monday to Saturday and 4pm to 1am Sunday. Pavla Hatza 14. © 01/481-48-78. www.globalclubzg.hr.

Sauna David This gay-owned bar/sauna is near the Botanical Gardens and main train station. Open 4 to 10pm Monday to Thursday; 2pm to midnight Friday; 4pm to midnight Saturday and Sunday. Maruličev Trg 13. © 01/533-65-07.

10

Excursions From Zagreb

Most visitors to Croatia, European and non-European alike, know something about the country's stunning Adriatic coastal playground and its sophisticated capital, Zagreb, but they know little about what lies beyond. In general, there is much less tourism chatter about Croatia's inland towns and treasures—both close to Zagreb and farther away —than they know about "going to the coast," even though these diverse inland geographic regions offer incredibly rich experiences as alternatives to the sun-and-fun culture.

Croatia away from Zagreb and the coast dances to a much less frenetic beat than its glamorous siblings: The atmosphere in the cool, green hills is more down-to-earth and much less commercial than it is on the white-hot Adriatic beaches. Inland Croatia is where you will find working towns and farms juxtaposed with castles and medieval fortresses built to protect the country from foreign invaders. This is where you will see pristine homes adjacent to houses bullet-pocked by wounds inflicted during the 1991 war.

The northern regions of Zagorje and Međimurje are places where many of Croatia's heroes were born and where many Croatian patriots died fighting for their country's freedom through the ages. Here hilltop towers stand sentry as if to protect the land against harm and tiny *klets* stand between crop rows to provide shelter for farmers and their tools.

Today towns among the rolling hills and flatlands outside Zagreb are beginning to actively court tourists as the capital spreads outward to meet fields of yellow sunflowers waving in the wind. So get out of town and take a trip to the country, where the roads less traveled will lead you to the "real" Croatia and the warm and genuine people who live there.

1 Orientation

You don't have to take a long road trip to sample Croatia's northern heartland: Many of the castles, wineries, historical sites, and natural wonders within a 161km (100-mile) radius of **Zagreb** can be visited on day trips depending on what you want to see. It takes just a few hours to see charming **Samobor** or rustic **Divlje Vode.** Even historic **Karlovač** is less than an hour from the capital. Excursions such as a day of hiking the trails at renowned **Plitvice Lakes National Park** with its waterfalls, karst gorges, and forests; or a day exploring the shops, cafes, and castle at the baroque town of **Varaždin,** are within easy reach of Zagreb. Whether you want to spend a few days driving through the Međimurje wine country in extreme northern Croatia, or if you have just half a day to wander around Tito's childhood village at **Kumrovec** in the **Zagorje,** you can do it without spending a lot of time in transit. Check with the **Zagreb County Tourist Association** at Preradovićeva 42 (*©* **01/487-36-65;** fax 01/ 487-36-70) for excursion possibilities. The office is open from 8am to 8pm Monday

Excursions from Zagreb

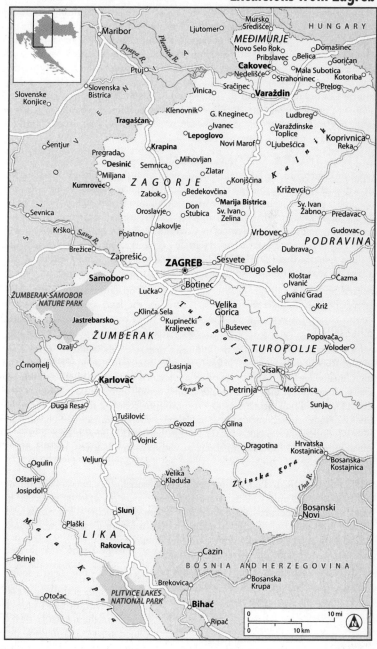

to Friday and from 9am to 1pm Saturday (closed Sun), late June through early September. Other times, office hours are from 8am to 4pm Monday to Friday. The association's website (http://zagzup.tripod.com/turizam/index.html) is handy for tourist contact information in Zagreb's outlying towns and for such statistics as the towns' distances from the capital. To get information on exploring the territory north of Zagreb in the Zagorje or in Međimurje regions, contact the **Tourist Board of Međâ imurje County** in Čakovec at R. Boškovića 3 (© **040/390-191;** www.tzm.hr).

We've put the sites in Zagreb's orbit into several itineraries according to routes out of the city, each of which can be used whole, broken into segments, or combined with other routes to suit individual interests.

GETTING THERE & GETTING AROUND

Once in Zagreb you can book guided excursions from the city in any direction. Multiple itineraries are available and especially useful if you are pressed for time, if you are unfamiliar with the region, if you are without your own transportation, or if you want an overview of the sites that ring Croatia's capital. Some excursions from Zagreb can be reached by train; for schedules, go to **Croatian Railways** (© **030/333-444;** www. hznet.hr). Another great way to travel outside Zagreb is by bus. Popular bus companies include **Croatia Bus** (© **01/235-23-33;** www.croatiabus.hr) and **Contus** (© **023/ 315-315;** www.contus.hr). No matter how you arrive at your destination, however, your adventure will involve a good bit of walking, as these destinations are compact and sometimes limited to pedestrians.

2 Excursions South of Zagreb

Most tourists who set out on the autocesta that stretches southwest from Zagreb toward Rijeka race across the 177km (110-mile) stretch of road as if they were wearing blinders. Usually that's because they are focused on getting to the Adriatic coast and nothing else. If they were to take a short detour onto the Jastrebarsko highway exit, they would find the gateway to a surprising collection of towns and terrains that offer wetlands, castles, upscale accommodations, wineries, and a mind-boggling array of outdoor activities, including river rafting, horseback riding, biking, hiking, and much more. Most of these destinations are within an hour's drive from Zagreb.

ESSENTIALS

VISITOR INFORMATION   Just about every tourist office in every city throughout Croatia offers tours of Plitvice Lakes. Tourist offices in Zagreb in particular have racks of maps, brochures, and information on most attractions and events within 161km (100 miles) of the city. In addition, most towns in Croatia have city tourist offices with more localized information plus commercial tourist agencies that run excursions and handle private accommodations.

GETTING THERE & GETTING AROUND   The area from Zagreb south to **Plitvice Lakes National Park (Plitvička Jezera)** ✺✺✺ can be accessed via the Zagreb-Rijeka autocesta. Each town along the way can be explored on a day trip as well, though the entire itinerary could take several days, especially if you decide to include the **Žumberak** region and **Samobor** (p. 285) on your list. The same applies if you linger at any destination, or if you are traveling by bus or train and have to wait for connections.

Of all the possible excursions from Zagreb, you probably need to allot the most time for a trip to Plitvice Lakes National Park, which is 2 hours from Zagreb and a place where most visitors take their time wandering trails and gazing at the gorgeous waterfalls. You might find that overnight stays in **Karlovac** or Plitvice are viable choices to slow the tempo of your travels, or you can speed things up and add itineraries farther afield. Rental cars are handy for such customization, especially if you are interested in visiting tiny hilltop wineries or searching for bird species in the **Crna Mlaka (Black Marsh)** wetlands. But rental cars are not absolutely necessary unless you plan to explore some of the more remote villages deep in the Žumberak region. Public transportation—buses, trains, and private tours from Zagreb, for example— also is available, but that can require some complicated logistical planning.

3 Samobor to the Žumberak

Picturesque, quaint, and full of cafes that serve the delicate but waist-expanding pastry known as *kremšnite,* Samobor is a favorite day trip for Zagrebačka and for tourists who have limited time but want to see a bit of the countryside. Samobor is just 26km (16 miles) west of Zagreb and linked to the capital by frequent bus service, good roads, and lots of tour operators, so it is a convenient destination.

Contemporary Samobor looks like an 18th-century postcard with its flower-bedecked pastel buildings and copper-domed church. During medieval times, the town was a hub for trades- and craftsmen who made a living with their hands. Today, Samobor mostly attracts weekend visitors who want to trek in the hills or stock up on local specialties such as *kremšnite,* a 4-inch-high square of custard meringue between sheets of crispy *mille-feuille* pastry; *samborska mustarda,* mustard made the same way it was made during the French occupation of the region; and Bermet, a distinctive, herb-infused aperitif wine that takes some getting used to. Once in Samobor, you can tour the town's museums, browse in its shops and galleries, or venture into more rural territory such as Zumberak Eko Selo, Divlje Vode, or the Samoborsko Gorje (Samobor Gorge).

Because of its close proximity to Zagreb, Samobor is rarely without tourists, but the liveliest time to be in town is during the **Samobor Carnival,** a pre-Lenten celebration that culminates with hordes of masked merrymakers swarming the streets and a huge fireworks display. Carnival has been a fixture in Samobor for more than a century, and the town really rocks while it's on. Samobor has a unique character, but logistically, it is almost a suburb of Zagreb, and its expansive cobbled town square lined with shops, cafes, and crafters could almost classify it as a theme park. You'll want to linger here for a while and with good reason. By contrast, the Žumberak is a vast area of forests, hills, rustic villages, and vestiges of the Greek Orthodox culture that once thrived there. There were almost no visible signs of tourism or construction activity there in the summer of 2007, perhaps because there isn't much to see between villages and historic sites, and much of this territory isn't accessible via public transportation. However, the Žumberak makes for a relaxing drive and lets you get a feel for life in Croatia's hinterlands. The northern part of the Žumberak is more mountainous than the southern part, where the landscape gives way to hillside vineyards in the Plešivica wine region.

ESSENTIALS

VISITOR INFORMATION   Samobor's **tourist office** is on the town's spacious main square at Trg Kralja Tomislava 5 (✆ **01/33-60-044;** www.samobor.hr). The staff is used to foreign tourists and can help with maps and information about transportation, accommodations, dining, and even area history for Samobor, the Žumberak, and beyond.

GETTING THERE   Samobor is about 26km (16 miles) west of Zagreb and adjacent to the hilly Žumberak. Buses to Samobor run every half-hour or so from Zagreb's main station (hourly on Sun), which allows for a quick excursion out of the city. (See contacts for the Zagreb Autobusni Kolodvor, p. 314.) Buses stop north of the main square, but the short walk to the center is easy and pleasant. If you are traveling by car from Zagreb, take A3 south and follow the signs. Parking is outside the center. We clocked our auto trip to Samobor from Zagreb's southern border at 11 minutes using minor roads. Buses to villages in the Žumberak region are infrequent, and some areas are not reasonably reached without a car, though avid cyclists may find the route challenging.

GETTING AROUND   From Samobor, it's easy to get to the Samobor Gorge on foot, where hiking trails abound. If you have your own transport, you can drive past the gorge into the Žumberak to challenging mountain trails in the north or to rustic villages, homes, and churches in the south.

WHAT TO SEE & DO

Samobor was a bustling center of commerce and agriculture during medieval times, but now it's an affluent bedroom community attached to Zagreb where many city folk have built large, expensive homes and others go on weekends to get away from metropolitan madness. Besides excellent access to hiking and cycling trails in the mountains west of town and in the Žumberak region, Samobor has several museums and galleries worth a look.

Museum Marton Practicality and craftsmanship are the themes at Croatia's first private museum, which has a nice collection of applied art. It's all housed in a restored granary where histories and explanations accompany the fine exhibits of antique crystal, china, furniture, and paintings.

Jurjevska 7, Samobor. 01/33-64-160. www.muzej-marton.hr. Admission 20kn ($4) adults, 15kn ($3) children and seniors. Sat–Sun 10am–1pm and 3–6pm.

Town Museum Displays in this former 18th-century "palace" chronicle Samobor's history. An ethnographic collection includes rustic farm implements and other vestiges of the area's way of life through the ages.

Livadićeva 7, Samobor. 01/33-36-214. Admission 5kn ($1). Tues–Thurs 8am–3pm; Fri 1–7pm; Sat–Sun 9am–1pm. Closed Mon.

Žumberačko Eko Selo To get to this ersatz dude ranch that opened in 1994, drive through Divlje Vode until you get to a fork in the road. Turn left. After a short distance, the road becomes a gravel track through the trees, and you won't see many signs, but continue for about 3km (2 miles) until you get to the camp complex, which consists of wooden cabins, a cowboy-style restaurant, a bubbling mountain stream, and an Old West saloon that plays almost nonstop country music. This is a family place where ducks, geese, chickens, donkeys, and other animals have free run of the property, a situation that encourages delightful animal "encounters" for the children. Horseback riding lessons, trail rides, and Western dress-up days are part of the program, too, and there are several interesting historical sites (a Roman cemetery, canyons and waterfalls, and Santa Gera, the Žumberak's highest mountain peak) that make good hikes.

Željko Milovanovic. d.o.o. zugostiteljstvo i turizam. R.J. "Klet." Kravljak bb, 10456 Kalje. 01/338-74-72. www.eko-selo.hr.

Samobor Castle

The spectacular ruins of Samobor Castle sit atop a hill right above the town of Samobor, which is only around 25 km (15½ miles) west of Zagreb. To reach the castle take the Zagreb–Ljubljana highway, get off at the Samobor exit, and follow the road with the concrete surface toward Samobor, taking the left fork into that town. Proceed right through the town center and start walking up from the park on the western edge of town (you can see the ruins immediately above). It is only about a 10- to 15-minute ascent on a switchback trail. As of this writing there was a locked gate at the main entrance to the ruins, but you could still gain access by walking around to the rear.

By the charter of King Bela IV in 1242, the town of Samobor was granted the privileges of a free market town. The castle was built around the same time, and various additions and renovations were made over the next 500 years. The castle was owned by a number of eminent families: the Babonićs, Counts Celjski, the Frankopans, the Ungnads, the Erdodys, the Kulmers, the Kiepachs, and the Allnochs. Samobor Castle was abandoned in the 18th century and gradually fell into ruins.

Courtesy of Tocher Mitchell

WHERE TO STAY

Samobor has several small hotels and pansions plus a slew of private accommodations that can be booked at any of the tourist agencies in town. For accommodations in Divlje Vode or Žumberačko Eko Selo, make arrangements directly with the facilities or at the Žumberak Nature Park office in Bregana (© **01/33-23-848;** pp.zsg@zg.hinet.hr).

Hotel Livadić (★)   The Livadić's location on the main square makes it a convenient choice, especially during Carnival, but it is the excellent **hotel** (★★) kavana and friendly atmosphere characteristic of Croatia's family-run hotels that make this a comfortable place to stay. Guest rooms are spacious and done in period decor, but with modern bathrooms. A plus: Guest rooms are off the square behind the restaurant, which minimizes noise from pedestrian traffic.

Trg Kralja Tomislava, Samobor. © **01/336-58-50.** Fax 01/332-55-88. www.hotel-livadic.hr. 17 units. From 465kn ($86) double. Rates include breakfast. AE, DC, MC, V. **Amenities:** Restaurant; terrace cafe. *In room:* TV, minibar.

Hotel Lavica   The Lavica is the ultimate renovation project: The hotel's history goes back nearly 250 years when it started out as a stable with hayloft on property belonging to a town official. Today, the Lavica is a rustic yet modern inn that combines the ambience of the past with conveniences of the present thanks to a 2003 renovation and ongoing improvements. Guest rooms are tastefully decorated with dark woods and cool colors; bathrooms have updated fixtures, and some have tubs rather than showers. The Lavica is lovely, low-key place to stay.

Ferde Livadićeva 5, Samobor. © **01/332-49-46.** Fax 01/336-66-11. www.lavica-hotel.hr. 22 units. From 314kn ($58) double. Rates include breakfast. AE, MC, V. **Amenities:** Restaurant. *In room:* TV, minibar.

View From the Top

Many marked trails and several challenging hikes originate in Samobor. Beginners can try a combo ride-walk technique to access a 4-story tower and platform erected in 2006. If you aren't afraid to climb this open steel structure (it has stairs), you will be treated to a spectacular 360-degree view of the Zumberak and beyond. From the main square, take the narrow, unmarked road next to the town museum and follow Sv. Ane Ulica to a sign that says "Vidikovac Turanj Tepec" (vantage point). Turn right on the gravel road immediately opposite the sign, park, and walk about 100 meters to the tower. There are other marked trails through the woods near the tower. Directions to more challenging routes can be obtained at the tourist office on the main square in Samobor.

Žumberačko Eko Selo ✦✦   Accommodations at this homage to the Wild West are unique in Croatia. Cabins are log-cabin rustic with touches of class: There are lace-curtains on the windows, Indian blankets on the beds, and lots of knotty pine on the walls. Guest rooms have the convenience of toilets and showers. Camping facilities are available, too. The "ranch" is open year-round, meals are hearty and delicious, and trail rides through the snow-covered forests are especially beautiful.

Koretići 13, 10456 Kalje. ✆ **01/338-74-73.** Fax 01/336-73-06. www.eko-selo.hr. From 50€ ($70) double. MC, V. **Amenities:** Restaurant; stable; excursions.

Pansion Divlje Vode   There are just seven basic rooms with French beds above the pink stucco trout restaurant on the hill overlooking the bio-park below. They come in handy if you don't want to drive back to Zagreb through the forest after dark.

Stojdraga 2. 10432 Bregana. ✆ **01/33-87-623.** 7 units. From 200kn ($40) double. Breakfast not included. AE, DC, MC, V.

WHERE TO DINE

Samobor is crammed with pastry cafes that serve its famous *kremšnite* and other guilty pleasures, but it also is known for fine dining and regional specials such as *češnjovke* (spicy sausage). The Žumberak itself is a dining destination with a rustic bent that includes hearty, homey fare. Either way, you won't go hungry in this region where heaping plates of game, freshwater fish, and decadent pastries are devoured with gusto.

Divlje Vode ✦✦ FISH   A long, almost-finished granite stairway leads up a steep hill to a pale pink mansion that is now part of this rustic restaurant. Divlje Vode serves diners on a beautiful terrace among pine trees overlooking the area trout farm where you can watch your dinner swim around before it lands on your plate. Trout is the dish of the day, and for 45kn ($8) you can have the freshly caught fish grilled, deep-fried, pan-fried, poached, or fried in corn flour. For a little more, you can order local specials like Zagorje soup, *štrukli*, or grilled meat, all of which are delicious and served in generous portions. Despite its out-of-the-way location, Divlje Vode can get crowded at lunchtime and on weekends. Those who venture to this out-of-the-way spot for a weekday dinner have the option of staying over in one of the restaurant's seven sobes.

Stojdraga 2, Žumberak. ✆ **01/33-87-629.** Entrees 35kn–75kn ($6–$13). AE, DC, MC, V. Daily 9am–11pm.

Kavana Lidivać ⭐⭐ PASTRY   Everything in this centrally located hotel coffee-house/restaurant is bright and welcoming in a meticulously furnished dining room augmented by adjacent garden seating fringed with beautiful container plantings in summer. The *palačinke* (crepes) filled with walnuts are delicious here, as are the *kremšnite* and other local specialties.

Trg Kralja Tomislava 1, Samobor. © 01/33-65-850. www.hotel-lidavic.hr. *Kremšnite* about $2. AE, DC, MC, V. Daily 8am–midnight.

Samoborski Slapovi ⭐⭐ INTERNATIONAL   Dinner in the woods is one of the attractions in this tiny hotel restaurant about 3.2km (2 miles) northwest of the Samobor center. The food here is substantial but uncomplicated, with grilled meat and regional specials showcased but supplemented by Italian and German-leaning choices. You might want to book one of the 12 rooms available for an overnight just so you can enjoy a few more meals in this pastoral setting.

Hamor 16, Samobor. © 01/33-84-063. Fax 01/33-84-062. Entrees 30kn–65kn ($6–$12). AE, DC, MC, V. Daily 7am–midnight.

4 Karlovac

54km (32 miles) SW of Zagreb; 90km (54 miles) N of Plitvice National Park

This leafy river town 54km (32 miles) and less than an hour from Zagreb has all the right elements to stand out as a model of baroque architecture and clever city planning. However, war and neglect have left their marks, and many of Karlovac's treasures are crumbling and in deplorable condition. The city of **Karlovac** was established by the Austro-Hungarians in 1579 as a military installation to defend against the encroaching Turks. Because of its strategic position between the **Kupa** and the **Korana rivers** and its proximity to the **Mrežnica** and **Dobra rivers,** Karlovac has been on the front line of battles spanning 4 centuries.

Many of Karlovac's stately baroque buildings still bear significant scars from Serbian artillery, and others are towering examples of the former socialist government's indifference to beauty, but the town is showing signs of renewal.

Originally, the city's medieval footprint was in the form of a six-pointed star set within a system of moats. Today the star-shaped layout is still intact, but it now is a green space that includes the Franjo Tuđman Promenade, a 2.4km-long (1.5-mile) path lined with chestnut trees that meanders around the central city.

When you approach Karlovac from any direction, it looks like a blue-collar industrial town ringed by middle-class suburbs. It's easy to miss the Old Town farther in, once a wealthy cluster of baroque homes and businesses. The Old Town is in various stages of dishabille, but it is worth seeing even though damage from the 1991 war is still visible almost everywhere you look. You'll see renovation projects going on here and there, though they seem inadequate in light of what needs to be done.

Even if some Karlovac residents have not come to terms with the war, there are signs that the town is emerging from hard times. There are two modern hotels in town **(Europa** and **Korana),** name-brand retailers **(Benetton, Levi's),** ubiquitous crowded cafes and pizza places, and even a few tourists taking in the sights before moving on to sun and fun on the coast.

The town's center comprises buildings that still suffer from battle blight, but they are clearly Frankopan or Hapsburg inspired; anyone wandering past them will think of the town's appearance before war left its ugly mark on the facades.

At the west end of town, **Karlovačko Brewery** might be the town's most recognizable brand name, but **Dubovac Castle** ❀ on a hill above it is probably its main tourist
attraction and can be reached in 10 minutes from the town center by car (or in 30
min. on foot). It once was possible to stay in one of the castle's 10 sobes (rooms), but
those have closed and the building is now being renovated. During construction, the
defensive tower is home to a permanent exhibition on the history of the castle and the
area around it. The banks of the Korana River also are popular and draw crowds at all
hours to swim, jog, walk their dogs, or enjoy the scenery.

Dining opportunities in the area range from homey *klets* (rustic restaurants serving
local cuisine) on deserted streets to the elegant **Dobra** ❀❀❀ in the Hotel Korana,
which also offers alfresco service on its handsome deck overlooking the river.

About 6km (10 miles) north of Karlovac, the town of **Ozalj** and its imposing hilltop castle offer spectacular views of the Z[az]umberak, a sight that is worth the ride
even if the still-under-renovation castle isn't. About 10km (6 miles) northwest of
Ozalj, the tiny village of **Krašić** has become a tourist destination because of the church
and museum there dedicated to the town's favorite son, **Alojzije Stepinac,** who was
archbishop of Zagreb during World War II and who is something of a folk hero in
Croatia. Stepinac was jailed by communists after being railroaded on charges of col-
laboration with the Nazis, and he spent the final years of his life under house arrest in
Krašić, the town where he was born. There is an imposing statue of Stepinac outside
the church, which is open for Mass and tour groups, and for anyone who happens to
meet up with the parish priest.

If you continue in the same northerly direction when you leave Krašić, you will see
rural villages almost untouched by time (and renovation). You will be in the part of
Croatia that is home to a strong Greek Orthodox culture, which is evident in some of
the architecture. When you get to **Pribić,** note the **Church of the Annunciation** just
outside the village: Its architecture is typical of the Orthodox genre.

From here, you can continue farther north into the Žumberak to **Sočice** to see
more churches and a small folk museum displaying farm implements and Greek ethnic garb; then proceed to **Žumberačko Eko Selo** (p. 286). You can then circle back
to Samobor and Zagreb.

ESSENTIALS

VISITOR INFORMATION   The **Karlovac Tourist Office** (✆ 047/615-115; fax
047/600-602) is located at Petra Zrinskog 3, diagonally across from the **Hotel Carlstadt** ❀. Hours are 8am to 3pm Monday through Friday; 8am to 1pm Saturday;
closed Sunday and holidays. A helpful staff, including a few who speak English, can
direct visitors to hotels and private accommodations and provide maps and brochures
about the city and surrounding areas. Commercial tourist agencies like **Generalturist**
at Zrinski Trg 4 (✆ 047/615-199; fax 047/615-398) can help you with excursions
from Karlovać and can help book rooms for you in town or at other destinations.

GETTING THERE   Karlovac is a little more than an hour from Zagreb by car on
the Zagreb-Rieka autocesta (A6). Buses and trains run to and from Zagreb with reg-
ularity almost every half-hour. In addition, there is connecting service to Rijeka and
some of the Kvarner islands. Train service to and from Zagreb runs with the frequency
of a commuter line (18 per day). There also is connecting train service to Rijeka.

GETTING AROUND   Karlovac is a walker's city, especially along the river and in
the town center. You can follow the "star," which is lined with trees and a popular

promenade, especially after dinner. You can even walk up to the medieval Dubovac Castle by setting out north from the Kupa, but this is a vigorous uphill hike and will take half an hour or more. There is a road for auto traffic to the castle, too.

WHAT TO SEE & DO

Besides people-watching from the town's many cafes, exploring the Old Town, tracing the "star," or strolling along the river, there are several notable attractions in Karlovac. Whether passing through or in town for a business meeting, visitors won't lack for things to see during downtime.

Dubovac Castle ✦ Originally built in the 13th century, the present castle underwent several redesigns at the hands of the Frankopans and the French, but the exterior has since been restored to some semblance of its former medieval splendor. Inside, the castle has seen better days, and renovation is afoot, but one hotelier says there are plans to eventually turn the building into a youth hostel. You can walk from town to the castle, which is a little over a mile due west of the center, but the steep grade can be challenging. The easiest way to get to Dubovac Castle is by car. Either way, the panoramic view of the city and the rivers that run through it is worth the effort.

2km (1¼ miles) west of the town center. ✆ 047/416-331. Castle admission 10kn ($2) for adults, half-price for children 7–18. Mon–Fri 5–9pm; weekends and holidays 9am–1pm and 5–9pm. For a curator-led tour (free) at other times, call the City Museum at ✆ 047/615-980.

City Museum (Gradski Muzej) Currently located on Trg Strossmayer, with some exhibits installed in Dubovac Castle, the museum has a large collection of Croatian cultural artifacts and a model of how Karlovac once looked. There are also historic photos of Croatian life and architecture and examples of pottery and other crafts. Descriptions are in Croatian only.

Trg Strossmayerov 7. ✆ 047/615-980. Admission 10kn ($2) for adults, half-price for children 7–18. Mon–Fri 8am–3pm; Sat–Sun 10am–noon. Special appointments available by calling the museum.

Holy Trinity Church & the Franciscan Monastery ✦ Holy Trinity Church and its attached Franciscan monastery are undergoing renovation, but it is still possible to see the church's interior during Mass. To see the monastery and its museum of sacred art, just knock on the door. Whoever is home will be happy to show you around.

Trg Bana Jelačića 7. ✆ 047/615-950.

WHERE TO STAY

Karlovač's hotel scene is looking up, thanks to two relatively new hotels and several others that have been updated. Private accommodations are also an option (contact the tourist office).

Hotel Korana-Srakovčić ✦✦✦ First-time Korana guests who follow the city's directional signs to this family-run hotel are inevitably taken aback when they approach a war-ravaged structure with broken windows and a burned HOTEL KORANA sign on the roof. Don't gasp and turn around. Instead, keep going about 91m (300 ft.) to the *real* Hotel Korana, a faithful re-creation of a historic 1896 building that was destroyed in the war with Serbia and lovingly rebuilt in 11 months according to the structure's original blueprints. The new Hotel Korana, which opened its doors in 2003, is a true boutique hotel in a park setting. Its personalized guest services sometimes find the staff organizing special events that range from corporate luncheons to hunts for wild mushrooms. The hotel can even set up a tour of the city's Karlovačko

Brewery or rafting on one of the nearby rivers. Guest rooms are spacious and airy, and each is themed to a different flower species, so if you forget your room number, you'll remember that you are in the Petunia Room. The hotel's **Restaurant Dobra** 🌟🌟 features nouvelle regional dishes that can be served on the wraparound deck, a perfect perch for watching the nightly promenade along the Korana riverwalk.

Perivoj Josipa Vrbanića 8. ℂ 047/609-090. Fax 047/609-091. www.hotelkorana.hr. 18 units. From 950kn ($175) double with balcony; from 1,350kn ($250) suite. Rate includes breakfast. AE, DC, MC, V. **Amenities:** Restaurant; bar; golf; tennis courts; wellness center w/sauna, solarium and massage; room for those w/limited mobility; shoeshine machine in lobby. *In room:* A/C, TV/SAT, dataport, minibar, hair dryer, safe.

Hotel Carlstadt 🌟   With the busiest street in town at its doorstep, the Hotel Carlstadt is convenient to sites and transport. The Carlstadt is in a state of ongoing update, though the objective is freshening rather than modernizing, so the guest rooms are still plain. They are, however, within easy reach of stores, cafes, and the city's green periphery with its promenade and public garden. In addition, the busy cafe/bar Carlstadt next door to the hotel at street level is the perfect place to rendezvous with friends or linger over a cup of kava.

Vraniczanyeva 1. ℂ 047/611-111. www.carlstadt.hr. 37 units. June 1–Sept 30: from 455kn ($84) double; Oct 1–May 31: from 415kn ($77) double. June 1–Sept 30: from 815kn ($150) suite; Oct 1–May 31: 740kn ($137) suite. Rates include breakfast. AE, DC, MC, V. Garage parking. **Amenities:** Coffee/bar; casino; fax and Internet service; currency exchange; laundry service. *In room:* A/C, TV, minibar.

Hotel Europa 🌟   The imposing stucco Hotel Europa is the first thing you see when you head for the Karlovac exit off the Zagreb-Rijeka autocesta. Opened in 2003, the Europa caters to tourists and businesspeople alike, and it is especially handy as a stopover if you want to visit nearby Plitvice Lakes National Park or if you want to take a leisurely trip to the Adriatic coast. Among the local excursions the hotel can arrange is a picnic along area wine roads, complete with a map and a basket full of locally grown/produced foods.

Banija 161. ℂ 047/609-666. Fax 047/609-667. www.hotel-europa.com.hr. 32 units. From 650kn ($120) double; from 980kn ($170) suite Rates include breakfast. AE, DC, MC, V. Video-monitored parking. **Amenities:** Restaurant; cafe/bar; sauna; solarium; excursions. *In room:* A/C, TV, dataport, minibar, hair dryer.

WHERE TO DINE

Karlovač is konoba country. Most of the city's dining spots are casual affairs that specialize in pizza, huge plates of grilled meats, and regional specialties such as platters of mixed grill (meat) and fish. However, a couple of restaurants go beyond the traditional to add a twist to the expected.

Restaurant Dobra 🌟🌟 *Value* NOUVELLE CROATIAN   The Dobra's dining room gleams with crystal, silver, and flowers at every table, but the wide porch overlooking the Korana River provides an even better show. No matter what time it is, diners on the deck can watch the river and an ever-changing kaleidoscope of strollers, dog-walkers, and joggers streaming past their table. The menu includes many Croatian standards such as *cevapčI (meat stew with paprika)* and a mixed grill, but the kitchen ventures out of the pantry, too. Try the wild quail chef de cuisine, grilled fresh trout with herbs, or grilled octopus served cold with fresh pineapple. In this area full of hunting enthusiasts, the quail could have been flying and the trout swimming a few hours earlier. Whether you go traditional or modern, you'll get to sample the chef's creativity with an *amuse bouche* before the meal. Ours was a delightful salmon tartar

> ## (Fun Fact What's a Konoba?
>
> A konoba is usually a family-run restaurant that specializes in regional cuisine made with local produce, homegrown and prepared meats, family-caught fish, and perhaps even family-made wines. Any dining spot that calls itself a konoba is usually casual and traditional, with family-style service, large portions at low prices, and a lot of regular local customers. Think Irish pub or neighborhood bistro.

served with homemade whole-grain toast slices. Service is gallant, and menus are in five languages, including English.

Perivoj Josipa Vrbaniča 8 (in the Hotel Korana). © 047/609-090. Fax 047/609-091. www.hotelkorana.hr. Entrees 45kn–80kn ($8–$15). AE, DC, MC, V. Daily 8am–10pm.

Restaurant Žganjer ⭐⭐ *(Finds* CREATIVE REGIONAL   This is one of those roadside places where you encounter food that you will remember forever. Grilled lamb and pig, bread from the *krusna pec* (brick stove), capon with olives, turkey baked with *mlinci* (noodles), mouthwatering local pastries, and local Vrbnička Žlahtina wine are among the offerings that will linger in your taste buds for a long time. You might even want to stay the night in the restaurant's 10-room pansion: Each room is nicely equipped with TV and minibar. If you do stay over, you'll have time to try a few more things on the menu.

Jelašl 41 (about 4.8km/3 miles from Karlovač center on State Rd. D-1 toward Split). © 047/641-333. Fax 047/641-304. Entrees 35kn–75kn ($6–$13). AE, DC, MC, V. 24 hr.

5 Plitvice Lakes National Park

The Plitvice Lakes National Park is Croatia's most touted natural wonder: Its majestic waterfalls, lakes, and forests have earned it a place on the UNESCO register of world natural heritage sites and made it Croatia's second biggest tourist attraction after the Adriatic coast and islands. The park's most compelling features are the waterfalls that interconnect its 16 clear turquoise lakes, which are set in dense forests of beech, fir, spruce, and soaring rock formations. The park's 4,856-hectares (12,000 acres) include 3,642 hectares (9,000 acres) of forest, 1,133 hectares (2,800 acres) of grassy areas and villages, and 36 hectares (88 acres) of water. Everywhere the water is crystal-clear thanks to deposits of travertine (powdery white limestone rock) under the water. The constant distribution of travertine creates the underwater mounds responsible for the waterfalls. The park is also rich with caves, springs, flowering meadows, the source of the River Korana (a gorge that looks like a green branch of the Grand Canyon), and several animal species including deer, wolves, wild boar, and the increasingly rare brown bear (though these animals rarely make an appearance during the hours when the park is open to visitors).

Plitvice became a national park in 1949. One of the Serb–Croat war's first casualties was a park policeman who was killed in an incident that is sometimes cited as one of the flashpoints for the 1991 war. The park was occupied for most of the war by Serb troops until 1995, and during that time, its offices and hotels were trashed, but the park itself was undamaged. Since then, the hotels and other buildings have been restored, and in the last 10 years visitors have returned to the park in droves. Plitvice now lures nearly a million visitors annually to its pristine acreage, which is crisscrossed with well-marked gravel paths and boardwalks that allow visitors to wander about for anywhere from 2 to 8 hours an outing, depending on how they structure their routes.

Park signs at the trail heads suggest itineraries and the length of time each would take, but in reality, you can make your own path and stay as long or as short a time as you like—provided you don't take a wrong turn and miss one of the bus or ferry stops. The in-park transportation system runs on eco-friendly fuel whisking visitors between sites.

ESSENTIALS

VISITOR INFORMATION   There are two entrances to the park, Ulaz 1 and Ulaz 2, each of which has a tourist info office, gift shop, and snack shop. The tourist office at Ulaz 1 is open daily from 8am to 8pm during July and August, from 9am to 5pm April to June and September, and from 9am to 4pm October to March. The office at Ulaz 2 is open from 8am to 7pm July and August, and from 9am to 5pm April to June and September. Here you can get brochures and advice about how to approach the park or how to find a hotel, but no decent free maps. The trails and directions to shuttle buses are clearly marked, but having a detailed map is a good idea to avoid detours, which could add hours and extra uphill climbs to your hike. An excellent, though unwieldy, map is available for 20kn ($4) at the ticket booth. Tickets are 85kn ($16) per day for adults and about 40kn ($8) for seniors and kids 7 to 18. Children 6 and under are free. Prices listed here are for high season and are lower other times.

GETTING THERE   Plitvice is conveniently located on the old road (E71) between Split and Zagreb, but you don't need a car to get there from anywhere in Croatia because almost every town and every hotel in the country either runs tours or connects visitors with tours that include Plitvice or focus on it. There is even a separate **Plitvice Tourism Office** in Zagreb at Trg Kralja Komislava 19 (© **01/461-35-86**) that will be happy to help you arrange a visit.

By Car   To get to Plitvice by car from Zagreb (trip time about 2 hr.), take the Zagreb-Rieka autocesta to Karlovac. From there, follow the signs to Plitvice via the old road to Split (E71).

By Bus   You can catch a bus from the main bus station in Zagreb (2½ hr.), from 8:20am to 1:45am for 48kn to 70kn ($9–$13) one-way, depending on the time of departure, bus line, and other factors. You can check schedules online at www.akz.hr, but you have to call reservations and info (© **060/313-333**) or stop at the main office at Avenue Marin Držića 4 in the town center to make a reservation or get a ticket. Make sure your bus stops at Plitvice and that it doesn't take the new highway and bypass the park on the way to Split; this is a possibility since the Zagreb-Split leg of the A1 autocesta opened in June 2005 and it is no longer necessary for anyone going to the coast to take the older road that passes the park.

GETTING AROUND   The delightfully Croatian **Lička Kuča restaurant** (p. 296) is at Ulaz 1, at the north end of the park and close to the bottom of the Lower Lakes, so stop there for lunch. Then hop in the car and drive about 2.4km (1½ miles) south to Ulaz 2 to begin your tour (if you are visiting anytime except Oct–Mar), because that entrance puts you in the middle of the property and gives you more options for exploring the park. Ulaz 2 is also the site of the park's three hotels (Jezero, Plitvice, and Bellevue; p. 295), in case you want to stay near the park and weren't lured by the ubiquitous SOBE signs on the roads leading to and from Plitvice.

WHAT TO SEE & DO

Plitvice is a hikers' paradise, but even couch potatoes can see most of the park's features by combining walking with riding on the Plitvice ferries and buses. Ulaz 2 is roughly in the middle of the park, so if you start there, you can easily get to **Prošćansko,** the highest and largest lake in the park, which is ringed by a hilly green landscape. No waterfalls here, as you are at the top of the cascade. From Ulaz 2 it is a quick downhill walk to a ferry, which will take you toward paths flanked by waterfalls you can almost reach out and touch. *Note:* Don't try this. Swimming is forbidden, as is walking on the travertine.

You can also follow the signs here to the foot of **Veliki Slap (Big Waterfall),** where slender streams of water zoom off the vertical granite face into **Korana Gorge.** Veliki Slap is the most dramatic waterfall in the park, and sometimes it seems that everyone is rushing to get there. However, there are smaller falls, series of falls, and clusters of falls in other parts of the park that are impressive, too.

WHERE TO STAY

Hotel Jezero ⍟   This is definitely a hotel for large tour groups: Rooms are small, the restaurant is big, and everything else is generic-looking. However, the restaurant is surprisingly good and the location couldn't be more convenient to the park.

Plitvička Jezera bb. ✆ 053/751-400 or -014. Fax 053/751-600. www.np-plitvicka-jezera.hr. 210 units. July–Aug: from 114€ ($160) double. June: 104€ ($145) double. Rest of year: 82€ ($115) double. 30% discount for kids 7–12; 50% discount for kids 6 and under. Kids stay free if they sleep in parent's bed. AE, DC, MC, V. Parking. **Amenities:** Restaurant; bar; pool; sauna; elevator; 5 rooms for those w/limited mobility. *In room:* TV, minibar, Internet line.

Hotel Plitvice   Farther away from the park than the Jezero, this smaller hotel also has fewer services, though it is in denser forest.

Plitvička Jezera bb. ✆ 053/751-100. Fax 053/751-013. www.np-plitvicka-jezera.hr. 52 units. July–Aug: 82€ ($115) double. June: 74€ ($104). Rest of year: 52€ ($73). AE, DC, MC, V. Kids stay free in parent's room. **Amenities:** Restaurant. *In room:* TV, minibar, Internet line.

Hotel Bellevue   This is the park's bare-bones hotel. It's where you stay if you get there late and are going to leave after you visit the lakes the next day.

Plitvička Jezera bb. ✆ 053/751-700. Fax 053/751-165. www.np-plitvicka-jezera.hr. 60 units. July–Aug: from 72€ ($100) double. June: 66€ ($92) double. Rest of year: 52€ ($73) double. AE, DC, MC, V. Parking.

WHERE TO DINE

Hundreds of dining spots pepper the road to and from Plitvice, most offering spit-roasted lamb or pig and other local specials. You can stop for a bite or buy your roasted meat by the kilo and picnic in the woods. There are a few sandwich concessions within the park itself as well as hotel restaurants, but there is only one free-standing restaurant within walking distance of the hotels.

Lička Kuča ⍟⍟ CROATIAN   This large, touristy restaurant is opposite Ulaz 1 and full of folk items, including an open wood-burning stove big enough to roast a whole cow. The restaurant serves regional dishes such as spit-roasted lamb, sausages, and *lička juha* (lamb soup with veggies).

Ulaz 1, Plitvice National Park. ✆ 053/751-024. Fax 053/751-026. Entrees 35kn–80kn ($6–$15). AE, DC, MC, V. Daily 11am–11pm. Closed Nov–Apr.

6 Excursions North of Zagreb

The green, rolling landscape of the Zagorje and Međimurje regions north of Zagreb could have been patterned on illustrations from *Grimm's Fairy Tales*. This is Croatia's storybook land, where each new vista reveals another gentle swell of green topped with cream-colored hilltop churches and gingerbread-brown brick cottages. In the troughs between these verdant agri-breakers, the villages of rural Croatia remain countryside repositories of the nation's early culture and customs, a source of larger-than-life heroes and historic events that helped shape the country and its unique character.

High in the hills, visitors can say a prayer to the Blessed Virgin at **Maria Bistrica** or wander the caves at **Krapina,** where signs of a Neanderthal settlement were discovered in 1899. Farther on, visitors can see the medieval fortresses of **Veliki Tabor** and **Trakošćan,** or marvel at the baroque town of **Varaždin** and its museums and castle. Even casual tourists will see that spas like **Terme Tuhelj** and **St. Martin** are turning their attention to guests looking for luxury rather than rehab, and that the aristocratic "palaces" like **Dvor Desinič** are attracting curious gourmets rather than indolent aristocrats. **Kumrovec,** Tito's rural birthplace, now looks like a Croatian version of Williamsburg, Virginia, USA, with blacksmiths forging iron, costumed guides explaining exhibits, and townspeople selling homemade *rakija* (brandy) and local honey.

At the top of the country, which skirts the Slovenian border, **Međimurje** wine roads curl through the hills near Čakovic, the region's center. There, family vineyards abound, and everyone from Grandma to the smallest of children pitches in to bring in the grapes.

The people of the Zagorje and Međimurje are known throughout Croatia as some of the nation's most industrious and frugal citizens. They also have reputations for generous hospitality, for serving exceptional meals made with local produce, and for loving their land and the fruit of their trees and vines. Just like the winegrowers in France's Beaujolais region who celebrate *le vin nouveau* on the third Thursday in November, the people in northern Croatia also have a designated day (Nov 11, St. Martin's Day) to taste and tout their new vintage. On that day, the wine is blessed and the whole area takes part in a festival of food, wine, and merrymaking, a celebration of a season's work that lasts well into the night, ending only with morning and the beginning of a new cycle of life.

7 Marija Bistrica, Kumrovec & Veliki Tabor

The route north from Zagreb past Mount Medvednica and through the Stubica Valley leads to the Zagorje region, home to some of Croatia's most beautiful vistas and the best castles, shrines, and historic sites in the country. On the way, you'll be immersed in the Zagorje's appealing rural atmosphere, which hasn't changed much over the centuries. The Catholic faithful will want to stop at **Marija Bistrica** 𝄢𝄢 to see where Pope John II put controversial Croatian Archbishop Alojzije Stepanic on the road to sainthood. History buffs will make a beeline for the ethno village of **Kumrovec (Staro Selo)** 𝄢𝄢𝄢, where Josip Brož Tito was born. Anyone game enough to venture into the Croatian countryside should be on the lookout for the lovingly restored 17th-century **Miljana Palace,** which you must admire from afar as it is closed to the public and not completely renovated. However, there's no problem exploring the very public **Veliki Tabor,** one of Croatia's best castles. This formidable stone keep comes complete with ghosts and a windswept perch on a hill overlooking grasslands and the winding road, and it, too is undergoing a face-lift.

ESSENTIALS

VISITOR INFORMATION Marija Bistrica's **tourist office** is at Zagrebač bb (© **049/468-380;** www.info-marija-bistrica.hr). Hours are 7am to 3pm Tuesday through Friday; and in summer, 8am to 2 pm Saturday and Sunday. The office can provide brochures, maps, and information on nearby accommodations. However, you might have to secure a room outside the center or in a farmhouse if any large tours are in town, and to reach them, you'll probably need a car. Try **Zagorje Tourist Agency** at Zagrebačka 88 (© **049/301-580**) for that. The **Kumrovec Tourist Board** is at Cesta Lijepe Naša 6A (© **049/502-044;** www.kumrovec.hr). You can also try the **Krapina-Zagorje County Tourist Board** at Zagrebačka 2 (© **049/233-653**).

GETTING THERE You can see all three of the above sites in a day if you are driving or taking a guided excursion, but it will take longer if you are using public transport, which is available from Zagreb and other parts of Croatia. Several public buses per day serve Marija Bistrica from Zagreb, and two per day run to Kumrovec. To get to Veliki Tabor, however, you'll have to take one of eight buses to Desinič and walk almost 2 miles to the castle from the bus stop. See "Getting There & Getting Around," in "Orientation," for bus schedule contact information.

GETTING AROUND Once you reach your destination, walking or biking are the only ways to explore this area. You can drive up to Veliki Tabor, but you must park outside the limits of Staro Selo and explore the village on foot.

WHAT TO SEE & DO

It's possible to fashion a castle tour, a winery tour, or even a Croatian "culture" tour to include the numerous sites in the Zagorje and Međimurje regions in the northwest territory. It's difficult to do justice to these beautiful areas without your own transportation or a focused, organized tour, because while public transportation is available, the time spent in transit and making connections is out of proportion to the time you need to see some of the sites. In this region, some places are destinations, and others are momentary pauses along the way.

Church of the Ascension ✦ Go through Sopot on your way out of Veliki Tabor to visit this incongruously large, double-steepled, neoclassical church in the middle of tiny Pregrada; it is known as the Zagorje Cathedral. You'll be even more surprised at the large amount of gilt inside, especially the gold embellishments on the oversize organ, purchased from the Zagreb Cathedral in 1854 when Zagreb decided it was not loud enough for its Herman Bollé church.

In the center of town (Pregrada).

Kumrovec ✦✦✦ When you park your car and walk the few steps to Staro Selo, just 40km (25 miles) from Zagreb but deep in the heart of rural Zagorje, you'll think you're going to market: It seems as if half the village is stationed at tables at the entrance selling homemade cakes, wine, rakija, and other foodstuffs with touristy "Tito" labels pasted on them. These entrepreneurs are taking advantage of the heavy traffic flow that leads to the birthplace of the late President Josip Broz Tito, who successfully put his own brand of ad hoc Communism on the former Yugoslavia in the years following World War II until his death in 1980. Staro Selo's main attractions are 19th- and 20th-century cottages and farm buildings that have been restored to look exactly as they did when Tito was born there in 1892 and the effect is that of an open-air ethnographic museum whose centerpiece is an authentic re-creation of the interior and exterior of

Tito's childhood home done by the Zagreb Museum of Arts and Crafts. You can walk from building to building, including a memorabilia room, where documents and photographs from Tito's time in office are on display. You can also watch blacksmithing and candle-making demonstrations on weekends. Throughout, docents in period costume can supplement the information in the printed English captions on displays.

Staro Selo. ⓒ **049/553-107**. www.mdc.hr/kumrovec. Admission 20kn ($4). Apr–Sept daily 9am–7pm; Oct–Mar daily 9am–4pm.

Marija Bistrica 🎭🎭 Just 37km (23 miles) from Zagreb, the little town is a draw for pilgrims on religious tours as well as others who want to see the shrine where a "miraculous" 15th-century statue of the Virgin Mary sits on the main altar of the 19th-century Herman Bollé **Pilgrimage Church of St. Mary** off the town center. According to legend, the statue was hidden behind a brick wall in the 17th century to protect it from desecration. It stayed that way until its whereabouts were revealed by a ray of light. The statue survived a fire in the late 19th century, which enhanced its reputed connection with the supernatural. The church itself is less interesting inside than out because of the huge outdoor "altar" and open-air auditorium behind the building. The expansive outdoor facility was built to accommodate John Paul II's visit to Marija Bistrica in 1998, when he beatified favorite son Archbishop Alojzije Stepinac. There is also a **Way of the Cross** on **Calvary Hill** behind the auditorium, which pilgrims sometimes climb on their knees to do penance. The town itself is quite mundane, but there are several good pizzerias and konobas if you arrive at mealtime.

Marija Bistrica. www.svetiste-mmb.hr. The church is open for Mass and choir practice.

Museum of Peasant Uprisings   This rather dry but significant collection of documents and visuals chronicles the 16th-century revolt organized by the agrarian Catholic population against the Protestant Hapsburg landowners of the time. The landowners took every opportunity to push the labor and financial burdens of their pursuits on the peasant population. The exhibit, located in the former Orsić Palace a mile north of Gornja Stubica, includes a few weapons and other artifacts.

Samci 63–64, Gornja Stubica. ⓒ **049/587-880**. Fax 049/587-882. www.mdc.hr/msb/seljacka-buna.htm. Admission 20kn ($4). Apr–Sept daily 9am–7pm; Oct–Mar daily 9am–5pm.

Our Lady of the Snows 🎭   You'll have to negotiate a bumpy, narrow road to get to this church in the tiny village of Belec north of Marija Bistrica, and you might be disappointed when you see the church's unremarkable facade. However, inside, you'll find yourself blinking at the fussy baroque furnishings and colliding colors that are downright distracting for anyone who wants to pray. The church was built in the 16th century by a noblewoman after she heard about an apparition of the Virgin Mary in a nearby town. The church is enclosed by a wall that provides a more serene courtyard setting.

Belec. Sun 8–11am.

Veliki Tabor 🎭   From a distance, Veliki Tabor looks like an impregnable fortress built on the highest point in the area. However, the large crane and blue tarp protruding from the castle's roof signaled the serious repairs going on at this 12th-century behemoth when we visited in the summer of 2007. Veliki Tabor was closed to visitors for 7 months because of the nature of the construction work going on there, but it reopened in October 2007 after a $7 million renovation. The castle is easily accessible because visitors can drive right up to the castle entrance. The interior courtyard with

Veronika of Desinić

According to legend, Veronika of Desinić was a beautiful girl who lived in the village at the foot of Veliki Tabor during the 15th century. During that time, the castle was owned by Count Herman II of Celje, a powerful Croatian governor who had a son named Friederich. One day while out riding, Friederich spotted the lovely village maiden and fell madly in love at first sight. However, Herman didn't approve of the liaison and forbade his son to see the low-born Veronika. As the young are wont to do, the couple defied Herman and eloped, but their time together was short. When the count found out what Veronika and his son had done, he had his soldiers hunt them down. Friederich was captured immediately and whisked away to a solitary cell where he was imprisoned for 4 years. Veronika was not so lucky. The count's minions found her and had her brought to Veliki Tabor, where she was jailed and tried as a witch. The judges found Veronika guilty of nothing more sinister than love and ordered her set free. However, Herman was still miffed about being defied and he ordered his servants to drown Veronika in a bucket of water before she left the courtroom. He then had Veronika's body bricked into the walls of the castle's pentagonal tower. In 1982, a female skull was found behind a Veliki Tabor wall during renovation, but there is no proof that it is Veronika's. The skull now resides in the castle's chapel and it is said that on stormy winter nights, a woman's screams can be heard at the castle.

its three floors of colonnades is impressive, as are the restored rooms, among them a wine cellar museum and a first-floor chapel that holds a skull reportedly belonging to the castle's resident ghost. Cosmetic improvements are ongoing

Near Desinic. www.veliki-tabor.hr. 10kn ($2).

WHERE TO STAY

There aren't any big resorts or many hotels (except for those attached to the area's thermal spa centers) in northwest Croatia, and with few exceptions, facilities resemble hospital housing rather than relaxing resort accommodations. Northwest Croatia also has many privately owned castles and mansions and, until recently, most lay unoccupied in disrepair. However, a few entrepreneurs have been restoring some of these mansions and converting them into boutique hotels. Consequently, the list of small hotels, family-run pansions, private accommodations, agri-tourism opportunities—and even spas retrofitted with luxuries—is growing.

Terme Tuhelj   Excellent pool facilities are among the draws for weekenders and daytrippers who patronize this newly renovated spa/hotel about an hour north of Zagreb. As of summer 2007, only 46 of the 136 rooms had been updated to include air-conditioning and satellite TV, so be sure to ask for a "new" room, even though it costs a little more. Since a Slovenian company known for converting aging spas took over in 2005, Tuhelj pool facilities have been transformed to rival those at a water park. Sections of the sprawling pool are connected by a "river current" so swimmers can float from water slide to water guns to covered water effortlessly. Besides a hotel, spa facilities, and an adrenaline park, Tuhelj has a small restaurant and bar, but swimmers also have the option of walking uphill to the more elaborate **Dvorac Mihanović** ✦✦ for meals. Tuhelj is jammed on summer weekends and holidays and parking can be difficult.

Ljudevita Gaja 4, Tuhelj. ✆ 049/556-224. Fax 049/556-216. www.terme-tuhelj.hr. 136 units. Renovated units from 750kn ($110/53€) double. Rates include breakfast, children's programs, and use of pools. AE, DC, MC, V. **Amenities:** Restaurant; bar; cafe; disco; pools; sauna; salon; massage; fitness classes. *In room:* Some A/C, TV, minibar, dial-up Internet connection.

Pansion Zelenjak ✦✦ *(Finds)*

You'll feel as if you're in your own castle in the hills in this gorgeous little inn 3.2km (2 miles) south of Kumrovec. The mustard-yellow building, which houses comfortable rooms and the **Zelenjak Restaurant** ✦✦ that specializes in local fare and fish, is the essence of Zagorje style. The whole effect is one of serenity. A rock garden, a pond and waterfall, and the forest-green backdrop complete the picture from your room's window. The only drawback is that you need your own transportation to reach Zelenjak.

Risvica 1, Kumrovec. ✆ 049/550-747. www.zelenjak.com. 7 units. From 300kn ($56) double. Rates include breakfast. No credit cards. Half-board available. **Amenities:** Restaurant; terrace cafe. *In room:* TV.

Dvorac Bežanec ✦

This country mansion is one of the finest privately owned homes in Croatia. It was built in the 17th century and underwent a complete restoration and conversion into a hotel from 1990 to 1999 after serving as an orphanage, a farm, a furniture shop, and a meat-processing plant. In its current incarnation, Dvorac Bežanec is a one-of-a-kind hotel with everything from tennis courts and hot-air balloon rides to archery and a small deer park. Except for the magnificent open-air courtyard, which is used for dining (the hotel's **Bežanec Restaurant** ✦✦ is excellent) and special events, the hotel's offbeat public rooms are chockablock with the owner's collection of Croatian artifacts and furniture, all of which coexist in planned clutter that spans the years since the hotel was built. The most current—and most impressive—display is made up of hundreds of original paintings and drawings (many of them naive art and all of it for sale). Guest rooms look like boudoir sets from a 1930s German movie and seem out of sync with the very modern bathrooms, but the effect is museum-chic. Bežanec is not for everyone, but it can be an acquired taste for those who want to experience Croatian kitsch.

Valentinovo bb, Pregrada. ✆ 049/376-800. Fax 049/376-810. www.bezanec.hr. 24 units. Doubles from 300kn 81€ ($100); suites from 450kn ($145/121€). Rates include breakfast. AE, DC, MC, V. Pets allowed. **Amenities:** Restaurant; wine cellar; tennis court; billiards room; lower-level nightclub; bicycle/moped rental; gallery excursions; zoo. *In room:* TV, radio, hair dryer.

Seljački Turizam Trsek

A farmhouse stay here includes fresh air, locally grown food, long walks in nature, and a lot of farm animals. The restaurant specializes in Zagorje dishes and uses a lot of "found" objects in its decor, including tables made of wine barrels. This is agri-tourism at its most authentic.

Trnovec Desinièki 23, Desineć. ✆ 049/343-464. www.trsek.hr. 6 units. From 245kn ($45) double. Rate includes breakfast. No credit cards. **Amenities:** Restaurant. *In room:* TV.

WHERE TO DINE

There is no shortage of restaurants in the Zagorje area, though most are very small, family-run affairs. Wherever you stop, it's almost impossible to get a bad meal, especially if you stick to local specialties.

Dvorac Mihanović ⭐⭐ REGIONAL Dvor means "castle" in Croatian, but the term is often loosely applied to manor houses (many of which are closed to the public) scattered in the Zagorje Hills. Mihanović is one of the exceptions. Inside this soft yellow building, the dining room is filled with crystal and dark wood as well as suits of armor and other doodads typical of the old aristocracy. Mihanović's menu is entirely in Croatian, and the cuisine is typically Zagorje (grilled meat, turkey *mlincima,* peasant plate of pork and veggies), but some dishes are vegetable-driven and designated "healthy" for those who are at Terme Tuhelj to shape up.

Ljudevita Gaja 6, Tuheljske Toplice. ℂ **049/556-214.** Fax 049/556-216. www.terme-tuhelj.hr. Entrees 40kn–70kn ($7–$12). AE, DC, MC, V. Daily 7am–midnight.

Bežanec (Pregrada) ⭐⭐ *Value* INTERNATIONAL Gourmet dining is the focus of Bežanec, the classy restaurant in its namesake hotel. The formal dining room exudes old-world formality, while courtyard tables are surrounded by flowers and open to the Zagorje sky. Hotel Bežanec specializes in the unusual, and the restaurant is no exception. Try the five-course tasting menu or choose such delicacies as ostrich in coconut sauce from the day's specials, and top it off with Bežanec's version of *štrukli.* Diners can choose a great bottle from a remarkable wine cellar stocked with Croatian and international wines.

Valentinovo bb. ℂ **049/376-800.** Fax 049/376-810. www.bezanec.hr. Entrees 50kn–130kn ($9–$23). 10% discount for cash. AE, DC, MC, V. 24 hr.

Zelenjak ⭐⭐ *Finds* REGIONAL CROATIAN Serving traditional Zagorje specialties has been a family business since 1936 at Zelenjak. Veal with mushrooms, cream, and cheese baked in a wooden stove originally used to bake bread *(Odrezak zapecen u Krusnoj peci)* is the restaurant's signature dish. Local wines are featured. Outside are playground, sports, and garden areas to keep the kids busy so parents can dine in peace. The restaurant has both a regular dining room with a winter garden and a larger facility that can accommodate crowds.

Risivica 1, Kumrovec. ℂ **049/550-747.** Fax 049/550-221. www.zelenjak.com. Entrees 40kn–60kn ($7-$11) with signature desserts such as štrukli at 15kn ($3). AE, DC, MC. Daily 8am–11pm.

Grešna Gorica ⭐ REGIONAL CROATIAN You get more than a meal when you travel to Grešna Gorica, less than a mile from Veliki Tabor and about 56km (35 miles) from Zagreb. Besides its rustic setting in the woods and its country decor, Grešna Gorica has a complement of barnyard animals and old farm implements (including antique winepresses) to add to the rural ambience. The menu continues the theme with simple Zagorje specials made with local produce and meat. Homemade sausages and cheeses, house-smoked ham, and Zagorje *štrukli* are among the offerings you can sample here. If you drive up to the restaurant, be aware that parking there is very limited. Most people park at the bottom of the hill on the road leading to Grešna Gorica and walk up a very steep path.

Desinić. ℂ **049/343-001.** Fax 049/343-001. www.gresna-gorica.com. Entrees 42kn–84kn ($8–$15). No credit cards. Daily(except during snowstorms) 10am–whenever the last guest leaves.

8 Trakošćan, Krapina, Lepoglava & Ludbreg

There are many interesting side trips possible along the road between Varaždan and Trakošćan. The sights require a few detours and perhaps venturing onto winding back roads, but they help complete the picture of the real Croatia.

ESSENTIALS

VISITOR INFORMATION   Information, maps, and lists of events in these three locations can be obtained at Varaždin's **Tourist Association** (p. 306).

GETTING THERE   Buses and trains serve both Krapina and Lepoglava, but there are no direct public buses from Zagreb to Trakošćan. However, even if you don't have your own transport, you can access Trakošćan by taking a bus to Varaždin and backtracking to Trakošćan.

GETTING AROUND   As with most sites in Croatia, walking is the method of choice for seeing these sites.

WHAT TO SEE

Majestic **Trakošćan Castle** is the main draw in this part of northern Croatia, but there are several towns worth exploring in this region.

Krapina's claim to fame involves the remains of a Neanderthal settlement discovered in the hills between Zagreb and Slovenia in 1899 by Dragutin Gorjanović Kramberger. Kramberger discovered more than 900 fossilized human bones—collectively known as Krapina Man—in caves on Hušnjakovo Hill, just west of the city. According to anthropologists' accounts, these remains belonged to around two dozen Neanderthals, thought to have lived 50,000 to 80,000 years ago. A museum with mock-ups of the famous prehistoric find is located just below the site where the originals were found, but construction of a new facility is under way. Entry is 10kn ($2). The museum is open 9am to 3pm Monday to Friday in summer, 8am to 3pm in winter.

Nineteen kilometers (12 miles) northeast of Krapina on the road between Varaždin and Trakošćan, the town of **Lepoglava** is best known as the site of Croatia's largest prison, and perhaps that single association is unfair. Since its beginning in the late 14th century and until the end of the 19th, Lepoglava was home to a Paulist monastery complex that also was a center of science, culture, education, and art—a reputation it earned when it was home to one of Croatia's first grammar schools and one of its first universities. The Paulist order in Croatia was disbanded by Austrian Emperor Joseph II in the mid–19th century. Shortly after that, the monks' cells were converted to prison cells where many Croatian patriots (Josip Broz Tito, Alojzije Stepinac, Franj Tuđman) were detained, mostly for political reasons. Another, more modern prison was built behind the monastery and still is in use though it is separated from the monastery by a wall. Lepoglava is also known as a center of lacemaking; its lace once was exported to the affluent European market and used in the fashions of the times. Today, Lepoglava still has a Lace Society, which hosts an International Lace Festival in early October. The Lepoglava Tourist Office is at Trg 1 Hrvatskog Sveučilišta 3 (© **042/791-190;** fax 042/791-389. www.lepoglava.hr).

Trakošćan Castle ✿✿   Trakošćan may be one of northern Croatia's most visited sites. As you approach it on the gravel switchback path to the entrance, it looks quite stately. Soaring white-and-yellow stone walls, red-tile capped turrets, a drawbridge, and palatial grounds create a fairy-tale illusion around the fortress, built in the 13th century. Trakošćan has seen hard times and gone through many owners since, the last being Juraj Drašković, who used the castle as a country getaway. Croatia's government took over the property after World War II and, in 1953, Trakošćan was opened to public

Hilltop Wonders

Croatia is world renowned for its beautiful Adriatic seacoast. Less known is the treasure trove of mountaintop castles scattered throughout the country. You can find castles in every part of Croatia, from Dalmatia to Istria to Zagorje (area north and west of Zagreb) and Slavonia. Most are in various stages of ruin while some have been restored. All of them are fascinating both historically and architecturally – no two castles are the same – and all have spectacular views of the surrounding countryside.

Most Croatian castles served not only as medieval residences but also as fortresses. They were built in the 12th or 13th centuries to defend against the Tartars (Mongols). In the 16th century they were expanded and refortified as bulwarks against the Ottoman Turk invasions. The Turks succeeded in capturing many of the castles, but some were so inaccessible or impenetrable that they held out. Still others experienced much fighting and changed hands several times. By the 17th century, advances in military technology had rendered castle fortresses obsolete. Besides, by that time noble ladies were refusing to live any longer in isolated, damp, drafty stone castles. So those not destroyed in battle were abandoned in favor of more luxurious, comfortable manor houses in the valleys.

There are approximately 200 visible castle/fortress ruins in Croatia. Unfortunately most of them are rather inaccessible and difficult to find. Usually there are no directional signs. **Medvedgrad** is neither—it's clearly visible from downtown Zagreb about a third of way up the slopes of Sljeme, the mountain just north of the city. It has been partially restored, some would say not according to historical records. There is a cafe/restaurant and a memorial to fallen Croatian soldiers. Nevertheless, the view of Zagreb to the south and west is very good and the grounds are worth exploring. The castle has a colorful, checkered history. Zagreb's Bishop Filip built the fortress in the 13th century, after King Bela IV granted him a deed authorizing its construction. The fortress had great strategic significance. It could be easily defended during times of war, and it was situated near the western border of the Hungarian-Croatian state. During the seven centuries after its construction, Medvedgrad had a total of 107 owners.

To reach the castle drive or take bus no. 102, which runs between Britanski Trg and Mihaljevac, and get off at the "Blue Church" in Šestine. Then take the paved road that runs up past the church cemetery toward the mountain. After you pass a restaurant on the right-hand side of the road, if you are walking, look for trail no. 12 going up into the forest on the left side of the road. The hike up from the bus stop takes 35-45 minutes and is moderately steep in places. You can also drive to the castle in about ten minutes on the paved road.

Courtesy of Tocher Mitchell

tours. Today, Trakošcan is still an imposing sight on its hill in Zagorje, but the exterior restoration is far more impressive than the improvements behind its walls. In fact, some of what's inside is downright tacky, though that doesn't mean the displays aren't worth seeing. The first floor is faithful to the 19th century, with period furniture, lots of wood, and portraiture. On higher floors, you'll find crude ancient weaponry, a mish-mash of furniture, walls with exposed patches of original wallpaper, and a couple of original tapestries. Note that each room has a unique, fed-from-behind stove, some with very ornate carvings. Also, among the dour, dark, and not particularly well-done portraits, a few by Julijana Erdody stand out as better than average. Unfortunately, that assessment doesn't apply to the painting techniques used on the walls. Heavy-handed *trompe l'oeil* and sponge-painting attempt to re-create period wallpaper designs, and the result is puzzling and bizarre. Trakošcan has much that is worth seeing, and a lot that destroys its restoration credibility.

© 042/796-422. www.trakoscan.hr. Admission 20kn ($4) adults, 10kn ($2) children. Apr–Sept daily 8am–6pm; Oct–March daily 9am–4pm.

Trakošcan Park ✿✿✿   The grounds in the immediate vicinity of Trakošcan Castle offer visitors a variety of activities in addition to Sunday afternoon strolls and picnics. Nearby Rava Gora offers good gusts and jumping-off points for paragliders, while rock climbers find the sheer cliffs challenging. Hikers and cyclers can scramble over miles of trails, and fishing enthusiasts can try their luck in the lake below the castle. Hunting still is a passion in this part of Croatia. The nearby Diana Hunting Grounds and lodge provide opportunities for gun enthusiasts in search of boar, deer, and game birds.

Adjacent to Trakošcan Castle.

WHERE TO STAY AND DINE

Motel Coning ✿   This modern (but bland) hotel within walking distance of Trakošcan Castle attracts tour buses and day-trippers who decide to stay over. Guest rooms are fine, though nothing special. A gaggle of exercise options helps you get the kinks out after a day of touring medieval towers.

Trakošcan 5, Trakošcan. © 042/796-224. Fax 042/796-205. www.coning.hr. 80 units. From 92€ ($110) double. AE, DC, MC, V. Parking. **Amenities:** Restaurant; bar; tennis courts; sauna; gym. *In room:* TV.

Hotel Raj ✿✿ *Value*   Guest rooms in this pink, flower-bedecked mansion across the road from the Holy Blood Chapel are just like home, with comfy beds and private bathrooms with showers. Situated in the southeast part of town, the hotel is walking distance to Ludbreg's center and its main attractions.

Alojzija Stepinca 2, Ludbreg. © 042/306-377. Fax 042/306-378. www.hotel-raj.com. 13 units. From 320kn ($55) double; from 400kn ($70) suite. Rates include breakfast. Half- and full board available. AE, DC, MC, V. **Amenities:** Restaurant. *In room:* A/C, TV, minibar.

Pivnica Mejaši ✿ CROATIAN   Loosely translated, Mejaši means "next door neighbor" and the pleasant eatery is next door to St. Joseph Church, where the origi-nal Ludbreg medallion resides. You'll find locals filling both the indoor and outdoor tables any time of day enjoying a beer or regional dishes like *suhi govedski jezici* (dried beef tongue), *srneći paprikaš* (venison paprikash), *dimljena prgica* (soft cheese smoked in the attic), or just an ordinary pizza.

Trg Sv. Trojstva 27. Ludbreg. © 042/810-510. Entrees 19kn–40kn ($4–$8); pizzas 20kn ($4) for a small to 60kn ($11) for a large. No credit cards. Sun–Fri 8am–11pm and Sat 8am–2am.

9 Varaždin

Eighteenth-century churches, houses, and public buildings are just some of the charms that make baroque Varaždin a popular excursion from Zagreb. **Stari Grad** ✺✺✺ is Varaždin's magnificent 12th-century castle and the centerpiece of any visit to the former Croatian capital, which today is one of northern Croatia's main cultural and economic centers. Varaždin owes its baroque character and its title of "Baroque Capital of Croatia" to an unfortunate 1776 fire that destroyed most of the town, though not its historic center—a tragedy the town turned to advantage when the ruined buildings were rebuilt as they appear today.

Trg Kralija Tomislava is Varaždin's main square and lined with the best baroque facades in town, which are conveniently identified with plaques that explain their lineage. Start at the 15th-century **Town Hall (Gradska Vijećnica),** with its 18th-century clock tower. Go south to the **Cathedral of the Assumption** ✺, the town's first baroque building. The cathedral was built in the mid–18th century by the Jesuits, who also built a monastery and other buildings in Varaždin. Just outside the Cathedral, you'll find **Herzer Palace (Dvor Herzer)** and the **Varaždin Insect Museum (Entomološki Odjel)** ✺✺, which has especially interesting displays of butterflies. There are other pleasing buildings and museums to visit in Varaždin, but Stari Grad is unquestionably the town's top attraction.

ESSENTIALS

VISITOR INFORMATION   Varaždin's **Tourist Association** is at Ivana Padovca 3 (© **042/210-987;** 049/210-985; www.tourism-varazdin.hr). The office is open April 15 through September 15 from 8am to 6pm Monday through Friday; from 9am to 1pm Saturday; and from 10am to 6pm Sunday. From September 16 through April 14, they are open from 8am to 4pm Monday through Friday; from 10am to 1pm Saturday; closed Sunday.

The very helpful and friendly office not only distributes maps, brochures, and suggestions about dining and accommodations in town, but they also have information about the entire area, including Međimurje to the north.

T-Tours at Ivana Gundulića 2 (© **042/200-991;** fax 042/210-990; www.t-tours.hr) puts together packages for day or overnight tours of Varaždin, Trakošćan, Ludbreg, or Međimurje. Packages include transport, museum tickets, and sometimes meals, rooms, or a wine tasting.

GETTING THERE   Varaždin is about an hour's drive northeast from Zagreb along well-marked highway. The town is also linked to the capital by frequent bus service (26 per day) and train service (14 per day).

GETTING AROUND   Varaždin's central district is a pedestrian area, so you'll have to park on the outskirts of Trg Ban Jelačića north of the sights and walk in. Stari Grad (castle) is a 5-minute walk from the center of town.

WHAT TO SEE & DO

Besides its stunning architecture, Varaždin has several good museums and interesting churches. Restoration is ongoing, but Varaždin is visitor-friendly, with plenty of historical and directional information as well as a large number of cafes, restaurants, and shops. The only drawback is the dearth of accommodations in the center of town.

Cathedral of the Assumption ✺✺   The cathedral originally was a combination church and gymnasium (school). It was built by the Jesuits in 1647 and its exterior was designed in the baroque style typical of the Society of Jesus of the time. Inside, you can see an elaborate altar with lots of gilt, statues, and marble columns backed by a painting of the Virgin's Assumption into Heaven as well as frescoes and woodcarvings. Because of its great acoustics, many concerts scheduled during **Varaždin's Baroque Evenings** are held here.

Pavlinska 5. (℃) **042/320-180.** Mon–Sat 9am–6pm; Sun for Masses (9am, 11am, 6pm).

Insect Museum (Entomološki Muzej) 𝕒𝕒 You can't visit Varaždin and not investigate the World of Insects display, an unusual collection of bugs and butterflies housed on the main floor of the baroque **Herczer Palace.** The extensive collection was donated by museum founder Franjo Košćec and dates to 1954. The museum includes 4,500 exhibits of central European insects, nests, habitats, models, and photographs, all of which are well-captioned and attractively presented.

Franjevački Trg 6. (℃) **042/210-474.** Admission 10kn ($2). Summer daily 10am–5pm daily. Winter Tues–Fri 10am–3pm; Sat 10am–1pm. Closed Mon.

Stari Grad 𝕒𝕒𝕒 Stari Grad is not only Varaždin's best attraction, it is also the town's cultural repository. It was designed in the mid–16th century by Domenico Dell'Allio as a defensive complex and it was used as a fortress against invading Turks. The Gothic/Renaissance compound was privately owned until 1925, when it became a museum. Today Stari Grad is one of the best-designed showcases of Croatian history in the nation, and a must-see for anyone who visits Zagreb and the Croatian interior. From the outside, Stari Grad almost looks like a group of medieval cluster homes, a solid block of white stone walls of various heights and rounded red-roofed towers. Inside the walls, courtyards, and arched walkways give the buildings a softer look and lead to eight rooms that house exhibits of aristocratic interiors and artifacts, all accompanied by marvelous explanations. The Varaždin **Town Museum** is also housed here. Multilingual docents are stationed throughout the building, ready to help anyone who wants further details about what he or she is seeing or who is interested in Varaždin lore.

Šetalište J.J. Strossmayera 7 (℃) **042/212-918.** Fax 049/310-519. Admission 20kn ($4) adults, 12kn ($2) children and retirees. Tues–Fri 10am–3pm; Sat–Sun 10am–1pm. Closed Mon.

Town Hall 𝕒 Varaždin's Town Hall is notable more for its exterior than for what's inside. The building's combination of Gothic and 18th-century stonework occupies a prominent position on the main square and it is a good meeting place or orientation point for visitors. From 10am to noon on Saturdays from May to October there is an added visual element: Guards in bright blue period uniforms stand outside the building.

In the center of town.

Town Cemetery 𝕒 This arboretum cum cemetery provides cooling respite after a day of touring the city's baroque treasures. Notable residents are few, but many varieties of the 7,000 cedars, maples, ash trees, red beeches, box trees, magnolias, and birches planted there starting in 1905 are rare.

West of Varaždin Castle (500m/500 yards). No phone. Free admission. May–Sept 7am–9pm; March–Apr 7am–8pm; Jan, Feb, Nov 7am–7pm.

WHERE TO STAY

Varaždin accommodations are mostly in pansions and private homes, though there is a fairly modern hotel within a few blocks of the town center and others on the town's periphery.

Hotel Varaždin 🏨🏨 This new entry (summer 2007) to the Varaždin hotel scene is a welcome addition. Not only does it expand accommodations choices, but it also is the only hotel in Varaždin's center. Guest rooms are comfortably sized and showers all have turbo spray. Hotel Varaždin isn't fancy, but it is a step up in convenience.

Kolodvorska 19. © **042/290-720.** Fax 042/201-916. www.hotelvarazdin.com. 27 units. Doubles from 600kn ($111). Rates include breakfast. **Amenities:** Restaurant; bar; pool; tennis court; Internet access; safe rental. *In room:* A/C, SAT/TV, minibar, hair dryer.

Hotel Turist Function triumphs over form in this generic block-style hotel half a mile from the town center. Most guest rooms are small and without personality, but the hotel is undergoing a long-term renovation and not all the rooms have been updated. Ask for one that has been redone. The Turist is increasing its list of amenities and adding excursions that cater to fishermen and hunters. (Kennels for hunting dogs are on the premises.) It will also offer guided mushroom hunts in the fall as well as food and wine events.

Aleja Kralja Zvonimira 1. © **042/395-395.** www.hotel-turist.hr. 104 units. From 500kn ($90) double. AE, DC, MC, V. Parking. **Amenities:** Restaurant; bar; disco; salon; excursions. *In room:* TV, minibar.

Pansion Garestin 🏨 Guest rooms are small and spartan in this little guesthouse. The restaurant serves wonderful fish and grilled meat dishes both in its meticulously turned-out dining room and on its lovely covered terrace.

Zagrebačka 34. © **042/214-314.** www.gastrocom.hr. 13 units. From 350kn ($60) double. Rates include breakfast. AE, DC, MC, V. Parking. **Amenities:** Restaurant. *In room:* A/C, TV, minibar.

WHERE TO DINE

Zlatna Guska 🏨🏨 REGIONAL CROATIAN Heraldry is the theme at Zlatna Guska (Golden Goose) restaurant in what once was the Inquisition Room on the lower level of a Zagorje palace. The stone walls and ceilings are covered with coats of arms belonging to the region's prominent families; dishes are named after them, too. Try the pork medallions St. Hebert, or the Bukan Buccaneers filet (a chicken breast stuffed with shrimp and covered with dill sauce). Service is accommodating. The wine list is filled with Croatian standards. Zlatna Guska is a perennial on Croatia's list of the 100 best restaurants in the country.

Jurija Habdelka 4. © **042/213-393.** Fax 042/200-377. Reservations recommended. Entrees 30kn–90kn ($5–$15). AE, DC, MC, V. Daily 8am–midnight.

Park 🏨🏨 REGIONAL CROATIAN As its name suggests, the Park is surrounded by greenery and flowers because its terrace opens to Varaždin's municipal gardens. This is an especially nice restaurant in summer, when you can dine outside on a variety of grilled meats or salads. Try a glass of local Grazevina (white wine) with the Varaždin Salad, a version of Waldorf salad with chicken.

J. Habdelića 6. © **042/211-499.** Fax 042/211-466. www.gastrocom.hr/park.htm. Entrees 35kn–100kn ($6–$17). AE, DC, MC, V. Daily 8am–11pm.

Kavana Korzo 🏨🏨 PASTRY Elaborate little cakes and coffee provide delightful treats at this Viennese-style cafe where old-world formality is the norm. The rolling pastry cart makes the experience authentic, though when things get crowded in summer, the cafe tosses out the rules and moves tables onto the square.

Trg Kralja Tomislava 2. © **042/390-914.** Pastries 10kn–40kn ($2–$7). AE, DC, MC, V. Daily 8am–11pm.

10 Međimurje

Međimurje is sometimes called the "flower garden of Croatia," not just because of its fertile land but because of its cultural, historical, and economic contributions to the nation's heritage. The region lies northeast of Varaždin and makes up the extreme northern part of Croatia where it borders Slovenia and Hungary. Međimurje's western half is characterized by gently rolling hills, vineyards, and orchards; in the east, flat, fertile farmland contributes a large portion of the country's grain and vegetable production.

The town of Čakovec is just 92km (55 miles) from Zagreb and it is Međimurje's largest population center. Međimurje's baronial 17th-century castle and exceptional Secessionist-style union building are quickly being eclipsed by a slickly updated town square ringed by lots of stores, restaurants, and bars. The square is enhanced by a conversation-piece fountain that spits arching streams of lighted water at night. But despite the town's new veneer, there still are many treasures waiting for discovery.

ESSENTIALS

VISITOR INFORMATION The **Tourist Board of Međimurje County** in Čakovec at R. Boškovića 3 (© **040/390-191;** www.tzm.hr) can provide you with a well-done map tracing Međimurje's wine road and points of interest. The map also indicates wineries where you can stop to taste or buy local vintages. You can get much of the same information at the **Čakovec Tourist Office** at Trg Kralja Tomislava 2 (© **040/313-319;** www.tourism-cakovec.hr).

GETTING THERE There are frequent bus and train services to Čakovec from Zagreb, plus one daily train to Budapest, but if you want to explore the wine road and areas in rural Međimurje, it is best to have your own transportation. Alternatively, people in the tourism office can arrange wine road tours. *Warning:* Međimurje's wineries are all family operations, so it is best to make arrangements in advance to ensure that vintners will be on premises when you arrive. For bus information, see "Orientation," earlier in this chapter.

GETTING AROUND Walking is the best way to tour Čakovec, but if you want to see any of rural Međimurje, you'll need a car and a good map.

WHAT TO SEE & DO

The Međimurje region is one of Croatia's most underrated treasures, virtually ignored by tourists and untouched by the 1991 war. In the northwestern corner of Međimurje County, you can meander around hilly, winding roads that end in family wineries of varying sizes. Međimurje is a place where you can walk the land with its owner and taste the wine he made there. This is where you can sit on the deck of a hilltop restaurant and see Slovenia, Hungary, and Austria (and sometimes the hills of the Czech Republic) beyond the restaurant's Croatian vineyard. **Međimurje's wine road** is a relatively new feature in the area, though many of the wineries listed on the vina cesta map have been there for generations. However, the county is now promoting its assets to tourists. You can stop at any of the wineries on the map, and you'll be offered a glass of wine and the opportunity to buy a bottle or two. In some cases, the wine tasting is more formal, but this is like being in Napa, California, before it became popular. (Pick up a map to the wineries at the Čakovec or Štrigova tourist offices.)

There is an order to things in Međimurje that isn't evident anywhere else in Croatia. People follow the tempo of planting and harvest times and they seem more in tune with nature than people in any other part of the country. Once you fall in step with the flow of things, you get it.

Dom Sindikata ⊕⊕   As an example of Secessionist architecture, this salmon-and-white building off the town center has no peers. It now houses the offices of the local workers' union and can't be ignored, as it is unlike anything else in Čakovec.

Trg Kralja Tomislava, Čakovec.

Muzej Meðimurja Čakovec ⊕   The original castle on this site at the edge of town was destroyed by a 1738 earthquake. The castle that stands in its place was built in the 18th century by Czech nobles. Many of the "New Castle's" 16th-century walls are still standing. The current baroque structure houses the Museum of Meðimurje, which opened in 1954. Displays include local costumes, paintings, and stone tombstones and sculpture, all from the region. The castle itself is currently undergoing renovation, so access is limited.

Trg Republike 5, Čakovec. ℂ 042/313-499. Admission 15kn ($3) adults, 12kn ($2) children. Tues–Fri 10am–3pm; Sat–Sun 10am–noon. Closed Mon.

St. Jerome Church ⊕⊕⊕   Štrigova is home to this baroque beauty, which was built by Paulist monks in the mid–18th century. The building fell into disuse during Tito's time, and it was roofless and full of chickens as recently as the 1970s. Currently, restoration is under way and access to the church is by appointment only. A visit is worth the phone call to the Strigova tourist office and the long climb up a steep staircase because inside you'll see the results of modern restoration and at least three partially recovered Ivan Ranger frescoes. There once was a commonly held belief that St. Jerome, a Bible translator, was born in Štrigova, and Pope Nicholas V continued that belief by issuing indulgences to anyone who made a pilgrimage there.

WHERE TO STAY

Accommodations in Meðimurje are mostly private, with some hotels attached to spas. This is a wonderful area to try a farmhouse stay.

Pansion Monika ⊕ (Value)   This six-room pansion in the Meðimurje wine country is the ideal place to use as a base for winery touring or as a place to crash after dinner at Dvorac Terbotz. The rooms above Monika's coffee shop/bar are immaculate. Each has access to a balcony with table and chairs for vineyard gazing. Rooms are available with breakfast, full board, or neither.

Železna Gora 183, Štrigova. ℂ 040/851-304. 6 units. From 240kn ($45) double. Rates include breakfast. www. apartmani-hrvatska.com/osobna.asp?BR=3583. No credit cards. Parking lot. **Amenities:** Restaurant; semi-private balconies. *In room:* A/C, TV, bidet.

Toplice Sveti Martin ⊕⊕   The spa's Apartment Village Regina opened to great fanfare in June 2005. The complex added a large block of economical condo-type accommodations that look like Colorado ski-country digs with living room, kitchenette, and pullout couch in addition to two beds, though some units are even larger. Think upgraded sports camp. Sveti Martin looks as if it is trying to be a full service resort with a variety of programs geared to weight loss, anti-aging, anti-cellulite, and general fitness. Most spa services are extra and can be purchased a la carte. Available special-interest tours include winery tours, hiking excursions, and hunting trips. Just-plain-relaxation vacations are also available. The complex itself is a village with shops,

Dragons and Devils

Dragons (*pozoj*) and devils are synonymous in the Međimurje, where tales of the scary beasts abound: There is one about a green pozoj from Čakovic that causes earthquakes and natural disasters, a black pozoj from Sv. Juraj na Bregu, that supposedly was killed by St. George, and a folk legend about a pit in Donja Dubrava where a *pozoj* (the devil) supposedly lives. The Donja Dubrava pozoj is closely associated with the mouths of three rivers, the Drava, the Mura, and the Trnava. The legend also mentions *kače*, serpents with 9 tails and heads that turn into princes if their wishes are fulfilled.

restaurants, and a market, which is good because most packages here are geared to 5- and 8-day stays, though one-night rates are available.

Grkaveščak bb, Sveti Martin na Muri. © 040/371-111. Fax 040/371-171. www.toplicesvetimartin.hr. 84 units. From 6,600kn, ($122/97€) double. Rates include buffet breakfast. AE, DC, MC, V. Parking. **Amenities:** 2 restaurants; pizzeria; pub; pools; sports facilities; aqua park; salon; massage; excursions. *In room:* A/C, TV, hair dryer, balcony/terrace.

WHERE TO DINE

Dining in Međimurje is always a treat, especially when you can pair fresh-off-the-farm foods with fresh-from-the-winery vintages. This is the ideal place to indulge in local specialties because the odds are they come from the restaurant's backyard.

Mala Hiza 🐥🐥🐥 *Finds* REGIONAL CROATIAN   In our opinion, Mala Hiza (little house) is one of the finest Croatian restaurants in the country. The building itself is an 1887 structure that once stood outside Zagreb. Thankfully, in 2002 owner Branimir Tomašić had the vision to dismantle and reassemble it in the village of Mačkovec, 4km (2.5 miles) outside Čakovic. He then surrounded it with a knock-out garden, created a Croatian interior with lots of wood, stone, and artifacts, and began serving guests a menu full of creative interpretations of regional Croatian cuisine. You can start with 3 kinds of kulen from Slavonia, proceed to turkey roulade with chestnut puree, Dalmatian prsut, and sour cherry sauce, and complement the lot with thumb-size portions of heavenly gnocchi stuffed with cheese and spinach. Or you can experiment with ostrich medallions smothered with mushrooms, green pepper, and cranberries. For dessert, try *zlevanka*, a special dessert of cornmeal cake topped with walnuts and poppyseed. A huge selection of off-menu old-time Croatian dishes and peka-cooked meats is available with notice, and the wine list is a showcase for Međimurje vintners. Service is delightfully helpful and friendly, and there is a well-protected nonsmoking section, a rarity in Croatia.

Mačkovec 107, Čakovec. © 040/341-101. www.mala-hiza.hr. Entrees 35kn–210kn ($6.50–$39). AE, DC, MC, V. Daily 9am–11pm.

Dvorac Terbotz 🐥🐥 REGIONAL CROATIAN   Just 5km (3 miles) from the Slovenian border, this restaurant is located in an elegant, renovated 18th-century mansion. Here you can sample wines from local producers and eat impeccably prepared local specialties. Try *cigansko pečenje*, spicy roast pork with roasted potatoes; or *sarma* with game, cranberries, and potato purée. Don't miss *Međimurska gebanica* for dessert. That's a cake made of layers of apples, walnuts, cheese, and poppy seeds. Terbotz is loaded with local dishes like these. Besides the food and the wine-tasting room, Terbotz has dining on its deck overlooking the restaurant's vineyards. On a clear day you can see Slovenia, Hungary, and Austria. Terbotz is in the process of adding pansion-style rooms.

Železna Gora 113, Štrigova. © **040/857-444**. Fax 040/857-445. www.terbotz.hr. Entrees 38kn–85kn ($6–$15). AE, DC, MC, V. Mon–Sat 11am–1am; Sun 11am–1pm.

Katarina ✿ REGIONAL CROATIAN   Located in the center of town in a historic cellar underneath the Millennium Shopping Center, Katarina turns out excellent grilled meat dishes and local specialties prepared from age-old recipes. The cellar's red-brick arches and heraldry-inspired decor create a nice backdrop for taste treats such as beef roulade or poached pears with cherry sauce. The restaurant has a good selection of locally produced wines.

Matice Hrvatske 6, Čakovec. © **040/311-990**. Entrees 35kn–90kn ($6–$16). AE, DC, MC, V. Daily 10am–11pm.

11

Inland Croatia

Tourists anticipating a trip to Croatia rarely include the regions east of Zagreb in their plans. That's too bad because frequently their reasons are based on misinformation or lack of accurate details. It is true that many of the towns between Zagreb and the country's eastern border on the Danube were battlegrounds during the 1991 war. And it is true that some of those towns have not completely recovered from the devastation. However, for anyone who tracks more than the brightest blips on the tourism radar screen, this delightfully relaxed area is a mother lode of experiences and attractions steeped in history and tradition.

If you are inclined to cross inland Croatia off your "places to visit" list because it doesn't offer the glitzy Dalmation beaches, exotic islands, or romantic ports of call that get most of Croatia marketing kunas, you could be missing out on a rich experience. Or, if you nix this region because you assume it lacks attractions comparable to Istria's knockout restaurants, Zagreb's lively nightlife, or Plitvice's stunning beauty, you could be passing on the opportunity to become acquainted with authentic, grassroots Croatia.

Inland Croatia is home to a collection of unique natural wonders, historic sites, and gastronomic delights capable of wowing even the most experienced traveler. If you go there, you can walk through Čigoć, a village in the Lonjsko Polje Nature Park where whole families of storks nonchalantly regard you from their mammoth nests atop centuries-old timber cottages. You can visit solemn Jasenovac and its

poignant monument to victims of World War II's ethnic violence and feel the sadness in the air. On the road to Đakovo, you can gawk at the horizon where redbrick bell towers of the Cathedral of St. Peter rise in the distance above acres of yellow sunflowers for miles before you get to town. In Osijek, you can take a turn around the promenade along the mighty Drava, walk the perimeter of the city along the top of what's left of the medieval walls surrounding the Old City, and smile at the ornate gewgaws that decorate the Austro-Hungarian mansions along Europska Avenue. It's almost a certainty that you'll cringe at the devastation still visible in Vukovar and you'll shake your head at the unspeakable cruelty that the town's citizens suffered when you visit the touching memorial to victims of a 1991 hospital massacre there. In Ilok, you'll feel exhilaration when you walk 30m (100 ft.) into the Earth to see the second-oldest winery in Europe. Its owners will tell you how they frantically bricked in bottles of the best vintages to save them from invading Serbs during the Homeland war. Then you can taste history in a glass of golden liquid poured from those precious bottles.

Inland Croatia isn't Las Vegas excitement or Disneyland illusion. It isn't an all-inclusive package of hedonistic services or an adrenalin rush of physical tests. Rather, inland Croatia's rewards are more subtle and lasting than frolicking in the sea or playing roulette.

This infrequently traveled region is the sum of all the "ah-ha!" moments that happen as you imagine the horror of war while gazing across the Danube at Serbia from a bluff in Ilok. It is the light bulb that goes off in your head while you stroll through Bjelovar's Norman Rockwell–perfect town square or as you stroke the soft gray muzzle of a horse at Đakovo's Lippizaner barn and stud farm. It is the amazing sensation that rolls over your tongue when you dig into a bowl of peppery *fiš paprikaš* (fish stew with peppers) in Osijek or when you sip a new vintage from a vineyard in Baranja wine country. It is also the grim realization that overtakes you when you see workers removing land mines along the road to fascinating Kopački Rit Nature Park. The payoff from a trip to inland Croatia isn't a transient thrill, but the total of many experiences that end in the understanding that something important happened there, something that formed Croatia's soul.

1 Orientation

VISITOR INFORMATION

All areas of inland Croatia are served by tourist information offices, though not all have local facilities. For general information about the country's interior, start with the **Croatian National Tourist Office** at 350 Fifth Ave., Suite 4003, New York, NY 10118 (© **212/279-8672;** fax 212/279-8683; www.croatia.hr). Travel agencies and tour operators also are good sources of information. Contact information for local tourist information offices is listed throughout below.

GETTING THERE

Except for the smallest and most remote villages, all the cities and towns of inland Croatia are served by bus and train routes linked to or originating in Zagreb. For bus schedules and ticket information, contact **Autobusni Kolodvor (Main Bus Station)** in Zagreb at Avenija M. Držića bb (© **060/313-333;** www.akz.hr). If you are at the station in Zagreb, window no. 14 is the 24-hour information center and is usually staffed by someone who can speak some English. For train information, contact the **Glavni Kolodvor (Main Train Station)** at Trg Kralja Tomislava 12 (© **060/333-444;** www.hznet.hr). For anyone with a car, the highway system that runs through inland Croatia is modern and efficient. Expect two-lane secondary roads to the smaller towns and some gravel roads in Lonjsko Polje Nature Park.

GETTING AROUND

Even tiny Čigoć is reachable by public bus , but once there, walking is the only way to see this nature reserve. Larger cities such as Osijek have tram systems that move people around the city efficiently. They also have connections to the rest of Croatia's larger population centers. However, travel to the rural areas of inland Croatia can be tedious and inconvenient on public transport, so it's better to tour the region by car, if possible.

2 Sisak & the Lonjsko Polje

The area between **Sisak** and **Jasenovac** is best known for **Lonjsko Polje Nature Park** its endangered wildlife, and 19th-century villages. The marshland area is also a favorite of bird-watchers, who hoist their binoculars at the **Krapke Dol** bird sanctuary near **Jasenovac.** But it is tiny, rustic **Čigoć** that attracts the most traffic. Čigoć is a designated European Stork Village and a living tribute to 19th-century Croatia.

ESSENTIALS

VISITOR INFORMATION The **Sisak Tourist Office** can provide maps of the town, and information on reaching Čigoć and Lonjsko Polje. It is at the west edge of the center at Rimska bb (Mali Kaptol) (© **044/522-655;** www.sisakturist.com). In Čigoć, the **Tourist Information Center** is at house no. 26 in the village (© **044/ 715-115**). It is open 9am to 4pm daily March through November. The staff there can provide knowledgeable, English-speaking park guides who will tell you about the village and nature park as well as direct you to the village's two ethnographic museums, which hold artifacts from Čigoć's early days. The guides can also direct you to *seoski turizam* (village tourism) houses where guests can stay overnight and share meals with a host family. The 20kn ($4) park-entry fee covers exploration of Čigoć; each stub will get you into either of the two museums without charge.

In Jasenovac, the **Jasenovac Tourist Office** is in the city library building (© **044/ 672-587**). The **Lonjsko Polje Nature Park Administration Office,** where you can get maps and information on the park, is at Trg Kralja Petra Svačića (© **044/672-080;** www.pp-lonjsko-polje.hr).

GETTING THERE From Sisak, you can take one of four daily buses or drive the 27km (17miles) of Sisak-Jasenovac road along the Lonja River to Mužilovćica, Lonja, and Krapje. For the next 3.2km (2miles) along the road past Čigoć, there is a string of villages similar to Čigoć, but without the large stork population. See "Orientation," above.

GETTING AROUND Sisak, Lonjsko Polje, Čigoć, and Jasenovac all are best explored on foot, though a car is handy to reach the Holocaust Museum from Jasenovac and to thoroughly explore Lonjsko Polje, which covers a huge area between Sisak and Jasenovac.

WHAT TO SEE & DO

Fortresses, storks, and some rural villages are the area's main attractions, and each is spectacular in its own way.

Sisak is a sleepy river town about 48km (30 miles) southeast of Zagreb and 23km (14 miles) west of the autocesta from the **Popovača** exit. Sisak is a good starting point for a tour of Croatia's eastern and southeastern cities as well as for the **Lonjsko Polje** (translation: field surrounding the Lonja) wetlands. It's worth a short walkabout, though not much more, if you have time. Situated near the confluence of the **Sava, Odra,** and **Kupa** rivers, Sisak has been a strategic site since Roman times. In fact, the remains of a Roman wall are preserved in front of the **St. Cross** church on Trg Bana Josip Jeličića in the center of town, which is the major population center in the region. Sisak has played a long and storied role in Croatian history. It is famous for a June 22, 1593, battle that ended in a Christian victory, preventing the Turks from advancing on Zagreb. Besides its war record, baroque buildings, and St. Cross church, Sisak is known for an annual Knightly Tournament held in June that includes a couple of days of feasting, jousting, and other colorful exhibitions and competitions to commemorate the 1593 victory.

Lonjsko Polje Nature Park The **Lonjsko Polje** is Europe's largest wetland nature park, stretching across more than 1,165 sq. km (450 sq. miles) and covering the area southeast from **Sisak** to **Jasenovac,** ending at the border with Bosnia. About 25% of this area is protected. Lonjsko Polje is a combination of forests and flatlands

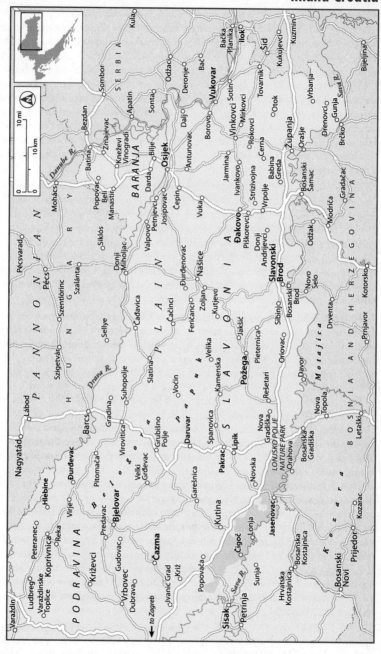

that are flooded half the year from approximately November to April. The other half of the year, part of Lonjsko Polje is a pasture that supports a herd of indigenous horses known as **Posavinas** (Posavina is translated as "the area around the Sava River"). The Posavina horses are a protected species of husky wild equines that roam this bio-diverse acreage when the waters recede from the pastureland. Besides Posavinas horses, the park is home to 238 bird species and 550 plant species. The area is 40% water and 60% woods and the largest protected wetland in the Danube Basin, Čigoć is part of this ecological area and you might run into a member of the environmental group Friends of Lonjsko Polje at Čigoć, who will explain environmental threats to this wet-land area to anyone who will listen. The group has launched an initiative promoting rural tourism aimed at allowing area citizens to prosper without ruining Lonjsko Polje's environmental balance.

Čigoć 🐦🐦🐦   A line of Hansel-and-Gretel Posavina houses made of 200-year-old low-land oak timbers comprise Čigoć, but the entrancing village is best known for the dozens of white storks that descend there in early spring to lay their eggs. Just 30km (19 miles) south of Sisak, Čigoć is also noteworthy as a historic military village where Austro-Hungarian troops set up a frontier against the Turkish invasion in the 17th century. However, it is the storks in their enormous nests atop the village's thatched roofs that entice most visitors to stop here and at a string of similar nearby villages (**Mužilovćica, Lonja,** and **Krapje**) on their excursions through **Lonsko Polje Nature Park,** where bird-watching, hiking in the forest, and communing with nature are the primary activities.

Jasenovac 🐦🐦   Jasenovac is a town, but this former concentration camp on the Drava near Bosnia is now a memorial to the tens of thousands of people who were put to death there during World War II. As you approach Jasenovac's outskirts, you can see a tall concrete sculpture that looks like an open tulip rising up from a huge empty field. Go past that and turn left at an unmarked road that leads to a low, flat building about 300 yards ahead. That is the Jasenovac museum and visitor center and well worth a stop.

Jasenovac was the largest concentration camp in the Balkans and many of the more than 70,000 known victims are buried in mass graves there and at the other four "work sites" that made up the camp. The museum and visitor center originally were built in the 1960s, but the facility was occupied by the Serbs during the Homeland War and it took until November 2006 to recover the items that were stolen during the conflict and to install a permanent exhibit inside.

The current multi-media installation is quite moving, with numerous screens lighting up the dark corners of the black painted space. A continuous slide show made up of period photos from the camps, footage and audio of survivors talking about their experiences at Jasenovac, and news footage from the 1940s that covers the camps' story are the bulk of the presentation. Three computers are hooked up to the memorial's database and visitors can use them to search family names, events—anything associated with Jasenovac. All captions are in Croatian and English and even the footage of survivor testimony is captioned in English. The ceiling is hung with clear acrylic panels engraved with the 70,000 names of known Jasenovac victims, and artifacts belonging to those victims are displayed in glass cases throughout the memorial.

Outside, there is a path that leads to a huge stone memorial sculpture about a quarter-mile from the visitor center. The path meanders past several train cars that were used to transport detainees to the camp. The train cars were a gift from Slovenia's rail-way. Along the way you will see models of what the camp looked like when it was

Smoke & Mirrors

If you look carefully at storks nesting on top of the wooden houses in Čigoć, you'll notice that the birds have built their nests on roofs rather than chimneys. That's because the houses here don't have chimneys. Instead, the structures' fireplaces are vented into the attic area, where the smoke collects and seeps out gradually. Because Croats waste nothing—not even smoke—residents use the area under the roof as a smoke house, where they cure ham, sausages, and some cheeses.

operating between 1941 and 1955. The museum has 5 curators, including Ms. Ines Sogonić who speaks English and who will be happy to answer your questions.

Tip: Take along a penlight to aid in reading some of the captions. Also, the memorial's database is not yet on the Web, so you can access its archives onsite only.

For more information on the memorial, go to www.jusp-jasenovac.hr. For historical information, on Jasenovac, go to www.ushmm.org/jasenovac, a very impressive website authored and maintained by the U.S. Holocaust Memorial Museum.

Braće Radić 147. 44 324 Jasenovac. ✆ 44/672-319. Admission to the Jasenovac Memorial Museum is free. Mon–Fri 9am–5pm; Sat and Sun 10am–4pm. Closed holidays.

WHERE TO STAY

Visitors to this region usually head for its rustic villages and wetlands; thus, accommodations are quite basic. There are few hotels with fewer services. Most overnight accommodations can be found in private homes and apartments.

Hotel i ✿ *Value* Hotel i is on Sisak's outskirts, but it's the best in town. The small inn opened in 2004, and while it offers modest accommodations, it has a comfy feel to it. Guest rooms still look brand new and all have bathrooms and individual A/C units. This isn't a destination hotel but it is a nice place to stay if you are exploring the area. Breakfast in Restaurant Gloria is a delight.

Obrtnička bb. ✆ 044/527-270. Fax 044/527-278. www.hotel-i-sisak.hr/index_en.php. 17 units, including 1 suite. Doubles from 450kn ($84), suite from 650kn ($120). Rates include breakfast. Half- and full board available. No credit cards. **Amenities:** Restaurant; Internet at reception; parking. *In room:* A/C, SAT TV, minibars in some rooms, hair dryer.

Hotel Panonija This basic hotel is serviceable and convenient for those who want to explore the part of the Lonjsko Polje that lies between Sisak and Jasenovac. Guest rooms are adequate and clean, but lack personality.

Sakcinskog 21, Sisak. ✆ 044/515-600. Fax 044/515-601. www.hotel-panonija.hr. 84 units. From 480kn ($85) double. AE, DC, MC, V. Rates include breakfast. Half- and full board available. **Amenities:** Restaurant; cafe; bar. *In room:* TV.

Park Prirode ✿✿ At Mužilovćica, Zlata and Jakša Ravlić serve hearty meals made from regional products in their timber house at no. 72. The Ravlićes will show you around their rural property and even take you for a ride on the river. Guest rooms in this Posavina timber structure have antique single beds and wall decorations that include 19th-century "couture."

Mužilovćica 72, 44213 Kratečko. ✆ 044/710/151. jaksa.ravlic@sk.htnet.hr. 4 units. Rates negotiable and may include some meals. No credit cards.

What Happened at Jasenovac?

According to United States Holocaust Memorial Museum records, Jasenovac was not just one big camp but a cluster of five detention centers established by the Ustaša-supported government of the "Independent State of Croatia" during World War II. Collectively, the Jasenovac facility was huge—the third-largest detention camp in Europe—and it was infamous for its deplorable living conditions, unspeakable torture methods, and mass killings. Between 1941 and April 1945, tens of thousands of Jews, Serbs, Roma (Gypsies), Croats, and miscellaneous political prisoners were brought to Jasenovac via trains from communities across Croatia to work if they had skills needed by the Axis regime or to be savagely tortured and/or murdered if they didn't, according to museum research reports. In addition, Jasenovac was especially notorious for its brutal execution methods—strangulation, live burning, live burial, murder by ax, ropes, chains—as well as for the alleged participation of local Catholic clergy in those executions.

Between the summer of 1942 and March 1943, Croatian authorities reportedly emptied the camp of remaining Croatian Jews (about 7,000) and sent them to Auschwitz-Birkenau, leaving only non-Jewish prisoners in the camp. There have been many debates about how many people died at Jasenovac, and there is no agreement on the number that perished here or even who some of them were. In April 1945 the Ustaša guards deliberately destroyed the camp buildings and all records of what went on at Jasenovac when they realized that Tito's Partisan troops were closing in on them. However, most estimates say those killed at Jasenovac's camps number "more than 200,000," including 18,000 Jews.

Hudi Seoski Turizam 🏕   Lonje is half a mile beyond Mužilovčica, followed by Krapje, where the Austrian sense of order is evident in the village layout. In fall 2004, Krapje entrepreneur Josip Hudi began offering rustic overnight accommodations that include bed, breakfast, and even a little fishing.

Krapje 76, 44325 Krapje. ✆ **044/611/202.** Rates negotiable and can include some meals. No credit cards.

WHERE TO DINE

There aren't many restaurants from Sisak to Jasenovac, and the cuisine in this stretch of the country is most aptly characterized as Croatian comfort food. Sisak has more than two dozen places where you can get a meal, but your best bet in the Lonjsko Polje area between Sisak and Jasenovac is to pack your own lunch with sausage and cheese from a local shop; or you can stop at one of the rural tourism spots in Čigoć or other villages along the way.

3 Podravina & Bjelovar-Bilogora

The north-to-southeast strip of territory from Hlebine to Daruvar runs through the Podravina and Bilogora regions of Croatia, where some of Croatia's richest farmland and most provincial towns and villages lie, each with its own claim to fame. This area is the equivalent of any stretch of small-town America and is just as colorful. You can buy big loaves of still-warm, crusty bread from the back of a bakery truck that makes early morning rounds of village streets. You can watch a twice-daily parade of farmers with silver cans full of fresh milk rushing to the dairy co-op station to have their creamy yields weighed and credited to their accounts. In this part of the country you still can see elderly goat herders using their staffs to urge their charges toward home. You can fall asleep to off-key group renditions of national songs filling the night air during almost weekly celebrations at the local church hall, an institution that marks life's defining moments. Here all get up with their roosters and go to bed before the 10pm news; and no one ever completely retires from his or her day job. This is the land of bountiful harvests and the heartbreak of war; of artists who interpret the vagaries of everyday life based on real people, and of men who gather each day to talk about what was and what might still be in Croatia. The towns in Podravina and Bilogora are segments of Croatia's solid backbone, independent but interconnected, and the people who live there are the salt of the earth.

ESSENTIALS

VISITOR INFORMATION The **Đurđevac Tourist Office** is at S. Radiča 1 (© **048/812-046**). Hlebine does not have its own tourist office, but information is readily available from the **Zagreb tourism bureau** (p. 250).

GETTING THERE See "Getting There" in "Orientation," earlier in this chapter.

GETTING AROUND Hlebine, Đurđevac, and Čazma are easily explored on foot. Bjelovar and Daruvar are a little larger, so a car is handy for those with limited time and endurance.

4 Hlebine & Đurđevac

Hlebine is famous for the naive art movement fostered by a group of 1930s peasant painters collectively known as the Hlebine School. Like the American artist known as Grandma Moses, artists from the Hlebine School portray the landscapes and people of the area in a straightforward, even crude way, depicting everyday activities and relationships with bold humor and even bolder imagery. Much art typical of this movement uses oil on glass as the medium, a technique that produces vivid color and great detail.

The town of Đurđevac, about 24km (15 miles) south of Hlebine, also has galleries dedicated to naive art, but Đurđevac is better known for its Picoki legend, a story about the rooster that saved Đurđevac.

ESSENTIALS

VISITOR INFORMATION The Đurđevac tourism offices can provide maps, brochures and general information about area attractions. Hlebine does not have a tourist office per se, but personnel at the Hlebine Gallery and other merchants around town are happy to help with directions and with pointing out sights worth a visit.

GETTING THERE To get to Hlebine via public transportation, you first must go to the provincial town of Koprivnica 13km (8 miles) to the west. Buses and trains from Zagreb stop there. Koprivnica is also where you transfer to one of the six weekday buses that go to Hlebine. However, bus service to Hlebine is infrequent on weekends, so it's best to have your own car if you visit then. See "Getting There" in "Orientation," earlier in this chapter, for contact information for trains and buses to

Koprivnica from Zagreb. Đurđevac is connected to Hlebine by infrequent bus service, but it is only 20 minutes away by car.

GETTING AROUND   Once in Hlebine or Đurđevac, walking is the most reasonable way to see the towns' sites.

WHAT TO SEE & DO
In reality, Hlebine is a big artists' colony of more than 200 painters and sculptors who work mostly in the Hlebine School style. Consequently, Hlebine's biggest attractions are its art galleries. Đurđevac, on the other hand, is a one-attraction wonder, and the "rooster castle" is its most visited sight.

Galerija Josip Generalić 𝕔𝕔𝕔   The former atelier of Ivan and Josip Generalić is easy to find because tour buses are usually parked in front of the two modest buildings that hold the artists' work. Ivan Generalić died in 1992 and his son Josip died in 2004. Paintings done by both Generalićes hang on the walls of Josip's workroom and in the small gallery. Some of it is for sale at very reasonable prices. *Tip:* There is a pictorial map of Hlebine's artists' whereabouts outside the Galeria Hlebine (below) that pinpoints the location of every atelier in town. It is best to make arrangements with individual artists before you arrive, but you can also take your chances with who's home and ask anyone at Galerija Hlebine to call ahead for you. Be sure to call ahead to make sure someone is on hand to open the gallery.

Gajeva 75—83, Hlebine. ⓒ 048/836-071. galerija.josip.generalic@kc.t-com.hr. Free admission. By appointment only.

Galerija Hlebine 𝕔𝕔   This modern gallery is more like a museum and it is filled with examples of naive art from a variety of painters. Revolving exhibits from the gallery's collection as well as some permanent installations are on display, too. There is even a room with nothing but works from Ivan Generalić, whose sense of humor is

A Bird in the Hand

During a fabled siege, the Turkish army under the command of Ulama-beg barricaded the people of Đurđevac behind the walls of the Old Town without food or water with the intention of starving them into submission. According to the legend, an old woman came up with the idea of shooting a rooster out of a cannon at the invading army to give the impression that the people of Đurđevac had so much food they could outlast the army. In reality, the rooster, or *picok,* was the last bit of food in the compound. The ploy worked and Ulama-beg and his army retreated, believing that the people had a huge store of food and that starving them out would be a losing battle. Before he left, Ulama-beg got in one last shot at Đurđevac by putting a curse on the townspeople, saying that from that day on they would be known as Picoki (roosters). Each year during the last week of June, the "Picoki" hold a big festival to commemorate their victory over the Turks. During this celebration, they re-enact the rooster shooting, though they purportedly now use a rubber chicken instead of a live rooster. In 2007, more than 30,000 people descended on Đurđevac for the annual rooster toss.

> **Fun Fact** **Cock-a-Doodle-Doo**
>
> As the story goes, when Ivan Generalić was a kid, his father would tiptoe into his room when he was sleeping and stick a squawking rooster in his face to wake him up. As a result of this poultry attack, Ivan developed a love-hate relationship with the birds, which usually are portrayed in an unflattering light in many of his works.

evident in his earthy representations of peasant life, especially those works that include demonic-looking roosters. Besides art by Generalić, the gallery has a selection of naive art from various artists for sale.

Trg Ivana Generalića 15, Hlebine. © **048/836-075**. Free admission. Mon–Fri 10am–4pm; Sat 10am–2pm. Closed Sun.

5 Čazma, Bjelovar, Daruvar

Čazma, Bjelovar, and Daruvar are typical towns in north-central Croatia. Not only are they noted as centers of agriculture, but they also are the sites of food-processing plants and other industries vital to the entire country's economy. Daruvar is also known for its large Czech population and as one of the towns that was on the front lines during the 1991 war with Serbia.

ESSENTIALS

VISITOR INFORMATION   The **Bjelovarsko-Bilogorska County Tourist Board** is at Trg Eugena Kvaternika 4 (© **043/243-944;** fax 043/241-229; tz.grada-bjelovar@bj.htnet.hr). Čazma's **Tourism Board** is at Milana Novačaća 13 (© **043/772-086;** tz-cazma@bj.htnet.hr). Daruvar's **Tourism Office** is at Julijev Park 1 (© **043/335-499;** fax 043/331-455). Each of these offices can provide maps, brochures, and suggestions about what to see, where to stay, and what to eat.

GETTING THERE   Čazma and Daruvar are linked to Zagreb via bus. Bjelovar has a train stop, but some routes entail multiple stops and transfers. For example, the railroad via Križevci connects Bjelovar with Zagreb, and another one via Virovitica connects it with Osijek. There is no train service to Čazma at this time. See "Getting There" in "Orientation," earlier in this chapter.

GETTING AROUND   Čazma, Bjelovar, and Daruvar all have compact cores, so walking is the best way to explore them.

WHAT TO SEE & DO

Each of the towns listed here is small and readily covered in a couple of hours, even on foot, and each has several pleasing sites worth checking out.

Čazma   This little town in Bjelovar-Bilogora County about 58km (36 miles) east of Zagreb is a sportsman's paradise. Hunters flock to the area for the deer, boar, pheasant, rabbit, and wild duck that freely roam the fields and gentle hills. Anglers are attracted by schools of freshwater fish teeming in the nearby Česma and Glogovnica rivers. For those who are into personal bests, Čazma has a large number of clay tennis courts and other sports venues. It is part of the **"Super-marathon Zagreb-Čazma"** itinerary, a 60km (36-mile) run held the first week of April that has been an annual event since 1976. History buffs can visit the unusually large Romanesque-style, twin-tower

Church of St. Mary Magdalene built in the 13th century. It was restored with baroque touches in the 18th. The church is noted for its incredibly ornate altar and pulpit, and for its 18th-century rococo organ decorated with lots of marble and gilt and topped by cherubs. The **Čazma Tourist Board** is at Milana Novačića 13 (© **043/772-086**).

Bjelovar ⊛⊛   Picturesque Bjelovar experienced just a few days of fighting during the 1991 civil war in Croatia, but it was a bona fide military town under the Empress Maria Theresa of Austria, who built a fort there in 1756. Today, the town's former army headquarters has been restored and serves as a branch of Zagreb University. Plans include converting the building to a business and cultural center plus galleries and an exhibition hall.

Bjelovar celebrates its military glory days every summer with **Terezijana,** a festival held the last full weekend in June. The celebration commemorates the empress's visit to inspect her city. During the festival, Maria Theresa's "entrance" to the town center is re-enacted with carriages, parades, and much fanfare; and includes fun, food, and an annual open-air spoof featuring locals portraying the empress and her subjects.

Every September, Bjelovar is the site of one of Croatia's largest livestock exhibitions, an event that draws farmers from all over the country and beyond. The rest of the year, life in Bjelovar, which is just 80km (50 miles) northeast of Zagreb, is fairly quiet and revolves around agriculture. Just about any time, you can stroll Bjelovar's beautiful town square, which twice was voted the best-designed and -maintained in Croatia by the Croatian National Tourism Board. You also can take a peek at the town's excellent civic museum, which has a good ethnographic collection. The **Bjelovar City Tourism Board** is at Trg Eugena Kvaternika 4 (© **043/243-944**).

Galeria '90 ⊛⊛ *(Finds)*   This small gallery on a side street off the main square is loaded with well-chosen pieces by local artists and craftspeople, including some who specialize in naive art. Sculpture, photography, ceramics, and paintings make up the bulk of the offerings, and almost anyone can find something here that is worth carrying home at prices that won't break the bank. The shop is run by the delightful Sonja Maletić. She also does custom framing and can ship your purchases home via DHL for a charge.

Ljudevta Gaja 10, Bjelovar. © **091/242-3622**. AE, DC, MC, V. Mon–Fri 8am–1pm and 5–8pm; Sat 8am–2pm. Closed Sun.

Bjelovar Market ⊛⊛   Almost every city, town, and village in Croatia has a market where local farmers and merchants sell produce, meat, cheeses, wines, and even household products and clothing. Bjelovar's is better than most, perhaps because of its location in the middle of Croatia's agricultural belt. You'll find gorgeous fruits and vegetables as well as fresh meats and sausages, cheeses, baked goods, plants, and some textiles. Don't miss the cheese section, where you can buy little pyramid-shaped mounds of cheese—fresh or smoked—called *prgica,* all homemade by vendors who will encourage you to taste their wares before buying.

Tip: Thursday and Saturday are the best days to hit this market. These are the traditional days *(sajmeni dan)* when the market has the most variety and vendors because producers from many parts of Croatia join locals to sell their wares. The practice started centuries ago when farmers brought their livestock to Bjelovar Thursdays and Saturdays each week.

Ivša Lebović. Mon–Sat 7am–4pm; Sun and holidays 7am–1pm.

Daruvar 🎯🎯   In Roman times, Daruvar was the site of baths called Aquae Balissae, which were named for the area's healing waters. Today, Daruvar still attracts tourists who want to soak in the town's mineral springs or who want to explore nearby **Papuk Mountain and National Park.** The town is also a gateway to the county's thriving hunting tourism. Roebuck, wild boar, and game birds are just some of the sought-after prizes that attract outdoorsmen.

Daruvar suffered moderate damage during the 1991 war, most notably at beautiful **Julijev Park** in the heart of town, but it has mostly recovered. Daruvar is also home to a large contingent of Croatia's Czech population, as testified to by the presence of **Staro Ceska Brewery.**

Daruvar Tourist Office. Julijev Park 1. ✆ **043/335-499.** Fax 043/331-455. komercialja@daruvarske-toplice.hr.

Papuk Mountain and National Park 🎯🎯   Papuk is the largest mountain in Slavonia. It and the land surrounding it were proclaimed protected areas in 1999. Papuk is geologically and ecologically diverse, and some of its rock formations are estimated to be 350 million years old. Besides of its geological significance, Papuk is home to cultural artifacts from the Iron Age and the remains of seven castles from the Middle Ages. It is also a recreational area frequented by hikers, skiers, and those who want to soak in Papuk's thermal pools and Orahovačko Lake.

S. Radića 46, 34330 Velika. ✆ **034/313-030.** Fax 034/313-027. www.pp-papuk.hr. Year-round.

WHERE TO STAY

Hotels in this part of Croatia are few and far between. Most are pretty basic because they generally cater to visiting farmers and hunters who don't demand much luxury. However, Daruvar's spa hotel is undergoing renovation, and some of the smaller places in town have been fixed up as well.

Hotel Balise 🎯   If you are passing through sleepy Daruvar, this pansion is a good, economical place in the center of town. The hotel was renovated in 2005 and is within easy reach of Julijev Park, the area's wineries, and Staro Ceška Brewery. From there you can go hiking to nearby **Petrov Peak** in the Papuk National Park or relax in the hotel's pleasant outdoor courtyard. Rooms are small but clean and comfortable, and the breakfast is top-notch.

Trg Kralja Tomislava 22, Daruvar. ✆ **043/440-220.** Fax 043/440-230. 19 units. From 500kn ($93) double. Kids 6 and under stay free in parent's room. AE, DC, MC, V. **Amenities:** Restaurant; bar; outdoor patio; excursions. *In room:* TV, hair dryer.

Hotel Termal/Daruvarske Toplice 🎯   Julijev Park, which is at the doorstep of this therapeutic spa resort, was damaged during the 1991 war, but the hotel was largely untouched. That is a mixed blessing in that the Termal's guest rooms were left intact but remain just as they were in the days when spartan accommodations and socialist drab were in style. However, the hotel still offers thermal waters and a host of fitness activities. The helpful staff will arrange hunting and fishing excursions and other tours for guests. The hotel/spa once was exclusively a rehab/medical center and is still popular among those who book rooms to access health services, but it now caters to tourists as well.

Julijev Park 8, Daruvar. ✆ **043/623-200.** Fax 043/331-455. www.daruvarske-toplice.hr. 161 units. From 540kn ($100) double; from 1,360kn ($252) suite. Rates include breakfast and are based on a 7-day stay. Half- and full board are available. AE, DC, MC, V. **Amenities:** Indoor, outdoor thermal pools; tennis courts; fitness center; sauna; bowling alley; hydromassage; room for those w/limited mobility.

WHERE TO DINE

Dining in Čazma, Bjelovar, and Daruvar tends to be casual; most local establishments are pizzerias or ma-and-pa affairs. However, a couple of restaurants offer sit-down food a cut above the rest.

Restoran Terasa ✻ CROATIAN   The dining room in this restaurant is just steps away from the Daruvarske Toplice hotel and has plenty of tall windows so diners can enjoy the view of leafy Julijev Park with their meals. The expansive wraparound terrace provides the best ambience for tasting the restaurant's Slavonian, Czech, and Dalmatian specialties.

Julijev Park 1, Daruvar. © **043/331-705.** Fax 043/331-455. Entrees 40kn–100kn ($8–$19). AE, DC, MC. Daily 9am–1pm.

Stara Ura ✻ *Value* CROATIAN   This plain-looking restaurant down the street from Bjelovar's military buildings looks like any small-town storefront in America. However, locals regularly choose Stara Ura (old clock) for their nights out because the chef has a reputation for his excellent preparations and adherence to traditional recipes. As at most restaurants in this part of Croatia, grilled meats are the menu mainstays.

V. Nazora 22, Bjelovar. © **043/244-870.** Entrees 40kn–60kn ($8–$11). No credit cards. Mon–Fri 8am–10pm; Sat 8am–midnight; closed Sun.

Slasticarna Zagorje ✻✻✻ ICE CREAM & PASTRY   Peach-colored walls, Biedermeier furniture, and a cheerful garden terrace are the setting for enjoying the best ice cream and cakes in town. There isn't a single local who hasn't sat down to a bowl of the creamy stuff here. This is where men stop to have coffee and read newspapers while their wives shop at the market, where kids beg their parents to take them for a special treat, and where teens take their first dates. In summer, head for the outdoor terrace where you can sit at wrought-iron garden tables with your honey while a delicate scent from the climbing roses creates a romantic cloud.

Ivana Viteza Trnskog 15, Bjelovar. © **043/244-678.** No credit cards. Daily 8am–11pm.

6 Western Slavonia: Lipik, Pakrac, Požega

Western Slavonia has its feet in two worlds: Its relative proximity to Zagreb provides a link to modern city life, while it also is part of the country's breadbasket, which stretches all the way to Croatia's eastern border. Farmland flows across the flat, fertile Pannonian plain as far as the eye can see. Here and there the endless horizon is broken up by a marshy nature area, national park, or steeple rising from one of the villages, towns, and cities that are Croatia's main agricultural producers. This part of Croatia also once had thriving industries that included flower-growing and a Lipizzan horse farm, but years of war and ethnic animosity sent the region's economy reeling, and it is just now starting to recover.

ESSENTIALS

VISITOR INFORMATION   Personnel in **Požega's Tourist Office** at Trg Svetog Trojstva 3 (© **034/274-900;** fax 034/274-901; www.pozega.hr) do not speak English, but they can provide English-language brochures and maps. Požega isn't worth an overnight, but if you must stay, accommodations are mostly B&B style and can be arranged at the Tourist Office. Lipik's tourist office is small but personnel are very willing to help. **Lipik's tourism office** is at Marija Terezija 27 (© **034/421-530;** grad-lipik@po.htnet.hr). Pakrac was on the front line during the Homeland War, and there isn't much left for a tourism office to talk about, but people there will be happy to tell you the town's history and what happened to it in the war. The **Pakrac tourism office** is at Trg Bana Jelačića 18 (© **034/411-454;** fax 034/411-081; www.pakrac.hr).

GETTING THERE   Pakrac is 27km (17 miles) south of Daruvar, and Lipik is just 5km (3 miles) south of Pakrac. Požega is 51km (33 miles) east of Pakrac. There is local bus service to Lipik, Pakrac, and Požega, but Požega has the only frequent service, with links to Osijek and beyond. Požega is also served by trains; both the bus and train stations are on the north side of town, a short walk from the center. All three towns can easily be reached by car from Osijek or Daruvar.

GETTING AROUND   You can see everything worth seeing in Pakrac on a drive-through and everything in Lipik by walking. Požega is a much bigger town and you might need a car or other transport to get to the 'burbs and peripheral attractions.

WHAT TO DO & SEE

The towns in this region are small and some are one-site wonders, but each has unique points of interest that might appeal to tourists intent on soaking up Croatia's history.

Lipik ✦   This quiet town is known for its medicinal spring and for the Lipizzaner horse farm that once flourished there. In the early 19th century, Daruvar's Count Izidor Janković built baths in Lipik to take advantage of the area's thermal waters. He also built a hotel to house the people who came to soak in them. The current spa buildings are part of a hospital that was built at the end of the 19th century, damaged in the 1991 war, and partially rebuilt in 2004. Several other nearby spa sites built by Janković (and the Lipizzaner farm) are still undergoing repair. Right now the only thermal pool in town is the hospital's; there is also a public pool [bazeni]. The Lipizzaner farm, which has been totally renovated, remains horseless at this time. The Lipizzaners that were moved to Serbia during the hostilities have not yet been returned to Croatia. Even though very few tourists choose to stay in Lipik these days, the entrepreneurial town has found a way to take its mineral water to the people: The water is bottled and sold all over Croatia under the Studenac brand. *Note:* Croatia was close to a deal with Serbia to return surviving stolen Lipizzaners. However, Serbia is demanding a $200,000 ransom to return the kidnapped horses.

Pakrac   Pakrac was on the front line during the 1991 war, but much of the damage done to the town was inflicted during its liberation. At that time, both armies on the front line went through the center of Pakrac with Serb forces on one side of the street and Croat forces on the other, shooting at each other. Today much of Pakrac is still in ruins, mostly because foreign aid to restore the town has dried up and war repairs have slowed. However, it is worth a drive-through just to see the devastation caused by the war. Many of the tumbled-down structures are still owned by Serbians, who once made up a large part of Pakrac, but most Serbs fled during the war and have not returned. If you do stop in Pakrac, be sure to see the palaces that belonged to Baron von Trenk, a Hapsburg officer who owned vast tracts of property in Slavonia. The exterior of his palace in town has undergone some renovation.

Požega ✦✦   About 145km (90 miles) east of Zagreb and 34km (21 miles) north of the Nova Gradiška exit off the autocesta (toll road), Požega is a busy market town in western Slavonia that was founded by the Romans in the 13th century, occupied by the Turks from 1536 to the last decade of the 17th century, and renovated in the baroque style in the 18th and 19th centuries.

Today's Požega is a combination of commerce and cafes, churches and memorials. Its **Stari Grad (Old Town),** on **Trg Svetog Trojstva (Holy Trinity Square)** in the southern part of the town, is the main tourist attraction. It has two churches on the south end of the square: the 14th-century **St. Lawrence Church (Crkva Sv Lovre),** which was redone in the baroque style in the 18th century; and the **Church of the Holy Ghost (Crkva Svetog Duha),** which was built in the 13th century and rebuilt in the 19th century after being destroyed by a fire in 1842. Holy Ghost is flanked by a **Franciscan monastery,** which contains many rare books and historical documents related to Požega. Archaeological finds dating back to the Romans and beyond can be seen in Požega's **City Museum (Gradski Muzej)** along with present-day exhibits. On the north side of the square you'll find an 18th-century **Plague Column** built in 1749 to honor the 798 citizens of Požega who died in the 6-month-long plague of 1739. Požega's **Cehovska (Guild) Street** is home to specialty shops and numerous cafes, as well as a gateway for visitors to **Papuk Nature Park** to the north, a 518-sq.-km (200-sq.-mile) area with diverse flora and fauna, the remains of seven medieval towns, and archaeological sites dating to the Bronze Age (700–200 B.C.).

WHERE TO STAY

Požega probably has the best options for lodging in this area, though Lipik has a small hotel which is quite pleasant.

Hotel Lipa 🏵🏵 This darling pink three-story is almost directly across the street from Lipik's spa hospital and is quite comfortable and clean. The hotel has undergone renovation (2004) since the war, when it was damaged, but it has emerged better than ever.

Marije Tereije 5, Lipik. ☎ 034/421-244. Fax 034/421-204. 20 units. From 475kn ($88) double. Rate includes breakfast. AE, DC, MC, V. Parking. **Amenities:** Restaurant. *In room:* TV.

Hotel Grgin Dol 🏵 The Grgin Dol is just southwest of Požega's town center off A. Kanižlića Street. It is a fine small-hotel option that offers guests excellent Slavonian food in its **restaurant** 🏵🏵. Guest rooms are tidy and a decent size, and the few amenities offered are the ones that are most important to guests.

Grgin Dol 20, Požega. ☎ 034/273-222. Fax 034/272-296. pozeska-dolina@po.t-com.hr. 17 units. From 50€ ($70) double. Rate includes breakfast; half-board available. MC. Parking. **Amenities:** Restaurant; bar; terrace. *In room:* TV.

WHERE TO DINE

You won't go hungry in Požega, where restaurants, bakeries, cafes, and bars stand cheek by jowl off the main square.

Caffe Bar Capitol 🏵 PASTRY & COFFEE This is just one of four coffeehouses in a row along busy Cehovska in Požega. On this street and others north of the main square, cafes, and bars are crammed together so you can take a breather from sightseeing with a frosty iced caffe served with a lemon slice, or a steaming *bijela* kava (coffee with milk). What sets Capitol apart is its restroom, which is exceptionally clean and modern.

Cehovska 5, Požega. ☎ 034/312-282. No credit cards. Daily 8am–11pm.

Restoran Grgin Dol 🏵🏵 SLAVONIAN Located in the hotel with the same name, this is a good place to try out *kulen* (spicy Slavonian sausage) and other regional treats. The restaurant specializes in such delicacies as goulash and *čobanac* (two meats and batter dumplings) and is, quite frankly, one of the best restaurants in Croatia.

Grgin Dol 20, Požega. ☎ 034/273-222. Entrees 40kn–90kn ($7–$17). MC. Daily 7am–11pm.

Restoran Tomislav ✦✦ REGIONAL CROATIAN   If you don't want pizza or a meal in a noisy konoba, head for Tomislav off the main square. This is the kind of place locals head for on special occasions, and while it isn't exactly formal, it is sit-down and more staid than most other places in town.

Vjekoslava Babukića 25, Požega. ✆ **034/274-066.** Fax 034/273-226. Entrees 50kn–95kn ($9–$17). AE, DC, MC, V. Daily 8am–11pm.

7 Eastern Slavonia

If you venture across the fertile expanse that stretches northeast from Nova Gradiša to Ilok, you'll eventually see evidence of the violence that affected almost every town and village in the region. Skeletal remains of hothouses once filled with lush flowers, and vegetable and fruit plants, as well as the burned-out Borovo tire plant stand silent witness to the conflict that left Vukovar and other eastern cities bullet pocked and destitute. As of summer 2007 most land-mine warnings had been replaced by red plastic strips on the ground, indicating removal is in progress. But the chilling skull and crossbones signs indicating land-mine danger still confront visitors occasionally, as if to reassert war's horror. Many jagged, more obvious scars from the violence are constant reminders that inland Croatia is still suffering from the effects of the Homeland War. However, there is good news. Besides broken glass and burned-out factories you'll see new shoots of hope sprouting, growing even flourishing—proof that the indomitable Croatian spirit is alive and well across the Pannonian plain.

8 Slavonski Brod, Đakovo & Nova Gradiška

Slavonski Brod   Slavonski Brod is Slavonia's second-largest town, and if either Đakovo or Osijek is on your itinerary, the easiest way to get there is to travel south from Požega, where you can rejoin the toll road at Slavonski Brod and continue on. However, you might want to spend an hour or so looking around Slavonski Brod before you hit the entrance ramp to the highway. Slavonski Brod was heavily damaged during the 1991 war and is slowly being restored. Earlier, it was an 18th-century, fortress-style town made almost entirely of wood. That changed late in the 19th century and in the 20th, when the town acquired some Hapsburg structures and later block-style high-rises to house workers in the local industries. Slavonski Brod isn't worth too much of your time, but the remains of the 18th-century Brod Fortress, which was built to stop the Turks from invading Slavonia, is an interesting pause, especially since an extensive restoration is in progress. Entrance to the buildings was prohibited as of summer 2007, but cycling around the property and imagining the fort in happier times is encouraged.

Đakovo ✦✦   Đakovo is a charming little town 35km (22 miles) from Osijek that is emerging from damage and a stagnant economy inflicted by the 1991 war. The city is best known for St. Peter the Apostle Cathedral, an imposing red-brick edifice built in 1882 under the sponsorship of Josip Juraj Strossmayer, Bishop of Đakovo, who was a patron of sacral art. Besides his attempts to unite the Slavic people, Strossmayer is remembered as the founder of the Yugoslav Academy of Arts and Sciences and its Strossmayer Gallery of Old Masters ✦✦ in Zagreb, to which he generously endowed his personal art collection. In addition to the cathedral, which has become almost synonymous with the city, Đakovo is known for its excellent white wines, a summer embroidery festival, and Državna Ergela Lipicanaca, its 500-year-old Lipizzaner barn *(ergela)* 🏇🏇🏇 in town and stud farm in Ivan Dvor where 225 of the majestic horses reside on 400 hectares (about 250 acres) just 5km (3 miles) northwest of town.

Nova Gradiška   is a town that is easily bypassed by tourists. There is no great cathedral, no landmark hotel, no chi-chi gourmet restaurant there. What Nova Gradiška does have is a couple of diamond-in-the-rough attractions. Nova Gradiška's proximity to the Bosnian border made it a shaky place to be during the Homeland War, but the town escaped relatively unscathed. Good thing, too, because that left St. Peter's Church, the church museum, and a 17th-century castle damage-free.

ESSENTIALS

VISITOR INFORMATION   If you stop at Slavonski Brod on your way east, the **tourist bureau** there will provide maps and brochures. That office is at Trg Pobjede 28/1 (© **035/447-721;** www.tzgsb.hr). The tourist office in Đakovo is staffed by volunteers, but it may be one of the most helpful and welcoming tourist offices in all of Croatia. Besides the cathedral and the museum, the Đakovo tourist rep told us about the Lipizzaner stable, restaurants, hotels, and celebrations in Đakovo, really rolling out the welcome mat. The **Đakovo office** is at Kralja Tomislava 3 (© **031/811-233**). In Nova Gradiška, head for Slavonskih Graničara 15 (© **035/361-495;** www.tzgng.hr) for tourist information.

GETTING THERE   Both trains and buses stop in Slavonski Brod, Đakovo, and Nova Gradiška. There are 14 buses and 15 trains daily from Zagreb to Slavonski Brod, which is connected to Požega, Nova Gradiška, and Đakovo by local routes. The Slavonski Brod bus station is at Trg Hrvatskog Proljeća (© **035/444-300**), while the train station (© **035/441-082**) is across the street from it. In Nova Gradaška, the train station is at Kolodvorska 5 (© **035/361-023**), and the bus station is almost next door at Kolodvorska 2 (© **035/361-219**). In Đakovo, the train station is less than a mile east of the center on Kralja Tomislava, and the bus station is less than a mile east of the cathedral on Splitska. See "Getting There," in "Orientation," earlier in this chapter, for transportation contact information.

GETTING AROUND   As with most inland Croatian cities, walking is the best way to navigate Đakovo, but right now Slavonski Brod is a one-attraction town and a car is handy to get to the fort in Slavonski Brod and the monastery in Nova Gradiška.

WHAT TO SEE & DO

Many visitors are drawn to Đakovo because of its awe-inspiring cathedral. Others stop there because Đakovo is the birthplace of Bishop Josip Juraj Strossmayer, who is a historic figure in Croatian politics, and who is especially remembered for his efforts to unite Serbs and Croats in a South Slav (Yugoslav) state. Strossmayer is also responsible for the city's distinctive cathedral, which he commissioned with funds generated by church properties in his see. For most people, however, Đakovo is just a pretty provincial town with a horse farm, a few architectural landmarks, and a nice pedestrian street (Korzo) lined with shops and restaurants.

Cathedral of St. Peter the Apostle 🏛🏛🏛   The neo-Gothic Cathedral of St. Peter the Apostle is enough reason to stop in Đakovo. You'll want to crane your neck to see the church's 84m (275-ft.) twin spires up close after looking at them for an hour or more while approaching the city on the highway from Zagreb. St. Peter the Apostle is the third iteration of a cathedral on this spot, and this one is magnificent. The enormous building was built between 1862 and 1882 by Viennese architect Baron Frederick Schmidt

The Treasure of Nova Gradiška

Nova Gradiška is an ordinary working class Croatian town in southeastern Slavonia that was just 3km (1.5 miles) from the fighting during the Homeland War. Today Nova Gradiška's citizens can enjoy a beautifully landscaped main square, a couple of decent restaurants, a hotel, and a Franciscan church and a monastery that is home to a trove of fascinating Bible treasures, one of which dates to the 12th century. The church was built by the Franciscans in 1734 and the museum is the result of one priest's passion for all things biblical. Inside you will find artifacts from the Holy Land, texts in various languages, and the marquee attraction, a hand-written, 12th-century Vatican Codex. Rev. Josip Grubišeć is a charming, English-speaking host who delights in sharing the church's treasure with interested tourists. Call ℂ 035/369-043 to arrange a tour at the church at Potočna 4.

at the behest of Bishop Josip Juraj Strossmayer. The cathedral's interior is full of fascinating statuary and artistic detail, from frescoes by Alexander and Ludwig Seitz to sculptures by noted Croatian artists of the times. The 19th-century park near the bishop's palace and the Mali (small) park nearby are both protected monuments.

Strossmayer Trg. Daily 7am–noon and 3–7pm.

Strossmayer Museum ☆☆
The Strossmayer Museum holds some of the bishop's artifacts and writings. It is immediately north of the cathedral in a pale yellow building.

Admission 5kn ($1). Tues–Fri 8am–7pm; Sat 8am–2pm. Closed Sun–Mon.

Korzo ☆
If you turn left after exiting the cathedral past the Strossmayer Museum, you will be on Ulica Papa Ivana Pavli II (Pope John Paul II St.). The pedestrian street is also known as the Korzo. Paved with red bricks, it is alive with shops and a midway that is a solid block of outdoor cafes.

Lipizzaner Stable and Stud Farm ☆☆☆
Đakovo's impressive Lipizzaner stable stud farm was founded in the early 16th century by the Hapsburgs, who were charged with providing quality horses for Vienna. Đakovo's is just one of several such farms in central Europe. Lipizzaners are prized for their intelligence and their ability to respond to commands as well as for their agility. The horses are brown when they are born but they turn mostly white in about 3 years. You can visit and even ride these beauties if you call ahead.

Tip: To get to the stud farm in Ivan Dvor, follow the signs toward Našice for about 5km (3 miles). About 100 yards from the road's intersection with Highway 7 you'll see a dirt road on the left that seems to go into the woods. Follow that for 2 more km (1.2 miles) to reach the farm. You will need a 4-wheel-drive vehicle for this if it has rained recently. For more details, go to www.ergela-djakovo.hr.

Augusta Šenoe 33. ℂ 031/813-286. www.ergela-djakovo.hr. Mon–Fri 9am–4pm. Weekend visits by appointment.

Đakovo Embroidery ☆☆☆
Đakovački Vezovi is a folklore festival celebrating traditions from the regions of Slavonia and Baranja. Traditional folk costumes, dancing, and singing groups characterize the celebration, which takes place the last weekend in

September. During the festival, the cathedral is the site of choir concerts, operatic performances, and art exhibitions; there is also a horse and wedding wagon. The highlight of the celebration is the show put on by pure white Lipizzaner horses from the city's stud farm, which has been a breeding center since the early 16th century.

WHERE TO STAY

Most accommodations in Slavonski Brod and Đakovo are private, but there are a few small hotels in the region that offer unique experiences.

Vinarija Zdelarević 𝖆𝖆𝖆   This lovely hotel in the middle of a vineyard is just 6km (4 miles) west of Slavonski Brod and 160km (100 miles) from Zagreb, off the A3 east-west autocesta. You'll get an enthusiastic welcome that includes a glass of wine when you arrive. Besides tastefully decorated rooms with modern showers and a dynamite **restaurant** 𝖆𝖆𝖆, Zdelarević offers tours of its winery, tastes of its vintages, and excellent Slavonian cuisine in its restaurant.

Vinogradska 102, Brodski Stupnik. ✆ 035/427-775. Fax 035/427-040. www.zdjelarevic.hr. 15 units. From 580kn ($108) double; from 750kn ($140) suite. Rates include breakfast. Half- and full board are available. AE, DC, MC, V. **Amenities:** Restaurant; bar; excursions; paintball; horseback riding; walking tours. *In room:* A/C, TV, hair dryers, anti-allergen bedding.

Hotel Blaža 𝖆𝖆   This relatively new (2002) but smallish hotel offers a higher level of comfort than most. Guest rooms, though not amenity-heavy, are outfitted with good-size modern bathrooms. Furnishings are plain but modern.

Starčević 158, Đakovo. ✆ 031/816-760. Fax 031/816-764. 20 units. From 470kn ($87) double. AE, DC, MC, V. Parking. **Amenities:** Restaurant; pool. *In room:* TV.

WHERE TO DINE

For the most part, dining is casual and plain in this part of Croatia, but things are looking up as the area's wine industry recovers and cuisine becomes more sophisticated without losing its regional flair.

Zdelarević 𝖆𝖆𝖆 *Value* SLAVONIAN   Slavonian cuisine meets nouveau gourmet in this winery restaurant that prides itself on creative cuisine. Whether you eat indoors with a view of the open kitchen or outdoors on the veranda near the vineyard, the experience will be unique and the food superb. Try the *ramstek na vinogradarski,* beef grilled with a frozen "brick" of butter flavored with wine and herbs. Add the *krumpir na Stupnicki,* potatoes baked in the oven with bacon and cream, and you have a very filling meal. The menu here is loaded with regional delights, all of them tweaked with expert additions. Pair your food with a bottle of Zdelarević wine from the restaurant winery, which was established in 1985 and is one of the first private wineries in Croatia. It produces chardonnay, Riesling, and other varietals.

Vinogradska 102, Brodski Stupnik in Vinarija Zdelarević. ✆ 035/427-775. Fax 035/427-040. www.zdjelarevic.hr. Entrees 35kn–90kn ($7–$17). AE, DC, MC, V. Daily 11am–11pm.

Gradski Podrum 𝖆 SLAVONIAN   Walk a few steps down to access this tidy cellar restaurant off the Korzo in Đakovo. The space has been a restaurant since 1945, but the building is 1880s vintage. The menu is tourist-friendly in that it is written in three languages, including English, and the space is blissfully air-conditioned. Stop for a pizza (10 varieties) or something more substantial like a Đakovo cutlet (veal filled with ham and kulen in a spicy sauce) or savor a mixed grill. The staff is friendly and can also help with directions around town.

H. Velikana 9. ℂ **031/813-199**. Entrees 25kn–120kn ($5–$22); pizzas 20kn–28kn ($4–$6). AE, MC, V. Daily 7am–midnight.

Slastica Korzo ICE CREAM & PASTRY   The street between Đakovo's cathedral and the rest of town is a solid block of umbrella tables and cafes. It's beyond almost everyone's willpower to navigate the strip without stopping for a "cold one." This little coffee shop serves delicious ice cream treats as well as more elaborate sweets and its air-conditioner blows cold air onto the tables outside, a plus.

H. Velikana 18. No phone. Ice cream from 6kn ($1). No credit cards. Daily 7am-9pm.

9 Osijek

Osijek is just 35km (22 miles) from Đakovo and 29km (18 miles) from the Hungarian border in the northeastern corner of Croatia. It is the largest city in Slavonia and the 4th largest in the country. More than 10 years after the end of the Homeland War, Osijek is finally recouping some of its former vigor. For the first decade after the end of the war, Osijek concentrated on repairing damage from the hostilities, but now the city has finished a $10-million face-lift of its main square while rehabbing older properties and building new ones. During the war, all but 15,000 of Osijek's 80,000 citizens fled the city and sought shelter with relatives in other parts of Croatia or in foreign countries. Many—but not all—have returned to their hometown, a sign that the local economy is on the upswing.

Osijek is also known as a "green city" because of the parks and tree-lined streets that link its three centers and shade its stately mansions. Osijek's western skyline, however, is a wall of socialist-era structures that belie the city's beauty. The city comprises three town centers: Tvrđa, Upper Town, and Lower Town, each of which has its own personality. The **Tvrđa** area is the most interesting, with its vestiges of Roman culture and Ottoman occupation; these days it looks like a construction zone because its buildings are being renovated. It is also the site of Osijek's summer cultural program, which opened with the very American Duke Ellington Orchestra in June 2007.

One of the city's best features is its riverwalk, a paved path flanking both banks of the Drava that is used by joggers, cyclists, in-line skaters, and people fishing or exercising their dogs. The riverwalk is quickly becoming a trendy nightlife and shopping spot because of a new adjacent shopping mall. A small bridge leads to Copacabana, the city's most popular beach, and on the river, the marina houses hundreds of powerboats and sculls. Other people-powered crafts can be seen cutting through the water at any time of the day.

ESSENTIALS

VISITOR INFORMATION   Osijek's **tourist office** is located at Županijska 2 (ℂ **031/203-755;** fax 031/203-947; www.tzosijek.hr). It can provide maps, brochures, and guidance about the city's sites and surrounding areas.

GETTING THERE   As the largest city in Slavonia, Osijek is served by regular bus and train services that link it to all parts of Croatia. The bus and train stations are adjacent to each other on Trg L. Ružička at the south end of the town center. See "Getting There" in "Orientation," earlier in this chapter.

GETTING AROUND   Osijek has a fast and efficient tram system. Once you're in the center of town, you can walk to the city's most interesting sites.

WHAT TO SEE & DO

There are 15 squares in Osijek, each with a different personality. Visitors can amble through Gornji Grad's 19th-century splendor in the city's northwestern quadrant to see architectural landmark buildings like the Croatian National Theater. Or you can go medieval in Tvrđa, the true center of town, where the fortress created by walls and former barracks is being transformed into a hip university center with trendy restaurants and a vibrant nightlife. Donji Grad is the quietest part of town and the most residential. It is on the northeastern edge of the city along the Drava, and there you can visit the baroque pilgrimage church of Our Lady of the Snows.

Church of Sts. Peter and Paul 𝕽𝕽   This church is often referred to as a cathedral, but it really is a parish church built between 1894 and 1898 according to plans drawn up by architects Franz Langenberg of Germany and Richard Jordan of Vienna. The massive red-brick neo-Gothic building is the biggest structure in town. Its huge footprint now covers the spot first occupied by a wooden chapel (1698) and then a small baroque church. The current structure covers nearly 1,062 sq. m (3,500 sq. ft.) and includes an 82m-tall (270-ft.) bell tower that is almost as high as the towers in Đakovo. The church on Osijek's main square has five Gothic altars. Its ceilings and walls are covered with sacral paintings.

Trg Marina Držica, Gornji Grad. 𝒞 031/369-626. Access during Mass; also daily noon–3pm and 5–5:30pm.

The Croatian National Theatre 𝕽𝕽𝕽   The building housing the theater was constructed in 1866, but the theater itself wasn't founded until 1907. The theater is a majestic example of Venetian-Moorish architecture, as well as a major cultural institution in Osijek even though it was heavily damaged during Croatia's 1991 war with Serbia. Today it is completely restored to its former glory, though a McDonald's on its street level isn't exactly in keeping with historic fidelity. Many purists resent even the tiny sign advertising the Golden Arches establishment, but in fact McDonald's contributed a significant amount of money to the theater's restoration after the war. Productions are staged at the theater from September to May.

Županijska 9, Osijevk. 𝒞 031/220-700.

Europska Avenue 𝕽𝕽   Osijek's broadest and most interesting street runs between Tvrđa (the Fort) to Gornji Grad (Upper Town) and intersects several city parks in between. Europska Avenue is also the street (from Kapucinska Ulica on the north end) where affluent Austrians built their Art Nouveau mansions between 1904 and 1905. Some of these structures have been repaired and restored, but others are sadly derelict. Note the single-story building at no. 24 (now home to the town's and university's library), as well as the bronze statue in Kralja Držislava Park. The building was a wedding gift from a wealthy citizen to his daughter. The statue was created by Robert Mihanović in 1898 as a memorial to fallen soldiers.

Tvrđa 𝕽𝕽𝕽   The partially walled former fort and center of Osijek is quickly becoming the hippest neighborhood in town. Originally built on the site of a Roman settlement, Tvrđa went through a series of rulers and attacks over the ages. It became the principal city in Pannonia in the 2nd century, was captured by the Avars and rebuilt by the Croats in the Middle Ages, before being leveled by Turkish forces in the 16th century. Finally, after routing the Turks in the 17th century, the Austrians rid the city of Turkish mosques and minarets and built a fortified compound incorporating the walls left over from Turkish rule—parts of these ancient fortifications still can be

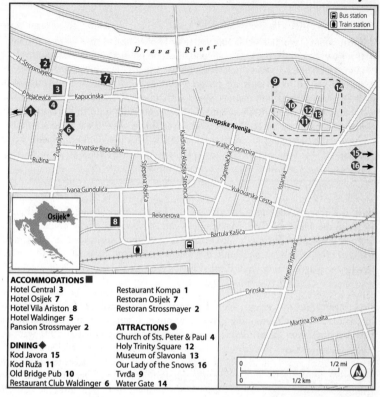

Bus station
Train station

ACCOMMODATIONS ■
Hotel Central **3**
Hotel Osijek **7**
Hotel Vila Ariston **8**
Hotel Waldinger **5**
Pansion Strossmayer **2**

DINING ◆
Kod Javora **15**
Kod Ruža **11**
Old Bridge Pub **10**
Restaurant Club Waldinger **6**

Restaurant Kompa **1**
Restoran Osijek **7**
Restoran Strossmayer **2**

ATTRACTIONS ●
Church of Sts. Peter & Paul **4**
Holy Trinity Square **12**
Museum of Slavonia **13**
Our Lady of the Snows **16**
Tvrđa **9**
Water Gate **14**

seen today. Even though Tvrđa has changed hands and personalities several times, it has retained its charm and old-world feel. Today, Tvrđa is a lovely area with cobblestone streets, lots of restaurants and galleries, and an artists' colony just inside the ramparts and the Water Gate. The Town Hall, Museum of Slavonia, and Osijek University are situated here.

Museum of Slavonia ⌘   There is a nice collection of archaeological finds from prehistoric to Roman times here. Housed in the City Magistrate Building on the southeastern corner of Holy Trinity Square, the 1702 structure is the oldest baroque building in Osijek. The museum moved there in 1946, and while the building was heavily shelled during the Homeland War, the collections escaped damage.

Trg Svetog Trojstva 6, Tvrđa. ℗ **031/122-505.** Fax 031/120-959. www.mdc.hr/osijek/eng/opci-podaci.html. Admission 10kn ($2) adults, 5kn ($1) children. Mon–Fri 7:30am–3:30pm; Sat–Sun 10am–1pm. Closed red-letter days (holidays).

Water Gate ⌘⌘   The Water Gate or Porta Aquatica led toward the Drava from the city fortifications when it was built in 1714. It still stands today as an entry to the walled part of the city. There once were five gates into the city, but the Water Gate is the only one that remains.

On the north side of the Tvrđa complex, right next to the Waldinger Gallery and near the Franciscan monastery and church.

Fun Fact **Homes, Sweet Homes**

Throughout Slavonia and Baranja you might notice houses that seem very small from the street but that resemble long, shotgun houses as they extend into the land. These houses, which have many entrances, are the result of the landowners' reluctance to divide their property among their sons. As the sons grew older and married, their parents would add groups of rooms for each son, each group with its own entrance. The additions were built onto the structure and into the property because the owners wanted to keep their acreage whole rather than parceling it out to their children. Thus the children became part owners of the family farm. The house facades face the street, but the buildings themselves jut into the land like a series of one-story motels.

Votive Pillar of the Holy Trinity 𝑅𝑅   This baroque plague pillar was built in 1729 by the widow of Gen. Maksimilijan Petraš, who died of the disease in 1728. Statuary decoration includes sculptures of Sts. Sebastian, Roch, Rosalia, and Catherine. The plague column was built as a prayer that "God have pity on Osijek and repulse the plague which ravaged the whole of Slavonia."

In the center of town (at Holy Trinity Square), Tvrđa.

Holy Trinity Square 𝑅𝑅𝑅   Holy Trinity is one of the most attractive town squares in Croatia. Besides the stunning **plague column** 𝑅𝑅, there is a round fountain with two red stone water basins. Restored historic buildings frame the square.

In the center of town. Tvrđa.

Our Lady of the Snows 𝑅   Our Lady of the Snows was built in 1895 based on a design of architect Franz Langenberg, who also designed the imposing Sts. Peter and Paul Church in Gornji Grad.

At the south end of Trg Bana Josip Jelačića, Donji Grad.

WHERE TO STAY

Osijek's hotel scene is improving, thanks to ambitious renovation projects that have restored or upgraded existing facilities.

Hotel Silver 𝑅   This privately owned hotel is about a mile from Osijek's center, but the walk into town is an easy one. Guest rooms are anything but cookie-cutter; some have slanted ceilings with skylights, while others are more conventional. Service is the main draw here, and room service is available from the hotel's small but excellent restaurant. The hotel can also arrange excursions to sites around town as well as trips to Kopački Rit Nature Park.

M. Divalta 84. ✆ 031/582-535. Fax 031/582-536. www.hotel-silver.hr. 18 units. Doubles from 690kn, ($112). AE, DC, MC, V. Limited guarded parking for 15 cars. **Amenities:** Restaurant; coffee bar; exchange office; room service. *In room:* A/C, TV, Internet access.

Hotel Waldinger 𝑅𝑅𝑅   The charming Hotel Waldinger is an oasis of elegance in the center of Osijek, a city that is still struggling to recover from the 1991 war. Named after 19th-century painter Adolf Igniat Waldinger and built in the center of town in 1904, this small hotel was completely renovated a century later in 2004. It now offers guests modern conveniences in an elegant, Secessionist-style interior, which is in stark contrast to the ultramodern high-rise Hotel Osijek a block away. Waldinger guest rooms are oversize and distinctive with soft colors, rich fabrics, and luxurious bathrooms. The paintings throughout the public and private spaces communicate the civilized air of a European manor. The English-speaking staff is helpful and courteous. Breakfast for Waldinger guests is in a private first-floor dining room, but the Kavana Waldinger ✿ at street level is open to the public. Besides its prime location steps away from one of the city's main squares, Trg Ante Starčevića, the Waldinger has a private lot with video-monitored free parking—a major perk for guests with cars. The elegant **Waldinger Restaurant Club** ✿✿✿ was added in 2007 just off the parking area.

Županijska 8, 31000 Osijek. ✆ **031/250-450.** Fax 031/250-453. 23 units, including 6 in the detached pansion. From 950kn ($176) double; from 1,200kn ($222) suite. Rates include breakfast. AE, DC, MC, V. **Amenities:** Restaurant; cafe; fitness center; sauna; exchange office; meeting rooms; library; art gallery; Internet; valet service. *In room:* A/C, TV, minibar, wake-up calls, Jacuzzi tub, hair dryer, safe.

Hotel Vila Ariston ✿   Everything is pristine in this butter-yellow hotel 15 minutes from Trg Ante Starčevića, Osijek's main shopping square. The English-speaking staff is eager to please and rooms are oversize with private balconies. Marble shines and parquet wood floors gleam in every corner of the building. The hotel is located just around the corner from the train station, which is convenient, but it's a shame that the tram tracks run less than 10 yards from the hotel's front door, making noise an issue. It's also too bad that the hotel's location takes it out of the riverfront action, and that the owner didn't think to put in an elevator when he built the 3-story Ariston in 2006. But, if you don't mind a little exercise (or a tram ride), and if you want a classy room with comfort and luxury at a moderate price, the Vila Ariston is the place for you.

Zrinjevac, Kačićeva 6. ✆ **031/251-351.** Fax 031/251-350. 8 units (6 doubles, 2 suites). Doubles from 777kn ($144); suites from 999kn ($185). Rates include breakfast. AE, DC, MC, V. Free video-monitored parking. **Amenities:** Restaurant; piano bar; valet service. *In room:* A/C, SAT TV, minibar, hair dryer, safe.

Hotel Osijek ✿ *Overrated*   The gleaming metal-and-glass Hotel Osijek soars 14 stories above the town's riverwalk as if flaunting its 2004 transformation from a socialist-style ugly duckling into a sleek capitalist swan. It is unabashedly trying to attract a clientele to match its new image and it has succeeded. The Osijek's lobby is minimalist chic and full of designer-clad guests, and its **Zimska Luka Restaurant** seems to attract yuppie corporate types and local celebs doing deals beside a panoramic view of the river. Add to that a lower-level watering hole for hip 20- and 30-somethings, an adjacent ice-cream/coffee shop for families, and a full-service salon, and you have the basics of a trendy hotel. Views from the riverside guest rooms are spectacular, but room size and amenities don't deliver what you'd expect for the expense-account prices charged here. In addition, the staff is cordial and efficient but not exceptionally helpful, and there is an extra charge for the use of bathrobes and slippers strategically placed in the rooms. If you want a hotel on the river, however, this is the only game in town.

Finds Ernestinovo

Ernestinovo is a little town between Osijek and Đakovo that is known for its fall sculpture festival during which sculptors, most of them Croatian, descend on the town and carve large wooden figures that they place along the side of the road from Ernestinovo to Vinkovci. The rest of the year a few of these large wooden figures can be seen positioned curbside throughout Ernestinovo.

Šamačka 4, 31000 Osijek. ℭ 031/230-333. Fax 031/230-444. www.hotelosijek.hr. 147 units. From 950kn ($176) double; from 1,490kn ($275) suite. Rates include breakfast. AE, DC, MC, V. 20 free parking spaces and adjacent city parking (free 8pm–7am). **Amenities:** Restaurant; pastry shop; bar; fitness center; business center; salon; shoeshine machine in lobby; valet service. *In room:* A/C, TV, wireless Internet on lower floors, minibar, hair dryer.

Hotel Central   The Central, which was built in 1899, is midway between the Waldinger and Osijek hotels, about a block from the river, and close to the city's tram line. The Central's lobby is a bit frayed around the edges, but the rooms are tidy and fairly priced. There are few room amenities here unless you count being able to walk to the river and the city's best sights in less than 15 minutes.

Trg Ante Starčevića. ℭ 031/283-399. Fax 031/283-891. www.hotel-central-os.hr. 39 units. From 786kn ($145) double; suites from 840kn ($156). AE, DC, MC, V. Rates include breakfast. Half- and full board available. **Amenities:** Restaurant; coffeehouse; solarium; excursions; bike rentals; salon. *In room:* TV, minibar.

Pansion Strossmayer 𝔄 *(Finds* Just 5 rooms above Restoran Strossmayer comprise Pansion Strossmayer, but you can't beat the location, the price, the amenities, or the breakfast crammed into the price of these immaculate units.

Strossmayerova 133. ℭ 031/375-888. 5 units. Doubles from 490kn ($90). Rate includes breakfast. AE, DC, MC, V. **Amenities:** Restaurant; bar. *In room:* A/C, SAT TV, hydromassage shower, toiletries that include toothbrush, paste, and shaving cream.

WHERE TO DINE

Osijek is a mecca for Slavonian cuisine and no matter where you dine, you won't leave hungry. Many restaurants in this part of Croatia are family style, so don't be surprised when huge platters of food arrive for all to share.

Waldinger Restaurant Club 𝔄𝔄𝔄 CONTINENTAL   The level of sophistication evident in the chic design of this restaurant in the middle of sausage-and-paprika Slovenia is as unexpected as Waldinger's inventive menu. Add culinary touches that would be at home in mid-town Manhattan and you have a gastronomic oasis worth a detour from any itinerary. WRC opened in January 2007 and since then diners have been drawn to the softly illuminated space filled with warm cherry floors, gauzy drapes, and lots of glass. Dishes like the "Black Widow," sirloin steak in blackberry-pimento sauce, wild filet of deer, bear, or doe in candied cherry sauce, or duck breast with green pepper and honey-orange sauce are the real draw, though. For dessert, we couldn't resist the restaurant's interpretation of Bananas Foster, a beautifully composed dish of flamed fruit, vanilla ice cream, and cinnamon. There is also a wine list deep in Croatian regionals.

Županuska 8. ℭ 031/214-671. Reservations recommended. Entrees 40kn ($7) (for pastas) to 150kn ($28). AE, DC, MC, V. Daily 11am–midnight.

Restoran Kompa 𝔄𝔄 *(Value* SLAVONIAN   Locals love this family-style restaurant where you can dine within feet of the mighty Drava. Very little English is spoken here and you will need your dictionary to figure out the menu, but the authentic Croatian dining experience is worth the effort. Fish is on the menu, but not exclusively, so start with local cheese and sausage and a bottle of the house wine *(Slavonski kulen, sir grbancijaš, vino buteljirano),* and you may not have enough room for dinner. Portions are enormous; do save a little room for the strudel. If you take a table outside after dark, bring along insect repellent.

Splavarska 1. ℭ 031/375-755. Fax 031/376-358. Entrees from 25kn ($5) for *sarma* (chopped meat and rice wrapped in marinated cabbage leaves) to 60kn ($11) for *šunka* and *sir* (ham and cheese). AE, DC, MC, V. Daily 9am–10pm.

Kod Javora 🍴🍴 SLAVONIAN   The atmosphere is kind of boisterous at this "din-ing hall" near the river, but the food is authentic Slavonian and well-prepared. Start with grilled pike filets wrapped in local *pršut* and served with a delicate thyme-scented tartar sauce that you'll want to put on everything else you order. Another good choice at this restaurant, whose name means "at the maple tree," is *perkelt,* a ragout variation of fish paprika with a spicy kick. For tamer tastes, *rezanci sa sirom* (noodles with cheese and bacon) is a good choice, though family-style service makes sampling easy. Wash it all down with a bottle of local Graševina, a crisp white wine that stands up to the intense flavors in most of the dishes here. Seating is available inside or on the river. When it's raining, the restaurant moves its outdoor tables into a big party tent.

Donjodravska obala 14. ✆ 031/506-950. Reservations recommended. Entrees 50kn–80kn ($9–$15). AE, MC, V. Daily 9am–11pm.

Restaurant Strossmayer 🍴 SLAVONIAN   The dining room is bright and cheer-ful in this cute all-purpose restaurant off Osijek's main square. Portions are huge and recipes authentic. Try the turkey shish kebob, which comes with a nice portion of grilled veggies. Or take a chance on the plat du jour, in our case, veal roulades in au natural gravy. There is a small outdoor terrace and, sadly, smoking is permitted in the restaurant.

Strossmayerova 133. ✆ 031/375-888. www.pizzastross.com. Entrees 25kn–75kn ($5–$14), more for meat and fish by the kilo. AE, DC, MC, V. Mon–Sat 10am–10pm; Sun 11am–3pm and 7–10pm.

Old Bridge Pub 🍴 CROATIAN/INTERNATIONAL   Many levels of dining com-prise the Old Bridge experience. Outside-inside, formal-bar-style, and everything in between is possible in this atmospheric spot near Tvrđa named after the 13km (8-mile) long oak bridge that linked Osijek and its marshy outposts in the 16th century. Try one of the restaurant's excellent pasta dishes—you can choose a pasta and match it with any sauce—or the Big Ben, a huge turkey shish kebab with grilled veggies. For dessert there is homemade štrukli or *knedle su šlivama,* plum dumplings that resemble sugar-covered jelly donuts filled with whole stewed plums. There is an extensive menu of Irish brews as well as lots of memorabilia from across the channel. Old Bridge offers live music in the downstairs room after 10 pm most days.

Kuhačeva 4. ✆ 031/211-611. www.oldbridgepub.hr. Entrees 34kn–85kn ($16–$46). AE, DC, MC, V. Mon–Thurs 7am–2am; Fri–Sat 7am–4am; Sun 9am–midnight.

Kod Ruže 🍴🍴 SLAVONIAN   Slavonia seems to have embraced the "back to our roots" movement in a big way and Kod Ruže (trans: At Rose's) is no exception. This restaurant housed in a vintage 1758 building near Tvrđa opened in January 2007 and it is full of taxidermed animals, ancient pottery, ancestral photos hanging in hand-carved frames on hand-painted patterned walls, and other regional antiques. Kod Ruže also tries to duplicate some of the recipes from Grandma's time on the menu. Start with a Slavonian plate for 2, generous portions of kulen, local cheese, and crack-ling "čvanci," or go for a filling bowl of game stew. In winter you can try *sarma,* sour cabbage leaves stuffed with meat and rice, and you can have grilled fish any time. Kod Ruže makes its own *ajvar,* a Croatian condiment made of red pepper and eggplant, but its pastries have a store-bought taste. The menu here changes seasonally and there is a nice list of Croatian wines.

Kuhačeva 25a. ✆ 031/206-066. Entrees 25kn–80kn ($5–$15). AE, DC, MC, V. Mon–Sat 9am–11pm and Sun 10am–4pm.

Fiš Paprikaš (Serves 10)

5 lb. cleaned carp	½ lb. stewed tomatoes
1 lb. cleaned catfish	2–3 hot chile peppers
½ lb. cleaned pike	3–4 onions, grated or chopped
2 tsp salt	1 tsp cayenne pepper
2 tsp paprika	1 qt. water

Place finely chopped or grated onion, sliced fish, tomato, and chile peppers in a 3-gallon pot. Cover with a quart of water and place over high heat. When the water comes to a boil, add salt, cayenne pepper, and paprika. Simmer for 30 minutes.

Fiš Paprikaš is usually served with wide homemade noodles cooked separately.

COFFEEHOUSES

Kavana Waldinger 𝄞𝄞 PASTRIES   The front of this coffeehouse next to the lobby of the Waldinger Hotel opens to the street. Besides mouth-watering pastries and ice-cream treats, patrons can linger over coffee while pedestrian traffic rolls by. Županijska 8. ✆ **031/250-470.** AE, DC, MC, V. Daily 8am–11pm.

Mala Kavana 𝄞𝄞 PASTRIES   There isn't a more advantageous spot for a coffeehouse than the corner of Gornji Grad's main square, which just underwent a 10-million€ makeover. Besides enjoying some of the best brews and people shows in town, patrons who sit at the outdoor tables can now amuse themselves with the sight of a modern water feature (fountain) and mall entrance. Županijska 2. No phone. No credit cards. Mon–Sat 6:30am–11pm; Sun 8am–11pm.

NIGHTLIFE

Clubbing and bar-hopping in Osijek have exploded in the last two years thanks to extensive riverfront development and the Tvrđa renovation. It is not unusual to find places for drinking and dancing that stay open until dawn.

Tufna 𝄞   This club opened in 2007 on the site of another club near Tvrđa and it was an instant success. Tufna offers two floors of music from disco to electro beats and it attracts all the beautiful people, provided they can prove that they are over 21. Open 8am to midnight Monday through Wednesday, 8am to 3am Thursday, 8am to 4am Friday and Saturday, and 10am to midnight on Sunday. Franje Kuhača 10. ✆ **031/215-020.** Fax: 031/215-021.

Cadillac CLUB   The acoustic performances from mostly local talent on center stage at Cadillac appeal to all age groups. The dark wood and mirrors give the place a cozy atmosphere that makes everyone feel at home. Open 8am to 3am daily. Kardinala Alojzija Stepinca 28. ✆ **031/209-138.** Acoustic performances Thurs; local rock groups Sat.

K 𝄞 BAR   The former Kesten Bar is in a new location near the train station as of 2007, but even with a new identity, the bar's followers have remained loyal. Tame by jet-set standards, the bar usually empties out by 11pm as hard-core partygoers move on to more raucous pastures. Open 9am to 11pm Monday through Friday, 8am to 11pm on Saturday, and 10am to 11pm Sunday. Kardinala Alojzija Stepinca 38a. © **098/843-078.**

Gen. Von Becker's ⚜⚜ BAR   Tvrđa's central square is a prime location for bars and restaurants these days and GVB's is sitting pretty there. The interior is reminiscent of the days when the Hapsburgs set the styles in town, though drinking, not history, is the focus here. Open 7am to midnight Monday through Thursday, 7am to 2am Friday and Saturday, and 10am to midnight Sunday. Franje Kuhača 13. No phone. No credit cards.

Old Bridge Pub ⚜ PUB   (above).

St. Patrick's Pub ⚜⚜ PUB   It's a mystery why Osijek has two Irish pubs, but the attraction of St. Patrick's on the main Tvrđa square is clear. Besides the welcoming interior, St. Pat's has a wonderful outdoor terrace where patrons can hoist a pint to summer—or whatever turns them on. Open 7am to midnight Monday through Wednesday, 7am to 1am Thursday, 7am to 2am Friday and Saturday, and 9:30am to midnight Sunday. Trg Svetog Trojstva. No phone. AE, DC, MC, V.

10 Baranja

Baranja extends beyond Croatia into Serbia and Hungary, but in Croatia, the Baranja land northeast of Osijek and up to Croatia's eastern border is mostly farm and vineyard country, with the Kopački Rit wetlands thrown in for good measure. Until recently, tourists tended to avoid Baranja because of land-mine threats, but today almost all land-mines have been removed and those that remain are underwater in inaccessible parts of Kopački Rit. Baranja is now coming into its own as a center for farm stays, wine tours, and sustainable tourism.

Kopački Rit Nature Park ⚜⚜⚜   Kopački Rit is a 168-sq.-m (65-sq.-mile) floodplain area of the Danube River, at the river's confluence with the Drava. According to park literature, it is also one of the largest alluvial plains in Europe and extends north into the Republic of Hungary. Kopački Rit was designated a nature park in 1967 to protect the flood-plain ecosystems. Today, the park is home to many wetland birds from early spring to fall when the Danube overflows its banks. White-tailed eagles, cormorants, great-crested grebes, white storks, and a few black storks can be seen here, when the plain is flooded and when wild boar, deer, and 40 species of fish inhabit the plains and the lakes and ponds that remain when the Danube waters pull back. Besides wildlife, attractions include Sakadaš and Kopačko lakes where more than 285 species of birds come to fish and nest; the 19th-century Tikveš Hunting Lodge, now home to meeting rooms and a restaurant; and Kopačevo, a traditional Slavonian settlement that has been frozen in time. Zelena Žava is a delightful restaurant that serves traditional specialties. Reservations are necessary if you want one of the English-language boat or Jeep tours.

Tip: There is a bicycle path that runs along the Osijek-Bilje road, which means you can stay in Osijek, just 10km (6 miles) southwest from the park, and pedal there. Or you can catch an Osijek-Bilje bus, which runs every half-hour or so, but you will have to walk 4km (2.5 miles) from the bus stop to the park's entrance.

Petefi Šandora 33, 31327 Bilje. © 031/752-350. Fax 031/752-351. www.kopacki-rit.com. 40kn ($7.50/5€) adults, 20kn ($4/3€) children Sun. 60kn ($11/8€) adults, 45kn ($8/6€) children other times. Park-guided boat trip 80kn ($15/11€); guided bird-watching tour 200kn ($37/27€). Daily 9am–5pm.

Restoran Tikveš ⚔⚔ You expect to see hunters in camouflage dining in this unpretentious restaurant nestled against Kopački Rit's vegetation. Usually, all you'll get is tourists and a fine meal from the nearby forest and rivers. Pheasant, venison, and boar are on the menu, as are carp Baranja and the Tikveš sandwich (kulen, cheese, salami). Desserts are homey (Grandma's sweet leaves, a concoction of filo, poppy seeds and walnuts) and there is a nice selection of Croatian wine.

Konpleks dvorca Tikveš, 31328 Lug. ℂ **031/752-901.** www.restoran-tikves.hr. Entrees 68kn–87kn ($13–$16). AE, DC, MC, V. Daily 9am–10pm.

Baranja Wine Road (Općina Kneževi Vinogradi) ⚔⚔⚔ There are more than 20 wineries listed on the Baranja wine route, and almost all serve food either as a complement to their wines or for those just out for a good meal. Some have lodging. Most of these wineries are family businesses with the owners living on the winery premises. It isn't difficult to arrange to visit any of these Baranja gems, but you should call ahead either to the Baranja Tourism Office or to the individual vintners to make sure they are home and prepared to serve you when you arrive.

Hrvatske Republike 3, Kneževi vinogradi. ℂ **031/730-938.** Fax 031/732-106. www.knezevi-vinogradi.hr.

BARANJA EXPERIENCES ⚔⚔⚔

Sklepić ⚔⚔⚔ Go back in time at this restored Baranja farmhouse complex 8km (5 miles) east of Beli Manastir at the top of Croatia. The owner says the food, activities, and accommodations in the rooms behind a porch decorated with fermenting cherries, geraniums, and drying peppers are as close to authentic as possible. Sklepić is a place where the bathrooms are indoors but TV and A/C are nonexistent. You can walk behind your unit to gather your own eggs and pick your veggies to use in your breakfast omelet and you can even help the family make bread or harvest crops. Lunch and dinner are not offered, but they are available a la carte at nearby Baranjska Kuča ⚔⚔.

Kolodvorska 58, Karanac. ℂ **098/739-159.** www.sklepic.hr. 8 units, including 2 quads. Doubles from 300kn ($55/41€). Quads from 150kn ($28/21€) per person. Rates include breakfast. **Amenities:** Fresh air.

Baranjska Kuča ⚔⚔ Everything is authentic and homemade in this rustic restaurant, which was a Karanac granary 120 years ago. It is just 15km (9 miles) northwest of Kopački Rit but a world away from ordinary. With every meal, the owner's wife serves *Šapsui sir* (farmers cheese with paprika) to spread on *lepinja*, little pitalike rolls baked in an oven made hot by burning wood, then removing it. Specialties include *čobanac* (soup with 3 kinds of meat) and *smud orly* (pike fried in beer). At night a gypsy band plays everything from rock to traditional Baranja folk music.

Kolodvorska 99, Karanac. ℂ **031/720-180.** Entrees 35kn–140kn ($7–$26). www.baranjskakuca.cjb.net or www.baranjskakuca.odmor.org.

WHERE TO STAY AND DINE

Hotel Patria The Patria is in Beli Manastir, as far as you can go into Baranja County without crossing over into Serbia. In fact, you can see the border from some parts of the property. The hotel opened in November 2006 and it is equipped to handle business travelers, families, even hunters. The hotel aspires to be a mini-resort, complete with a petting zoo, barbecue kiosk, dorm facility that sleeps 27, and a kennel for almost two dozen dogs. Most rooms have tubs in the bathroom and a blue plastic elliptical in case you can't make it to the well-equipped fitness center. Did we mention that the hotel's exterior is painted a "can't-miss-it" shade of deep lilac?

A Pair of Podrumi

- **Kolar Wine Cellar** ✦✦✦ Produces 80,000 liters from its century-old cellar. The facility includes a restaurant and some of the most immaculate sobes we've seen anywhere in Croatia. Maršala Tita 139, Suza. ✆ **031/733-184**. 3 units. Doubles from 360kn (50€)/$67). Rates include breakfast. **Amenities:** A/C; SAT TV. *In room:* Bath w/shower; 1 w/tub, terrace.

- **Gerštmajer Wine Cellar** ✦✦✦ Four generations of winemakers have worked the land that supplies this 150-year-old winery. Gerštmaijer sells much of his production in bulk to restaurants and for parties, but if you can snag one of his bottles of Rajnski rizling, it is sublime. Maršala Tita 152, Zmajevac. ✆ **091/351-55-86**.

Tip: The hotel offers an attractive detached hostel with rooms that sleep 4 to 7 guests. Prices are lower than the hotel (150kn/21€/$28] per person without breakfast), but the bathroom is down the hall.

Osječka 1C. 31300 Beli Manastir. ✆ **031/710-710**. Fax 031/710-720. www.hotelpatria.hr. 42 units, including 2 suites. Deluxe doubles from 700kn ($130/95€). Rates include breakfast. AE, DC, MC, V. **Amenities:** Restaurant; lobby bar; terrace dining; hostel; fitness center; free parking; dog kennel; children's area. *In room:* A/C SAT TV, minibar, hair dryer, safe, elliptical.

11 Vukovar & Ilok

From a historical point of view, **Vukovar** is an important stop on any tour of Croatia and until recently there wasn't much for tourists to see except ravaged structures languishing after the Homeland War. That has changed dramatically in the last two years thanks to an infusion of grant money from the Croatian government in recognition of the area's historical and archaeological significance. Today Vukovar is teeming with archaeologists working to uncover significant vestiges of long-gone civilizations, including Bronze Age settlements on the Danube. Vukovar once was known for its elegance and culture, and until 2006 it looked like a powerful, living, antiwar advertisement because of the rubble left over from the almost total devastation it suffered during the war that swept through Slavonia in 1991. Some say the city was served up to the Serbs and the Yugoslav People's Army (JNA) as a sacrificial lamb and left in shambles for years as a reminder of that event.

Before the war, Vukovar was a center of industry and manufacturing in Croatia thanks to the huge Borovo tire factory and other businesses. The city also enjoyed a modest tourism trade thanks to its baroque center, its lovely riverfront location, and its vibrant society. However, Vukovar's position just across the river from Serbia and its large Serbian population (37%) also made it a prime target during the war. The result was a 3-month-long siege in 1991 that all but leveled the city and emptied it of people.

Vukovar finally was returned to Croatia in 1998, but not all its citizens have come back, perhaps because there isn't much to return to. Many local businesses and homes lie in ruins, jobs are scarce, and some say the government has been slow to rebuild Vukovar because it wants the ravaged city to remain a physical symbol of the brutal siege.

About 39km (24 miles) east of Vukovar, **Ilok** is the easternmost city in Croatia and home to a 13th-century fortress and palace that is being excavated. It also has an 18th-century Franciscan monastery that was built inside the walls where St. Ivan Kapestran (St. John Capistrano), a Franciscan warrior monk, successfully defended the banks of the Danube against invading Turks.

St. Ivan died at the monastery after a battle in 1456, but in 1526 another wave of Turks attacked and eventually prevailed. They held Ilok until 1697, when Austria took over. Subsequently, the Hapsburgs gave the entire town—perhaps as a reward—to Livio Odescalchi, an Italian military officer who helped defeat the Ottoman forces.

Ilock's Fruška Gora area has been known since Roman times for its microclimate, which supports lush vineyards and robust wine production. Ilok was taken by the Serbs during the Homeland War, but it was not as badly damaged as Vukovar because almost all its citizens were given the opportunity to flee before the attack. Today, several high-powered investors have become interested in Ilok and recently have been acquiring its vineyards and wineries. Ilok's wine industry is approaching pre-war production levels.

ESSENTIALS

VISITOR INFORMATION   Vukovar's **tourism office** is at J. J. Strossmayera 15 on the way to the Eltz Palace. You can pick up brochures and maps here, but you need to arrive during weekday office hours 7am to 3pm (✆ **032/441-762;** fax 032/442-889; turisticka-zajednica-grada-vukovara@vk.htnet.hr)—and you need to know where to look. The **Ilok tourism office** is in the town center at Trg Nikole Iločkog 2 (✆ **032/ 590-020;** tz-grada-iloka@vk.htnet.hr).

GETTING THERE   Buses run through flat farmland and vineyards from Osijek and Vinkovci to Vukovar with convenient frequency. There isn't much to see but corn and wheat during the 35km (22-mile) trip. However, the 40km (25-mile) trip from Vukovar is much more scenic whether you take a bus from Vukovar or drive your own car as it follows the Danube through vineyards and the Fruška Gora range.

GETTING AROUND   Both Vukovar and Ilok are best explored on foot, though Vukovar covers a much larger area. If you want to visit Ilok's wineries, you'll need your own transportation.

WHAT TO SEE & DO

Parts of Vukovar have been restored, but except for the remnants of war, there is little to see besides the City Museum in restored Eltz Palace and the waterfront war monument. Ilok and its vineyards suffered less damage in the war, so that city has much more to offer at this time.

Ovčara Memorial Center ⭒⭒⭒   The memorial 5km (3 miles) south of Vukovar opened Nov. 20, 2006, 15 years to the day when 261 Croat men, women, and children—some hospital patients—were executed in 1991. Ovčara was a series of storage hangars used to keep Croat prisoners en route to Serbian work camps. It is in the same building (restored) where soldiers seeking sanctuary in the Vukovar hospital were taken, then shot and buried in a mass grave northeast of the facility. The memorial's interior is painted black while photos of the identified dead fade in and out of view on them. There is an eerie memorial flame in a circular stone frame in the floor, which is "carpeted" with actual bullets found on the property after the massacre. Tip Ovčara does not charge an entrance fee, but there is a small shop at the exit where books and

The Vučedol Dove

This ceramic archaeological find was uncovered in the early 20th century about 5km (3 miles) south of Vukovar on the Danube. The little pot made around 2500 B.C. is the most famous and popular artifact of Vučedol culture in southeastern Europe. It has been reproduced and kept in almost every home in Croatia since the 1991 war, when it came to symbolize peace for those fighting for freedom in Croatia. The original is displayed at the Archaeological Museum in Zagreb (p. 274).

replicas of the Vučedal dove are sold to support the memorial. A TV looping news footage of Serb soldiers celebrating the destruction of Vukovar and showing Vukovar residents slowly leaving the city carrying their belongings is chilling.

3km (1.8 miles) southeast of Vukovar on the Ovčara-Brabovo road. Daily 10am–5pm.

Civic Museum 🍴🍴 In 1736, after the Turks had been routed from Vukovar, the city was given to the Eltz nobles, who built churches and an elaborate baroque palace. The 18th-century Eltz Palace, like many other buildings in Croatia, was nationalized after World War II, after which it became the site of the Vukovar Civic Museum. The building was heavily damaged in 1991 and its treasures whisked away to safety in other parts of Croatia. Today most of the pieces from the collections are back and the damaged areas of the palace are being restored.

L. Ribara 2, Vukovar. ☎ 032/441-270. Mon–Sat 8am–4pm.

Iločki Podrumi Winery 🍴🍴🍴 This winery on the banks of the Danube is one of the region's largest. It also is the second-oldest winery in Europe. The winery was raided by the Serbs in the 1991 war, when most of its barrels were damaged and its stores confiscated, but the owners were able to hide some of the winery's older vintages, which are now for sale. The winery resumed production in 1999 after the 7-year occupation ended in 1998. It now produces more than 4 million liters of traminac, graševina, chardonnay, Rhine riesling, and other varietals annually. It also offers tours, tastings, and meals, and sells retail from the facility. English-speaking guides are available for tours if you make reservations in advance, or you can drop in. The winery also serves Slavonian meals to groups on tour or others with advance notice. The Iločki Podrum winery and its wines are well known and respected throughout Europe. In fact, Ilok wines were served at the coronation of Queen Elizabeth II in 1953.

Dr. Franje Tudmana 72, Ilok. ☎ 032/590-003. Fax 032/590-047. www.ilocki-podrumi.hr.

Mathias Kulen 🍴🍴 *Kulen,* Slavonia's spicy wood-smoked sausage, has many producers in Slavonia, but Mathias is the best there is. You can get Mathias kulen in higher-end grocery stores. This little retail store about 16km (10 miles) southeast of Vukovar is the best place to find the delicacy, which is made only in Slavonia. Kulen production is a fairly complicated and expensive affair; Mathias's kulen sells for about 100kn ($20) per pound.

Gustava Krkleca 15, Vinkovci. ☎ 032/367-848. Fax 032/366-107. mathias@email.htnet.hr. No credit cards. Mon–Fri 8am–3pm; Sat 8am–1pm. Closed Sun.

Church and Monastery of Sv. Ivan Kapistran ✦✦✦ This church and monastery hold a treasure-trove of history and artifacts from the area. The Franciscan monks booby-trapped the church and monastery with mines during the 1991 war to keep the Serbs out. The head monk stayed inside, though the buildings were damaged. The church is also home to St. John Capistrano's relics, which are on display in a glass case. You can see the church's painstaking restoration in progress in a monastery studio, which also holds a large collection of sacral art. Knock on the monastery door, and the church's affable pastor will be happy to show you the church, the monastery, and the treasures hidden there during the war.

Ilok. ✆ **032/344-034.** Visits by appointment.

WHERE TO STAY

Neither Vukovar nor Ilok merits an overnight stay unless you have business in the area. Until recently there has been a dearth of acceptable accommodations in both cities, but that is changing. Both towns are now regular stops for Danube cruise ships which drop their passengers at the dock in Vukovar to see the town's monument to fallen soldiers. Hotels in both towns are trying hard to respond.

Hotel Lav ✦✦ Built on the site a hotel that overlooked the storied river, the Lav's opening in the spring of 2005 is a hopeful sign that Vukovar finally may be on the road to recovery from the Homeland War. The neighborhood around the Lav still shows the effects of the devastating shelling that all but leveled Vukovar, but right now the hotel stands above it like a gleaming promise on the Danube. Guest rooms are comfortably furnished with nice touches like magnifying mirrors and Pascal Morabity toiletries in the bathrooms. Most have great views of the river and Serbia on the opposite bank, especially from the lavishly outfitted suites. The hotel uses environmentally safe operating methods when possible and it is "art friendly" by displaying the work of local artists in its public spaces. *Tip:* Lav management has implemented a "Bike and Bed" initiative to serve an increasing number of cyclists who take advantage of the area's 100km (60 miles) of bike routes. Besides a hotel room, the Lav provides bike storage.

J. J. Strossmayera 18, Vukovar. ✆ **032/297-111.** Fax 032/445-110. www.hotel-lav.hr. 42 units, including 4 suites. From 970kn ($180) double; from 2,470kn ($458) suite. Rates include breakfast. Half- and full board available. AE, DC, MC, V. Parking. **Amenities:** Restaurant; bar; cafe; bike storage; laundry; parking. *In room:* A/C, SAT TV, wireless Internet, safe.

Hotel Dunav ✦ The Dunav was built as a package hotel and despite several updates, it still is. Rooms and public spaces still have that dark, socialist aura and infrastructure like the elevators and bathrooms is very basic. One bright spot: The Dunav has a lovely terrace where you can enjoy drinks and light snacks during the day.

Trg Republike. Hrvratske 1. ✆ 032/441-285. Fax 032/441-762. 57units. Doubles from 812kn ($153); suites from 904kn ($168). Rates include breakfast. AE, DC, MC, V. Amenities: Restaurant; bar. In room: Phone.

WHERE TO DINE

Dining options in Vukovar and Ilok are improving but almost as thin as hotel options. Casual places serve pizza and simple grilled meat and fish dishes. However, there is a surge in agri-tourism, which includes home-cooked meals in very small rural wineries and inns, and the area's Graševina white wine is excellent.

Tri Vrške ✦ SLAVONIAN Dining options in Vukovar are mostly limited to cafes and pizzerias, but if you happen to be staying at the Hotel Lav overnight, this casual riverside restaurant, whose name means "Three Fishnets," is just steps away. Besides good Slavonian food, the restaurant has a view of the Serbian landscape from its tables

Sv. Ivan Kapistran

Sv. Ivan Kapistran (St. John Capistrano) was born to a former German knight and his wife in Italy in 1385. John became a lawyer in Perugia and was appointed governor of that Italian city by King Ladislas of Naples. During Perugia's war with another Italian town in 1416, John was taken prisoner, and while confined, he promised God that he would become a priest if he got out alive. John kept his promise to God and became a priest, then traveled across Italy establishing new Franciscan communities and spreading the word of God. In 1455, at the age of 70, John was asked by Pope Callistus II to lead troops against invading Turks. Thus, he became the leader of 70,000 Crusaders who in 1456 won the Battle of Belgrade against the enemy. John died 3 months later in Ilok, Croatia, where he is buried. The Mission of San Juan Capistrano founded by Franciscan Brother Juniperro Serra in 1776 in Orange County, California, is named after this 15th-century hero, who is the patron saint of jurists.

on the banks of the Danube. Most dishes lean toward seafood. A schnitzel option is served with rice and vegetables. Pike, seafood paprika, grilled calamari, and a fried seafood platter are other possibilities. In the afternoon you can stop here for a coffee and pastry break.

Parobrodska 3, Vukovar. ✆ 032/441-788. Entrees 28kn–58kn ($5–$10). AE, DC, MC, V. Daily 8am–10pm.

Restaurant Lav ✿✿   The Hotel Lav's restaurant serves surprisingly sophisticated cuisine in a space that is bright, tastefully decorated, and generously enhanced with original artwork from local talent. Dig into the Slavonian feast, a platter of grilled pork chops, bacon, and sausage, or go lighter with beef with truffles. There are many local specialties on the menu, a trend that extends to the dessert cart.

J. J. Strossmayera 18, Vukovar. ✆ 032/297-111. Fax 032/445-110. www.hotel-lav.hr. Entrees 35kn–130kn ($7–$24). AE, DC, MC, V. Daily 7am–11pm.

Restoran Iločka Kuća ✿✿ SLAVONIAN   Even though restaurants and cafes almost completely line Dr. F. Tuđmana in Ilok, seek out Restoran Iločka Kuća, because it stands a little taller than its neighbors. Pizza, grilled meat, and home-cooked specialties are the order of the day at this typical Slavonian dining spot, whose servers are very friendly, even if they speak very little English.

Dr. F. Tuđmana 7, Ilok. ✆ 032/590-402. Entrees 30kn–65kn ($6-$12). No credit cards. Daily 7am–midnight.

Appendix:
Croatia in Context

Contemporary Croatia is a land of contrasts and contradictions: Primitive Stone Age settlements, glittering seaside resorts, vestiges of Greek and Roman antiquity, pristine natural wonders, and newly cosmopolitan cities all coexist in a framework of geographic and cultural diversity. Croatia is famous and infamous—it is a popular sun-drenched tourist destination and, at the same time, an ethnic battlefield that was the site of one of the most vicious European wars in modern times.

Despite serial invasions by foreign nations, Croatia successfully protected its heritage and kept it alive in its citizens' hearts and homes. Modern Croats are fiercely independent survivors, who have again and again emerged from ethnic conflicts and foreign occupations to reassert their national identity.

Fortunately, Croatia's wars are in the past and the newly vibrant nation is facing the 21st century poised to embrace progress, global commerce, tourism, and independence as it pushes forward to claim a place in the European Union.

To understand how far Croatia has come and to find the source of its strength, look to the Croatian people. Shared hardship and fierce solidarity are the catalysts that make the Croatians eager to proclaim their heritage after having spent much of the last thousand years or so anticipating war, at war, or recovering from war. Contemporary Croatia is confidently racing toward prosperity, shaking off its underdog image as it focuses on the future and builds on its past.

1 History 101

PREHISTORY

At the turn of the 20th century (1899) the remains of a type of Neanderthal who lived in caves some 30,000 years ago were discovered at Krapina, a tiny town north of Zagreb. These early cave dwellers' bones were dubbed "Krapina Man," and they established a time line that put humans in Croatia in the middle of the Stone Age. Traces of other prehistoric cultures also have been found at the island of Hvar and Vukovar in extreme eastern Croatia, but none is older or more significant than Krapina Man.

ILLYRIANS

Recorded Croatian history begins around 1200 B.C., when the people occupying the region that is now Croatia, Bosnia, Albania, and Serbia began to form a coalition of tribes known as the Illyrians. The Illyrian tribes shared similarities, such as burial customs and dwelling styles, but there is no concrete evidence that any one tribe was assimilated by any other. In fact, each Illyrian tribe had its own name based on where it settled, and at least some of them became regional powers and established cities that survive today.

THE GREEK COLONISTS

The Greeks began colonizing the Adriatic coast of Croatia in the 4th century B.C., beginning with Issa (the island of Vis), a colony founded by residents of Syracuse (Sicily). Other settlements followed, including Paros (Hvar) and Tragurion (Trogir). The Illyrians traded oil, wine, salt, metals and other commodities with the Greeks but nonetheless tried to get rid of foreign settlements. In the 3rd century B.C., the Illyrians attempted to form an independent state under the leadership of one of its pirate tribes. In 229 B.C. the Greeks, alarmed by this turn of events, asked the Romans for help in containing Illyrian lawlessness. When the Romans sent messengers to negotiate peace with the Illyrian Queen Teuta, she had them executed. This touched off a series of wars that lasted more than 60 years, ending with the defeat of the Illyrians and the creation of the Roman province of Illyricum.

THE ROMAN OCCUPATION

The spread of Roman colonies across Croatia continued until A.D. 9, when the Adriatic coast and interior lands were annexed by the Emperor Tiberius to create three Roman provinces: Dalmatia (Adriatic seacoast), Noricum (northern territory/Austria), and Pannonia (Hungary). The Romans built fortresses, roads, bridges, aqueducts, and sparkling new cities that overtook Illyrian culture or drove it away. The main Roman cities of that time were Pola (Pula), Jader (Zadar), Salona (Solin) near Split, and Epidaurum (Cavtat). The Roman propensity for building roads linked northeast Italy to Byzantium (Istanbul) and opened lines of communication that facilitated trade and troop movements and the spread of Roman culture.

Those same roads brought Christianity to the area, and with it persecution, primarily at the hand of the Emperor Diocletian, whose "retirement home" at Split is one of Croatia's best-preserved vestiges of the Roman era, which flourished until the end of the 4th century.

From about A.D. 395 until the 7th century, Croatia suffered a series of invasions by the Ostrogoths, Slavs, and other barbarians. But it was the Avars, a warlike Asian tribe, who allegedly brought the Slavic Croats—ancestors to today's Croatians—to the area.

According to the 10th-century Byzantine Emperor Constantine Porphyrogenitus, the Emperor Heraclius asked the Croats to come to the region to help him get rid of the Avars and to protect Rome's interests, though the Croats didn't stop at saving the Roman occupation.

THE CROAT MIGRATION

Porphyrogenitus's account of the Croats' arrival has been disputed, partly because it was written 300 years after the fact. Other accounts differ about the Croats' appearance in southeastern Europe. Some experts say the Croats came from the Ukraine; others pinpoint Poland; and some say the Croats migrated from Iran because the name "Hvrat" has Persian origins. The trail leading back to the Croats is further clouded because the name Croat (Hvrat) was used by other Slavic tribes of the times (White Croats in Poland; Croats in the Czech Republic area; and other groups from nearby Slovenia, Slovakia, and Macedonia). Either way, it is likely that there were several waves of Croat migration, with the first group settling the part of the Roman province of Pannonia that is now southern Hungary. Subsequent migrations settled land all the way to Dalmatia.

Eventually, the Croat émigrés organized into two dukedoms, and at the same time they began to accept Roman-rite Christianity and Roman culture. But the existence of two distinct centers of culture—Mediterranean (Dalmatia) and central European (Pannonia)—served to form a dueling Croatian psyche, which lingers today. Croats continued to live under a series of foreign and Croatian administrations until A.D. 924, when the country was united under the leadership of Tomislav I, the first King of Croatia.

MEDIEVAL CROATIA

Tomislav was crowned around A.D. 924 and united the Pannonian and Dalmatian duchies, which included what is much of present-day Slavonia, Dalmatia, Istria, and Bosnia/Herzegovina. He disappears from history around A.D. 928, but no one disputes that he had a profound effect on Croatia. He was succeeded by a series of monarchs who enjoyed relative stability for almost the next 2 centuries. Among them were King Petar Krešimir IV (1058–74) and King Dmitar Zvonimir (1075–89). Zvonimir's reign is notable because he entrenched Catholicism in Croatia and strengthened the country's relationship with the Roman Church. His reign is immortalized on the Baška Tablet, a kind of Croatian Rosetta stone engraved with the oldest known Croatian text. The tablet is on display in Zagreb's archaeological museum.

HUNGARY & VENICE

After Zvonimir's death in the 11th century, the monarchy withered, and Croatia and Hungary formed a common kingdom guided by a parliament (Sabor). During this time, the wealth and power of the landed nobility grew, and an increase in the feudal obligations of the agrarian population followed.

Free cities (Dubrovnik, among others) were founded along the coast, increasing trade and political strength in the region. Many made trade agreements with Venice, which by now was a contender for control of Croatia's ports.

Trade increased, and northern Croatian cities also saw rapid development, but a Tatar invasion in 1242 diverted the government's attention to the country's defense as invaders razed Zagreb and everything else in their path. Ultimately, Hungarian King Bela IV outmaneuvered the Tatars and retained control, but the country's growing strength from its alliance with Hungary fueled Venice's determination to control Istria and Dalmatia and ultimately access to the sea.

Venice began a long-term campaign to take over the Croatian coast early in the 13th century: They captured Zadar in 1202 and Dubrovnik in 1205. For the next century, the Venetian influence along the coast increased until they achieved their objective. During the period of Venetian acquisition, the counts of Anjou came to the Croatian throne, and in 1358 they reasserted Hungarian control of Dalmatia thanks to Louis of Anjou. King Louis expelled the Venetians, but disarray in the House of Anjou ultimately resulted in the sale of rights over Dalmatia back to the Venetians in 1409.

THE OTTOMANS & HAPSBURGS

During the 15th century the Ottoman Turks advanced on Croatian lands, taking Bulgaria and Bosnia and leaving the rest of Croatia vulnerable. During the battle against the Turks at Mohács, Hungarian King Louis II was killed in action, leaving the Turk Sultan Suleyman the Magnificent in control of much of southern Croatia. Louis did not have an heir, and the throne went to his designated successor, Ferdinand I of Hapsburg, a move that put Croatia in the Hapsburg Empire.

The first Hapsburg rulers were determined to defend Croatia against the Turks, who continued to gobble up Croat land until the mid–17th century despite efforts to contain them. During this time, Croatia lost 75% of its territory and people, but by the mid–17th century, the Hapsburgs had retaken Croatia and pushed the Turks out of the region. Subsequently, Hapsburg armies gradually drove the Turks out of the rest of central Europe (except for Bosnia and Herzegovina). The decrease in Turk strength opened the door for the Venetians to once again surge in Dalmatia.

In 1671, the Croats made a push for self-rule, but the Hapsburgs would have none of it and quashed the movement. During the next century, the Hapsburgs gradually squeezed out Croatian authority, which further made Croatia a takeover target.

By this time many Orthodox Serbs who were living in Catholic Croatia and Russia began to show an interest in the region. This raised the question of who would take control, Catholic Austria or Orthodox Russia. Thus began the so-called Eastern Question, which was one of the precipitators of World War I.

THE NAPOLEON EFFECT

During the 18th century, Austria, Hungary, and Venice all continued to vie for pieces of Croatia and for imposition of their own cultures. The Hapsburgs pushed to install German customs and language; the Hungarians proposed that Hungarian be accepted as the official language and claimed that Slavonia belonged to Hungary; the Venetians extended their territories to the Dinara mountains and beyond, thanks to the Treaty of Požarevac; and the Turks retained control of Bosnia and Herzegovina. The Požarevac treaty made it difficult to define Croatia's geography, but in 1808 Napoleon "solved" the problem by capturing coastal towns, uniting Dalmatia with parts of Slovenia and Croatia, and renaming the joint territories the Illyrian Provinces. Napoleon's influence was profound but short-lived. He promoted agriculture and commerce, raised the status of the Orthodox population, and started a reawakening of Croatian nationalism. But with his defeat in 1815 at the hands of the English navy, control of Dalmatia once again reverted to the Hapsburgs, who immediately reasserted authority over Croatia.

ILLYRIANISM

After the fall of Napoleon, Austria created the Kingdom of Illyria, an administrative unit designed to thwart Hungarian nationalism and unification of the South Slavs. Dalmatia, however, was not part of this reorganization, as Austria decided to keep this gold mine as its vacation playground. Eventually, the Hapsburgs' attempts to exert absolute control over every aspect of Croatian life backfired. Croatian leaders began stirring up nationalism by promoting the Croatian language and culture and by forming a Slavic kingdom under the Hapsburgs' noses. In 1832, Ljudevit Gaj, a Croatian noble, tried to elbow the Hungarians aside by addressing the Sabor in the Croatian language, which was daring at the time. Gaj, who was a journalist and linguist, pushed a South Slavic literary language, engineered a Latin-based script, and in 1836 founded an anti-Hungarian journal that called for cultural and political unity. The Hungarians were understandably angered by these developments and tried to impose Hungarian as the official language of Slavonia. The Croatians responded by sending any correspondence written in Hungarian back to Hungary unread.

THE AUSTRO-HUNGARIAN INFLUENCE

In 1848, Hungary challenged Austria during the revolution that was sweeping across Europe. Croatians, who feared another wave of domination from Hungary and who had hoped for unification, sided with Austria and began to call for self-determination. Austria yielded to Croatian pressure and raised Josip Jelačić to the position of Ban (viceroy) of Croatia. Jelačić immediately convened the Croatian Sabor to consolidate his support. He suspended relations with Hungary and declared war, but his Austrian allies reasserted their authority over Croatia after defeating the Hungarians with Jelačić's help.

Austria ended absolute rule over Croatia in 1860, and in 1866 the Austro-Hungarian Empire was near collapse. In an effort to save it, Emperor Franz Joseph united Austria and Hungary in a dual monarchy. In a Sabor dominated by pro-Hungarian officials, a compromise on Croatia was reached that acknowledged the country as a distinct political entity within the empire.

Croatia increased its autonomy within the empire and in 1868 established a political/cultural base in Zagreb. However, the Croatian leadership was divided between those advocating a South Slav union and those favoring a Greater Croatia. In addition, animosity between the Croats and Serbs was on the rise. Bishop Josip Strossmayer attempted to reduce the religious differences between the Croats and Serbs to defuse the growing tensions.

Ante Starčević represented the opposition to Strossmayer's initiatives and was suspicious of any conciliatory moves directed at the Serbs. Both movements were sabotaged by Ban (which means "lord" or "master") Károly Khuen-Héderváry when he ignored a compromise that allowed home rule for Croatia and promoted Hungarian language and culture by provoking conflict between Croats and Serbs.

Despite Héderváry's treachery, in 1906, Serbs and Croats again came together to create the Croat-Serb Coalition, which immediately came under attack from Vienna, which feared a loss of Austrian influence.

WORLD WAR I & ITS AFTERMATH

In 1908, Austria-Hungary annexed Bosnia and its diverse population of Catholic Croats, Orthodox Serbs, and Muslims. This move set back the Serb goal of creating a Serbian state and reignited tensions between Croats and Serbs. Thus, when Hapsburg heir Franz Ferdinand visited the Bosnian capital of Sarajevo in 1914, the mood of the city was hostile.

On June 28, Bosnian Serb Gavrilo Princip assassinated Franz Joseph and his wife, and a month later Austria-Hungary declared war on Serbia. Germany sided with Austria; Russia, France, and Great Britain countered by forming an alliance of their own, thus drawing a line in the sand for World War I.

For a time, the Croats sided with the Hapsburg contingent, but on December 1, 1918, after the Austro-Hungarian empire had been defeated, Serb Prince Aleksandar Karadordević broke ranks and created the Kingdom of Serbs, Croats, and Slovenes. The unification seemed reasonable in theory, but it did not allow for autonomy of any of the nations or provide any guidelines to facilitate cooperation among diverse people suddenly thrown together under a single umbrella.

Only one Croat raised an alarm about the ramifications of unification. Stjepan Radić, leader of the Croatian Peasant's Party, urged caution, but his pleas went unheeded. In 1927, after the new Croatian government failed to move in the direction of autonomy, Radić and Serbian Svetozar Pribićević of the Independent Democratic Party joined forces to unite the Serbs and Croats. But on June 20, 1928, extremists from Belgrade fatally shot Radić and two members of the Peasant's Party while parliament was in session. Fearing that the assassination would incite further ethnic violence, King Aleksandar dissolved parliament, established a dictatorship, and changed the name of the state to the Kingdom of Yugoslavia (South Slavia).

WORLD WAR II

Aleksandar's dictatorship resembled a police state in which 90% of the police and government officials were Serbian, a situation that invited trouble. As a reaction to this state of affairs, in 1929 Croat Ante Pavelič founded the Ustaše, an organization dedicated to the overthrow of Aleksandar's state. Five years later, in 1934, the Ustaše, with Italy's help, assassinated the king in Marseilles, an act that threw Yugoslavia into turmoil and made it vulnerable to Nazi exploitation.

Yugoslavia tried to remain neutral at the start of World War II, but pressure to support the Axis was great, and on March 25, 1941, Yugoslavia's Prince Pavle aligned the country with the fascists.

Within 2 days the prince was overthrown and the pact nullified, but the Nazis would not let the cancellation stand. On April 6, they bombed Belgrade and invaded Yugoslavia. It took the Nazis just 10 days to defeat the Yugoslav army. Shortly after that, the Ustaše formed the Independent State of Croatia (Nezavisna Država Hrvatska, NDH), leaving the rest of Yugoslavia to fend for itself.

The Ustaše at first attempted to drive the Serbs out of Croatia, but when that proved impossible, they set up several concentration camps, the most infamous being the camps at Jasenovac, about 97km (60 miles) south of Zagreb on the Sava River. No one knows how many people died in Jasenovac at the hands of the Ustaše, but reports did chronicle acts of inhumanity and barbarism in the camps. Not all Croats condoned the Ustaše and their methods.

THE RESISTANCE MOVEMENT

A resistance movement to counter the Ustaše was organized almost immediately after Germany invaded in 1941, but it was divided between the pro-Serbian Četniks and the pro-Communist Partisans led by Josip Broz "Tito." Committed as these groups were, they were not very effective in combating the Ustaše because they were more intent on competing with and killing each other. However, the Allies recognized Tito's Partisans as the official resistance at the Tehran Conference and funneled all aid to the Communist group, which helped liberate Belgrade.

Ironically, the internal conflict between opposing resistance groups in Yugoslavia helped the Allied victory because it tied up hundreds of thousands of Axis troops, who then were unavailable to fight the Allies. Even so, when the war ended in 1944, more than 1.7 million Yugoslavs had died as a result of the fighting, a number that represented a staggering 10% of the country's population.

TITO & POSTWAR YUGOSLAVIA

After the war, Tito's Communist Party won the Yugoslav election with 90 percent of the vote, but Tito was not in lockstep with Stalin and declared Yugoslav non-alignment in 1948, which allowed him to function as a cafeteria Communist.

Non-alignment was a double-edged sword for Yugoslavia. On the one hand, the country had to endure a Soviet blockade in the 1950s as a result of Tito's non-conformity, but on the other, Tito's position helped tourism flourish along the Adriatic coast. His approval of site management allowed competition and created efficiencies in the workplace. He also gave each of Yugoslavia's six republics—Croatia, Serbia, Slovenia, Bosnia/Herzegovina, Macedonia, and Montenegro—control over its own internal affairs.

Tito's largesse had its limits. In 1967 the Croatian economy was booming, which buoyed national sentiment. The first expression of renewed nationalism surfaced in the cultural realm: The Croatian intelligentsia, worried by attempts to create a single Serb-Croat literary language, issued a declaration stating that Croatian was a language distinct from Serbian. Croatian Serbs issued a retort stating that they had a right to their own language, too, and that they wanted to use the Cyrillic script. Tito quickly suppressed both sides of the argument, which put an end to the nascent nationalist movement dubbed "Croatian Spring."

For a while, other efforts at liberalization—demands for autonomy, student strikes, calls for government reform—were attempted, but in 1971 Tito cracked down on those reformers, too, effectively putting an end to the Croatian Spring once and for all. Tito's hard line had a chilling effect on reform efforts not only in Croatia but also in the rest of Yugoslavia, though his iron hand didn't stop Yugoslavs outside the country from criticizing his style of government.

YUGOSLAVIA IN TURMOIL

On May 4, 1980, after decades of balancing Communist ideology with Western capitalism in Yugoslavia, Josip Broz "Tito" died at the age of 88. His funeral in Belgrade was attended by thousands of Yugoslavs and more than 100 heads of state.

Unfortunately, like many authoritarian leaders, Tito had not developed a plan of succession, which left the Yugoslav state without a strong leader. To complicate matters, the region's economy was deteriorating in the wake of the 1970s oil crisis, a huge national debt, and the disappearance of foreign credit sources. The republics once again became restless, and old problems resurfaced.

The first hot spot was Kosovo, a region in southwest Serbia with a large Muslim Albanian population. Kosovo, which had enjoyed a modicum of autonomy, decided in 1981 that it wanted republic status. Six years later, the emboldened Serb minority in Kosovo took the position that the Albanians there were a threat to them. That inspired Serbs in Croatia to almost simultaneously express the same sentiment about the Croats. A collective angst spread, pushing Yugoslavia to crack along national, religious, and ethnic lines.

In 1987, a relatively unknown Serb politician named Slobodan Milošević began to proclaim Serb superiority while working toward installing a Communist government in Yugoslavia. Two years after Milošević's debut as a champion of Serbs, the Berlin Wall came down, leaving him holding an unpopular position while the rest of Europe raced off in the opposite ideological direction.

WAR IN CROATIA

Despite Milošević's efforts to expand his bloc of followers, Croatia and other Yugoslav republics were trying to make the transition to democracy. In May 1989 the Croatian Democratic Union (HDZ), led by former general and historian Franjo Tuđman, became one of the first non-Communist organizations in Croatia, and in less than a year began campaigning for Croatia's secession from Yugoslavia. By April, free elections were held in Croatia and Tuđman was sworn in as president the next month. He promptly declared Croatian statehood, a preliminary stage before independence. At the same time Stjepan Mešić was chosen as Croatia's first post-Communist prime minister, and a constitution was written that declared the Serbs in Croatia a national minority rather than a unique nation within the republic.

This classification fomented outrage in the Serb community. In 1991, Milošević, seeing that the breakup of Yugoslavia was inevitable, began gathering support for a Greater Serbia, which would include all the areas of Croatia and Bosnia/Herzegovina where Serbs were in residence. Worse, Milošević developed a plan to "ethnically cleanse" Eastern Croatia of Croats living there. Under such conditions, civil war was inevitable.

Hostilities broke out in 1991 with Milošvić pulling Serb forces into Croatia from all over Yugoslavia. During the violence, cities such as Dubrovnik, Vukovar, and Osijek suffered heavy damage, thousands of Croatians were forced to leave their homes, and thousands more were killed. The fighting also spread to other republics in Yugoslavia—most notably Bosnia—as Milošević and the Serbs kept advancing and pressuring Croats and Muslims in Bosnia to fight each other.

Finally, hostilities between the Croats and the Muslims in Bosnia were ended by the U.S., and peace was declared in northern Yugoslavia in 1995. But it was 3 more years before the last Serb military units left Croatia. A year later, Tuđman died, paving the way for the election of Stjepan Mešić, who had opposed Tuđman's war policies in Bosnia/Herzegovina, and he has served as President of Croatia ever since.

POSTWAR CROATIA

Croatia's economy was a shambles as the war drew to a close: Employment hovered at 20%; industry was almost non-existent; agricultural output was drastically low; and some companies were unable to pay their workers even the depressed average monthly wage of $400.

In some business sectors, the country's economy is still struggling, but tourism and service industries are reviving as people return to Croatia's captivating landscape.

The bad taste from the Croat-Serb civil war hasn't completely disappeared, and many people are still trying to recover from the horrors of ethnic cleansing, poverty, and loss. In April 2001, Slobodan Milošević, architect of the campaign to "cleanse" certain areas of all but Serbs, was arrested and charged with corruption after a 26-hour armed standoff with police at his Belgrade home. Two months later Milošević was turned over to the United Nations and charged with committing crimes against humanity in Kosovo and Croatia.

In November of that year, the U.N. War Crimes Tribunal charged Milošević with genocide stemming from his alleged activity during the 1992–95 Bosnian war. Milošević, known as the "Butcher of the Balkans," is the first head of state to face an international war-crimes court. He died March 12, 2006, while in custody at The Hague, while his trial was in progress and before a verdict could be reached.

THE 21ST CENTURY & BEYOND

After a decade of war, Croatia is still rebuilding its image as a tourist destination and as a democratic nation. At the same time, the country is determined to take its place at the world table. Signs of economic recovery are everywhere, from packed luxury hotels on the Adriatic coast to the thriving upscale shopping malls and gourmet restaurants in Zagreb. Croatia is beginning to show signs that it is shaking off its down-in-the-mouth persona and presenting a more sophisticated, savvy face to the world.

The Croatian government is working to reduce foreign debt, boost the economy, and promote the country's natural treasures while it waits for admittance to the European Union, an event that is expected to occur by 2010. If Croatia achieves its economic and social goals, there are no limits to its future.

2 A Taste of Croatia

Croatia's cuisine reflects widely diverse cultural and geographic influences. Some culinary traditions are a result of Croatia's proximity to the sea and fertile farmland, and some are the result of foreign occupiers who imported their tastes and recipes. Croatians are very proud of their gastronomic traditions, and while there are regional differences, you'll find that freshness, grilling, and daily baking are consistent across the country.

You will find a distinct Italian trend in cuisine on the coast, thanks to centuries of occupation by Rome and Venice; and a bent toward dishes heavy in meat and sauces in continental Croatia, thanks to years of Austrian, Hungarian, and Turkish domination. Wherever you go, you'll find that the result is a wonderfully diverse Croatian cuisine rooted in family and friends, the seasons, and the bounty of Croatia's soil and sea.

MEALS & DINING CUSTOMS

BREAKFAST & GABLEC Western-style breakfast *(doručak)* (eggs, pastries, meats, cereals) is served at larger hotels and restaurants throughout Croatia. In smaller towns and in homes, a glass of *rakija* (fruit brandy), a cup of coffee, and perhaps bread or a roll hot from the local bakery is the normal early-morning meal.

However, around 10am Croatians sometimes stop for *gablec* (*marenda* on the coast), literally "breakfast eaten with cutlery." This meal is a smaller version of lunch, Croatia's main meal, but it sometimes substitutes.

Sitting down to gablec around 10am was common among people all over the former Yugoslavia—including Croatia—because back then people started work and school around 6 or 7am, which didn't allow time for breakfast. Thus, they got hungry around 10am and a meal of home-style food like *sarma* (stuffed sour cabbage), *goulash*, or *fis paprikas* customarily was offered in factories, schools, and local restaurants. (People didn't have time to go home for a meal, and carryout and fast food were nonexistent.) Today gablec is still popular, but many places start serving around noon instead of 10am and continue serving late into the afternoon, to correspond with later job starts.

LUNCH   Lunch (*ručak*) generally is Croatia's main meal. It often begins with a bowl of soup followed by an entree of roasted meat, vegetable or salad, potatoes or noodles, and dessert. Croatians eat lunch anywhere from 10am (gablec) to late afternoon, and if they eat dinner at all, it usually is a light meal.

DINNER   Dinner (*večera*) for Croatians often consists of a very thin-crusted pizza or a shared plate of munchies such as *čevapi* (spicy grilled sausage), *pršut* (smoked ham), and cheese or grilled sardines, usually served well after 8pm. If they aren't eating at home, Croatians dine at **restorans** or **konobas,** both of which serve a wide range of dishes but differ in levels of formality, with restorans being the fancier. In cities and large tourist areas, all dining establishments offer full menus to accommodate foreign eating habits, which frequently revolve around eating the biggest meal of the day at dinner rather than lunch.

COFFEE & ICE CREAM   Drinking coffee is a social event in Croatia. You can find places full of people sipping java on almost every street in every Croatian town at any time of day. Sometimes these establishments are cafes attached to restaurants or pastry shops, and sometimes they are free-standing shops that serve only drinks (alcoholic or nonalcoholic). Ice-cream shops—almost as ubiquitous as coffee shops—serve coffee and mostly nonalcoholic beverages plus a huge array of ice-cream concoctions ranging from basic cones to multi-layered sundaes, as well as a selection of cakes and pastries.

TIPPING   Tipping in Croatia is becoming more commonplace, especially in upscale restaurants. In the past, tipping was welcome but not expected. Today, however, in newer, upscale places, an extra 10% or 15% is considered polite. In informal restaurants in smaller towns and coffee shops, tipping is rare and not expected, but most people leave any coins they receive in change. Croatian waiters work for salaries and benefits by law and do not depend on tips for living wages.

COUVERT   Adding a *couvert* to the bill is a relatively new practice in Croatian restaurants and is not uniformly imposed. The couvert is a "cover charge" that is a prima facie charge for bread, which is brought to the table automatically in most cases. Menus will usually list the couvert and its cost, which can range from 5kn ($1) to 35kn ($7) or more. You can refuse the bread and escape the couvert, but once the bread basket lands on your table, you have to pay the charge.

REGIONAL SPECIALTIES

Dining is a national sport in Croatia. Across-the-board, food is surprisingly good in all regions of the country. However, besides consistent quality and an ever-present offering of grilled meat and fish and pizza from north to south, each part of the country prides itself on specific traditional dishes.

CONTINENTAL CROATIA (Zagreb, Bilogora, Zagorje, Podravina, Međimurje) Food traditions in this region were influenced by a seasonal climate, fertile farmland, and the rural lifestyle of the common people, plus the lavish gastronomy of the nobility (Austrian, Hungarian, and so forth) who lived in castles dotting the terrain. Consequently, cuisine in this part of Croatia is more substantial than in other regions. For example, the need to store meat safely inspired *lodrica ili tiblica* (big wooden bowl), baked meats kept in bowls full of lard in cool places for later use. Smoking and drying, also methods used to preserve meats, extended to cheese *(prgica),* still a popular item in regional markets. *Žganci,* a kind of grits topped with cheese, sour cream, yogurt, or bacon, is a common breakfast dish. Turkey or duck with *mlinci* (baked noodles), *sarma* (ground meat in sour cabbage leaves), and *krvavice* (blood sausage with sauerkraut) are popular mains. Favorite desserts in this region are *štrukle* (phyllo filled with fresh cheese, apples, cherries, or other fruit) and *palačinke* (crepes filled with honey and walnuts or jam). *Knedle sa šljivama* (potato dumplings stuffed with plums) are on almost every restaurant menu. In Međimurje, *prekomurska gibanica* (yeast cake layered with fresh cheese, apples, walnuts, poppy seeds, and raisins) is a must-try sweet after dinner.

GORSKI KOTAR & LIKA The area southwest of central Croatia (including the Plitvice Lakes) but not on the coast is a combination of forests, hills, and pastures where winters are long and summers (and the growing season) quite short. The food is similar to that of continental Croatia, with a few notable additions. You'll see a lot of roadside stalls selling homemade cheeses and fruit brandies as well as spit-roasted lamb and pork. Look for *janjetina* (lamb) or janjetina baked under a peka.

Lika-style sauerkraut is another specialty that consists of marinated cabbage and smoked sausage served with potatoes boiled in their skins. *Pijane pastrve* (drunken trout) is fish cooked in wine sauce and served with potatoes and other veggies, while *lički lonac* (Licki pot) is a stew of fresh cabbage, potatoes, root vegetables, and meat.

SLAVONIA & BARANJA Cuisine in this region in the eastern part of continental Croatia commonly has a Hungarian influence: The food is quite heavy and seasoned with a lot of paprika. Specialties include *čobanac* (goulash made from several kinds of meat and seasoned with hot paprika, garlic, and bay leaves), *ribli paprikaš* (paprika-based stew with a variety of fish and served with pasta), *punjene paprikaš* (paprika peppers stuffed with minced pork, rice, and bacon), and freshwater fish grilled on a spit over an open fire. *Kulen* (spicy paprika sausage), *rezanci* (broad egg noodles topped with sweetened walnuts or poppy seeds), and *breskvice* (dough balls filled with walnuts, sugar, chocolate, and fruit brandy, colored red to resemble peaches) are other regional delights. And the red stuff served with meat is called *ajvar,* a kind of red-pepper tapenade that can be mild or hot.

KVARNER & ISTRIA These two regions offer the most diverse cuisine in Croatia, perhaps because they combine both inland and coastal tastes. Here the *peka* (a metal, bell-shaped lid) covers food placed on a ceramic slab during cooking. The lid is also covered with hot ash during the process. The peka is used extensively for both meat and fish. In the Kvarner, try *Creska janjetina* (lamb from the island of Cres) and *škampi* (shrimp dishes cooked under the bell); or try any of the game stews infused with bay leaves that grow in the mountainous part of Cres island. In Lovran and along Kvarner Bay, *maruni* (chestnuts) are used in almost everything, including *kroštule* (fried strips of dough made with flour, eggs, lemon zest, and grape brandy) for dessert. On Pag, try *paški sir* (Pag cheese), lamb, and *pršut*(Dalmatian ham) all infused with flavor because of the animals' diet of local herbs. Istria has the most refined cuisine in Croatia and is also the source of some of the country's best wines. Try *riblja juha* (fish soup), *riblji složenac* (fish stew), *kuhane kozice* (boiled prawns), *crni rižoto sa plodovima mora* (black and white seafood risotto), and any dish with *tartufe* (truffles). *Istarski fuži sa tartufima* (a special Istrian pasta with truffles) and *Istarski fuži sa gulasom od divljači* (Istrian fuzi with game goulash) are both worth trying. *Fritaja sa divljim šparogama* (omelet with wild asparagus) and all sorts of snacks that include Istarski *pršut* (Istrian ham), *ovčji* and *kravlji sir* (sheep and cow's cheeses), and *slane srdele* (salted sardines), are also popular. Wines to try in this region are the whites, *Malvazija* and *Vrbnička žlahtina;* and the reds, *Teran* and *Borgonja.*

DALMATIA Freshness and simplicity are the watchwords that most aptly characterize Dalmatian cuisine. Main meals typically start with *pršut* and *paški sir,* both often scattered with olives that have different flavors, depending on the Dalmatian village that grows and processes them. *Kamenice* (oysters) from Ston on the Pelješac Peninsula are also prized, as is anything from the sea. *Riba na lešo* (fish grilled with olive oil) and served with *blitva* (boiled Swiss chard and potatoes) is a common main course, as is *školjke i škampi na buzaru* (shellfish and shrimp stew). There are as many recipes and spellings for *buzara* as there are restaurants, but common ingredients in this sauce seem to be oil, garlic, parsley, wine, and shellfish. *Pašticada* (larded beef or pork roasted in wine and spices) is another good choice, as is *ribe na sajur* (fish grilled after marinating in olive oil and wine vinegar). Wines to seek out in this region include *Bogdanuša* and *Postup* (white); and *Kaštelet* and *Plavac* (red).

ORDERING A MEAL (& PAYING FOR IT)

English	Croatian	Pronunciation
Menu	**jelovnik**	Yay-*lohv*-neek
Order	**naručiti**	Nah-roo-*chee*-tee
Waiter	**konobar**	*koe*-noe-bar
I am hungry.	**Ja sam gladan.**	Ya-sahm-*glah*-dahn
Menu, please.	**Molim vas jelovnik.**	*Moe*-leem vahss yay-*lohv*-neek
Do you serve food here?	**Da li poslužujete hranu ovdje?**	Dah lee poe-*sloozh*-oo-yay-tay *ha*-ra-noo *ohv*-day?
What would you like to order?	**Što bi ste željeli naručiti?**	*Shtoe* bee stay *zjehl*-yay-lee nah-roo-*chee*-tee?
We would like to order . . .	**Željeli bi smo naručiti . . .**	*Zjehl*-yay-lee bee smaw nah-roo *chee*-tee
Table for two (three, four)	**stol za dvoje (troje, četvoro)**	Stall za *dvo*-ye, (*troe*-ye, chet-*voe*-roe)
We would like to pay.	**Željeli bi smo platiti.**	*Zjehl*-yay-lee bee some *plah*-tee-tee.
Check/bill, please.	**Račun molim.**	*Rah*-choon, *moe*-leem.

BASICS

English	Croatian	Pronunciation
breakfast	**doručak**	*doe*-roo-chahk
lunch	**ručak**	*roo*-chahk
dinner	**večera**	*veh*-chair-ah

English	Croatian	Pronunciation
knife	nož	noezh
fork	viljuška	*vee*-loosh-kah
spoon	žlica	*zhlee*-tsa
plate	tanjur	*tah*-nyoor
cold	hladno	*hah*-lahd-noe
hot	vruće	*vrooch*-eh
warm	toplo	*toe*-ploe
sugar	šećer	*shay*-chair
without sugar	bez šećera	bayz *shay*-chair
salt	sol	soal
pepper	papar	*pah*-pahr
bread	kruh	crew
pastry	pecivo	*pay*-tsee-voe
meat	meso	*may*-soe
I am a vegetarian.	Ja sam vegetarijanac.	Yah sahm vay-gay-tahr-ee-*yah*-nahts

BEVERAGES

English	Croatian	Pronunciation
white wine	bijelo vino	bee-*yeh*-lo *vee*-noe
tea	čaj	chai
red wine	crno vino	*tser*-noe *vee*-noe
(fruit) juice	đus	juice
coffee	kava	*kah*-vah
coffee with milk/cream	kava sa mlijekom/ vrhnjem	*kah*-vah sah ml-*yay*-kum/ *ver*-nyem
ice	led	layd
lemonade	limunada	lee-moo-*nah*-dah
milk	mlijeko	ml-*yay*-koe
beer (cold)	pivo	*pee*-voe
brandy (usually homemade)	rakija	*rah*-kee-yah
hot chocolate	topla čokolada	*toe*-plah choe-koe-*lah*-dah
water	voda	*voe*-dah

SOUPS & STARTERS

English	Croatian	Pronunciation
Swiss chard boiled with potatoes	blitva	*bleet*-vah
sausage	kobasica	koe-*bah*-see-tsa
goat cheese	kozji sir	*koezh*-yee seer
Zagorje potato soup	juha od krumpira na zagorski način	*Yoo*-ha ode kroom-*peer*-ah nah zah-*gore*-ski *na*-cheen.
spicy sausage from Slavonia	kulen	*koo*-len
bean and veggie soup from Istria	maneštra	mah-*nay*-strah
mixed salad	miješana salata	mee-*yeh*-shah-na sa-*lah*-tah

English	Croatian	Pronunciation
hard sheep's cheese with olive oil from Pag	paški sir	*pahsh*-kee seer
smoked ham	pršut	per-*shoot*
stuffed red peppers	punjene paprika	*poon*-yen-ay *pah*-pre-kah
shish kabob	ražnijiči	*rahz*-nyee-chee
spicy fish stew with paprika	riblji paprikaš/ fis paprikas	*reeb*-lyee *pah*-pre-kash/ fish *pah*-pre-kash
ham	šunka	*shoon*-kah

FISH/PASTA

English	Croatian	Pronunciation
fish stew	brodet/brodetto	*bro*-debt/*bro*-debt-toe
black risotto made with squid ink, olive oil, onion, and garlic	crni rižot	*tser*-nee ree-*zhote*
mussels	dagnje	*dahg*-nyay
Istrian egg pasta in a special twisted shape	fuži	*foo*-zhee
pasta with truffles	fuži i tartufi	*foo*-zhee ee tar-*too*-fee
goulash	gulaš	*goo*-lahsh
octopus	hobotnica	*hoe*-boat-nee-tsa
scallops	jakopove kapice	*yah*-koe-poe-vay kah-*pee*-tsa
lobster	jastog	*yah*-stoeg
shrimp	kozice	koe-*zee*-tsay
squid	lignje	*leeg*-nyeh
baked noodles	mlinci	*mleen*-tsee

MEAT

English	Croatian	Pronunciation
spicy grilled meatballs	ćevapčići/čevapi	cheh-*vahp*-chee-chee/cheh-*vahp*-ee
meat stew with paprika	čobanec	*choe*-bah-nayts
beef	govedina	*goe*-vay-dee-na
lamb	janjetina	*yah*-nyay-tee-nah
liver	jetra	*yay*-trah
cutlet (beef/pork)	kotlet	*cot*-let
meat stew with paprika	mučkalica	*mooch*-kah-lee-tsa
beef stew with wine and dried fruit	pašticada	pash-tee *sah*-dah
rotisserie roasted meat	pečenje	*pay*-chay-nyay
turkey	purica	*poo*-ree-tsa
grilled meat on a skewer	ražnjiči	*rahz*-nyee-chee
marinated cabbage leaves stuffed with rice and/or chopped meat	sarma	*sahr*-mah
bacon	slanina	*slah*-nee-nah

English	Croatian	Pronunciation
venison	**srnetina**	*ser*-nay-tee-nah
pork	**svinjetina**	s*veen*-yay-tee-nah
veal	**teletina**	*tay*-lay-tee-nah

DESSERTS

English	Croatian	Pronunciation
cake or cookies	**kolač**	*koe*-lahtch
custard-filled pastry	**kremešnite**	*krehm*-shnit-eh
crepes filled with jam or sweet walnuts	**palačinke**	pah-lah-*cheen*-kay
ice cream	**sladoled**	*slah*-doe-layd
Dubrovnik flan	**rožata**	*roe*-zhah-tah
cheese-filled blintzes	**štrukli**	*shtrook*-lee
cake	**torta**	*tor*-tah

3 Glossary of Useful Croatian Terms & Phrases

Language is the most daunting aspect of a trip to Croatia for any English-speaking tourist. Signs in Croatian look like gibberish to many English speakers, and conversations often sound like it, too. Even with an English-Croatian dictionary, it is difficult to understand what is being said and even more difficult to figure out how to form the words for a response. Croatians realize that theirs is a complicated language. Consequently, most are fluent in at least one other language besides Croatian, usually German, Italian, or English. However, if you try to learn at least a few rudimentary words and phrases in this Slavic variant, you will be richly rewarded for your efforts.

Pronunciation is not as difficult as it looks when you're staring at a word that appears to be void of vowels. With a few guidelines and a little practice, you should be able to make yourself understood.

PRONUNCIATION GUIDE
All letters are pronounced.
c sounds like "ts" in cats
č sounds like "ch" in chew
ć sounds like "tu" in picture
đ sounds like "dj" in adjunct
g sounds like "g" in god
j sounds like "y" in your
š sounds like "sh" in shut
ž sounds like "z" in azure
e sounds like "e" in bet
i sounds like "ee" in meet
o sounds like "o" in dog
u sounds like "oo" in loot
r is trilled

BASIC VOCABULARY

English	Croatian	Pronunciation
Yes	**Da**	dah
No	**Ne**	nay

English	Croatian	Pronunciation
good	**dobro**	*doe*-broe
bad	**loše**	*losh*-eh
I don't know.	**Ne znam.**	Nay znahm
I don't understand.	**Ne razumijem.**	Nay ra-*zoo*-mee-yem
to	**do**	doh
from	**od**	ode
day	**dan**	dahn
week	**tjedan**	*tyay*-dahn
month	**mjesec**	*myes*-ets
year	**godina**	*goe*-dee-nah
why	**zašto**	*zah*-shtoe
where	**gdje**	*gd*-yay
when	**kada**	*kah*-dah
how	**kako**	*kah*-koe
left	**lijevo**	lee-*yay*-voe
right	**desno**	*days*-noe
early	**rano**	*rah*-noe
late	**kasno**	*kahz*-noe
behind	**iza**	*ee*-zah
in front of	**ispred**	*ee*-spread
far	**daleko**	dah-*lay*-koe
close	**blizu**	*blee*-zoo
Where is . . . ?	**Gdje je . . . ?**	*Gd*-yay yay. . . niceties
Good day.	**Dobar dan.**	*Doe*-bar dahn.
Hi/bye.	**Bok** (corresponds to Italian "ciao")	boke
Thank you.	**Hvala.**	*Huh*-vah-lah
You're welcome.	**Nema na. Čemu or molim.** (response to hvala)	*Nay*-ma nah *chay*-moo / *moe*-leem.
Good morning.	**Dobro jutro.**	*Doe*-broe *you*-troe.
Good evening.	**Dobra večer.**	*Doe*-brah *vay*-chair.
Good night.	**Laku noć.**	*Lah*-koo noech.
Goodbye.	**Doviđenja.**	Doe-vee-*djen*-ya.
See you later.	**Vidimo se poslije.**	*Vee*-dee-moe say *poes*-lee-yay.
How are you?	**Kako sta?**	*Kah*-koe stah?
Fine, thank you.	**Dobro, hvala.**	*Doe*-broe, *huh*-vah-lah.
No, thank you.	**Ne hvala.**	Nay, *huh*-vah-lah.
Please	**Molim**	*Moe*-leem
Please come in.	**Izvolite uđite.**	*Eez*-vole-ee-tay udge-*ee*-teh.

English	Croatian	Pronunciation
Excuse me/sorry.	**Oprostite.**	*O-pro*-stee-tay.
Let's go.	**Hajdemo.**	*I*-day-moe.
Please, sit down.	**Izvolite, sjednite.**	*Eez*-vole-ee-tay *syed*-nee-teh.
Can you help me, please?	**Da li mi možete pomoći, molim?**	Dah lee mee *moe*-zay-tay poe *moeche*-ee *moe*-leem?
Do you speak English?	**Da li govorite engleski?**	Dah lee *goe*-vore-ee-tay Eng-*lay*-skee?
French	**Francuski**	Frahn-*tsu*-skee
German	**Njemački**	Nye-*match*-kee
Italian	**Italijanski**	Ee-tal-ee-*yan*-skee
I understand.	**Razumijem.**	Rah-*zoo*-mee-yem.
I don't understand.	**Ne razumijem.**	Nay rah-*zoo*-mee-yem.
What's your name?	**Kako se zovete?**	*Kah*-koe say *zoe*-vay-tay?
My name is_____.	**Zovem se_____.**	Zoe-vehm say_____.time
today	**danas**	*day*-nahs
tomorrow	**sutra**	*soo*-trah
yesterday	**jučer**	*you*-chair
every day	**svaki dan**	*svah*-kee dahn
week	**tjedan**	tee-*yay*-dahn
now	**sad**	sahd
soon	**uskoro**	oos-core-roe
later	**kasnije/poslije**	*kahs*-nee-yay/*poe*-slee-yay.
always	**uvijek**	*oo*-vee-yeck
What time is it?	**Koliko je sati?**	*Koh*-lee-koh yay *sah*-tee?

GETTING AROUND

English	Croatian	Pronunciation
Excuse me, I am looking for . . .	**Oprostite, tražim . . .**	O-*pro*-stee-tay, *trazh*-eem . . .
I want to go to . . .	**Želio(he)/Željela (she) bih ići . . .**	Zhel-ee-o/*zhel*-yay-lah bee *ee*-chee . . .
Is it far?	**Da li je daleko?**	Dah lee yay dah-lay-ko?
How many kilometers from here?	**Koliko kilometara odavde?**	Koe-lee-koe *kee*-loe-maytah-rah ode-*ahv*-day?
Turn back.	**Vratite se nazad.**	*Vrah*-tee-tay say *nah* zahd.
Turn/Go . . .	**Vratite se/okrenite/idite . . .**	*Vrah*-tee-tay say/oh-*kray* nee-tay/ee-*dee*-tay . . .
left	**lijevo**	lee-*yay*-voe
right	**desno**	*days*-noe
straight ahead	**ravno**	*rahv*-noe
street	**ulica**	*oo*-lee-tsah

English	Croatian	Pronunciation
square	**trg**	*tur*-ig-ah
next to	**pored**	*poe*-red
there	**tamo**	*tah*-moe
map	**karta**	*kar*-tah
I would like to buy a ticket.	**Želio/Željela bih kupiti kartu.**	*Zhel*-ee-o/*zhel*-yay-lah bee koo-pee-tee *kar*-too.
ticket	**(putna) karta**	(*poot*-nah)*kar*-tah
one-way ticket	**jednosmjerna karta**	*yed*-nose-myair-na *kar*-tah.
round-trip ticket	**povratna karta**	*poe*-vraht-nah *ka*r-tah
ticket	**ulaznica** (for movies, museum)	*oo*-lahz-neetsa
Where is the . . . ?	**Gdje se nalazi . . . ?**	Ga dyay say *nah*-lah-zee . . .
beach	**plaža**	*plah*-zha
bank	**banka**	*ban*-ka
church	**crkva**	*tserk*-vah
drugstore	**ljekarna**	*lee*-yay-car-nah
market	**tržnica**	*terzh*-nee-tsa
museum	**muzej**	*moo*-zay
park	**park**	park
police station	**policijska postaja**	poe-*leets* ee-ska *poe*-shta-ya
post office	**poštanski ured, pošta**	*poe*-stan-skee *oo*-raid, *poe*-shtah
tourist office	**turistički ured**	too-*ree*-steech-kee *oo*-raid
train station (If central station in town, then	**željeznička stanica/ postaja centra željeznički kolodvor.)**	*zhel*-yay-zneech-kah sta-*nee*-tsa/ *poe*-stah-ya *tsen*-trah *zhel*-yay-zneech-kee *koe*-loe-dvoar
bus station	**autobusna**	ow-*toe*-boos-nah
airport	**zračna luka**	*zrach*-na *loo*-kah
taxi stand	**taksi stajalište**	*tahk*-see *stye*-ya-lees-tay
Is the (post office) open?	**Da li je pošta otvorena?**	Dah lee yay *poe*-shta oat-*voar*-ray-nah?
I would like to change some money.	**Želio/Željela bih promijeniti novac.**	*Zhel*-ee-oh/*zhel*-yay-la bee proh-mee-yay-nee-tee *no*-vats.
exchange office	**mjenjačnica**	myay-nyats-*nee*-tsa
exchange rate	**tečajna lista**	*tay*-chai-nyah *leest*-ah
Where can I find a (good) . . . ?	**Gdje mogu naći (dobrog) . . .?**	Gd-yay *moe*-goo *nah*-chee (*doe*-broeg)
dentist	**zubara**	*zoo*-bah-rah
doctor	**liječnika**	lee-*yaych*-nee-kah
hospital	**bolnica**	bole-*nee*-tsa

SIGNS

English	Croatian	Pronunciation
entry	**ulaz**	*oo*-lahz
exit	**izlaz**	*eez*-lahz
toilets/WC		
toilets (men)	**muskarci**	moosh-*kar*-tsi
toilets (women)	**žene**	*zhe*-neh
hospital	**bolnica**	bole-*nee*-tsa
police	**policija**	poe-*lee*-tsee-yah
prohibited	**zabranjeno**	zah-brah-*nyay*-noe
not allowed	**nije dopušteno**	*nee*-yay *doe*-poos-tay-no

HEALTH

English	Croatian	Pronunciation
I am sick.	**Bolestan sam/ bolesna sam.**	*Boe*-less-than sahm/ *boe*-less-nah sahm.
I need a doctor.	**Potreban mi je liječnik.**	Poe-*tray*-bahn mee yay lee-*yaych*-neek.
fever	**groznica**	*growz*-nee-tsa
headache	**glavobolja**	glah-*voe*-bowl-yay
stomachache	**bol u trbuhu**	bowl oo *ter*-boo
dentist	**zubar**	*zoo*-bar
I have a headache.	**Imam glavobolju.**	*Eee*-mom glah-*voe*-bowl-yoo.
I am allergic to antibiotics.	**Alergičan/allergična sam na antibiotike.**	Ah-*lure*-gee-chan/ah-*lure*-geech-nah sam *ahn*-tee-bee-oh-teek.
antibiotic	**antibiotic**	*ahn*-tee-bee-oh-teek
penicillin	**penicillin**	peh-nee-*tsee*-leen
pill	**tableta**	tah-*bleh*-tah
aspirin	**aspirin**	ah-*spee*-reen
I am on medications for (asthma/diabetes/ epilepsy).	**Pijem lijekove protiv (astme, dijabetesa, epilepsije).**	*Pee*-yem lee-*yay*-koe-vay pro-*teev* (*ast*-may, dee-yah-*bay*-tay-sah, ep-ee-*lep*-see-yeh).
virus	**virus**	*vee*-roos

ATTRACTIONS

English	Croatian	Pronunciation
bridge	**most**	most
cathedral	**katedrala**	kah-tay-*dra*-lah
church	**crkva**	*tserk*-vah
island	**otok**	*oh*-toke
lake	**jezero**	*yeh*-zeh-roe
Old Town	**Stari Grad**	*star*-ee grahd
ruins	**ruše vine**	*roo*-sheh-vee-neh
sea	**more**	*moe*-reh

SHOPPING

English	Croatian	Pronunciation
How much/How many?	**Koliko?**	*Koe*-lee-koe
What is the time?	**Koliko je sati?**	*Koe*-lee-koe yeh *sah*-tee?
a little	**malo**	*mah*-loe
a lot	**puno**	*poo*-noe
enough	**dosta**	*doe*-stah
(too) expensive	**(pre) skupo**	(pray) *scoo*-poe

GETTING A ROOM

English	Croatian	Pronunciation
room	**soba**	*soe*-bah
Excuse me, is there a hotel nearby?	**Oprostite, da li postoji hotel u blizini?**	Oh-*proe*-stee-tay, dah lee *poe*-stoy-ee *hoe*-tel oo *blee*-zee-nee?
Do you have a free room?	**Da li imate slobodnu sobu?**	Dah lee *ee*-mah-tay *slow*-bode-new *soe*-boo?
We would like a double room.	**Željeli bi smo jednu dvokrevetnu sobu.**	*Zhel*-yay-lee bee some *yay*-dnoo *dvoe*-kray-vayt-noo *soe*-boo.
I would like a room with a:	**Želio/željela (she) bih sobu sa:**	*Zhel*-ee-oh/*zhel*-yay-lah bee *soe*-boo sah:
shower	**tušem**	*toosh*-em
bathtub	**kadom**	*kah*-dome
balcony	**balkonom**	*bal*-koe-nome
air-conditioning	**klimom**	*klee*-mome
telephone	**telefonom**	teh-*leh*-phone-ohm
How much is the room per night?	**Koliko košta soba za jednu noć?**	*Koe*-lee-koe *koe*-shtah *soe*-bah zah *yayd*-noo noech?
per person	**po osobi**	poe *oh*-*soe*-bee
per week	**za tjedan dana**	zah *tyay*-dahn *dah*-nah
Okay, I will take the room.	**Uredu, uzet ću sobu.**	*Oo*-ray-doo, *oo*-zayt choo *soe*-boo.
I would like to make a reservation for a room.	**Želio/željela bih rezervirati sobu.**	*Zhel*-ee-oh/*zhel*-yay lah bee ray-zer-*veer*-ah-tee *soe*-boo.
I will stay for 2 nights.	**Ostat ću dvije noći.**	*Oh*-staht choo dvee-yay *noe*-chee.
Can I look at the room?	**Da li mogu pogledati sobu?**	Dah lee *moe*-goo *poe*-glay-dah-tee *soe*-boo?
Do you have any other rooms?	**Da li imate još koju sobu?**	Dah lee *ee*-mah-tay yoesh *koe*-yoo *soe*-boo?

Index

CLOSED
due to
accidental demolition

WEGEN BISSIGEN
EICHHÖRNCHEN GESCHLOSSEN

CERRADO

CABRAS

Κλειστό
Μετεωρίτες

プール も

POOL CLOSED

ELECTRIC EELS

閉
鎖
中

Hotel
closed for
facelifting

FERMÉ POUR
RAISON
DE GRÈVE
DES BONNES

FECHADO!
POR CAUSA DE
ATAQUES DOS CROCODILOS

— I don't speak
sign language.

A hotel can close for all kinds of reasons.
Our Guarantee ensures that if your hotel's undergoing construction, we'll
let you know in advance. In fact, we cover your entire travel experience.
See www.travelocity.com/guarantee for details.

⁂ travelocity®
You'll never roam alone.®